February 2011

Ref.
973   v.3

Milestone Documents in African American History

Exploring the Essential Primary Sources

MILESTONE DOCUMENTS IN AFRICAN AMERICAN HISTORY

Exploring the Essential Primary Sources

Volume 3
1901 – 1964

Paul Finkelman, Editor in Chief

Schlager Group
Dallas, Texas

Milestone Documents in African American History
Copyright © 2010 by Schlager Group Inc.

All rights reserved. No part of this book may be reproduced or utilized in any form or by any means, electronic or mechanical, including photocopying, recording, or by any information storage or retrieval systems, without permission in writing from the publisher. For information, contact:

Schlager Group Inc.
2501 Oak Lawn Avenue, Suite 440
Dallas, Tex. 75219
USA

You can find Schlager Group on the World Wide Web at
http://www.schlagergroup.com
Text and cover design by Patricia Moritz

Printed in the United States of America

10 9 8 7 6 5 4 3 2 1

ISBN: 978-1-935306-05-4

This book is printed on acid-free paper.

Contents

Editorial and Production Staff ix
Contributors x
Acknowledgments xii
Reader's Guide xiii
Introduction xiv

Volume 1: 1619–1852

John Rolfe's Letter to Sir Edwin Sandys 2
Virginia's Act XII: Negro Women's Children to Serve according to the Condition of the Mother .. 17
Virginia's Act III: Baptism Does Not Exempt Slaves from Bondage 27
"A Minute against Slavery, Addressed to Germantown Monthly Meeting" 36
John Woolman's *Some Considerations on the Keeping of Negroes* 47
Lord Dunmore's Proclamation 63
Petition of Prince Hall and Other African Americans to the Massachusetts General Court 72
Pennsylvania: An Act for the Gradual Abolition of Slavery 84
Thomas Jefferson's *Notes on the State of Virginia* 96
Slavery Clauses in the U.S. Constitution 112
Benjamin Banneker's Letter to Thomas Jefferson 130
Fugitive Slave Act of 1793 140
Richard Allen: "An Address to Those Who Keep Slaves, and Approve the Practice" 151
Prince Hall: *A Charge Delivered to the African Lodge* 163
Ohio Black Code 175
Peter Williams, Jr.'s "Oration on the Abolition of the Slave Trade" 187
Samuel Cornish and John Russwurm's First *Freedom's Journal* Editorial ... 200
David Walker's *Appeal To The Coloured Citizens of the World* 213
State v. Mann 231
William Lloyd Garrison's First *Liberator* Editorial 242
The Confessions of Nat Turner 255
United States v. Amistad 270
Prigg v. Pennsylvania 284
Henry Highland Garnet: "An Address to the Slaves of the United States of America" 306
William Wells Brown's "Slavery As It Is" 320
First Editorial of the *North Star* 338
Roberts v. City of Boston 351

Fugitive Slave Act of 1850 366
Narrative of the Life of Henry Box Brown, Written by Himself 381
Sojourner Truth's "Ain't I a Woman?" 394
Frederick Douglass's "What to the Slave Is the Fourth of July?" 404
Martin Delany: The Condition, Elevation, Emigration, and Destiny of the Colored People
   of the United States 425

Volume 2: 1853–1900

Twelve Years a Slave: Narrative of Solomon Northup 444
Dred Scott v. Sandford 456
John S. Rock's "Whenever the Colored Man Is Elevated, It Will Be by His Own Exertions" 496
Virginia Slave Code 509
Harriet Jacobs's Incidents in the Life of a Slave Girl 522
Osborne P. Anderson: A Voice from Harper's Ferry 534
Emancipation Proclamation 552
Frederick Douglass: "Men of Color, To Arms!" 564
War Department General Order 143 574
Thomas Morris Chester's Civil War Dispatches 584
William T. Sherman's Special Field Order No. 15 598
Black Code of Mississippi 611
Thirteenth Amendment to the U.S. Constitution 622
Testimony before the Joint Committee on Reconstruction on Atrocities in the
   South against Blacks 633
Fourteenth Amendment to the U.S. Constitution 650
Henry McNeal Turner's Speech on His Expulsion from the Georgia Legislature 662
Fifteenth Amendment to the U.S. Constitution 676
Ku Klux Klan Act 686
United States v. Cruikshank 698
Richard Harvey Cain's "All That We Ask Is Equal Laws, Equal Legislation, and Equal Rights" 715
Civil Rights Cases 728
T. Thomas Fortune: "The Present Relations of Labor and Capital" 762
Anna Julia Cooper's "Womanhood: A Vital Element in the Regeneration and
   Progress of a Race" 772
John Edward Bruce's "Organized Resistance Is Our Best Remedy" 792
John L. Moore's "In the Lion's Mouth" 802
Josephine St. Pierre Ruffin's "Address to the First National Conference
   of Colored Women" 815
Booker T. Washington's Atlanta Exposition Address 824
Plessy v. Ferguson 836
Mary Church Terrell: "The Progress of Colored Women" 858
Ida B. Wells-Barnett's "Lynch Law in America" 872

Volume 3: 1901–1964

George White's Farewell Address to Congress 887
W. E. B. Du Bois: *The Souls of Black Folk* 898
Niagara Movement Declaration of Principles 917
Theodore Roosevelt's Brownsville Legacy Special Message to the Senate 930
Act in Relation to the Organization of a Colored Regiment in the City of New York 944
Monroe Trotter's Protest to Woodrow Wilson 954
Guinn v. United States 964
William Pickens: "The Kind of Democracy the Negro Expects" 981
Thirty Years of Lynching in the United States 992
Cyril Briggs's *Summary of the Program and Aims of the African Blood Brotherhood* 1011
Walter F. White: "The Eruption of Tulsa" 1022
Marcus Garvey: "The Principles of the Universal Negro Improvement Association" 1034
Alain Locke's "Enter the New Negro" 1046
James Weldon Johnson's "Harlem: The Culture Capital" 1063
Alice Moore Dunbar-Nelson: "The Negro Woman and the Ballot" 1077
John P. Davis: "A Black Inventory of the New Deal" 1088
Robert Clifton Weaver: "The New Deal and the Negro: A Look at the Facts" 1102
Charles Hamilton Houston's "Educational Inequalities Must Go!" 1115
Walter F. White's "U.S. Department of (White) Justice" 1128
Mary McLeod Bethune's "What Does American Democracy Mean to Me?" 1140
A. Philip Randolph's "Call to Negro America to March on Washington" 1152
To Secure These Rights 1162
Executive Order 9981 1182
Ralph J. Bunche: "The Barriers of Race Can Be Surmounted" 1192
Sweatt v. Painter 1204
Haywood Patterson and Earl Conrad's *Scottsboro Boy* 1216
Brown v. Board of Education 1234
Marian Anderson's *My Lord, What a Morning* 1246
Roy Wilkins: "The Clock Will Not Be Turned Back" 1260
George Wallace's Inaugural Address as Governor 1270
Martin Luther King, Jr.: "Letter from Birmingham Jail" 1284
John F. Kennedy's Civil Rights Address 1302
Martin Luther King, Jr.: "I Have a Dream" 1316
Civil Rights Act of 1964 1328
Fannie Lou Hamer's Testimony at the Democratic National Convention 1358

Volume 4: 1965–2009

Malcolm X: "After the Bombing" 1370
Moynihan Report 1386

South Carolina v. Katzenbach	1406
Stokely Carmichael's "Black Power"	1424
Bond v. Floyd	1444
Martin Luther King, Jr.: "Beyond Vietnam: A Time to Break Silence"	1460
Loving v. Virginia	1478
Kerner Commission Report Summary	1492
Eldridge Cleaver's "Education and Revolution"	1516
Jesse Owens's *Blackthink: My Life as Black Man and White Man*	1532
Angela Davis's "Political Prisoners, Prisons, and Black Liberation"	1548
Clay v. United States	1566
Jackie Robinson's *I Never Had It Made*	1583
Final Report of the Tuskegee Syphilis Study Ad Hoc Advisory Panel	1600
FBI Report on Elijah Muhammad	1614
Shirley Chisholm: "The Black Woman in Contemporary America"	1630
Thurgood Marshall's Equality Speech	1644
Jesse Jackson's Democratic National Convention Keynote Address	1658
Anita Hill's Opening Statement at the Senate Confirmation Hearing of Clarence Thomas	1674
A. Leon Higginbotham: "An Open Letter to Justice Clarence Thomas from a Federal Judicial Colleague"	1686
Colin Powell's Commencement Address at Howard University	1704
Louis Farrakhan's Million Man March Pledge	1716
One America in the 21st Century	1726
Clarence Thomas's Concurrence/Dissent in *Grutter v. Bollinger*	1740
Barack Obama: "A More Perfect Union"	1762
Barack Obama's Inaugural Address	1778
U.S. Senate Resolution Apologizing for the Enslavement and Racial Segregation of African Americans	1792
Barack Obama's Address to the NAACP Centennial Convention	1802
Teacher's Activity Guides	1817
List of Documents by Category	1827
Subject Index	1831

Milestone Documents in African American History

Exploring the Essential Primary Sources

George H. White's Farewell Address to Congress

1901

"You may tie us and then taunt us for a lack of bravery, but one day we will break the bonds."

Overview

George Henry White's Farewell Address to Congress was delivered to the House of Representatives on January 29, 1901. White was a two-term Republican congressman from North Carolina's Second Congressional District (known as the Black Second because of its large African American majority). During his years in the Fifty-fifth and Fifty-sixth Congresses, he had been the only black man among 357 representatives and 84 senators from 42 states. On the day White spoke, his legislative service was drawing to a close because he had chosen not to run for a third term in the November 1900 election, a decision he had made known in a speech on June 30 of that year. In consequence, he would leave the House of Representatives on March 4, 1901, the last African American to serve in Congress in the three and a half decades following the Civil War. Because of changes in the southern political landscape, there was little likelihood that another African American would soon succeed him.

White was a proud and stubborn man, and his four years in the House had been contentious and far from satisfying. He was the twenty-second African American since 1870 to hold congressional office, and like most of his predecessors (nineteen of them in the House, two in the Senate, and all of them Republicans), he was subjected to the institutional bias of white representatives and senators, who openly denigrated African Americans as ignorant, inferior, and incompetent; mocked them with "darky stories"; and mimicked them with an affected "plantation" dialect. In the weeks before his farewell speech, White had attempted on several occasions to call his white colleagues to account for such behavior but had been denied the opportunity. His efforts, for example, to introduce legislation on behalf of African Americans who, in the late 1890s, faced disenfranchisement by state legislatures and mob violence from white supremacy groups, brought immediate objection from southern Democrats that effectively left his proposals stillborn. When he boldly proposed reducing southern representation in Congress proportionate to the number of African Americans denied the vote, Democratic newspapers in North Carolina accused him of inciting racial unrest. These were matters that weighed heavily on White's mind as he prepared his valedictory address.

Context

White was the last of twenty African Americans elected to the House of Representatives in the nineteenth century, who collectively served thirty-eight two-year terms between 1870 and 1901. (The two African Americans elected to the Senate in the 1870s served a total of seven years.) They were all among the most visible beneficiaries of Radical Reconstruction policies that extended the suffrage to black males and other civil rights to the African American population in the South in the aftermath of the Civil War. That extension of rights generated opposition from powerful forces in the defeated South, and by the end of the century the personal freedoms of African Americans had been reduced or replaced by Jim Crow laws that, in turn, created a harsh segregated world in the American South.

The Civil War ended with the question of how to return the southern states to the Union unresolved and a matter of some confusion as a result of President Abraham Lincoln's assassination. Lincoln in 1862 had used his executive authority to appoint provisional military governors for the southern states recaptured by the Union army. His plan for Reconstruction was simplicity itself: States would be readmitted when at least 10 percent of the voters in 1860 took an oath of allegiance to the United States. After Lincoln's death, a struggle emerged in Congress between those who urged a continuation of the 10 percent plan and the antislavery wing of the Republican Party, who demanded a program of black civil rights to protect African Americans throughout the South. The Radicals, as they came to be known, gained control of the Congress and immediately clashed with President Andrew Johnson, whose policies seemed to support white supremacy.

In the 1866 congressional elections the Radical Republicans gained two-thirds of the seats in Congress and immediately passed, over President Johnson's veto, the Reconstruction Acts of 1867 that divided the old Confederacy into five military districts. To secure readmission, each state had to accept the Thirteenth Amendment to the Constitution, which outlawed slavery, and the Fourteenth Amendment, which extended a broad range of civil and political rights to African Americans. A key provision required the states to revise their constitutions to include

Time Line	
1852	■ **December 18** George Herbert White is born in Rosindale, North Carolina.
1865	■ **December 6** The Thirteenth Amendment to the U.S. Constitution ends slavery.
1868	■ **April** North Carolina voters approve the constitution of 1868, which grants African Americans the right to vote. ■ **July 9** The Fourteenth Amendment grants African Americans full citizenship in the United States.
1869	■ **November** Voters in Tennessee replace their Republican biracial Reconstruction state government with a white-only Democratic "redeemer" government.
1870	■ **February 3** The Fifteenth Amendment gives the vote to African American males. ■ **February 25** Hiram Rhodes Revels, Republican of Mississippi, is elected by the state legislature to fill a one-year vacancy in the U.S. Senate, becoming the first African American to serve in Congress. ■ **December 12** Joseph Rainey, Republican from South Carolina, becomes the first African American to serve in the U.S. House of Representatives.
1877	■ **March 4** Rutherford B. Hayes is inaugurated president of the United States following a disputed election, settled by the Compromise of 1877.

extending the vote to black males. The Freedmen's Bureau was authorized to oversee the implementation of the new laws and ensure that the rights of African Americans were protected. In 1868 most of southern states revised their constitutions to include, among other rights, the franchise (the vote) for blacks. They eliminated the earlier legislatures' Black Codes, which restricted or denied the postwar civil rights of the newly freed African Americans and controlled a broad range of personal freedoms, including employment, education, housing, and the right to move about freely after dark. In the fall elections Republican-dominated legislatures comprising a loose coalition of African Americans and whites emerged. The whites, if from the North, were called carpetbaggers, and if from the South they were labeled scalawags by their Democratic opposition. In due course they enacted major civil rights programs in their states, including universal public education and revisions to the judicial system that included placing blacks on trial juries.

Beginning in 1870, Congress passed the Enforcement Acts, a series of laws that protected black voting rights, office holding, and jury service and (in 1871) outlawed the Ku Klux Klan, which had waged a campaign of violence and death against African Americans in the rural South. (Although the Klan disbanded in 1872—to be revived in 1915—white violence in the form of lynchings continued against blacks through the remainder of the nineteenth century and into the next.) The Radical Republicans passed the Civil Rights Act of 1875, prohibiting discrimination in hotels, trains, and other public spaces. By then, there was a growing movement among southern whites opposed to racial equality that sought to restore southern white rule in the old Confederacy. Known as the "Redeemers," they enjoyed a major success with the election of Wade Hampton, a former Confederate general dedicated to white supremacy, to the governorship of South Carolina in 1876. Another victory came with the formal end of Reconstruction starting in April 1877 with the withdrawal of federal troops from South Carolina and Louisiana, fulfilling the terms of the Compromise of 1877 that settled the disputed presidential election of 1876. In that election the winner of the popular vote, Samuel J. Tilden, a Democrat, fell one vote short of a majority in the Electoral College because of confusing ballot counts from three southern states. After days of wrangling, the Democrats in Congress (most of them southerners) agreed to make the Republican Rutherford B. Hayes president. In return, Hayes promised to restore civilian rule in the two states still under military control. Shortly after his swearing-in, Hayes ordered all remaining federal troops out of the South.

During the next two decades, the largely Democratic Redeemers replaced the biracial Republican governments throughout the South and gradually stripped away the hard-won rights of African Americans. In consequence, Jim Crow laws, which in time denied blacks access to transportation, housing, employment, recreation, and education, created a racially segregated society that lasted until the middle of the next century. The laws were given legal sanction by the U.S.

Supreme Court in 1883 when it declared the Civil Rights Act of 1875 unconstitutional on the ground that Congress did not have the power to regulate the conduct and transactions of individuals. In 1896 the Court gave racial segregation constitutional standing in *Plessy v. Ferguson*.

The final assault by southern whites on African American empowerment began with the Mississippi Plan in 1890. Developed in the state's constitutional convention, the plan was manifested in a "purity" clause that expressly stated in the constitution that "blacks must no longer be allowed to vote." The means of enforcement (in order to circumvent the Fifteenth Amendment) was to apply a property requirement and a poll tax or a literacy test or both as a basis for voting. The literacy test over time evolved into an "understanding" test, in which the would-be voter would be required to interpret a passage from the state's constitution. The Mississippi Plan spread through the South and by 1910 had been adopted in seven states. Its constitutionality was affirmed by the Supreme Court in 1898 in *Williams v. Mississippi*. That same year the Louisiana legislature provided the last refinement to eliminating the black vote by adding a grandfather clause to the state constitution specifically exempting from the property, poll tax, and literacy tests "any individuals whose fathers or grandfathers were legally entitled to vote prior to January 1, 1867." No African American, of course, could meet that requirement. With variations in the date, the clause was soon added to other state constitutions in the South.

Most of these limitations on African Americans were in place in North Carolina in time for the fall election in 1900. Added to them were the internal political conflicts that divided the Democratic majority in the state from the once-dominant Republicans. Examining the possibility of his winning a third term in Congress and well aware of the defeats he had met in the House—his antilynching bill had died in the Judiciary Committee—George White decided not to seek reelection.

About the Author

George Henry White was born on December 18, 1852, in Rosindale, North Carolina, to Wiley F. White, a free African American farmer, and his wife, Mary, a slave. (Under North Carolina law George White was free at birth because of his father's status.) Wiley White could read and write and apparently passed those skills on to his son, who at the end of the Civil War attended black public schools in nearby Columbus county. In 1873 he entered Howard University in Washington, D.C., earning a normal school (teaching) certificate in 1877. White qualified for the North Carolina bar in 1879 and practiced law while serving as the principal of several public schools, including the New Bern normal school for training black teachers. He gradually assumed leadership roles in the communities where he taught and became in time a respected public official.

White entered politics in 1880 when he was elected as a Republican to the first of two terms in the lower house of

Time Line

1880
- **November**
  At age twenty-eight, White is elected to the North Carolina General Assembly—his first political office.

1890
- **August 12**
  The Mississippi constitutional convention systematically disenfranchises African Americans by imposing a poll tax requirement and literacy tests for voters.

1896
- **May 18**
  In *Plessy v. Ferguson* the Supreme Court rules that segregation by race is constitutional.

1897
- **March 15**
  White takes his seat as a Republican in the Fifty-fifth Congress of the United States.

1898
- **May 12**
  Louisiana amends its state constitution with a grandfather clause that effectively limits the franchise to white males having the vote prior to January 1, 1867, and their descendants, a provision adopted by six other southern states by 1910.

- **August 12**
  In *Williams v. Mississippi* the Supreme Court upholds the constitutionality of the Mississippi Plan's poll taxes and literacy tests for voters.

1899
- **March 4**
  White begins his second term as the only African American in the Fifty-sixth Congress of the United States.

1900
- **August**
  North Carolina voters approve by a wide margin a constitution that "grandfathers" illiterate whites but effectively bars all African Americans from voting.

Time Line

1901
- **January 29** White delivers his Farewell Address to Congress.

1928
- **November 6** Oscar Stanton De Priest, Republican from Illinois, is the first African American elected to serve in the U.S. House of Representatives in the twentieth century.

1964
- **January 24** The Twenty-fourth Amendment to the U.S. Constitution prohibits the use of poll taxes in national elections.

1965
- **August 6** The Voting Rights Act enforces the Fifteenth Amendment and outlaws literary tests as a prerequisite for voting.

1966
- **March 24** In *Harper v. Virginia State Board of Elections*, the U.S. Supreme Court declares the use of a poll tax in state and local elections is unconstitutional.

2009
- **September 26** President Barack Obama invokes George White's Farewell Address during brief remarks delivered at the Congressional Black Caucus Foundation's annual Phoenix Awards Dinner in Washington, D.C.

---

the North Carolina General Assembly. As a member of the legislature's Education Committee, he proposed improvements in teacher training, mandatory schooling for the young, and increased funding for white and black public schools. He took on important duties in the county Republican Party, served in the upper house of the General Assembly, and was a delegate to several Republican National Conventions. In 1886, White was elected to the prestigious and politically powerful position of solicitor (public prosecutor) for the Second Judicial District, thereby setting the stage for his entrance onto the national scene. Possessing a shrewd political mind, he bided his time for a decade, building public support in the predominantly African American "Black Second" congressional district, which elected him to the House of Representatives in 1896—the lone African American in the Fifty-fifth Congress but a part of the Republican majority brought into office with the winning Republican presidential candidate, William McKinley.

White was assigned to the House Agriculture Committee. He supported most Republican-backed foreign policy measures. His major focus, however, during his four years in Congress was on civil rights for African Americans. He was unsuccessful in both terms in securing federal action against the southern states' continuing disenfranchisement of black voters. Reelected to the House in 1898, White continued on the Agriculture Committee and served as well on the District of Columbia Committee, which oversaw Washington's municipal government. In his second term he repeatedly sought antilynching legislation that would make mob violence a potential capital offense, but found little support from either the president or his fellow Republicans.

Although White considered himself a national spokesperson for African Americans (and the black newspapers seemed to agree), his positions were increasingly viewed as too radical by his House colleagues and by Republicans in his home district, where changes in the election law in his second term denied the ballot to many of his black supporters. In 1900 he made it known he would not run for reelection. In interviews with northern newspapers, he said that he could not live in North Carolina and be treated as a man, and he urged his black constituents to emigrate to the North or to the West in search of a better life.

Following his dramatic and powerful Farewell Address and his retirement from Congress in March 1901, White opened a successful private law practice in Washington, D.C., moving his office to Philadelphia four years later. As an entrepreneur, he developed Whitesboro, a town for African Americans on the New Jersey shore at Cape May, and established the People's Savings Bank in Philadelphia to provide banking services, including home and business loans, to the city's African Americans. In the summer of 1917, after the People's Savings Bank became insolvent and closed its doors, White was appointed assistant city solicitor, his first public position since his years in Congress. He died in his sleep on December 28, 1918, ten days after his sixty-sixth birthday.

Explanation and Analysis of the Document

The document reproduced here is the speech George H. White delivered on the floor of the U.S. House of Representatives on January 29, 1901, now known as his Farewell Address. The topic before the House that day was the annual appropriation bill of the House Agriculture Committee, a bill that included the continuation of a free seed program to the nation's farmers and payment of the salaries of scientists and other experts in the Department of Agriculture. Given the complexity and importance of the bill (H.R. 13801), the House was sitting as a Committee of the Whole, which means, in parliamentary terms, that the usual rules of procedure for legislative action are suspended, allowing any member of the House, who chooses to attend, to speak freely. A chairman chosen from the majority presides (rather than the speaker), and any vote is by a simple majority (rather than a specified quorum). The House in regular session may vote to overturn any decisions made in this way.

Because the House was meeting on January 29, 1901, as a Committee of the Whole, White was free to ignore H.R. 13801 and turn, if he wished, to more personal concerns. In his opening remarks, which are not included here, White acknowledged the importance of the bill's contents and then boldly seized the opportunity to deliver a strong defense of his African American constituents and offer a profoundly moving farewell to the Congress he has faithfully served for four years.

White's eloquent opening sentences in paragraph 1 are among the best-known lines in his address. They provide a powerful introduction to the reasons he is ignoring the bill before the House and introduce his indictment of his colleagues, who have consistently slandered his race by linking "the unfortunate few" who commit crimes or lead less than exemplary lives to the majority of hard-working, responsible African Americans. Their calumnies intensified during the last weeks of the Fifty-sixth Congress as the House took up the reapportionment bill, which would increase the size of the House in 1903 by twenty-nine seats, bringing the chamber's total membership to 386 from 357. The debate gave White an opportunity to urge Congress to overturn the disenfranchisement provisions that several southern states had added to their constitutions or their election laws, thereby removing African Americans from the voting roles. White points out that because of parliamentary rulings he was denied the opportunity during the debate to respond to his white southern colleagues' demeaning statements.

White in paragraph 2 singles out his fellow representative from North Carolina, William W. Kitchin, a Democrat and a long-time political rival, as a particular scourge of African Americans, whose right to vote has been stripped away through a state constitutional amendment in August 1900. White deplores the unfairness of the amendment, which permits illiterate white men to vote if they register before 1908 and their ancestors were qualified to vote in 1867 or earlier, a qualification that is denied to African Americans, who are subject to a literacy test (including an interpretation of the state constitution) and a poll tax.

In paragraphs 3 and 4, White announces that he will leave the House in the next five weeks. He explains that William Kitchin's younger brother, Claude, would succeed him as a result of questionable vote counts. White carefully avoids charging fraud and says only that the returns went unchallenged in North Carolina's general election in August 1900.

In paragraphs 6 through 10 White directs his audience's attention to Stanyarne Wilson, a Democrat from South Carolina, who earlier took a leading role in the debate on reapportionment and disenfranchisement in the southern states. An example of White's biting wit is in paragraph 6, where he neatly insults his colleague without openly breaking the House rule that requires the chamber's members to treat each other with courtesy and respect. The veiled insult continues in paragraph 7 as White seems to accept Wilson's assertions that the Reconstruction government in South Carolina was corrupt and ineffective because of its Republican, biracial composition. What White is saying, however, is that if corruption existed (he concedes there may have been a few ignorant and gullible blacks in the legislature), it was not due to the African Americans in the legislature but to the work of unscrupulous whites from the North (carpetbaggers) who exploited the unstable institutions of the postwar South and then retreated to their northern homes or, White says in a witty aside, remained in the South and became Democrats.

White continues his assault on Wilson's argument in paragraph 8. He suggests that Wilson is probably correct in saying that southern whites are working to lift southern blacks and that he is grateful, but he quickly points out that it is black laborers who make it possible for their white "friends" to contribute the "stinty [limited or meager] pittance" that supports black education. White adds in paragraph 9 that for all the self-congratulation implicit in the Democrats' asserting that they are aiding African Americans to help themselves, statistics show that far greater sums are spent per capita on white schools than on black schools in South Carolina.

As he continues to rebut Wilson in paragraph 10, White's initial reference to "the musty records of 1868" is to the records of the several state constitutional conventions that year called to organize new governments during Reconstruction. Most of those constitutions provided universal education, suffrage to all males over twenty-one, and the right to hold public office regardless of race. The opponents of such measures then and in subsequent years argued that African Americans were unprepared for such responsibilities. In their view, most blacks were and continued to be ignorant, illiterate, or indolent, a caricature White rejects out of hand. He pointedly suggests that the condition of the freed slaves and of African Americans generally has changed significantly in the thirty-two years since the state constitutions were written. In paragraphs 10 and 11, he catalogs the advances that the race, despite obstacles imposed by the white world, have achieved in every area of life. It should be noted that the property values and other monetary references are in line with American averages in the nineteenth century.

Paragraphs 12 and 13 provide a stirring challenge to Congress and to white America to understand who African Americans are by moving past skin color and race to see them as human beings like themselves. White's language and his argument here are crystal clear: African Americans want what all Americans want: freedom, equality, family, and work. (The federation of labor White refers to in the last line of paragraph 12 is the recently organized American Federation of Labor, which was a cooperative composed of many independent trades, some of them identified as black or colored unions of, say, carpenters or plumbers, that united in the federation to seek common wages, rights, and

Governor Wade Hampton (Library of Congress)

protections.) Paragraph 13 carries White's defense of his people into the social and civic world, arguing that African Americans are denied full participation there not because of their own indifference but rather because of white prejudice and race hatred.

Paragraph 14 is White's eloquent valedictory. His first sentence is a bold prediction that references the phoenix, the fabulous bird of ancient myth that is eternally renewed through death. The second offers in a dozen or so words his brilliant refutation of white America's hate-filled stereotypes of African Americans. Together they make up the most quoted passage from the speech in the twentieth century and, to many African Americans, the most memorable.

The anecdote that White relates in paragraphs 15 and 16—a transition to his concluding remark—never happened. The English philosopher Sir Francis Bacon's bribery trial took place in 1621; he was found guilty, removed from office as attorney general, and fined. The English courtier and navigator Sir Walter Raleigh was executed in 1618 for disobeying King James I's orders not to invade Spanish territory in North America. In his first trial for treason in 1603, Raleigh, defending himself, unsuccessfully pleaded with the court to have his accusers brought to face him because "I am here for my life!"

White's speech comes full circle in paragraph 17 in a single-sentence summary of his argument, echoing the opening lines and reiterating his term-long struggle to get the House to respond to both the white supremacy violence and the disenfranchisement of African Americans in the southern states.

Audience

There were 357 congressmen from forty-five states in the Fifty-sixth Congress. The division of the House was 187 Republicans, 161 Democrats, 5 Populists, and 4 members of splinter parties. Since the measure before the House of Representatives was the annual agricultural appropriation bill—under the existing rules the House was sitting as a Committee of the Whole, and members could choose not to attend—it is likely that not all of the members were present. An unknown number of spectators were in the galleries, but because White was known to be speaking that day, a goodly number of African Americans were probably present. (A gifted and forceful speaker, White had drawn such an audience on past occasions.)

White's full speech was printed twice in 1901: in the *Congressional Record* (56th Congress, 2nd session, volume 34, part 2) and as a stand-alone fourteen-page booklet entitled *Defense of the Negro Race—Charges Answered. Speech of Hon. George H. White, of North Carolina, in the House of Representatives, January 29, 1901*. According to White's biographer, Benjamin H. Jutesen, portions of the Farewell Address were reprinted in such contemporary African American newspapers as the Washington, D.C. *Colored American*, the *Cleveland Gazette*, and the *New York Age*, the most widely read black paper in the country. The address later appeared in several anthologies of black writing, giving it wide circulation well into the twentieth century. Its closing words—particularly "Phoenix-like he will rise up some day and come again"—resonated among African Americans for the next fifty years.

Impact

Because White had already forgone the 1900 election and thus given up his seat in the House, his Farewell Address had little impact on Congress—not that day or in the years following. His words did nothing to lessen the institutional racism that he and his African American predecessors had experienced in the House and Senate, and Congress failed to halt the southern states' violations of the Fifteenth Amendment that denied the vote to generations of African Americans until the 1960s. As for White himself, the southern Democrats were happy to be rid of him, as were many Republicans, who had been uncomfortable with the North Carolinian's outspoken and unapologetic ways. Congressmen of both parties from the North and West well into the twentieth century remained indifferent to the second-class status of African Americans, 90 percent of whom lived in the South in 1901.

White continued in the House without incident for another month and quietly withdrew into his Washington home on March 3, 1901, in advance of the swearing-in of his successor from North Carolina, a white man who had been the beneficiary of the state's changed voting standards that barred most African Americans from voting. The next day, at noon on March 4, both houses of the North Carolina legislature marked the official end of White's term in

Essential Quotes

> "You may tie us and then taunt us for a lack of bravery, but one day we will break the bonds."
>
> (Paragraph 11)

> "This, Mr. Chairman, is perhaps the negroes' temporary farewell to the American Congress; but let me say, Phoenix-like he will rise up some day and come again."
>
> (Paragraph 14)

> "I am pleading for the life, the liberty, the future happiness, and manhood suffrage for one-eighth of the entire population of the United States."
>
> (Paragraph 17)

office by passing resolutions of thanksgiving that heralded a new era in which no black man would be serving in the U.S. Congress. The principal newspaper in the state hailed the departure of its "insolent negro" as a blessing not only to the state but to the nation as well.

For nearly three decades there were no African Americans in Congress until, as a consequence of the Great Migration of thousands of black men and women out of the South to the North, Oscar Stanton De Priest, a Republican from the South Side of Chicago, entered the Seventy-first Congress in March 1929—the first African American elected to the House of Representatives in the twentieth century. Through the following years the number of black men and women in Congress increased, especially in the years after 1950. In the 1960s, as a result of peaceful demonstrations by black students and others throughout the South, the barriers that had prevented African Americans from voting (and that had discouraged George White from seeking reelection in 1890) were removed. In January 1964 the Twenty-fourth Amendment to the U.S. Constitution barred the use of a poll tax as a prerequisite to voting in national elections. The use of a poll tax in state and local elections was declared unconstitutional by the U.S. Supreme Court in March 1966 in *Harper v. Virginia State Board of Elections*. President Lyndon Johnson signed the historic Voting Rights Act in August 1965, outlawing the use of literacy tests in voter registration and providing the federal government with powers to enforce the Fifteenth Amendment.

Additional milestones are worth noting: In November 1968 Edward W. Brooke, a Republican from Massachusetts, was elected to the Ninetieth Congress and served two terms in the U.S. Senate—the first African American elected to that chamber in eighty-five years. And in 1973 Andrew Young, Democrat of Georgia, and Barbara Jordan, Democrat of Texas, entered the Ninety-third Congress as the first African Americans from the Deep South to be elected to the House since White bid the chamber farewell in 1901. Since 1870 a total of 119 African Americans have been elected to the House, six to the Senate. When the 111th Congress convened in January 2009, there were forty-one African Americans in the House of Representatives and one in the Senate, and Barack Obama was president of the United States. Nine months later, speaking at the Congressional Black Caucus Foundation's annual Phoenix Awards Dinner in Washington, D.C., President Obama saluted his audience, telling them that they were the fulfillment of White's prophecy that "Phoenix-like," African American men and women would "rise up and come again" to serve the nation in the national government.

See also Thirteenth Amendment to the U.S. Constitution (1865); Fourteenth Amendment to the U.S. Constitution (1868); Fifteenth Amendment to the U.S. Constitution (1870); Civil Rights Cases (1883); *Plessy v. Ferguson* (1896).

Further Reading

- **Articles**

"Southern Negro's Plaint." *New York Times*, August 26, 1900.

- **Books**

Anderson, Eric. *Race and Politics in North Carolina, 1872–1901: The Black Second*. Baton Rouge: Louisiana State University Press, 1981.

Dray, Philip. *Capitol Men: The Epic Story of Reconstruction through the Lives of Black Congressmen*. Boston: Houghton Mifflin, 2008.

Hahn, Steven. *A Nation Under Our Feet: Black Political Struggles in the Rural South, from Slavery to the Great Migration*. Cambridge, Mass.: Belknap Press of Harvard University Press, 2003.

Jutesen, Benjamin R. *George Henry White: An Even Chance in the Race of Life*. Baton Rouge: Louisiana State University Press, 2001.

White, George Henry. *In His Own Words: The Writings, Speeches, and Letters of George Henry White*, ed. Benjamin R. Jutesen. Lincoln, Nebr.: iUniverse, Inc., 2004.

■ Web Sites

"Black Americans in Congress." Web site of the Office of the Clerk of the U.S. House of Representatives.
http://baic.house.gov/.

"Defense of the Negro Race—Charges Answered." Documenting the American South Web site.
http://docsouth.unc.edu/nc/whitegh/whitegh.html.

"North Carolina History Project." John Locke Foundation Web site.
http://www.northcarolinahistory.org/.

—Allan L. Damon

Questions for Further Study

1. In the years after the Civil War, a number of African Americans served in the U.S. Senate and House of Representatives. Why did their numbers dwindle until White was the last one before the 1960s?

2. Define "Radical Republicans." In what sense were they "radical"? What impact did they have on the Reconstruction period following the Civil War?

3. Trace the history of black voting rights in the post–Civil War decades. What specific events led to White's decision not to run again in North Carolina?

4. W. E. B. Du Bois's *The Souls of Black Folk* appeared just two years after White's address. Compare the two documents. To what extent do both make similar arguments and express similar hopes?

5. What were "carpetbaggers"? What role did they play in the political landscape of the post–Civil War South?

George H. White's Farewell Address to Congress

I want to enter a plea for the colored man, the colored woman, the colored boy, and the colored girl of this country. I would not thus digress from the question at issue and detain the House in a discussion of the interests of this particular people at this time but for the constant and the persistent efforts of certain gentlemen upon this floor to mold and rivet public sentiment against us as a people and to lose no opportunity to hold up the unfortunate few who commit crimes and depredations and lead lives of infamy and shame, as other races do, as fair specimens of representatives of the entire colored race. And at no time, perhaps, during the Fifty-sixth Congress were these charges and countercharges, containing, as they do, slanderous statements, more persistently magnified and pressed upon the attention of the nation than during the consideration of the recent reapportionment bill, which is now a law. As stated some days ago on this floor by me, I then sought diligently to obtain an opportunity to answer some of the statements made by gentlemen from different States, but the privilege was denied me; and I therefore must embrace this opportunity to say, out of season, perhaps, that which I was not permitted to say in season.

In the catalogue of members of Congress in this House perhaps none have been more persistent in their determination to bring the black man into disrepute and, with a labored effort, to show that he was unworthy of the right of citizenship than my colleague from North Carolina, Mr. Kitchin. During the first session of this Congress, while the Constitutional amendment was pending in North Carolina, he labored long and hard to show that the white race was at all times and under all circumstances superior to the Negro by inheritance if not otherwise, and the excuse for his party supporting that amendment, which has since been adopted, was that an illiterate Negro was unfit to participate in making the laws of a sovereign State and the administration and execution of them; but an illiterate white man living by his side, with no more or perhaps not as much property, with no more exalted character, no higher thoughts of civilization, no more knowledge of the handicraft of government, had by birth, because he was white, inherited some peculiar qualification, clear, I presume, only in the mind of the gentleman who endeavored to impress it upon others, that entitled him to vote, though he knew nothing whatever of letters. It is true, in my opinion, that men brood over things at times which they would have exist until they fool themselves and actually, sometimes honestly, believe that such things do exist....

I might state as a further general fact that the Democrats of North Carolina got possession of the state and local government since my last election in 1898, and that I bid adieu to these historic walls on the 4th day of next March, and that the brother of Mr. Kitchin will succeed me. Comment is unnecessary. In the town where this young gentleman was born, at the general election last August for ... state and county officers, Scotland Neck had a registered white vote of 395, most of whom of course were Democrats, and a registered colored vote of 534, virtually if not all of whom were Republicans, and so voted. When the count was announced, however, there were 831 Democrats to 75 Republicans; but in the town of Halifax, same county, the result was much more pronounced.

In that town the registered Republican vote was 345, and the total registered vote of the township was 539, but when the count was announced it stood 990 Democrats to 41 Republicans, or 492 more Democratic votes counted than were registered votes in the township. Comment here is unnecessary....

It would be unfair, however, for me to leave the inference upon the minds of those who hear me that all of the white people of the State of North Carolina hold views with Mr. Kitchin and think as he does. Thank God there are many noble exceptions to the example he sets, that, too, in the Democratic party; men who have never been afraid that one uneducated, poor, depressed Negro could put to flight and chase into degradation two educated, wealthy, thrifty white men. There never has been, nor ever will be, any Negro domination in that state, and no one knows it any better than the Democratic party. It is a convenient howl, however, often resorted to in order to consummate a diabolical purpose by scaring the weak and gullible whites into support of measures and men suitable to the demagogue and the ambitious office seeker, whose crave for office overshadows and puts to flight all other considerations, fair or unfair....

Document Text

I trust I will be pardoned for making a passing reference to one more gentleman — Mr. Wilson of South Carolina—who, in the early part of this month, made a speech, some parts of which did great credit to him, showing, as it did, capacity for collating, arranging, and advancing thoughts of others and of making a pretty strong argument out of a very poor case.

If he had stopped there, while not agreeing with him, many of us would have been forced to admit that he had done well. But his purpose was incomplete until he dragged in the reconstruction days and held up to scorn and ridicule the few ignorant, gullible, and perhaps purchasable negroes who served in the State legislature of South Carolina over thirty years ago. Not a word did he say about the unscrupulous white men, in the main bummers who followed in the wake of the Federal Army and settled themselves in the Southern States, and preyed upon the ignorant and unskilled minds of the colored people, looted the States of their wealth, brought into lowest disrepute the ignorant colored people, then hied away to their Northern homes for ease and comfort the balance of their lives, or joined the Democratic party to obtain social recognition, and have greatly aided in depressing and further degrading those whom they had used as easy tools to accomplish a diabolical purpose.

These few ignorant men who chanced at that time to hold office are given as a reason why the black man should not be permitted to participate in the affairs of the government which he is forced to pay taxes to support. He insists that they, the Southern whites, are the black man's best friend, and that they are taking him by the hand and trying to lift him up; that they are educating him. For all that he and all Southern people have done in this regard, I wish in behalf of the colored people of the South to extend our thanks. We are not ungrateful to friends, but feel that our toil has made our friends able to contribute the stinty pittance which we have received at their hands.

I read in a Democratic paper a few days ago, the Washington Times, an extract taken from a South Carolina paper, which was intended to exhibit the eagerness with which the Negro is grasping every opportunity for educating himself. The clipping showed that the money for each white child in the State ranged from three to five times as much per capita as was given to each colored child. This is helping us some, but not to the extent that one would infer from the gentleman's speech.

If the gentleman to whom I have referred will pardon me, I would like to advance the statement that the musty records of 1868, filed away in the archives of Southern capitols, as to what the Negro was thirty-two years ago, is not a proper standard by which the Negro living on the threshold of the twentieth century should be measured. Since that time we have reduced the illiteracy of the race at least 45 percent. We have written and published nearly 500 books. We have nearly 800 newspapers, three of which are dailies. We have now in practice over 2,000 lawyers, and a corresponding number of doctors. We have accumulated over $12,000,000 worth of school property and about $40,000,000 worth of church property. We have about 140,000 farms and homes, valued in the neighborhood of $750,000,000, and personal property valued about $170,000,000. We have raised about $11,000,000 for educational purposes, and the property per-capita for every colored man, woman and child in the United States is estimated at $75.

We are operating successfully several banks, commercial enterprises among our people in the South land, including one silk mill and one cotton factory. We have 32,000 teachers in the schools of the country; we have built, with the aid of our friends, about 20,000 churches, and support 7 colleges, 17 academies, 50 high schools, 5 law schools, 5 medical schools and 25 theological seminaries. We have over 600,000 acres of land in the South alone. The cotton produced, mainly by black labor, has increased from 4,669,770 bales in 1860 to 11,235,000 in 1899. All this was done under the most adverse circumstances. We have done it in the face of lynching, burning at the stake, with the humiliation of "Jim Crow" laws, the disfranchisement of our male citizens, slander and degradation of our women, with the factories closed against us, no Negro permitted to be conductor on the railway cars, whether run through the streets of our cities or across the prairies of our great country, no Negro permitted to run as engineer on a locomotive, most of the mines closed against us. Labor unions—carpenters, painters, brick masons, machinists, hackmen and those supplying nearly every conceivable avocation for livelihood—have banded themselves together to better their condition, but, with few exceptions, the black face has been left out. The Negroes are seldom employed in our mercantile stores. At this we do not wonder. Some day we hope to have them employed in our own stores. With all these odds against us, we are forging our way ahead, slowly, perhaps, but surely, You may tie us and then taunt us for a lack of bravery, but one day we will break the bonds. You may use our labor for two and a half centuries and then taunt us for our

Document Text

poverty, but let me remind you we will not always remain poor! You may withhold even the knowledge of how to read God's word and learn the way from earth to glory and then taunt us for our ignorance, but we would remind you that there is plenty of room at the top, and we are climbing....

Mr. Chairman, before concluding my remarks I want to submit a brief recipe for the solution of the so-called "American Negro problem." He asks no special favors, but simply demands that he be given the same chance for existence, for earning a livelihood, for raising himself in the scales of manhood and womanhood, that are accorded to kindred nationalities. Treat him as a man; go into his home and learn of his social conditions; learn of his cares, his troubles, and his hopes for the future; gain his confidence; open the doors of industry to him; let the word "Negro," "colored," and "black" be stricken from all the organizations enumerated in the federation of labor.

Help him to overcome his weaknesses, punish the crime-committing class by the courts of the land, measure the standard of the race by its best material, cease to mold prejudicial and unjust public sentiment against him, and ... he will learn to support ... and join in with that political party, that institution, whether secular or religious, in every community where he lives, which is destined to do the greatest good for the greatest number. Obliterate race hatred, party prejudice, and help us to achieve nobler ends, greater results and become satisfactory citizens to our brother in white.

This, Mr. Chairman, is perhaps the negroes' temporary farewell to the American Congress; but let me say, Phoenix-like he will rise up some day and come again. These parting words are in behalf of an outraged, heart-broken, bruised, and bleeding, but God-fearing people, faithful, industrious, loyal people—rising people, full of potential force.

Mr. Chairman, in the trial of Lord Bacon, when the court disturbed the counsel for the defendant, Sir Walter Raleigh raised himself up to his full height and, addressing the court, said:

Sir, I am pleading for the life of a human being.

The only apology that I have to make for the earnestness with which I have spoken is that I am pleading for the life, the liberty, the future happiness, and manhood suffrage for one-eighth of the entire population of the United States.

Glossary

bummers	foragers or marauders during the Civil War
Fifty-sixth Congress	the congressional term from 1899 to 1901, following the practice of numbering two-year congressional terms
hackmen	the drivers of hacks, or cabs
Jim Crow	the informal term used to designate laws and social customs that deprived African Americans of their liberties and rights
Lord Bacon	Francis Bacon, seventeenth-century scientist, jurist, statesman, and philosopher, tried by Parliament for corruption
Mr. Kitchin	William W. Kitchin, White's political rival, whose younger brother, Claude, would succeed White in office
Mr. Wilson	Stanyarne Wilson, a U.S. congressional representative from South Carolina
musty records of 1868	the records of the state constitutional conventions during Reconstruction
Phoenix	a legendary Arabian bird that was said to burn itself to death and then rise from the ashes
Sir Walter Raleigh	an English aristocrat and courtier of the late sixteenth and early seventeenth centuries who was a favorite of Queen Elizabeth I

W. E. B. Du Bois (Library of Congress)

W. E. B. Du Bois: *The Souls of Black Folk*

1903

"[Booker T.] Washington represents in Negro thought the old attitude of adjustment and submission."

Overview

In 1903, W. E. B. Du Bois published the classic book for which he is most remembered, *The Souls of Black Folk: Essays and Sketches*. A groundbreaking study of the African American community from a sociological perspective, the book outlines for both black and white readers the position of African Americans at the turn of the twentieth century. *The Souls of Black Folk* was in large part a repudiation of the views of Booker T. Washington, the black leader who urged other blacks to pursue economic equality before trying to gain political and social equality. Du Bois, in contrast, urged African Americans to develop a "black consciousness" based on an appreciation of their own unique art, culture, religious views, and history and to continue to pursue civil rights. In Chapter III, "Of Mr. Booker T. Washington and Others," Du Bois takes on the rift between Washington's accommodationist views and a more assertive, militant view of African American aspirations. *The Souls of Black Folk* was a key early doctrine of the Harlem Renaissance, the flowering of black culture and art that centered on the Harlem district of Manhattan in New York City, and it remains a central document in the seismic shift of African American consciousness at the start of the twentieth century.

Context

Du Bois came of age during the Reconstruction era that followed the Civil War, "Reconstruction" referring to the political process of reintegrating the rebellious Confederate states into the Union. Confederate soldiers returning to ruined homes found themselves in tenuous financial and political circumstances. The defeated South entered a period of economic chaos. In the midst of this postwar turmoil, the U.S. Congress, led by the Radical Republicans (the loose faction of the Republican Party that before the war opposed slavery and after the war defended the rights of African Americans and wanted to impose harsh terms on the rebellious South), enacted the Thirteenth Amendment, which abolished slavery and other forms of involuntary servitude throughout the United States.

What followed was a flood of legislation and constitutional amendments designed to reshape the racial landscape of the United States. The Civil Rights Act of 1866 gave blacks the right to buy and sell property and to make and enforce contracts to the same extent as white citizens. The Fourteenth Amendment, which was ratified in 1868, affirmed the citizenship rights of former slaves and guaranteed "due process" and "equal protection" to all citizens under the law. The four Reconstruction Acts (1867–1868) created military districts in the South to ensure order during the states' return to the Union, required congressional approval for new state constitutions (a requirement for Confederate states to rejoin the Union), gave voting rights to all men in the former Confederacy, and stipulated that Confederate states had to ratify the Fourteenth Amendment. The Fifteenth Amendment, which took effect in 1870, guaranteed the voting rights of all citizens. The Ku Klux Klan Act of 1871 gave the U.S. president sweeping powers to combat the Klan and similar organizations in the South that were using violence and intimidation to deprive African Americans of their rights and that often directed their violence against white Republicans who supported equal rights for blacks. The Civil Rights Act of 1875 made it unlawful for inns, restaurants, theaters, and other public facilities to deny access to any individual based on race.

The Hayes-Tilden Compromise of 1877 represented the turning point in the fate of black Americans in the South. The most disputed presidential election in American history took place in 1876. After the votes were counted, Democrat Samuel Tilden held a narrow lead in both the popular vote and in the Electoral College over Republican Rutherford B. Hayes, but a number of electoral votes were in dispute. In the Compromise of 1877, Democrats (whose stronghold was in the South) agreed to recognize Hayes as president on the condition that he withdraw federal troops from Florida, South Carolina, and Louisiana, the only three southern states where postwar troops remained. This event marked the end of the Reconstruction era and allowed whites to reassert their dominance using violence, intimidation, and fraud.

Matters worsened in the years that followed. A series of U.S. Supreme Court cases undermined the Fourteenth and Fifteenth Amendments. In the 1876 case *United States v.*

Time Line

1868
- **February 23**
  William Edward Burghardt Du Bois is born in Great Barrington, Massachusetts.

1885
- Du Bois enrolls at Fisk University in Nashville, Tennessee.

1888
- Du Bois enrolls at Harvard University and receives a bachelor's degree in 1890.

1895
- Du Bois receives a PhD in history from Harvard.
- **September 18**
  Booker T. Washington delivers his "Atlanta Compromise" speech at the Atlanta Cotton States and International Exposition.

1897
- Du Bois begins teaching at Atlanta University, where he remains until 1910.

1903
- Du Bois's controversial essay collection *The Souls of Black Folk* is published.

1905
- **July**
  Du Bois cofounds the Niagara Movement.

1910
- Du Bois becomes director of publicity and research and a member of the board of directors of the National Association for the Advancement of Colored People (NAACP); he also founds and edits *The Crisis*, the association's official periodical.

1915
- **November 14**
  Booker T. Washington dies in Tuskegee, Alabama.

1934
- Du Bois resigns from the NAACP and returns to Atlanta University as chair of the Department of Sociology.

Reese, the Court rejected an African American's challenge to a poll tax, holding that the Fifteenth Amendment did not affirmatively assure the right to vote and that the poll tax was racially neutral. *United States v. Cruikshank*, decided the same year, involved an action against a group of whites who used lethal force to break up a political rally that blacks had organized. The Court held that the blacks who brought the case had not established that they were denied any rights based on their color. In the Civil Rights Cases of 1883, which was a consolidation of several cases that presented similar issues, the Court declared that the 1875 Civil Rights Act was unconstitutional. The decision established the "state action" doctrine by holding that Congress did not have the authority to regulate private acts of discrimination. In 1896 segregation was affirmed when the Supreme Court ruled in *Plessy v. Ferguson* that laws requiring segregation in public transportation did not violate the Fourteenth Amendment as long as the separate facilities provided for blacks were equal to those available to whites. Yet another case upheld the outcome of Mississippi's 1890 state constitutional convention, which had the express purpose of disenfranchising black voters. In *Williams v. Mississippi*, the Supreme Court held in 1898 that because Mississippi's voter registration laws were not explicitly discriminatory, they did not violate the Fourteenth Amendment.

In *The Souls of Black Folk*, Du Bois reacted to the rising tide of segregation and racial subordination and established himself as one of the most prominent African American intellectuals and leaders of the early twentieth century. It also set off a heated debate that still reverberates in some circles. A few years before the book was published, the white South found what it believed would be a resolution of the still unsettled question of the status of the black population. The answer to the dilemma came from an unlikely source, a former slave who became perhaps the most powerful person of color in the history of the Republic. The bearer of this solution, Booker T. Washington, spent his childhood in Virginia assisting his family in a series of menial jobs. After he graduated from Hampton Normal and Agricultural Institute (now Hampton University), Washington received an offer to establish a school in rural Alabama. At what became the Tuskegee Institute, Washington developed a program emphasizing industrial education. He trained brick masons, carpenters, and other student artisans who constructed several of Tuskegee's buildings. Women were taught the domestic arts. Tuskegee's program was based on Washington's belief that black students would be served best by training for vocations in the industrial sphere rather than for professions.

In 1895 Washington delivered a historic speech in Atlanta, Georgia, before a large and mainly white audience—the so-called "Atlanta Compromise" speech. Invoking a metaphor that would be seen as the solution for race relations, Washington, in a statement Du Bois quotes in Chapter III of *The Souls of Black Folk*, held out one hand and said, "In all things purely social we can be as separate as the fingers, yet as one hand in all things essential to mutual progress." He then closed his fingers into a fist to buttress his point. The implication of Washington's words was clear: African Americans would be trained to be obedient and reliable workers who would not challenge white supremacy. The speech received national acclaim and made Washington the preeminent leader of black America, particularly among white Americans but among many black Americans as well.

Despite his success, there was much about Washington's philosophy that rankled many African Americans. In addition to preaching accommodation, Washington's speeches included numerous references to the shortcoming of blacks. These comments were often couched in humorous anecdotes that delighted his white audiences but were demeaning to blacks. Washington ridiculed classical education as "sheer folly" because it would not prepare African Americans for practical occupations.

The lines were drawn. Largely in response to Washington's popularity, Du Bois wrote *The Souls of Black Folk*, a collection of incisive essays, several of which had been previously published in the *Atlantic* magazine.

About the Author

William Edward Burghardt Du Bois was born on February 23, 1868, in Great Barrington, Massachusetts, where he was raised by his mother, Mary Silvina Burghardt, whose English roots could be traced back to the American Revolution. She raised her son after his father, Alfred Du Bois, deserted the family when William was two years old. After completing public schooling in Great Barrington, Du Bois enrolled at Fisk University in Nashville, Tennessee, in 1885. He graduated in 1888 and was admitted to Harvard University as a junior.

After earning a bachelor's degree at Harvard, Du Bois remained to pursue graduate studies. He also studied at the University of Berlin and traveled extensively across Europe. He returned to the United States in 1894 and taught briefly at Wilberforce University in Ohio and then at Atlanta University until 1910. Du Bois helped organize the Niagara Movement in 1905 and was one of the founding members of the National Association for the Advancement of Colored People (NAACP), which was established in 1909. He also edited the organization's journal, *The Crisis*, until his departure in 1934.

Du Bois returned to Atlanta University as the head of the sociology department, but in 1944 he rejoined the NAACP as director of publicity and research. His increasing impatience with the lagging advancement of African American rights and ideals, however, alienated his colleagues at the NAACP, and in 1948 he was discharged from his position. During this period Du Bois associated with a number of left-wing organizations. From 1949 to 1955 he was vice chair of the Council on African Affairs, which was cited by the U.S. attorney general as a "subversive" organization. In 1950 he became the chair of the Peace Information Center in New York City. That year, at the age of eighty-two, he ran unsuccessfully for the U.S. Senate as the Progressive Party's candidate.

Time Line

1944 — Du Bois returns to the NAACP as director of publicity and research but is dismissed in 1948.

1950 — Du Bois runs for the U.S. Senate in New York on the Progressive Party ticket.

1951 — Du Bois is indicted, tried, and acquitted on a charge of failing to register as a foreign agent.

1961 — Du Bois becomes a member of the American Communist Party and is invited to Ghana by President Kwame Nkrumah.

1963 — Du Bois becomes a citizen of Ghana and dies there on August 27.

In the 1950s the United States was in the midst of the cold war. Fears of espionage and Communist influence abounded. The infamous McCarthy hearings, led by Wisconsin senator Joseph McCarthy, were held to root out suspected Communists in the government and elsewhere. Du Bois's association with leftist groups made him suspect, and NAACP officials distanced themselves from him. In 1951 Du Bois was indicted and tried on the charge of failing to register as a foreign agent. Although he was acquitted, he remained in the eye of government agencies, and the State Department revoked his passport. Du Bois officially joined the American Communist Party in 1961. That year, the president of Ghana, Kwame Nkrumah, invited him to visit Africa and edit the *Encyclopedia Africana*. Du Bois accepted and later became a citizen of Ghana, where he died on August 27, 1963, at the age of ninety-five.

Explanation and Analysis of the Document

The Souls of Black Folk advances the thesis that "the problem of the Twentieth Century is the problem of the color-line." Du Bois traces what he calls the "double-consciousness" of African Americans, the "sense of always looking at one's self through the eyes of others." The book assesses the progress of blacks, the obstacles that blacks face, and the possibilities for progress in the future. Chapter III, "Of Mr. Booker T. Washington and Others," directly addresses Washington's assimilationist views. The cleavage between Washington and Du Bois is one that still reverberates in American race relations.

◆ **The Ascendancy of Mr. Booker T. Washington**

In the first eight paragraphs of Chapter III, Du Bois outlines the rise of Booker T. Washington to prominence. He points to the growth and industrial development of the United States, what other authors have called the "Gilded Age," when business was expanding and fortunes were being made in the decades following the Civil War. He notes that in the antebellum years, efforts to provide blacks with industrial training had taken place under the auspices of organizations such as the American Missionary Association and individuals such as William G. Price, an African American educator whose career mirrored that of Washington. Du Bois refers to these efforts at industrial education as a "by-path" that Washington was able to turn into a "Way of Life." Du Bois continues by noting that Washington's program won applause in the South and admiration in the North, though not necessarily among blacks.

Du Bois then goes into more detail about Washington and his program. He refers to Washington's efforts in creating Tuskegee Institute and cites the "Atlanta Compromise" speech of 1895, where Washington advocated (to a largely white audience) that blacks abandon the quest for social and political equality until they have achieved economic equality. Many blacks saw the speech as a surrender, but many whites applauded it, making Washington—in the words of Du Bois—the "most distinguished Southerner since Jefferson Davis," the president of the Confederate States of America during the Civil War. In paragraph 4, Du Bois begins his critique of Washington by suggesting that he had "grasped the spirit of the age which was dominating the North" and that he had learned the speech of "triumphant commercialism," where manual skills were more important than something as presumably esoteric as French grammar. In paragraph 5, Du Bois ironically refers to Washington as a "successful man" in gathering a "cult" of followers, but he also indicates that the time has come to point out Washington's mistakes and shortcomings.

Du Bois hints at the nature of the criticism that Washington has encountered. In his position, Washington has had to "walk warily" to avoid offending his patrons and the South in general. Du Bois notes that at the National Peace Jubilee at the end of the Spanish-American War, Washington alluded to racial prejudice, and he appears to have done so at a White House dinner he had with President Theodore Roosevelt in 1901—a highly publicized and controversial event. These events attracted some criticism, but Washington has generally managed adroitly to avoid giving offense, says Du Bois. In paragraph 7, Du Bois asserts that Washington has encountered opposition, some of it bitter, among his own people, particularly "educated and thoughtful colored men." While these men might admire Washington's honest efforts to do something positive, they feel "deep regret, sorrow, and apprehension" because of the popularity of Washington's views. Paragraph 8 notes, however, that people are hesitant to criticize Washington openly. This, says Du Bois, is "dangerous," and he raises the question of whether African Americans are submitting to a leader who has been imposed on them by external pressure.

◆ **The History of the American Black Leadership**

Paragraph 9 begins to examine the history of leadership in the African American community. Du Bois observes that these leaders emerge from the environment in which the people lived, and when that environment consists of "sticks and stones and beasts," people will oppose it. Thus, in paragraph 10, he discusses black leadership before 1750. He makes reference to the "Maroons," the name given to escaped slaves in Haiti and throughout the Caribbean who formed gangs that lived in the forests. These gangs, which were generally small but sometimes grew to thousands of men, repeatedly attacked French plantations. "Danish blacks" refers to a group of slaves who, in 1723, gained control of Saint John in the Virgin Islands (then the Danish West Indies) for six months. Cato of Stono is a reference to the Stono Rebellion of 1739 (also called Cato's Rebellion), a slave revolt in South Carolina. By the end of the century, however, it was thought that "kindlier relations" would replace rebellion, as exemplified in the poetry of "Phyllis" (that is, Phillis Wheatley) and the heroism of blacks such as Crispus Attucks, Peter Salem, and Salem Poor during the Revolutionary War. James Durham was the first African American doctor in the colonies, and Benjamin Banneker was an accomplished scientist, mathematician, and surveyor who helped lay out Washington, D.C. "Cuffes" is a reference to Paul Cuffe and his followers, who wanted to establish a free colony in West Africa.

Du Bois then turns to the worsening condition of American slaves in the late eighteenth and early nineteenth century. Notable events included the revolt in Haiti led by Toussaint-Louverture that resulted in an independent Haiti in 1803. Back in the United States, significant slave revolts were headed by Gabriel Prosser in Virginia in 1800, Denmark Vesey in South Carolina in 1822, and Nat Turner in Virginia in 1831. Meanwhile, in the North, African Americans were segregating themselves in black churches at a time when white mainstream churches were ignoring their needs. Paragraph 12 alludes to David Walker's highly influential *Appeal to the Coloured Citizens of the World*, written in 1829. Du Bois goes on to point out instances of prominent northern men who "sought assimilation and amalgamation with the nation on the same terms with other men," but says that they continued to be regarded as "despised blacks."

Accordingly, during the abolition era prior to the Civil War, numerous black leaders, including Charles Lenox Remond, William Cooper Nell, William Wells Brown, and Frederick Douglass, launched a new period of self-assertion. The logic of self-assertion reached its extreme with John Brown's raid on Harpers Ferry, Virginia, in 1859. After the Civil War, leadership in the African American community passed to Douglass and several others: Robert Brown Elliott, a black congressman; Blanche Kelso Bruce, the first black senator to serve a full term; Charles Langston, a black activist (and grandfather of the poet Langston Hughes); Alexander Crummell, an abolitionist and pan-Africanist; and Daniel Payne, a bishop in the African Methodist Episcopal Church and one of the founders of Wilberforce

A Harper's Weekly cartoon representing Republican disaffection with the Compromise of 1877, suggesting that Democrats were coercing and not compromising (Library of Congress)

University, where he became the first African American college president in the nation's history.

In paragraph 14, Du Bois uses the term "Revolution" to refer to the disputed presidential election of 1876, which led to the end of the Reconstruction era. In the post-Reconstruction climate, Douglass and Bruce carried on, but Bruce died in 1898 and Douglass was aging. Booker T. Washington arose to fill the vacuum they left, becoming the leader not of one race but of two, both blacks and whites. Some blacks resented Washington's ascendancy, but their criticisms were hushed because of the potential of economic gains as northern businesses were investing in southern enterprises. All were weary of the race problem, and Washington's views seemed to provide a way out.

◆ **The Old Attitude of Adjustment and Submission**

Beginning with paragraph 15, Du Bois takes on Washington directly. He describes Washington's program as one of "adjustment and submission" and one that "practically accepts the alleged inferiority of the Negro races." Washington "withdraws" the demands of African Americans for equality as citizens. He calls for African Americans to surrender political power, civil rights, and higher education and instead to "concentrate all their energies on industrial education, and accumulation of wealth, and the conciliation of the South." The result, however, has been the "disfranchisement" (usually spelled "disenfranchisement") of blacks, legalized civil inferiority, and loss of opportunities for higher education. In paragraph 17, Du Bois asks whether it is even possible for blacks to achieve economic equality when they have been denied political power, civil rights, and access to education. He then goes on to point out the paradoxes: that black artisans and workingmen cannot defend their rights without the vote, that submission will "sap" the manhood of any race, and that an institution like Tuskegee itself could not remain open without a class of African Americans who have pursued higher education. The result of these paradoxes has been the creation of two classes of blacks: those who "represent the attitude of revolt and revenge" and those who disagree with Washington but cannot say so. These people, according to Du Bois, are obligated to demand of the nation the right to vote, civic equality, and access to education. In paragraph 20, Du Bois acknowledges that the "low social level" of many African Americans leads to discrimination, but he also argues that "relentless color-prejudice is more often a cause than a result of the Negro's degradation." He insists that there is a demand for educational institutions to provide training for African American teachers, professionals, and leaders.

Du Bois continues in paragraph 21 by obliquely criticizing those, particularly blacks, who accept Washington and his views. He acknowledges that they see in Washington an effort to conciliate the South, no easy task. But he also insists that the issue is one that has to be approached honestly. They recognize that the right to vote, civic rights, and the right to be educated will not come easily, and that the prejudice of the past will not disappear overnight. But they also know that the path to progress will not open by throwing away rights; a people cannot gain respect by "continually belittling and ridiculing themselves."

◆ **The Thinking Classes of American Negroes**

With paragraph 22, Du Bois begins to build toward a conclusion. He insists that "the thinking classes of American Negroes" are obliged to oppose Washington. While acknowledging that there has been some progress in relations between North and South after the Civil War, he states that if reconciliation has to be bought at the price of "industrial slavery and civic death" or by "inferiority," then patriotism and loyalty demands disagreement with Washington. He maintains that it is necessary to judge the South with discrimination, to recognize that it is a place in ferment and undergoing social change. He concedes in paragraph 24 that the attitude toward blacks in the South is not uniform; ignorant people want to disenfranchise blacks, but not all southerners are ignorant. Among those who are ignorant, he mentions North Carolina governor Charles Aycock, a white supremacist; Thomas Nelson Page, who wrote sentimental novels idealizing pre–Civil War plantation life; and Ben Tillman, an open racist who fought Republican government in South Carolina as a member of a paramilitary group known as the Red Shirts.

Du Bois acknowledges that Washington has opposed injustice to people of color. Nevertheless, he calls Washington's views "propaganda" that justifies the South in its attitude toward African Americans, that blacks are responsible for their own degraded condition, and that only through their own efforts can blacks rise in the future. Du Bois counters these "half-truths" by arguing that race prejudice is still a potent force in the South, that earlier systems of education could not succeed without a class of educated blacks, and that blacks can rise only if the culture at large encourages and arouses this effort. The key mistake Washington makes is to impose the burden of the "Negro problem" on blacks without recognizing that it is a national problem, one that it will take the united efforts of North and South to solve. Indeed, says Du Bois, industrial training, along with virtues such as thrift and patience, are to the good, but without fighting for the right and duty to vote, eliminating the "emasculating effects of caste distinctions," and striving for higher education, the promise of the Founding Fathers that "all men are created equal" will never be realized.

Audience

The audience for *The Souls of Black Folk* was broad. Several of the essays had already appeared in the *Atlantic* magazine, one of the nation's leading mainstream publications. Accordingly, the book attracted attention from both the black and the white intelligentsia and went through several editions. The author's purposes were to convince white readers of the essential humanity of African Americans and to promote among black readers a new consciousness. Virtually any writer, white or black, writing on race issues during the early decades of the twentieth century would have read and paid tribute to Du Bois and his book, and even in the twenty-first century the book is still regarded as a classic—and its ideas are still debated.

Impact

In *The Souls of Black Folk*, Du Bois boldly challenged Booker T. Washington and his accommodationist approach to race relations. Du Bois emphasized the need to develop a "Talented Tenth"—an educated vanguard that would serve as the teachers and leaders in the black community. Demanding political and civil rights for Americans, in 1905 he organized the Niagara Movement, a group of black militants who were adamantly opposed to segregation. Regarded as a forerunner of the NAACP, the nation's oldest, most influential, and highly venerable civil rights organization, the Niagara Movement met annually in Buffalo, New York, through 1909. Around this time, the philosophical differences between Washington and Du Bois grew into a bitter personal animosity. Washington used his influence to block financial support for Atlanta University, and he intimated to the university's president that further support would not be forthcoming as long as Du Bois remained on the faculty. Consequently, Du Bois and Atlanta University parted company in 1910.

Du Bois went on to pursue a career as a distinguished activist, editor, and scholar. As one of the cofounders of the NAACP, he fought unceasingly for social change. The formation of the NAACP was fueled in part by a 1908 race riot in Springfield, Illinois. Violence of this sort was not new, as the lynching of African Americans had been increasing with alarming frequency throughout the late nineteenth century. The riot in Springfield was one of several episodes of brutality inflicted by white mobs against black communities. What was alarming about the Springfield riots was that they erupted outside the South in the birthplace of Abraham Lincoln. Many worried that the "race war" in the South would be transported to northern cities.

These events spurred Mary Ovington, a social worker who had been active in the Niagara Movement, to contact William English Walling, a Socialist who supported progressive causes, and Dr. Henry Moskowitz, another well-known progressive. The group issued a call for the formation of a political movement that would develop a program aimed at securing racial equality. A conference of the newly formed NAACP was held on May 12–14, 1910, in New York City, where the organization outlined its goals. In *The Souls of Black Folk*, Du Bois had insisted on voting rights, civic equality, and access to higher education. These principles were incorporated into the fledgling organization's mission, which was to ensure the political, educational, social, and economic equality of people of color and to

Essential Quotes

> "Mr. Washington represents in Negro thought the old attitude of adjustment and submission."
>
> (Paragraph 15)

> "Is it possible, and probable, that nine millions of men can make effective progress in economic lines if they are deprived of political rights, made a servile caste, and allowed only the most meagre chance for developing their exceptional men? If history and reason give any distinct answer to these questions, it is an emphatic No."
>
> (Paragraph 17)

> "[Washington's] doctrine has tended to make the whites, North and South, shift the burden of the Negro problem to the Negro's shoulders and stand aside as critical and rather pessimistic spectators; when in fact the burden belongs to the nation, and the hands of none of us are clean if we bend not our energies to righting these great wrongs."
>
> (Paragraph 26)

> "But so far as Mr. Washington apologizes for injustice, North or South, does not rightly value the privilege and duty of voting, belittles the emasculating effects of caste distinctions, and opposes the higher training and ambition of our brighter minds,—so far as he, the South, or the Nation, does this,—we must unceasingly and firmly oppose them."
>
> (Paragraph 28)

eliminate racial prejudice. Du Bois was appointed director of publicity and research for the NAACP.

By November 1911 a sixteen-page magazine under Du Bois's editorship was ready for distribution. For a title, Du Bois settled on *The Crisis: A Record of the Darker Races*. A thousand copies were printed, and the magazine was immediately successful. After *The Crisis* was established as the voice of the NAACP, Du Bois's stature rose rapidly. Within a short period of time, the magazine's circulation reached a thousand issues per month. As the periodical's reputation grew, Du Bois became the most well-known black intellectual of his time. When Booker T. Washington died in 1915, the power of the Tuskegee machine faded rapidly. Its influence was replaced by the NAACP, which by 1919 had more than eighty-eight thousand members.

Over the next decade the NAACP continued its fight against segregation, using lobbying, public education, and demonstrations as its primary tools. Between 1918 and 1922, the NAACP campaigned for the adoption of antilynching laws by Congress. Such legislative measures failed to gain ground, however, even when argued on the basis of the fundamental Fourteenth Amendment right to due process. Du Bois viewed this and other barriers to equality for blacks as reprehensible, and he began to rethink the integrationist goals of the NAACP. In 1934 controversy erupted over an editorial Du Bois authored that argued that African Americans should adopt a program of self-segregation in which black-owned economic institutions would be encouraged and developed. Frustrated with the NAACP's inability to make progress toward eliminating segregation, Du Bois contended that integration would likely take a long time to achieve. During the interim, instead of focusing all of its energies on demands for integration, the black community would be better served by developing and relying on its own institutions.

Du Bois's editorial was perceived as acquiescing to continued segregation. A vigorous debate ensued. To many observers, Du Bois appeared to be advocating a return to Washington's philosophy. Du Bois's editorial independence was tolerated as long as *The Crisis* was self-supporting. But during the Great Depression years of 1930s, the publication lost money. In the wake of the controversy, the NAACP's board of directors took steps to rein in Du Bois by adopting a formal resolution requiring editorials to reflect the NAACP's institutional views and requiring advance approval by the board. This was more than Du Bois could take. In June 1934 he announced his resignation.

See also Fourteenth Amendment to the U.S. Constitution (1868); Fifteenth Amendment to the U.S. Constitution (1870); Ku Klux Klan Act (1871); *United States v. Cruikshank* (1876); Civil Rights Cases (1883); Booker T. Washington's Atlanta Exposition Address (1895); *Plessy v. Ferguson* (1896); Niagara Movement Declaration of Principles (1905).

Further Reading

■ Books

Crouch, Stanley, and Playthell Benjamin. *Reconsidering the Souls of Black Folk: Thoughts on the Groundbreaking Classic Work of W. E. B. Du Bois*. Philadelphia: Running Press, 2002.

Du Bois, W. E. B. *Dusk of Dawn: An Essay toward an Autobiography of a Race Concept*. New York: Harcourt, Brace, 1940.

———. *The Autobiography of W. E. B. Du Bois: A Soliloquy on Viewing My Life from the Decade of Its First Century*. New York: International Publishers, 1969.

Lewis, David Levering. *W. E. B. Du Bois: Biography of a Race, 1868–1919*. New York: Henry Holt, 1993.

———. *W. E. B. Du Bois: The Fight for Equality and the American Century: 1919–1963*. New York: Henry Holt, 2009.

Marable, Manning. *W. E. B. Du Bois: Black Radical Democrat*. Boston: Twayne, 1986.

Rampersad, Arnold. *The Art and Imagination of W. E. B. Du Bois*. New York: Schocken Books, 1990.

■ Web Sites

"About the NAACP—History." NAACP Web site. http://www.naacp.org/about/history.

"W. E. B. Du Bois: Online Resources." Library of Congress Web site. http://www.loc.gov/rr/program/bib/dubois.

—Leland Ware and Michael J. O'Neal

Questions for Further Study

1. What role did Du Bois play early on in the Harlem Renaissance? In what way did he help create a climate of thought that led to the renaissance?

2. Du Bois and Booker T. Washington are often thought of as representing the opposite poles of black thought during this era. See Booker T. Washington's Atlanta Exposition Address (1895) and summarize the points of view of each figure. Explain how their views were in opposition to each other.

3. What did Du Bois mean by the "double-consciousness" of African Americans? How did he attempt to overcome that double consciousness?

4. Du Bois used expressions such as "the thinking classes of American Negroes." He was, in fact, highly educated and by any measure an intellectual. Do you think that Du Bois was an elitist? Did he look down on classes of blacks who, presumably, were not "thinking"? Do you think you would have enjoyed sitting down to have lunch with a figure such as Du Bois?

5. Read this document in conjunction with the Niagara Movement Declaration of Principles (1905). To what extent did the latter document, written just two years later, embody principles that Du Bois articulated in *The Souls of Black Folk*?

W. E. B. Du Bois: *The Souls of Black Folk*

III. Of Mr. Booker T. Washington and Others

> From birth till death enslaved; in word, in deed, unmanned!
>
> * * * * * * * * *
>
> Hereditary bondsmen! Know ye not
> Who would be free themselves must strike the blow?
>
> —Byron

Easily the most striking thing in the history of the American Negro since 1876 is the ascendancy of Mr. Booker T. Washington. It began at the time when war memories and ideals were rapidly passing; a day of astonishing commercial development was dawning; a sense of doubt and hesitation overtook the freedmen's sons,—then it was that his leading began. Mr. Washington came, with a simple definite programme, at the psychological moment when the nation was a little ashamed of having bestowed so much sentiment on Negroes, and was concentrating its energies on Dollars. His programme of industrial education, conciliation of the South, and submission and silence as to civil and political rights, was not wholly original; the Free Negroes from 1830 up to war-time had striven to build industrial schools, and the American Missionary Association had from the first taught various trades; and Price and others had sought a way of honorable alliance with the best of the Southerners. But Mr. Washington first indissolubly linked these things; he put enthusiasm, unlimited energy, and perfect faith into his programme, and changed it from a by-path into a veritable Way of Life. And the tale of the methods by which he did this is a fascinating study of human life.

It startled the nation to hear a Negro advocating such a programme after many decades of bitter complaint; it startled and won the applause of the South, it interested and won the admiration of the North; and after a confused murmur of protest, it silenced if it did not convert the Negroes themselves.

To gain the sympathy and cooperation of the various elements comprising the white South was Mr. Washington's first task; and this, at the time Tuskegee was founded, seemed, for a black man, well-nigh impossible. And yet ten years later it was done in the word spoken at Atlanta: "In all things purely social we can be as separate as the five fingers, and yet one as the hand in all things essential to mutual progress." This "Atlanta Compromise" is by all odds the most notable thing in Mr. Washington's career. The South interpreted it in different ways: the radicals received it as a complete surrender of the demand for civil and political equality; the conservatives, as a generously conceived working basis for mutual understanding. So both approved it, and to-day its author is certainly the most distinguished Southerner since Jefferson Davis, and the one with the largest personal following.

Next to this achievement comes Mr. Washington's work in gaining place and consideration in the North. Others less shrewd and tactful had formerly essayed to sit on these two stools and had fallen between them; but as Mr. Washington knew the heart of the South from birth and training, so by singular insight he intuitively grasped the spirit of the age which was dominating the North. And so thoroughly did he learn the speech and thought of triumphant commercialism, and the ideals of material prosperity, that the picture of a lone black boy poring over a French grammar amid the weeds and dirt of a neglected home soon seemed to him the acme of absurdities. One wonders what Socrates and St. Francis of Assisi would say to this.

And yet this very singleness of vision and thorough oneness with his age is a mark of the successful man. It is as though Nature must needs make men narrow in order to give them force. So Mr. Washington's cult has gained unquestioning followers, his work has wonderfully prospered, his friends are legion, and his enemies are confounded. To-day he stands as the one recognized spokesman of his ten million fellows, and one of the most notable figures in a nation of seventy millions. One hesitates, therefore, to criticise a life which, beginning with so little, has done so much. And yet the time is come when one may speak in all sincerity and utter courtesy of the mistakes and shortcomings of Mr. Washington's career, as well as of his triumphs, without being thought captious or envious, and without forgetting that it is easier to do ill than well in the world.

The criticism that has hitherto met Mr. Washington has not always been of this broad character. In the South especially has he had to walk warily to avoid the harshest judgments,—and naturally so, for he is dealing with the one subject of deepest sensitiveness to that section. Twice—once when at the Chicago celebration of the Spanish-American War he alluded to the color-prejudice that is "eating away the vitals of the South," and once when he dined with President Roosevelt—has the resulting Southern criticism been violent enough to threaten seriously his popularity. In the North the feeling has several times forced itself into words, that Mr. Washington's counsels of submission overlooked certain elements of true manhood, and that his educational programme was unnecessarily narrow. Usually, however, such criticism has not found open expression, although, too, the spiritual sons of the Abolitionists have not been prepared to acknowledge that the schools founded before Tuskegee, by men of broad ideals and self-sacrificing spirit, were wholly failures or worthy of ridicule. While, then, criticism has not failed to follow Mr. Washington, yet the prevailing public opinion of the land has been but too willing to deliver the solution of a wearisome problem into his hands, and say, "If that is all you and your race ask, take it."

Among his own people, however, Mr. Washington has encountered the strongest and most lasting opposition, amounting at times to bitterness, and even today continuing strong and insistent even though largely silenced in outward expression by the public opinion of the nation. Some of this opposition is, of course, mere envy; the disappointment of displaced demagogues and the spite of narrow minds. But aside from this, there is among educated and thoughtful colored men in all parts of the land a feeling of deep regret, sorrow, and apprehension at the wide currency and ascendancy which some of Mr. Washington's theories have gained. These same men admire his sincerity of purpose, and are willing to forgive much to honest endeavor which is doing something worth the doing. They cooperate with Mr. Washington as far as they conscientiously can; and, indeed, it is no ordinary tribute to this man's tact and power that, steering as he must between so many diverse interests and opinions, he so largely retains the respect of all.

But the hushing of the criticism of honest opponents is a dangerous thing. It leads some of the best of the critics to unfortunate silence and paralysis of effort, and others to burst into speech so passionately and intemperately as to lose listeners. Honest and earnest criticism from those whose interests are most nearly touched,—criticism of writers by readers,— this is the soul of democracy and the safeguard of modern society. If the best of the American Negroes receive by outer pressure a leader whom they had not recognized before, manifestly there is here a certain palpable gain. Yet there is also irreparable loss,—a loss of that peculiarly valuable education which a group receives when by search and criticism it finds and commissions its own leaders. The way in which this is done is at once the most elementary and the nicest problem of social growth. History is but the record of such group-leadership; and yet how infinitely changeful is its type and character! And of all types and kinds, what can be more instructive than the leadership of a group within a group?—that curious double movement where real progress may be negative and actual advance be relative retrogression. All this is the social student's inspiration and despair.

Now in the past the American Negro has had instructive experience in the choosing of group leaders, founding thus a peculiar dynasty which in the light of present conditions is worth while studying. When sticks and stones and beasts form the sole environment of a people, their attitude is largely one of determined opposition to and conquest of natural forces. But when to earth and brute is added an environment of men and ideas, then the attitude of the imprisoned group may take three main forms,—a feeling of revolt and revenge; an attempt to adjust all thought and action to the will of the greater group; or, finally, a determined effort at self-realization and self-development despite environing opinion. The influence of all of these attitudes at various times can be traced in the history of the American Negro, and in the evolution of his successive leaders.

Before 1750, while the fire of African freedom still burned in the veins of the slaves, there was in all leadership or attempted leadership but the one motive of revolt and revenge,—typified in the terrible Maroons, the Danish blacks, and Cato of Stono, and veiling all the Americas in fear of insurrection. The liberalizing tendencies of the latter half of the eighteenth century brought, along with kindlier relations between black and white, thoughts of ultimate adjustment and assimilation. Such aspiration was especially voiced in the earnest songs of Phyllis, in the martyrdom of Attucks, the fighting of Salem and Poor, the intellectual accomplishments of Banneker and Derham, and the political demands of the Cuffes.

Stern financial and social stress after the war cooled much of the previous humanitarian ardor. The disappointment and impatience of the Negroes at the persistence of slavery and serfdom voiced itself in two movements. The slaves in the South, aroused undoubtedly by vague rumors of the Haytian revolt, made three fierce attempts at insurrection,—in 1800 under Gabriel in Virginia, in 1822 under Vesey in Carolina, and in 1831 again in Virginia under the terrible Nat Turner. In the Free States, on the other hand, a new and curious attempt at self-development was made. In Philadelphia and New York color-prescription led to a withdrawal of Negro communicants from white churches and the formation of a peculiar socio-religious institution among the Negroes known as the African Church,—an organization still living and controlling in its various branches over a million of men.

Walker's wild appeal against the trend of the times showed how the world was changing after the coming of the cotton-gin. By 1830 slavery seemed hopelessly fastened on the South, and the slaves thoroughly cowed into submission. The free Negroes of the North, inspired by the mulatto immigrants from the West Indies, began to change the basis of their demands; they recognized the slavery of slaves, but insisted that they themselves were freemen, and sought assimilation and amalgamation with the nation on the same terms with other men. Thus, Forten and Purvis of Philadelphia, Shad of Wilmington, Du Bois of New Haven, Barbadoes of Boston, and others, strove singly and together as men, they said, not as slaves; as "people of color," not as "Negroes." The trend of the times, however, refused them recognition save in individual and exceptional cases, considered them as one with all the despised blacks, and they soon found themselves striving to keep even the rights they formerly had of voting and working and moving as freemen. Schemes of migration and colonization arose among them; but these they refused to entertain, and they eventually turned to the Abolition movement as a final refuge.

Here, led by Remond, Nell, Wells-Brown, and Douglass, a new period of self-assertion and self-development dawned. To be sure, ultimate freedom and assimilation was the ideal before the leaders, but the assertion of the manhood rights of the Negro by himself was the main reliance, and John Brown's raid was the extreme of its logic. After the war and emancipation, the great form of Frederick Douglass, the greatest of American Negro leaders, still led the host. Self-assertion, especially in political lines, was the main programme, and behind Douglass came Elliot, Bruce, and Langston, and the Reconstruction politicians, and, less conspicuous but of greater social significance, Alexander Crummell and Bishop Daniel Payne.

Then came the Revolution of 1876, the suppression of the Negro votes, the changing and shifting of ideals, and the seeking of new lights in the great night. Douglass, in his old age, still bravely stood for the ideals of his early manhood,—ultimate assimilation through self-assertion, and on no other terms. For a time Price arose as a new leader, destined, it seemed, not to give up, but to re-state the old ideals in a form less repugnant to the white South. But he passed away in his prime. Then came the new leader. Nearly all the former ones had become leaders by the silent suffrage of their fellows, had sought to lead their own people alone, and were usually, save Douglass, little known outside their race. But Booker T. Washington arose as essentially the leader not of one race but of two,—a compromiser between the South, the North, and the Negro. Naturally the Negroes resented, at first bitterly, signs of compromise which surrendered their civil and political rights, even though this was to be exchanged for larger chances of economic development. The rich and dominating North, however, was not only weary of the race problem, but was investing largely in Southern enterprises, and welcomed any method of peaceful cooperation. Thus, by national opinion, the Negroes began to recognize Mr. Washington's leadership; and the voice of criticism was hushed.

Mr. Washington represents in Negro thought the old attitude of adjustment and submission; but adjustment at such a peculiar time as to make his programme unique. This is an age of unusual economic development, and Mr. Washington's programme naturally takes an economic cast, becoming a gospel of Work and Money to such an extent as apparently almost completely to overshadow the higher aims of life. Moreover, this is an age when the more advanced races are coming in closer contact with the less developed races, and the race-feeling is therefore intensified; and Mr. Washington's programme practically accepts the alleged inferiority of the Negro races. Again, in our own land, the reaction from the sentiment of war time has given impetus to race-prejudice against Negroes, and Mr. Washington withdraws many of the high demands of Negroes as men and American citizens. In other periods of intensified prejudice all the Negro's tendency to self-assertion has been called forth; at this period a policy of submission is advocated. In the history of nearly all other races and peoples the doctrine preached at such crises has been that manly self-respect is worth more than lands and houses, and that a people who voluntarily surrender such respect, or cease striving for it, are not worth civilizing.

In answer to this, it has been claimed that the Negro can survive only through submission. Mr. Washington distinctly asks that black people give up, at least for the present, three things,—

First, political power,
Second, insistence on civil rights,
Third, higher education of Negro youth,—

and concentrate all their energies on industrial education, and accumulation of wealth, and the conciliation of the South. This policy has been courageously and insistently advocated for over fifteen years, and has been triumphant for perhaps ten years. As a result of this tender of the palm-branch, what has been the return? In these years there have occurred:

1. The disfranchisement of the Negro.
2. The legal creation of a distinct status of civil inferiority for the Negro.
3. The steady withdrawal of aid from institutions for the higher training of the Negro.

These movements are not, to be sure, direct results of Mr. Washington's teachings; but his propaganda has, without a shadow of doubt, helped their speedier accomplishment. The question then comes: Is it possible, and probable, that nine millions of men can make effective progress in economic lines if they are deprived of political rights, made a servile caste, and allowed only the most meagre chance for developing their exceptional men? If history and reason give any distinct answer to these questions, it is an emphatic *No*. And Mr. Washington thus faces the triple paradox of his career:

1. He is striving nobly to make Negro artisans business men and property-owners; but it is utterly impossible, under modern competitive methods, for workingmen and property-owners to defend their rights and exist without the right of suffrage.
2. He insists on thrift and self-respect, but at the same time counsels a silent submission to civic inferiority such as is bound to sap the manhood of any race in the long run.
3. He advocates common-school and industrial training, and depreciates institutions of higher learning; but neither the Negro common-schools, nor Tuskegee itself, could remain open a day were it not for teachers trained in Negro colleges, or trained by their graduates.

This triple paradox in Mr. Washington's position is the object of criticism by two classes of colored Americans. One class is spiritually descended from Toussaint the Savior, through Gabriel, Vesey, and Turner, and they represent the attitude of revolt and revenge; they hate the white South blindly and distrust the white race generally, and so far as they agree on definite action, think that the Negro's only hope lies in emigration beyond the borders of the United States. And yet, by the irony of fate, nothing has more effectually made this programme seem hopeless than the recent course of the United States toward weaker and darker peoples in the West Indies, Hawaii, and the Philippines,—for where in the world may we go and be safe from lying and brute force?

The other class of Negroes who cannot agree with Mr. Washington has hitherto said little aloud. They deprecate the sight of scattered counsels, of internal disagreement; and especially they dislike making their just criticism of a useful and earnest man an excuse for a general discharge of venom from small-minded opponents. Nevertheless, the questions involved are so fundamental and serious that it is difficult to see how men like the Grimkes, Kelly Miller, J. W. E. Bowen, and other representatives of this group, can much longer be silent. Such men feel in conscience bound to ask of this nation three things:

1. The right to vote.
2. Civic equality.
3. The education of youth according to ability.

They acknowledge Mr. Washington's invaluable service in counselling patience and courtesy in such demands; they do not ask that ignorant black men vote when ignorant whites are debarred, or that any reasonable restrictions in the suffrage should not be applied; they know that the low social level of the mass of the race is responsible for much discrimination against it, but they also know, and the nation knows, that relentless color-prejudice is more often a cause than a result of the Negro's degradation; they seek the abatement of this relic of barbarism, and not its systematic encouragement and pampering by all agencies of social power from the Associated Press to the Church of Christ. They advocate, with Mr. Washington, a broad system of Negro common schools supplemented by thorough industrial training; but they are surprised that a man of Mr. Washington's insight can-

Document Text

not see that no such educational system ever has rested or can rest on any other basis than that of the well-equipped college and university, and they insist that there is a demand for a few such institutions throughout the South to train the best of the Negro youth as teachers, professional men, and leaders.

This group of men honor Mr. Washington for his attitude of conciliation toward the white South; they accept the "Atlanta Compromise" in its broadest interpretation; they recognize, with him, many signs of promise, many men of high purpose and fair judgment, in this section; they know that no easy task has been laid upon a region already tottering under heavy burdens. But, nevertheless, they insist that the way to truth and right lies in straightforward honesty, not in indiscriminate flattery; in praising those of the South who do well and criticising uncompromisingly those who do ill; in taking advantage of the opportunities at hand and urging their fellows to do the same, but at the same time in remembering that only a firm adherence to their higher ideals and aspirations will ever keep those ideals within the realm of possibility. They do not expect that the free right to vote, to enjoy civic rights, and to be educated, will come in a moment; they do not expect to see the bias and prejudices of years disappear at the blast of a trumpet; but they are absolutely certain that the way for a people to gain their reasonable rights is not by voluntarily throwing them away and insisting that they do not want them; that the way for a people to gain respect is not by continually belittling and ridiculing themselves; that, on the contrary, Negroes must insist continually, in season and out of season, that voting is necessary to modern manhood, that color discrimination is barbarism, and that black boys need education as well as white boys.

In failing thus to state plainly and unequivocally the legitimate demands of their people, even at the

Glossary

"Atlanta Compromise"	the informal name of a speech given by Booker T. Washington in 1895
Attucks, Salem, and Poor	African Americans Crispus Attucks, Peter Salem, and Salem Poor, who fought in the Revolutionary War
Aycock	North Carolina governor Charles Aycock, a white supremacist
Banneker	Benjamin Banneker, an accomplished African American scientist, mathematician, and surveyor who helped lay out Washington, D.C.
Barbadoes	James G. Barbadoes, one of the founders of the American Anti-Slavery Society
Ben Tillman	an open racist who fought Republican government in South Carolina as a member of a paramilitary group known as the Red Shirts
Bruce	Blanche Kelso Bruce, the first black U.S. senator to serve a full term
Byron	George Gordon Lord Byron, a prominent British Romantic poet of the early nineteenth century; the quotation is from his long narrative poem *Childe Harold's Pilgrimage*
Cato of Stono	a reference to the Stono Rebellion of 1739 (also called Cato's Rebellion), a slave revolt in South Carolina
Crummell	Alexander Crummell, a prominent abolitionist and pan-Africanist
Cuffes	a reference to Paul Cuffe and his followers, who wanted to establish a free colony in West Africa
Danish blacks	a group of slaves who, in 1723, gained control of Saint John in the Virgin Islands (then the Danish West Indies) for six months
Derham	James Derham, the first African American doctor in the colonies
Douglass	Frederick Douglass, the preeminent abolitionist of the nineteenth century

Document Text

cost of opposing an honored leader, the thinking classes of American Negroes would shirk a heavy responsibility,—a responsibility to themselves, a responsibility to the struggling masses, a responsibility to the darker races of men whose future depends so largely on this American experiment, but especially a responsibility to this nation,—this common Fatherland. It is wrong to encourage a man or a people in evil-doing; it is wrong to aid and abet a national crime simply because it is unpopular not to do so. The growing spirit of kindliness and reconciliation between the North and South after the frightful difference of a generation ago ought to be a source of deep congratulation to all, and especially to those whose mistreatment caused the war; but if that reconciliation is to be marked by the industrial slavery and civic death of those same black men, with permanent legislation into a position of inferiority, then those black men, if they are really men, are called upon by every consideration of patriotism and loyalty to oppose such a course by all civilized methods, even though such opposition involves disagreement with Mr. Booker T. Washington. We have no right to sit silently by while the inevitable seeds are sown for a harvest of disaster to our children, black and white.

First, it is the duty of black men to judge the South discriminatingly. The present generation of Southerners are not responsible for the past, and they should not be blindly hated or blamed for it. Furthermore, to no class is the indiscriminate endorsement of the recent course of the South toward Negroes more nauseating than to the best thought of the South. The South is not "solid"; it is a land in the ferment of social change, wherein forces of all kinds are fighting for supremacy; and to praise the ill the South is today perpetrating is just as wrong as to condemn the good. Discriminating and broad-minded criticism is what the South needs,—

Glossary

Du Bois of New Haven	probably a reference to Du Bois's ancestor, Alexander Du Bois, who was disowned by his family because his mother was a black Haitian
Elliott	Robert Brown Elliott, a black congressman
Forten	James Forten, an early abolitionist and businessman
Gabriel	Gabriel Prosser, who led a slave revolt in Virginia in 1800
Grimkes	a reference to the half-brothers of prominent white abolitionists Sarah and Angelina Grimke, born of their father's liaison with a slave woman
Haytian revolt	the revolution that led to a free Haiti in 1803
J. W. E. Bowen	John Wesley Edward Bowen, a Methodist clergyman, university educator, one of the first African Americans to earn a Ph.D. degree in the United States, and the first African American to receive a Ph.D. from Boston University
Jefferson Davis	the president of the Confederate States of America during the Civil War
Joshua	in the Old Testament, the leader of the Israelites after the death of Moses
Kelly Miller	a scientist, mathematician, essayist, and newspaper columnist; the first black admitted to The Johns Hopkins University
Langston	Charles Langston, a black activist and grandfather of the poet Langston Hughes
Maroons	escaped slaves in Haiti and throughout the Caribbean who formed gangs that lived in the forests and attacked French plantations
Nat Turner	leader of a slave rebellion in Virginia in 1831
Nell	William Cooper Nell, an abolitionist, author, journalist, and civil servant
Payne	Daniel Payne, a bishop in the African Methodist Episcopal Church and one of the founders of Wilberforce University

Document Text

needs it for the sake of her own white sons and daughters, and for the insurance of robust, healthy mental and moral development.

Today even the attitude of the Southern whites toward the blacks is not, as so many assume, in all cases the same; the ignorant Southerner hates the Negro, the workingmen fear his competition, the money-makers wish to use him as a laborer, some of the educated see a menace in his upward development, while others—usually the sons of the masters—wish to help him to rise. National opinion has enabled this last class to maintain the Negro common schools, and to protect the Negro partially in property, life, and limb. Through the pressure of the money-makers, the Negro is in danger of being reduced to semi-slavery, especially in the country districts; the workingmen, and those of the educated who fear the Negro, have united to disfranchise him, and some have urged his deportation; while the passions of the ignorant are easily aroused to lynch and abuse any black man. To praise this intricate whirl of thought and prejudice is nonsense; to inveigh indiscriminately against "the South" is unjust; but to use the same breath in praising Governor Aycock, exposing Senator Morgan, arguing with Mr. Thomas Nelson Page, and denouncing Senator Ben Tillman, is not only sane, but the imperative duty of thinking black men.

It would be unjust to Mr. Washington not to acknowledge that in several instances he has opposed movements in the South which were unjust to the Negro; he sent memorials to the Louisiana and Alabama constitutional conventions, he has spoken against lynching, and in other ways has openly or silently set his influence against sinister schemes and unfortunate happenings. Notwithstanding this, it is equally true to assert that on the whole the distinct impression left by Mr. Washing-

Glossary

Phyllis	Phillis Wheatley, an eighteenth-century slave poet
President Roosevelt	Theodore Roosevelt, who earlier had led forces in the Spanish-American War
Price	William G. Price, an African American educator
Purvis	Robert Purvis, a nineteenth-century abolitionist who was three quarters white but chose to identify with the black community
Remond	Charles Lenox Remond, an orator and abolitionist
Revolution of 1876	a reference to the disputed presidential election of 1876, which led to the end of the Reconstruction era
Senator Morgan	John Tyler Morgan, a segregationist Alabama senator after the Civil War
Shad	probably a reference to Abraham Shadd, a free black who opposed African colonization by U.S. blacks
Socrates	an ancient Greek philosopher
St. Francis of Assisi	a Catholic saint who founded the Franciscan order of priests
Thomas Nelson Page	an author of sentimental novels idealizing pre–Civil War plantation life
Toussaint	Toussaint L'Ouverture, the leader of the Haitian Revolution
Tuskegee	Tuskegee Institute, the educational institution, stressing occupational skills, founded by Booker T. Washington
Vesey	Denmark Vesey, who led a slave revolt in South Carolina in 1822
Walker's wild appeal	David Walker's influential *Appeal to the Coloured Citizens of the World*
Wells-Brown	William Wells Brown, a prominent historian, lecturer, playwright, and novelist

ton's propaganda is, first, that the South is justified in its present attitude toward the Negro because of the Negro's degradation; secondly, that the prime cause of the Negro's failure to rise more quickly is his wrong education in the past; and, thirdly, that his future rise depends primarily on his own efforts. Each of these propositions is a dangerous half-truth. The supplementary truths must never be lost sight of: first, slavery and race-prejudice are potent if not sufficient causes of the Negro's position; second, industrial and common-school training were necessarily slow in planting because they had to await the black teachers trained by higher institutions,—it being extremely doubtful if any essentially different development was possible, and certainly a Tuskegee was unthinkable before 1880; and, third, while it is a great truth to say that the Negro must strive and strive mightily to help himself, it is equally true that unless his striving be not simply seconded, but rather aroused and encouraged, by the initiative of the richer and wiser environing group, he cannot hope for great success.

In his failure to realize and impress this last point, Mr. Washington is especially to be criticised. His doctrine has tended to make the whites, North and South, shift the burden of the Negro problem to the Negro's shoulders and stand aside as critical and rather pessimistic spectators; when in fact the burden belongs to the nation, and the hands of none of us are clean if we bend not our energies to righting these great wrongs.

The South ought to be led, by candid and honest criticism, to assert her better self and do her full duty to the race she has cruelly wronged and is still wronging. The North—her co-partner in guilt—cannot salve her conscience by plastering it with gold. We cannot settle this problem by diplomacy and suaveness, by "policy" alone. If worse come to worst, can the moral fibre of this country survive the slow throttling and murder of nine millions of men?

The black men of America have a duty to perform, a duty stern and delicate,—a forward movement to oppose a part of the work of their greatest leader. So far as Mr. Washington preaches Thrift, Patience, and Industrial Training for the masses, we must hold up his hands and strive with him, rejoicing in his honors and glorying in the strength of this Joshua called of God and of man to lead the headless host. But so far as Mr. Washington apologizes for injustice, North or South, does not rightly value the privilege and duty of voting, belittles the emasculating effects of caste distinctions, and opposes the higher training and ambition of our brighter minds,—so far as he, the South, or the Nation, does this,—we must unceasingly and firmly oppose them. By every civilized and peaceful method we must strive for the rights which the world accords to men, clinging unwaveringly to those great words which the sons of the Fathers would fain forget: "We hold these truths to be self-evident: That all men are created equal; that they are endowed by their Creator with certain unalienable rights; that among these are life, liberty, and the pursuit of happiness."

Niagara Movement Declaration of Principles

1905

"Any discrimination based simply on race or color is barbarous."

Overview

The Niagara Movement Declaration of Principles outlined a philosophy and political program designed to address racial inequality in the United States. It had its origin on July 11, 1905, when twenty-nine African American men began deliberations at the Erie Beach Hotel in Fort Erie, Ontario, just across the border from Buffalo and Niagara, New York. When they adjourned three days later, the Niagara Movement had been born. The Niagara Movement had a limited impact on race relations in the United States. Within five years it would cease to exist, and in the history of the struggle for equal rights it has long been overshadowed by the more successful, long-lived, biracial National Association for the Advancement of Colored People (NAACP). Nevertheless, the Niagara Movement was an important landmark in U.S. and African American history.

Several factors distinguish the movement. First, it was a purely African American effort to address discrimination and racial inequality. No whites were involved in its creation, organization, or operation. Second, it enunciated a clearly defined philosophy and political program, embodied in the Declaration of Principles that was drafted and approved at the 1905 meeting. While rephrased and modified somewhat, the sentiments and tone of the Declaration of Principles would outlive the Niagara Movement and help define the agenda of the NAACP and the civil rights movement of the 1950s and early 1960s. Finally, the gathering in Fort Erie pointedly excluded the most prominent African American leader of the day, Booker T. Washington, as well as anyone perceived to be allied with him. In addition to confronting American racism, the Niagara Movement and its Declaration of Principles were also a challenge to Booker T. Washington's leadership and his program for the advancement of African Americans.

Context

There is no question that the racial situation in the United States in the first decade of the twentieth century called out for a strong and assertive civil rights organization. Race relations in the country had deteriorated steadily since the end of Reconstruction following the Civil War. By the turn of the century the promise of equality incorporated in the Reconstruction Amendments to the U.S. Constitution and the Civil Rights Acts of 1866 and 1875 had been undone by state action and by the U.S. Supreme Court. A series of state laws and local ordinances segregating blacks and whites received sanction in the Supreme Court, culminating with the *Plessy v. Ferguson* decision in 1896. In this case the Supreme Court legitimized "separate but equal facilities" and provided the legal basis for segregation for the next half-century. At the same time, southern states began to place limits on the right of African Americans to vote, using tactics such as the grandfather clause, white primaries, literacy tests, residency requirements, and poll taxes to prevent blacks from voting. In 1898 the Supreme Court upheld so-called race-neutral restrictions on black suffrage in *Williams v. Mississippi*. The effect was virtually to eliminate black voting in the states of the South. African Americans did not fare much better in the North, where segregation, if not disenfranchisement, grew increasingly common.

Accompanying segregation and disenfranchisement was a resurgence in racial violence. While the Reconstruction Ku Klux Klan had been effectively suppressed by the mid-1870s, the late nineteenth century and early twentieth century experienced an unprecedented wave of racially motivated lynchings and riots. During the first decade of the twentieth century, between fifty-seven and 105 African Americans were lynched by white mobs each year. Lynch mobs targeted blacks almost exclusively, and any pretense of legalism and due process vanished. Furthermore, blacks increasingly became victims of the more generalized racial violence of race riots. Race riots during this period typically involved whites rioting against blacks. Some, such as the 1898 riot in Wilmington, North Carolina, were linked to political efforts to stir up racial hostility as part of a campaign to disenfranchise blacks; others, such as the New York race riot of 1900 and the Atlanta race riot of 1906, grew out of resentment of the presence of blacks. To the degree that the rage they unleashed had an objective, it was to destroy the black community and put blacks in "their place."

As the racial scene deteriorated, African Americans faced a transition in leadership. Frederick Douglass, who had symbolized the African American struggle against slav-

Time Line

1895

- **February 20**
  Frederick Douglass dies at his home in Washington, D.C.

- **September 18**
  Washington delivers his Atlanta Exposition Address during the opening ceremonies of the Cotton States and International Exposition, which in the eyes of most Americans elevates him to the leadership of the African American community.

1896

- **May 18**
  In *Plessy v. Ferguson*, the Supreme Court rules that a Louisiana law segregating passengers on railroads was legal because it provided "separate but equal" facilities; this became the legal basis for the segregation of African Americans.

1898

- **April 25**
  In *Williams v. State of Mississippi*, the Supreme Court rules that a Mississippi law that allowed poll taxes and literacy tests to be used as voter qualifications is legal, legitimizing the efforts of southern states to deny African Americans the right to vote.

- **November 10**
  A race riot erupts in Wilmington, North Carolina, following a local election, as Democrats force blacks and Republicans to resign from their elected offices. A confirmed fourteen blacks are killed, although estimated deaths were several times that many; a number of leading black citizens are banished from the town.

1900

- **August 15**
  White mobs, with the support of police, attack blacks in the Tenderloin district of New York City. Scores of blacks are beaten, with many requiring hospitalization.

---

ery and had been an outspoken advocate for equal rights in the post–Civil War period, died in 1895. That same year Booker T. Washington rose to national prominence with his speech at the Cotton States and International Exposition in Atlanta. The southern-based Washington focused on the economic development of African Americans as the surest road to equality, and while he opposed segregation and black disenfranchisement, he eschewed militant rhetoric and direct confrontation. Washington essentially believed that rational argument and an appeal to southerners' self-interest would defeat prejudice. As time passed and the racial situation worsened, many blacks, especially college-educated northerners, grew impatient with Washington's leadership. By the early twentieth century, such critics as the Boston newspaper editor William Monroe Trotter had become increasingly outspoken about Washington's failures. After 1903 W. E. B. Du Bois emerged as the most respected opponent of Washington and his Tuskegee political machine, the loose coalition of friends and allies through which Washington exercised his political influence on the African American community.

About the Author

Most people assume that W. E. B. Du Bois was the author of the Declaration of Principles. Actually the authorship is not that simple or clear. The final form of the document would be approved by the twenty-nine delegates at the Fort Erie meeting. The actual drafting of the declaration was a collaboration between Du Bois and William Monroe Trotter.

W. E. B. Du Bois was born February 23, 1868, in Great Barrington, Massachusetts, and raised by his mother in an environment characterized by varying degrees of poverty. Despite these limitations, Du Bois excelled in school and achieved one of the most impressive educations of his generation. He took bachelor degrees at Fisk and then Harvard, pursued graduate work at Harvard and the University of Berlin, and earned his Ph.D. in history from Harvard in 1895. He held faculty positions at Wilberforce University and then Atlanta University and spent a year working for the University of Pennsylvania on a study of blacks in Philadelphia. In 1903 he published *The Souls of Black Folk*, his third book and the one that propelled him to the forefront of African American intellectuals; shortly thereafter he emerged as the most respected critic of Booker T. Washington. In 1905 he made his first major foray into racial politics when he assumed a major role in the creation and operation of the Niagara Movement.

William Monroe Trotter was born on April 7, 1872, in Chillicothe, Ohio, but was raised in Boston among the city's black elite. He attended Harvard, where he met Du Bois. After graduating Phi Beta Kappa, he worked in insurance and real estate. In 1901 he cofounded and became editor of the *Guardian*, a Boston newspaper noted for its militant, uncompromising, and often intemperate support of African American civil rights and racial justice and for its criticism and attacks on Booker T. Washington. In July 1903 he was the principal organizer of the "Boston riot," when he and his allies disrupted a Booker T. Washington speech at the Columbus Avenue AME Zion Church. He was sentenced to thirty days in jail for provoking the incident. While Du Bois was the leading African American intellectual of his day, Trotter was the race's most outspoken polemicist.

Although they were of different temperaments, Du Bois and Trotter worked well together on the Declaration of Principles. The document combined Du Bois's more scholarly approach with Trotter's more polemical style. The partnership did not last long. The two clashed over leadership issues, especially the role that whites should play in the Niagara Movement. Trotter withdrew from the organization and founded the National Equal Rights League in 1908. Although he participated in the creation of the NAACP, he objected to the dominant roles whites played in the organization. He continued to agitate for racial equality and publish the *Guardian* until his death in 1934. Du Bois assumed a major role in the NAACP, especially as editor of *The Crisis* from its founding in 1910 until he returned to Atlanta University in 1934. Du Bois was the premier African American intellectual of the twentieth century as well as a civil rights advocate and an advocate of pan-Africanism. He died in Ghana in 1963.

Explanation and Analysis of the Document

The Declaration of Principles was approved by the assembly of African American men who met July 11–13, 1905, in Fort Erie, Ontario. The document drafted by W. E. B. Du Bois and William Monroe Trotter contains eighteen short paragraphs, each raising and briefly addressing a specific issue. The style of the declaration is that of a list or an outline rather than an analytical discussion of the status of African Americans. The first seventeen paragraphs contain a manifesto of grievances and demands; the eighteenth is a list of duties. Together they summarize the issues confronting African Americans in the early twentieth century and define the purpose and agenda of the Niagara Movement.

The first section of the declaration, "Progress," comments on the gathering of the Niagara Movement and congratulates African Americans on the progress they had achieved in the preceding ten years. These ten years essentially covered the time period since the death of Frederick Douglass and the rise to power of Booker T. Washington, and the Niagarites viewed this as a period of failed leadership and a decline in the rights of African Americans. The progress cited—the increase in intelligence and in the acquisition of property and the creation of successful institutions—omits reference to the political and civil rights of African Americans.

◆ "Suffrage," "Civil Liberty," and "Economic Opportunity"

The next three paragraphs address in sequence "Suffrage," "Civil Liberty," and "Economic Opportunity"—areas in which African Americans faced clear and increasing discrimination. Here the declaration lists grievances for the

Time Line

1901
- **November 9**
  The *Guardian* (Boston) debuts under the editorship of William Monroe Trotter. The paper quickly becomes recognized for its radical support for equal rights and its attacks, often personal in nature, on the leadership of Booker T. Washington.

1903
- **April 18**
  W. E. B. Du Bois emerges as a major African American leader with the publication of *The Souls of Black Folk*. In this book Du Bois initiates his criticism of Washington's leadership with the chapter "Of Mr. Booker T. Washington and Others."
- **July 30**
  William Monroe Trotter and his allies disrupt a Booker T. Washington speech at the Columbus Avenue AME Zion Church in Boston. In the ensuing melee Trotter and one of his associates are arrested for inciting a riot. The incident deepens the rift between Washington and Du Bois.

1905
- **July 11**
  Twenty-nine African Americans, including W. E. B. Du Bois, meet in Fort Erie, Ontario, for three days to organize the Niagara Movement. Their Declaration of Principles outlines a new civil rights agenda.

1906
- **September 22–25**
  Atlanta race riot erupts as white mobs attack blacks and black neighborhoods, resulting in the deaths of at least ten blacks and leaving scores injured.

1908
- **August 14**
  A race riot erupts in Springfield, Illinois, as a white mob attacks, beats, and lynches blacks and burns black residences. The violence lasts two days, leaving two blacks dead and forty black families homeless. Sporadic violence against blacks continues for several weeks.

Time Line

1909
- **May 31**
  A biracial committee, dominated by white liberals, meets in New York City and establishes the Negro National Committee to address racial violence and civil rights. Du Bois plays a major role in this meeting and the new organization.

1910
- **May 12–14**
  The Negro National Committee meets again in New York and reorganizes itself as the National Association for the Advancement of Colored People. Du Bois is the only black on the board of directors and also assumes the paid position of director of publications and research.
- **November**
  Du Bois publishes the inaugural issue of *The Crisis*, the NAACP's monthly journal. Du Bois will serve as editor of *The Crisis* for twenty-four years.

1915
- **November 14**
  Booker T. Washington dies at his home in Tuskegee, Alabama.

1916
- **August 24–26**
  Amenia Conference, hosted by the NAACP president Joel E. Spingarn, brings together fifty prominent white and African American civil rights leaders in an effort to heal the breach between the followers of the late Booker T. Washington and W. E. B. Du Bois.

---

first time and evokes protest as an appropriate response to these grievances. The declaration asserts the importance of manhood suffrage and then notes that black political rights have been curtailed and that blacks cannot afford to place their political fate in the hands of others. This argument did not address the specifics of the strategies used to disenfranchise blacks—literacy tests, the grandfather clause, or similar practices. Instead, it asserted that all men deserve the right to vote. This approach distinguished the Niagarites from Booker T. Washington, who supported suffrage and attacked disenfranchisement on the basis that it treated blacks differently than whites. The declaration sees universal manhood suffrage as a fundamental right of all men and calls on blacks to protest "empathically and continually" as long as their political rights are violated. This introduces a theme that runs through the declaration: that discrimination is a violation of the rights of African Americans and that the response to these violations must be agitation and protest (not negotiation and patience).

The declaration continues this argument in its examination of civil liberty. It defines civil liberty as civil rights—rights shared equally by all citizens. It broadens the concept to include the right to "equal treatment in places of public entertainment," that is, restaurants, theaters, hotels, and other places of public accommodation. Exclusion from such places must not be based on race or color but instead on the individual's behavior and demeanor. The declaration demands equal access not to residences or other private spaces but to places open to the public, the same places blacks finally achieved access to in the Civil Rights Act of 1964. Furthermore, to gain their civil rights, blacks must be willing to protest.

As it turns to economic opportunity, the Declaration of Principles directly confronts the heart of Washington's program for African American advancement. Washington believed that the acquisition of property and prosperity would earn blacks the respect of whites and equal rights and that this prosperity could most easily be achieved in the South. The declaration rejects this, noting that African Americans are denied equal economic opportunity in the South and that prejudice and inequity in the law in that region undermine black economic efforts. Specifically, it protests the spread of peonage that has returned blacks to virtual slavery in large areas of the rural South and the practice of discrimination in hiring, wages, and credit that has "crushed" black labor and small businesses.

◆ **"Education"**

Education was a key issue for the Niagara Movement. Most of the delegates who attended the gathering were from the college-educated black elite, the group that Du Bois termed the "Talented Tenth" and the group that most Niagarites believed would provide the leadership for African American advancement. Generally, this group denigrated Booker T. Washington and his Tuskegee Institute for their focus on job training and practical education. However, the section on education in the Declaration of Principles recognizes the need for all forms of education in the African American community. It focuses its complaints on the lack of equal access to education for blacks, especially in the South. Specifically, it calls for "common" schools (basically elementary schools) to be free and compulsory for all children, regardless of race. It also calls for blacks to have access to high schools, colleges and universities, and trade and technical schools, and it calls for the U.S. government to aid common-school education, especially in the South.

What is striking about the statement on education is that it does not call for the desegregation of education. It specifi-

Tuskegee Institute students in mattress-making class (1902) (Library of Congress)

cally asks for an increase in the number of public high schools in the South, where blacks rarely had access to them, and it requests white philanthropists to provide adequate endowments for black institutions of higher education. The focus is clearly on improving black access to educational facilities of all types and at all levels. The language of this section is also much more conciliatory; agitation is suggested only to pressure the U.S. government to provide aid to black common schools. To understand this, it is important to remember that public school systems did not appear in most southern states prior to the period of Reconstruction, and in 1905 schools throughout the South were very poorly funded. Educational facilities for African Americans received significantly less support than did those for white students.

◆ "Courts," "Public Opinion," and "Health"

The next three paragraphs address three seemingly unrelated topics. The statement on courts begins with a "demand" for fair and honest judges, the inclusion without discrimination of blacks on juries, and fair and equitable sentencing procedures. It then lists additional needed reforms ranging from social service institutions such as orphanages and reformatories and an end to the convict-lease system. In contrast, the statement on health begins, "We plead for health—for an opportunity to live in decent houses and localities." There was a connection between the two issues, although it was somewhat tenuous. Bringing justice to the criminal justice system extended to providing a decent environment for orphans, dependent children, and children in the court system; health was extended to include a healthy environment, both physically and morally, in which to raise children. While these concerns were not always at the forefront of civil rights agitation, these issues, especially those that relate to child welfare, reflected the social agenda voiced by white progressive reformers in the early years of the century.

The paragraph on public opinion introduces a new concern, a perceived shift away from the ideals of democracy that were voiced in the eighteenth century by the Founding Fathers. The last sentence, with its reference to "all men ... created free and equal" and "unalienable rights," echoes the language of the Declaration of Independence. The Niagara delegates were not ignorant of the slavery and racial prejudice that were central to the founding of the

Charles Darwin, whose ideas about the "survival of the fittest" underpinned "scientific racism" (Library of Congress)

United States, but their alarm over the "retrogression" was justified. Racial violence was rampant; democracy seemed challenged by labor wars and fears of unrestricted immigration; and the arts, sciences, and social sciences embraced a new scientific racism that was based on the application of Charles Darwin's "survival of the fittest" to efforts to categorize and rank human races.

◆ **"Employers and Labor Unions"**

The declaration's earlier discussion of economic opportunity focuses completely on conditions in the South. Here it turns to economic opportunity in the North, especially the abuses blacks suffered at the hands of racially prejudiced labor unions and the exploitation of blacks by white employers in using them as strike breakers. This situation, and especially the restrictive behavior of white labor unions, characterized the African American experience with organized labor throughout much of the twentieth century. It ran counter to the belief of many progressives and Socialists that class unity would defeat racial prejudice. The declaration denounces the practices of both employers and unions in strong terms and blames them for contributing to class warfare.

◆ **"Protest"**

Protest, along with agitation, were central tenets of the Niagara Movement's strategy for achieving racial justice, and both terms appear frequently in the Declaration of Principles. In contrast to Booker T. Washington's Atlanta Exposition Address, with its ambiguity on the effectiveness of agitation, the Declaration of Principles is crystal clear—protest and agitation are necessary tools to combat injustice. However, the language and tone in the section specifically discussing protest are exceptionally mild. The term *agitation* is not used, and the word *protest* is used only once. The argument is that blacks must not "allow the impression to remain" that they assented to inferiority, were "submissive" to oppression, or were "apologetic" when faced with insults, and the argument is worded to suggest that Washington was both apologetic and submissive. But there is little power or threat in this language beyond the assurance that although blacks may of necessity submit to oppression, they must continue to raise their voices in protest.

◆ **"Color-Line"**

Beginning with this paragraph the Declaration of Principles returns to the issue of discrimination and its impact on African Americans. "Color-Line" discusses legitimate and illegitimate discrimination. The former included discrimination based on intelligence, immorality, and disease (for example, quarantining someone with a highly infectious disease to protect public health). In contrast, discrimination based on physical conditions such as place of birth (immigrants) and race was never justified. The color line—segregation and discrimination based on race or skin color or both—is described in harsh terms, as barbarous and as a relic of unreasoning human savagery. According to the Declaration of Principles, the fact that the color line is sanctioned by law, custom, or community standards does nothing to legitimize it or to diminish the evil and injustice that it manifests.

◆ **"'Jim Crow' Cars," "Soldiers," and "War Amendments"**

These three paragraphs briefly address three specific issues related to discrimination. "'Jim Crow' cars" refers to the segregation of African Americans on railroads. This issue had both practical and symbolic importance. Railroads were by far the chief means of intercity transportation at the beginning of the twentieth century. Policies that restricted black passengers to overcrowded, rowdy Jim Crow cars affected all black passengers, especially women and the black elite. Virtually every African American who traveled through the South suffered this indignity. Du Bois himself had been victimized by this practice and sought Washington's help in an unsuccessful effort to seek redress from the Southern Railway Company. The issue of Jim Crow segregation on railroads was the subject of the *Plessy v. Ferguson* case; the Supreme Court ruling legitimizing separate-but-equal segregation provided the legal basis for segregation in schools, parks, public accommodations, and almost all areas of life. The Declaration of Principles condemns Jim Crow cars as effectively crucifying "wantonly our manhood, womanhood and self-respect."

"Soldiers" puts the Niagara Movement on record protesting the inequity experienced by African Americans serving in the armed forces. This issue took on additional meaning a year later as blacks reacted to the harsh treatment of the black soldiers following a racial clash with local civilians in the so-called Brownsville incident in Brownsville, Texas, and it was revived again during World War I as black troops suffered from systematic discrimination and mistreatment.

One of the most frustrating issues facing African Americans was that along with abolishing slavery, the three Civil War Amendments wrote civil rights and voting rights into the U.S. Constitution. The Fourteenth Amendment guaranteed all citizens, including blacks, equal protection under the law and equal rights and privileges; the Fifteenth Amendment provided that no citizen could be denied the right to vote "on account of race, color, or previous condition of servitude." What the declaration calls for is legislation from Congress to enforce these provisions.

♦ "Oppression" and "The Church"

In examining the broad issue of oppression, the declaration presents a litany of crimes perpetrated on African Americans, from their kidnapping in Africa to their ravishment and degradation in America; as they have struggled to advance themselves, again and again they have encountered criticism, hindrance, and violence. In a thinly veiled attack on Booker T. Washington, the Niagarites also place blame on African American leadership for providing in the face of oppression only cowardice and apology, essentially leaving it to the oppressor to define the rights of the oppressed. Finally, in the brief paragraph "The Church," the declaration charges churches and organized religion with acquiescence to racial oppression and condemns them as "wrong, unchristian and disgraceful."

♦ "Agitation"

Following this litany of grievances, the Declaration of Principles reaffirms its commitment to protest and agitation. The delegates vow to voice their grievances "loudly and insistently" and note that "manly agitation is the way to liberty." As in the section on "Protest," the language is clear but measured and temperate rather than threatening.

♦ "Help" and "Duties"

The Declaration of Principles concludes with a section recognizing with gratitude the valuable assistance that African Americans had received throughout their history from their white friends and allies. It then lists eight duties that it expects blacks to follow as they pursue their rights. These duties include civic responsibilities, such as the duty to vote, work, and obey the law, as well as personal obligations, such as the duty to be clean and orderly and to educate their children. These last two sections softened the impact of the declaration and were intended to assure whites that the Niagara Movement was neither revolutionary nor antiwhite. Ironically, the tone of these concluding paragraphs is more that of Booker T. Washington than W. E. B. Du Bois. The final sentence of the declaration notes that the document, characterized as a "statement, complaint and prayer," is being submitted to the American people and to God.

Taken as a whole, the Declaration of Principles is both an interesting and a compelling document. It is a comprehensive list of issues, concepts, grievances, and statements about the conditions confronting blacks at the beginning of the last century. What is compelling is that this was the most successful effort to date to express all of this in one place and do so in language that was pointed and uncompromising yet restrained. At the same time, the declaration is interesting for what it did not say. By the standards of the twenty-first century it is not a particularly radical document. Although the Niagara Movement was an all-black organization, there is no hint of black nationalism or separatism in its Declaration of Principles. Rather, it serves as a restrained, moderate document outlining a program of desegregation, equal rights, and racial justice. It praises white friends and allies for their support, and it reminds blacks that they have the duty and responsibility to be hardworking and law-abiding citizens who embody the values and habits of middle-class America. Despite the anti–Booker T. Washington nature of the Niagara Movement and its members and Washington's open hostility to both the Niagara Movement and its Declaration of Principles, there is little in the document with which the Tuskegeean could take issue.

Audience

The authors of the Declaration of Principles concluded by submitting the document to the American people. While this may have represented the wishes of the group assembled at Fort Erie, the actual audience was much more modest. The initial audience for the document was that group of twenty-nine men assembled at the inaugural meeting of the Niagara Movement. The secondary audience was the four hundred or so men and women who would join the Niagara Movement before its demise in 1909. Of course, the intended audience was much larger. It included the African American community, especially in the North, and the intention was that blacks from all parts of the United States would hear about and read the document and join the Niagara Movement. The document was also crafted for a white audience. The language and moderate tone, as well as the specific statement of appreciation to white friends and allies, were intended to attract financial and political support for the agenda and the movement and convince progressive whites that they offered a realistic and palatable alternative to the racial agenda of Booker T. Washington.

In the short term the audience was quite small, as press coverage of the Fort Erie meeting and the Declaration of Principles was limited. It is not clear how much coverage a small meeting of African Americans in Ontario would receive in the white press in ordinary circumstances, but in July 1905 a very effective campaign by the Tuskegee machine kept press coverage to a minimum. News of the Fort Erie events was kept out of most of the white press when a Washington ally went to the Buffalo Associated Press office and persuaded it not to forward the news of the Fort Erie meeting. There was some reporting in the African American press,

Essential Quotes

> "Any discrimination based simply on race or color is barbarous, we care not how hallowed it be by custom, expediency or prejudice."
> (Color-Line)

> "The Negro race in America stolen, ravished and degraded, struggling up through difficulties and oppression, needs sympathy and receives criticism; needs help and is given hindrance, needs protection and is given mob-violence, needs justice and is given charity, needs leadership and is given cowardice and apology, needs bread and is given a stone."
> (Oppression)

> "Of the above grievances we do not hesitate to complain, and to complain loudly and insistently. To ignore, overlook, or apologize for these wrongs is to prove ourselves unworthy of freedom."
> (Agitation)

especially in Atlanta and Washington, where there was widespread support for the Niagarites, and, of course, in Boston, where Trotter's *Guardian* pushed the story. But on the whole the black press remained loyal to Washington and withheld news of the meeting. Eventually the audience grew significantly. The Declaration of Principles and much of the agenda of the Niagara Movement were picked up by the NAACP and influenced its approach to civil rights.

Impact

Much like its audience, the impact of the Declaration of Principles grew over time. Initially, the influence of the Niagara Movement and its Declaration of Principles was limited. Membership never exceeded about four hundred, and the dream of a vibrant organization with chapters nationwide was never realized. Feuding leadership and the failure to secure adequate funding doomed the organization, and membership and attendance at its annual meeting began to decline. The Niagara Movement shut down following its 1909 meeting. During its short life the declaration accomplished one thing: It defined the terms of the Du Bois–Washington debate. As the writer and civil rights activist James Weldon Johnson noted, the animosity between these two factions reached an intensity that is difficult to comprehend today.

The principal impact of the document followed the demise of the Niagara Movement, when it essentially set the agenda of the NAACP. The focus of the Declaration of Principles on voting rights and discrimination and segregation were also the focus of the NAACP for its first fifty years; protest and agitation were its tools. Perhaps the clearest example of this impact is the use of the declaration's statement on the Civil War Amendments and its call for Congress to enforce the provisions of these amendments. This is exactly what the NAACP did, using the courts instead of Congress. In 1915 the NAACP scored one of its first major victories when it filed a brief in *Guinn v. United States*, the case in which the Supreme Court overturned Oklahoma's use of the grandfather clause to restrict black suffrage. In the 1930s the NAACP launched its legal assault on the continuing restrictions on black suffrage, provisions that kept blacks from serving on juries, and segregation, especially in public and higher education. Ultimately, this campaign led to the reversal of *Plessy v. Ferguson* and separate-but-equal segregation. In the 1950s and 1960s the civil rights movement used the declaration strategy by successfully lobbying for a series of civil rights acts, finally enforcing provisions of the Fourteenth Amendment to attack segregation, and enacting the Voting Rights Act to enforce the Fifteenth Amendment.

See also Fourteenth Amendment to the U.S. Constitution (1868); Fifteenth Amendment to the U.S. Constitution (1870); Ku Klux Klan Act (1871); Booker T. Washington's Atlanta Exposition Address (1895); *Plessy v. Ferguson* (1896); Monroe Trotter's Protest to Woodrow Wilson (1914).

Further Reading

Books

Fox, Stephen R. *The Guardian of Boston: William Monroe Trotter*. New York: Atheneum, 1970.

Harlan, Louis R. *Booker T. Washington: The Wizard of Tuskegee, 1901–1915*. New York: Oxford University Press, 1983.

Lewis, David Levering. *W. E. B. Du Bois: Biography of a Race, 1868–1919*. New York: Henry Holt, 1993.

Marable, Manning. *W. E. B. Du Bois: Black Radical Democrat*. Boston: Twayne, 1986.

Meier, August. *Negro Thought in America, 1880–1915*. Ann Arbor: University of Michigan Press, 1968.

Moore, Jacqueline M. *Booker T. Washington, W. E. B. Du Bois, and the Struggle for Racial Uplift*. Wilmington, Del.: Scholarly Resources, 2003.

Rampersad, Arnold. *The Art and Imagination of W. E. B. Du Bois*. Cambridge, Mass.: Harvard University Press, 1976.

Rudwick, Elliott M. *W. E. B. Du Bois: Propagandist of the Negro Protest*. New York: Atheneum, 1969.

Wolters, Raymond. *Du Bois and His Rivals*. Columbia: University of Missouri Press, 2002.

Web Sites

Du Bois, W. E. B. "Address to the Nation." Wake Forest University Web site.
http://www.wfu.edu/~zulick/341/niagara.html.

———. "Chapter III. Of Mr. Booker T. Washington and Others." In *The Souls of Black Folk*.
http://etext.virginia.edu/etcbin/toccer-new2?id=DubSoul.sgm&images=images/modeng&data=/texts/english/modeng/parsed&tag=public&part=3&division=div1.

———. "The Talented Tenth (Excerpts)." The Gilder Lehrman Center for the Study of Slavery, Resistance, and Abolition at Yale University.
http://www.yale.edu/glc/archive/1148.htm.

Manly, Howard. "Black History: The Niagara Movement." *Boston-Bay State Banner* Web site.
http://www.baystate-banner.com/issues/2007/10/11/news/local10110711.htm.

"The Niagara Movement." African American History of Western New York Web site.
http://www.math.buffalo.edu/~sww/0history/hwny-niagara-movement.html.

—Cary D. Wintz

Questions for Further Study

1. In what ways did the Declaration of Principles represent a new and different African American approach to prejudice, discrimination, and racism? Explain exactly what was new and different and what was not.

2. Was the Declaration of Principles a radical or a conservative document? Explain your answer both in the context of 1905 and in terms of concepts of radical and conservative and civil rights today.

3. What is the difference between the Niagara Movement and the NAACP? Explain how the Declaration of Principles relates to each of these organizations.

4. The Declaration of Principles called upon Congress for the "enactment of appropriate legislation for securing the proper enforcement of those articles of freedom, the thirteenth, fourteenth and fifteenth amendments of the Constitution of the United States." In what sense were these three amendments "articles of freedom"? What freedoms did they guarantee? To what extent had they not been enforced? Since Congress had initially approved these amendments, why had they not been enforced?

5. "Agitation" and "protest" are recurring themes in the Declaration of Principles. What did the Niagara Movement mean by these terms? What did most Americans at the time think about African American agitation and protest? Explain how the Niagara Movement and later the NAACP utilized agitation and protest.

Niagara Movement Declaration of Principles

Progress: The members of the conference, known as the Niagara Movement, assembled in annual meeting at Buffalo, July 11th, 12th and 13th, 1905, congratulate the Negro-Americans on certain undoubted evidences of progress in the last decade, particularly the increase of intelligence, the buying of property, the checking of crime, the uplift in home life, the advance in literature and art, and the demonstration of constructive and executive ability in the conduct of great religious, economic and educational institutions.

Suffrage: At the same time, we believe that this class of American citizens should protest emphatically and continually against the curtailment of their political rights. We believe in manhood suffrage; we believe that no man is so good, intelligent or wealthy as to be entrusted wholly with the welfare of his neighbor.

Civil Liberty: We believe also in protest against the curtailment of our civil rights. All American citizens have the right to equal treatment in places of public entertainment according to their behavior and deserts.

Economic Opportunity: We especially complain against the denial of equal opportunities to us in economic life; in the rural districts of the South this amounts to peonage and virtual slavery; all over the South it tends to crush labor and small business enterprises; and everywhere American prejudice, helped often by iniquitous laws, is making it more difficult for Negro-Americans to earn a decent living.

Education: Common school education should be free to all American children and compulsory. High school training should be adequately provided for all, and college training should be the monopoly of no class or race in any section of our common country. We believe that, in defense of our own institutions, the United States should aid common school education, particularly in the South, and we especially recommend concerted agitation to this end. We urge an increase in public high school facilities in the South, where the Negro-Americans are almost wholly without such provisions. We favor well-equipped trade and technical schools for the training of artisans, and the need of adequate and liberal endowment for a few institutions of higher education must be patent to sincere well-wishers of the race.

Courts: We demand upright judges in courts, juries selected without discrimination on account of color and the same measure of punishment and the same efforts at reformation for black as for white offenders. We need orphanages and farm schools for dependent children, juvenile reformatories for delinquents, and the abolition of the dehumanizing convict-lease system.

Public Opinion: We note with alarm the evident retrogression in this land of sound public opinion on the subject of manhood rights, republican government and human brotherhood, and we pray God that this nation will not degenerate into a mob of boasters and oppressors, but rather will return to the faith of the fathers, that all men were created free and equal, with certain unalienable rights.

Health: We plead for health—for an opportunity to live in decent houses and localities, for a chance to rear our children in physical and moral cleanliness.

Employers and Labor Unions: We hold up for public execration the conduct of two opposite classes of men: The practice among employers of importing ignorant Negro-American laborers in emergencies, and then affording them neither protection nor permanent employment; and the practice of labor unions in proscribing and boycotting and oppressing thousands of their fellow-toilers, simply because they are black. These methods have accentuated and will accentuate the war of labor and capital, and they are disgraceful to both sides.

Protest: We refuse to allow the impression to remain that the Negro-American assents to inferiority, is submissive under oppression and apologetic before insults. Through helplessness we may submit, but the voice of protest of ten million Americans must never cease to assail the ears of their fellows, so long as America is unjust.

Color-Line: Any discrimination based simply on race or color is barbarous, we care not how hallowed it be by custom, expediency or prejudice. Differences made on account of ignorance, immorality, or disease are legitimate methods of fighting evil, and against them we have no word of protest; but discriminations based simply and solely on physical peculiarities, place of birth, color of skin, are relics of that unreasoning human savagery of which the world is and ought to be thoroughly ashamed.

Document Text

"Jim Crow" Cars: We protest against the "Jim Crow" car, since its effect is and must be to make us pay first-class fare for third-class accommodations, render us open to insults and discomfort and to crucify wantonly our manhood, womanhood and self-respect.

Soldiers: We regret that this nation has never seen fit adequately to reward the black soldiers who, in its five wars, have defended their country with their blood, and yet have been systematically denied the promotions which their abilities deserve. And we regard as unjust, the exclusion of black boys from the military and naval training schools.

War Amendments: We urge upon Congress the enactment of appropriate legislation for securing the proper enforcement of those articles of freedom, the thirteenth, fourteenth and fifteenth amendments of the Constitution of the United States.

Oppression: We repudiate the monstrous doctrine that the oppressor should be the sole authority as to the rights of the oppressed. The Negro race in America stolen, ravished and degraded, struggling up through difficulties and oppression, needs sympathy and receives criticism; needs help and is given hindrance, needs protection and is given mob-violence, needs justice and is given charity, needs leadership and is given cowardice and apology, needs bread and is given a stone. This nation will never stand justified before God until these things are changed.

The Church: Especially are we surprised and astonished at the recent attitude of the church of Christ—of an increase of a desire to bow to racial prejudice, to narrow the bounds of human brotherhood, and to segregate black men to some outer sanctuary. This is wrong, unchristian and disgraceful to the twentieth century civilization.

Agitation: Of the above grievances we do not hesitate to complain, and to complain loudly and insistently. To ignore, overlook, or apologize for these wrongs is to prove ourselves unworthy of freedom. Persistent manly agitation is the way to liberty, and toward this goal the Niagara Movement has started and asks the cooperation of all men of all races.

Help: At the same time we want to acknowledge with deep thankfulness the help of our fellowmen from the Abolitionist down to those who today still stand for equal opportunity and who have given and still give of their wealth and of their poverty for our advancement.

Duties: And while we are demanding, and ought to demand, and will continue to demand the rights

Glossary

Abolitionist	a person who advocated the complete, immediate, and unconditional abolition of slavery, especially in the United States, prior to and during the Civil War
artisans	skilled craftsmen or workers
civil rights	rights guaranteed to all citizens by law or the Constitution regardless of such differences as race
common school	a free public elementary school
convict-lease system	a system of labor in which prisoners are leased to an employer by the court or the prison system
execration	vehement denunciation
hallowed	sacred; respected; venerated beyond question
iniquitous	unjust
"Jim Crow" car	a segregated railroad coach, usually of inferior quality, set aside for African Americans
peonage	a system of agricultural labor in which workers are bound to their job, often against their will, by economic debt or other means; virtual bondage
retrogression	a reversal in development of condition; moving backward or becoming worse
suffrage	the right to vote

Document Text

enumerated above, God forbid that we should ever forget to urge corresponding duties upon our people:

    The duty to vote.
    The duty to respect the rights of others.
    The duty to work.
    The duty to obey the laws.
    The duty to be clean and orderly.
    The duty to send our children to school.
    The duty to respect ourselves, even as we respect others.

This statement, complaint and prayer we submit to the American people, and Almighty God.

Theodore Roosevelt (Library of Congress)

Theodore Roosevelt's Brownsville Legacy Special Message to the Senate

1906

"The act was one of horrible atrocity, and ... unparalleled for infamy in the annals of the United States Army."

Overview

President Theodore Roosevelt's Special Message to the U.S. Senate of December 19, 1906, explained his summary dismissal of 167 members of the segregated Twenty-fifth Infantry Regiment from the U.S. Army. The dismissals resulted from charges that the soldiers had engaged in a conspiracy of silence after some members of their regiment had attacked the Mexican-border city of Brownsville, Texas, on the night of August 13, 1906. Reported shootings by the military took the life of a civilian and seriously wounded a police officer. The message was a response to two Senate information-gathering resolutions that had been submitted to Secretary of War William Howard Taft, and it was presented together with several documents, including a letter from General A. B. Nettleton and memoranda demonstrating precedents for the summary discharges. The dismissals involved virtually all members of Companies B, C, and D (the only companies of the regiment that went to Brownsville); they also led to the expulsion of black troops from Texas and the heightening of racial tension in the United States.

The president's Special Message caused a heated controversy within the government and across the nation. Republican Senator Joseph B. Foraker of Ohio, who perhaps was eyeing a presidential campaign, argued the innocence of the accused on the chamber floor as well as in public speeches and magazine articles. A report released in March 1908 by the Senate Committee on Military Affairs, however, supported Roosevelt's action, although a supplementary report recommended a policy of leniency toward the men that would allow them to reenlist, which the president himself had also urged earlier. With respect to the possibility that certain townspeople might have staged the attack on Brownsville and framed the regiment, Senator Foraker was able to obtain the support of only Senator Morgan G. Bulkeley of Connecticut. The perceived image of black soldiers attacking a town embittered racial relations in many garrison towns. It would not be until 1970 that the regiment's innocence would be reconsidered in a scathing study by the historian John D. Weaver that condemned Roosevelt's handling of the Brownsville affray. That book prompted California Democratic Representative Augustus Hawkins to introduce legislation signed by President Richard M. Nixon in 1972 that granted honorable discharges, nearly all of them posthumous, to the 153 cashiered servicemen who had not been allowed to reenlist.

Context

The Twenty-fifth Infantry was one of six African American U.S. Army regiments organized by Congress in July of 1866 (two cavalry and four infantry). These regiments served in Texas and other western frontier areas for much of the late nineteenth century. They were often assigned frontier duty because of the need for security in the West and the Great Plains; furthermore, many military towns in the East were reticent about welcoming black soldiers. In the West, African American regiments not only offered protection to often ungrateful civilians from attacks by outlaws and Native Americans but also performed more mundane operations, such as stringing and maintaining telegraph lines, building roads, aiding travelers, delivering federal mail, performing agricultural experiments, and compiling weather records. Black soldiers patrolled reservations to ensure that Native Americans stayed on them. They also protected reservation residents from white intruders, occasionally arrested white buffalo hunters, and acted as translators and even agents for some tribes. For these services, Native Americans gave them a respected name, "Buffalo Soldiers."

From the outset, African American soldiers had to confront racial prejudice along with other obstacles. Customary indignities and occasional violence directed toward troops seldom drew retaliation. Two incidents, however, broke the sullen calm of garrison towns in the 1880s. At San Angelo, Texas, white citizens shot to death two Tenth Cavalry soldiers stationed at Fort Concho within ten days. Irate troopers scattered handbills around the community, protesting the unpunished murders and threatening to mete out justice. Some soldiers unleashed a volley of gunfire toward a suspected culprit, an act that prompted intervention by the Texas Rangers, punishment of the soldiers, and removal of the companies from Fort Concho. A similar incident played out at Sturgis City, Dakota Territory, in August 1885. The lynching of a black soldier provoked members of the Twenty-fifth Infantry from Fort Meade to

Time Line

1866
- **July 28** By act of Congress, six black regiments are established.

1867–1881
- African American troops, dubbed "Buffalo Soldiers" by the Plains Indians, serve in Texas, generally without incident.

1899
- **October 18** Members of the Tenth Cavalry attack a Laredo peace officer after complaints of abuse.
- **November 20** Members of the Ninth Cavalry fire on Rio Grande City, allegedly to repel an attack on Fort Ringgold.

1900
- **February 7** An El Paso lawman is killed when soldiers of the Twenty-fifth Infantry attempt to free a jailed comrade.

1906
- **July 28** Companies B, C, and D of the Twenty-fifth Infantry arrive at Fort Brown, Texas, along the Mexican border.
- **August 13** Around midnight, shots ring out in the town of Brownsville and the neighboring garrison, resulting in one death and two injuries.
- **November 4** Following several military investigations into the Brownsville raid, President Theodore Roosevelt summarily dismisses 167 members of the regiment from the military for having refused to provide information about the alleged instigators of the incident.
- **December 3** Senator Joseph B. Foraker of Ohio introduces a resolution for a Senate investigation of the Brownsville raid.

---

fire into a saloon, killing a customer. In this instance the War Department resisted public demands to remove the troops after having charged four soldiers with the shooting.

Black troops faced both indifference from town officials toward enforcing their safety and swift reprisals from the military for alleged transgressions. White officers, frequently hoping for a fast track to promotion, commanded the soldiers; indeed, West Point graduated only three African Americans over the course of the nineteenth century. Post commanders keenly felt the obligation to maintain good relationships with the citizenry of garrison towns, and the army never considered itself a laboratory for social experimentation. Whether the military meted out harsher justice for black troops than white troops in similar circumstances is a matter of debate among historians, but African Americans clearly worked under more difficult conditions, often in areas such as Texas, which once had been part of the Confederacy.

The transfer of black troops to the South after the Spanish-American War in 1898 sparked more frequent racial clashes between forts and towns than in preceding years. The higher incidence of conflict derived from opposing movements that had gained momentum after the war: an attempt in the southern states to further isolate blacks and remove them entirely from political participation and a determination on the part of black soldiers, many of whom had received commendations for valor in the recent war, to validate their constitutional rights. Partly as a reaction to the Populist movement, which threatened the establishment and brought whites and blacks together tentatively during political campaigns of the 1890s, southern legislatures enacted laws that stipulated stricter property qualifications and literacy tests for African American voters. Many southern states, including Texas, also required poll taxes for black voters and established all-white Democratic primaries. After the Supreme Court's *Plessy v. Ferguson* ruling (1896), many communities began to enforce segregationist practices even more strictly, such as requiring separate seating on newly introduced electric streetcars. Incidents of lynching reached an all-time high in the South in the early 1900s, with Texas ranking third in frequency, and black community groups complained of excessive use of force by police.

Members of all the African American regiments encountered hostility from whites after the end of the Spanish-American War. A group of Floridians booed the soldiers while cheering their Spanish military prisoners. Snipers fired at troop trains passing through Alabama and departing from Houston, Texas. National Guardsmen scuffled with black soldiers at Huntsville, Alabama. A constable in Texarkana, Texas, almost provoked retaliation when he attempted to arrest a soldier on a troop train after a disturbance at a local brothel. Some of the soldier's comrades, unaware of the circumstances, silently drew weapons at the sight of an armed civilian accosting a member of their unit. Their reaction allowed the soldier to disappear aboard the train, escaping arrest and identification. The most serious clashes, however, awaited the troops' arrival at their Texas posts in 1899.

Prior to the Brownsville affray, Texas clashes between soldiers and townspeople, often law officers, had erupted at

Laredo, Rio Grande City, and El Paso. The events preceding these conflicts bore a dismal similarity to conditions in Brownsville. Predominantly Hispanic populations, governed by a white political and business establishment, greeted the arriving troops with suspicion followed by minor disturbances. Soldiers complained of discrimination and price gouging from the business community as well as harassment by local police. Some civilians plainly hoped that the War Department could be persuaded to remove the black troops and replace them with white units—a virtual impossibility in light of the strained resources of the military command. At Fort McIntosh, Laredo, Company D of the Twenty-fifth Infantry felt victimized by a local peace officer. Mistaking another officer for the man, a number of enlisted men assaulted him with rifle butts and then fired their arms in the streets. The mayor protested to the governor, who strongly supported the stance of the local official. The War Department resolved the matter by evacuating the post.

Almost simultaneously, another incident broke the peace at Fort Ringgold, Rio Grande City, a hundred miles to the south. After a ruckus in a gambling hall involving the citizenry and members of Troop D, Ninth Cavalry, rumors reached the post of an impending attack from the town. The disabled post commander gave credence to his men's reports of snipers by allowing the firing of a Gatling gun toward Rio Grande City. Mercifully, there were no casualties, but a major row ensued between officials of the town and the fort over culpability, each claiming attack by the other. Texas governor Joseph D. Sayers involved himself in the controversy, engaging in a dispute with the army over legal jurisdiction. The matter dissipated when an angry grand jury failed to return indictments against any soldier.

In the most serious civilian-military rift before Brownsville, a sergeant from Company A of the Twenty-fifth Infantry was charged with murder in 1900 for having led a group of soldiers to the El Paso jail to release a jailed comrade, who they believed had been unjustly detained. In the scuffle a popular lawman received fatal wounds. Because of heated emotions in El Paso, a change of venue was ordered for the ensuing trial. A Dallas court sentenced Sergeant John Kipper to fifty years at hard labor, further embittering race relations between the military and civilians in the state.

Only the magnitude of the controversy that surrounded the Brownsville incident separated it from its lesser-known predecessors. The Twenty-fifth Infantry passed a productive six years abroad and stateside after its partial involvement in the Rio Grande City imbroglio. After the outbreak of the Philippine insurrection in 1899, all of the regiment's companies were shipped to the islands within one year. The regiment demonstrated the same combat efficiency in the Pacific as it had in Cuba, drawing accolades from Brigadier General A. S. Burt. Filipinos themselves praised the troops' decorum. These same heroics failed to impress Brownsville residents, who for whatever reasons refused to accept the troops, regardless of their stellar military campaign record. Among those who objected to the troops' presence were outright bigots, residents with an antimilitary bias, Latinos challenged by a new minority group, and the lawless. The

Time Line

1906
- **December 19**
  President Roosevelt issues a Special Message to the Senate about the Brownsville raid, in which he justifies his dismissal of the soldiers.

1908
- **March 11**
  The Senate Committee on Military Affairs issues a report on the Brownsville raid and dismissals; the committee supports the presidential decision by a vote of nine to four.

1972
- **September 28**
  President Richard M. Nixon issues honorable discharges and pensions to the dismissed soldiers, following a resolution by Democratic California representative Augustus Hawkins.

highly publicized murder at El Paso had also promoted a feeling of apprehension among some of the citizenry. Disappointing news from Austin, Texas, elicited resentment from the soldiers as well; the War Department rescinded the regiment's participation in maneuvers at Camp Mabry after Texas National Guardsmen threatened the black soldiers with violence if they were to appear.

Tensions at Brownsville quickly mounted. Some residents wired Washington, D.C., to complain about the First Battalion even before it was garrisoned at Fort Brown on July 28. Departing white troops acknowledged that they had heard threats against the incoming blacks. Although the city administration sought to maintain a constructive relationship with the army for defensive and financial reasons, federal authorities showed no concern. Fred Tate, a customs inspector, clubbed Private James W. Newton for supposedly jostling Tate's wife and another white woman on a sidewalk. Another customs officer, A. Y. Baker, pushed Private Oscar W. Reed into the Rio Grande. Baker claimed that he was trying to quiet the soldier, who allegedly had returned from Matamoras, Mexico, drunk and boisterous. Locals voiced racial slurs at the soldiers on the streets. Payday, August 11, passed without the confrontation that some had feared, but the following night a report of an attack on a white woman by a black soldier jolted the community. Mrs. Lon Evans, who lived near the red-light district, complained that a uniformed black man had grabbed her hair and thrown her to the ground. The incident had caused Mrs. Evans little physical pain, and she could not swear that her assailant had worn a military uniform. Nevertheless, claims of blacks assaulting white women were known to incite lynch mobs. Accordingly, Mayor Frederick J. Combe and post commander Major Charles W. Penrose hastily met to defuse the situation. Penrose subsequently imposed an eight o'clock curfew on his men.

Around midnight shots rang out near the garrison wall separating the town from the fort. Various Brownsville residents later testified that they saw a shadowy group of nine to twenty persons who divided into two groups and charged up an alley toward town, firing several hundred shots at random into lighted areas. The shooters killed the bartender, Frank Natus, and shattered the arm of M. Y. Dominguez, a police lieutenant, necessitating its amputation. Alleged witnesses never were able to identify the culprits and insisted that the raiders had worn military uniforms or that the shots had emanated from military rifles. Daylight searches located spent army-type cartridges in the streets. Soldiers, contrarily, protested their innocence until the death of the last surviving serviceman over seventy years later. Major Penrose echoed the sentinel's belief that the post had been under attack, particularly after a roll call found all servicemen present or accounted for and a weapons and ammunition inspection revealed none missing. A morning visit from Mayor Combe, brandishing empty cartridges from the streets, convinced the commanding officer of the garrison's guilt, a view quickly adopted by Brownsville residents, newspapers, Texas congressmen, and Governor S. W. T. Lanham, who demanded removal of all African American soldiers from the state.

After an initial investigation, the U.S. government accepted the widely held conviction of the soldiers' guilt. President Roosevelt sent Major General Augustus P. Blocksom to Brownsville several days after the raid. Eleven days later he submitted a report to the White House that differed from the view of the black regiment's guilt only in his conclusion that both sides had exaggerated the facts, that Tate probably had overreacted in his beating of Private Newton, and that some of the citizenry were racially prejudiced. Stating that black soldiers had adopted an aggressive stance, Blocksom posited a scenario in which some soldiers began firing between barracks and the wall, others fired into the air to create an alarm, and nine to fifteen men scaled the wall and rushed through an alley into the streets. The attackers subsequently returned to camp to clean and reassemble their weapons while duping their officers into believing they had not left the garrison. Blocksom also noted that the men's motivation for the raid was questionable, since some bars had served the soldiers and Natus had never quarreled with the troops. Nevertheless, he considered the accusers' testimony as more reliable than that of the soldiers. Blocksom also declared that the discovery of the empty cartridges, which did not fit the recently assigned Springfield rifles, was not pertinent to his decision. He recommended the discharge of every man in the battalion. Each soldier would be granted the option to reenlist only if he identified the guilty by a date determined by the War Department. Roosevelt, adhering to the demands of Texas officials and press, ordered the transfer of the First Battalion to Fort Reno, Oklahoma, except for those held as suspects involved in the raid. Captain William J. "Bill" McDonald of the Texas Rangers and Major Penrose settled on a dozen defendants, based strictly on conjecture, who were grudgingly not indicted by the Cameron County grand jury for lack of evidence. The War Department scheduled Fort Brown for temporary closure.

Determined to uncover the guilty, Roosevelt sent Brigadier General Ernest A. Garlington, inspector general of the U.S. Army, to Fort Reno and Fort Sam Houston in San Antonio, Texas, to interrogate the suspects. Following Blocksom's suggestion, the president instructed Garlington to threaten all members of the battalion with dismissal without honor. When the mere threat proved ineffective, Garlington urged Roosevelt to proceed with its execution. Roosevelt complied on November 4 with War Department Special Order No. 266, an edict that escalated the Texas controversy to national stature and sparked criticism from African Americans and some whites. The *Richmond Planet* and *Atlanta Independent* accused Roosevelt of having delayed until after the congressional elections to assure a black Republican vote in key northern states. Black ministers joined the fray, and the scholar-activist W. E. B. Du Bois urged his followers to vote Democratic in the 1908 elections. Booker T. Washington, the widely publicized White House guest and administration patron to the African American constituency, continued to support Roosevelt and took his own share of criticism together with the chief executive and Secretary of War Taft, the front-runner for the Republican presidential nomination in 1908. An interracial organization, the Constitutional League, raised the argument of the troops' innocence. The director of the league, John Milholland, a white Progressive, assailed the reports of Blocksom and Garlington for racism, haste, and inconsistencies. Republican senator Joseph B. Foraker took up the argument and carried it to a larger stage.

Ordinarily the most stalwart of conservatives, Foraker may have acted from principle, presidential ambitions, or personal dislike of Roosevelt. In any case, he became the cashiered soldiers' most celebrated advocate. His Senate resolution called for an investigation of the raid and summoned the War Department to provide the evidence it had used in its decision. On December 19, Roosevelt countered with a Special Message defending the summary dismissals.

About the Author

Theodore Roosevelt, the twenty-sixth president of the United States, was born October 27, 1858, to a wealthy family in Oyster Bay, New York. The second of four children, Roosevelt was a sickly child and required homeschooling. A voracious reader and experienced world traveler even as a boy, Roosevelt entered Harvard at age eighteen. He excelled with the Harvard boxing team, among other sporting endeavors, and graduated in 1880. He ranched for several years in the Dakota Territory, where he built up his physique and developed a lifelong passion for nature.

Roosevelt served two years in the New York State Assembly, unsuccessfully campaigned for mayor of New York City, served on the U.S. Civil Service Commission, became president of the New York City Board of Police Commissioners, and accepted an appointment as assistant secretary of the U.S. Navy. In all of these positions he displayed a marked enthusiasm for efficiency and public service. Along the way he wrote several books, including *The Naval War of 1812* (1882) and the four-volume series *The Winning of the West* (1889–1896).

The Spanish-American War of 1898 defined Roosevelt for many Americans. His war plan dispatched Commodore George Dewey to a victory over the Spanish navy in the Philippines. At the start of the war, Roosevelt accepted the commission of lieutenant colonel and led the flamboyant "Rough Riders," or the First U.S. Volunteer Cavalry, to fame in Cuba. The forty-year-old Roosevelt emerged from the war as "the Hero of San Juan Hill," where he had fought alongside troops that had included African Americans from the Twenty-fourth Infantry Regiment. For his heroism, he was posthumously awarded the Congressional Medal of Honor in 2001. Roosevelt's popularity brought the governorship of New York within his grasp; he easily won election and instituted several policies of reform during his two-year term. In 1900 he received the Republican vice presidential nomination. The assassination of William McKinley only six months into his second term catapulted Roosevelt to the presidency. At the time he was only forty-two, the youngest man ever to have become president of the United States.

Roosevelt's presidency brought Progressivism to the national scene. He articulated a philosophy of a strong presidency as he took the lead in conservation and labor-management relations. He signed into law many pieces of reform legislation, such as the Hepburn Act, which strengthened the Interstate Commerce Commission Act, the Meat Inspection Act, and the Pure Food and Drug Act. In an unusual display of racial tolerance for the period, the president hosted the African American leader Booker T. Washington at a White House luncheon. He pursued a strong foreign policy, including intervention in the Panamanian insurrection against Colombia, which facilitated the construction of the Panama Canal. In a more diplomatic fashion, he arranged debt payments by the Dominican Republic to European creditor nations and won the Nobel Peace Prize in 1906 for his moderation of the Portsmouth Peace Conference in 1905, which had brought the Russo-Japanese War to an end.

In 1908 Roosevelt denied himself renomination as the Republican presidential candidate and appeared to have left the political arena once his chosen successor, William Howard Taft, won the election. However, he grew impatient with Taft's apparent caution and mounted a third-party campaign against him in 1912, running on the Progressive Party ticket. The division of the vote between Taft and Roosevelt assured the victory of Democrat Woodrow Wilson. Roosevelt then devoted much of his time to travel and writing until World War I. Frustrated in his attempts to strengthen American policy against Germany and, later, to revive his military career, Roosevelt died in his sleep on January 6, 1919.

Explanation and Analysis of the Document

President Roosevelt addresses Senate inquiries to him and Secretary of War William Howard Taft in his Special Message of December 19, 1906. In addition to his defense of his summary dismissal of almost all members of Companies B, C, and D of the Twenty-fifth Infantry, Roosevelt also submitted a Department of War report, a letter from General A. B. Nettleton, a memorandum on precedents supporting the action, and other documents. In his message, the president calls attention to his constitutional power as commander in chief of the armed forces, evidence of the guilt of the unit members, and the existence of a conspiracy of silence among the men to protect the known guilty. Roosevelt denies color as having been a factor in his decision and cites precedents that upheld the dismissals.

Obviously sensitive to the allegation of racial discrimination, Roosevelt defends the record of his investigators in the opening paragraphs of his message and his own record in his conclusion. The president attacks the premise that General Garlington had acted as a southerner; he also emphasizes that Lieutenant Colonel Leonard A. Lovering was a native of New Hampshire, while Major Blocksom had been born in Ohio and General Nettleton in Illinois. He notes that Blocksom had judged the men guilty in his report, while Garlington had acted to protect the innocent from the guilty soldiers. (Garlington and Roosevelt's views were that the guilty soldiers would be named by the innocent soldiers and escape dismissal. The townspeople considered all the soldiers guilty. The soldiers considered none of them guilty.)

He dismisses the notion of birthplace as having played any role in the investigation; all those involved had displayed professional honor and loyalty to the flag and the service. On his own behalf, Roosevelt recalls his condemnation of lynching in his message to the opening session of Congress, his appointment of African Americans to federal offices in both the North and South, and a determined policy to treat people as individuals, regardless of race.

Roosevelt emphasizes that the evidence, reports of federal investigators, and sworn testimony determined his decision, which was corroborated by the discovery of ammunition and other items in the streets of Brownsville. In taking this position, the president skirts the observation that some of the discovered military equipment was not of the type used by the army at that time; he also appears to give more credence to testimony of the Brownsville residents than that of the soldiers. In Roosevelt's view, the most trustworthy reports, of course, came from his appointed investigators. He acknowledges previous incidents that had involved the members of the Twenty-fifth Infantry, ascribing blame to both the soldiers and Brownsville civilians, but he denies any possible justification for the attack on the town. Roosevelt considers the testimony of civilians as consistent except for minor details and dismisses the possibility of collusion on their part. He also rejects as absurd the claim that townsmen shot one another to frame the soldiers; later studies, however, would propose the likelihood of that scenario. In Roosevelt's view,

Buffalo soldiers on the western frontier (Library of Congress)

nine to twenty soldiers climbed over the fort's walls, hurried through an area near the fort, and shot at whomever they saw entering lighted buildings or otherwise moving about. Policemen, the target of fire, identified the shooters as soldiers. The culprits returned the short distance to the barracks, which was not more than 350 yards, within less than ten minutes and thus escaped discovery. Officers, believing the fort was under siege, became aware of the situation only several hours later, which gave the shooters sufficient time to return to their routines. Roosevelt oversaw the War Department's investigation of the white officers, which recommended that two be court-martialed.

The president focuses his frustration and anger on the noncommissioned officers, all of them African Americans, whom he considered the leaders of the alleged cover-up. He saw them as responsible primarily for the discipline and good conduct of the men. They held the keys to the arms room and must have known the whereabouts of the soldiers and suspected their guilt. Roosevelt felt no sympathy for the dismissal of the most senior noncommissioned officers, since supposedly they should have acted to prevent mutiny and murder. He left no room for the possibility of ignorance on the part of any of the dismissed soldiers. They were warned to separate themselves from the guilty or face expulsion from the army with no opportunity for future government employment. Roosevelt denied, however, that dismissal constituted punishment, for the proper punishment for murder was death.

Almost one quarter of President Roosevelt's message is devoted to precedents supporting his action, and he repeatedly denies that race had been a factor in reaching his decision. He cites a district attorney's letter about cases that had involved misconduct by white soldiers; every member of those units had cooperated in the investigations, which ended in findings of guilt for some soldiers and innocence for others. The Civil War presented numerous instances of summary dismissals for misconduct or desertion. In one case, General Ulysses S. Grant mustered two officers out of the service and forced the other brigade members to repay the loss of money to the victim of an unsolved robbery. Roosevelt observes that in the 1906 fiscal year the War Department had discharged 352 enlisted men for misconduct without trial or court martial. He reserves the concluding paragraph to recount his record as an advocate of racial equality in matters of education, opportunity, and employment.

Audience

Roosevelt's immediate audience was the U.S. Senate, which had requested information supporting his decision of November 4, 1906, to summarily discharge 167 members of the First Battalion of the Twenty-fifth Infantry. However, because of the public controversy waged in the media, he was also addressing a national audience. Aside from African Americans and a few sympathetic whites, most of the nation plainly agreed with the president's position and explanation.

Impact

The Senate Committee on Military Affairs, on which Joseph Foraker served, conducted hearings on the Brownsville incident between February 1907 and March 1908. The sessions followed speeches by Foraker, who denounced the absence of trials and suggested that outside forces had raided Brownsville. Despite popularizing the controversy, Foraker's crusade on behalf of the soldiers met the same dismal fate as his campaign for the Republican presidential nomination. By a vote of nine to four, the committee sustained Roosevelt's action, with all five Democrats and four Republican members affirming it. A supplementary report signed by four senators provided for the reenlistment of men who had proved their innocence, a motion supported by Roosevelt. Senator Nathan B. Scott of West Virginia wrote a report that was signed by three other Republican members, including Foraker, which stated that the government had not proved its case. Foraker, in turn, issued a report with Senator Morgan Bulkeley of Connecticut that maintained the men's innocence since they lacked a motive for the crime. On a note to be echoed six decades later, Foraker and Bulkeley asserted that members of the citizenry stood to gain from the soldiers' disgrace and removal. Foraker continued his assault on the decision in an article in the *North American Review* one year later.

The government investigations resulted in courts-martial of two officers of the First Battalion. Major Penrose and Captain Edgar Macklin were tried for dereliction of duty but found not guilty. The War Department permitted fourteen of the cashiered soldiers to reenlist in 1910 but never stated its criteria for that determination. Although no new evidence had come to light, the First Battalion was exonerated more than a half century later. President Richard Nixon, acting on the proposal of Democratic Representative August Hawkins

Essential Quotes

"The act was one of horrible atrocity, and as far as I am aware, unparalleled for infamy in the annals of the United States Army."

"It has been supplemented by another, only less black, in the shape of a successful conspiracy of silence for the purpose of shielding those who took part in the original conspiracy of murder."

---

of California, granted an honorable discharge and a pension of $25,000 to each of the 153 dismissed servicemen in 1972, without ascribing any blame for the Brownsville attack. Nixon's decision came two years after the publication of a history of the incident, *The Brownsville Raid* by John D. Weaver, which convincingly presented Foraker's argument of innocence. Only one member of the battalion, Dorsey Willis, had survived to receive the pardon. Willis had continued to maintain the innocence of all the soldiers and their lack of knowledge about the raid. Most historians today believe that justice was not served in Roosevelt's action—from the lack of due process, the absence of certain evidence, or the likelihood of a conspiracy against the black soldiers.

Further Reading

■ Articles
Tinsley, James A. "Roosevelt, Foraker, and the Brownsville Affray." *Journal of Negro History* 41 (January 1956): 43–65.

■ Books
Christian, Garna L. *Black Soldiers in Jim Crow Texas, 1899–1917.* College Station: Texas A&M University Press, 1995.

Hearings before the Committee on Military Affairs, United States Senate, concerning the Affair at Brownsville, Tex., on the Night of August 13 and 14, 1906. Washington, D.C.: Government Printing Office, 1907.

Lane, Ann J. *The Brownsville Affair: National Crisis and Black Reaction.* Port Washington, N.Y.: Kennikat Press, 1971.

Weaver, John D. *The Brownsville Raid.* New York: W. W. Norton, 1970.

—Garna L. Christian

Questions for Further Study

1. Using this document and Thomas Morris Chester's Civil War Dispatches (1864), trace the history of African American participation in the military during the late nineteenth century.

2. Summarize the events surrounding the Brownsville disturbance. Why was it so difficult at the time to affix blame where it belonged?

3. Theodore Roosevelt was a military commander during the Spanish-American War, in which black soldiers and units acquitted themselves with valor. Yet Roosevelt defended his dismissal of the African American troops. Why?

4. Why were the dismissed soldiers exonerated in 1972?

5. How did the incident at Brownsville illustrate the Jim Crow system in the South—and, indeed, throughout much of the country—at the turn of the twentieth century?

Theodore Roosevelt's Brownsville Legacy Special Message to the Senate

To the Senate:

In response to Senate resolution of December 6 addressed to me, and to the two Senate resolutions addressed to him, the Secretary of War has, by my direction, submitted to me a report which I herewith send to the Senate, together with several documents, including a letter of General Nettleton and memoranda as to precedents for the summary discharge or mustering out of regiments or companies, some or all of the members of which had been guilty of misconduct.

I ordered the discharge of nearly all the members of Companies B, C, and D of the Twenty-fifth Infantry by name, in the exercise of my constitutional power and in pursuance of what, after full consideration, I found to be my constitutional duty as Commander in Chief of the United States Army. I am glad to avail myself of the opportunity afforded by these resolutions to lay before the Senate the following facts as to the murderous conduct of certain members of the companies in question and as to the conspiracy by which many of the other members of these companies saved the criminals from justice, to the disgrace of the United States uniform.

I call your attention to the accompanying reports of Maj. Augustus P. Blocksom, of Lieut. Col. Leonard A. Lovering, and of Brig. Gen. Ernest A. Garlington, the Inspector-General of the United States Army, of their investigation into the conduct of the troops in question. An effort has been made to discredit the fairness of the investigation into the conduct of these colored troops by pointing out that General Garlington is a Southerner. Precisely the same action would have been taken had the troops been white—indeed, the discharge would probably have been made in more summary fashion. General Garlington is a native of South Carolina; Lieutenant-Colonel Lovering is a native of New Hampshire; Major Blocksom is a native of Ohio. As it happens, the disclosure of the guilt of the troops was made in the report of the officer who comes from Ohio, and the efforts of the officer who comes from South Carolina were confined to the endeavor to shield the innocent men of the companies in question, if any such there were, by securing information which would enable us adequately to punish the guilty. But I wish it distinctly understood that the fact of the birthplace of either officer is one which I absolutely refuse to consider. The standard of professional honor and of loyalty to the flag and the service is the same for all officers and all enlisted men of the United States Army, and I resent with the keenest indignation any effort to draw any line among them based upon birthplace, creed, or any other consideration of the kind. I should put the same entire faith in these reports if it had happened that they were all made by men coming from some one State, whether in the South or the North, the East or the West, as I now do, when, as it happens, they were made by officers born in different States.

Major Blocksom's report is most careful, is based upon the testimony of scores of eye-witnesses—testimony which conflicted only in non-essentials and which established the essential facts beyond chance of successful contradiction. Not only has no successful effort been made to traverse his findings in any essential particular, but, as a matter of fact, every trustworthy report from outsiders amply corroborates them, by far the best of these outside reports being that of Gen. A. B. Nettleton, made in a letter to the Secretary of War, which I herewith append; General Nettleton being an ex-Union soldier, a consistent friend of the colored man throughout his life, a life-long Republican, a citizen of Illinois, and Assistant Secretary of the Treasury under President Harrison.

It appears that in Brownsville, the city immediately beside which Fort Brown is situated, there had been considerable feeling between the citizens and the colored troops of the garrison companies. Difficulties had occurred, there being a conflict of evidence as to whether the citizens or the colored troops were to blame. My impression is that, as a matter of fact, in these difficulties there was blame attached to both sides; but this is a wholly unimportant matter for our present purpose, as nothing that occurred offered in any shape or way an excuse or justification for the atrocious conduct of the troops when, in lawless and murderous spirit, and under cover of the night, they made their attack upon the citizens.

The attack was made near midnight on August 13. The following facts as to this attack are made clear by Major Blocksom's investigation and have not been, and, in my judgment, can not be, successfully controverted. From 9 to 15 or 20 of the colored soldiers took part in the attack. They leaped over the walls from the barracks and hurried through the town. They shot at whomever they saw moving, and they shot into houses where they saw lights. In some of these houses there were women and children, as the would-be murderers must have known. In one house in which there were two women and five children some ten shots went through at a height of about 4 1/2 feet above the floor, one putting out the lamp upon the table. The lieutenant of police of the town heard the firing and rode toward it. He met the raiders, who, as he stated, were about 15 colored soldiers. They instantly started firing upon him. He turned and rode off, and they continued firing upon him until they had killed his horse. They shot him in the right arm (it was afterwards amputated above the elbow). A number of shots were also fired at two other policemen. The raiders fired several times into a hotel, some of the shots being aimed at a guest sitting by a window. They shot into a saloon, killing the bartender and wounding another man. At the same time other raiders fired into another house in which women and children were sleeping, two of the shots going through the mosquito bar over the bed in which the mistress of the house and her two children were lying. Several other houses were struck by bullets. It was at night, and the streets of the town are poorly lighted, so that none of the individual raiders were recognized; but the evidence of many witnesses of all classes was conclusive to the effect that the raiders were negro soldiers. The shattered bullets, shells, and clips of the Government rifles, which were found on the ground, are merely corroborative. So are the bullet holes in the houses; some of which it appears must, from the direction, have been fired from the fort just at the moment when the soldiers left it. Not a bullet hole appears in any of the structures of the fort.

The townspeople were completely surprised by the unprovoked and murderous savagery of the attack. The soldiers were the aggressors from start to finish. They met with no substantial resistance, and one and all who took part in that raid stand as deliberate murderers, who did murder one man, who tried to murder others, and who tried to murder women and children. The act was one of horrible atrocity, and so far as I am aware, unparalleled for infamy in the annals of the United States Army.

The white officers of the companies were completely taken by surprise, and at first evidently believed that the firing meant that the townspeople were attacking the soldiers. It was not until 2 or 3 o'clock in the morning that any of them became aware of the truth. I have directed a careful investigation into the conduct of the officers, to see if any of them were blameworthy, and I have approved the recommendation of the War Department that two be brought before a court-martial.

As to the noncommissioned officers and enlisted men, there can be no doubt whatever that many were necessarily privy, after if not before the attack, to the conduct of those who took actual part in this murderous riot. I refer to Major Blocksom's report for proof of the fact that certainly some and probably all of the noncommissioned officers in charge of quarters who were responsible for the gun-racks and had keys thereto in their personal possession knew what men were engaged in the attack.

Major Penrose, in command of the post, in his letter (included in the Appendix) gives the reasons why he was reluctantly convinced that some of the men under him—as he thinks, from 7 to 10—got their rifles, slipped out of quarters to do the shooting, and returned to the barracks without being discovered, the shooting all occurring within two and a half short blocks of the barracks. It was possible for the raiders to go from the fort to the farthest point of firing and return in less than ten minutes, for the distance did not exceed 350 yards.

Such are the facts of this case. General Nettleton, in his letter herewith appended, states that next door to where he is writing in Brownsville is a small cottage where a children's party had just broken up before the house was riddled by United States bullets, fired by United States troops, from United States Springfield rifles, at close range, with the purpose of killing or maiming the inmates, including the parents and children who were still in the well-lighted house, and whose escape from death under such circumstances was astonishing. He states that on another street he daily looks upon fresh bullet scars where a volley from similar Government rifles was fired into the side and windows of a hotel occupied at the time by sleeping or frightened guests from abroad who could not possibly have given any offense to the assailants. He writes that the chief of the Brownsville police is again on duty from hospital, and carries an empty sleeve because he was shot by Federal soldiers from the adjacent garrison in the course of their murderous foray; and not far away is the fresh grave of an unoffending citizen of the place, a boy in years, who was wantonly shot down by these United States soldiers while unarmed and attempting to escape.

Document Text

The effort to confute this testimony so far has consisted in the assertion or implication that the townspeople shot one another in order to discredit the soldiers—an absurdity too gross to need discussion, and unsupported by a shred of evidence. There is no question as to the murder and the attempted murders; there is no question that some of the soldiers were guilty thereof; there is no question that many of their comrades privy to the deed have combined to shelter the criminals from justice. These comrades of the murderers, by their own action, have rendered it necessary either to leave all the men, including the murderers, in the Army, or to turn them all out; and under such circumstances there was no alternative, for the usefulness of the Army would be at an end were we to permit such an outrage to be committed with impunity.

In short, the evidence proves conclusively that a number of the soldiers engaged in a deliberate and concerted attack, as cold blooded as it was cowardly; the purpose being to terrorize the community, and to kill or injure men, women, and children in their homes and beds or on the streets, and this at an hour of the night when concerted or effective resistance or defense was out of the question, and when detection by identification of the criminals in the United States uniform was well-nigh impossible. So much for the original crime. A blacker [crime] never stained the annals of our Army. It has been supplemented by another, only less black, in the shape of a successful conspiracy of silence for the purpose of shielding those who took part in the original conspiracy of murder. These soldiers were not school boys on a frolic. They were full-grown men, in the uniform of the United States Army, armed with deadly weapons, sworn to uphold the laws of the United States, and under every obligation of oath and honor not merely to refrain from criminality, but with the sturdiest rigor to hunt down criminality; and the crime they committed or connived at was murder. They perverted the power put into their hands to sustain the law into the most deadly violation of the law. The noncommissioned officers are primarily responsible for the discipline and good conduct of the men; they are appointed to their positions for the very purpose of preserving this discipline and good conduct, and of detecting and securing the punishment of every enlisted man who does what is wrong. They fill, with reference to the discipline, a part that the commissioned officers are of course unable to fill, although the ultimate responsibility for the discipline can never be shifted from the shoulders of the latter.

Under any ordinary circumstances the first duty of the noncommissioned officers, as of the commissioned officers, is to train the private in the ranks so that he may be an efficient fighting man against a foreign foe. But there is an even higher duty, so obvious that it is not under ordinary circumstances necessary so much as to allude to it—the duty of training the soldier so that he shall be a protection and not a menace to his peaceful fellow-citizens, and above all to the women and children of the nation. Unless this duty is well performed, the Army becomes a mere dangerous mob; and if conduct such as that of the murderers in question is not, where possible, punished, and, where this is not possible, unless the chance of its repetition is guarded against in the most thoroughgoing fashion, it would be better that the entire Army should be disbanded. It is vital for the Army to be imbued with the spirit which will make every man in it, and above all, the officers and non-commissioned officers, feel it a matter of highest obligation to discover and punish, and not to shield, the criminal in uniform.

Yet some of the noncommissioned officers and many of the men of the three companies in question have banded together in a conspiracy to protect the assassins and would-be assassins who have disgraced their uniform by the conduct above related. Many of these non-commissioned officers and men must have known, and all of them may have known, circumstances which would have led to the conviction of those engaged in the murderous assault. They have stolidly and as one man broken their oaths of enlistment and refused to help discover the criminals.

By my direction every effort was made to persuade those innocent of murder among them to separate themselves from the guilty by helping bring the criminals to justice. They were warned that if they did not take advantage of the offer they would all be discharged from the service and forbidden again to enter the employ of the Government. They refused to profit by the warning. I accordingly had them discharged. If any organization of troops in the service, white or black, is guilty of similar conduct in the future I shall follow precisely the same course. Under no circumstances will I consent to keep in the service bodies of men whom the circumstances show to be a menace to the country. Incidentally I may add that the soldiers of longest service and highest position who suffered because of the order, so far from being those who deserve most sympathy, deserve least, for they are the very men upon whom we should be able especially to rely to prevent mutiny and murder.

People have spoken as if this discharge from the service was a punishment. I deny emphatically that such is the case, because as punishment it is utterly inadequate. The punishment meet for mutineers and murderers such as those guilty of the Brownsville assault is death; and a punishment only less severe ought to be meted out to those who have aided and abetted mutiny and murder and treason by refusing to help in their detection. I would that it were possible for me to have punished the guilty men. I regret most keenly that I have not been able to do so.

Be it remembered always that these men were all in the service of the United States under contracts of enlistment, which by their terms and by statute were terminable by my direction as Commander in Chief of the Army. It was my clear duty to terminate those contracts when the public interest demanded it; and it would have been a betrayal of the public interest on my part not to terminate the contracts which were keeping in the service of the United States a body of mutineers and murderers.

Any assertion that these men were dealt with harshly because they were colored men is utterly without foundation. Officers or enlisted men, white men or colored men, who were guilty of such conduct, would have been treated in precisely the same way; for there can be nothing more important than for the United States Army, in all its membership, to understand that its arms cannot be turned with impunity against the peace and order of the civil community.

There are plenty of precedents for the action taken. I call your attention to the memoranda herewith submitted from The Military Secretary's office of the War Department, and a memorandum from The Military Secretary enclosing a piece by ex-Corporal Hesse, now chief of division in The Military Secretary's office, together with a letter from District Attorney James Wilkinson, of New Orleans. The district attorney's letter recites several cases in which white United States soldiers, being arrested for crime, were tried, and every soldier and employee of the regiment, or in the fort at which the soldier was stationed, volunteered all they knew, both before and at the trial, so as to secure justice. In one case the soldier was acquitted. In another case the soldier was convicted of murder, the conviction resulting from the fact that every soldier, from the commanding officer to the humblest private, united in securing all the evidence in their power about the crime. In other cases, for less offense, soldiers were convicted purely because their comrades in arms, in a spirit of fine loyalty to the honor of the service, at once told the whole story of the troubles and declined to identify themselves with the criminals.

During the civil war numerous precedents for the action taken by me occurred in the shape of the summary discharge of regiments or companies because of misconduct on the part of some or all of their members. The Sixtieth Ohio was summarily discharged, on the ground that the regiment was disorganized, mutinous, and worthless. The Eleventh New York was discharged by reason of general demoralization and numerous desertions. Three companies of the Fifth Missouri Cavalry and one company of the Fourth Missouri Cavalry were mustered out of the service of the United States without trial by court-martial by reason of mutinous conduct and *disaffection of the majority of the members of these companies* (an almost exact parallel to my action). Another Missouri regiment was mustered out of service because it was in a state bordering closely on mutiny. Other examples, including New Jersey, Maryland, and other organizations, are given in the enclosed papers.

I call your particular attention to the special field order of Brig. Gen. U. S. Grant, issued from the headquarters of the Thirteenth Army Corps on November 16, 1862, in reference to the Twentieth Illinois. Members of this regiment had broken into a store and taken goods to the value of some $1,240, and the rest of the regiment, including especially two officers, failed, in the words of General Grant, to "exercise their authority to ferret out the men guilty of the offenses." General Grant accordingly mustered out of the service of the United States the two officers in question, and assessed the sum of $1,240 against the said regiment as a whole, officers and men to be assessed pro rata on their pay. In its essence this action is precisely similar to that I have taken; although the offense was of course trivial compared to the offense with which I had to deal.

Ex-Corporal Hesse recites what occurred in a United States regular regiment in the spring of 1860. (Corporal Hesse subsequently, when the regiment was surrendered to the Confederates by General Twiggs, saved the regimental colors by wrapping them about his body, under his clothing, and brought them north in safety, receiving a medal of honor for his action.) It appears that certain members of the regiment lynched a barkeeper who had killed one of the soldiers. Being unable to discover the culprits, Col. Robert E. Lee, then in command of the Department of Texas, ordered the company to be disbanded and the members transferred to other companies and

Document Text

discharged at the end of their enlistment, without honor. Owing to the outbreak of the Civil War, and the consequent loss of records and confusion, it is not possible to say what finally became of this case.

When General Lee was in command of the Army of Northern Virginia, as will appear from the enclosed clipping from the *Charlotte Observer*, he issued an order in October, 1864, disbanding a certain battalion for cowardly conduct, stating at the time his regret that there were some officers and men belonging to the organization who, although not deserving it, were obliged to share in the common disgrace because the good of the service demanded it.

In addition to the discharges of organizations, which are of course infrequent, there are continual cases of the discharge of individual enlisted men without honor and without trial by court-martial. The official record shows that during the fiscal year ending June 30, last, such discharges were issued by the War Department without trial by court-martial in the cases of 352 enlisted men of the Regular Army, 35 of them being on account of "having become disqualified for service through own misconduct." Moreover, in addition to the discharges without honor ordered by the War Department, there were a considerable number of discharges without honor issued by subordinate military authorities under paragraph 148 of the Army Regulations, "where the service has not been honest and faithful—that is, where the service does not warrant reenlistment."

So much for the military side of the case. But I wish to say something additional, from the standpoint of the race question. In my message at the opening of the Congress I discussed the matter of lynching. In it I gave utterance to the abhorrence which all decent citizens should feel for the deeds of the men (in almost all cases white men) who take part in lynchings and at the same time I condemned, as all decent men of any color should condemn, the action of those colored men who actively or passively shield the colored criminal from the law. In the case of these companies we had to deal with men who in the first place were guilty of what is practically the worst possible form of lynching—for a lynching is in its essence lawless and murderous vengeance taken by an armed mob for real or fancied wrongs—and who in the second place covered up the crime of lynching by standing with a vicious solidarity to protect the criminals.

It is of the utmost importance to all our people that we shall deal with each man on his merits as a man, and not deal with him merely as a member of a given race; that we shall judge each man by his conduct and not his color. This is important for the white man, and it is far more important for the colored man. More evil and sinister counsel never was given to any people than that given to colored men by those advisers, whether black or white, who, by apology and condonation, encourage conduct such as that of the three companies in question. If the colored men elect to stand by criminals of their own race because they are of their own race, they assuredly lay up for themselves the most dreadful day of reckoning. Every farsighted friend of the colored race in its efforts to strive onward and upward, should teach first, as the most important lesson, alike to the white man and the black, the duty of treating the individual man strictly on his worth as he shows it. Any conduct by colored people which tends to substitute for this rule the rule of standing

Glossary

Col. Robert E. Lee	later a general who commanded the Army of Northern Virginia during the Civil War
disaffection	disloyalty to the government
Judge Jones	U.S. District Court Judge Thomas Goode Jones, who heard a number of peonage cases in 1903
Judge Speer	Emory Speer, a judge in Georgia who ruled against the use of chain gangs and upheld the constitutionality of laws against peonage
noncommissioned officers	those of the rank of sergeant who command troops but are not commissioned as lieutenants, captains, and the like
peonage	the practice of requiring a debtor to work for his creditor until the debt is discharged

by and shielding an evil doer because he is a member of their race, means the inevitable degradation of the colored race. It may and probably does mean damage to the white race, but it means ruin to the black race.

Throughout my term of service in the Presidency I have acted on the principle thus advocated. In the North as in the South I have appointed colored men of high character to office, utterly disregarding the protests of those who would have kept them out of office because they were colored men. So far as was in my power, I have sought to secure for the colored people all their rights under the law. I have done all I could to secure them equal school training when young, equal opportunity to earn their livelihood, and achieve their happiness when old. I have striven to break up peonage; I have upheld the hands of those who, like Judge Jones and Judge Speer, have warred against this peonage, because I would hold myself unfit to be President if I did not feel the same revolt at wrong done a colored man as I feel at wrong done a white man. I have condemned in unstinted terms the crime of lynching perpetrated by white men, and I should take instant advantage of any opportunity whereby I could bring to justice a mob of lynchers. In precisely the same spirit I have now acted with reference to these colored men who have been guilty of a black and dastardly crime. In one policy, as in the other, I do not claim as a favor, but I challenge as a right, the support of every citizen of this country, whatever his color, provided only he has in him the spirit of genuine and farsighted patriotism.

Theodore Roosevelt

Poster of African American soldiers fighting German soldiers in World War I, with portrait of Abraham Lincoln above (Library of Congress)

Act in Relation to the Organization of a Colored Regiment in the City of New York

"The adjutant-general shall organize and equip a colored regiment of infantry in the city of New York."

Overview

In 1913 the New York State Legislature passed An Act to Amend the Military Law, in Relation to the Organization and Equipment of a Colored Regiment of Infantry in the City of New York, creating an African American National Guard unit, later known as the "Harlem Hell Fighters." The regiment played a crucial role in World War I. During the German spring offensive of 1918, the Harlem Hell Fighters were often the only regiment between the Germans and Paris, France. The New York law was a key legislative milestone in the struggle for African Americans to have equal opportunities to serve in the armed forces.

Article XI of New York's fourth constitution, passed in 1894, required that the state maintain a military force of "not less than ten thousand enlisted men, fully uniformed, armed, equipped, disciplined and ready for active service." In response to an incursion into New Mexico by the renegade Mexican revolutionary general Pancho Villa in March 1916, almost all of New York's military forces were mustered into federal service and started leaving the state in June. Governor Charles Whitman realized that New York would thus be left with fewer soldiers than the constitutional requirement. Whitman; his military secretary, Lorillard Spencer; and the public service commissioner, William Hayward, a long-time Whitman associate, discussed the options for increasing the state's troop strength. Spencer had recently discovered the 1913 law authorizing an African American regiment for New York's National Guard. Whitman decided to create the regiment after the federal War Department requested that the state provide more troops. Whitman appointed Hayward as colonel and commander of the regiment and directed him to organize it immediately.

Context

African Americans have served in every American war. In wars against the Indians in the early eighteenth century, blacks fought along with white militiamen in defending colonial settlements. During the French and Indian War (1754–1763), African Americans again provided a significant number of soldiers and support troops. Many enslaved blacks in the northern states achieved their freedom through military service during those times. At the battles of Lexington and Concord, the first military engagements of the American Revolution (1775–1783), there were African Americans among the minutemen who fought the British. But early in the American Revolution there was also resistance among many slave owners, including George Washington, to arming blacks because they feared an armed slave revolt. Ironically, the British offered freedom and land to any slave who fought on the British side. Although the British lost the war, they honored their commitment and settled their black soldiers and families on land grants in Nova Scotia (today, a province in Canada). In the War of 1812 (lasting until 1815), African Americans fought in the Battle of New Orleans. In 1815, two battalions of blacks helped inflict the worst defeat ever experienced by the British Army.

The Civil War (1861–1865) brought thousands of African Americans into the Union army. In Massachusetts, Fredrick Douglass, an escaped slave who became a famous orator and writer, was involved in organizing and recruiting for a volunteer regiment of African Americans (led by white officers), the Fifty-fourth Massachusetts Volunteer Regiment. Douglass's two sons joined that regiment. Following the Civil War, an act of congress made four African American regiments—two cavalry and two infantry—a permanent part of the regular army. During the Spanish-American War (1898), many African Americans joined volunteer regiments and were accepted into the army. Despite forgotten promises, these former soldiers remembered their service with great pride. So it was that African Americans came to view military service as a right and an obligation of American citizens, allowing visible recognition of their participation as full members of society. Several states, including Massachusetts, Maryland, Tennessee, and Ohio, as well as the District of Columbia, had organized all-black militia and National Guard units; Illinois had an African American regiment based in Chicago. These units traced their beginnings to volunteer units that had fought in the Civil War. Despite the large number of African Americans from New York City who served in the Civil War and, later, the Spanish-American War, the city had no black militia or National Guard unit.

Early in 1911, a group of influential African American business and social leaders known as the Equity Congress

Time Line

1913

- **March 28**
  The state senator Henry Salant introduces a bill for a "colored battalion of infantry in the city of New York."

- **April 1**
  The assemblyman Thomas Kane submits a bill for a full "colored regiment of infantry in the city of New York."

- **June 2**
  Governor William Sulzer signs the Colored Regiment of Infantry Act into law, consolidating the two related bills to call for an African American regiment of infantry in New York City.

1914

- **August 1**
  Following the assassination of the Austrian archduke Franz Ferdinand on June 28, Germany declares war on Russia. Because of a series of complex mutual defense treaties, most European nations joined the war on one side or another.

- **August 4**
  President Woodrow Wilson declares the United States to be a neutral nation.

1916

- **June 16**
  Governor Charles Whitman appoints William Hayward as colonel of the Fifteenth Infantry Regiment, with orders to organize the regiment and begin recruiting.

- **October 1**
  Whitman presents the regimental colors to the Fifteenth Infantry in a ceremony at the Union League Club in New York City.

1917

- **April 6**
  The United States declares war on Germany.

- **July 25**
  The Fifteenth Infantry Regiment enters active federal service.

---

decided to actively encourage the formation of an African American militia regiment in New York City. However, creating a new militia unit would require an act of the New York legislature. Pending such action, the Equity Congress supported organizing a provisional regiment. In April 1911, Louis Cuvillier, a white New York assemblyman whose district included a large African American population, introduced a bill in the New York Assembly to authorize "a colored regiment of infantry in the city of New York." The state adjutant general strongly opposed the bill and was quoted in the *New York Times* of February 8, 1911, as saying "that it would take $50,000 to equip the regiment, $20,000 a year to support it, and that there would be prejudice in the guard against it." The bill was very detailed and specified the organization of the regiment down to the level of providing a precise number of officers, but it was not well structured. It repeated entire sections of existing law verbatim. Nonetheless, the bill was approved by both houses of the legislature and, in late July, was sent to Governor John Dix to be signed into law. Dix, however, did not approve the bill. In July, the *New York Times* reported that the bill's opponents in the legislature considered it to be "so loosely and badly drawn that the high hopes entertained by the colored men whose political influence won votes for it are sure to be disappointed." Cuvillier was aware of the opposition within the governor's staff and told the Equity Congress that the bill had failed because of the adjutant general's opposition.

The assemblyman Dean Nelson introduced a less specific bill on January 18, 1912. According to the *Assembly Introductory Number Record*, it was amended with minor revisions but was then sent back to the Military Affairs Committee. The assembly record shows that the bill was not reported out of the committee. There was no further action taken to establish an African American regiment until 1913, after Dix was defeated in his bid for a second term as governor of New York in the 1912 election. William Sulzer, a Democratic congressman from New York City, became governor in January 1913. The state senator Henry Salant then introduced a bill on March 28, 1913, to authorize "the organization and equipment of a colored battalion of infantry in the city of New York." On April 1, Thomas Kane, a Democrat who had defeated Nelson in the 1912 election, introduced another bill with wording similar to Salant's, but rather than calling for a battalion, the bill specified organizing a full regiment. (At the time, a regiment in the New York National Guard comprised three battalions.) Salant's bill also provided funding for an armory, while Kane's bill did not. In committee, the two bills were resolved into one that authorized a regiment but provided no funding.

The amended bill was passed by the assembly on April 29, 1913, and by the senate on May 2. The bill went to Sulzer for signature on May 7, and he signed the bill into law on June 2. That law required the New York adjutant general to organize and equip the regiment no later than three months after the effective date of the act. Although the law specified that it was to take effect immediately, Sulzer was impeached and removed from office before the law could be implemented. Finally, in 1916, Governor

Charles Whitman ordered the regiment to be formed and designated it the Fifteenth Infantry Regiment, New York National Guard. In 1918, while the unit was assigned to the French Army, the War Department changed its designation to the 369th Infantry Regiment.

About the Author

The legislation creating New York City's African American infantry regiment was first introduced in both houses of the New York State Legislature. These two bills, differing slightly, were ultimately consolidated into a single bill, signed by Governor Sulzer. Thomas Kane introduced the bill in the New York State Assembly. Kane had immigrated to the United States from Ireland in 1887 when he was nineteen years old. He was a skilled amateur athlete who was president of the Clipper Athletic Club for seven years and worked in industrial marketing. He was one of the first to support building public playgrounds in New York City. With support from Tammany Hall, he defeated the Republican incumbent Dean Nelson by a 25 percent margin in the 1912 election. Henry Salant introduced similar legislation in the New York State Senate. He was a native New Yorker who ran as a National Progressive in the 1912 election. Salant had been a very successful real estate lawyer in New York City. He was removed from office in late April 1913 following an election protest and ballot recount. Afterward Salant continued his active law practice and appeared as counsel in a number of important cases. He remained active in New York Republican Party politics through the 1920s but held no further significant political office.

Explanation and Analysis of the Document

Although legislation intended to create an African American regiment for New York City had been introduced and passed by the legislature before, first in 1911 and again in 1912, the governor did not sign those bills into law. On June 2, 1913, the newly elected Governor Sulzer signed into law the Colored Regiment of Infantry Act.

The 1913 act amended Article 2 of Chapter 41, "Military Law," of the 1909 laws of New York State, which defined the command, organization, and administration of the state National Guard. Legislation similar to the enacted bill had been proposed in 1911, but that bill contained additional language that duplicated provisions in the existing military law. In 1912 a much shorter version of the 1911 bill was proposed, but that bill also contained redundant language. The final bill was pared down to the language essential to require the adjutant general—the senior New York State military administrative authority—to create a regiment no later than three months after the bill became law. However, the law inadvertently contained a provision that allowed the adjutant general to delay creation of the regiment: It required the officers of the regiment to be commissioned according to the military law provisions for

Time Line

1917
- **August 5**
  The entire New York National Guard is mustered into the U.S. Army.

1918
- **March 1**
  The Fifteenth Infantry is designated the 369th Infantry Regiment and assigned to the French Sixteenth Division for training and service before being sent to the front lines for two years.
- **July 15–18**
  The 369th Infantry reverses a German attack and becomes known as the Harlem Hell Fighters.
- **November 11**
  The armistice ends the war at 11:00 AM.
- **December 13**
  The Croix de Guerre is pinned to the colors of the 369th, awarding the decoration to every member.

1919
- **February 17**
  Soon after returning to New York, the 369th marches down Fifth Avenue in its own victory parade.

eligibility and examination. The adjutant general interpreted the law to require that the regiment's officers be black, but black officers of the provisional regiment did not have sufficient military education to pass the examinations.

Audience

There were two main audiences for the law. First, the New York State adjutant general and the New York National Guard were responsible for executing its provisions. Second, and perhaps politically more important, were the African American community in New York City and the politically active Equity Congress, backers of the provisional regiment.

Impact

Despite the law's provision that the African American regiment be created within three months, the adjutant general and other state authorities took no action. There were conflicting loyalties among those political appointees who

William Hayward (Library of Congress)

owed allegiance to Tammany Hall and those who supported Governor Sulzer. Tammany Hall was the name given to the political organization that dominated the Democratic Party in New York State and New York City during the nineteenth and early twentieth centuries. Originally it had dominated Irish American politics but in the late nineteenth century encompassed the larger immigrant community. In the early twentieth century, it worked to divert African Americans from their traditional support of the Republican Party. Tammany maintained its control through a system of patronage appointments, illegal payments and kickbacks, and generally corrupt political practice. Sulzer had received political support from Tammany Hall for a large part of his career, but when he became governor, he refused to follow Tammany instructions for political appointments. In October 1913, Tammany Hall politicians whom Sulzer had opposed started impeachment proceedings, alleging he had misappropriated campaign funds; he was forced out of office in 1913. Lieutenant Governor Martin H. Glynn, who supported the Tammany Hall political machine, then became governor. Glynn had no interest in pursuing the formation of an African American regiment and took no action despite inquiries from the black community.

The *New York Times* reported on May 11, 1914, that "C. Franklin Carr of New York, a candidate for Colonel of the negro regiment" had written a letter to the state's adjutant general on May 1 expressing the provisional regiment's impatience with the delay in mustering the unit into the New York National Guard. The letter continued to state that if an interpretation of the authorization law meant that the regiment would need to have white officers, the regiment would be willing to accept that condition. On May 9, an assistant to the adjutant general replied that since "not a sufficient number of officers succeeded in passing the prescribed examination to officer one company, the organization of the colored regiment has been temporarily postponed." The *Annual Report of the Adjutant General of the State of New York* covering the year 1914 states that fifty-seven candidates for commissions were tested: "The result was so disappointing as to make it obviously improper to expend public funds any further in the attempt to comply with the act." The same report mentions that the state had thirteen regiments, four more than the War Department required—with the implication that forming a new regiment would drain scarce funds from the rest of the state's National Guard. The adjutant general, in sum, was not favorably disposed toward the creation of a new black regiment; no further action was taken for almost two more years.

When Charles Whitman defeated Glynn in New York's 1914 gubernatorial election, the U.S. government was cautiously watching events in Europe. The previous August, Germany had declared war on Russia and France, followed by Great Britain's declaration of war on Germany. In Mexico, the revolutionary Pancho Villa was waging war for control of the Mexican government. Villa saw the U.S. government's transition of support from him to his opponent, Venustiano Carranza, as a betrayal and a personal affront. Consequently, in March 1916, Villa crossed the border into New Mexico and killed seventeen citizens in the town of Columbus. In April, the War Department mobilized the National Guard in response to Villa's attack, and almost all of the New York National Guard entered federal service. When the New York National Guard was mobilized, it fielded an entire division.

On June 16, 1916, Governor Whitman appointed William Hayward as colonel in the New York National Guard with orders to start organizing and recruiting for the new African American unit, named the Fifteenth Infantry Regiment. Many wondered why Hayward was selected to command the Fifteenth rather than Charles Fillmore, who was the acting colonel of the provisional regiment; it is probable that Hayward's appointment was a political reward from Whitman, as was the appointment of Lorillard Spencer as the adjutant of the regiment. Both Hayward and Spencer were close to the governor and had previously been provided with political appointments. Spencer held the rank of captain in the New York National Guard Coast Artillery Corp but was promoted to major when he became Whitman's military secretary. Conveniently, Hayward, who had been public service commissioner, still held the rank of colonel in the Nebraska National Guard, albeit on the excess inactive list; it was thus a simple administrative act to have him transferred to the New York National Guard's excess inactive list and then detailed to active service.

In the first weeks of their efforts, Colonel Hayward and his adjutant, Major Spencer, ran into great difficulties finding recruits in New York's African American community. Although they were pleased to finally have the regiment, they were especially concerned that it might have only white officers. Hayward advertised that the color line would not be

Essential Quotes

"The adjutant-general shall organize and equip a colored regiment of infantry in the city of New York."

"Such regiment when organized and equipped shall become a part of the national guard of the state of New York, and subject to all the statutes, rules and regulations governing such national guard."

---

drawn in the Fifteenth Infantry and that colored men who qualified would be commissioned as officers. He opened the doors to the Fifteenth Infantry Regiment's first recruiting office on June 27, 1916. A few prospective recruits came by, and several were enlisted that night. Later in the week the *New York Age*, a popular African American weekly newspaper in New York City, printed two related articles on its front page: one about the heroic actions of the all-black Tenth Cavalry Regiment in Mexico and the other on the recruiting efforts for New York's Fifteenth Infantry. Those two articles brought hundreds of recruits into the regiment; by the middle of July, the first battalion had been filled.

While the regiment continued to attract a number of highly qualified African Americans, there were not enough to fill the large number of officer positions, and Hayward was indeed forced to bring in a number of white officers. Hamilton Fish III, a New York assemblyman and well-connected socialite, was appointed a captain, as was Arthur Little, a well-known insurance broker. Most of the enlisted personnel came from Harlem, the Bronx, and Brooklyn; Hayward recruited and formed one battalion in each of the three locations. For the most part, the men he recruited were ordinary laborers, such as porters, doormen, and the like. Needham Roberts, a former bellhop, had tried to enlist in the navy but had been turned down. Henry Johnson had been a railroad porter in Albany, New York, but went to New York City to enlist. Horace Pippin had been a metalworker, a molder in a brake-shoe foundry. He had shown some artistic talent as a child, and his war diary is illustrated with his drawings. In the 1930s Pippin gained fame as one the leading American "naive" artists of the century.

Another enlistee was James Reese Europe, who joined New York's Fifteenth on September 18, 1916, and recruited his friend and colleague Noble Sissle to join ten days later. Europe was a famous bandleader whose music was well known across the country. He joined the regiment to be a soldier, not a musician, but when Hayward was having problems recruiting, he turned to Europe to form a band that would bring in men to join the regiment. Europe scoured New York for skilled musicians; when he exhausted the supply, he went to Chicago to recruit Frank DeBroit, a famous black cornet player. Because there was a shortage of clarinet and saxophone players at the time, Europe persuaded Hayward to fund a trip to Puerto Rico. Europe returned with a group of eighteen highly skilled musicians he had somehow persuaded to enlist and go to New York.

The Fifteenth New York was mobilized into federal service on July 25, 1917. On August 5, along with all the other units of the National Guard of the United States, the Fifteenth New York entered the U.S. Army. After two months of guard duty in the New York area, the regiment was sent to Camp Wadsworth in Spartanburg, South Carolina, for additional training. Race relations at Camp Wadsworth were extremely tense, and there were a number of violent incidents. The commander of Camp Wadsworth, Brigadier General Charles Phillips, believed the situation to be so critical that he arranged a private meeting between Colonel Hayward and Secretary of War Newton Baker on October 22, just seven days after the regiment had arrived there. Two days later, the regiment left Spartanburg by train for New York to await transportation by ship to France in November. After a number of mishaps, including a return to New York for engine repair, the regiment landed in Brest, France, on December 27, 1917.

Rather than being sent into combat training as they had expected, the regiment was unceremoniously boarded onto freight cars and sent to Saint-Nazaire to be a labor and construction unit. While the rest of the regiment was building railroads and unloading cargo, the regimental band directed by Europe was sent on a tour across France. A visiting American theatrical producer, Winthrop Ames, and the Broadway actor E. H. Sothern had been touring France to find entertainment for American troops when they heard Europe's band. In their opinion, it was the best band they had ever heard. It may have been their recommendation that led the army to order the band to play at a rest and recuperation area at Aix-les-Bains, a resort area near the French Alps. On February 12, 1918, the band boarded a train and played their way across the southeastern quarter of France; everywhere the train stopped, the band played. The French had never heard a jazz band before and embraced the music with great enthusiasm.

General John J. Pershing, the commanding general of the American Expeditionary Force, was then being pressured by the French and British commanders to assign American forces to fill in losses in both armies. Pershing adamantly refused, insisting that Americans command Americans. When Germany launched its spring offensive in March 1918, Pershing made an exception to his policy and agreed to loan three regular U.S. Army divisions and two National Guard regiments to back up the French and British forces. The German offensive stalled, and the American units were never assigned—except for the Fifteenth New York, which was given to the French Fourth Army; Pershing had no confidence in the combat skills of African Americans but had found a way to satisfy French requests for American units and get rid of what he saw as a problem. Under French leadership, Pershing's African American "problem" became one of the most decorated American regiments in the war.

When the regiment reported for duty with the French Army, it learned it had been designated as the "369th Infantry Regiment." Because the regiment was to be part of the French Army, it had to exchange American equipment for French-issued items. They were given the distinctive helmet worn by the French soldiers, with a crest that ran from front to back, as well as French leather belts and strappings to hold their ammunition, gas masks, and grenade bags. They were armed with the same rifles as were the other French troops deployed in the same sector. After three weeks' training with French infantry weapons and tactics, the regiment was assigned to a 2.8-mile sector of frontline trenches. The 369th Infantry Regiment's first combat experience occurred late on April 14 when the regiment came under a German artillery attack. The shelling lasted only a short time, and there were no casualties. The 369th commanded the frontline trenches from April 29 until July 4, when it was relieved and sent to the second-line trenches.

In mid-July, the last phase of the German spring offensive began in the Champagne-Ardenne, as the Germans attempted to widen their front on the Marne River. After helping stop the German attack, the French attached the 369th to the 161st Division, which had been pushed back from its frontline trenches by the German attack. The 369th counterattacked on July 18 and recaptured the frontline trenches. Portions of the regiment were then parceled out to support other French units from July 21 through August 19. Once the sector was quiet and the regiment was reunited, it resumed training. The regiment was permanently reassigned to the 161st Division on September 9, prior to the French Fourth Army's Meuse-Argonne offensive, started on September 26. That day the 369th, assigned to support the French attack, discovered a gap in the front lines and advanced to capture the town of Ripont. The following day they advanced about three-quarters of a mile. While the rest of the 161st was being delayed by German resistance, the regiment captured Séchault and advanced three-quarters of a mile further. After the heavy fighting abated and the front was consolidated, the 161st Division, including the 369th, was relieved and returned to a rehabilitation area around October 8. On October 14 the regiment, as part of the 161st, began occupation of the Thur sector, northeast of Belfort. Because of their remarkable record in combat, the men of the 369th were accorded the honor of being the first American troops to cross the Rhine into Germany.

Despite the regiment's accomplishments, once the 369th was reassigned from the French Army back to the U.S. Army, it once again faced racial prejudices. The U.S.

Questions for Further Study

1. Compare this document with Thomas Morris Chester's Civil War Dispatches (1864). What do you think Chester's reaction to the new law would have been?

2. Using this document in conjunction with Chester's Civil War Dispatches and Harry Truman's Executive Order 9981 desegregating the military in 1948, trace the history of African American involvement in the military and efforts to desegregate it.

3. Describe the role that the Harlem Hell Fighters played in World War I.

4. What role did local politics have in the formation of the Colored Regiment of Infantry Act and in delays in its implementation?

5. In the twentieth century numerous African American leaders called on black men to resist the military draft. See, for example, Stokely Carmichael's "Black Power" (1966). What changed in attitudes toward the military between the early twentieth century and the later decades of the century?

Army refused to allow the Harlem Hell Fighters to march in the Paris victory parade and quickly shipped them back to New York. Yet Colonel Hayward promised his men a victory parade of their own and, using his many political connections, arranged a remarkable event. On February 17, 1919, the Harlem Hell Fighters, led by Europe and the regimental band, marched down Fifth Avenue from the victory arch being built at 24th and Broadway to Harlem.

In a larger sense, the full impact of the 369th Harlem Hell Fighters and other black regiments' service in World War I was not realized until President Harry S. Truman integrated the U.S. military forces in 1948. Starting with the Korean War, as African Americans began to be accepted into the military on an equal basis with whites and other races, a renewed consciousness emerged of a uniquely black military heritage of service. That heritage, service despite racial prejudice and inequality, is a heritage of honor, courage, and sacrifice that continues to inspire African American youth.

See also Executive Order 9981 (1948).

Further Reading

■ Articles

"Against Negro Regiment: Adjt. Gen. Verbeck Says One in Brooklyn Would Be Costly." *New York Times,* February 8, 1911.

"Colored Regiment to Wait: Not Enough Candidates Have Passed to Officer Provisional Infantry." *New York Times,* May 11, 1914.

"Topics of the Times." *New York Times,* July 13, 1911.

■ Books

Annual Report of the Adjutant General of the State of New York for the Year 1914. Albany, N.Y.: J. B. Lyon, 1915.

Barbeau, Arthur E., and Florette Henri. *The Unknown Soldiers: Black American Troops in World War I.* Philadelphia: Temple University Press, 1974.

Foner, Jack D. *Blacks and the Military in American History: A New Perspective.* New York: Praeger, 1974.

Harris, Stephen L. *Harlem's Hell Fighters: The African-American 369th Infantry in World War I.* Washington, D.C.: Potomac Books, 2003.

Kennedy, David M. *Over Here: The First World War and American Society.* New York: Oxford University Press, 1980.

Little, Arthur W. *From Harlem to the Rhine: The Story of New York's Colored Volunteers.* New York: Covici, Friede, 1936.

Slotkin, Richard. *Lost Battalions: The Great War and the Crisis of American Nationality.* New York: Henry Holt, 2005.

Whitman, Charles. *Public Papers of Charles Seymour Whitman, Governor: 1915.* Albany, N.Y.: J. B. Lyon, 1916.

———. *Public Papers of Charles Seymour Whitman, Governor: 1916.* Albany, N.Y.: J. B. Lyon, 1919.

■ Web Sites

"Integration of the Armed Forces." Redstone Arsenal Web site.
   http://web.archive.org/web/20070203164944/www.redstone.army.mil/history/integrate/welcome.html.

"*Horace Pippin's Autobiography, First World War,* ca. 1921." Smithsonian Institution "Archives of American Art" Web site.
   http://www.aaa.si.edu/collections/searchimages/images/item_7434.htm.

"93d Division Summary of Operations in the World War." U.S. Army Center of Military History Web site.
   http://www.history.army.mil/topics/afam/93div.htm.

"WWI—African American Soldiers." New York State Archives "Remembering World War I, 1914–1918" Web site.
   http://iarchives.nysed.gov/Gallery/gallery.jsp?id=147&ss=WWI.

—William S. Pettit

Act in Relation to the Organization of a Colored Regiment in the City of New York

Became a law June 2, 1913, with the approval of the Governor. Passed, three-fifths being present.

The People of the State of New York, represented in Senate and Assembly, do enact as follows:

Section 1. Article two of chapter forty-one of the laws of nineteen hundred and nine, entitled "An act in relation to the militia, constituting chapter thirty-six of the consolidated laws," is hereby amended by adding at the end thereof a new section, to be section forty, to read as follows:

§40. Colored regiment of infantry. Within three months after this section takes effect, the adjutant-general shall organize and equip a colored regiment of infantry in the city of New York. Such regiment when organized and equipped shall become a part of the national guard of the state of New York, and subject to all the statutes, rules and regulations governing such national guard. The officers of such regiment shall be commissioned by the governor, subject to the provisions of this chapter, in relation to eligibility and examination. The armory board of the city of New York shall provide quarters for such regiment.

§2. This act shall take effect immediately.

Woodrow Wilson (Library of Congress)

Monroe Trotter's Protest to Woodrow Wilson

1914

"As equal citizens and by virtue of your public promises we are entitled at your hands to freedom from discrimination."

Overview

As a candidate for the presidency of the United States in 1912, Woodrow Wilson proposed a platform based on what he characterized as "new freedom." In doing so, Wilson made promises to African Americans that he could be counted on to provide fairness if elected. However, upon his election, Wilson reneged on his original promise and instituted a policy of racial segregation in both the Department of the Treasury and the Post Office Department. The National Association for the Advancement of Colored People (NAACP), the leading civil rights group in the nation at that time, forwarded a letter of protest to Wilson, but their efforts were ignored. On November 6, 1913, and again on November 12, 1914, President Wilson met with a delegation of African American leaders from the National Independent Equal Rights League. Their spokesman, the uncompromising *Boston Guardian* editor William Monroe Trotter, challenged Wilson in his opening remarks at the second meeting to live up to his promises to provide equality for African Americans. Trotter's message was characteristically direct, even blunt. It led to a tense encounter that garnered much public attention.

Context

The 1910s were a time of racial volatility in the United States, evidenced by numerous urban race riots, notably in East St. Louis and Chicago. The historian Rayford Logan has characterized this period as the nadir of race relations in America. Terrifying violence against African Americans included numerous lynchings and other hostile attacks. Racial segregation had become entrenched in American life. The doctrine of "separate but equal" had even obtained legal status in the Supreme Court's *Plessy v. Ferguson* decision of 1896, and in his famous Atlanta Exposition Address in 1895 the most prominent black leader of the day, Booker T. Washington, advocated a "gradualist" program of self-improvement that other African Americans came to consider inadequate to the troubled times. The Niagara Movement and the subsequent founding of the NAACP in 1909 represented a more activist response. A broader effect of southern violence was the northward migration of black Americans. Beginning in earnest in 1910, this persistent shift saw millions of African Americans move to the industrial north in search of jobs and, they hoped, a better life. To assist in meeting the numerous social, economic, cultural, and political challenges posed by the recently arriving black southerners, the National Urban League was formed in New York City in 1910.

The death of Frederick Douglass in 1895 left Booker T. Washington as the most prominent representative of national black leadership. Washington, a former slave, was known for his gradualism, a strategy of improving poor southern blacks' conditions through industrial education and hard work. His status as the first president of the influential Tuskegee Institute in Alabama, his prominent Atlanta address, and his recognition by several U.S. presidents cemented Washington's image as the nation's foremost African American. However, a number of northern blacks, including Monroe Trotter's camp of radical intellectuals, took a more assertive stance and waged an intense public and private debate with the "Bookerites." This ideological struggle came to a head on July 30, 1903, when Washington spoke at an event sponsored by the National Negro Business League at the Columbus Avenue African Methodist Episcopal Zion Church in Boston. Trotter and several of his associates protested so vigorously that they were ejected and arrested. Also in 1903, W. E. B. Du Bois published *The Souls of Black Folk*, with a chapter, "Of Mr. Booker T. Washington and Others," that represented an additional challenge to the "Tuskegee Machine" and its hold on black leadership. Washington died in 1915, a year after Trotter's confrontation with President Wilson, leaving a leadership vacuum that Du Bois, Trotter, and others intended to fill.

In 1912, Woodrow Wilson, a Democrat, had appealed to blacks (who were mainly Republicans) for their votes, offering promises of equal treatment should he be elected president. Frustrated with the incursion of segregation into the federal bureaucracy, Trotter requested meetings with Wilson in November 1913 and again in November 1914. In this time of great travail, the election of Wilson to the presidency of the United States offered hope for African Americans. In fact, a number of black leaders, including Trotter,

Time Line

1895
- Frederick Douglass dies, and Booker T. Washington delivers his Atlanta Exposition Address.

1896
- **May 18**
  The Supreme Court's *Plessy v. Ferguson* decision legitimates racial segregation in American life, law, and culture.

1898
- **November 10**
  A race riot occurs in Wilmington, North Carolina.

1903
- The historian W. E. B. Du Bois publishes *The Souls of Black Folk*.

1905
- The Niagara Movement is founded in Niagara Falls, Ontario, in call for opposition to racial segregation and disenfranchisement as well as policies of accommodation.

1906
- Racial disturbances and riots occur in Brownsville, Texas, and Atlanta, Georgia.

1908
- **August 14–15**
  A race riot occurs in Springfield, Illinois.

1909
- **February 12**
  The National Association for the Advancement of Colored People is founded.

1910
- The National Urban League is founded in New York City.

1912
- Monroe Trotter, Du Bois, and other black leaders endorse Woodrow Wilson for president.

publicly supported Wilson's candidacy, breaking with their traditional Republican allegiance. Wilson was known in many circles as a progressive, but his concerns did not extend to African Americans and their condition. Like his early foreign policy, Wilson's approach to African American demands for equality could well be described as noninterventionist. Adding to the tensions that flared in the meeting, Wilson was still grieving at the time over the death of his wife, Ellen Axson Wilson, on August 6.

About the Author

William Monroe Trotter, son of the noted Union army soldier and activist James Monroe Trotter, was born on April 7, 1872, at his grandparents' farm in Springfield Township, Ohio, and raised in a middle-class neighborhood in Boston. He graduated from Harvard with Phi Beta Kappa honors in 1895 and earned his master's there the following year. Primarily known as a journalist, he served in various activist organizations and, in 1901, founded (along with George W. Forbes) the influential newspaper the *Boston Guardian*, which served as an important news vehicle promoting equal rights for African Americans. Defiant and uncompromising on issues of race, he went on to become a militant civil rights advocate and one of the most influential African American leaders of the early twentieth century. He accomplished much in his career before the age of forty.

Along with W. E. B. Du Bois, Trotter also played a leading role in the founding of the Niagara Movement in 1905, serving as head of the Press and Public Opinion Committee. Du Bois and Trotter together drafted the organization's radical "Declaration of Principles," which was supported by the movement membership. Trotter also played a leading role in the NAACP, attending the founding meeting in 1909 and maintaining contact with the group until disputes occurred with leaders such as Oswald Garrison Villard and Du Bois. During these years, Trotter was also an important figure in the National Independent Equal Rights League. Both Trotter and Du Bois endorsed Woodrow Wilson for president in 1912. However, they soon realized that the new president was less supportive of equal rights for African Americans than he had promised to be as a candidate. Wilson's actions, such as outright rejection of black advisers, support of segregation in federal office buildings, and exclusion of blacks from important civil service posts, garnered a sharp response from notable black leaders, including Trotter.

Trotter opposed D. W. Griffith's film *The Birth of a Nation* (based on Thomas Dixon's novel and play *The Clansman*), which was shown at the White House in 1915. President Wilson praised the film, while Trotter stridently opposed the film's glorification of the Ku Klux Klan. Indeed, Trotter was arrested, with others, while picketing the stage production in Boston, which eventually was forced to close. The film was banned in Ohio, Chicago, St. Louis, and some areas of Massachusetts but continued to be shown in a number of Boston theaters for several months. Trotter's death is still somewhat of a mystery. On his sixty-second birthday, he reportedly fell (or, some say, jumped) from a window of his home to his death.

Explanation and Analysis of the Document

In the first paragraph, Trotter reminds the president that, a year earlier, he and other black leaders had presented a petition, signed by persons from thirty-eight states, "protesting against segregation of employees of the National government whose ancestry could be traced in whole or in part to Africa." The focus of the group's concerns was the U.S. Treasury and Post Office, where "all the forms of segregation … are still practiced." Trotter reminds Wilson that the group had urged him to undo this racial segregation and that "there could be no freedom, no respect from others, and no equality of citizenship under segregation for races," particularly when such segregation was so rampant in the federal bureaucracy. Trotter highlights the social, political, and personal damage of such an arrangement, noting how the implied labeling of African Americans as "a lower order of beings" consigned them to an "inferiority of status." Trotter then proceeds to list the segregated areas of the federal government, drawing specific attention to facilities for dining, dressing, and washing. The effect of this policy, he says, is "a public humiliation and degradation" that has far-reaching consequences. He calls this continued segregation "a gratuitous blow" against those who had supported Wilson's candidacy to lead America for all Americans.

Trotter next reminds Wilson of his promise to investigate these conditions himself. One year later, he notes that segregation persists in all the areas of initial concern and has, in fact, spread to other federal buildings. Obviously, this finding greatly alarmed Trotter and the delegation, as they had invested much public capital in supporting Wilson. In part, therefore, the occasion represented an opportunity for Trotter and other leaders to save face among skeptical African Americans. More centrally, his words represent genuine frustration and anger at the turn of events.

In the third paragraph, Trotter details the specifics of racial segregation in federal government buildings. Segregated facilities then existed in the Treasury Department, the Bureau of Engraving and Printing, and the Navy Department for dressing rooms, working positions, eating arrangements, and even lavatories. The repetition of this last word, mentioned eleven times in this paragraph alone, illustrates the level of humiliation and dehumanization to which African Americans were being subjected.

That such high hopes were followed by such worsening outcomes a year later was too much for the delegation, especially Trotter, to stomach. To the fiery activist it was unbearable that African American employees who dared to use the public facilities on the floors where they worked would be accused of "insubordination." In one particularly ridiculous case, African Americans were forbidden from even entering an adjoining room occupied by white clerks. Black men working on the sixth floor were forced to use public facilities on the eighth floor. In Trotter's mind there seemed to be no rational or substantial explanation for such debased and mortifying treatment for any human beings, especially for African Americans who had staunchly pledged their support for the nation, and (in many cases) for Wilson himself, at the behest of Trotter. As he puts it (in paragraph 9), "Consider that any passerby on the streets of the national capital, whether he be black or white, can enter and use the public lavatories in government buildings while citizens of color who do the work of the government are excluded."

Time Line

1914
- **November 12** Trotter and other African American leaders meet with President Wilson in the White House, where Trotter delivers his protest concerning segregation; their acrimonious confrontation is widely reported the following day.

1915
- Booker T. Washington dies.
- Trotter campaigns to have D. W. Griffith's film *The Birth of a Nation* (praised by President Wilson) banned in Boston for its positive portrayal of the Ku Klux Klan.

1916
- Woodrow Wilson is reelected president.

1917
- Race riots occur in East St. Louis, Illinois, and Houston, Texas.

1918
- **November 11** The Armistice brings World War I to an end.

1919
- Race riots occur in Chicago, Illinois, and Elaine, Arkansas.

1921
- Massive rioting in Tulsa, Oklahoma, destroys the city's black neighborhood.

1934
- Trotter dies in Boston.

Charles Evans Hughes (standing center), Republican Party presidential candidate campaigning in New York City
(Library of Congress)

Such matters were not petty for Trotter. The overt and underlying message they sent to African Americans all around the country was indicative of the value that their federal government placed on them. Black citizens were already devastated by the degree to which the party of Abraham Lincoln had abandoned its forthright championing of the interests of African Americans for nearly two decades, even while African Americans remained loyal to the Republicans. Now, searching for some sense of hope in Wilson as emblematic of a new Democratic Party, black people were intensely disappointed. That African Americans were undergoing one of the worst periods in their history at this time, owing to the rampant harassment, violence, and lynchings, made the added insult of toilet segregation too much to bear.

Trotter unequivocally states, in paragraph 4, that the delegation has come to "renew the protest," asking the president once again to "abolish segregation of Afro-American employees in the executive department." Striking here, in addition to the use of the term *Afro-American*, is his inclusive concern for African American women and men. (Trotter opposed use of the term *Negro*, choosing instead to use terms such as *Colored American* and *Afro-American*.) In both these instances, Trotter was ahead of his time, indicating a truly progressive character to his leadership and personality.

In paragraph 5, Trotter makes one of his most poignant statements, one that had overarching and far-reaching implications for African Americans for the remainder of the century and beyond. Trotter predicts that if the government of the United States of America can be allowed to segregate African Americans, it will encourage the rest of the nation to continue to do the same, permitting segregation to spread from the White House to every part of the nation. Inaction on the part of Wilson was sending a disturbing message to every African American citizen and potentially giving whites a license to continue their inhumane treatment of blacks. In this policy Trotter foresaw danger for the entire nation, potentially leading to its unraveling. American citizenship thus would become extremely precarious, even to the point of placing into question the promises of the founding documents and the structure of American democracy itself. This point was a prophetic warning from Trotter that would soon possess clear meaning as the United States entered World War I in 1917 to make the world "safe for democracy," in Wilson's words.

Trotter, a master strategist, proceeds in paragraph 6 to recount the delegation's strategy to date, reminding Wilson of the serious and organized manner of their protest. That protest had graduated from the national antisegregation petition offered in 1913 to protests at the voting polls whereby African Americans, as a sign of their heightened disdain for inaction, voted "against every Democratic candidate save those outspoken against segregation." Trotter noted that David Walsh of Massachusetts, the only Democrat elected governor in the eastern part of the country, had publicly appealed to Wilson to end segregation. Mere lip service or empty promises could not allay the frustrations of African Americans. Only tangible, concerted actions by governmental leaders would do that. The clear message to the president was that he should reverse course and make good on his promise or else potentially face the same fate as many of his Democratic colleagues around the nation. With the next presidential election just two years away, this message was no idle threat. Just as we publicly supported you, we can also publicly denounce you, Trotter and the delegation seem to imply, unless you end segregation in the federal bureaucracy once and for all.

Trotter underscores the power of the African American vote in the recent shift of black political allegiance that helped to elect Wilson. This historic shift away from the Republican Party resulted from the Republicans' disregard for African American concerns at a crucial period of the nation's history. Here the race leader demonstrates that the shift was not a matter that blacks took lightly. African Americans were not wedded to Wilson or the Democrats any more than they were to the Republican Party, should either turn its back on African American efforts for equality. Wilson may have been touted as the "second Lincoln," says Trotter, but his actions and inactions placed African American representatives, like Trotter himself, in the compromising position of being labeled as false leaders and race traitors. This was not the kind of change that African Americans could believe in or had hoped for when voting for Wilson.

In the final sections of his address, Trotter, using Wilson's own words, reminds the president of the promise he made to African American people. Then, in paragraph 9, comes an argument linking fellow citizenship with "congregation," by which he means a united community, one that is subverted by segregation.

As "equal citizens and by virtue of your public promises," African Americans are "entitled" to "freedom from discrimination, restriction, imputation and insult in government employ." The parting shot that surely rang throughout the entire room asks if Wilson had instituted a "new freedom for white Americans and new slavery for your Afro-American fellow citizens." Trotter concludes with the delegation's specific policy proposal: that the president issue an executive order banning all racial segregation of government employees on account of race. "We await your reply." According to an article published that day in the Philadelphia *Evening Ledger*, Wilson reportedly replied to Trotter that he had spoken "as no other man has spoken since I assumed the Presidency" and said that he would no longer receive him as part of a future delegation.

Much has been made of Trotter's militant tone during this meeting. However, this opening statement to the president evidences a degree of decorum and respect. He maintains a reasonable attitude in expressing the hope that Wilson will be a man of his word. But Trotter and the delegation also offered a warning that the people whom they represented were greatly alarmed at the lack of progress, especially the further encroachment upon their movement for equality. Furthermore, the symbolism of the president of the United States seeming to condone racial segregation in the very citadel of democracy could not go unchallenged. Neither could Wilson's professed dedication to making the world "safe for democracy" while he directly and indirectly denied African Americans their rights and full citizenship.

Audience

William Monroe Trotter delivered this address directly to Woodrow Wilson in the White House on November 12, 1914. It was the second meeting for the two men. In attendance were Trotter and a number of other black leaders from the National Independent Equal Rights League. The spirited and heated discussion lasted for forty-five minutes, before Wilson ordered the delegation to leave. News of the controversial meeting was featured in various newspapers including the Philadelphia *Evening Ledger*, the *New York Times*, the *Boston Evening Transcript*, and the African American newspaper the *New York Age*. Copies of the opening address were reprinted in numerous newspapers, including the black press. The president himself was the direct focus of frustration and criticism, since his reneging on campaign pledges had angered and embarrassed his black supporters out of hand.

Impact

The meetings of November 1913 and November 1914 demonstrated the serious difficulties African Americans had with the administration of Woodrow Wilson, in particular with the president himself. At the time of the second meeting, Wilson was undergoing severe strain and grief owing to the tragic death of his wife of thirty years. Considering the commensurate strain felt by Trotter, the delegation, and African American people across the country, this meeting had the makings of a truly volatile encounter, which ended with Wilson's ordering Trotter and the delegation out of his office. The second exchange was characterized as a confrontation by the White House, dismissing any idea that the meeting held any level of civility at all. Trotter's anger at Wilson and the Democrats did not subside after the meeting. In protest, he left the Democratic Party in 1916 and supported the Republican candidate, Charles Evans Hughes. At the same time, Trotter maintained his vigilant struggle for African Americans' equal rights.

A huge cloud of protest resulted from the confrontation between Trotter and Wilson. The national mainstream press was highly critical of Wilson. The *Nation* characterized racial segregation as "a sad blot upon the Wilson administration." The *New Republic* chided Wilson for confirming the emptiness of his pre-election promises to African Americans. The black press was even more critical of the government tolerance for racial segregation. Still, in the pages of the *New York Age* the writer and civil rights advocate James Weldon Johnson—considered a moderate

Essential Quotes

> "Such segregation was a public humiliation and degradation, entirely unmerited and far-reaching in its injurious effects, a gratuitous blow against ever-loyal citizens and against those many of whom aided and supported your elevation to the presidency of our common country."
>
> (Paragraph 1)

> "Because we cannot believe you capable of any disregard of your pledges we have been sent by the alarmed American citizens of color. They realize that if they can be segregated and thus humiliated by the national government at the national capital the beginning is made for the spread of that persecution and prosecution which makes property and life itself insecure in the South, the foundation of the whole fabric of their citizenship is unsettled."
>
> (Paragraph 5)

> "Fellow citizenship means congregation. Segregation destroys fellowship and citizenship."
>
> (Paragraph 9)

> "As equal citizens and by virtue of your public promises we are entitled at your hands to freedom from discrimination, restriction, imputation and insult in government employ. Have you a 'new freedom' for white Americans and a new slavery for your Afro-American fellow citizens? God forbid!"
>
> (Paragraph 10)

on issues of racial justice who worked actively within the "system" to achieve justice and equality for African Americans—praised Trotter's stance in principle while disagreeing with his particular tactics. Although segregation continued in the departments of the federal government, scholars credit Trotter with blunting its spread in bringing national attention to the subject. The Wilson administration retreated in the encounter's aftermath.

Although no substantial change in federal segregation policy occurred in the immediate aftermath of the meeting, it was evident that a clear message had been sent to the White House. The Wilson administration, in the period following the meeting, recoiled regarding matters of race, while the black press focused less and less on the subject for about two years. The race question slipped into the background in the years leading up to World War I, as African Americans hoped that their support for America's participation in the war would demonstrate their patriotism and win for them equality and acceptance. In the interim, Booker T. Washington died in 1915, leaving somewhat of a leadership vacuum in black America. Then, by 1916, the United States was drawing closer to the ongoing European war, reopening national discussion regarding race matters and American citizenship.

See also Booker T. Washington's Atlanta Exposition Address (1895); *Plessy v. Ferguson* (1896); W. E. B. Du Bois: *The Souls of Black Folk* (1903); Niagara Movement Declaration of Principles (1905).

Further Reading

■ Articles

Lunardini, Christine. "Standing Firm: William Monroe Trotter's Meetings with Woodrow Wilson, 1913–1914." *Journal of Negro History* 64, no. 3 (Summer 1979): 244–264.

"President Resents Negro's Criticism." *New York Times*, November 13, 1914, p. 11. Available online. New York Times Web site. http://query.nytimes.com/gst/abstract.html?res=9C01E0DC1738E633A25750C1A9679D946596D6CF.

■ Books

Bartlett, Bruce. *Wrong on Race: The Democratic Party's Buried Past*. New York: Palgrave Macmillan, 2008.

Bennett, Lerone, Jr. *Pioneers in Protest*. Baltimore, Md.: Penguin, 1969.

Cooper, John Milton. *Reconsidering Woodrow Wilson: Progressivism, Internationalism, War, and Peace*. Baltimore, Md.: Johns Hopkins University Press, 2008.

———. *Woodrow Wilson: A Biography*. New York: Alfred A. Knopf, 2009.

Fox, Stephen R. *The Guardian of Boston: William Monroe Trotter*. New York: Atheneum, 1970.

———. "William Monroe Trotter." In *Dictionary of American Negro Biography*, ed. Rayford W. Logan and Michael R. Winston. New York: W. W. Norton, 1982.

Logan, Rayford W. *The Betrayal of the Negro: From Rutherford B. Hayes to Woodrow Wilson*. New York: Da Capo Press, 1997.

Maynard, William Barksdale. *Woodrow Wilson: Princeton to the Presidency*. New Haven, Conn.: Yale University Press, 2008.

Smith, Jessie Carney. "William Monroe Trotter." In *Notable Black American Men*. Detroit: Gale Research, 1999.

—Zachery Williams

Questions for Further Study

1. What circumstances do you think might have led to so much racial unrest during the 1910s? Why do some historians regard this decade as among the worst in the nation's history with regard to race?

2. Describe the ideological struggle between such figures as Booker T. Washington and William Monroe Trotter. What was the source of this struggle? What impact did it have on African Americans?

3. Historians regard Woodrow Wilson as a "progressive" president, but his progressivism did not appear to extend to issues of race. What do you think might explain that? What would make a "progressive" president praise a movie glorifying the Ku Klux Klan?

4. A century-plus earlier, another African American leader directly challenged his president. Compare this document to Benjamin Banneker's Letter to Thomas Jefferson, written in 1791. What do you think Banneker's attitude toward Trotter's protest would have been? What differing tactics did the two writers use in addressing their presidents?

5. In what ways did World War I complicate race relations in the United States? How might these complications have influenced both Trotter and Wilson in their meetings?

Monroe Trotter's Protest to Woodrow Wilson

One year ago we presented a national petition, signed by Afro-Americans in thirty-eight states, protesting against the segregation of employees of the National government whose ancestry could be traced in whole or in part to Africa, as instituted under your administration in the treasury and post-office departments. We then appealed to you to undo this race segregation in accord with your duty as president and with your pre-election pledges. We stated that there could be no freedom, no respect from others, and no equality of citizenship under segregation for races, especially when applied to but one of many racial elements in the government employ. For such placement of employes means a charge by the government of physical indecency or infection, or of being a lower order of beings, or a subjection to the prejudices of other citizens, which constitutes inferiority of status. We protested such segregation as to working conditions, eating tables, dressing rooms, rest rooms, lockers and especially public toilets in government buildings. We stated that such segregation was a public humiliation and degradation, entirely unmerited and far-reaching in its injurious effects, a gratuitous blow against ever-loyal citizens and against those many of whom aided and supported your elevation to the presidency of our common country.

At that time you stated you would investigate conditions for yourself. Now, after the lapse of a year, we have come back having found that all the forms of segregation of government employes of African extraction are still practiced in the treasury and postoffice department buildings, and to a certain extent have spread into other government buildings.

Under the treasury department, in the bureau of engraving and printing there is segregation not only in dressing rooms, but in working positions, Afro-American employes being herded at separate tables, in eating, and in toilets. In the navy department there is herding at desks and separation in lavatories. In the postoffice department there is separation in work for Afro-American women in the alcove on the eighth floor, of Afro-American men in rooms on the seventh floor, with forbidding even of entrance into an adjoining room occupied by white clerks on the seventh floor, and of Afro-American men in separate rooms just instituted on the sixth floor, with separate lavatories for Afro-American men on the eighth floor; in the main treasury building in separate lavatories in the basement; in the interior department separate lavatories, which were specifically pointed out to you at our first hearing; in the state and other departments separate lavatories; in marine hospital service building in separate lavatories, though there is but one Afro-American clerk to use it; in the war department in separate lavatories in the postoffice department building separate lavatories; in the sewing and bindery divisions of the government printing office on the fifth floor there is herding at working positions of Afro-American women and separation in lavatories, and new segregation instituted by the division chief since our first audience with you This lavatory segregation is the most degrading, most insulting of all. Afro-American employes who use the regular public lavatories on the floors where they work are cautioned and are then warned by superior officers against insubordination.

We have come by vote of this league to set before you this definite continuance of race segregation and to renew the protest and to ask you to abolish segregation of Afro-American employes in the executive department.

Because we cannot believe you capable of any disregard of your pledges we have been sent by the alarmed American citizens of color. They realize that if they can be segregated and thus humiliated by the national government at the national capital the beginning is made for the spread of that persecution and prosecution which makes property and life itself insecure in the South, the foundation of the whole fabric of their citizenship is unsettled.

They have made plain enough to you their opposition to segregation last year by a national anti-segregation petition, this year by a protest registered at the polls, voting against every Democratic candidate save those outspoken against segregation. The only Democrat elected governor in the eastern states, was Governor Walsh of Massachusetts, who appealed to you by letter to stop segregation. Thus have the Afro-Americans shown how they detest segregation.

In fact, so intense is their resentment that the movement to divide this solid race vote and make

Document Text

peace with the national Democracy, so suspiciously revived when you ran for the presidency, and which some of our families for two generations have been risking all to promote, bids fair to be undone.

Only two years ago you were heralded as perhaps the second Lincoln, and now the Afro-American leaders who supported you are hounded as false leaders and traitors to their race. What a change segregation has wrought!

You said that your "Colored fellow citizens could depend upon you for everything which would assist in advancing the interests of their race in the United States." Consider this pledge in the face of the continued color segregation! Fellow citizenship means congregation. Segregation destroys fellowship and citizenship. Consider that any passerby on the streets of the national capital, whether he be black or white, can enter and use the public lavatories in government buildings while citizens of color who do the work of the government are excluded.

As equal citizens and by virtue of your public promises we are entitled at your hands to freedom from discrimination, restriction, imputation and insult in government employ. Have you a "new freedom" for white Americans and a new slavery for your Afro-American fellow citizens? God forbid!

We have been delegated to ask you to issue an executive order against any and all segregation of government employes because of race and color, and to ask whether you will do so. We await your reply, that we may give it to the waiting citizens of the United States of African extraction.

Glossary

bureau of engraving and printing	a federal agency, part of the Treasury Department, that produces paper currency, government bonds, postage stamps, and various other official documents
Governor Walsh	David Ignatius Walsh, the isolationist governor of Massachusetts who argued for film censorship in his state in response to *The Birth of a Nation*, a film glorifying the Ku Klux Klan that Wilson had approved of
this league	the National Independent Equal Rights League

Edward White (AP/Wide World Photos)

GUINN V. UNITED STATES

"While ... the [Fifteenth] Amendment gives no right of suffrage, ... its prohibition might measurably have that effect."

Overview

In the 1915 Supreme Court case *Frank Guinn and J. J. Beal v. United States,* Chief Justice Edward White held that the grandfather clause, an amendment to Oklahoma's constitution, limited black suffrage and was therefore invalid. The case also applied to Maryland's constitution, which had a similar clause. The grandfather clause worked in conjunction with a literacy test to deprive African Americans of the right to vote. The literacy test stipulated that all voters be able to read, but the grandfather clause lifted literacy test requirements for anyone who was otherwise qualified to vote anywhere in the United States on January 1, 1866. The clause was particularly galling to African Americans in Oklahoma, as that state had not even existed in 1866. The literacy test additionally discriminated against African Americans, since it was very subjective and was applied by white southern registrars.

The U.S. Supreme Court held that Oklahoma's grandfather clause was unconstitutional, because it violated the spirit of the Fifteenth Amendment, ratified in 1870, which granted former slaves the right to vote. The Court's ruling had little direct effect on the extension of voting rights to African Americans in Oklahoma, however: The state simply passed a new statute, disenfranchising all those who did not register to vote during a brief, two-week window in 1916, except those who had voted in 1914. Thus, all voting whites could still vote, but all of the previously disenfranchised blacks were still disenfranchised, unless they had been able to work their way through the system in a two-week period.

Context

The *Guinn* case was one of the first major court cases in which the National Association for the Advancement of Colored People (NAACP) played a role, filing a brief, and represented one of the few times in the early twentieth century when the federal government appeared on the side of African Americans in a legal battle. *Guinn* was also one of the first challenges to discriminatory voting laws, which had been restricting voting rights to certain segments of American society for more than forty years. The first such laws appeared in the post–Civil War Reconstruction period. African Americans and poor whites gained allies in the White House when the Republican Party—the party of Abraham Lincoln—took power in 1860; meanwhile, southern Democrats—supporters of segregationist policies at that time—vowed to wrest their power back using any and all means to achieve their ends. Despite the fact that the ratification of the Fifteenth Amendment to the U.S. Constitution in the spring of 1870 had granted all male citizens the right to vote regardless of race, color, or prior slave status, violence and threats of violence were often used and suggested by Democrats over the next decade to keep Republicans, particularly black Republicans, from voting. As a result, all of the southern states had Democratic legislatures by the late 1870s.

Efforts continued in subsequent years to eliminate all African Americans and many poor whites from the voting ranks, leading to the growth of the Populist movement. This biracial groundswell stemmed from a financial crisis and labor unrest in the United States that resulted in the failure of businesses throughout the country, particularly many small farms in the South and the West. Channeling the anger of America's small farmers and other laborers who wanted reform, the Populist movement pushed for policy changes that would empower the nation's workers, both black and white, and protect small businesses from corrupt corporate interests. Reform and Fusion tickets won often in the South (and the West) in the early 1890s. Fusion politics refers to the combined power of the Republican and Populist parties at the end of the nineteenth century. In response, wealthy whites interested in seeing a resurgence of the Democratic Party organized mobs to drive African Americans from the polls. Many states adopted constitutional amendments in the late 1890s and early 1900s designed specifically to disenfranchise blacks and to limit the voting of poor whites. All of the previous restrictions on voting rights were retained and even more were added.

It was in the midst of this political clash that Oklahoma became the forty-sixth state in the Union in late 1907. The region came late into statehood, because much of its land had been set aside for Native American reservations until the 1890s. In 1910 Oklahoma adopted a constitutional amendment that tied the voting rights of its citizens to the

Time Line

1860
- **November 6**
  Abraham Lincoln is the first Republican to be elected president of the United States.

1865
- The end of the Civil War leads to Reconstruction in the American South.

1870
- **Spring**
  The Fifteenth Amendment to the U.S. Constitution is ratified, giving all male citizens the right to vote regardless of race, color, or previous slave status; most African American men are able to vote for a time.

1877
- The Compromise of 1877 removes federal troops from the South and ends any chance that African Americans will receive fair treatment; the South effectively becomes a one-party state, with the Democratic Party being fully behind white supremacy.

1896
- **May 18**
  In its decision in the case of *Plessy v. Ferguson*, the U.S. Supreme Court upholds the legality of "separate but equal" segregation adopted throughout the South.

1898
- **April 25**
  In the case of *Williams v. Mississippi*, the U.S. Supreme Court upholds literacy and understanding qualifications established by some states to determine voter eligibility, because on their face the clauses do not discriminate against African Americans.

1907
- **November 16**
  Oklahoma becomes a state.

1910
- Although the Fifteenth Amendment guarantees all black men the right to vote, an amendment to the Oklahoma constitution effectively bars African Americans from voting in that state.

---

successful completion of a literacy test. However, certain individuals—almost always whites—were able to circumvent the literacy test requirement because of an exception known as the grandfather clause, which guaranteed descendants of eligible voters the right to vote without question. The amendment used a date of January 1 of the year after the end of the Civil War as the date for which a voter was required to prove that an ancestor—presumably a grandfather—was qualified to vote. Prospective voters who were unable to satisfy the terms of the grandfather clause were forced to prove their literacy. Maryland's grandfather clause, tested also in the case of *Guinn v. United States*, was adopted in 1908, just a couple of years before Oklahoma's.

The grandfather clause had little effect on the right to vote for most whites, but it served as a barrier to the ballot box for African American voters. Freedmen and all men of color were not guaranteed the right to vote until the passage of the Fifteenth Amendment in 1870—four years after the date specified in the grandfather clause. The Oklahoma state government claimed that the clause did not discriminate against voters on the basis of their race; the term *race* was not even mentioned in the text. Clearly, however, the voting rights of African Americans, not whites, were most threatened by the terms of the statute. In fact, the grandfather clause and similar voting restrictions generally had loopholes to protect white voters. Typically, a person who owned property or paid sufficient taxes was considered exempt from the clause; because the rate of property ownership was higher among whites than blacks, this exception adversely affected potential black voters.

It should be noted, however, that the grandfather clause (and the literacy test used in Oklahoma) were not the only methods employed to disenfranchise blacks. Among other techniques was the poll tax, an annual per-person fee that had to be paid before a ballot could be cast in any election. In effect, the poll tax added an economic dimension to the social inequities encountered by African Americans seeking to exercise their right to vote. At about a dollar per person, the tax placed a financial burden on a segment of the population with little or no money to spare. In addition to making the payment, voters were required to prove that they had paid the tax each year for as long as they had resided in the state; however, records and receipts for those members of the black community who managed to pay the poll tax were often lost or never entered in official logs. Taken together, these provisions effectively denied the right of suffrage to African Americans in the South.

It was in this context that the case of *Guinn v. United States* came to the Supreme Court. Black citizens of Oklahoma had voiced complaints to the U.S. Justice Department concerning the enormous amount of racial violence surrounding the Oklahoma elections of 1910, which served to discourage blacks from voting. In light of the brutal and discriminatory atmosphere of the elections, U.S. Attorney John Embry, along with fellow U.S. Attorney William R. Gregg, indicted two Oklahoma elections officials, J. J. Beal and Frank Guinn, on criminal charges of depriving people of their rights under the Constitution and federal law. Contrary to most expectations, the officials were convicted of civil rights violations on September 29, 1911—despite the fact that they had been enforcing an amendment to the Oklahoma state constitution. The two officials took the case to the U.S. Court of Appeals, claiming that they should not be prosecuted for upholding the law of their state. The Court of Appeals sent the case on to the Supreme Court in 1913, and it was decided on June 21, 1915.

About the Author

Chief Justice Edward Douglass White, Jr., was born November 3, 1845, in Louisiana and served in the Confederate army during the Civil War. After that service, he returned to his parents' sugarcane plantation and began to study law. Practicing in Louisiana after joining the bar in 1868, he briefly served in the state senate and then on the Louisiana Supreme Court before returning to his legal practice in 1880. In 1891, White was elected to the U.S. Senate; three years later he was appointed to the U.S. Supreme Court, and in 1910 he became the Court's chief justice. A southern Democrat, White was the second Catholic to serve as a Supreme Court justice.

Although White had sided with the majority in the 1896 case of *Plessy v. Ferguson*, which upheld segregation in public transportation and in general by establishing the "separate but equal" clause, he went on to author the *Guinn v. United States* decision in 1915. In 1917, White agreed with the majority in *Buchanan v. Warley*, a decision that held a residential segregation law in Louisville, Kentucky, illegal. The common thread between the latter two cases, and the difference between them and *Plessy*, is that the law in the cases of both *Buchanan* and *Guinn* directly and clearly discriminated against African Americans, whereas in *Plessy* the law was explained away by the majority as being unbiased on its face. After *Guinn*, White served as chief justice for another six years. He died on May 19, 1921.

Explanation and Analysis of the Document

At issue in the U.S. Supreme Court case of *Guinn v. United States* was whether grandfather clauses had been deliberately enacted by state governments to deny African Americans their right to vote. Two Oklahoma election officials, Frank Guinn and J. J. Beal, had been charged with violating federal law by conspiring to deprive black Oklahomans of their voting rights in a general election held in 1910. Following the convictions of both men by a jury in an Oklahoma district court a year later, the *Guinn* case was brought before the Supreme Court on appeal in 1913. *Guinn v. United States* forced the highest court in the nation to examine the combined use of grandfather clauses and literacy tests as prerequisites to voting; specifically, the application of such tests in Oklahoma and Maryland was analyzed for fairness amid charges that black voters had been subjected to racial discrimination at the ballot box.

Time Line

1915
- **June 21** In *Guinn v. United States*, the Supreme Court voids the grandfather clause as a violation of the Fifteenth Amendment.

1916
- Oklahoma gets around the meaning of the *Guinn* decision by allowing all people who voted in 1914 to be automatically reregistered, while forcing all who had not—namely, African Americans—to register within a two-week window or face a permanent bar to the registration process.

1944
- **April 3** In one of the first voting rights victories since the *Guinn* case, the Supreme Court, in *Smith v. Allwright*, strikes down the whites-only primary in Texas, which had made blacks ineligible to vote for the nomination of Democratic Party candidates for the U.S. Senate, the House of Representatives, and the office of governor.

1964
- **January 23** The passage of the Twenty-fourth Amendment leads to the end of the poll tax in federal elections.
- **July 2** The Civil Rights Act of 1964 is signed by President Lyndon Baines Johnson.

1965
- **August 6** The Voting Rights Act of 1965 is passed to enforce the Fifteenth Amendment to the U.S. Constitution.

1966
- **March 24** The Supreme Court, endorsing a sweeping view of federal power in *Harper v. Virginia Board of Elections*, holds that the poll tax at the state level violates the equal protection clause of the Fourteenth Amendment.

Before voting, a black voter had to prove his literacy to the satisfaction of a white registrar. Whites were generally exempt from the test by the grandfather clause, which waived the need for a voter to display his literacy if his grandfather had been eligible to vote in 1866. African American voters could not satisfy this requirement because suffrage had not yet been granted to freedmen in 1866. And so blacks, at the discretion of a white registrar, might be asked to read a book in Greek or submit to a general knowledge test about a provision in either the state's constitution or the U.S. Constitution. In some southern states, general knowledge provisions were imposed by election officials, with registrars asking prospective voters such questions as "How many bubbles are there in a bar of soap?" The adequacy of a black voter's response to such questions was determined solely by the registrar.

Before the text of Chief Justice Edward White's opinion in *Guinn v. United States* is a syllabus summarizing the key points of the lower court's decision. Justice White then quotes the laws backing up the Fifteenth Amendment, discusses the election officials' trial, reiterates the jury instructions given at that trial, and lays out the responsibility of the Supreme Court in the case: "Let us at once consider and sift the propositions of the United States, on the one hand, and of the plaintiffs in error, on the other, in order to reach with precision the real and final question to be considered." That question, according to White, boils down to whether or not the state amendment creating the grandfather clause was valid and whether the law itself was invalid because it violated the Fifteenth Amendment. White examines the arguments on each side of the case and ends with justifications for his conclusions.

Justice White's opinion begins by noting that two election officials were charged with violating the federal law by denying "certain negro citizens" the right to vote based on the color of their skin. The Thirteenth Amendment, passed in late 1865, had abolished slavery in the United States, but the South's refusal to guarantee basic human rights to emancipated slaves forced the adoption of the Fourteenth Amendment, granting citizenship to all freedmen. Abuses continued, however, and the Republican Party in the South was seriously weakened because its large African American voting base was being denied the right to vote on a variety of technicalities. The Fifteenth Amendment to the U.S. Constitution was designed to further safeguard the rights of newly freed slaves by removing obstacles to their voting. The chief justice quotes the language of the Fifteenth Amendment, which was ratified soon after the end of the Civil War: "The right of citizens of the United States to vote shall not be denied or abridged by the United States or by any State on account of race, color, or previous condition of servitude." Black suffrage seems to be spelled out quite clearly by the text of this amendment, but that was not the case. *Guinn v. United States* tested the power of the Fifteenth Amendment against the rights of states to establish their own standards for suffrage.

After stating the law, the Court then looks back at the claims of each side represented in the original case. Representing the United States was U.S. solicitor general John Davis, who appeared before the Court to challenge the Oklahoma amendment. Davis argued that Oklahoma's provision had the effect of denying the right to vote based on race and should be struck down as a violation of the Fifteenth Amendment, regardless of whether the law was explicitly in violation of that constitutional provision. The defense, however, argued for state sovereignty—not state sovereignty in terms of states being allowed to ignore the Fifteenth Amendment, but sovereignty in terms of their being able to set their own qualifications for voting. As the law in question did not specifically use race as a standard, the state contended that it should be allowed. The federal government, the defendants argued, should not be able to read a motive into the act or state that the effect of the law made an otherwise lawful act invalid. The defendants also claimed that the fact that no blacks qualified to vote under the law was not due to the law but due to their inability to read. It should be noted that no defense was noted by the Supreme Court as to why a date of January 1, 1866, was picked if the point were not to force all black voters to take the test.

The Supreme Court argues here that suffrage and qualifications put upon suffrage were state issues and that their position in this case did not limit that state power in any way. Of course, state regulations like this one that blatantly violated the Fifteenth Amendment were still being challenged, but otherwise the federal government left most decisions to the states alone. The Court then considers the literacy test, stating that it would not challenge the state's right to administer such a test. The only challenge was the use of the law to try to bypass the intended meaning of the Fifteenth Amendment.

Justice White continues his opinion with the enumeration of three key questions: Did the grandfather clause law violate the Fifteenth Amendment? Did the amendment, choosing January 1, 1866 as the date to use for the grandfather clause, mean what the government said it did? And would the striking down of the grandfather clause make the rest of the literacy test invalid? The rest of Justice White's opinion sought to answer to those questions.

The Court, in answering the first question, notes that the Fifteenth Amendment still allows room for the state to manage the business of voting; state-imposed literacy tests, then, remain lawful. It is important to evaluate this decision in the proper context: It embodies an era during which states wielded great power. The reach of the Fourteenth Amendment to prohibit racial bias at the state level was still very limited, and the use of the amendment to curtail the actions of state legislatures, unless they were directly and blatantly biased, did not occur for another three decades, when the Supreme Court decided *Shelley v. Kraemer* (1948), holding that courts could not enforce racially based private restrictive covenants.

In his explanation of what the Fifteenth Amendment says about suffrage, White holds that the state still has full power over suffrage qualifications, with the exception of those qualifications based on "race, color, or previous condition of servitude." He goes on to say that while no right

Commemorative print marking the enactment on March 30, 1870, of the Fifteenth Amendment (Library of Congress)

to vote is directly created by the amendment, that right might still result when discriminatory rules are struck down by the amendment, which the Court held to be self-executing. White takes exception to the intent of Oklahoma's grandfather clause, pointing out that for a brief period of time prior to the adoption of the clause the hurdles to African American suffrage, while still present, were actually lower. According to White, there was no doubt that the statute had been adopted as an attempt to get around the Fifteenth Amendment. For that reason, the amendment to the Oklahoma constitution ran into direct conflict with the federal constitutional amendment.

Regarding the date the amendment to the Oklahoma Constitution was adopted, White again theorizes that the only possible reason for using the date of January 1, 1866, was to bypass the rights implied in the Fifteenth Amendment. Although the language of the grandfather clause does not refer to skin color or prior slave status, its clear purpose was to avoid granting suffrage to former slaves. As White puts it, the very use of that date shows a "direct and positive disregard of the 15th Amendment." The Court also considered whether anything had occurred in 1866 other than the granting of the right to vote to blacks in some areas (and throughout the nation four years later with the passage of the Fifteenth Amendment) that would cause a state to return its voting status to a time prior to that date. In other words, the opinion states that there was no legal change to suffrage in 1866 other than granting slaves the right to vote. If the date had been based on some other, potentially more reasonable (in the eyes of the Court) state intention, the Court might still have considered the grandfather clause law valid. No such reason was found, however.

Finally the Court examined the literacy test, but not to determine whether it disparately affected African Americans, as that was not a concern of the court at the time. Actually, at this point in history, the Court also ignored laws that produced obvious disadvantages for black voters, such as the white primary created in Texas and other states. There, the Democratic Party was by far the majority party, and so the primary to nominate party candidates was even more important than the election, in which candidates from the various parties squared off against each other. In other decisions, the

Essential Quotes

"The suffrage and literacy tests in the amendment of 1910 to the constitution of Oklahoma are so connected with each other that the unconstitutionality of the former renders the whole amendment invalid."

"Beyond doubt the Amendment does not take away from the state governments in a general sense the power over suffrage which has belonged to those governments from the beginning.... In fact, the very command of the Amendment recognizes the possession of the general power by the state, since the Amendment seeks to regulate its exercise as to the particular subject with which it deals."

"While in the true sense, therefore, the [Fifteenth] Amendment gives no right of suffrage, it was long ago recognized that in operation its prohibition might measurably have that effect."

"We seek in vain for any ground which would sustain any other interpretation but that the provision ... [makes the date of 1866] the basis of the right to suffrage conferred in direct and positive disregard of the 15th Amendment."

Supreme Court allowed the Democratic Party to limit primary voting to whites and ignored the connection of the party to the state. It was not until 1944 that the white primary was finally struck down. Thus, the court's decision here to consider the literacy test in the abstract is not surprising.

In *Guinn v. United States*, the literacy test used in Oklahoma was directly intertwined with the state's grandfather clause, and so the question was whether the grandfather clause could be struck down while allowing the literacy test to still operate. Justice White states that, in general, the Court would rely on state court decisions in areas like this, but he also points out that no such decision had yet been made. He asks what the impact of the decision already announced—striking down the grandfather clause—would be on the literacy test. The Court holds that the statute contradicted itself once the grandfather clause was removed, as without the grandfather clause all people would be subjected to the literacy test, which was the exact opposite of the stated goal of the legislation. The stated goal of the legislation was to limit the number of people who had to take the literacy test, and the elimination of the grandfather clause would have once again forced everyone to take the literacy test. Thus, since the legislation, as necessarily amended by the Supreme Court decision, contradicted itself, it must be struck down as a whole, even though literacy tests generally would be allowed.

Literacy tests were used to deprive African Americans of their right to suffrage through the early 1960s, as were comprehension tests covering the federal and state constitutions. Employed unfairly and disproportionately against blacks but rarely given to whites, these tests swayed the results of elections for decades. A half century after the 1915 decision in *Guinn v. United States*, the Voting Rights Act of 1965 did away with impediments to voting by allowing the federal government to appoint registrars in any state where a significant racial disparity in voting registration existed. After the passage of this law, millions more African Americans registered to vote. In 1915, though, such advances were still fifty years in the future.

At the end of his opinion, Justice White addresses an objection made by the defendants to the charge made against them in court. This argument basically states that since the charge had presumed that the suffrage amendment to the Oklahoma constitution was unconstitutional, it should be thrown out because it had presumed their guilt. However, the Supreme Court replies that since the Fifteenth Amendment was self-executing and clearly in conflict with the suffrage amendment to the Oklahoma constitution, the charge would be allowed. The final complaint was against a conspiracy statute under which the men were arrested. However, that same day the U.S. Supreme Court had upheld the same statute in another case dealing with Oklahoma—one concerning election officials who refused to count the votes cast by African Americans. The officials were convicted, and the conviction was upheld, which in turn meant that the statute was acceptable; therefore, the conviction of the defendants in the *Guinn* case was also upheld. It should be noted that the aforementioned cases involving Oklahoma election officials were rooted somewhat in political considerations. The Republican Party was losing political ground, so party officials pushed for the thorough investigation of alleged voting rights abuses. By the end of the nineteenth century, the Republican Party had practically died out throughout the South; the adoption of new constitutions by some southern states around 1900 compounded the party's woes and proved that their concern was not an idle one. Whether motivated by the fear of the party's demise or by a real concern for the rights of those not being allowed to vote, the Republican Party's escalation of suffrage cases to the U.S. Supreme Court was a necessary step in black enfranchisement.

Audience

There are several different audiences for this Supreme Court decision, the most obvious being the parties involved: the U.S. government and the two Oklahoma election officials named in the case, Frank Guinn and J. J. Beal, who had been convicted of civil rights violations. A broader audience was the South as a whole as well as the state of Maryland, which also had a grandfather clause. The nation's black community and the lawyers and members of the NAACP (who, as noted, had filed a brief) were no doubt interested parties, and this case stands as the first twentieth-century victory for African Americans at the Supreme Court level. Historians, scholars, and students of African American culture represent a modern-day audience, one that can see how the nation took its first halting steps toward equality and how limited those steps really were.

Impact

The decision in the case of *Guinn v. United States* had a limited impact on black voting rights at the time it was handed down. Only a few states had such grandfather clauses, as most preferred to restrict African American suffrage more subtly. Even national leaders who supported segregation were opposed to these clauses owing to their deliberate disregard for the spirit of the law. The voters in Oklahoma were not affected by the decision; the Oklahoma state government simply adopted a law allowing all people who had voted in 1914 to vote again, along with whoever could survive a rigorous registration process that was open for only two weeks. Those states with literacy tests could breathe a sigh of relief as well, since the Supreme Court refused to challenge them directly and generally granted full rights to the state to create their own standards for suffrage, as long as they did not blatantly challenge the Fifteenth Amendment.

The more important effect was a long-term one, as the NAACP and others saw that they could win at the Supreme Court level and so continued to press cases to the highest court. *Guinn* also saw the first brief filed by the NAACP, which helped to validate the group's efforts. The NAACP would come to be the premier organization fighting for African Americans' rights through the court system.

Questions for Further Study

1. What is a grandfather clause as it pertains to voting rights, and how did grandfather clauses interfere with the voting rights of African Americans? What was particularly unfair about Oklahoma's grandfather clause?

2. What methods besides grandfather clauses were used to interfere with black voting rights during this era and beyond?

3. On what basis did the U.S. Supreme Court find the Oklahoma statute in question unconstitutional?

4. What was the short-term effect of the Court's decision? What, if any, was the long-term effect?

5. What role, if any, did party politics play in the events surrounding *Guinn v. United States*. Consider not only the Republican and Democratic parties but the Populist Party as well.

See also Thirteenth Amendment to the U.S. Constitution (1865); Fourteenth Amendment to the U.S. Constitution (1868); Fifteenth Amendment to the U.S. Constitution (1870); *Plessy v. Ferguson* (1896); Civil Rights Act of 1964.

Further Reading

■ Books

Kotz, Nick. *Judgment Days: Lyndon Baines Johnson, Martin Luther King, Jr., and the Laws That Changed America*. Boston: Houghton Mifflin, 2005.

Pratt, Walter F., Jr. *The Supreme Court under Edward Douglass White, 1910–1921*. Columbia: University of South Carolina Press, 1999.

Rush, Mark E., ed. *Voting Rights and Redistricting in the United States*. Westport, Conn.: Praeger, 1998.

Shoemaker, Rebecca S. *The White Court: Justices, Rulings, and Legacy*. Santa Barbara, Calif.: ABC-CLIO, 2004.

Valley, Richard M. *The Two Reconstructions: The Struggle for Black Enfranchisement*. Chicago: University of Chicago Press, 2004.

Zelden, Charles. *Voting Rights on Trial*. Indianapolis, Ind.: Hackett, 2004.

—Scott A. Merriman

GUINN V. UNITED STATES

Syllabus

The so-called Grandfather Clause of the amendment to the constitution of Oklahoma of 1910 is void because it violates the Fifteenth Amendment to the Constitution of the United States.

The Grandfather Clause being unconstitutional, and not being separable from the remainder of the amendment to the constitution of Oklahoma of 1910, that amendment as a whole is invalid.

The Fifteenth Amendment does not, in a general sense, take from the States the power over suffrage possessed by the States from the beginning, but it does restrict the power of the United States or the States to abridge or deny the right of a citizen of the United States to vote on account of race, color or previous condition of servitude. While the Fifteenth Amendment gives no right of suffrage, as its command is self-executing, rights of suffrage may be enjoyed by reason of the striking out of discriminations against the exercise of the right.

A provision in a state constitution recurring to conditions existing before the adoption of the Fifteenth Amendment and the continuance of which conditions that amendment prohibited, and making those conditions the test of the right to the suffrage, is in conflict with, and void under, the Fifteenth Amendment.

The establishment of a literacy test for exercising the suffrage is an exercise by the State of a lawful power vested in it not subject to the supervision of the Federal courts.

Whether a provision in a suffrage statute may be valid under the Federal Constitution if it is so connected with other provisions that are invalid as to make the whole statute unconstitutional is a question of state law, but, in the absence of any decision by the state court, this court may, in a case coming from the Federal courts, determine it for itself.

The suffrage and literacy tests in the amendment of 1910 to the constitution of Oklahoma are so connected with each other that the unconstitutionality of the former renders the whole amendment invalid.

The facts, which involve the constitutionality under the Fifteenth Amendment of the Constitution of the United States of the suffrage amendment to the constitution of Oklahoma, known as the Grandfather Clause, and the responsibility of election officers under § 5508, Rev.Stat., and § 19 of the Penal Code for preventing people from voting who have the right to vote, are stated in the opinion.

Mr. Chief Justice White delivered the opinion of the court

This case is before us on a certificate drawn by the court below as the basis of two questions which are submitted for our solution in order to enable the court correctly to decide issues in a case which it has under consideration. Those issues arose from an indictment and conviction of certain election officers of the State of Oklahoma (the plaintiffs in error) of the crime of having conspired unlawfully, willfully and fraudulently to deprive certain negro citizens, on account of their race and color, of a right to vote at a general election held in that State in 1910, they being entitled to vote under the state law and which right was secured to them by the Fifteenth Amendment to the Constitution of the United States. The prosecution was directly concerned with §5508, Rev.Stat., now §19 of the Penal Code which is as follows:

"If two or more persons conspire to injure, oppress, threaten, or intimidate any citizen in the free exercise or enjoyment of any right or privilege secured to him by the Constitution or laws of the United States, or because of his having so exercised the same, or if two or more persons go in disguise on the highway, or on the premises of another, with intent to prevent or hinder his free exercise or enjoyment of any right or privilege so secured, they shall be fined not more than five thousand dollars and imprisoned not more than ten years, and shall, moreover, be thereafter ineligible to any office or place of honor, profit, or trust created by the Constitution or laws of the United States."

We concentrate and state from the certificate only matters which we deem essential to dispose of the questions asked.

Suffrage in Oklahoma was regulated by §1, Article III of the Constitution under which the State was admitted into the Union. Shortly after the admission, there was submitted an amendment to the Constitution making a radical change in that article which was adopted prior to November 8, 1910. At an election for members of Congress which followed the adoption of this Amendment, certain election officers, in enforcing its provisions, refused to allow certain negro citizens to vote who were clearly entitled to vote under the provision of the Constitution under which the State was admitted, that is, before the amendment, and who, it is equally clear, were not entitled to vote under the provision of the suffrage amendment if that amendment governed. The persons so excluded based their claim of right to vote upon the original Constitution and upon the assertion that the suffrage amendment was void because in conflict with the prohibitions of the Fifteenth Amendment, and therefore afforded no basis for denying them the right guaranteed and protected by that Amendment. And upon the assumption that this claim was justified and that the election officers had violated the Fifteenth Amendment in denying the right to vote, this prosecution, as we have said, was commenced. At the trial, the court instructed that, by the Fifteenth Amendment, the States were prohibited from discriminating as to suffrage because of race, color, or previous condition of servitude, and that Congress, in pursuance of the authority which was conferred upon it by the very terms of the Amendment to enforce its provisions, had enacted the following (Rev.Stat., §2004):

"All citizens of the United States who are otherwise qualified by law to vote at any election by the people of any State, Territory, district, … municipality, … or other territorial subdivision, shall be entitled and allowed to vote at all such elections, without distinction of race, color, or previous condition of servitude; any constitution, law, custom, usage, or regulation of any State or Territory, or by or under its authority to the contrary notwithstanding."

It then instructed as follows:

"The State amendment which imposes the test of reading and writing any section of the State constitution as a condition to voting to persons not on or prior to January 1, 1866, entitled to vote under some form of government, or then resident in some foreign nation, or a lineal descendant of such person, is not valid, but you may consider it insofar as it was in good faith relied and acted upon by the defendants in ascertaining their intent and motive. If you believe from the evidence that the defendants formed a common design and cooperated in denying the colored voters of Union Township precinct, or any of them, entitled to vote, the privilege of voting, but this was due to a mistaken belief sincerely entertained by the defendants as to the qualifications of the voters—that is, if the motive actuating the defendants was honest, and they simply erred in the conception of their duty—then the criminal intent requisite to their guilt is wanting, and they cannot be convicted. On the other hand, if they knew or believed these colored persons were entitled to vote, and their purpose was to unfairly and fraudulently deny the right of suffrage to them, or any of them entitled thereto, on account of their race and color, then their purpose was a corrupt one, and they cannot be shielded by their official positions."

The questions which the court below asks are these:

"1. Was the amendment to the constitution of Oklahoma, heretofore set forth, valid?"

"2. Was that amendment void insofar as it attempted to debar from the right or privilege of voting for a qualified candidate for a Member of Congress in Oklahoma, unless they were able to read and write any section of the constitution of Oklahoma, negro citizens of the United States who were otherwise qualified to vote for a qualified candidate for a Member of Congress in that State, but who were not, and none of whose lineal ancestors was entitled to vote under any form of government on January 1, 1866, or at any time prior thereto, because they were then slaves?"

As these questions obviously relate to the provisions concerning suffrage in the original constitution and the amendment to those provisions which forms the basis of the controversy, we state the text of both. The original clause, so far as material, was this:

"The qualified electors of the State shall be male citizens of the United States, male citizens of the State, and male persons of Indian descent native of the United States, who are over the age of twenty-one years, who have resided in the State one year, in the county six months, and in the election precinct thirty days, next preceding the election at which any such elector offers to vote."

And this is the amendment:

"No person shall be registered as an elector of this State or be allowed to vote in any election herein, unless he be able to read and write any section of the constitution of the State of Oklahoma; but no person who was, on January 1, 1866, or at any time prior thereto, entitled to vote under any form of government, or who at that time resided in some foreign nation, and no lineal descendant of such person, shall be denied the right to register and vote because of his inability to so read and write sections of such constitution. Precinct election inspectors having in charge the registration of electors shall enforce the provisions of this section at the time of registration, provided registration be required. Should registration be dispensed with, the provisions of this section shall be enforced by the precinct election officer when electors apply for ballots to vote."

Considering the questions in the right of the text of the suffrage amendment, it is apparent that they are two-fold, because of the two-fold character of the provisions as to suffrage which the amendment contains. The first question is concerned with that provision of the amendment which fixes a standard by which the right to vote is given upon conditions existing on January 1, 1866, and relieves those coming within that standard from the standard based on a literacy test which is established by the other provision of the amendment. The second question asks as to the validity of the literacy test and how far, if intrinsically valid, it would continue to exist and be operative in the event the standard based upon January 1, 1866, should be held to be illegal as violative of the Fifteenth Amendment.

To avoid that which is unnecessary, let us at once consider and sift the propositions of the United States, on the one hand, and of the plaintiffs in error, on the other, in order to reach with precision the real and final question to be considered. The United States insists that the provision of the amendment which fixes a standard based upon January 1, 1866, is repugnant to the prohibitions of the Fifteenth Amendment because, in substance and effect, that provision, if not an express, is certainly an open, repudiation of the Fifteenth Amendment, and hence the provision in question was stricken with nullity in its inception by the self-operative force of the Amendment, and, as the result of the same power, was at all subsequent times devoid of any vitality whatever.

For the plaintiffs in error, on the other hand, it is said the States have the power to fix standards for suffrage, and that power was not taken away by the Fifteenth Amendment, but only limited to the extent of the prohibitions which that Amendment established. This being true, as the standard fixed does not in terms make any discrimination on account of race, color, or previous condition of servitude, since all, whether negro or white, who come within its requirements enjoy the privilege of voting, there is no ground upon which to rest the contention that the provision violates the Fifteenth Amendment. This, it is insisted, must be the case unless it is intended to expressly deny the State's right to provide a standard for suffrage, or, what is equivalent thereto, to assert: a, that the judgment of the State exercised in the exertion of that power is subject to Federal judicial review or supervision, or b, that it may be questioned and be brought within the prohibitions of the Amendment by attributing to the legislative authority an occult motive to violate the Amendment or by assuming that an exercise of the otherwise lawful power may be invalidated because of conclusions concerning its operation in practical execution and resulting discrimination arising therefrom, albeit such discrimination was not expressed in the standard fixed or fairly to be implied, but simply arose from inequalities naturally inhering in those who must come within the standard in order to enjoy the right to vote.

On the other hand, the United States denies the relevancy of these contentions. It says state power to provide for suffrage is not disputed, although, of course, the authority of the Fifteenth Amendment and the limit on that power which it imposes is insisted upon. Hence, no assertion denying the right of a State to exert judgment and discretion in fixing the qualification of suffrage is advanced, and no right to question the motive of the State in establishing a standard as to such subjects under such circumstances or to review or supervise the same is relied upon, and no power to destroy an otherwise valid exertion of authority upon the mere ultimate operation of the power exercised is asserted. And, applying these principles to the very case in hand, the argument of the Government, in substance, says: no question is raised by the Government concerning the validity of the literacy test provided for in the amendment under consideration as an independent standard, since the conclusion is plain that that test rests on the exercise of state judgment, and therefore cannot be here assailed either by disregarding the State's power to judge on the subject or by testing its motive in enacting the provision. The real question involved, so the argument of the Government insists, is the repugnancy of the standard which the amendment makes, based upon the conditions existing on January 1, 1866, because, on its face and inherently, considering the substance of things, that standard is a mere denial of the restrictions imposed by the prohibitions of the Fifteenth Amendment, and by necessary result, recreates and perpetuates the very conditions which the Amendment was intended to destroy.

Document Text

From this, it is urged that no legitimate discretion could have entered into the fixing of such standard which involved only the determination to directly set at naught or by indirection avoid the commands of the Amendment. And it is insisted that nothing contrary to these propositions is involved in the contention of the Government that, if the standard which the suffrage amendment fixes based upon the conditions existing on January 1, 1866, be found to be void for the reasons urged, the other and literacy test is also void, since that contention rests not upon any assertion on the part of the Government of any abstract repugnancy of the literacy test to the prohibitions of the Fifteenth Amendment, but upon the relation between that test and the other as formulated in the suffrage amendment, and the inevitable result which it is deemed must follow from holding it to be void if the other is so declared to be.

Looking comprehensively at these contentions of the parties, it plainly results that the conflict between them is much narrower than it would seem to be because the premise which the arguments of the plaintiffs in error attribute to the propositions of the United States is by it denied. On the very face of things, it is clear that the United States disclaims the gloss put upon its contentions by limiting them to the propositions which we have hitherto pointed out, since it rests the contentions which it makes as to the assailed provision of the suffrage amendment solely upon the ground that it involves an unmistakable, although it may be a somewhat disguised, refusal to give effect to the prohibitions of the Fifteenth Amendment by creating a standard which it is repeated, but calls to life the very conditions which that Amendment was adopted to destroy and which it had destroyed.

The questions then are: (1) giving to the propositions of the Government the interpretation which the Government puts upon them and assuming that the suffrage provision has the significance which the Government assumes it to have, is that provision, as a matter of law, repugnant to the Fifteenth Amendment? which leads us, of course, to consider the operation and effect of the Fifteenth Amendment. (2) If yes, has the assailed amendment, insofar as it fixes a standard for voting as of January 1, 1866, the meaning which the Government attributes to it? which leads us to analyze and interpret that provision of the amendment. (3) If the investigation as to the two prior subjects establishes that the standard fixed as of January 1, 1866, is void, what, if any, effect does that conclusion have upon the literacy standard otherwise established by the amendment? which involves determining whether that standard, if legal, may survive the recognition of the fact that the other or 1866 standard has not, and never had, any legal existence. Let us consider these subjects under separate headings.

1. *The operation and effect of the Fifteenth Amendment.* This is its text:

"Section 1. The right of citizens of the United States to vote shall not be denied or abridged by the United States or by any State on account of race, color, or previous condition of servitude."

"Section 2. The Congress shall have power to enforce this article by appropriate legislation."

(a) Beyond doubt, the Amendment does not take away from the state governments in a general sense the power over suffrage which has belonged to those governments from the beginning, and without the possession of which power the whole fabric upon which the division of state and national authority under the Constitution and the organization of both governments rest would be without support and both the authority of the nation and the State would fall to the ground. In fact, the very command of the Amendment recognizes the possession of the general power by the State, since the Amendment seeks to regulate its exercise as to the particular subject with which it deals.

(b) But it is equally beyond the possibility of question that the Amendment, in express terms, restricts the power of the United States or the States to abridge or deny the right of a citizen of the United States to vote on account of race, color or previous condition of servitude. The restriction is coincident with the power, and prevents its exertion in disregard of the command of the Amendment.

But, while this is true, it is true also that the Amendment does not change, modify or deprive the States of their full power as to suffrage except, of course, as to the subject with which the Amendment deals and to the extent that obedience to its command is necessary. Thus, the authority over suffrage which the States possess and the limitation which the Amendment imposes are coordinate, and one may not destroy the other without bringing about the destruction of both.

(c) While, in the true sense, therefore, the Amendment gives no right of suffrage, it was long ago recognized that, in operation, its prohibition might measurably have that effect; that is to say, that, as the command of the Amendment was self-executing and reached without legislative action the conditions of discrimination against which it was aimed, the result might arise that as a consequence of the striking down of a discriminating clause a right of suffrage would be enjoyed by reason of the generic character of the provision which would remain after the discrimination was stricken out. *Ex parte Yarbrough*; *Neal v. Delaware*. A familiar illustration of this doctrine resulted from the effect of the adoption of the Amendment on state constitutions in which, at the time of the adoption of the Amendment, the right of suffrage was conferred on all white male citizens, since, by the inherent power of the Amendment, the word white disappeared, and therefore all male citizens, without discrimination on account of race, color or previous condition of servitude, came under the generic grant of suffrage made by the State.

With these principles before us, how can there be room for any serious dispute concerning the repugnancy of the standard based upon January 1, 1866 (a date which preceded the adoption of the Fifteenth Amendment), if the suffrage provision fixing that standard is susceptible of the significance which the Government attributes to it? Indeed, there seems no escape from the conclusion that to hold that there was even possibility for dispute on the subject would be but to declare that the Fifteenth Amendment not only had not the self-executing power which it has been recognized to have from the beginning, but that its provisions were wholly inoperative, because susceptible of being rendered inapplicable by mere forms of expression embodying no exercise of judgment and resting upon no discernible reason other than the purpose to disregard the prohibitions of the Amendment by creating a standard of voting which on its face was, in substance, but a revitalization of conditions which, when they prevailed in the past, had been destroyed by the self-operative force of the Amendment.

2. *The standard of January 1, 1866, fixed in the suffrage amendment and its significance.*

The inquiry, of course, here is, does the amendment as to the particular standard which this heading embraces involve the mere refusal to comply with the commands of the Fifteenth Amendment as previously stated? This leads us for the purpose of the analysis to recur to the text of the suffrage amendment. Its opening sentence fixes the literacy standard, which is all-inclusive, since it is general in its expression and contains no word of discrimination on account of race or color or any other reason. This, however, is immediately followed by the provisions creating the standard based upon the condition existing on January 1, 1866, and carving out those coming under that standard from the inclusion in the literacy test which would have controlled them but for the exclusion thus expressly provided for. The provision is this:

"But no person who was, on January 1, 1866, or at any time prior thereto, entitled to vote under any form of government, or who at that time resided in some foreign nation, and no lineal descendant of such person, shall be denied the right to register and vote because of his inability to so read and write sections of such constitution."

We have difficulty in finding words to more clearly demonstrate the conviction we entertain that this standard has the characteristics which the Government attributes to it than does the mere statement of the text. It is true it contains no express words of an exclusion from the standard which it establishes of any person on account of race, color, or previous condition of servitude prohibited by the Fifteenth Amendment, but the standard itself inherently brings that result into existence, since it is based purely upon a period of time before the enactment of the Fifteenth Amendment, and makes that period the controlling and dominant test of the right of suffrage. In other words, we seek in vain for any ground which would sustain any other interpretation but that the provision, recurring to the conditions existing before the Fifteenth Amendment was adopted and the continuance of which the Fifteenth Amendment prohibited, proposed by, in substance and effect, lifting those conditions over to a period of time after the Amendment to make them the basis of the right to suffrage conferred in direct and positive disregard of the Fifteenth Amendment. And the same result, we are of opinion, is demonstrated by considering whether it is possible to discover any basis of reason for the standard thus fixed other than the purpose above stated. We say this because we are unable to discover how, unless the prohibitions of the Fifteenth Amendment were considered, the slightest reason was afforded for basing the classification upon a period of time prior to the Fifteenth Amendment. Certainly it cannot be said that there was any peculiar necromancy in the time named which engendered attributes affecting the qualification to vote which would not exist at another and different period unless the Fifteenth Amendment was in view.

While these considerations establish that the standard fixed on the basis of the 1866 test is void, they do not enable us to reply even to the first question asked by the court below, since, to do so, we must consider the literacy standard established by

Document Text

the suffrage amendment and the possibility of its surviving the determination of the fact that the 1866 standard never took life, since it was void from the beginning because of the operation upon it of the prohibitions of the Fifteenth Amendment. And this brings us to the last heading:

3. *The determination of the validity of the literacy test and the possibility of its surviving the disappearance of the 1866 standard with which it is associated in the suffrage amendment.*

No time need be spent on the question of the validity of the literacy test, considered alone, since, as we have seen, its establishment was but the exercise by the State of a lawful power vested in it not subject to our supervision, and, indeed, its validity is admitted. Whether this test is so connected with the other one relating to the situation on January 1, 1866, that the invalidity of the latter requires the rejection of the former, is really a question of state law, but, in the absence of any decision on the subject by the Supreme Court of the State, we must determine it for ourselves. We are of opinion that neither forms of classification nor methods of enumeration should be made the basis of striking down a provision which was independently legal, and therefore was lawfully enacted because of the removal of an illegal provision with which the legal provision or provisions may have been associated. We state what we hold to be the rule thus strongly because we are of opinion that, on a subject like the one under consideration, involving the establishment of a right whose exercise lies at the very basis of government, a much more exacting standard is required than would ordinarily obtain where the influence of the declared unconstitutionality of one provision of a statute upon another and constitutional provision is required to be fixed. Of course, rigorous as is this rule and imperative as is the duty not to violate it, it does not mean that it applies in a case where it expressly appears that a contrary conclusion must be reached if the plain letter and necessary intendment of the provision under consideration so compels, or where such a result is rendered necessary because to follow the contrary course would give rise to such an extreme and anomalous situation as would cause it to be impossible to conclude that it could have been upon any hypothesis whatever within the mind of the lawmaking power.

Does the general rule here govern, or is the case controlled by one or the other of the exceptional conditions which we have just stated, is then the remaining question to be decided. Coming to solve it, we are of opinion that, by a consideration of the text of the suffrage amendment insofar as it deals with the literacy test, and to the extent that it creates the standard based upon conditions existing on January 1, 1866, the case is taken out of the general rule and brought under the first of the exceptions stated. We say this because, in our opinion, the very language of the suffrage amendment expresses, not by implication nor by forms of classification nor by the order in which they are made, but by direct and positive language, the command that the persons embraced in the 1866 standard should not be under any conditions subjected to the literacy test, a command which would be virtually set at naught if on the obliteration of the one standard by the force of the Fifteenth Amendment the other standard should be held to continue in force.

The reasons previously stated dispose of the case and make it plain that it is our duty to answer the first question No, and the second Yes; but before we

Glossary

Ex parte	a Latin term referring to a legal proceeding in which only one party is represented
necromancy	sorcery, usually involving the dead
nullity	the condition of being void
occult	secret or hidden
plaintiff in error	the plaintiff in a case on appeal, who may or may not be the plaintiff in the lower court case whose decision is being appealed
self-executing	a law that does not require further legislative or court action to take effect
Syllabus	the portion of a Supreme Court decision that summarizes the key findings and rulings

direct the entry of an order to that effect, we come briefly to dispose of an issue the consideration of which we have hitherto postponed from a desire not to break the continuity of discussion as to the general and important subject before us.

In various forms of statement not challenging the instructions given by the trial court, concretely considered, concerning the liability of the election officers for their official conduct, it is insisted that as, in connection with the instructions, the jury was charged that the suffrage amendment was unconstitutional because of its repugnancy to the Fifteenth Amendment, therefore, taken as a whole, the charge was erroneous. But we are of opinion that this contention is without merit, especially in view of the doctrine long since settled concerning the self-executing power of the Fifteenth Amendment, and of what we have held to be the nature and character of the suffrage amendment in question. The contention concerning the inapplicability of §5508, Rev.Stat., now §19 of the Penal Code, or of its repeal by implication, is fully answered by the ruling this day made in *United States v. Mosley*, No. 180, post.

We answer the first question, No, and the second question, Yes.

And it will be so certified.

WILLIAM PICKENS: "THE KIND OF DEMOCRACY THE NEGRO EXPECTS"

1918

"There should be no 'colored' wages and no 'white' wages."

Overview

"The Kind of Democracy the Negro Expects" is a speech that was first given by the activist William Pickens in 1918 and on a number of occasions in the years immediately after World War I. The entry of the United States into the World War I in April 1917 presented a number of challenges for civil rights organizations like the National Association for the Advancement of Colored People (NAACP). Many African Americans had little enthusiasm for the war effort. They were forced to make use of inferior, segregated facilities and subjected to the wholesale denial of their political and civil rights across most of the South, and the war at best seemed far removed from their daily concerns. At worst, the rhetoric of President Woodrow Wilson, that the conflict was a war for democracy to free oppressed peoples overseas, could be seen as little more than hypocrisy, given the way African Americans were treated at home. Moreover, America's wartime allies, such as Britain, France, and Belgium, had imposed colonial rule on nonwhite countries across Africa and Asia, with little concern or respect for the democratic rights of the indigenous peoples.

Given this environment, civil rights campaigners had to maintain a careful balance, drawing attention to the grievances of African Americans but without appearing unpatriotic. Pickens, an African American educator, civil rights activist, and future field secretary of the NAACP, attempted to reconcile these competing objectives in "The Kind of Democracy the Negro Expects." Seeking to promote black support for the war, he suggested that this backing was also conditional. In the postwar world, African Americans would expect to enjoy the same democratic rights enjoyed by other Americans, and such rights also had to be extended to other nonwhite populations around the world.

Context

At the turn of the twentieth century, the best-known African American spokesperson in the United States was Booker T. Washington. Born a slave in 1856, Washington sought to avoid confrontation with southern whites over issues of civil and political rights by arguing for economic self-help as the most effective form of racial uplift for African Americans. In 1881 he founded Tuskegee Institute in Alabama, which promoted a curriculum of industrial education with an emphasis on training in practical vocational skills, such as building and woodworking, as opposed to academic subjects like English literature or history.

Washington's philosophy reflected not just his own beliefs but also the social and racial climate of his day. The last decades of the nineteenth century and early years of the twentieth century were a time of worsening race relations in the United States, with the political disfranchisement of African Americans and segregation in almost all aspects of daily life becoming commonplace across the South. Black southerners enjoyed little protection under the law, and as late as World War I an average of one African American a week was killed by white lynch mobs in the region, often under horrifying circumstances.

Arguably, Washington achieved the best that was possible under such conditions. Even so, by the early years of the twentieth century a growing number of African Americans in the North began to question his leadership. In particular, the Massachusetts-born educator, scholar, and civil rights advocate W. E. B. Du Bois argued that Washington's program of industrial education condemned African Americans to second-class citizenship as servants and menial laborers. Instead, the most able black students needed to have access to higher education to be trained for careers in law, medicine, teaching, and other professions. Collectively such individuals would be a "talented tenth" (about one-tenth of the population), becoming the leaders of African American communities at national, state, and local levels.

In July 1905 Du Bois and a small group of like-minded individuals formed the Niagara Movement to voice their opposition to Washington. An all-black organization, the movement also sought to protest the denial of black civil and political rights in the United States. From the start, the Niagara group struggled to achieve its objectives because of internal divisions within the movement, the ambitious nature of its program, and the hostility of Washington and his allies. In 1909 the movement folded, but it was succeeded by a new biracial civil rights organization, the National Association for the Advancement of Colored People. Supported by influential liberal whites, like the New

Time Line

1905
- **July**
  The Niagara Movement, an African American civil rights protest organization and forerunner of the NAACP, is formed.

1908
- **August 14**
  Race riots take place in Springfield, Illinois.
- **September 3**
  William Walling publishes an article on the riots, "The Race War in the North," and calls for a new biracial organization to address America's racial problems.

1909
- **February 12**
  The National Negro Committee, forerunner of the NAACP, is formed in New York City in response to Walling's call.

1910
- **May 30**
  The National Association for the Advancement of Colored People is chosen as the name for the new organization.

1910–1930
- During this period, known as the Great Migration, 1.25 million African Americans leave the South, mostly to seek employment in cities of the North, like Chicago, Detroit, New York, and Pittsburgh.

1912
- **November**
  Woodrow Wilson is elected president of the United States.

1914
- **August**
  World War I breaks out.

1915
- **November**
  Booker T. Washington, the most influential African American spokesperson in the United States since the death of Frederick Douglass in 1895, dies.

York newspaper proprietor Oswald Garrison Villard, the association grew steadily over the next decade. This growth reflected the fact that by this time increasing numbers of African Americans had begun to see Washington's leadership as outdated and overly accommodating to the views of white southerners.

World War I (1914–1918) brought further evidence of this mood of increased black assertiveness, a climate that can be attributed to a number of factors. The death of Booker T. Washington in 1915 resulted in the breakup of his network of advisers and supporters known as the Tuskegee Machine. In 1916 the Amenia Conference, held to reconcile Tuskegee supporters with the NAACP, led a number of Washington's allies to join the association. The years from 1910 to 1930 saw the onset and development of what became known as the Great Migration. During this time, some 1.25 million African Americans left the South for the factories of the North, to take advantage of employment opportunities created by the effective end to immigration from Europe in the war years. The migration can also be seen as a sign of generational change, as younger African Americans, further removed from slavery, sought to escape the repressive living conditions of the South in favor of the comparatively more enlightened pattern of race relations that existed in the North.

The war also prompted greater awareness by African Americans of the importance of racial issues in an international context. More than four hundred thousand black Americans enlisted in the U.S. armed forces during the war, many of whom served overseas, mostly in France. Du Bois played a leading role in the organization of four Pan-African Congresses in 1919, 1921, 1923, and 1927. The congress movement sought to work with European imperial powers to improve the economic and political rights of colonial peoples. More controversially, the Universal Negro Improvement Association of Marcus Garvey campaigned for the establishment of an independent black state in Africa, with the implicit threat of the use of force to expel European colonial powers from the continent if necessary. First organized in the United States in 1917, the Universal Negro Improvement Association rapidly gathered support in African American communities, achieving a following of around a million at its peak in the early 1920s, as well as establishing branches in Africa, Latin America, and the Caribbean.

About the Author

William Pickens was born in Anderson County, South Carolina, on January 5, 1881. Both his parents were former slaves. From 1899 to 1902 he attended Talladega College, an African American educational institution in Alabama run by the American Missionary Association. The predominantly white faculty at Talladega sought to instill Christian values in students and trained them to be leaders in racial uplift in the black community. After going on to study the classics at Yale University from 1902 to 1904, Pickens returned to Talladega to take up a teaching post. At this stage he supported the teachings of Booker T. Washington.

In July 1905 the formation of the Niagara Movement reflected growing opposition to Washington's program by some members of the African American community, particularly in the North. Although he never joined the movement, Pickens was increasingly drawn to the ideas put forward by the new radicals. In doing so, he incurred the displeasure of Washington. The influence of the latter, combined with Pickens's mounting disagreements with what he saw as the excessive paternalism of some white teachers at Talladega, led to his being dismissed from Talladega in 1914.

In June 1915 Pickens secured a position as dean at Morgan College, a Methodist Episcopal Church–run school for African Americans in Baltimore. There he became increasingly associated with the NAACP, the biracial civil rights organization that succeeded the Niagara Movement in 1909. In these years Pickens developed a growing reputation as a speaker on civil rights issues. He first delivered "The Kind of Democracy the Negro Expects" in 1918 and gave the speech again on a number of occasions in the early postwar years."

In 1920 Pickens left Morgan to take up a post first as assistant field secretary and later as full field secretary in the NAACP, with responsibility for maintaining and expanding the association's membership. His oratorical skills made him well suited to this position. At the same time, he experienced ongoing difficulties in his relationship with the NAACP's board of directors. He felt he was underpaid and the importance of his work undervalued. This contributed to his briefly considering taking a position with the rival Universal Negro Improvement Association of Marcus Garvey.

Such tensions notwithstanding, Pickens remained with the NAACP until April 1941, when he accepted a temporary position in the U.S. Treasury Department to promote the sale of government bonds to African Americans during World War II. He never returned to the NAACP. Pickens's personal differences with the association's national secretary, Walter White, together with his disagreement with the association's opposition to the establishment of a segregated air base for African American pilots at Tuskegee, Alabama, led the board of directors to terminate his employment with the NAACP in June 1942. Pickens remained with the Treasury Department until his retirement in December 1950. He was buried at sea on April 6, 1954, after suffering a fatal heart attack returning from a holiday cruise to Latin America and the Caribbean on the SS *Mauritania*.

Explanation and Analysis of the Document

In this speech Pickens seeks to explain what African Americans, who had collectively fought for the United States in World War I, had come to expect in a democratic society. In the introduction he considers the term *democracy* and notes that it can mean different things to different groups and individuals. The main body of the speech is divided into five sections: "Democracy in Education," "Democracy in

Time Line

1916
- **November** Wilson is reelected as president.

1917
- **April 6** The United States enters World War I.
- **May** A segregated African American officer training camp is established in Des Moines, Iowa.
- **October 5** Emmett J. Scott, former personal secretary to Booker T. Washington, is appointed as special assistant to the secretary of war, to advise on race-related issues.

1918
- Pickens first delivers his speech "The Kind of Democracy the Negro Expects."
- **July** W. E. B. Du Bois, NAACP director of publicity and research, publishes "Close Ranks," an editorial in the association journal, *The Crisis*, calling on African Americans to support the U.S. war effort.
- **November 11** World War I ends.

1919
- **May** Du Bois publishes "Returning Soldiers," an editorial in *The Crisis*, urging African American servicemen returning home from Europe to fight racism in the United States as vigorously as they had fought imperialism abroad.
- **June–December** A series of race riots, dubbed the Red Summer by NAACP field secretary James Weldon Johnson, takes place in some twenty-five cities across the United States.

1920
- **August 26** Certification of the Nineteenth Amendment to the U.S. Constitution gives equal voting rights to women.

Industry," "Democracy in State," "Democracy without Sex-preferment," and "Democracy in Church." In two concluding paragraphs he discusses the contradictions between democracy and racial segregation and the need to view the "Negro question" in the American South in a global context.

◆ **Introduction**

Pickens reflects on the widespread use of the term *democracy* in the first paragraph. He notes that "by the extraordinary weight of the presidency of the United States many undemocratic people have had this word forced upon their lips." This is a reference to the stated war aims of President Woodrow Wilson. In his war message to Congress in April 1917, Wilson asked the U.S. Senate and House of Representatives to support his call for a declaration of war against Germany and its allies. He used idealistic language to justify this request. The conflict would be more than just a military struggle. It would bring about a new world order based on peace, freedom, and democracy. He frequently repeated such claims during both the course of the war and the negotiations for the Versailles peace settlement in 1919.

The "undemocratic people" who "have not yet had the right ideal forced upon their hearts" might at first sight be taken as a reference to the governments of Germany and its recently defeated military allies. However, Pickens makes clear that this description also applies to groups and individuals closer to home, referring to an American woman whom he recently heard expressing "alarm" at the thought that democracy might mean that "colored women would have the right to take any vacant seat or space on a street car." Such a person is someone who "believes in a democracy of me-and-my kind, which is no democracy." The phrase *of me-and-my kind* can be seen as a critical observation by Pickens on the campaign for the passage of the Nineteenth Amendment to the U.S. Constitution in 1919–1920, giving women equal voting rights. Some supporters of the amendment argued for white women to be given the vote, while ignoring the rights of their African American counterparts.

This kind of conduct is not only inconsistent but is indeed similar to the values of the German aristocracy, the "Prussian junker" who "has no doubt that he and the other junkers should be free and equal" but denies these rights to others. Pickens thus restates his earlier suggestion that Americans who oppose democratic rights for African Americans at home are no better than the autocratic German regime that the United States has been striving to overthrow.

In a short second paragraph, Pickens reminds his listeners of the loyal support of African Americans for the war effort by referring to the kind of democracy "he is fighting for." This language also conveys the idea that the African American struggle for democracy within the United States is comparable to the struggle for democracy overseas in the war against Germany.

◆ **"First: Democracy in Education"**

In his first point, Pickens highlights the importance of "equal right and opportunity" in education for all. These rights are the "foundation stones of democracy." "How can we ever hope for democracy," he argues, "if men are artificially differentiated at the beginning, if we try to educate a 'working class' and a 'ruling class,' forcing different race groups into different lines without regard to individual fitness?" This can be seen as a criticism of the industrial education movement associated with Booker T. Washington. At Tuskegee Institute in Alabama, Washington promoted the teaching of practical skills and trades, such as carpentry and bricklaying for male students and cookery and sewing for women. This contrasted with the teaching of traditional academic subjects, such as languages and the humanities, as was practiced at other institutions, like Talladega College, Alabama, attended by Pickens himself. Washington believed industrial education provided the majority of African Americans with the immediate vocational skills they needed to prosper in life. However, this viewpoint was criticized by Pickens and others for neglecting the need to train black students for careers in higher professions, such as law and medicine.

◆ **"Second: Democracy in Industry"**

Pickens then turns his attention to industry. From around 1910 onward, increasing numbers of African Americans left the South as part of the Great Migration to take advantage of employment opportunities in the factories of the North. Before the war such options had been severely limited because of racial prejudice on the part of both employers and trade unions and competition from large-scale immigration from southern and eastern Europe. Where African Americans were able to get factory jobs, it was often only as strikebreakers or at lower rates of pay than those of white workers. Pickens's comments in this section reflect his concern that such practices must not be allowed to return now that the war is over: "There should be no 'colored' wages and no 'white' wages; no 'man's' wage and no 'woman's' wage."

He argues that the right to equal employment opportunities is not just a matter of fairness but also is in the national interest: "For every man to serve where he is most able to serve is public economy and is to the best interest of the state." He cites Mississippi as an example of a region where this right does not exist. In the Magnolia State, "a caste system" holds African Americans, "the majority of the population," in the "triple chains of ignorance, semi-serfdom and poverty." This is a reference to the sharecropping system, which was widely used in agriculture across the South at this time. Large landowners or planters provided tenant farmers, or sharecroppers, with land for cultivation, together with food and accommodation throughout the year until their crops, usually cotton, were harvested and sold. In theory, landlord and tenant then shared the profits realized. In reality, the high markup and interest rates charged by planters for goods and services meant that tenants typically received little or no reward. In many instances they were compelled to enter into further sharecropping agreements with planters for the following year, in a vain attempt to pay off debts they still owed. Over time this meant that share-

African American infantry unit marching northwest of Verdun, France, in World War I (Library of Congress)

croppers, for the most part African Americans but also including poor whites, became trapped in peonage, or "semi-serfdom" of the kind that Pickens describes.

Pickens suggests that such unjust labor practices damage the economic well-being of the United States. If allowed to prevail throughout the country, these practices would result in the nation's being either "the unwilling prey or the golden goose for the Prussian." He thus implies that the actions of southern planters are not only unjust but also unpatriotic. Similarly, the personal fortunes amassed by wealthy industrialists in the North at the expense of low-paid workers is a form of "industrial junkerism," comparable to the excesses of the Prussian aristocracy.

◆ "Third: Democracy in State"

Here Pickens links the civil rights struggle of African Americans in the United States with that of colonial populations around the world. Equality before the law is "as much for South Africa as for South Carolina." In this section's second paragraph he argues that the denial of civil and political equality is not only wrong but also encourages "other evils," for "discriminating laws are the mother of the mob spirit." This is an obvious reference to the practice of lynching, the unlawful killing of a person by parties unknown. For much of the nineteenth century, lynching was associated with a form of rough justice meted out on the western frontier. From the 1880s onward, it became a crime increasingly confined to the southern states, with the large majority of lynch victims being African Americans.

On July 26, 1918, President Wilson publicly spoke out against "mob actions." At the same time he presided over the spread of segregation in the federal government bureaucracy and the introduction of new measures that required civil service applicants to provide information on their racial ancestry. During Wilson's two terms of office, from 1913 to1921, there was a marked fall in the number of African Americans employed by the civil service. Pickens observes that "if being a Negro unfits a man for holding a government office for which he is otherwise fit," then in the eyes of "an ignorant white man in Tennessee" it also "unfits the same man for claiming a 'white man's' chance in the courts." In making this observation, he tacitly accuses

Essential Quotes

> "There should be no 'colored' wages and no 'white' wages; no 'man's' wage and no 'woman's' wage."
>
> ("Second: Democracy in Industry")

> "The Negro cannot consistently oppose color discrimination and support sex discrimination in democratic government."
>
> ("Fourth: Democracy without Sex-preferment")

> "Like many other questions our domestic race question, instead of being settled by Mississippi and South Carolina, will now seek its settlement largely on the battlefields of Europe."
>
> ("Finally")

the Wilson administration of hypocrisy by suggesting that there is a link between this trend and the persistence of lynching, or "mob actions," in the South.

◆ "Fourth: Democracy without Sex-preferment"

Pickens next declares his support for women's rights, noting that "the Negro cannot consistently oppose color discrimination and support sex discrimination in democratic government." He cites the example of the nineteenth-century African American leader Frederick Douglass. A former slave, Douglass consistently campaigned both for the abolition of slavery and in support of women's rights.

Pursuing a by now familiar theme, Pickens continues to link the African American civil rights struggle with high-profile democratic causes of the day. He thus concludes that "the argument against the participation of colored men and of women in self-government is practically one argument." By logical implication, campaigners who favor equal voting rights for women must also support political equality for African Americans.

◆ "Fifth: Democracy in Church"

Turning to religion, Pickens warns that the Christian church is "no place for the caste spirit or for snobs." This concern reflects Pickens's own life experience as both a student and a teacher in church-funded schools and colleges for African Americans. During his time as a teacher at Talladega College, Alabama, he supported a 1914 strike by African American students against the perceived patronizing attitudes of some white teachers employed by the American Missionary Association. Referring to church missionary work overseas, he implicitly questions the ability of the American churches to win new nonwhite converts when their congregations at home are segregated along racial lines. Simply put, "colored races the world over will have even more doubt in the future than they have had in the past of the real Christianity of any church which holds out to them the prospect of being united in heaven after being separated on earth."

◆ "Finally"

In a concluding section, Pickens develops his attack on racial segregation, or "Jim-Crowing." Held to be lawful under the Constitution by the U.S. Supreme Court in the 1896 landmark ruling of *Plessy v. Ferguson*, by this time the use of segregated facilities in public transport and accommodations was widespread across the South. The wartime influx of African American migrants prompted the further spread of segregationist practices to cities of the North.

In the final paragraph Pickens reminds his audience of the patriotism of African Americans during the war. He also returns to the theme of internationalism that runs throughout the speech, arguing that the "Negro question" in the southern United States is part of a wider "world question."

Audience

The speech was intended to simultaneously convey a variety of messages to different audiences. In addressing African Americans, Pickens sought to promote patriotic support for the nation's war effort by stressing that this support was conditional on more respect for the democratic rights of African Americans, and of nonwhite peoples globally, when the conflict ended. With respect to the Wilson administration, the speech highlighted that emphasis on democratic freedoms for oppressed peoples overseas had to be matched by greater concern for the rights of persecuted minorities at home. Speaking to whites who are working for the advancement of African Americans, Pickens aimed to point out that such endeavors had to be undertaken in a spirit of genuine equality, rather than one of patronizing condescension. For present-day audiences, the document serves as a timeless reminder to the governments and peoples of all democratic societies that involvement in any war or conflict must be undertaken in a way that is consistent with their core ideals and values.

Impact

Pickens's speech had limited impact in its day. The return to peacetime conditions at the end of 1918 saw few gains for African Americans as a result of their support for the war effort. A southerner with conservative views on race relations, Woodrow Wilson made no effort to secure greater civil and political rights for African Americans. In the South, inferior, segregated schooling continued to be the norm for African Americans until May 1954, when the U.S. Supreme Court ruled it unconstitutional in the *Brown v. Board of Education* decision. In the cities of the North, the growing numbers of African Americans living there as a result of the Great Migration led to increased racial tensions and the spread of segregationist practices. Although women secured equal voting rights in the United States with the passage of the Nineteenth Amendment to the U.S. Constitution in 1920, this advance can be attributed to factors other than the efforts of Pickens and the NAACP.

In the longer term, the speech has taken on greater significance. During World War II, from 1939 to 1945, memories of the painful experiences of World War I contributed to a greater sense of militancy in many African American communities. This new mood was encapsulated in the Double V campaign promoted by the NAACP during the war. First popularized by the African American newspaper the *Pittsburgh Courier*, the slogan called on black communities to fight against both Nazism abroad and racial injustice at home.

Viewed in historical perspective, the document is important as a sign of an increased assertiveness on the part of African American civil rights campaigners during and immediately after World War I. The continuing work of Pickens and other NAACP activists in the interwar years sowed the seeds for the later successes of the civil rights movement in the 1950s and 1960s. The document is also ahead of its time in depicting the campaign for black civil rights within the United States as part of the wider global struggle for independence and equality by nonwhite colonial populations.

See also Niagara Movement Declaration of Principles (1905); *Plessy v. Ferguson* (1896); *Brown v. Board of Education* (1954).

Questions for Further Study

1. Why were African Americans in general indifferent to American participation in World War I? To what extent would that same indifference arise in connection with the Vietnam War, as reflected in Stokely Carmichael's "Black Power" (1966)?

2. What impact did the Great Migration of the early twentieth century have on race relations? To what extent did the migration contribute to the social, political, and intellectual climate that gave rise to Pickens's speech?

3. Pickens tried to walk a fine line between asserting the goals of African Americans for democracy at home without appearing to be unpatriotic. Did he accomplish this goal? If so, how?

4. Pickens places emphasis on democracy in education and on equal rights for women. Compare his views on these issues with those expressed in W. E. B. Du Bois's *The Souls of Black Folk* (1903) and Anna Julia Cooper's "Womanhood: A Vital Element in the Regeneration and Progress of a Race" (1892).

5. Using this document in conjunction with Thomas Morris Chester's Civil War Dispatches (1864) and the events surrounding A. Philip Randolph's "Call to Negro America to March on Washington" (1941), prepare a time line of events bearing on segregation and finally integration of the U.S. armed forces.

Further Reading

■ Books

Avery, Sheldon. *Up from Washington: William Pickens and the Negro Struggle for Equality, 1900–1954*. Newark: University of Delaware Press, 1989.

Barbeau, Arthur E., and Florette Henri. *The Unknown Soldiers: Black American Troops in World War I*. Philadelphia: Temple University Press, 1974.

Ellis, Mark. *Race, War, and Surveillance: African Americans and the United States Government during World War I*. Bloomington: Indiana University Press, 2001.

Kornweibel, Theodore. *"Investigate Everything": Federal Efforts to Ensure Black Loyalty during World War I*. Bloomington: Indiana University Press, 2002.

Lewis, David L. *W. E. B. Du Bois: Biography of a Race, 1868–1919*. New York: Henry Holt, 1993.

Patler, Nicholas. *Jim Crow and the Wilson Administration: Protesting Federal Segregation in the Early Twentieth Century*. Boulder: University of Colorado Press, 2004.

Sullivan, Patricia. *Lift Every Voice: The NAACP and the Making of the Civil Rights Movement*. New York: New Press, 2009.

■ Web Sites

"African-American Soldiers in World War I: The 92nd and 93rd Divisions." National Endowment for the Humanities EDSITEment Web site.
http://edsitement.neh.gov/view_lesson_plan.asp?id=497.

—Kevern J. Verney

William Pickens: "The Kind of Democracy the Negro Expects"

Democracy is the most used term in the world today. But some of its uses are abuses. Everybody says "Democracy"! But everybody has his own definition. By the extraordinary weight of the presidency of the United States many undemocratic people have had this word forced upon their lips but have not yet had the right ideal forced upon their hearts. I have heard of one woman who wondered with alarm whether "democracy" would mean that colored women would have the right to take any vacant seat or space on a street car, even if they had paid for it. That such a question should be asked, shows how many different meanings men may attach to the one word Democracy. This woman doubtless believes in a democracy of me-and-my-kind, which is no democracy. The most autocratic and the worst caste systems could call themselves democratic by that definition. Even the Prussian junker believes in that type of democracy; he has no doubt that he and the other junkers should be free and equal in rights and privileges. Many have accepted the word Democracy merely as the current password to respectability in political thinking. The spirit of the times is demanding democracy; it is the tune of the age; it is the song to sing. But some are like that man who belonged to one of the greatest political parties: after hearing convincing arguments by the stump-speaker of the opposite party, he exclaimed: "Wa-al, that fellow has convinced my judgment, but I'll be d—d if he can Change My Vote!"

It is in order, therefore, for the Negro to state clearly what he means by democracy and what he is fighting for.

First. Democracy in Education. This is fundamental. No other democracy is practicable unless all of the people have equal right and opportunity to develop according to their individual endowments. There can be no real democracy between two natural groups, if one represents the extreme of ignorance and the other the best of intelligence. The common public school and the state university should be the foundation stones of democracy. If men are artificially differentiated at the beginning, if we try to educate a "working class" and a "ruling class," forcing different race groups into different lines without regard to individual fitness, how can we ever hope for democracy in the other relations of these groups? Individuals will differ, but in democracy of education peoples living on the same soil should not be widely diverged in their training on mere racial lines. This would be illogical, since they are to be measured by the same standards of life. Of course, a group that is to live in Florida should be differently trained from a group that is to live in Alaska; but that is geography and general environment, and not color or caste.—The Negro believes in democracy of education as first and fundamental: that the distinction should be made between individual talents and not between color and castes.

Second. Democracy in Industry. The right to work in any line for which the individual is best prepared, and to be paid the standard wage. This is also fundamental. In the last analysis there could be very little democracy between multi-millionaires and the abject poor. There must be a more just and fair distribution of wealth in a democracy. And certainly this is not possible unless men work at the occupations for which they are endowed and best prepared. There should be no "colored" wages and no "white" wages; no "man's" wage and no "woman's" wage. Wages should be paid for the work done, measured as much as possible by its productiveness. No door of opportunity should be closed to a man on any other ground than that of his individual unfitness. The cruelest and most undemocratic thing in the world is to require of the individual man that his whole race be fit before he can be regarded as fit for a certain privilege or responsibility. That rule, strictly applied, would exclude any man of any race from any position. For every man to serve where he is most able to serve is public economy and is to the best interest of the state. This lamentable war that was forced upon us should make that plain to the dullest of us. Suppose that, when this war broke out, our whole country had been like Mississippi (and I refer to geography unividiously),—suppose our whole country had been like Mississippi, where a caste system was holding the majority of the population in the triple chains of ignorance, semi-serfdom and poverty. Our nation would be now either the unwilling prey or the golden goose for the Prussian. The long-headed thing for any state is to let every man do his best all of the time. But

Document Text

some people are so short-sighted that [they] only see what is thrust against their noses. The Negro asks American labor in the name of democracy to get rid of its color caste and industrial junkerism.

Third. Democracy in State. A political democracy in which all are equal before the laws; where there is one standard of justice, written and unwritten; where all men and women may be citizens by the same qualifications, agreed upon and specified. We believe in this as much for South Africa as for South Carolina, and we hope that our American nation will not agree with any government, ally or envy, that is willing to make a peace that will bind the Africa[n] Negro to political slavery and exploitation.

Many other evils grow out of political inequality. Discriminating laws are the mother of the mob spirit. The political philosopher in Washington, after publishing his opinion that a Negro by the fault of being a Negro is unfit to be a member of Congress, cannot expect an ignorant white man in Tennessee to believe that the same Negro is, nevertheless, fit to have a fair and impartial trial in a Tennessee court. Ignorance is too logical for that. I disagree with the premises but I agree with the reasoning of the Tennesseean: that if being a Negro unfits a man for holding a government office for which he is otherwise fit, it unfits the same man for claiming a "white man's" chance in the courts. The first move therefore against mob violence and injustice in the petty courts is to wipe out discriminating laws and practices in the higher circles of government. The ignorant man in Tennessee will not rise in ideal above the intelligent man in Washington.

Fourth. Democracy without Sex-preferment. The Negro cannot consistently oppose color discrimination and support sex discrimination in democratic government. This happened to be the opinion also of the First Man of the Negro race in America,—Frederick Douglass. The handicap is nothing more nor less than a presumption in the mind of the physically dominant element of the universal inferiority of the weaker or subject element. It is so easy to prove that the man who is down and under, deserves to be down and under. In the first place, he is down there, isn't he? And that is three-fourths of the argument to the ordinary mind; for the ordinary mind does not seek ultimate causes. The argument against the participation of colored men and of women in self-government is practically one argument. Somebody spoke to the Creator about both of these classes and learned that they were "created" for inferior roles. Enfranchisement would spoil a good field-hand,—or a good cook. Black men were once ignorant,—women were once ignorant. Negroes had no political experience—women had no such experience. The argument forgets that people do not get experience on the outside. But the American Negro expects a democracy that will accord the right to vote to a sensible industrious woman rather than to a male tramp.

Fifth. Democracy in Church. The preachings and the practices of Jesus of Nazareth are perhaps the greatest influence in the production of modern democratic ideas. The Christian church is, therefore, no place for the caste spirit or for snobs. And the colored races the world over will have even more doubt in the future than they have had in the past of the real Christianity of any church which holds out to them the prospect of being united in heaven after being separated on earth.

Finally. The great colored races will in the future not be kinder to a sham democracy than to a "scrap-of-paper" autocracy. The private home, private right

Glossary

Prussia	now part of Germany, a formerly independent kingdom with a reputation for a strong militaristic ethos
junker	a member of the Prussian aristocracy
Frederick Douglass	a prominent nineteenth-century African American author, speaker, and abolitionist
"scrap-of-paper" autocracy	probably a reference to the common notion that the Axis powers before and during World War I created governments ruled by one man by routinely invalidating treaties with other nations
Jim-Crowing	a reference to "Jim Crow," the name given to laws and social customs that kept African Americans in inferior segregated positions

and private opinion must remain inviolate; but the commonwealth, the public place and public property must not be appropriated to the better use of any group by "Jim-Crowing" and segregating any other group. By the endowments of God and nature there are individual "spheres"; but there are no such widely different racial "spheres." Jesus' estimate of the individual soul is the taproot of democracy, and any system which discourages the men of any race from individual achievement, is no democracy. To fix the status of a human soul on earth according to the physical group in which it was born, is the gang spirit of the savage which protects its own members and outlaws all others.

For real democracy the American Negro will live and die. His loyalty is always above suspicion, but his extraordinary spirit in the present war is born of his faith that on the side of his country and her allies is the best hope for such democracy. And he welcomes, too, the opportunity to lift the "Negro question" out of the narrow confines of the Southern United States and make it a world question. Like many other questions our domestic race question, instead of being settled by Mississippi and South Carolina, will now seek its settlement largely on the battlefields of Europe.

Moorfield Storey, first president of the National Association for the Advancement of Colored People (Library of Congress)

Thirty Years of Lynching in the United States, 1889–1918

1919

"The United States has for long been the only advanced nation whose government has tolerated lynching."

Overview

The unlawful killing of a person or persons by parties unknown, lynching reputedly had its origins in the American Revolution when Charles Lynch of Bedford County, Virginia, formed a vigilante association to rid the region of Tories, or British sympathizers. For much of the nineteenth century it was seen as a form of rough justice meted out to outlaws in frontier communities in the absence of effective legal authorities. Between 1889 and 1918 at least 3,224 people were killed by lynch mobs in the United States; 2,522 were black and 702 white.

After reaching a peak in the late 1880s and early 1890s, the number of lynchings began to decline. At the same time, the lynchings became increasingly shocking in nature, with victims often subjected to prolonged torture before being put to death. One of the most horrifying of such incidents was the 1916 lynching of Jesse Washington in Texas. A mentally impaired African American teenager, Washington was mutilated and burned to death over several hours. The "Waco Horror," as it became known, prompted the National Association for the Advancement of Colored People (NAACP) to set up a committee to initiate an antilynching campaign. NAACP staffers were given the task of collecting details on all reported lynchings since 1889 with a view to book publication. The resulting work, *Thirty Years of Lynching in the United States, 1889–1918*, was intended to provide statistical and factual information to support the association's campaign.

Context

The period 1889–1918 is commonly viewed by scholars as the nadir in the history of U.S. race relations since the end of the Civil War in 1865. In the last decades of the nineteenth century, African Americans lost many of the rights they had secured in the early Reconstruction era, 1865–1877. During this time the passage of the Thirteenth, Fourteenth, and Fifteenth amendments to the U.S. Constitution, in 1865, 1868, and 1870, respectively, had confirmed the abolition of slavery and sought to secure equal citizenship and voting rights for former slaves, or freedmen as they were known. Such safeguards proved ineffective.

By 1877 the white-dominated Democratic Party had regained political power across the South. State Republican Party administrations—composed of northern whites, called "carpetbaggers"; southern white unionists, called "scalawags"; and African Americans—were ousted at the polls by a combination of fraud, intimidation, and violence. Southern Democrats cited the ignorance and corruption of Republican incumbents as justification for such actions. Although there was only limited substance to such claims, successive Republican administrations from 1877 to 1885 chose not to intervene at the federal level.

Beginning in the late 1880s and early 1890s southern Democrats sought to exclude African Americans from political life on a permanent basis through the passage of new state election laws. Although the Fifteenth Amendment prevented U.S. citizens from being denied the vote on account of "race, color or previous condition of servitude," Democratic state governments found ways to get around such provisions. Instead, they passed laws requiring prospective voters to pass literacy tests or demonstrate a "good understanding" of selected passages from state constitutions. In the case of *Williams v. Mississippi* (1898) the U.S. Supreme Court ruled that such measures were lawful under the Constitution, as they supposedly applied to all voters. In practice, the new laws were used almost exclusively against black voters, and as a result the large majority of African Americans in the South were disfranchised until as late as the early 1960s.

In a previous ruling, *Plessy v. Ferguson* (1896), the Supreme Court had approved state laws requiring racial segregation. Using the concept of "separate but equal," it held that such measures did not violate the equal citizenship rights guaranteed by the Fourteenth Amendment. The reality was very different. The *Plessy* ruling effectively condemned African Americans in the South to greatly inferior facilities and services in almost every aspect of daily life, including schools, theaters, hospitals, public transportation, and even cemeteries.

By this time the economic opportunities open to African Americans in the region were also severely restricted, largely through the widespread use of the sharecropping system in southern agriculture. First introduced in the early postwar years, sharecropping was ostensibly a market compro-

Time Line

1892
- *Southern Horrors: Lynch Law in All Its Phases* is published by the African American antilynching campaigner Ida B. Wells. This and her later booklet, *A Red Record* (1895), are among the first works to draw public attention to the issue of lynching.

1908
- **August 14**
  Race riots in Springfield, Illinois, result in seven deaths, including the lynching of two black men.
- **September 3**
  William Walling publishes an article on the riots, "The Race War in the North," and calls for a new biracial organization to address America's racial problems.

1909
- **February 12**
  The National Negro Committee is formed in New York City in response to Walling's call.

1910
- **May 30**
  The National Association for the Advancement of Colored People (NAACP) is chosen as the name for the new organization.

1915
- D. W. Griffith's epic film *The Birth of a Nation* is released and enjoys extraordinary popularity. Scenes depicting an African American being put to death by the Ku Klux Klan for the attempted rape of a white woman evoke black protests. The NAACP joins a nationwide campaign to have the film banned or censored but achieves only partial success.

1916
- **July**
  The lynching of Jesse Washington in Texas prompts formation of an NAACP antilynching committee.

mise between freed slaves and the former slave-owning planter aristocracy. Lacking the financial resources to hire wage laborers, planters instead provided plots of land for cultivation to freedmen together with food and accommodation over the course of the year. This was on the understanding that when the crops, almost invariably cotton, were harvested, landowner and tenant would divide the proceeds. In practice, the high markups and interest rates charged by planters for the goods supplied meant that black sharecroppers were by then so deeply in debt that they received no share of the profits at all. Worse, money still owed meant they were obliged to continue working for the same landlord in the forthcoming year in a vain attempt to clear their account. By this means large numbers of black farmers in the South became trapped into a permanent system of debt peonage under which they were little better off than in their former slave condition.

The deteriorating status of African Americans was reflected in changing white racial attitudes. Although white southerners had always viewed African Americans as racially inferior, during slavery they were also widely perceived as faithful family retainers. In the early postwar years southern mythology depicted slaves as loyal protectors of the families of planters when the male members of the household were absent in the service of the Confederacy. During the 1880s and 1890s this image began to change. In southern white popular culture African Americans were increasingly depicted as less than human, even bestial in nature. Black men were portrayed as vicious sexual predators, intent on forcing their attentions on white women. This image hardened into the potent myth of the black rapist. Across the South, white communities became increasingly obsessed by the need to protect women from such a threat by any means necessary. It was in this context that a sharp rise in the number of lynchings occurred in the region in the late 1880s and early 1890s.

About the Author

The book has no single author but is rather a digest of factual information and statistical data collected by NAACP researchers on all lynchings in the United States between 1889 and 1918. One of the prime movers of this initiative was John R. Shillady, who became national secretary of the NAACP in January 1918. Born in 1875, the middle-aged Shillady was a veteran social worker and administrator when he joined the association. In addition to experience, he brought considerable energy and enthusiasm to his new job, increasing branch memberships from nine thousand to forty thousand within a year. He took particular interest in the NAACP's antilynching campaign and wrote the foreword for *Thirty Years of Lynching*.

Within a year of the book's publication Shillady narrowly avoided becoming a lynch victim himself. During a visit to Texas in August 1920 he was badly beaten by a white mob. Although Shillady managed to escape, he never fully recovered from the physical and mental trauma. Within months he resigned his position with the NAACP, despairing of the prospects for any meaningful advance in the nation's troubled race relations. He died in 1943. Shillady was succeeded as national secretary by James Weldon Johnson, the first African American to occupy the position on a permanent full-time basis.

Explanation and Analysis of the Document

The document extract is made up of three parts: a foreword by NAACP secretary John R. Shillady; a "Summation of the Facts Disclosed in Tables," providing a brief overview of the statistical data on lynching in the United States, 1889–1918; and "The Story of One Hundred Lynchings." Not reprinted here are two appendixes: "Analysis of Number of Persons Lynched" and "Chronological List of Persons Lynched in United States 1889 to 1918, Inclusive, Arranged by States." (The various tables referred to in the pamphlet are also not reproduced.) Most of the book thus takes the form of the presentation of statistical information together with press accounts or reports by NAACP researchers on individual lynchings. There is little analytical commentary. A conscious decision was taken to present the information in this way, so as to let the facts speak for themselves.

◆ **Foreword**

Shillady sets out the moral case against lynching in his foreword. He notes that the United States is the only advanced modern country that tolerates the crime and stresses the need for the rule of law. Such arguments provide strong justification for the NAACP's antilynching campaign.

Shillady concentrates on the case against lynching rather than suggesting measures to solve the problem. This is because any such discussion would have raised difficult legal and political issues. Many Americans shared Shillady's views on lynching, but the NAACP's preferred solution, the passage of a federal antilynching law, was controversial. Some legislators, whose support the association needed, were reluctant to endorse such a measure. These legislators included Republican William Borah of Idaho, chairman of the Senate Judiciary Committee. Borah believed that a federal antilynching law would be unconstitutional. Legal experts consulted by the NAACP expressed similar doubts. This view was initially shared by Moorfield Storey, the first president of the biracial association and a leading constitutional lawyer.

Although Storey ultimately overcame his misgivings and came to support such a law, others did not. Under the U.S. Constitution, murder is a state, rather than a federal, crime. A federal antilynching law could thus be seen as a violation of state sovereignty. Moreover, at this time the new medium of radio was in its infancy and the introduction of television almost three decades in the future. Many Americans perceived their national political leaders as comparatively remote figures. Before America's experience of the New Deal in the 1930s and World War II (1941–1945), there was an expectation that the federal

Time Line

1917
- **July 28** The NAACP sponsors a silent parade against lynching in New York City. Up to fifteen thousand people take part.

1918
- **January** John R. Shillady is appointed NAACP national secretary.
- **April** The Dyer bill introduced in the U.S. House of Representatives attempts to make lynching a federal crime. The NAACP makes repeated unsuccessful attempts to secure the passage of a federal antilynching law.
- **July 26** President Woodrow Wilson publicly speaks out against mob actions.

1919
- **April** *Thirty Years of Lynching in the United States* is published.

1920
- **August 20** John Shillady is badly beaten by a white mob in Austin, Texas, and never fully recovers.

1923
- In the case of *Moore v. Dempsey* the U.S. Supreme Court rules that federal courts can intervene to protect the procedural rights of defendants tried and convicted in mob-dominated areas.

1929
- *Rope and Faggot: A Biography of Judge Lynch* by NAACP assistant secretary Walter White is published. The book is one of the first scholarly studies on the causes of lynching.

1930
- **November 1** The Association of Southern Women for the Prevention of Lynching, headed by Jessie Daniel Ames, holds its first meeting in Atlanta, Georgia.

government would exercise only limited authority over Americans' daily lives. A federal antilynching law, in this view, would have set a dangerous precedent for the creeping centralization of political power.

Shillady is careful to avoid such issues. In the third paragraph he thus cites President Woodrow Wilson's public condemnation of mob actions as support for the NAACP's position. Significantly, however, Wilson here stresses that it is the responsibility of state governors, law-enforcement officers, and local communities to put an end to such actions. He does not endorse the idea of a federal antilynching law.

Wilson, himself a southerner, differed from members of the NAACP on race relations. One of the founding principles of the association was its opposition to racial segregation and a commitment to reversing the 1896 *Plessy* decision. Wilson, in contrast, believed segregation to be a positive good, as did leading members of his administration. He actually presided over the introduction of segregationist practices in the civil service during his two terms of office (1913–1921).

Although educated white southerners like Wilson opposed lynching, they did not support the passage of an antilynching law, which they feared would be but a first step toward further federal intervention to regulate the daily life of citizens in the South. Over time such actions might interfere with other established customs of the region, most notably the system of racial segregation. The Wilsonian alternative to federal action was for southern states themselves to accept responsibility for the suppression of lynching. Unfortunately, as Shillady points out, there was little evidence that this would be effective. In 1918 alone sixty-three African Americans and four whites were lynched in the United States, yet not a single member of any of the lynch mobs was convicted. In only two instances did cases even go to trial, one of which involved the lynching of a white man in the northern state of Illinois.

The principal reason for this failure to prosecute was that many white southerners tacitly supported the actions of lynch mobs. Even in cases of extreme violence, they were unwilling, as witnesses or jurors, to assist in the conviction of a white defendant for the murder of an African American. Shillady notes that lynching still has its apologists. Although they are perhaps less numerous and less vocal than in recent years, he says, they are to be found in all sections of southern society and include individuals held in the highest esteem in the community. James Vardaman, governor of Mississippi (1904–1908), had stated that "if it is necessary every Negro in the state will be lynched; it will be done to maintain white supremacy." Similarly, the renowned Atlanta newspaper publisher John Temple Graves proclaimed before a University of Chicago audience that a lynch mob was an "engine of vengeance, monstrous, lawless, deplorable, but under the uncured defects of the law the fiery terror of the criminal and the chief defense of woman."

This last comment reflects the fact that the most common justification put forward by apologists for lynchings was the need to protect white women from sexual assault by African American men. By this logic, the lynch mob was preferable to a formal trial, where the rape victim would have to relive the horror of her ordeal in court. Moreover, the time-consuming nature of the legal process meant that the conviction and hanging of a rapist was a less effective deterrent to such outrages than the summary public retribution meted out by a lynching party.

◆ **Summation of the Facts Disclosed in Tables**

The Summation in *Thirty Years of Lynching* highlights key findings from detailed statistical tables contained in the first appendix. These statistics show that in the period 1889–1918, at least 3,224 people were killed by lynch mobs in the United States, of which 2,522, or 78.2 percent, were African Americans. The footnotes (omitted here) point out that a further 181 probable victims have been excluded from this total because of the limited data available on them. This can be seen as an attempt by the authors of the document to avoid allegations of exaggeration or sensationalism. All information provided is based on verifiable fact.

DISTRIBUTION OF THE LYNCHINGS This section notes that most lynchings occurred in the South. The facts are presented with little comment. Readers are left to draw their own conclusions. However, this information, together with that already provided on the racial background of lynch victims, dispels any notion that lynching is predominantly a form of rough justice associated with western frontier states. Similarly, the fact that fifty lynch victims were African American women may cast some doubt on any suggestion that nearly all lynchings in the South were related to the crime of rape. The decline in the incidence of lynching from 1914 to 1918, most notably in northern and western states, reinforces the fact that it is now almost exclusively a racially motivated crime confined to the southern states.

DECREASE IN LYNCHING DURING PAST THIRTY YEARS This section seems designed to suggest that as of 1919, lynching is regarded as unacceptable by the vast majority of Americans and that, compared with the rest of the nation, the South is lacking in respect for the rule of law and recognition of what constitutes acceptable behavior in a civilized modern society. The numbers of Mexican lynch victims cited for Texas highlights the extent to which other nonwhite groups were vulnerable to the crime. By implication, not just African Americans but also other ethnic minorities could become a potential target for lynch mobs.

ALLEGED OFFENSES WHICH APPEAR AS "CAUSES" FOR THE LYNCHINGS The statistics show that most lynchings are for alleged offenses other than rape. Moreover, even in the rape-related cases the evidence is weak. Although southern apologists for lynching, like Graves and Vardaman, are not mentioned by name, the arguments put forward by such leaders are here effectively discredited.

◆ **The Story of One Hundred Lynchings**

The narratives here act to counterbalance the impersonal analysis of the summation by providing details on the

Cartoon depicting "Judge Lynch" (Library of Congress)

suffering of lynch victims. They remind readers that the numerical data on lynching represent more than just statistical information. Every lynching reported is also a personal tragedy for the victim and his or her family.

All cases are well documented. For the most part the information provided is in the form of accounts of lynching as reported in respected newspapers and journals. These accounts often reveal shocking details of individual lynchings. Nonetheless, with the exception of two brief introductory paragraphs that "give concreteness and make vivid the facts of lynching," they are presented without any accompanying commentary expressing horror or moral outrage. The NAACP editors are again careful to avoid any suggestions of bias or sensationalism. In any case, no additional comments are needed. The reports in themselves provide the most compelling testimony for the Association's anti-lynching campaign.

The first introductory paragraph refers to the "lynching sport." The justification for this description is borne out by the accounts that follow, which show that many lynchings clearly occurred with the approval and even active participation of much of the local white community. Lynchings were often public spectacles of entertainment, with large crowds of up to fifteen thousand in attendance (Georgia, 1899; South Carolina, 1911; Texas, 1912; Texas, 1916; Tennessee, 1917; Tennessee, 1918).

In the South Carolina lynching of Will Jackson (1911), the white mob was led by Joshua W. Ashleigh, a local member of the state legislature. Victor B. Chesire published a special edition of the local newspaper he edited, *The Intelligencer*, to provide coverage of the event. He admits that he "went out to see the fun without the least objection to being a party to help lynch the brute." In the 1912 lynching of Dan Davis in Texas, "the crowd jeered the dying man and uttered shocking comments suggestive of a cannibalistic spirit." Some spectators "danced and sang to testify to their enjoyment of the occasion." At the 1917 burning to death of Ell Person in Memphis, Tennessee, the fifteen thousand onlookers included "women, even little children," who "cheered as they poured the gasoline on the axe fiend and struck the match." The mob "fought and screamed and crowded to get a glimpse of him." When the victim died sooner than expected, a "complaint on all sides" went around that "they burned him too quick! They burned him too quick!"

The use of language in the reports is often matter of fact, with no expressions of disapproval or a sense that what has taken place is in any way unusual or wrong. This is despite the fact that lynchings often involved prolonged, sadistic torture. Victims were frequently burned alive and suffered physical mutilation, such as castration and the cutting off of ears, fingers, and toes (Texas, 1897; Georgia,

Essential Quotes

> "The United States has for long been the only advanced nation whose government has tolerated lynching. The facts are well known to students of public affairs. It is high time that they became the common property, since they are the common shame, of all Americans."
>
> (Foreword)

> "Lynching has had, and to some degree still has, its apologists, who have alleged one or another excuse for it in given cases. But, none of the several pleas which has been made to explain or excuse it can stand the light of reason or find the slightest real justification in a nation governed by law."
>
> (Foreword)

1899; Delaware, 1903; Mississippi, 1904; Georgia, 1904; Texas, 1912; Texas, 1916; Tennessee, 1917; Tennessee, 1918; Georgia, 1918). Neither the journalistic reports nor the crowds of onlookers at lynchings showed any compassion for the suffering of victims. The reporting of phrases such as "slowly roasting" (Tennessee, 1918) and "meat on a hot frying pan" (Tennessee, 1917) has the effect of dramatizing the dehumanization of the victims. After death, their remains were afforded no respect, with body parts being cut off and taken as souvenirs (Georgia, 1899; South Carolina, 1911; Texas, 1916; Tennessee, 1917).

Although some lynch victims stood accused of rape, or attempted rape (Texas, 1897; Georgia, 1899; Delaware, 1903; West Virginia, 1912; Texas, 1912; Texas, 1916), most were alleged to have committed other crimes. A number of these crimes were minor and even trivial offenses. In Louisiana (1901), Louis Thomas was lynched because he "stole six bottles of soda pop" and then struck his white accuser. Five years later, also in Louisiana, William Carr was hanged for "killing a white man's cow," while in 1911 in Georgia another African American was killed for "loitering in a suspicious manner."

Sometimes, lynch victims were either innocent third parties or clearly not guilty of the crimes they were alleged to have committed (Tennessee, 1901; Mississippi, 1904; West Virginia, 1912). Female victims were shown no more compassion than their male counterparts. Mary Turner (Georgia, 1918) and Alma Howze (Mississippi, 1918) were both lynched even though they were both clearly pregnant. In Oklahoma in 1911, Laura Nelson was "raped by members of the mob" before being hanged. Although the members of the lynch mobs were commonly referred to in the press as "parties unknown," it is clear that in many cases they were well-known figures in the community. Still, the account contains only one case, in North Carolina in 1918, where any members of the mob were brought to trial and convicted for their actions.

Audience

Thirty Years of Lynching was widely distributed and addressed all law-abiding Americans, in the North and in the South, in the hope that it would generate public support for the NAACP's antilynching campaign. More specifically, it was aimed at winning the support of members of the United States Senate and House of Representatives for the passage of a federal antilynching law. Within the South it sought to influence moderate political leaders and law-enforcement officers to make greater efforts to reduce the incidence of lynching and to make members of lynch mobs subject to punishment before the law. It provided accurate factual and statistical information for use by NAACP activists at the national, state, and local level and served as a counter to the propaganda disseminated by apologists for lynching.

Impact

The book failed to achieve its immediate objectives. Despite a prolonged campaign by the NAACP for most of the 1920s and 1930s, the passage of a federal antilynching law was never achieved. In the South it continued to be the exception rather than the rule for participants in lynch mobs to be brought to justice before state courts. In other respects, however, *Thirty Years of Lynching* was more successful. Together with the efforts of campaigning groups like the Association of Southern Women for the Prevention of Lynching, founded in 1930, and the NAACP itself, the book helped change public attitudes. By the end of the 1930s the number of lynchings had dramatically declined, and the crime was increasingly seen as unacceptable in a civilized society. At the state level, southern political leaders and law-enforcement officers made greater efforts to prevent lynchings. Although they were still unlikely to face legal sanctions, members of lynch mobs could no longer take it for granted that they would enjoy community approval for their actions.

Today documented instances of lynching in the United States are rare, but occasional cases are still reported. The perpetrators of such crimes are invariably subject to the full force of the law. In this context the NAACP book is more than just testimony to the memory and suffering of lynch victims of the past. It also serves as a reminder of the potential consequences of extralegal actions by vigilante groups in any society at any time.

See also Emancipation Proclamation (1863); Thirteenth Amendment to the U.S. Constitution (1865); Fourteenth Amendment to the U.S. Constitution (1868); Fifteenth Amendment to the U.S. Constitution (1870); Plessy v. Ferguson (1896); Ida B. Wells-Barnett's "Lynch Law in America" (1900).

Further Reading

■ Books

Allen, James. *Without Sanctuary: Lynching Photography in America*. Santa Fe, N.M.: Twin Palms, 2000.

Bernstein, Patricia. *The First Waco Horror: The Lynching of Jesse Washington and the Rise of the NAACP*. College Station: Texas A&M University Press, 2005.

Brundage, William F. *Lynching in the New South: Georgia and Virginia, 1880–1930*. Urbana: University of Illinois Press, 1993.

Dray, Philip. *At the Hands of Persons Unknown: The Lynching of Black America*. New York: Random House, 2002.

Hall, Jacquelyn D. *Revolt against Chivalry: Jessie Daniel Ames and the Women's Campaign against Lynching*. New York: Columbia University Press, 1979.

Litwack, Leon F. *Trouble in Mind: Black Southerners in the Age of Jim Crow*. New York: Alfred A. Knopf, 1998.

Pfeifer, Michael J. *Rough Justice: Lynching and American Society, 1874–1947*. Urbana: University of Illinois Press, 2004.

Sullivan, Patricia. *Lift Every Voice: The NAACP and the Making of the Civil Rights Movement*. New York: New Press, 2009.

Tolnay, Stewart E., and E. M. Beck. *A Festival of Violence: An Analysis of Southern Lynchings, 1882–1930*. Urbana: University of Illinois Press, 1995.

Waldrep, Christopher. *The Many Faces of Judge Lynch: Extralegal Violence and Punishment in America*. New York: Palgrave Macmillan, 2002.

White, Walter. *Rope and Faggot: A Biography of Judge Lynch*. Notre Dame, Ind.: University of Notre Dame Press, 2001.

Zangrando, Robert L. *The NAACP Crusade against Lynching, 1909–1950*. Philadelphia: Temple University Press, 1980.

—Kevern J. Verney

Questions for Further Study

1. Compare this document with Ida B. Wells-Barnett's "Lynch Law in America" (1900). To what extent do the two documents share similar views? How do the documents differ in the way the authors make their cases?

2. Why did many people during this era want to see Congress pass a federal antilynching bill? Why were state laws against murder regarded as inadequate to stop lynching? Why were some people simultaneously horrified by lynching and yet opposed to the passage of such a bill?

3. What conditions led to the emergence and, later, the reemergence of the Ku Klux Klan? For insight, see the entry on the Ku Klux Klan Act (1871).

4. What role did the NAACP play in the campaign against lynching, other than preparation of this document?

5. Woodrow Wilson is often regarded as a progressive president, yet he opposed passage of a federal antilynching bill. What political considerations did Wilson face that led him to take this position?

THIRTY YEARS OF LYNCHING IN THE UNITED STATES, 1889–1918

Foreword

Until the recent outbreaks in Germany, where, under revolutionary conditions, a few lynchings have taken place, the United States has for long been the only advanced nation whose government has tolerated lynching. The facts are well known to students of public affairs. It is high time that they became the common property, since they are the common shame, of all Americans.

The National Association for the Advancement of Colored People, within the limits of its financial resources, has been carrying on an educational and publicity campaign in the public press, through its own pamphlet publications and the columns of *The Crisis*, and through public meetings, to bring home to the American people their responsibility for the persistence of this monstrous blot upon America's honor. Lynching has had, and to some degree still has, its apologists, who have alleged one and another excuse for it in given cases. But, none of the several pleas which has been made to explain or excuse it can stand the light of reason or find the slightest real justification in a nation governed by law, which has found ample means to cope with lawlessness whenever and wherever the public authorities have taken seriously their oaths of office.

On July 26, 1918, when the nation was at war with the Central Powers, President Wilson appealed to "the governors of all the states, the law officers of every community and, above all, the men and women of every community in the United States, all who revere America and wish to keep her name without stain or reproach, to cooperate, not passively merely, but actively and watchfully, to make an end of this disgraceful evil," saying, "It cannot live where the community does not countenance it."

Despite President Wilson's earnest appeal, made under such extraordinary circumstances, lynchings continued during the remaining period of the war with unabated fury. Sixty-three Negroes, five of them women, and four white men fell victims to mob ruthlessness during 1918 and in no case was any member of the mobs convicted in any court and in only two instances were trials held. In both of these instances the mob members were acquitted. One case was that of the lynchers of the white man, Robert P. Praeger, in Illinois, the other that of the lynchers of a Negro, Will Bird, in Alabama.

The present publication, "Thirty Years of Lynching in the United States, 1889–1918," sums up the facts for this period. It is believed that more persons have been lynched than those whose names are given in Appendix II following. Only such cases have been included as were authenticated by such evidence as was given credence by a recognized newspaper or confirmed by a responsible investigator.

In presenting this material we have refrained from editorial comment, restricting our text to a brief summary of the facts which are more fully illustrated in the tables printed in Appendix I. In addition to the two appendices named, and to the summary of the facts disclosed in the tables, we have included a short summary of the actual happenings in the cases of one hundred persons lynched, as taken from press accounts and, in a few cases, from the reports of our own investigators. These data appear under the heading, *The Story of One Hundred Lynchings*.

Acknowledgment is made to Miss Martha Gruening and to Miss Helen Boardman, who assisted her, for work done in examining the files of leading newspapers and other records for a period of thirty years and in compiling data from which *The Story of One Hundred Lynchings* has been taken.

John R. Shillady, *Secretary*.

National Association for the Advancement of Colored People.

Summation of the Facts Disclosed in Tables

More or less accurate records of lynchings have been kept by the Chicago *Tribune*, Tuskegee Institute and, since 1912, *The Crisis* and the National Association for the Advancement of Colored People. These records go back to 1885. In the present study of the subject, we have confined ourselves to the story of the past thirty years, from 1889 to 1918 inclusive. During these years 3,224 persons have been killed by lynching mobs. Seven hundred and two white persons and 2,522 Negroes have been victims. Of the whites lynched, 691 have been men and 11 women;

of the colored, 2,472 were men and 50 were women. For the whole period, 78.2 per cent, of the victims were Negroes and 21.8 per cent, white persons.

Distribution of the Lynchings

For the thirty years' period as a whole, the North has had 219 victims, the South, 2,834, the West, 156, and Alaska and unknown localities, 15 victims. An examination of Table No. 3 will show that the eight South Atlantic States are responsible for 862 of the total of 2,834 for the South as a whole; the four East South Central States have had 1,014 victims, and the four West South Central States 958. Georgia leads in this unholy ascendancy with 386 victims, followed closely by Mississippi with 373 victims, Texas with 335, Louisiana with 313, Alabama with 276, Arkansas with 214, Tennessee with 196, Florida with 178 and Kentucky with 169. The nine states above named are those which, for the thirty years' period, have each a percentage of the total number of lynchings in excess of five per cent.

Fifty colored women and 11 white women were lynched in 14 states. Thirteen of the 14 states in which women fell victims to mobs were Southern states, Nebraska being the only state outside the South which lynched women....

While in all sections of the country there has been a progressive decrease in the number of lynchings at each of the five years' periods, this decrease in the North and West has far outrun the decrease in the South. The North and West together have lynched 21 persons during the last five years' period, whereas during the same time 304 persons were lynched in the South.

Georgia began the first five years' period with 61 lynchings and ended the last five years' period with exactly the same number. This number, by the way, was the lowest, with one exception, which Georgia reached during the thirty years. Alabama, on the contrary, began with 84, a number one-third greater than Georgia's, which had been reduced during the last five years' period to 19. Mississippi began with 91 for the first period and ended with 28 in the latter five years' period. Georgia and Texas alone, of all the states, have made no proportionate decrease in the number of lynchings during the thirty years' period. Texas shows an increase during the last five years over her record for three preceding five years' periods.

In considering these facts it should be borne in mind that the number of lynchings has steadily been decreasing. When, therefore. Georgia and Texas show no decrease in the former state and only a small decrease in the latter state, it means that relative to the country as a whole, lynchings have been on the increase in these two states.

Decrease in Lynching during Past Thirty Years

Table No. 8 shows the percentage of decrease in the number of persons lynched during each five years' period. Comparing the five years, 1914–1918, with the five years, 1889–1893, the table shows a decrease of 61.3 per cent, in the total number of persons lynched. The percentage of decrease in the number of whites lynched was 77.6 and of colored, 54.4. Since 1903 the number of whites lynched has been decreasing steadily. The increase for the period 1914–1918 to 61 white persons lynched is largely accounted for by the fact that in 1915, 43 whites were lynched. Twenty-seven of these were Mexicans who were lynched in the state of Texas. Many citizens of Texas look upon Mexicans in somewhat the same way as they look upon Negroes (alas for democracy), so that the lynching of this number of Mexicans would not be regarded by them in the same light as would the lynching of so many white Texans or other white citizens of the United States.

Except in 1915 and in 1909 and 1910, the number of whites lynched in any year since 1903 has been less than ten. The percentage of whites lynched in the first ten years' period of our study was 30 per cent; in the second ten years' period, 12.4 per cent, and in the third ten years' period, 15 per cent.

Alleged Offenses which Appear as "Causes" for the Lynchings

Table No. 6 sums up the known facts regarding the alleged offenses committed by the men and women lynched. It is to be remembered that the alleged offenses given are pretty loose descriptions of the crimes charged against the mob victims, where actual crime was committed. Of the whites lynched, nearly 46 per cent were accused of murder; a little more than 18 per cent were accused of what have been classified as miscellaneous crimes, *i.e.*, all crimes not otherwise classified; 17.4 per cent were said to have committed crimes against property; 8.7 per cent crimes against the person, other than rape, "attacks upon women," and murder; while 8.4 per cent were accused of rape and "attacks upon women."

Among colored victims, 35.8 per cent were accused of murder; 28.4 per cent of rape and "attacks upon women" (19 per cent of rape and 9.4 per cent of "attacks upon women"); 17.8 per cent of crimes against the person (other than those already mentioned) and against property; 12 per cent were charged with miscellaneous crimes and in 5.6 per cent of cases no crime at all was charged. The 5.6 per cent, classified under "Absence of Crime" does not include a number of cases in which crime was alleged but in which it was afterwards shown conclusively that no crime had been committed. Further, it may fairly be pointed out that in a number of cases where Negroes have been lynched for rape and "attacks upon white women," the alleged attacks rest upon no stronger evidence than "entering the room of a woman" or brushing against her. In such cases as these latter the victims and their friends have often asserted that there was no intention on the part of the victim to attack a white woman or to commit rape. In many cases, of course, the evidence points to *bona fide* attacks upon women.

An examination of Table No. 7 shows that the decreases in succeeding five years' periods in the number of victims charged with rape and "attacks upon women" have been more pronounced than for any other alleged cause....

It is apparent that lynchings of Negroes for other causes than the so-called "one crime" have for the whole period been a large majority of all lynchings and that for the past five years, less than one in five of the colored victims have been accused of rape or "attacks upon women" (rape, 11 per cent; attacks upon women, 8.8 per cent; total, 19.8 per cent).

The Story of One Hundred Lynchings

To give concreteness and to make vivid the facts of lynching in the United States, we give below in chronological order an account of one hundred lynchings which have occurred in the period from 1894 to 1918. These "stories," as they are technically described in newspaper parlance, have been taken from press accounts and, in a few cases, from the reports of investigations made by the National Association for the Advancement of Colored People. Covering twenty-five years of American history, these accounts serve to present a characteristic picture of the lynching sport, as it was picturesquely defined by Henry Watterson.

The last of the "stories" describes one of the rare events in connection with lynchings, that of the conviction of members of a mob involved in such affairs. In this case no lynching was consummated, it having been prevented by the prompt and public-spirited action of the mayor of the city (Winston-Salem, North Carolina), and members of the "Home Guard" and Federal troops who defended the jail against a mob.

Alabama, 1894

Three Negroes, Tom Black, Johnson Williams and Tony Johnston, were lynched at Tuscumbia, Alabama. They were in the local jail, awaiting trial on the charge of having burnt a barn. A mob of two hundred masked men entered the jail. after having enticed away the jailer with a false message, took the keys from the jailer's wife and secured the three prisoners. They were carried to a near-by bridge. Here a rope was placed around the neck of each victim, the other end being tied to the timbers of the bridge, and they were compelled to jump.

New York *Tribune*, April 23, 1894....

Texas, 1897

Robert Henson Hilliard, a Negro, for a murder to which he confessed and for alleged rape, was burned to death by a mob at Tyler, Texas. Hilliard confessed the murder but stated that he killed his victim because he had unwittingly frightened her and feared that he would be killed.

A report of the crime and its punishment was written by an eye-witness and printed by a local publishing house. It ended as follows:

"Note: Hilliard's power of endurance was the most wonderful thing on record. His lower limbs burned off before he became unconscious and his body looked to be burned to the hollow. Was it decreed by an avenging God as well as an avenging people that his sufferings should be prolonged beyond the ordinary endurance of mortals?"

The End

"We have sixteen large views under powerful magnifying lenses now on exhibition. These views are true to life and show the Negro's attack, the scuffle, the murder, the body as found, etc. With eight views of the trial and burning. For place of exhibit see street bills. Don't fail to see this."

Breckenridge-Scruggs Co.

Document Text

No indictments were found against any of the mob's members.

Georgia, 1899

Sam Hose, a Negro farm laborer, was accused of murdering his employer in a quarrel over wages. He escaped. Several days later, while he was being hunted unsuccessfully, the charge was added that he raped his employer's wife. He confessed the murder, but refused, even under duress, to confess the other crime.

The following account of the lynching is taken from the New York *Tribune* for April 24, 1899.

"In the presence of nearly 2,000 people, who sent aloft yells of defiance and shouts of joy, Sam Hose (a Negro who committed two of the basest acts known to crime) was burned at the stake in a public road, one and a half miles from here. Before the torch was applied to the pyre, the Negro was deprived of his ears, fingers and other portions of his body with surprising fortitude. Before the body was cool, it was cut to pieces, the bones were crushed into small bits and even the tree upon which the wretch met his fate was torn up and disposed of as souvenirs."

"The Negro's heart was cut in several pieces, as was also his liver. Those unable to obtain the ghastly relics directly, paid more fortunate possessors extravagant sums for them. Small pieces of bone went for 25 cents and a bit of the liver, crisply cooked, for 10 cents."

No indictments were ever found against any of the lynchers....

Tennessee, 1901

Ballie Crutchfield, a colored woman, was lynched by a mob at Rome, Tennessee, because her brother stole a purse.

The mob took Crutchfield from the custody of the sheriff, and started with him for the place of execution, when he broke from them and escaped.

"This," says the despatch, "so enraged the mob, that they suspected Crutchfield's sister of being implicated in the theft and last night's work was the culmination of that suspicion."

The Coroner's jury found the usual verdict that the woman came to her death at the hands of parties unknown.

New York *Tribune*, March 16, 1901.

Louisiana, 1901

Louis Thomas, at Girard, La., a Negro, broke into a local store and stole six bottles of soda-pop. He was later found by a white man named Brown, disposing of its contents, and on being accused of theft, struck his accuser. Brown procured a rifle and shot the Negro twice through the body, but as neither wound proved fatal, a mob of white men took the Negro from the house where he lay wounded and strung him up.

New York *Tribune*, July 16, 1901....

Delaware, 1903

George White, a Negro, accused of rape and murder, was taken out of jail at Wilmington, Del., dragged to the scene of his alleged crime and forced to confess. He was tied to a stake, burned and riddled with bullets, even as he was being burned. The Chamber of Commerce of Wilmington, which met a few days later, refused to pass a resolution condemning the lynching but passed one against forest fires.

New York *Tribune*, June 23, 24, 1903....

Mississippi, 1904

Luther Holbert, a Doddsville Negro, and his wife were burned at the stake for the murder of James Eastland, a white planter, and John Carr, a Negro, The planter was killed in a quarrel which arose when he came to Carr's cabin, where he found Holbert, and ordered him to leave the plantation. Carr and a Negro, named Winters, were also killed.

Holbert and his wife fled the plantation but were brought back and burned at the stake in the presence of a thousand people. Two innocent Negros had been shot previous to this by a posse looking for Holbert, because one of them, who resembled Holbert, refused to surrender when ordered to do so. There is nothing in the story to indicate that Holbert's wife had any part in the crime.

New York *Tribune*, February 8, 1904....

Georgia, 1904

For the brutal murder of a white family (the Hodges family) at Statesboro', Georgia, two Negroes, Paul Reed and Will Cato, were burned alive in the presence of a large crowd. They had been duly convicted and sentenced, when the mob broke into the courtroom and carried them away, in spite of the plea of a brother of the murdered man, who was present in the court, that the law be allowed to take its course. None of the lynchers were ever indicted.

Ray Stannard Baker, "Following the Color Line," Chicago *Tribune*, December 31, 1904.

Georgia, 1904

Because of the race prejudice growing out of the Hodges murder by Reed and Cato and their lynching, Albert Roger and his son were lynched at Statesboro', Ga., August 17, for being Negroes. A number of other Negroes were whipped for no other offense.

Ray Stannard Baker, "Following the Color Line," Chicago *Tribune*, December 31, 1904.

Georgia, 1904

On account of the race riots which grew out of the above murder (Hodges) and lynching, McBride, a respectable Negro of Portal, Ga., was beaten, kicked and shot to death for trying to defend his wife, who was confined with a baby, three days old, from a whipping at the hands of a crowd of white men.

Ray Stannard Baker, "Following the Color Line," Chicago *Tribune*, December 31, 1904….

Louisiana, 1906

For the crime of killing a white man's cow, William Carr, a Negro, was killed at Planquemines, Louisiana. The lynching was conducted in a most orderly manner, Carr being taken from the Sheriff without resistance by a mob of thirty masked men, hurried to the nearest railroad bridge and hanged without Ceremony.

Despatch to New York *Tribune*, March 18, 1906….

Oklahoma, 1911

At Okemah, Oklahoma, Laura Nelson, a colored woman, accused of murdering a deputy sheriff who had discovered stolen goods in her house, was lynched together with her son, a boy about fifteen. The woman and her son were taken from the jail, dragged about six miles to the Canadian River, and hanged from a bridge. The woman was raped by members of the mob before she was hanged.

The Crisis, July, 1911….

South Carolina, 1911

Will Jackson was lynched at Honeapath, S. C., for an alleged attack on a white child. He was hanged to a tree by his feet and his body riddled with bullets. His fingers were cut off for souvenirs. The mob was led by Joshua W. Ashleigh, a local member of the State Legislature, and his son, while Victor B. Chesire, editor of a local newspaper, *The Intelligencer*, after taking part in the lynching, got out a special edition telling about it in the following words: "*The Intelligencer* man went out to see the fun without the least objection to being a party to help lynch the brute." The then Governor of the State, Cole Blease, absolutely refused to use the power of his office to bring the lynchers to justice, and the Coroner's jury found that the Negro came to his death "at the hands of parties unknown."

The Crisis, December, 1911.

Georgia, 1911

Two colored men, Allen and Watts, were lynched in Monroe, Georgia, one for an alleged attack on a white woman, the other for "loitering in a suspicious manner." Judge Chas. H. Brand ordered Allen brought to Monroe for trial although it was known that the citizens had organized a mob to lynch him. The Judge was offered troops by the Governor to protect the prisoner but refused. Allen was sent to Monroe in charge of two officers. The train was stopped and he was taken off and shot. The mob then proceeded to Monroe where they stormed the jail, took out Watts and hanged and shot him. The same Judge had refused to ask for troops on a previous occasion, saying that he "would not imperil the life of one man to save the lives of a hundred Negroes."

No indictments were found against the lynchers.

The Crisis, August, 1911….

Georgia, 1911

T. W. Walker, a colored man of Washington, Ga., killed C. S. Hollinshead, a wealthy planter of the same place. It was stated that there was no apparent cause for the crime, but a Northern colored paper published the charge that Walker killed Hollinshead for attacking his wife and an Atlanta paper reprinted it. A crowd of white men tried to lynch Walker, who had been sentenced to death, but were so drunk that he succeeded in escaping. He was caught and resentenced to instant execution. Before he could be taken from the court room, a brother of Hollinshead shot and severely wounded him. He was then taken out and hanged, the court announcing that the brother would not be prosecuted. The only arrest made in connection with the affair was that of the Negro editor who published the charge against Hollinshead.

The Crisis, January, 1912....

West Virginia, 1912

In Bluefield, W. Va., September 4, 1912, Robert Johnson was lynched for attempted rape. When he was accused he gave an alibi and proved every statement that he made. He was taken before the girl who had been attacked and she failed to identify him. She had previously described very minutely the clothes her assailant wore. When she failed to identify Johnson in the clothes he had, the Bluefield police dressed him to fit the description and again took him before her. This time she screamed on seeing him, "That's the man." Her father had also failed to identify him but now he declared himself positive that he recognized Johnson as the guilty man. Thereupon Johnson was dragged out by a mob, protesting his innocence, and after being severely abused, was hung to a telegraph pole. Later his innocence was conclusively established.

"The Lynching of Robert Johnson," James Oppenheim in *The Independent*, October 10, 1912....

Texas, 1912

Dan Davis, a Negro, was burned at the stake at Tyler, Texas, for the crime of attempted rape, May 25, 1912.

There was some disappointment in the crowd and criticism of those who had bossed the arrangements, because the fire was so slow in reaching the Negro. It was really only ten minutes after the fire was started that smoking shoe soles and twitching of the Negro's feet indicated that his lower extremities were burning, but the time seemed much longer. The spectators had waited so long to see him tortured that they begrudged the ten minutes before his suffering really began.

The Negro had uttered but few words. When he was led to where he was to be burned he said quite calmly, "I wish some of you gentlemen would be Christian enough to cut my throat," but nobody responded. When the fire started, he screamed "Lord, have mercy on my soul," and that was the last word he spoke, though he was conscious for fully twenty minutes after that. His exhibition of nerve aroused the admiration even of his torturers.

A slight hitch in the proceedings occurred when the Negro was about half burned. His clothing had been stripped off and burned to ashes by the flames and his black body hung nude in the gray dawn light. The flesh had been burned from his legs as high as the knees when it was seen that the wood supply was running short. None of the men or boys were willing to miss an incident of the torture. All feared something of more than usual interest might happen, and it would be embarrassing to admit later on not having seen it on account of being absent after more wood.

Something had to be done, however, and a few men from the edge of the crowd, ran after more dry-goods boxes, and by reason of this "public service" gained standing room in the inner circle after having delivered the fuel. Meanwhile the crowd jeered the dying man and uttered shocking comments suggestive of a cannibalistic spirit. Some danced and sang to testify to their enjoyment of the occasion.

Special correspondence of the St. Louis *Post-Despatch*. *The Crisis*, June, September, 1912....

Texas, 1916

Jesse Washington, a defective Negro boy, of about nineteen, unable to read and write, was employed as farm hand in Robinson, a small town near Waco, Texas. One day, the wife of his employer found fault with him, whereupon he struck her on the head with a hammer and killed her. There is some, but not conclusive, evidence that he raped her. He was arrested, tried, found guilty and sentenced to death by hanging within ten days of the commission of the crime. As the sentence was pronounced, a mob of fifteen hundred white men, who feared the law's delays, broke into the courtroom and seized the prisoner. He was dragged through the streets, stabbed, mutilated and finally burned to death in the presence of a crowd of

15,000 men, women and children. The Mayor and Chief of Police of Waco also witnessed the lynching.

After death what was left of his body was dragged through the streets and parts of it sold as souvenirs. His teeth brought $5 apiece and the chain that had bound him 25 cents a link. No one was ever indicted for participating in the lynching.

Investigation by the National Association for the Advancement of Colored People....

Tennessee, 1917

On April 30, Antoinette Rappal, a sixteen-year-old white girl, living on the outskirts of Memphis, disappeared on her way to school. On May third her body was found in a river, her head severed from it. On May 6 a Negro wood chopper, Ell Person, was arrested on suspicion. Under third degree methods he confessed to the crime of murder. The Grand Jury of Shelby County immediately indicted him for murder in the first degree.

The prisoner was taken secretly to the State penitentiary at Nashville. It was known that he would be brought back for trial to Memphis. Each incoming train was searched, and arrangements were made for a lynching.

On May 15 the sheriff disappeared from Memphis. He returned on May 18, announcing that he was informed that several mobs were between Arlington and Memphis. The men were reported to be drinking. "I didn't want to hurt anybody and I didn't want to get hurt," he said, "so I went South into Mississippi."

The press did nothing to quell the mob spirit, and on May 21 announced that Ell Person would be brought to Memphis that night. Thousands of persons on foot and in automobiles went to the place that had been prepared for the lynching.

With a knowledge of these conditions, Person was brought back from Nashville, guarded only by two deputies. Without difficulty he was taken from the train, placed in an automobile, and driven to the spot prepared for his death.

The Memphis *Press* reported the lynching in full. We give a few of its statements.

"Fifteen thousand of them—men, women, even little children, and in their midst the black-clothed figure of Antoinette Rappal's mother—cheered as they poured the gasoline on the axe fiend and struck the match.

"They fought and screamed and crowded to get a glimpse of him, and the mob closed in and struggled about the fire as the flames flared high and the smoke rolled about their heads. Two of them hacked off his ears as he burned; another tried to cut off a toe but they stopped him.

"The Negro lay in the flames, his hands crossed on his chest. If he spoke no one ever heard him over the shouts of the crowd. He died quickly, though fifteen minutes later excitable persons still shouted that he lived when they saw the charred remains move as does meat on a hot frying pan.

"'They burned him too quick! They burned him too quick!' was the complaint on all sides."

Investigation of the burning of Ell Person at Memphis, by James Weldon Johnson. Published by the National Association for the Advancement of Colored People.

Tennessee, 1918

Jim McIlherron was prosperous in a small way. He was a Negro who resented the slights and insults of white men. He went armed and the sheriff feared him. On February 8 he got into a quarrel with three young white men who insulted him. Threats were made and McIlherron fired six shots, killing two of the men.

He fled to the home of a colored clergyman who aided him to escape, and was afterwards shot and killed by a mob. McIlherron was captured and full arrangements made for a lynching. Men, women and children started into the town of Estill Springs from a radius of fifty miles. A spot was chosen for the burning. McIlherron was chained to a hickory tree while the mob howled about him. A fire was built a few feet away and the torture began. Bars of iron were heated and the mob amused itself by putting them close to the victim, at first without touching him. One bar he grasped and as it was jerked from his grasp all the inside of his hand came with it. Then the real torturing began, lasting for twenty minutes.

During that time, while his flesh was slowly roasting, the Negro never lost his nerve. He cursed those who tortured him and almost to the last breath derided the attempts of the mob to break his spirit.

Walter F. White, in *The Crisis*, May, 1918.

Georgia, 1918

Hampton Smith, a white farmer, had the reputation of ill treating his Negro employees. Among those whom he abused was Sidney Johnson, a Negro peon,

Document Text

whose fine of thirty dollars he had paid when he was up before the court for gaming. After having been beaten and abused, the Negro shot and killed Smith as he sat in his window at home. He also shot and wounded Smith's wife.

For this murder a mob of white men of Georgia for a week, May 17 to 24, engaged in a hunt for the guilty man, and in the meantime lynched the following innocent persons: Will Head, Will Thompson, Hayes Turner, Mary Turner, his wife, for loudly proclaiming her husband's innocence, Chime Riley and four unidentified Negroes. Mary Turner was pregnant and was hung by her feet. Gasoline was thrown on her clothing and it was set on fire. Her body was cut open and her infant fell to the ground with a little cry, to be crushed to death by the heel of one of the white men present. The mother's body was then riddled with bullets. The murderer, Sidney Johnson, was at length located in a house at Valdosta.

The house was surrounded by a posse headed by the Chief of Police and Johnson, who was known to be armed, fired until his shot gave out, wounding the Chief. The house was entered and Johnson found dead. His body was mutilated. After the lynching more than 500 Negroes left the vicinity of Valdosta, leaving hundreds of acres of untilled land behind them.

The Lynchings of May, 1918, in Brooks and Lowndes Counties, Georgia, by Walter F. White. Published by the National Association for the Advancement of Colored People.

Mississippi, 1918

On Friday night, December 20, 1918, four Negroes, Andrew Clark, age 15; Major Clark, age 20; Maggie Howze, age 20; and Alma Howze, age 16, were taken from the little jail at Shubuta and lynched on a bridge over the Chickasawha River. They were suspected of having murdered a Dr. E. L. Johnston, a dentist.

An investigation disclosed the following facts: That Dr. Johnston was living in illicit relations with Maggie Howze and Alma Howze. That Major Clark, a youth working on Johnston's plantation wished to marry Maggie. That Dr. Johnston went to Clark and told him to leave his woman alone. That this led to a quarrel, made the more bitter when it was found that Maggie was to have a child by Dr. Johnston; and that the younger sister was also pregnant, said to be by Dr. Johnston.

Shortly after this Johnston was mysteriously murdered. There were two theories as to his death; one that he was killed by Clark, the other that he was killed by a white man who had accused him of seducing a white woman. It was generally admitted that Johnston was a loose character.

Alma Howze was so near to motherhood when lynched that it was said by an eye-witness at her burial on the second day following, that the movements of her unborn child could be detected.

Investigation by the National Association for the Advancement of Colored People.

North Carolina, 1918

Mob Leaders Go To Prison

Realizing that if a lyncher is permitted to remain unpunished the decency of the community is greatly endangered, Judge B. F. Long of the Superior Court sentenced fifteen white men, indicted for participa-

Glossary

"at the hands of parties unknown"	a phrase the authorities commonly used in investigations of lynchings to avoid assigning guilt
bona fide	Latin for "in good faith"; authentic or genuine
Central Powers	in World War I, the German Empire, the Austro-Hungarian Empire, Bulgaria, and the Ottoman Empire
Henry Watterson	a late-nineteenth to early-twentieth-century journalist, editor of the *Louisville Courier-Journal*, and opponent of lynching
posse	from the Latin phrase *posse comitatus*, meaning "power of the county," used to refer to a temporary police force but often associated with mob violence

tion in a riot in Winston-Salem, Nov. 17, to serve from fourteen months to six years in prison. The men were found guilty of attempting to lynch Russell High, a prisoner in the city jail.

The fifteen men were a part of a mob that for a night and morning terrorized Winston-Salem, and in their efforts to lynch a black man, innocent of the crime of assault for which he had been arrested on suspicion, put life and property in peril and incidentally killed four people, one a little white girl. The Mayor of the city acted with promptitude and courage, railing out the Home Guards and the fire department which played water on the mob. Nearly every policeman was hurt. The Governor rushed troops from Camp Green at Charlotte. For many days cannon guarded the streets. "We don't mean to be sentimental on this matter," a prominent business man is quoted as saying, "but we aren't going to have our city's good name spoilt by a lynching."

Condensed from reports of the North Carolina press.

Cyril Briggs's Summary of the Program and Aims of the African Blood Brotherhood

"The Negroes in the United States ... are destined to play a vital part in a powerful world movement for Negro liberation."

Overview

The 1920 *Summary of the Program and Aims of the African Blood Brotherhood* remains one of the first documents to successfully merge black nationalism and international Communism, making it a key document in the history of both African Americans and the Left. Written by a West Indian immigrant named Cyril V. Briggs, the *Summary* enumerates eight goals for the African Blood Brotherhood for African Liberation and Redemption (ABB), a secret, all-black society founded by Briggs to unite people of African descent and counter what Briggs perceived to be the menacing forces of capitalism and white racism.

In his *Summary*, Briggs argues for united opposition of diverging black organizations against lynching and the Ku Klux Klan (KKK), both treacherous outgrowths of white racism in the United States. He also suggests that black children be educated in black history, outlining an early approach to an Afrocentric black studies curriculum. Essential to this project was an emphasis on recovering the history of Africa, even showing how African civilizations rivaled if not surpassed those of Europe.

In addition, Briggs calls for the organization of labor against unfettered, free-market capitalism. Here, however, he suspends his emphasis on race to include white Communists. Briggs's affinity for white Communists led him to break from the other most notable proponent of black nationalism at the time, Marcus Garvey, and forge his unique brand of race-based, class-oriented politics. Briggs's *Summary of the Program and Aims of the African Blood Brotherhood* thus serves as both a thematic link to other insurgent nationalist movements at the time, including Ireland's struggle for independence from Britain in the Irish Easter Rising, and a bold response to white Anglo-Saxon Protestant nativism, embodied most forcefully in the resurgence of the notorious white supremacist group the KKK during World War I.

Context

Issued in 1920, the *Summary of the Program and Aims of the African Blood Brotherhood* came on the heels of one of the most violent years of racial conflict in the United States. Following the end of World War I, returning black soldiers confronted remarkable levels of white violence, all sparked by war-related fears. One such fear was that African American soldiers might upset white political rule in the American South, no longer subordinating themselves to the humiliations of Jim Crow segregation. Partly owing to such fears, more than thirty riots—all instigated by whites—broke out against blacks in what became known as Red Summer, while lynchings of individual blacks spread across the South.

Another fear that influenced racial politics at the time, one that was more prominent in the North, was that African Americans might steal white jobs. In the second two decades of the nineteenth century, upwards of five hundred thousand African Americans left the South in what has since been termed the Great Migration, seeking jobs. Once white soldiers returned from Europe, however, the black newcomers employed in northern factories were viewed as unwanted intruders who threatened to permanently displace the returning GIs. Not surprisingly, blacks became the target of white working-class violence as early as 1917, when a white mob killed more than two hundred African American workers in East St. Louis, Illinois. Two years later, white mobs attacked African Americans in Chicago after a black swimmer wandered onto a white beach; the incident resulted in over thirty deaths and five hundred injuries.

Compounding racial violence in the Midwest was a surge in nativist sentiment nationally, spearheaded by rural whites fearful of alien immigration. Prior to the 1890s, most immigrants to the United States hailed from northern Europe, a region tending to be Nordic, Protestant, and otherwise culturally similar to the English and Scotch-Irish settlers of the colonial era. Beginning in 1891, however, immigration patterns shifted toward non-Protestant, southern Europeans, including Catholics and Jews from Italy, Poland, Russia, Hungary, and Greece. Afraid of such aliens, a group of Harvard University alumni formed the Immigration Restriction League in 1894, lobbying successfully for quotas on all immigrants to the United States.

Perhaps the most extreme anti-immigrant group in the United States at the time of Cyril Briggs's *Summary* was

Time Line

1914
- **July 28**
  World War I officially begins with Austria-Hungary's declaration of war against Serbia.

1916
- **April 24**
  Irish Republicans in Dublin seek independence for Ireland, beginning a weeklong rebellion against British oppression known as the Easter Rising.

1917
- **November**
  Eight months after the overthrow of the Russian czar, the Communist Party gains control of the former empire in the Russian Revolution.

1918
- **January 8**
  U.S. President Woodrow Wilson unveils his Fourteen Points.
- **September**
  Cyril Briggs founds *The Crusader*.
- **November 11**
  World War I ends as Germany signs an armistice with the Allied forces.

1919
- Briggs founds a secret society called the African Blood Brotherhood for African Liberation and Redemption.
- **March**
  The Communist International (Comintern) forms in Moscow.

1920
- Briggs issues his *Summary of the Program and Aims of the African Blood Brotherhood*.

1921
- Congress passes the first Emergency Quota Act.

1922
- Claude McKay travels to Russia to address the Fourth Comintern.

1925
- The Ku Klux Klan reaches the height of its influence.

---

the KKK. First organized by Confederate officers intent on restoring white rule to the South after the Civil War, the Klan lost support after the collapse of Reconstruction, only to regain backing in 1915. That year, a group of white southerners angry over the alleged 1914 rape of a white girl by a Jewish pencil factory manager named Leo Frank, and inspired by a romantic movie about the first Klan entitled *Birth of a Nation*, met at Stone Mountain, Georgia, to resurrect the second KKK. Under the leadership of a Texas dentist named Hiram W. Evans, the Klan expanded its target list to include not just African Americans but Jews, Catholics, and immigrants in general. Declared an imperial wizard in 1922, Evans made the Klan's motto "100 per cent Americanism," actively working to cull recruits not simply from the South but from the Midwest and the West. During his tenure, the KKK became a powerful force of hatred in the state politics of Georgia, Texas, Indiana, Colorado, and Oregon. Klansmen even made it to the 1924 Democratic National Convention, forming the extreme right wing of the Democratic Party at the time.

At least some of the Klan's violence stemmed from fears that the white race, and specifically Anglo-Saxon Protestants, risked extinction; this phobia was encouraged by academics who espoused what quickly came to be known as scientific racism. Perhaps foremost among them was Madison Grant, a conservationist who worked to save the redwoods of the Pacific Northwest at the same time that he worked to save the Anglo-Saxon Protestants of the Atlantic Northeast, both groups facing what Grant believed to be impending extinction. The popularity of Grant's book *The Passing of the Great Race*, a celebration of Anglo-Saxon achievements published in 1916, convinced some that the United States would never, in fact, achieve true assimilation. The cultural theorist Randolph S. Bourne penned an essay in 1916 entitled "Trans-National America," arguing that even European immigrants from places like Germany, Scandinavia, and Poland were not assimilating into American society, but rather clinging to older, Continental identities. For Bourne, such reluctance indicated a problem with prevailing notions of America as a liberal, democratic nation-state based not on ethnic or racial identity but on democratic idealism. Such idealism was precisely what President Woodrow Wilson endorsed during his administration, using it to rationalize American involvement in World War I. Bourne opposed American entry into the war and countered Wilsonian idealism with pluralism, or the acceptance and appreciation of ethnic and cultural differences, an idea that also appealed to Cyril Briggs.

Even though Briggs joined Bourne in failing to see an American melting pot, he did see hope for cross-cultural alliances under Communism. The Russian Revolution of 1917 convinced many, including Briggs, that Communism was a viable political alternative to free-market capitalism. After deposing the Russian czar, Communist revolutionaries pulled Russia out of World War I—designating it a capitalist war—and immediately went about establishing an egalitarian, antiproperty state. By the end of 1919, the newly formed Soviet government established the Communist International, or Comintern, an agency dedicated to spreading Communist ideals of revolution worldwide. That same year, the American Communist Party formed, inspiring Briggs to synthesize Communist theory with his own interests in racial pluralism and, more specifically, black nationalism. Although he was hardly the first person of color to be inspired by Communism in the United States, Briggs forged a critical link between Communism and black nationalist thought at a moment when most white Communists did not recognize the salience of racial allegiance—or racial difference.

Conversely, Briggs's interest in Communism separated him from other proponents of black separatism in the 1920s, perhaps the best known of whom was Marcus Garvey, the father of the Back to Africa movement. In 1922 the African American writer Claude McKay took Briggs's ideas with him to the Soviet Union, addressing the Fourth Comintern in Moscow and initiating the beginnings of a formal relationship between the Soviet Union and the black Left. Raised on black-majority islands and schooled in European political thought, West Indian immigrants to places like Harlem brought with them a militant class politics that coincided with the New Negro Movement, a domestic campaign challenging white cultural hegemony that would absorb some but not all West Indian immigrant intellectuals. In the aftermath of the Russian Revolution of 1917, black West Indians in Harlem joined together to form leftist political groups that would serve as the foundation for a much more radical, Communist-oriented West Indian culture in New York. Briggs saw great potential in coupling the struggle for equality in the United States with the revolutionary spirit of Communism. The idea of black liberation as a global effort informs his *Summary of the Program and Aims of the African Blood Brotherhood*.

About the Author

Born on the small Caribbean island of Nevis on May 28, 1888, Cyril V. Briggs personally confronted many of the same tensions that drove anticolonialist sentiment in the first half of the twentieth century. The illegitimate son of a woman of color and a white overseer, Briggs was dark skinned enough to be rejected from Caribbean white society, yet light skinned enough to earn the description "Angry Blond Negro," noted Mark Solomon in *The Cry Was Unity: Communists and African Americans, 1917–1936*. Frustrated by a lack of opportunity on his home island, Briggs immigrated to the United States in 1905 and settled in New York City, gravitating toward Harlem's growing West Indian community. There, he found others who had grown up in the West Indies with a deep resentment toward European—and particularly British—imperialism, factors that contributed to an emerging politics of racial solidarity and anticapitalism.

In 1912, Briggs landed a job with the *New York Amsterdam News*, a weekly periodical devoted to issues of interest among the city's African Americans. He took heart in President Woodrow Wilson's Fourteen Points plan issued in January 1918, particularly the promise that colonized peoples be granted "a voice in their own government." That September, Briggs founded *The Crusader*, a magazine dedicated, in Briggs's words, to promoting "Negro power and culture throughout the world," including the idea that human civilization began in Africa, that black achievements were underemphasized in American schools, and that African Americans would be better served by an "independent, separate existence" from whites.

Inspired by the success of *The Crusader* and disappointed in Wilson's failure to work actively for colonial independence, Briggs abandoned hope in traditional struggles for civil rights and social equality, taking inspiration instead from global outbreaks of racial and ethnic nationalism, most notably the Irish Easter Rising of 1916. To Briggs, Ireland's attempt to free itself from British oppression in the Easter Rising indicated that ethnic and racial nationalism was, in fact, a logical strategy for black advancement. He shared this sentiment with Marcus Garvey, a Jamaican stonemason who immigrated to the United States in 1916 and quickly established one of the most dynamic black organizations in American history, the Universal Negro Improvement Association. Both Garvey and Briggs took the Easter Rising to mean that a possible answer to racial injustice in the United States was black nationalism, a position that Briggs articulated forthrightly in 1917, when he identified African Americans as nothing less than a "nation within a nation."

While Garvey adopted a view of black nationalism similar to the one held by Briggs, Briggs differed from Garvey in that he also took an interest in the Russian Revolution, finding Soviet internationalism an attractive model upon which to build his own version of black transnationalism. Briggs attempted to fuse Communism with black nationalism by founding a secret society called the African Blood Brotherhood for African Liberation and Redemption in 1919. Garvey, on the other hand, rejected Communism in favor of black capitalism, which led to a rift between the two activists.

In defiance of Garvey, Briggs joined the Communist Party in 1921, and the ABB merged with the party in 1925, becoming the American Negro Labor Congress. By 1929, Briggs himself was elevated to the central executive committee of the Communist Party of the United States. Though expelled for his black nationalist views, Briggs continued to side with Communist policies, eventually rejoining the Communist Party of the United States in 1948. He died on October 18, 1966.

Explanation and Analysis of Document

The *Summary of the Program and Aims of the African Blood Brotherhood* by Cyril V. Briggs can be viewed as an attempt to rethink the concept of nationhood itself, suggesting that nations need not be bounded by language or geography but can be formed around a shared past or expe-

Barricades in Petrograd, Russia, during the Russian Revolution (Library of Congress)

rience. Issued at its first conference in 1920, the *Summary* outlines the goals of the self-declared secret brotherhood. The document itself is a relatively short list that enumerates nine political objectives, the first of which declares the need for a "liberated race" free from "alien political rule." Here, alien political rule implies both rule by whites over blacks in the United States and rule by colonial powers over the colonized generally. Indeed, one of the more remarkable attributes of the *Summary* is that it foreshadowed the Trinidadian-born activist Stokely Carmichael's Black Power thesis declaring that African Americans lived in what was essentially a domestic colony in 1967. Almost half a century earlier, Briggs had implied as much, drawing a not-so-subtle connection between imperial rule over blacks in the West Indies—Briggs's home—and white rule over blacks in the United States.

Like Carmichael, Briggs focuses on economic inequality or, as he puts it, the "crushing weight of exploitation." Although Jim Crow segregation might easily have been included in this section, the *Summary* concentrates more on economic inequality, or that which keeps "the many in degrading poverty" so that others—presumably white elites—can "wallow in stolen wealth." Continued poverty in the otherwise wealthy United States, implies the *Summary*, ties American blacks to blacks around the world. In an interesting refusal to distinguish between, on the one hand, African Americans who could trace their lineage to slavery and recent West Indian immigrants on the other, Briggs notes in his first point that blacks in America, "both native and foreign born," are particularly well suited to play a "vital part" in a larger, global "movement for Negro liberation." Briggs's merger of black natives and immigrants here reflects a larger pan-African sensibility, one that does not place reparations for domestic slavery any higher than general redress for wrongs done to people of African descent generally. Unlike the National Association for the Advancement of Colored People, in other words, Briggs does not see a domestic struggle for civil rights to be as important as a larger, global struggle to achieve a free America and a "free Africa." Although it is subtle, this distinction is important, as it demonstrates a strategic advance in the direction of a true but fledgling black nationalism, one that did not differentiate between blacks from one country or another but rather viewed all people of African descent as comprising their own country.

To make the claim that all people of African descent essentially belonged to the same oppressed nation, Briggs necessarily had to occlude any mention of divisions that existed and had existed over time between African peoples, along with discrimination and injustice imposed by Africans against other Africans. Indeed, implicit in Briggs's claims of black subjugation at the hands of Europeans was a profound de-emphasis on the importance of history in the determination of events— particularly any mention of the longstanding role that slavery had played in African societies. That large West African empires like Asante and Dahomey owed their existence to slavery was ignored, as was the fact that African slavery predated slavery in the New World.

The second point of the *Summary* demands racial equality in the political, social, and economic realms. Briggs does not elaborate on whether economic equality means equality of opportunity or result, but given his Socialist leanings the latter was probably the more likely. For political equality, Briggs could have meant equal access to the vote, a right that eluded African Americans in the South, or he might have been referencing the U.S. Supreme Court's distinction between social and political equality, a differentiation it made in *Plessy v. Ferguson* in 1896. In that case, the Court declared that while the Constitution protected political equality, such as the right to vote, it did not guarantee social equality—meaning that state laws requiring racial segregation in public places were entirely legal. Of course, such laws did not exist in the northeastern United States, where segregation tended to be de facto (discrimination that occurred in real-life situations) rather than de jure (discrimination stipulated by law), but Briggs's reference to them indicates that he envisioned African Americans in the South eventually joining his Brotherhood.

The third objective of the *Summary* calls for the "fostering of racial self-respect" through increased awareness of the contribution that blacks had made both to "modern civilization" and to the ancient world. Briggs had discussed such contributions at length in *The Crusader*, including notions that Africa was the cradle of civilization and that African people, including Egyptians, had inspired the Greeks. Although Briggs does not elaborate more in his *Summary*, his was clearly a call for Afrocentrism in education, a prescient move, given that black studies departments would not be formed until the late 1960s. Closely tied to this emphasis on education is the eighth point of the *Summary*, which declares that "knowledge is power" and concedes that no racial advancement can occur without overcoming "ignorance." To further the ends of black education, Briggs proposes to send lecturers "throughout America," teaching African Americans, establishing forums, and publishing newspapers.

Even as blacks needed to strive for education, maintains Briggs, so too did they need to unite against the KKK, a white supremacist group that blamed white America's economic and employment woes on the various waves of immigrants—among them blacks, Jews, and European Catholics—to the United States. Both points 4 and 5 of the *Summary* reference the need to counter the Klan, as the terrorist organization experienced a resurgence upon the return of black soldiers to the United States following World War I. The KKK eschewed cities like New York, opting instead to focus its efforts on rural America, where segregationist sentiment had gone wild. But just as Briggs indicates an interest in ending segregation in the American South (for its denial of social equality), so too does he seem interested in aiding African Americans battling the Klan in the Midwest and West.

To fight the Klan, Briggs advocates organizing the "Negro masses" and establishing a federation of black groups capable of presenting a united front. What precisely Briggs thought this united front might do is unclear, though he does indicate an interest in reaching out to other groups targeted by the KKK, particularly Catholics and Jews. Here, Briggs makes sure to emphasize that any potential alliance between blacks, Catholics, and Jews does not necessarily have to compromise his earlier interest in black nationalism, nor, as he points out in the fifth objective of the *Summary*, would it have to compromise black "identity" or "autonomy." Indeed, "not love or hatred," argues Briggs in point 4, "but IDENTITY OF INTERESTS AT THE MOMENT," warranted reaching across racial lines and bringing in white minorities suffering from violence and discrimination.

Although he is adamant that black/white alliances would not compromise the essentially nationalist character of the ABB, Briggs indicates a much greater interest in reaching out to whites than his stated emphasis on Afrocentrism seems to indicate. In the ninth section of the *Summary*, for example, Briggs calls both for "fellowship and coordination" with "other dark races," presumably people of Asian and South American descent, as well as with "truly class-conscious white workers." Here, Briggs's Communism arguably shines through his racial nationalism, indicating a potentially subversive aspect of his ABB agenda. While it is couched in nationalist terms of blood that might have attracted Garveyites, Briggs's *Summary* could easily have been an attempt to rob Garvey of support, diverting his sheep into the Communist fold. Only white Communists, after all, would be "truly class-conscious," a perspective that Garvey, a black capitalist, did not value.

Further indication of Briggs's dissatisfaction with Garvey was his notion that political struggles and business ventures needed to be kept separate. In objective 6 of the *Summary*, Briggs makes it clear that "individual and corporation enterprises" should not be joined with "mass movements." In all likelihood this was an allusion to Garvey's Black Star Line of ships, funded through the donations of poor black Harlemites, with the ultimate goal of linking blacks throughout the Atlantic world. Ruined by mismanagement and inadequate funding, Garvey's cruise line probably disturbed Briggs, both for its reliance on the meager funds of the black poor and its similarity to a capitalist business venture. Instead, Briggs advocated the endorsement of "cooperative enterprises"—not large-scale business ventures, but grassroots organizations that directly benefited the participants.

For blacks caught up in big business, Briggs recommends "industrial unionism," another indication of his Communist leanings. Well aware of the discrimination that black workers suffered at the hands of white-dominated unions, Briggs calls not for the formation of separate, black unions, but rather for the reform of white unions corrupted by greedy, manipulative employers. In point 7, Briggs alludes to a potential alliance between blacks and whites, particularly those "radical and progressive" white union leaders who promised to lead the charge in labor reform.

Audience

The *Summary of the Program and Aims of the African Blood Brotherhood* targeted several audiences. First, it

Essential Quotes

> "The Negroes in the United States—both native and foreign born—are destined to play a vital part in a powerful world movement for Negro liberation."
>
> (1)

> "Not love or hatred, but IDENTITY OF INTERESTS AT THE MOMENT, dictates the tactics of practical people."
>
> (4)

> "For the purpose of waging an effective struggle and weakening our enemies wherever possible, we must (a) establish fellowship and coordination of action within the darker masses and (b) between these masses and the truly class-conscious White Workers who seek the abolition of human exploitation."
>
> (9)

sought to sway African Americans in the urban North, the very same blacks who might be tempted to join Marcus Garvey's Universal Negro Improvement Association. Although Briggs and Garvey had not finalized their ideological split by 1920, Briggs's criticism of merging protest with business, something that Garvey succeeded in doing with his Black Star Line, indicates that Briggs hoped to siphon support from Garvey's political machine. Even if blacks did not quit the Universal Negro Improvement Association, for example, they could still work to nudge it away from capitalism and toward Briggs's Socialist nationalism. Only later would Briggs and Garvey become open enemies, decrying one another in the public sphere.

Other targets of Briggs included African Americans in the South and the West. The *Summary*'s opposition to lynching—a largely southern phenomenon—promised to win support from African Americans in the South, even as Briggs's opposition to the KKK promised to extend the reach of the ABB to the Midwest and West, particularly as the Klan spread its membership to western states like Oregon.

Finally, Briggs's *Summary* appealed to Communists. Although he was interested in black nationalism, Briggs made it clear that an interracial alliance between blacks and "truly class-conscious White Workers" would only help black interests, an appeal that inspired young, black Communists like the writer Claude McKay to merge racial nationalism with Soviet internationalism. Anyone interested in rethinking the boundaries of nationhood, in de-coupling them from geography and linking them to ethnic or racial identity, joined the intended audience of Briggs's *Summary of the Program and Aims of the African Blood Brotherhood*.

Impact

One of the first documents to articulate a pan-African national identity, Cyril Briggs's *Summary of the Program and Aims of the African Blood Brotherhood* had a profound, if subtle, effect on theories of race formation in twentieth-century America. To take just a few examples, Briggs did much to inspire the Communist position that African Americans should form their own nation in the Deep South, a surprising position that became official Soviet policy in 1928. Soviets learned of Briggs's views thanks to the Harlem Renaissance poet Claude McKay, a black Communist who joined the ABB before traveling to Moscow in 1922. Inspired by Briggs, McKay used his position as a reporter for the radical newspaper *The Liberator* to arrange interviews between Briggs and white Communists in New York, hoping to cobble together an interracial Left. When McKay arrived in the Soviet Union in 1922, he was hailed as a hero, toasted by Russian Communist leader Leon Trotsky, and made an honorary member of the Moscow government hierarchy. From this position, McKay successfully spread Briggs's views to the highest echelons of Soviet leadership.

While protégés like McKay spread his views abroad, Briggs's ideas also prefigured black politics at home. Writing at the same time as many of the luminaries of the Harlem Renaissance, Briggs contributed to the then-radical notion that African American culture was unique and valuable and that African civilization itself predated and in many cases prefigured European civilization. Such claims not only coincided with the New Negro Movement but also foreshadowed the explosion of Afrocentrism that would emerge in the United States following the devolution of the civil rights movement in the 1960s.

Briggs's emphasis on the distinctive nature and contribution of black culture to Western civilization would become a core axiom of black nationalism, foreshadowing the formation of African American studies departments at colleges across the United States in the 1960s and 1970s. By the close of the twentieth century, prominent black scholars such as Cornel West were advocating a merger of black culture and Socialism reminiscent of Briggs, while scholars such as Paul Gilroy were reframing the concept of black studies around a transnational, diasporic portrait of people of African descent across the Atlantic world, much like Briggs had advocated. Even Briggs's emphasis on the African roots of Western civilization reemerged as a topic of intense scholarly debate in the 1980s and 1990s, following the publication of Cornell University historian Martin Bernal's book *Black Athena*. Although it was criticized by some, the book presented a case very similar to the one that Briggs had endorsed in 1920, suggesting that much of Greek culture came from Egypt.

See also *Plessy v. Ferguson* (1896); Marcus Garvey: "The Principles of the Universal Negro Improvement Association" (1922); Alain Locke's "Enter the New Negro" (1925); Stokely Carmichael's "Black Power" (1966).

Further Reading

■ Articles

Bourne, Randolph S. "Trans-National America." *Atlantic Monthly* 118, no. 1 (July 1916): 86–97.

Briggs, Cyril. "The American Race Problem." *The Crusader* 1, nos. 1–4 (September–December 1918). Available online. Marxists Internet Archive. http://www.marxists.org/history/usa/groups/abb/1918/0900-briggs-amraceproblem.pdf.

Guterl, Matthew Pratt. "The New Race Consciousness: Race, Nation, and Empire in American Culture, 1910–1925." *Journal of World History* 10, no. 307 (1999): 307–352.

Stephens, Michelle A. "Black Transnationalism and the Politics of National Identity: West Indian Intellectuals in Harlem in the Age of War and Revolution." *American Quarterly* 50, no. 3 (September 1998): 592–608.

■ Books

Gilroy, Paul. *The Black Atlantic: Modernity and Double Consciousness*. Cambridge, Mass.: Harvard University Press, 1993.

Grant, Madison. *The Passing of the Great Race; or, The Racial Basis of European History*. New York: Scribner's, 1921.

Maxwell, William J. *New Negro, Old Left: African American Writing and Communism between the Wars*. New York: Columbia University Press, 1999.

Solomon, Mark. *The Cry Was Unity: Communists and African Americans, 1917–1936*. Oxford: University of Mississippi Press, 1998.

Questions for Further Study

1. To what extent would Cyril Briggs have approved of Eldridge Cleaver's "Education and Revolution," written in 1969?

2. Using this document in connection with Martin R. Delany's *The Condition, Elevation, Emigration, and Destiny of the Colored People of the United States* (1852) and such documents as Malcolm X's "After the Bombing" speech (1965) and Stokely Carmichael's "Black Power" (1967), trace the history of black nationalism in the United States. Do you believe that black nationalism is still a potent force in the twenty-first century? Why or why not?

3. What impact did the events surrounding World War I have on Briggs and on the black nationalist movement?

4. What objections did Briggs and the African Blood Brotherhood have to capitalism? What was the appeal of Communism to the brotherhood?

5. What do you think the attitude of W. E. B. Du Bois (*The Souls of Black Folk*) and Alain Locke ("Enter the New Negro") would have been to Briggs's *Summary*? Why?

Van Deburg, William L., ed. *Modern Black Nationalism: From Marcus Garvey to Louis Farrakhan*. New York: New York University Press, 1997.

West, Cornel. "Marxist Theory and the Specificity of Afro-American Oppression." In *Marxism and the Interpretation of Culture*, ed. Cary Nelson and Lawrence Grossberg, Urbana: University of Illinois Press, 1988.

▪ Web Sites

"Early American Marxism." marxisthistory.org Web site. http://www.marxisthistory.org/subject/usa/eam/index.html.

—Anders Walker

Cyril Briggs's Summary of the Program and Aims of the African Blood Brotherhood

1) **A Liberated Race**—in the United States, Africa, and elsewhere. Liberated not merely from alien political rule, but also from the crushing weight of exploitation, which keeps the many in degrading poverty that the few may wallow in stolen wealth. The Negroes in the United States—both native and foreign born—are destined to play a vital part in a powerful world movement for Negro liberation. Just as the Negro in the United States can never hope to win genuine equality with his white neighbors under the system of exploitation, so, too, a free Africa is impossible until commercial exploitation is abolished. The ABB proposes (1) to develop and organize the political and economic strength of the Negro in the North for the purpose of eliminating peonage, disfranchisement, etc., in the South and raising the status of the Negro in that section of the country, and (2) to organize the national strength of the entire Negro group in America for the purpose of extending moral and financial aid and, where necessary, leadership to our blood-brothers on the continent of Africa and in Haiti and the West Indies in their struggle against white capitalist exploitation.

2) **Absolute Race Equality.** In this question are inextricably bound the issues of Political Equality, Social Equality, and Economic Equality. Let one be denied and the whole principle of racial equality is denied.

3) **The Fostering of Racial Self-Respect** by the dissemination of the true facts concerning the Negro's contributions to modern civilization and the predominant party played in the ancient world by the African peoples.

4) **Organized and Uncompromising Opposition to the Ku Klux Klan** and all other movements or tendencies inimical to the true interests of the Negro masses. To effectively oppose the bigotry and prejudice of the Ku Klux Klan we must (a) organize the Negro masses; (b) create a strong Negro Federation out of the existing organizations that we may present a United Front; and (c) for the purpose of fighting the Klan ally ourselves with all groups opposed to its vicious activities, viz: the workers, particularly the Jewish workers and the Catholic workers, at whom, with the Negro, the Klan's activities are especially directed. As for the purpose of throwing off our oppression, the enemies of the Imperialist system are our natural allies by virtue of being in the same camp and opposed to the same enemy, so the enemies of the Klan are our friends in that they fight the foe we fight. The Negro masses must get out of their minds the stupid idea that it is necessary for two groups to love each other before they can enter into an alliance against their common enemy. Not love or hatred, but IDENTITY OF INTERESTS AT THE MOMENT, dictates the tactics of practical people.

5) **A United Negro Front** with which to oppose the Ku Klux Klan and all other organizations and tendencies antagonistic to the Negro. This can be done only by bringing all Negro organizations into a Federation with a program to which any serious and intelligent Negro organization could subscribe. Their identity would not be lost. Their autonomy practically unimpaired. And the race organized and effective for the first time in its history.

6) **Industrial Development** along genuine cooperative lines whereby the benefits will be equally distributed among the masses participating, and not appropriated by a few big stockholders and dishonest and inefficient officials drawing exorbitant salaries. The ABB is sternly opposed to the foisting of individual and corporation enterprises upon mass movements for the reason that (a) such procedure is manifestly dishonest and misleading. Enterprises supported by mass movements should be of such a nature as to equally benefit everyone in the movement, not merely a handful of officials; (b) the ABB does not consider any commercial enterprise good enough to base the sacred Liberation Movement upon the mere chances of success or failure. No movement so based can long survive the collapse of its commercial enterprises. We believe in fostering and encouraging cooperative enterprises that will benefit the many rather than the few, but without basing the movement upon them.

7) **Higher Wages for Negro Labor, Shorter Hours, and Better Living Conditions.** To gain for Negro Labor the full reward of its toil and to prevent exploitation either on the job or at the source of supplies we must encourage industrial unionism among our people and at the same time fight to break down the prejudice in the unions which is stimulated and

Document Text

encouraged by the employers. This prejudice is already meeting the attack of the radical and progressive element among white union men and must eventually give way before the united onslaught of Black and White Workers. Wherever it is found impossible to enter the existing labor unions, independent unions should be formed, that Negro labor be enabled to protect its interests.

8) **Education**. That "Knowledge is Power" was never more true than today when on every hand it is being demonstrated that races or groups advance by virtue of their acquirement of knowledge or lag behind because of their failure to overcome ignorance. The ABB proposes to send lecturers throughout America, establish forums, newspapers, etc., etc.

9) **Cooperation with Other Darker Races and with the Class-Conscious White Workers**. For the purpose of waging an effective struggle and weakening our enemies wherever possible, we must (a) establish fellowship and coordination of action within the darker masses and (b) between these masses and the truly class-conscious White Workers who seek the abolition of human exploitation.

The ABB submits the above summary of its program and aims, confident that it will receive the earnest attention of the race and that it will earn their active support.

Glossary

Ku Klux Klan	formed in the wake of the Civil War, a group that promoted white supremacy through lynching, violence, and intimidation
peonage	a system by which debtors can pay off their debt by working for their creditors

A Ku Klux Klan parade down Pennsylvania Avenue in Washington, D.C., in the mid-1920s (Library of Congress)

Walter F. White: "The Eruption of Tulsa"

1921

"All that was lacking to make the scene a replica of modern 'Christian' warfare was poison gas."

Overview

The race riot in Tulsa, Oklahoma, of May 31–June 1, 1921, "the night Tulsa died," stands as one of the more disgraceful episodes in American history. Among its first chroniclers was Walter F. White, whose article "The Eruption of Tulsa" appeared in *The Nation* magazine on July 29 that year. The riot was sparked by a rumor of a sexual assault that was picked up by a city newspaper. Events quickly spiraled out of control as mobs gathered. On the night of May 31 and continuing until noon the following day, gangs of white and black citizens waged open warfare on one another, with white gangs shooting black citizens in public and torching and vandalizing homes and businesses in Tulsa's black Greenwood district. Roughly thirty-five blocks in Greenwood, including more than twelve hundred homes and numerous businesses, were destroyed by fire, and some ten thousand people were left homeless. Although the official death toll was put at thirty-nine, few who have studied the event, including White, believe this figure. According to an American Red Cross investigation, the number was at least three hundred, and some investigators place the number much higher, perhaps in the thousands. Suspicions remain that many of those killed in the rioting were buried in mass graves.

Context

The broad context for the Tulsa race riot was the legacy of slavery in the United States and the complex racial politics of the post–Civil War era, when so-called Black Codes enforced racial segregation and a crucial U.S. Supreme Court case, *Plessy v. Ferguson* (1896), provided legal justification for segregation. But in the early years of the twentieth century, several more specific developments conspired to create the conditions that would erupt in violence in Tulsa. White alludes to many of these conditions in his article.

One development was the reemergence of the Ku Klux Klan. The Klan had been formed in 1866 in Tennessee and in the ensuing years opposed Reconstruction in the South and launched efforts to deny African Americans their rights under the Civil Rights Act of 1866 and other legislation.

The Klan's power ebbed in later decades as many of its leaders were arrested, tried, and convicted for crimes against African Americans. The Klan experienced a rebirth after 1915, however, in part because of the enormous popularity of D. W. Griffith's film *The Birth of a Nation*, based on a 1905 book by Thomas Dixon titled *The Clansman*. The movie, still considered a classic for its technical brilliance if not its message, romanticized the Klan by depicting its members as defenders of a white American way of life and portraying African Americans as drunkards and rapists.

By the early 1920s the Klan had some three million members, many of them prominent representatives of the middle class, and the group successfully influenced the election of public officials in Indiana, Oregon, and other states, including Oklahoma. In Tulsa, numerous judges, lawyers, doctors, teachers, entertainers, bankers, and businessmen were Klan members. The Klan and its sympathizers enforced their views through violence and intimidation, particularly lynching. The actions of lynch mobs are often thought of as spontaneous outbreaks of violence, but in fact many were planned events, with newspapers announcing their time and place, agents selling train tickets to the sites, and families packing picnic lunches to watch the gruesome spectacles. This lynch-mob mentality would play a major role in the Tulsa riot.

A second development was the newfound voice of the African American community. In 1905 black leaders began the Niagara Movement to combat segregation, disenfranchisement, and lynchings. The movement gained prominence in 1908 after a race riot broke out in Springfield, Illinois, when a white woman claimed that a black man had tried to rape her—a charge she later recanted. These and other events led to the formation of the National Association for the Advancement of Colored People (NAACP) in 1909. At roughly the same time, Marcus Garvey, a black nationalist, was gaining prominence as the founder of the Universal Negro Improvement Association, which by the early 1920s boasted nearly a million members and was the largest nonreligious black organization in the United States. Garvey's central message was one of black pride and self-help—the belief that only blacks could improve their own condition through enterprise. Then, in 1919, the African Blood Brotherhood, a black liberation and self-

Time Line

1901
- Oil is first discovered near Tulsa, Oklahoma, laying the foundation for black economic prosperity.

1908
- **August**
  Racial violence erupts in Springfield, Illinois, after a white woman claims that she was raped by a black man.

1909
- **February 12**
  The National Association for the Advancement of Colored People is formed in part as a response to the Springfield riot.

1917
- **April 6**
  The United States declares war on Germany, entering World War I; four hundred thousand African Americans serve in the military during the war.

1918
- **November 11**
  The armistice ending hostilities of World War I is signed.

1919
- **May 10**
  Racial violence breaks out in Charleston, South Carolina, beginning the "Red Summer" of 1919; racial riots erupt in numerous U.S. cities into October.

1921
- **May 31**
  The Tulsa race riot erupts, continuing into June 1.
- **July 29**
  Walter F. White publishes "The Eruption of Tulsa" in *The Nation*.

1997
- **April**
  Oklahoma House Joint Resolution 1035 creates the Oklahoma Commission to Study the Tulsa Race Riot of 1921.

---

defense organization with ties to the Communist Party, was formed. Many white Americans looked on these developments with trepidation.

This emphasis on black economic development would play a role in the Tulsa riot. Many African Americans were leaving the Deep South to find greater economic opportunity in the North and Midwest, often placing themselves in competition with whites for jobs at a time when the nation was experiencing unemployment, inflation, and a sharp economic downturn. (The U.S. gross domestic product—the total value of goods and services—was just shy of $90 billion in 1920; in 1921 the figure was down to $74 billion.) Many black Oklahomans were enjoying some measure of prosperity because of the state's oil boom, which had begun in 1901 with the discovery of oil in the state, accelerated after 1905 with further oil strikes, and in the span of just two decades turned Tulsa from a backwater village into a thriving city. The Greenwood section of northeast Tulsa was a prosperous black commercial and residential district—so prosperous that the black leader Booker T. Washington called it the "Negro Wall Street." The relative affluence in Tulsa's black district, with its groceries, restaurants, shops, professional offices, newspapers, churches, hospitals, a library, and even a few millionaires, was a source of racial tension born of jealousy and a belief among many whites that African Americans living in Tulsa's "Little Africa" did not know their "proper" place.

A third development was World War I. After the United States declared war on Germany in April 1917, the administration of President Woodrow Wilson did a masterly job of convincing Americans that war was the only option. They responded enthusiastically to his calls for sacrifice. But one of the side effects of the war was an exaggerated patriotism. Anyone who looked different, spoke with an accent, or had a German name was looked on with suspicion. The wave of immigration to the United States that preceded the war—immigration from such places as Italy, eastern Europe, and Russia—contributed to a growing sense that America was being "overrun" by potentially subversive elements. The Russian Revolution of 1917 did not help, for many Americans feared that Communists were infiltrating the United States. Labor unrest in the years immediately after World War I was ascribed to Jews, Bolsheviks (Communists), and people who were not white and not Protestant; radical labor organizations often targeted disaffected African Americans for recruitment. In this climate, Tulsa's African American community was barely tolerated prior to the night of May 31, 1921.

Adding to the resentment and climate of hostility was the large number of race riots that had taken place in the war's immediate aftermath—when some blacks were lynched while still wearing their military uniforms and ships bearing blacks returning from the war were attacked by mobs. Tensions ran particularly high in 1919. Between May and October, racial violence broke out in at least thirty-four American cities—a period that the African American author and NAACP director James Weldon Johnson called the Red Summer of 1919. Many of these riots were relatively small in scale, but others—in Charleston, South Carolina; Longview, Texas; Philadelphia, Pennsylvania; Washington, D.C.; Knoxville, Tennessee; Norfolk, Virginia; Omaha, Nebraska; Chicago, Illinois; and Elaine, Arkansas—were major events, with loss of life and widespread property damage. These events, combined with labor agitation and bombings perpetrated by Communists and anarchists, fueled a climate of fear and suspicion that could erupt in violence anywhere.

The fuse in Tulsa was lit on the late afternoon of May 30. A nineteen-year-old shoe shiner named Dick Rowland needed to use a restroom. The only one available for a "colored" person was on the top floor of the nearby Drexel Building in downtown Tulsa. He entered an elevator operated by seventeen-year-old Sarah Page, who was white. It is unclear what exactly happened in the elevator, for no copy of Page's statement to the police exists, but it appears that Rowland may have tripped upon entering the elevator—or may have accidentally stepped on Page's foot—and in an effort to regain his balance, he threw out his hand and grabbed her arm. Another version of the story is that Page somehow slipped, and Rowland reached out to steady her. In either case, Page apparently cried out. A clerk in a clothing store on the first floor of the building heard the cry, saw a young black man hurriedly leaving the building, found Page in a distraught frame of mind, and summoned the police. The police did not regard the incident as serious, but the following morning they pursued Rowland to his mother's home in Greenwood and took him to the Tulsa County Courthouse for questioning.

Matters might have ended there, but in its afternoon edition of May 31 the *Tulsa Tribune* ran a story with the headline "Nab Negro for Attacking Girl in an Elevator." The incident, thus, tapped into the "rape myth," common at the time, which perpetuated the notion that white women needed to be protected from black sexual predators. Additionally, the paper ran a second story claiming that a lynch mob was forming, though it is unknown what the paper's source of information was. Interestingly, the second story was removed from the paper's later edition and then removed from its archives; no copy of the story has been found. In response, a crowd of white people began gathering at the courthouse. Many were just curious onlookers, but many others were outraged at what they believed had been an assault on a white woman by a black man. By early evening the growing crowd had all the earmarks of a lynch mob.

Over the next several hours, white and black citizens began arming themselves. Small teams of armed blacks appeared at the courthouse and in the surrounding area, offering to help the sheriff protect Rowland from the mob, but they were turned away. In response to what appeared to be a "Negro uprising," bands of whites took up arms, and the size of the crowd around the courthouse swelled to perhaps two thousand. Sometime after 10:00 PM a shot rang out, sparking gunfire that left several whites and blacks dead on the streets. Matters escalated as bands of whites pursued blacks to the Greenwood section, looting stores for guns and ammunition along the way and attempting to seize weapons from the National Guard armory. Meanwhile, Greenwood's residents were panicking, either gathering weapons or fleeing north away from the city. Throughout the night, groups of whites and blacks fired on each other across the railroad tracks that separated Greenwood from the white part of town. Fires were set in two dozen black-owned businesses at the edge of Greenwood. Some white and Hispanic Tulsans took up arms to come to the defense of the black community, but the sheer number of rioters overwhelmed them.

Matters escalated again after sunup at about 5:00 AM on June 1. White gangs gathered to launch an all-out assault on Greenwood, firing indiscriminately on any blacks who had not yet fled. There were reports that planes were dropping firebombs into the community, and throughout the early morning, fires spread throughout Greenwood. Meanwhile, African Americans, many of them injured, were being held at detention centers, and local hospitals treated some eight hundred people who were injured in the rioting, near-

Time Line

2000
- **February 5**
  The Oklahoma Commission recommends that reparations be paid to the survivors of the Tulsa race riot.

2001
- **February 28**
  The Oklahoma Commission issues its report, *Tulsa Race Riot: A Report by the Oklahoma Commission to Study the Tulsa Race Riot of 1921.*
- **April 7**
  The Tulsa Reparations Commission is formed.

2003
- **April 28**
  A lawsuit on behalf of the survivors of the Tulsa riot is filed in U.S. District Court; the case is dismissed in 2004.

2004
- **June 21**
  The U.S. Tenth Circuit Court of Appeals hears an appeal of the 2003 lawsuit; on September 8 the court rules that the statute of limitations has passed.

2009
- The John Hope Franklin Tulsa-Greenwood Race Riot Claims Accountability bill is introduced to the U.S. Congress.

ly all of them white. People in the city's white section were threatened with violence and vandalism if they did not turn over black cooks and housekeepers to the rioters.

Finally, at about 9:00 AM on June 1, Oklahoma National Guard troops began arriving from Oklahoma City. Tulsa was placed under martial law, and by noon the violence had come to an end. Greenwood, though, was a smoking war zone. On June 7, the Tulsa City Commission passed a fire ordinance saying that the Greenwood commercial district could not be rebuilt, but the district was, in fact, later rebuilt. A grand jury was convened with a view to charging the perpetrators of the riot, but, as quoted in the "Tulsa Race Riot" Web site by Scott Ellsworth, the grand jury concluded that "there was no mob spirit among the whites, no talk of lynching and no arms. The assembly was quiet until the arrival of armed Negroes, which precipitated and was the direct cause of the entire affair." Many white Tulsans were horrified by what had been wrought in their city and opened their homes to homeless blacks, and the American Red Cross provided food and tents for the homeless. But a sense of shame settled over the city, and the Tulsa riot became a largely forgotten event until the 1990s.

About the Author

Walter Francis White, one of the most prominent civil rights leaders of the first half of the twentieth century, was born on July 1, 1893, in Atlanta, Georgia. After graduating from Atlanta University in 1916, he joined the staff of the NAACP in New York City in 1918. He worked under James Weldon Johnson as the NAACP's assistant national secretary until 1931, when he became the executive director—a position he held until his death. Throughout his career, he led the NAACP's fight against discrimination, lynching, disenfranchisement, and segregation. He was instrumental in creating the organization's Legal Defense Fund, which sought equal justice in the courts. He was the motivating force behind President Harry Truman's order to desegregate the military after World War II, and under his direction the Legal Defense Fund led the efforts to erase segregated schooling that culminated in the 1954 U.S. Supreme Court case *Brown v. Board of Education*.

White was the author of numerous essays that appeared in national magazines. During his early years in the NAACP, he investigated lynchings and riots, often traveling incognito to the sites of these events and putting himself in great personal danger in the process, though his ability to "pass" as white because of his light complexion helped gain him access to the police, politicians, and others. In 1919, for example, he traveled to Arkansas to investigate the riot that had taken place in Elaine in October of that year—and fled the town in the face of threats. Seventy-nine African Americans were arrested, tried, and convicted for their role in that riot. As a result of White's efforts, the U.S. Supreme Court eventually overturned the convictions on the ground that armed observers in the courtroom and an armed mob outside the courthouse had a tendency to intimidate the jury.

White was also a prominent figure in the Harlem Renaissance, the flowering of black culture and art that was centered in the Harlem neighborhood of New York City in the 1920s and 1930s. He was the author of several books, including *Fire in the Flint* (1924), *Flight* (1926), *Rope and Faggot* (1929), *A Rising Wind* (1945), and *How Far the Promised Land* (1955). His autobiography, *A Man Called White*, was published in 1948. A novel titled *Blackjack* was left unfinished when he died on March 21, 1955, in New York City.

Explanation and Analysis of the Document

White begins his article by sketching in broad strokes the events that happened in Tulsa. He notes that the incident was sparked by the report of a "hysterical white girl" and suggests that her account of what happened in the elevator was dubious, given that she was of "doubtful reputation" and that the alleged attack occurred in "open daylight" in a city of one hundred thousand people (though he later acknowledges the 1920 U.S. Census figure of seventy-two thousand). White ironically refers to "100-per-cent Americans" who acted on the report without bothering to verify it, causing death and destruction. In the second paragraph, White laments the "grip" that mob violence can have on the "throat of America," where that violence can break out anywhere and at any time.

Beginning with the third paragraph, White traces the backdrop for the event. He provides statistics on Tulsa, including its dramatic population growth and its prosperity as a result of the state's oil boom. In the fifth paragraph he notes that African Americans had shared in the prosperity, to the "bitter resentment" of "the lower order of whites," who believed that the city's African Americans were "presumptuous" in their prosperity. Many of these whites, immigrants from southern states, were themselves "lethargic and unprogressive by nature." White then proceeds to detail that prosperity, noting that Tulsa was home to at least three black millionaires and several others with substantial assets. Because of changes in the value of the dollar from inflation, $25,000 in 1921 is equivalent to about $287,000 today.

White goes on to discuss the supposed "radical" views of Tulsa's black population—and dismisses this belief by noting that the community simply wanted an end to "'Jim-Crow' [railroad] cars, lynching, peonage." "Jim Crow" is the informal name given to laws designed to keep African Americans in subservient positions, such as laws requiring them to ride in separate railroad cars. "Peonage" refers to a system that requires debtors to work for their creditors until the debt is discharged. Although White provides no particulars about peonage, it was well known at the time that many blacks in the surrounding area and throughout Oklahoma were virtual slaves on their own land because of debts owed to the white establishment. White asserts that black efforts to emancipate themselves from these conditions fostered resentment on the part of whites.

The seventh paragraph details the rough-and-tumble nature of life in Tulsa at that time, where justice was as like-

Black detainees are led to the Convention Hall following the race riot in Tulsa, Oklahoma. (AP/Wide World Photos)

ly to be enacted at the end of a gun or noose as in the courtroom. White notes that corruption and vice permeated the city and that large numbers of people were interested not in the community's civic life but in making money and getting away with illegal activities. He claims that 6 percent of the county's residents were under indictment, with little likelihood that their cases would ever come to trial. White provides further startling facts in the eighth paragraph. When a white man charged with murder was lynched, the police directed traffic so that onlookers could get a view of the event. Insurance companies refused to do business in Tulsa because the risk was too great. All of this, in White's view, fostered disrespect for the law among both blacks and whites.

Paragraphs 9 through 12 detail the events of the riot: the incident in the elevator, the newspaper account of the alleged assault, the gathering of a lynch mob and the fears in the black community that Rowland would fall into the hands of the mob, and the escalating violence. White repeats the claim that airplanes were used to drop incendiary bombs on the Greenwood community, a charge that would later be investigated and found to likely have been true. White makes his account more graphic and dramatic by focusing on the fates of individuals, such as an aged couple who were shot in their home and a prominent doctor who was shot to death while being taken to a detention center. This man had been described by the "Mayo brothers" (Charles and William Mayo, famous as the founders of the Mayo Clinics) as "the most able Negro surgeon in America."

In the thirteenth paragraph, White addresses the number of casualties. He rejects the official body count and calls attention to the activities of gravediggers, which suggest that the death toll was much greater than that given by the authorities. He notes that at least some victims of the riot were "incinerated" in their homes and that there were reports of truckloads of bodies being dumped in the nearby Arkansas River, though he acknowledges that this rumor could not be confirmed. In more recent years, the charge that the dead were hastily buried in mass graves has been raised. Some efforts have been made to investigate the matter using archaeological methods, but no systematic search for these graves has been made, and the results have been inconclusive.

In the final paragraph White grows more rhetorical. He refers to the riot's "horrible carnage" and suggests that it was worse than the crimes being ascribed to the "Bolsheviki," or Bolsheviks, referring to the political party in Russia regarded as synonymous with Communism. He uses the word "pogroms," referring to organized or spontaneous rioting directed against a religious or ethnic group and again associated with Russia. White concludes by noting the willingness of Tulsa's black population (which he asserts to be fifteen thousand but which most sources put at ten or eleven thousand) to come to the defense of Dick Rowland, and he suggests that a "nationwide Tulsa" might be necessary to "wake" the United States to racial injustice.

Audience

White's account was published in *The Nation*, which had been founded in 1865 and, in the twenty-first century, remains the oldest continuously published weekly magazine in America. It was founded in New York City at the end of the Civil War to celebrate the North's victory, and throughout its history the magazine has espoused liberal and progressive causes. Thus, White's article would have been read by Americans who likely sympathized with the magazine's stand on such issues as civil rights, imperialism,

Essential Quotes

"[Tulsa's] reign of terror stands as a grim reminder of the grip mob violence has on the throat of America, and the ever-present possibility of devastating race conflicts where least expected."
(Paragraph 2)

"The Negroes of Tulsa and other Oklahoma cities are pioneers; men and women who have dared, men and women who have had the initiative and the courage to pull up stakes in other less-favored States and face hardship in a newer one for the sake of greater eventual progress. That type is ever less ready to submit to insult."
(Paragraph 6)

"All that was lacking to make the scene a replica of modern 'Christian' warfare was poison gas."
(Paragraph 11)

"One story was told me by an eye-witness of five colored men trapped in a burning house. Four burned to death. A fifth attempted to flee, was shot to death as he emerged from the burning structure, and his body was thrown back into the flames. There was an unconfirmed rumor afloat in Tulsa of two truck loads of dead Negroes being dumped into the Arkansas River, but that story could not be confirmed."
(Paragraph 13)

"There is a lesson in the Tulsa affair for every American who fatuously believes that Negroes will always be the meek and submissive creatures that circumstances have forced them to be during the past three hundred years."
(Paragraph 14)

---

war, trade unionism, and other issues of concern to liberals and progressives. During its history, most of its editors have drawn the attention of the FBI and other authorities, who have suspected the magazine of subversive tendencies. It is noteworthy that an African American was able to publish his article in a "white" magazine at a time when the work of African American writers usually appeared in organs published by and for African Americans.

Impact

It is difficult to assess any particular impact that White's article had at the time. The article was one of a flurry of reports about the events in Tulsa, and it was one small piece of the mosaic of efforts on the part of White, the NAACP, and other African American leaders to call the nation's attention to violence and injustice against their race. Ultimately, White's article, along with oral histories of the riot and other documents, would have an effect. For decades, the riot had merited barely a mention in history books, and in Oklahoma the event was seemingly purged from the state's collective memory. Few efforts were made at an official level to right the wrongs done in 1921. Although Greenwood was rebuilt (and became a thriving center for jazz music), most of the African Americans who had lived there fled. In the shadow of the event's utter shamefulness, the riot was forgotten, at least as far as any official commemoration was concerned. But as the seventy-fifth anniversary of the riot approached in 1996, many Oklahomans came to believe that it was time to document the riot and set the record straight. The goal was to improve race relations and, possibly, provide reparations for the riot's survivors and the descendants of those who lost their lives. Approximately 124 survivors were known at that time, 45 of them living in Tulsa. Many of them had been young boys who had passed ammunition to adults attempting to fend off the assaults.

In April 1997, Oklahoma House Joint Resolution 1035 created the Oklahoma Commission to Study the Tulsa Race Riot of 1921. On February 28, 2001, the commission delivered its report, *Tulsa Race Riot: A Report by the Oklahoma Commission to Study the Tulsa Race Riot of 1921*. On one level, the report achieved its aim. The state legislature went on record as accepting moral responsibility for the Tulsa riot. The report created a comprehensive record of the riot, and, in connection with the commission's investigation, numerous books were published, Web sites and physical exhibits about the riot were created, a documentary film titled *Before They Die!* was produced, and the occurrence of the riot was brought to the nation's attention through television and newspaper reports, news radio stories, magazine articles, talk shows, and other documentaries.

The Oklahoma legislature, however, declined to pay reparations. While deploring the events, members of the legislature argued that the state's taxpayers should not be forced to pay reparations for events they did not cause. They further argued that the riot was not the result of government action. Although the sheriff, other local authorities, and the National Guard may have been culpable in failing to prevent the riot or may have been slow to respond, the rioters, the legislature argued, were private citizens, not government actors. In this way they distinguished the matter from the government's payment of reparations to the survivors of the Japanese internment during World War II, an action of the federal government.

The Tulsa Reparations Commission, formed shortly after the report was released in 2001, thought differently. In 2003 the new commission filed suit in U.S. District Court, asking for reparations and naming the city of Tulsa, its police chief and police department, and the state of Oklahoma as defendants. In March 2004, U.S. District Court Judge James O. Ellison dismissed the suit, ruling that the statute of limitations had long passed. Ellison made clear that the event was a horrible tragedy and indicated that he was not happy about his ruling, but the law, he said, gave him no choice. The plaintiffs in the case, led by Harvard lawyer Charles J. Ogletree, Jr., argued that the statute of limitations should run from the time the commission issued its report. Most of the riot's survivors were unaware of the full scope of the riot and had been barred from pursuing legal claims in the past. Ellison rejected this argument.

In response to the district court's ruling, the plaintiffs appealed to the U.S. Tenth Circuit Court of Appeals. The court heard the appeal on June 21, 2004, and issued its ruling on September 8 of that year. The court affirmed the district court's ruling, holding that while the statute of limitations can be recalibrated under extraordinary circumstances, such conditions did not exist in this case. On March 9, 2005, the plaintiffs petitioned the U.S. Supreme Court to hear the case on appeal, but the Court declined to do so. In 2007 the

Questions for Further Study

1. Summarize the social, economic, and political events that laid the foundation for the eruption of violence in Tulsa, Oklahoma.

2. Racial violence was sometimes sparked by competition for jobs, particularly during tough economic times. To what extent were the concerns of labor, sometimes expressed by the radical labor movement, involved in the violence that erupted in Tulsa?

3. Why do you think people in the state of Oklahoma decided to revisit the Tulsa race riot after so many years? Do you believe that doing so was a positive step, or did it just reopen old wounds?

4. What is your position on the issue of paying reparations to the survivors of those affected by the Tulsa riot?

5. Why do you believe that so much racial violence erupted in the wake of World War I?

Tulsa-Greenwood Race Riot Claims Accountability bill was submitted to the U.S. House of Representatives with a view to providing legislative relief to the survivors. After the death of John Hope Franklin, a prominent black historian and the son of one of the riot's survivors, the bill was renamed the John Hope Franklin Tulsa-Greenwood Race Riot Claims Accountability bill of 2009. As of 2010, the bill was in committee in the House of Representatives. Walter F. White's dramatic account of the events in Tulsa became part of the historical record in efforts to heal the wounds the riot opened nearly a century ago.

See also Niagara Movement Declaration of Principles (1905); *Plessy v. Ferguson* (1896); *Brown v. Board of Education* (1954).

Further Reading

■ Books

Brophy, Alfred L. *Reconstructing the Dreamland: The Tulsa Race Riot of 1921: Race, Reparations, and Reconciliation*. New York: Oxford University Press, 2002.

Ellsworth, Scott. *Death in a Promised Land: The Tulsa Race Riot of 1921*. Baton Rouge: Louisiana State University Press, 1982.

Halliburton, R. *The Tulsa Race War of 1921*. San Francisco: R and E Research Associates, 1975.

Hirsch, James S. *Riot and Remembrance: The Tulsa Race War and Its Legacy*. Boston: Houghton Mifflin, 2002.

Hower, Bob, and Maurice Willows. *1921 Tulsa Race Riot and the American Red Cross, "Angels of Mercy."* Tulsa, Okla.: Homestead Press, 1993.

Johnson, Hannibal B. *Black Wall Street: From Riot to Renaissance in Tulsa's Historic Greenwood District*. Austin, Tex.: Eakin Press, 1998.

Madigan, Tim. *The Burning: Massacre, Destruction, and the Tulsa Race Riot of 1921*. New York: St. Martin's Press, 2001.

Parrish, Mary E. Jones. *Race Riot 1921: Events of the Tulsa Disaster*. Tulsa, Okla.: Out on a Limb Publishers, 1998.

Williams, Lee E., and Lee E. Williams II. *Anatomy of Four Race Riots: Racial Conflict in Knoxville, Elaine (Arkansas), Tulsa, and Chicago, 1919–1921*. Hattiesburg: University and College Press of Mississippi, 1972.

■ Web Sites

Ellsworth, Scott. "The Tulsa Race Riot." Tulsa Reparations Coalition Web site.
http://www.tulsareparations.org/TulsaRiot.htm.

"Tulsa Race Riot." Oklahoma Historical Society "Encyclopedia of Oklahoma History and Culture" Web site.
http://digital.library.okstate.edu/encyclopedia/entries/T/TU013.html.

University of Tulsa, McFarlin Library, "Tulsa Race Riot of 1921 Archive—Photographs" Web site.
http://www.lib.utulsa.edu/Speccoll/collections/RaceRiot/indexphotos.htm.

—Michael J. O'Neal

Walter F. White: "The Eruption of Tulsa"

A hysterical white girl related that a nineteen-year-old colored boy attempted to assault her in the public elevator of a public office building of a thriving town of 100,000 in open daylight. Without pausing to find whether or not the story was true, without bothering with the slight detail of investigating the character of the woman who made the outcry (as a matter of fact, she was of exceedingly doubtful reputation), a mob of 100-per-cent Americans set forth on a wild rampage that cost the lives of fifty white men; of between 150 and 200 colored men, women and children; the destruction by fire of $1,500,000 worth of property; the looting of many homes; and everlasting damage to the reputation of the city of Tulsa and the State of Oklahoma.

This, in brief, is the story of the eruption of Tulsa on the night of May 31 and the morning of June 1. One could travel far and find few cities where the likelihood of trouble between the races was as little thought of as in Tulsa. Her reign of terror stands as a grim reminder of the grip mob violence has on the throat of America, and the ever-present possibility of devastating race conflicts where least expected.

Tulsa is a thriving, bustling, enormously wealthy town of between 90,000 and 100,000. In 1910 it was the home of 18,182 souls, a dead and hopeless outlook ahead. Then oil was discovered. The town grew amazingly. On December 29, 1920, it had bank deposits totaling $65,449,985.90; almost $1,000 per capita when compared with the Federal Census figures of 1920, which gave Tulsa 72,076. The town lies in the center of the oil region and many are the stories told of the making of fabulous fortunes by men who were operating on a shoe-string. Some of the stories rival those of the "forty-niners" in California. The town has a number of modern office buildings, many beautiful homes, miles of clean, well-paved streets, and aggressive and progressive business men who well exemplify Tulsa's motto of "The City with a Personality."

So much for the setting. What are the causes of the race riot that occurred in such a place?

First, the Negro in Oklahoma has shared in the sudden prosperity that has come to many of his white brothers, and there are some colored men there who are wealthy. This fact has caused a bitter resentment on the part of the lower order of whites, who feel that these colored men, members of an "inferior race," are exceedingly presumptuous in achieving greater economic prosperity than they who are members of a divinely ordered superior race. There are at least three colored persons in Oklahoma who are worth a million dollars each; J. W. Thompson of Clearview is worth $500,000; there are a number of men and women worth $100,000; and many whose possessions are valued at $25,000 and $50,000 each. This was particularly true of Tulsa, where there were two colored men worth $150,000 each; two worth $100,000; three $50,000; and four who were assessed at $25,000. In one case where a colored man owned and operated a printing plant with $25,000 worth of printing machinery in it, the leader of the mob that set fire to and destroyed the plant was a linotype operator employed for years by the colored owner at $48 per week. The white man was killed while attacking the plant. Oklahoma is largely populated by pioneers from other States. Some of the white pioneers are former residents of Mississippi, Georgia, Tennessee, Texas, and other States more typically southern than Oklahoma. These have brought with them their anti-Negro prejudices. Lethargic and unprogressive by nature, it sorely irks them to see Negroes making greater progress than they themselves are achieving.

One of the charges made against the colored men in Tulsa is that they were "radical." Questioning the whites more closely regarding the nature of this radicalism, I found it means that Negroes were uncompromisingly denouncing "Jim-Crow" [railroad] cars, lynching, peonage; in short, were asking that the Federal constitutional guaranties of "life, liberty, and the pursuit of happiness" be given regardless of color. The Negroes of Tulsa and other Oklahoma cities are pioneers; men and women who have dared, men and women who have had the initiative and the courage to pull up stakes in other less-favored States and face hardship in a newer one for the sake of greater eventual progress. That type is ever less ready to submit to insult. Those of the whites who seek to maintain the old white group control naturally do not relish seeing Negroes emancipating themselves from the old system.

A third cause was the rotten political conditions in Tulsa. A vice ring was in control of the city, allowing open operation of houses of ill fame, of gambling joints, the illegal sale of whiskey, the robbing of banks and stores, with hardly a slight possibility of the arrest of the criminals, and even less of their conviction. For fourteen years Tulsa has been in the absolute control of this element. Most of the better element, and there is a large percentage of Tulsans who can properly be classed as such, are interested solely in making money and getting away. They have taken little or no interest in the election of city or county officials, leaving it to those whose interest it was to secure officials who would protect them in their vice operations. About two months ago the State legislature assigned two additional judges to Tulsa County to aid the present two in clearing the badly clogged dockets. These judges found more than six thousand cases awaiting trial. Thus in a county of approximately 100,000 population, six out of every one hundred citizens were under indictment for some sort of crime, with little likelihood of trial in any of them.

Last July a white man by the name of Roy Belton, accused of murdering a taxicab driver, was taken from the county jail and lynched. According to the statements of many prominent Tulsans, local police officers directed traffic at the scene of the lynching, trying to afford every person present an equal chance to view the event. Insurance companies refuse to give Tulsa merchants insurance on their stocks; the risk is too great. There have been so many automobile thefts that a number of companies have canceled all policies on care in Tulsa. The net result of these conditions was that practically none of the citizens of the town, white or colored, had very much respect for the law.

So much for the general causes. What was the spark that set off the blaze? On Monday, May 30, a white girl by the name of Sarah Page, operating an elevator in the Drexel Building, stated that Dick Rowland, a nineteen-year-old colored boy, had attempted criminally to assault her. Her second story was that the boy had seized her arm as he entered the elevator. She screamed. He ran. It was found afterwards that the boy had stepped by accident on her foot. It seems never to have occurred to the citizens of Tulsa that any sane person attempting criminally to assault a woman would have picked any place in the world rather than an open elevator in a public building with scores of people within calling distance. The story of the alleged assault was published Tuesday afternoon by the Tulsa Tribune, one of the two local newspapers. At four o'clock Commissioner of Police J. M. Adkison reported to Sheriff [Willard] McCullough that there was talk of lynching Rowland that night. Chief of Police John A. Gustafson, Captain Wilkerson of the Police Department, Edwin F. Barnett, managing editor of the Tulsa Tribune, and numerous other citizens all stated that there was talk Tuesday of lynching the boy.

In the meantime the news of the threatened lynching reached the colored settlement where Tulsa's 15,000 colored citizens lived. Remembering how a white man had been lynched after being taken from the same jail where the colored boy was now confined, they feared that Rowland was in danger. A group of colored men telephoned the sheriff and proffered their services in protecting the jail from attack. The sheriff told them that they would be called upon if needed. About nine o'clock that night a crowd of white men gathered around the jail, numbering about 400 according to Sheriff McCullough. At 9:15 [PM] the report reached "Little Africa" that the mob had stormed the jail. A crowd of twenty-five armed Negroes set out immediately, but on reaching the jail found the report untrue. The sheriff talked with them, assured them that the boy would not be harmed, and urged them to return to their homes. They left, later returning, 75 strong. The sheriff persuaded them to leave. As they complied, a white man attempted to disarm one of the colored men. A shot was fired, and then—in the words of the sheriff—"all hell broke loose." There was a fusillade of shots from both sides and twelve men fell dead—two of them colored, ten white. The fighting continued until midnight when the colored men, greatly outnumbered, were forced back to their section of the town.

Around five o'clock Wednesday morning the [white] mob, now numbering more than 10,000, made a mass attack on Little Africa. Machine-guns were brought into use; eight aeroplanes were employed to spy on the movements of the Negroes and according to some were used in bombing the colored section. All that was lacking to make the scene a replica of modern "Christian" warfare was poison gas. The colored men and women fought gamely in defense of their homes, but the odds were too great. According to the statements of onlookers, men in uniform, either home guards or ex-service men or both, carried cans of oil into Little Africa, and, after looting the homes, set fire to them. Many are the stories of horror told to me—not by colored people— but by white residents. One was that of an aged colored couple, saying their evening prayers before retiring in their little home on Greenwood Avenue. A mob broke into the house, shot both of the old peo-

Document Text

ple in the backs of their heads, blowing their brains out and spattering them over the bed, pillaged the home, and then set fire to it.

Another was that of the death of Dr. A. C. Jackson, a colored physician. Dr. Jackson was worth $100,000; had been described by the Mayo brothers "the most able Negro surgeon in America"; was respected by white and colored people alike, and was in every sense a good citizen. A mob attacked Dr. Jackson's home. He fought in defense of it, his wife and children and himself. An officer of the home guards who knew Dr. Jackson came up at that time and assured him that if he would surrender he would be protected. This Dr. Jackson did. The officer sent him under guard to Convention Hall, where colored people were being placed for protection. En route to the hall, disarmed, Dr. Jackson was shot and killed in cold blood. The officer who had assured Dr. Jackson of protection stated to me, "Dr. Jackson was an able, clean-cut man. He did only what any red-blooded man would have done under similar circumstances in defending his home. Dr. Jackson was murdered by white ruffians."

It is highly doubtful if the exact number of casualties will ever be known. The figures originally given in the press estimate the number at 100. The number buried by local undertakers and given out by city officials is ten white and twenty-one colored. For obvious reasons these officials wish to keep the number published as low as possible, but the figures obtained in Tulsa are far higher. Fifty whites and between 150 and 200 Negroes is much nearer the actual number of deaths. Ten whites were killed during the first hour of fighting on Tuesday night. Six white men drove into the colored section in a car on Wednesday morning and never came out. Thirteen whites were killed between 5:30 AM and 6:30 AM Wednesday. O. T. Johnson, commandant of the Tulsa Citadel of the Salvation Army, stated that on Wednesday and Thursday the Salvation Army fed thirty-seven Negroes employed as grave diggers and twenty on Friday and Saturday. During the first two days these men dug 120 graves in each of which a dead Negro was buried. No coffins were used. The bodies were dumped into the holes and covered over with dirt. Added to the number accounted for were numbers of others—men, women, and children—who were incinerated in the burning houses in the Negro settlement. One story was told me by an eyewitness of five colored men trapped in a burning house. Four burned to death. A fifth attempted to flee, was shot to death as he emerged from the burning structure, and his body was thrown back into the flames. There was an unconfirmed rumor afloat in Tulsa of two truck loads of dead Negroes being dumped into the Arkansas River, but that story could not be confirmed.

What is America going to do after such a horrible carnage—one that for sheer brutality and murderous anarchy cannot be surpassed by any of the crimes now being charged to the Bolsheviki in Russia? How much longer will America allow these pogroms to continue unchecked? There is a lesson in the Tulsa affair for every American who fatuously believes that Negroes will always be the meek and submissive creatures that circumstances have forced them to be during the past three hundred years. Dick Rowland was only an ordinary bootblack with no standing in the community. But when his life was threatened by a mob of whites, every one of the 15,000 Negroes of Tulsa, rich and poor, educated and illiterate, was willing to die to protect Dick Rowland. Perhaps America is waiting for a nationwide Tulsa to wake her. Who knows?

Glossary

Bolsheviki	usually spelled Bolsheviks, referring to the political party in Russia regarded as synonymous with Communism
Citadel	the name given to any church building used by the Salvation Army
forty-niners	gold prospectors who migrated to California during the gold rush of 1849
Mayo brothers	Charles and William Mayo, famous as the founders of the Mayo Clinic
peonage	a system that requires debtors to work for their creditors until the debt is discharged
pogroms	organized or spontaneous rioting directed against a religious or ethnic group, usually associated with Communist Russia

Marcus Garvey (Library of Congress)

Marcus Garvey: "The Principles of the Universal Negro Improvement Association"

"We represent a new line of thought among Negroes."

Overview

Long before the term *Black Power* became a rallying cry for dispossessed communities throughout the African diaspora, the noted Jamaican activist Marcus Mosiah Garvey gained international recognition for opposing power arrangements that adversely affected the life chances and experiences of African-descended peoples. Presenting universal truths that transcended geographical, class, and national boundaries, Garvey built a global, Pan-African movement that galvanized blacks from the dirt roads of Clarksdale, Mississippi, to the impoverished streets of Kingston, Jamaica. No small factor in Garvey's massive appeal was the self-determinist impulse, a dominant theme in his classic 1922 speech "The Principles of the Universal Negro Improvement Association" (UNIA). Over the course of this energetic and impassioned address, which Garvey delivered in New York City on November 25, 1922, the UNIA leader assails the arrogance of white privilege, decries those who embrace a politics of apathy, and reminds his followers of the transformative power of self-love and self-respect. Three important aspects of the UNIA political agenda can be gauged from this text: the strong emphasis Garvey placed on the need for blacks both to pursue a political agenda independent of whites and to engage in the politics of statecraft and nation building and the strong humanist impulse undergirding the Garvey movement.

Context

Commonly referred to as the New Negro era, the 1920s was a time of great political and cultural upheaval in black America. The massive migration of southern blacks to the urban North, the explosion of artistic expression associated with the Harlem Renaissance, and the meteoric rise of Marcus Garvey's UNIA transformed the contours of black political thought, as well as African Americans' and West Indians' expectations of what was politically possible in the contemporary world. No leader benefited more from the growing militancy of African Americans than Marcus Garvey. To capture the attention of black Americans disgruntled that their sacrifices during World War I had not brought racial democracy to the United States or the rest of the West, Garvey preached a message of race pride, Pan-African unity, and self-determination. Transformative change for people of African descent, he regularly informed his followers, could be achieved only through their own initiatives. "It is of no use for the Negro," Garvey once remarked (as quoted in *Marcus Garvey Papers*), "to continue to depend on the good graces of the other races of the world, because we are living in a selfish, material age, when each and every race is looking out for itself." Toward the goal of empowering his race, Garvey organized the UNIA, formed various economic cooperatives and initiatives, hosted international conventions, and started a newspaper, *The Negro World*, with a large readership that spanned the globe. Such endeavors gave Garvey a huge following, particularly in the United States, where hundreds of thousands of African Americans and West Indians championed his program.

Garvey's message, though, was not entirely new. In the nineteenth century, one of the earliest proponents of black nationalism was Henry Highland Garnett, an abolitionist and orator who supported the emigration of African Americans to Mexico, the West Indies, or the African nation of Liberia. At about the same time, Edward Wilmot Blyden, an educator, writer, and diplomat, traveled to Liberia, where he came to believe that the only hope for African Americans was for them to return to Africa. One of the most prominent black nationalists from the same time period was Martin R. Delany. Delany, born in Virginia in 1812, pursued numerous careers throughout his life: physician, educator, political candidate, journalist, author, and African explorer. He edited one of the earliest African American newspapers, *The Mystery*, and worked briefly alongside Frederick Douglass on *The North Star* newspaper. Early on he adopted Douglass's integrationist approach, but he later broke with Douglass by proposing a program of black separatism and black emigration, most of these views developed in his 1852 book *The Condition, Elevation, Emigration, and Destiny of the Colored People of the United States, Politically Considered*. Later, after the Civil War, Henry McNeal Turner, a bishop in the African Episcopal Methodist Church, faced entrenched racism in his native Georgia. He and a number of other African Americans were elected to the Georgia legislature in 1868.

Time Line

1887
- **August 17** Malchus Mosiah Garvey, Jr., is born in St. Ann's Bay, Jamaica.

1914
- **August** Garvey founds the Universal Negro Improvement Association (UNIA).

1917
- **May** Garvey founds the New York division of the UNIA.

1919
- **June 27** The Black Star Line is incorporated by the members of the UNIA with Garvey as president.
- **November** The Bureau of Investigation, forerunner of the FBI, launches an investigation of Garvey and UNIA.

1922
- **January 12** Garvey, along with other Black Star Line officials, is arrested on mail fraud charges.
- **November 25** Garvey delivers his address "The Principles of the Universal Negro Improvement Association" to an audience in Liberty Hall in New York City.

1923
- **June 23** Garvey is sentenced to five years in prison for using the mails to deceive the public.

1925
- **February 8** Garvey begins serving a five-year sentence in the Atlanta Federal Penitentiary.

1927
- **November** President Calvin Coolidge commutes Garvey's sentence, and he is released from prison and deported to Jamaica.

Initially, the legislature refused to seat them, backing down only under protests from Washington, D.C. Turner became so discouraged about the lack of racial progress that he supported the Back to Africa movement and black nationalism. He often shocked listeners with his fiery oratory and his belief that God was black.

Thus, when Marcus Garvey created the UNIA in Jamaica in 1914 (under the name Universal Negro Improvement and Conservation Association and African Communities League), the foundations for the black nationalism he espoused had already been laid. He returned to New York City to create the New York division of the UNIA, which originally had just thirteen members. Three months later the organization had 3,500 members. On August 17, 1918, Garvey founded *The Negro World*, a weekly newspaper that published articles of interest not only to African Americans but to members of the African diaspora around the world. By 1920 the organization had more than eleven hundred divisions in at least forty countries and claimed four million members. On August 13, 1920, at the organization's first convention, it published the "Declaration of Rights of the Negro Peoples of the World."

Garvey was of the opinion that the political and economic freedom of blacks in the West depended on their connection to an African nation-state with the political leverage to protect the rights of African-descended peoples regardless of their nationality. Accordingly, he directed his attention to helping Liberia develop into a world power. Late in the spring of 1920, he dispatched Elie Garcia, the auditor-general of the UNIA, to Monrovia, Liberia, where he communicated the organization's Pan-African goals to government officials, queried about the possibility of forming a UNIA colony on unsettled land, and stated the association's willingness to lend financial support to the country. Liberia's secretary of state, Edwin Barclay, informed Garcia of the government's interest in giving the association facilities for promoting industry, agriculture, and business projects.

The Liberian agenda, however, proved to be problematic. Even though the country had its share of financial and political problems, Garvey had faith that Liberia could develop into a world power if its leaders embraced a partnership with the UNIA. To realize his agenda, Garvey created the Liberian Construction Loan in the fall of 1920 with the purpose of building colleges, universities, industrial plants, railroad tracks, and roads and to provide opportunities for artisans and craftsmen to develop industries. An industrially developed Liberia, Garvey believed, would give men and women who wanted to start off independently the opportunity to build fortunes. Many women and men in the UNIA were interested in leaving the United States for Liberia, but several things stood in their way. The UNIA lacked the resources to facilitate the migration of interested parties to Liberia.

By 1921, Garvey's Black Star Line (BSL), a steamship line, faced serious financial trouble owing to the postwar recession, its ships' constant mechanical troubles, and administrative ineptitude. Even if the BSL had the capital to purchase vessels capable of making trips from the United States to West Africa, the UNIA would have still had problems overcoming certain diplomatic concerns. Garvey's Pan-African vision included not only a more economically and politically stable Liberia but also a continent loosened from England's and France's colonial yoke. As was to be expected, France and England saw Garvey's political agenda as antithetical to their imperialistic designs and activities. Not wishing to provoke these powers, Liberia's president, C. D. B. King, protected his country's national interest by gradually disassociating itself from the UNIA. Nevertheless, Garvey continued to place Liberia at the center of his political program, spreading his Pan-African message as he toured various sections of the United States.

Garvey also met with resistance from elements of the black American community, some of whom dismissed him as a racist demagogue and were contemptuous of his political style, approach, and plans. W. E. B. Du Bois, James Weldon Johnson, and A. Philip Randolph, among other leaders, dismissed his program as impractical, impossible, and detrimental to the black liberation struggle in America. In their writings and in their speeches, these leaders attacked Garvey's physical characteristics, his Jamaican background, and his working-class followers. On rare occasions, some critics managed to speak honestly about Garvey's strengths and weaknesses. Garvey's goals, Du Bois admitted in 1921, were feasible, but his methods according to Du Bois were wasteful, ineffective, and possibly illegal. So disturbed were some black activists by Garvey's political agenda, his focus on race pride, and his ruminations on color divisions within the black community that they happily assisted the federal government in its effort to have Garvey deported after he was convicted of mail fraud.

Garvey delivered many of his orations at Liberty Hall in New York City; the UNIA required each branch of the organization to maintain a "Liberty Hall" for its members so that by 1927 there were some fourteen hundred Liberty Halls throughout the world. Garvey delivered his address to UNIA members on November 25, 1922, in an effort to boost the spirits and determination of the UNIA.

About the Author

Garvey was born Malchus Mosiah Garvey on August 17, 1887, in St. Ann's Bay, Jamaica, where he excelled as a student at the local Anglican Church school. Not until the age of fourteen did Garvey begin to view the world in black and white. One of his closest playmates had been a white girl. Her parents, according to Garvey, sent her to Edinburgh and informed their daughter that she was never to communicate with Garvey because of his race.

Garvey moved to Kingston, Jamaica, in 1906. Over the next four years, he gained invaluable political experience as vice president of the Kingston Typographical Union, publisher of *Garvey's Watchman*, and assistant secretary of the National Club. These activities fed his desire to explore the world, so he followed a path trodden by many West Indians by embarking for Latin America. There he labored as a

Time Line

1929
- **September**
  Garvey founds the People's Political Party, the first modern political party in Jamaica.

1940
- **June 10**
  Garvey dies in London after having two strokes.

timekeeper on a banana plantation in Costa Rica, started two newspapers, and stayed abreast of the condition of Jamaican workers. Further travel would enrich Garvey's Pan-African consciousness. A brief return to Jamaica in 1911 was followed by a two-year stay in London, where he attended classes at Birkbeck College, formed a relationship with the noted Pan-Africanist Duse Muhammad Ali, and built contacts with West African students. As Garvey traveled and engaged the world, he increasingly envisioned himself as the one who could lead his people toward the path of true liberation and freedom.

Upon his return to Jamaica, Garvey and his future wife, Amy Ashwood, formed the UNIA with the express purpose of improving the material and educational conditions of blacks in Jamaica and the world over. Foremost on their agenda was creating an industrial school in Kingston in the vein of Booker T. Washington's Tuskegee Institute. Unable to persuade locals to aid his endeavor, Garvey departed for the United States in 1916 in the hope of raising funds for the UNIA's proposed industrial school. Two months after settling in New York, he embarked on an extensive tour of black communities in various parts of the country. Nothing impressed him more than African Americans' entrepreneurial accomplishments in the face of Jim Crow segregation and economic hardships. After a year on the road, Garvey returned to Harlem in May 1917. After his return, he concentrated less on the development of an industrial school in Jamaica and more on building an international movement with the economic and political capacity to lift African-descended peoples the world over.

Garvey incorporated the New York chapter of the UNIA in June 1918. Two months later he launched the organization's official organ, *The Negro World*, one of the most successful papers in the black world, with subscribers in the United States, the West Indies, Latin America, and Africa. Garvey was a powerful speaker, as his listeners learned when he delivered "The Principles of the Universal Negro Improvement Association" in 1922. He had less success as a business entrepreneur. In 1919 he started the BSL, but the company was plagued by problems that eventually led to his indictment and conviction for mail fraud in 1923. According to U.S. law, any immigrant convicted of criminal activity could be immediately deported to his or her country of origin. So starting in 1919, the Justice Department planted agents in the New York UNIA and in other major divisions and branches across the country in order to uncover any criminal activity committed by Garvey. Because of the UNIA's shoddy bookkeeping practices, Bureau of Investigation assistant director J. Edgar Hoover and his associates focused on the BSL's promotional practices. On January 12, 1922, Garvey, along with other BSL officials, was arrested on mail fraud charges for allegedly advertising and selling stock in a nonexistent ship supposedly purchased to transport prospective colonists to Liberia. Garvey vehemently denied cheating his people, but he was nevertheless convicted in 1923.

In 1925 Garvey began serving a five-year prison sentence, but President Calvin Coolidge commuted his sentence in 1927 and he was deported to Jamaica. Over the next decade Garvey continued to travel, speak, and write, and he attained elective office in Jamaica. He returned to London in 1935, where he lived and worked until his death on June 10, 1940.

Explanation and Analysis of the Document

Garvey's address gives voice to the deep humanism that pervaded his political ideas. Contrary to the opinion of his opponents, Garvey asserts that his message of race pride should not be interpreted as antiwhite. One of his first points of emphasis is that the UNIA aims not simply to improve the life chances and experiences of African-descended peoples but also to create a more humane and just world. He notes in the first paragraph that the "association adopts an attitude not of hostility to other races and peoples of the world, but an attitude of self respect, of manhood rights on behalf of 400,000,000 Negroes of the world." He goes on to emphasize this message in the second paragraph, stating that "we represent peace, harmony, love, human sympathy, human rights and human justice, and that is why we fight so much." Here Garvey lends support to such contemporary writers as Anthony Bogues, Tony Martin, and Sylvia Winters, who argue that one of the central elements of the black radical tradition has been its deep humanism, that is, its focus on eliminating all forms of human oppression.

In the second paragraph, Garvey also highlights the fact that people of African descent fought in the Revolutionary War, the Civil War, the Spanish American War, and World War I, thereby reminding his audience that African Americans have long been loyal Americans, willing to fight and even die for their country. He makes reference to the "heights of Mesopotamia," a region that corresponds roughly to modern-day Iraq, but it is unclear what precise location he means. The region had not been called Mesopotamia for centuries, so perhaps he is referring to the struggles for ascendancy in the region in the early medieval period. More likely, he is thinking of the efforts of black soldiers in the Middle East during World War I, using "Mesopotamia" as a kind of figure of speech for the region. He regards the fight for emancipation of the race as analogous to these conflicts.

In the third paragraph, Garvey suggests that recent expressions of African consciousness represent a "new line of thought." He continues by saying that it does not make any difference whether this line of thought is seen as "reactionary" or "advanced," for in either case it represents a quest for liberty and freedom. Again, he stresses that the organization's goal is uplift for all people, yet he acknowledges that the role of government, in his view, is to "place race in control, even as other races are in control of their own governments." In the fourth paragraph, he suggests that this goal is by no means unreasonable. It was not unreasonable for George Washington or for the "Liberals of France," a reference to the French Revolution in the late eighteenth century. Nor was it unreasonable for the people of Russia, led in part by Leo Tolstoy, one of czarist Russia's greatest novelists and a prominent proponent of anarchism, to "sound the call of liberty" in their nation. In paragraph 5, Garvey seems to momentarily digress by noting that the UNIA does not promote church building or building new social institutions (such as the Young Men's Christian Association or the Young Women's Christian Association), noting that these institutions already exist. Further, he states that the UNIA has little interest in politics, observing that already there are enough politicians. Rather, he says, the UNIA is "engaged in nation building."

In paragraph 6, Garvey returns to the theme of human rights. He states that "misunderstanding" has arisen about the goals and aims of the UNIA. He emphasizes that the organization believes in the rights not only of the "brown race" but of all races, and he stresses that the rights of whites, the yellow race (Asians), and others are worthy of consideration. He goes on, though, to suggest that the other races have denied those of African descent their proper place in the civilizations of the world. The UNIA's goal is not to disrupt existing societies or governments but to "free our motherland from the grasp of the invader," leading to "industrial, political, social and religious emancipation." To that end, the organization aims to unite the world's 400,000,000 blacks—a figure that he uses repeatedly in the speech—to enable them "to give expression to their own feeling." He stresses that a key goal is political freedom in Africa.

In paragraph 8, Garvey turns to the distinction between the UNIA and other black movements. The UNIA, he says, seeks "independence of government." Other organizations "seek to make the Negro a secondary part of existing governments." He argues that these other movements would leave blacks in a secondary position, without constitutional rights. Having lived in London, he is equipped to talk about British institutions that claim to be trying to improve the condition of blacks, but he asserts that equality will never be achieved until a black has the same chance as any other person to become a president or premier—or to become a street cleaner.

Here he lays out why the New Negro must be concerned with nation building: "You and I can live in the United States of America for 100 more years," he explains to the audience, "and our generations may live for 200 years or for 5000 more years, and so long as there is a black and white population, when the majority is on the side of white race, you and I will never get political justice or get political equality in this country." Consequently, he maintained that the UNIA would focus its attention on nation-building in Africa: "The U.N.I.A. refuses to recognize any political or social system in Africa except that which we are about to establish for ourselves."

Garvey reiterates that he is not preaching a message of hate, what he calls in paragraph 9 "propaganda of hate." He even goes so far as to say "we love the white man" and that "we love all humanity." He acknowledges that just as Africa has things that Europeans want, so too does Europe have things that Africans want. Garvey wants to ensure, though, that if Africa sells its oil, diamonds, precious metals, and rubber to Europeans, it does so under the terms of a fair deal, not colonial exploitation. In paragraph 10, he emphasizes that if it takes power, scientific intelligence, and education to "redeem a race," then the world's 400 million blacks have what it takes for that redemption.

In paragraph 11, Garvey turns to a martial metaphor. Again he refers to the sacrifices of blood that blacks have offered "fighting for the white man." He asserts that blacks will make similar sacrifices to fight for a free Africa under the UNIA's Pan-African flag whose colors were red, black, and green. He continues the martial metaphor in paragraphs 12 and 13, where he insists that blacks will "march out" to redeem their motherland. African Americans, he says, will not forget the blessings of America and those of civilization. He alludes to the nation's history of slavery, with its "bloody carnage and massacre," but he insists that a united black race will now be able to defend itself. He concludes with a cry to the people of Africa, telling them to "hold the fort, for we are coming."

Audience

Written during a period of great upheaval for the UNIA, which had seen its primary economic venture, the Black Star Line, collapse in April of 1922, Garvey's address was designed to lift the spirits of the UNIA's loyal rank and file. Times had been extremely rough for the UNIA in recent months. Combined with the BSL's collapse, Garvey had been arrested for mail fraud, the UNIA's Liberian plans had been suspended, and the organization's 1922 convention had been rife with internal debates. Thus, in addition to clarifying the UNIA's political agenda, Garvey was attempting to rally his troops. "We should say to the millions who are in Africa to hold the fort," he thundered in the concluding paragraph, "for we are coming 400,000,000 strong."

Impact

Garvey's followers fed off his determined spirit, whose essence is captured in this 1922 speech. Notwithstanding various trials and tribulations, the Garvey movement remained strong for the remainder of the decade. Vibrant chapters were formed throughout the United States, making the UNIA the most visible and active organization of

Edwin Barclay, president of Liberia (Library of Congress)

the New Negro era. To many of his enemies Garvey was a racist demagogue who profited from the emotions and ignorance of his people, but for many women and men suffering under an oppressive and unyielding order Garvey was a divinely chosen leader whose racial program blazed a path toward political freedom and self-consciousness.

Long after Garvey's address and his 1927 deportation from the United States, his influence still bore an imprint on African American political culture. Supporters followed Garvey's activities in Jamaica and then London through careful reading of *The Negro World* and Garvey's second paper, *The Blackman*. Finding an audience receptive to a race-first analysis proved difficult for Garvey during the Great Depression years as more blacks shifted toward the left of the political spectrum, but Garvey's ideas enjoyed a revival as decolonization, civil rights, and Black Power struggles intensified in the 1950s and 1960s. Now claiming their native son, Jamaica celebrated the UNIA leader as a national hero who raised the consciousness of African people. Noted Pan-Africanist and Ghanaian president Kwame Nkrumah named the nation's first fleet of ships after Garvey's Black Star Line. A profound love and appreciation for Garvey's life, work, and dedication was also evident in black communities across the United States as his influence surfaced in the activities of Elijah Muhammad's Nation of Islam, in the political rhetoric of Malcolm X, and in the nationalist lyrics of hip-hop

Essential Quotes

> "We represent peace, harmony, love, human sympathy, human rights and human justice, and that is why we fight so much."
> (Paragraph 2)

> "We represent a new line of thought among Negroes. Whether you call it advanced thought or reactionary thought, I do not care. If it is reactionary for people to seek independence in government, then we are reactionary. If it is advanced thought for people to seek liberty and freedom, then we represent the advanced school of thought among the Negroes of this country."
> (Paragraph 3)

> "The Universal Negro Improvement Association stands for the Bigger Brotherhood; the Universal Negro Improvement Association stands for human rights, not only for Negroes, but for all races. The Universal Negro Improvement Association believes in the rights of not only the black race, but the white race, the yellow race and the brown race."
> (Paragraph 6)

> "We are not preaching a propaganda of hate against anybody. We love the white man; we love all humanity, because we feel that we cannot live without the other. The white man is as necessary to the existence of the Negro as the Negro is as necessary to his existence. There is a common relationship that we cannot escape."
> (Paragraph 9)

activists like Public Enemy and the aptly named group Black Star (comprised of Mos Def and Talib Kweli). Popular black bookstores in New York, Atlanta, Philadelphia, Washington, D.C., and other metropolises sell hundreds of Garvey books and posters to black women and men, young and old, who still carry and hold on to his vision of a world in which the children of Africa will one day experience complete political, social, and economic freedom.

See also Henry Highland Garnet's Address to the Slaves of the United States of America (1843); Martin R. Delany: *The Condition, Elevation, Emigration, and Destiny of the Colored People of the United States* (1852); Henry McNeal Turner's Speech on His Expulsion from the Georgia Legislature (1868).

Further Reading

■ **Books**

Garvey, Amy Jacques. *Garvey and Garveyism*. New York: Collier, 1970.

Grant, Colin. *Negro with a Hat: The Rise and Fall of Marcus Garvey and His Dream of Mother Africa*. London: Jonathan Cape, 2008.

Hill, Robert A., ed. *Marcus Garvey, Life and Lessons: A Centennial Companion to the Marcus Garvey and Universal Negro Improvement Association Papers*. Berkeley: University of California Press, 1987.

———. *The Marcus Garvey and Universal Negro Improvement Association Papers*. Vols. 1–10. Los Angeles: University of California Press, 1983–2006.

Lewis, Rupert, and Patrick Bryan, eds. *Garvey: His Work and Impact*. Mona, Jamaica: Institute of Social and Economic Research and Department of Extra-Mural Studies, University of the West Indies, 1988.

Martin, Tony. *Race First: The Ideological and Organizational Struggles of Marcus Garvey and the Universal Negro Improvement Association*. Westport, Conn.: Greenwood Press, 1976.

Stein, Judith. *The World of Marcus Garvey: Race and Class in Modern Society*. Baton Rouge: Louisiana State University Press, 1986.

■ **Web Sites**

"Garvey, Marcus (1887–1940)." BlackPast.org Web site. http://www.blackpast.org/?q=aah/garvey-marcus-1887-1940.

—Claudrena N. Harold

Questions for Further Study

1. Describe the social, economic, and political circumstances that gave rise to Garvey and the UNIA.

2. Summarize the intellectual foundations of the black nationalist movement that were in place by the time Garvey delivered his address. Who were some of Garvey's predecessors in espousing black nationalism?

3. Why do you think that prominent African Americans such as W. E. B. Du Bois, A. Philip Randolph, and James Weldon Johnson opposed Garvey? What strain of thinking did Garvey represent that was opposed to that of these other figures?

4. Garvey was known as a highly flamboyant figure who, for example, affected military uniforms. He was also convicted of mail fraud. To what extent do you believe these personal factors undermined his message? Do you believe that Garvey was a serious figure or a gadfly?

5. How did the UNIA resemble—or differ from—other African American organizations such as the NAACP? What goals did the UNIA pursue that Garvey may have felt were not being pursued by other black organizations?

Marcus Garvey: "The Principles of the Universal Negro Improvement Association"

Over five years ago the Universal Negro Improvement Association placed itself before the world as the movement through which the new and rising Negro would give expression of his feelings. This Association adopts an attitude not of hostility to other races and peoples of the world, but an attitude of self respect, of manhood rights on behalf of 400,000,000 Negroes of the world.

We represent peace, harmony, love, human sympathy, human rights and human justice, and that is why we fight so much. Wheresoever human rights are denied to any group, wheresoever justice is denied to any group, there the U.N.I.A. finds a cause. And at this time among all the peoples of the world, the group that suffers most from injustice, the group that is denied most of those rights that belong to all humanity, is the black group of 400,000,000. Because of that injustice, because of that denial of our rights, we go forth under the leadership of the One who is always on the side of right to fight the common cause of humanity; to fight as we fought in the Revolutionary War, as we fought in the Civil War, as we fought in the Spanish American War, and as we fought in the war between 1914–18 on the battle plains of France and of Flanders. As we fought on the heights of Mesopotamia; even so under the leadership of the U.N.I.A., we are marshaling the 400,000,000 Negroes of the world to fight for the emancipation of the race and of the redemption of the country of our fathers.

We represent a new line of thought among Negroes. Whether you call it advanced thought or reactionary thought, I do not care. If it is reactionary for people to seek independence in government, then we are reactionary. If it is advanced thought for people to seek liberty and freedom, then we represent the advanced school of thought among the Negroes of this country. We of the U.N.I.A. believe that what is good for the other folks is good for us. If government is something that is worthwhile; if government is something that is appreciable and helpful and protective to others, then we also want to experiment in government. We do not mean a government that will make us citizens without rights or subjects with no consideration. We mean a kind of government that will place race in control, even as other races are in control of their own governments.

That does not suggest anything that is unreasonable. It was not unreasonable for George Washington, the great hero and father of the country, to have fought for the freedom of America giving to this great republic and this great democracy; it was not unreasonable for the Liberals of France to have fought against the anarchy to give to the world French Democracy and French Republicanism; it was no unrighteous cause that led Tolstoi to sound the call of liberty in Russia, which has ended in giving to the world the social democracy of Russia, an experiment that will probably prove to be a boon and a blessing to mankind. If it was not an unrighteous cause that led Washington to fight for the independence of this country, and led the Liberals of France to establish the Republic, it is therefore not an unrighteous cause for the U.N.I.A. to lead 400,000,000 Negroes all over the world to fight the liberation of our country.

Therefore the U.N.I.A. is not advocating the cause of church building, because we have a sufficiently large number of churches among us to minister to the spiritual needs of the people, and we are not going to compete with those who are engaged in so splendid a work; we are not engaged in building any new social institutions, and Y.M.C.A.'s or Y.W.C.A.'s, because there are enough social workers engaged in those praise-worthy efforts. We are not engaged in politics because we have enough local politicians, Democrats, Socialists, Soviets, etc., and the political situation is well taken care of. We are not engaged in domestic politics, in church building or in social uplift work, but we are engaged in nation building....

I desire to remove the misunderstanding that has been created in the minds of millions of peoples throughout the world in their relationship to the organization. The Universal Negro Improvement Association stands for the Bigger Brotherhood; the Universal Negro Improvement Association stands for human rights, not only for Negroes, but for all races. The Universal Negro Improvement Association believes in the rights of not only the black race, but the white race, the yellow race and the brown race. The Universal Negro Improvement Association believes that the white man has as much right to be considered, the yellow man has as much right to be considered, the brown man has as much right to be considered as well as the black man of Africa. In view of the fact that the black man of Africa has contributed as much to the world as the white man of Europe, and the brown man and yellow man of Asia, we of the Universal Negro Improvement Association demand that the white, yellow and brown races give to the black man his place in the civilization of the world. We ask for nothing more than the rights of 400,000,000 Negroes. We are not seeking, as I said before, to destroy or disrupt the society or the government of other races, but we are determined that 400,000,000 of us shall unite ourselves to free our motherland from the grasp of the invader. We of the Universal Negro Improvement Association are determined to unite 400,000,000 Negroes for their own industrial, political, social and religious emancipation.

We of the Universal Negro Improvement Association are determined to unite the 400,000,000 Negroes of the world to give expression to their own feeling; we are determined to unite the 400,000,000 Negroes of the world for the purpose of building a civilization of their own. And in that effort we desire to bring together the 15,000,000 of the United States, the 180,000,000 in Asia, the West Indies and Central and South America, and the 200,000,000 in Africa. We are looking toward political freedom on the continent of Africa, the land of our fathers....

The difference between the Universal Negro Improvement Association and the other movements of this country, and probably the world, is that the Universal Negro Improvement Association seeks independence of government, while the other organizations seek to make the Negro a secondary part of existing governments. We differ from the organizations in America because they seek to subordinate the Negro as a secondary consideration in a great civilization, knowing that in America the Negro will never reach his highest ambition, knowing that the Negro in America will never get his constitutional rights. All those organizations which are fostering the improvement of Negroes in the British Empire know that the Negro in the British Empire will never reach the height of his constitutional rights. What do I mean by constitutional rights in America? If the black man is to reach the height of his ambition in this country—if the black man is to get all of his constitutional rights in America—then the black man should have the same chance in the nation as any other man to become president of the nation, or a street cleaner in New York. If [the] black man in the British Empire is to have all his constitutional rights it means that the Negro in the British Empire should have at least the same right to become premier of Great Britain as he has to become [a] street cleaner in the city of London. Are they prepared to give us such political equality? You and I can live in the United States of America for 100 more years, and our generations may live for 200 years or for 5000 more years, and so long as there is a black and white population, when the majority is on the side of white race, you and I will never get political justice or get political equality in this country. Then why should a black man with rising ambition, after preparing himself in every possible way to give expression to that highest ambition, allow himself to be kept down by racial prejudice within a country? If I am as educated as the next man, if I am as prepared as the next man, if I have passed through the best schools and colleges and universities as the other fellow, why should I not have a fair chance to compete with the other fellow for the biggest position in the nation? I have feelings, I have blood, I have senses like the other fellow; I have ambition, I have hope. Why should he, because of some racial prejudice, keep me down and why should I concede to him the right to rise above me and to establish himself as my permanent master? That is where the U.N.I.A. differs from other organizations. I refuse to stultify my ambition, and every true Negro refuses to stultify his ambition to suit any one, and therefore the U.N.I.A. decides if America is not big enough for two presidents, if England is not big enough for two kings, then we are not going to quarrel over the matter; we will leave one president in America, we will leave one king in England, we will leave one president in France and we will have one president in Africa. Hence, the Universal Negro Improvement Association does not seek to interfere with the social and political systems of France, but by the arrangement of things today the U.N.I.A. refuses to recognize any political or social system in Africa except that which we are about to establish for ourselves.

We are not preaching a propaganda of hate against anybody. We love the white man; we love all humanity, because we feel that we cannot live without the other. The white man is as necessary to the existence of the Negro as the Negro is as necessary to his existence. There is a common relationship that we cannot escape. Africa has certain things that Europe wants, and Europe has certain things that Africa wants, and if a fair and square deal must bring white and black with each other, it is impossible for us to escape it. Africa has oil, diamonds, copper, gold and rubber and all the minerals that Europe wants, and there must be some kind of relationship between

Document Text

Africa and Europe for a fair exchange, so we cannot afford to hate anybody....

The question often asked is what does it require to redeem a race and free a country? If it takes man power, if it takes scientific intelligence, if it takes education of any kind, or if it takes blood, then the 400,000,000 Negroes of the world have it....

If we have been liberal minded enough to give our life's blood in France, in Mesopotamia and elsewhere, fighting for the white man, whom we have always assisted, surely we have not forgotten to fight for ourselves, and when the time comes that the world will again give Africa an opportunity for freedom, surely 400,000,000 black men will march out on the battle plains of Africa, under the colors of the red, the black and the green.

We shall march out, yes, as black American citizens, as black British subjects, as black French citizens, as black Italians or as black Spaniards, but we shall march out with a greater loyalty, the loyalty of race. We shall march out in answer to the cry of our fathers, who cry out to us for the redemption of our own country, our motherland, Africa.

We shall march out, not forgetting the blessings of America. We shall march out, not forgetting the blessings of civilization. We shall march out with a history of peace before and behind us, and surely that history shall be our breastplate, for how can man fight better than knowing that the cause for which he fights is righteous? How can man fight more gloriously than by knowing that behind him is a history of slavery, a history of bloody carnage and massacre inflicted upon a race because of its inability to protect itself and fight? Shall we not fight for the glorious opportunity of protecting and forever more establishing ourselves as a mighty race and nation, never more to be disrespected by men? Glorious shall be the battle when the time comes to fight for our people and our race.

We should say to the millions who are in Africa to hold the fort, for we are coming 400,000,000 strong.

Glossary

breastplate	a piece of armor that covers and protects the chest
Liberals of France	the leaders of the late-eighteenth-century French Revolution
Mesopotamia	a region in the Middle East that corresponds roughly with modern-day Iraq
Tolstoi	Leo Tolstoy, a nineteenth-century Russian novelist and anarchist
West Indies	the islands of the Caribbean
Y.M.C.A.	Young Men's Christian Association
Y.W.C.A.	Young Women's Christian Association

A band at the Savoy Ballroom (Library of Congress)

Alain Locke's "Enter the New Negro"

1925

"The intelligent Negro of today is resolved not to make discrimination an extenuation for his shortcomings in performance, individual or collective."

Overview

In March 1925, Alain Locke edited "Harlem: Mecca of the New Negro," a special issue of the journal *Survey Graphic*. In addition to work by a number of prominent African American writers, the issue contained his own essay "Enter the New Negro," which highlighted the social, cultural, and artistic growth of African Americans, urged black artists and writers to look to African and African American history for inspiration, and expressed his belief that art and literature could break down racial barriers. Locke was eminently qualified to speak to this subject. He was America's first black Rhodes Scholar and later earned a PhD in philosophy from Harvard University. In 1925 Locke was early in a long and distinguished career as a professor at Howard University, and he would go on to write several highly regarded books and scholarly articles about African American culture and art. He was one of the leading figures in the Harlem Renaissance, the term given to the flourishing of African American culture in the 1920s and 1930s, much of it centered in the Harlem district of Manhattan in New York City—and, in fact, he is often referred to as the "Father of the Harlem Renaissance." His passion and profound intellect contributed significantly to the vitality of the movement.

Locke's essay is not to be confused with his book *The New Negro*, which was also published in 1925. This anthology, an expansion of the *Survey Graphic* issue, included literary works by writers such as Jean Toomer, Zora Neale Hurston, Countee Cullen, Langston Hughes, and Claude McKay. Additionally, it included political and social analysis by James Weldon Johnson, E. Franklin Frazier, Walter White, and W. E. B. Du Bois. Because of Locke's essay and anthology expounding the achievements and aspirations of the "New Negro," the Harlem Renaissance is sometimes referred to as the New Negro Movement.

Context

Two major developments in African American history formed the backdrop for Locke's essay. One was the Great Migration, the term given to the movement of African Americans to northern and midwestern cities during the 1910s and 1920s, in part to escape the entrenched racism in the South, in part to seek employment in burgeoning industrial cities. During the Civil War, only about 8 percent of blacks lived in the North or Midwest. In 1900 still only about 10 percent lived in states that were not formerly slave states. That would change dramatically in the first decades of the new century. From 1910 to 1920, for example, the black population of Chicago grew from 44,000 to 110,000. In 1914 the black population of New York City was 50,000; in 1930 it was 165,000. In 1910 the black population of Detroit was 6,000; by 1929 the figure was 120,000. Cleveland, Boston, Baltimore, Cincinnati, Indianapolis, and other major cities experienced similarly rapid black population growth; so did smaller cities such as Dayton and Toledo in Ohio; Omaha, Nebraska; and Flint, Michigan. This growth was part of a national urbanizing trend and a corresponding decline in the rural population. In 1910 the majority of Americans lived in rural areas, defined at the time as communities with populations under 2,500. Thus, 49.9 million people lived in rural areas, while 42 million lived in urban areas; by 1920 the balance had shifted, with 54.1 million living in urban areas and 51.5 million living in rural areas. This trend continued throughout the 1920s so that by 1930, 68.9 million lived in urban areas to just 53.8 million in rural areas.

Typifying this urbanization was a city like Tulsa, Oklahoma. When Oklahoma achieved statehood in 1907, the city's population was a mere 7,000; by 1920 the city's population had increased more than tenfold, to 72,000. Included in that population were 11,000 African Americans, who were enjoying some measure of prosperity because of the state's oil boom. The black section of Tulsa, called the Greenwood district, was so prosperous that the black leader Booker T. Washington called its commercial district, with its restaurants, groceries, stores, professional offices, newspapers, churches, hospitals, and a library, the "Negro Wall Street."

Oil contributed to Tulsa's growth, but a number of other factors conspired to shift the nation's black population northward and westward. In the late 1910s, for example, a boll weevil infestation devastated southern cotton crops, forcing many black sharecroppers off their land. Then the outbreak of World War I opened large numbers of jobs in

Time Line

1885
- **September 13**
  Alain Locke is born in Philadelphia, Pennsylvania.

1910
- The Great Migration begins; in time, over four million African Americans would leave the South for the North and Midwest.

1904
- Large numbers of African Americans begin moving to Harlem in New York City.

1909
- **February 12**
  The National Association for the Advancement of Colored People is formed.

1913
- The building that would become the Apollo Theater is built in Harlem.

1917
- **April 6**
  The United States declares war on Germany, entering World War I; four hundred thousand African Americans serve in the military during the war.

1918
- Locke joins the philosophy faculty of Howard University in Washington, D.C.
- **November 11**
  The armistice ending World War I is signed.

1919
- Race riots plague numerous American cities, including Cleveland, Ohio; Omaha, Nebraska; and Elaine, Arkansas.

1922
- Claude McKay publishes *Harlem Shadows*, a poetry collection regarded as among the first major literary productions of the Harlem Renaissance.

1923
- Blues singer Bessie Smith revives the failing Columbia Record Company with her album *Down Hearted Blues*; Club De Luxe in Harlem reopens as the Cotton Club.

---

northern defense industry plants. The war, plus the Immigration Act of 1924, curtailed the flow of immigrants to the United States, increasing the demand for labor in northern factories. In 1927 major flooding in Mississippi again forced many southern blacks off their land. Often, black families heading north simply purchased the cheapest available train ticket, explaining why, for example, many Mississippians ended up in Chicago. In all, from 1910 to 1930 about 4.1 million African Americans left the South for opportunities in the North and Midwest.

The result of the Great Migration was the urban concentration of African Americans who had previously lived in relative isolation from one another in rural areas. Many who migrated were by definition ambitious and energetic, looking for a better life for themselves and their families. In their new communities, they formed a critical mass of culture in the broadest sense of the term: art, literature, music, church life, and dance as well as political and social awareness. Organizations such as the National Association for the Advancement of Colored People and Marcus Garvey's Universal Negro Improvement Association, along with new periodicals such as *Opportunity: A Journal of Negro Life*, were giving voice to the aspirations of African Americans. The new communities provided an audience for African American achievement. The result was the emergence of a black artistic and intellectual class under the leadership not only of Locke but also of W. E. B. Du Bois, James Weldon Johnson, and Walter White. In addition to a flowering of poetry and fiction—by such writers as Langston Hughes, Jean Toomer, Countee Cullen, Zora Neale Hurston, Claude McKay, Arna Bontemps, and numerous others—more popular forms of black culture flourished, led by a roster of black jazz and blues singers and musicians whose names are still recognized today: Billie Holiday, Duke Ellington, Count Basie, Louis Armstrong, Eubie Blake, Fats Waller, Josephine Baker, Billy Strayhorn, Lena Horne, and dozens more. Much of this popular culture was centered in New York City's Harlem neighborhood, the site of such cultural magnets as the Apollo Theater, the Savoy Ballroom, and the Cotton Club. Black Swan Records recorded the work of numerous black musicians.

Ironically, Harlem, with its stately homes and facilities such as the Polo Grounds (home of the New York Giants) and an opera house, had been a bedroom community for Manhattan's white upper class in the nineteenth century. It became a largely black community after a financial crash caused real estate values in Harlem to plummet and Philip Payton, Jr., the owner of the Afro-American Realty Company, opened the district to black tenants. Some white property barons resisted this demographic shift by buying up apartment buildings and evicting black tenants; Payton and others retaliated by buying up buildings of their own and evicting whites.

The Harlem Renaissance was by no means a unified movement with a manifesto and shared aims. On the one hand, the Harlem Renaissance encompassed those who were drawn to popular forms of entertainment and culture and who sought patrons exclusively among the emerging black middle class. More conservative elements, though, wanted to see greater integration of black culture with mainstream white culture and sought white patrons for their work; one of the key events in the Harlem Renaissance was a 1924 gathering hosted by the journal *Opportunity* that included a number of white publishers who were taking an interest in black literature and wanted to publish it. The conservative element feared that a great deal of black popular literature and entertainment played into stereotypes about African Americans. They were also troubled by the militancy of many blacks, especially those who espoused the doctrines of Socialism and Communism. This tension between the black intelligentsia and those who preferred "Stompin' at the Savoy" (the name of a 1930s big-band hit song), rather than undermining the movement, contributed to its vitality, for the spirit of the Harlem Renaissance reached throughout the entire black community, from the Harvard-trained professional to the factory worker—though that spirit would be dampened by the onset of the Great Depression in 1929.

Such a movement demanded intellectual underpinnings. These underpinnings were provided by such writers as Du Bois, the author of the 1903 book *The Souls of Black Folk*, and, later, Alain Locke. "Enter the New Negro," along with *The New Negro*, was a key document in the flowering of black culture during the 1920s. The essay was published in the same year as other important events affecting African Americans. That year, A. Philip Randolph organized the Brotherhood of Sleeping Car Porters, the first largely African American labor union; Cullen, one of the finest black poets in this era, published his first collection, *Color*; and the singer and dancer Josephine Baker performed overseas in *La revue nègre*, expanding the audience for African American artists to France, where she was wildly popular.

About the Author

Alain Locke was born on September 13, 1885, in Philadelphia. His given name was Allen, but he changed it to the French "Alain" because of his love of French literature. His father had earned a law degree at Howard University but worked as a postal clerk in the city; his mother was a schoolteacher. He was raised in a cultured environment and as a child attended the progressive Ethical Cultural School and then graduated second in his class from Philadelphia's Central High School. An early bout with rheumatic fever left him with heart damage, so he spent much of his time in sedentary activities such as reading and playing the violin and piano.

After studying at the Philadelphia School of Pedagogy, Locke entered Harvard University, graduating magna cum laude in just three years. At Harvard he was a member of Phi Beta Kappa, a prestigious national honorary society for top students, and won the Bowdoin Prize for the best essay in English. He did not feel much of a connection with other African American students at Harvard. Biographers Leonard Harris and Charles Molesworth report that in a letter to his mother he said that he could not understand

Time Line

1925
- **March** Locke publishes "Enter the New Negro" in the journal *Survey Graphic*.
- Locke publishes *The New Negro*, an anthology of work by African American writers.

1954
- **June 9** Alain Locke dies in New York City.

how they could "come up here in a broad-minded place like this and stick together like they were in the heart of Africa." He also wrote that he found his black peers "coarse." It was this separateness that would motivate him to stress America's multiculturalism and come to regard art as a way of dissolving racial barriers.

In 1907 Locke became the first African American Rhodes Scholar, a prestigious award that entitles the recipient to study at England's Oxford University. At Oxford's Hertford College—the only one that would accept a black student—he studied literature, Greek, Latin, and philosophy and earned a bachelor's degree in literature in 1910. Afterward he studied philosophy for a year at the University of Berlin in Germany. In 1912 he took a position teaching literature at Howard University, but in 1916 he returned to Harvard to study philosophy, completing a PhD in 1918. He returned to Howard, where he was appointed chair of the philosophy department and remained there until 1953.

During his distinguished career at Howard, Locke was the author of numerous books and journal articles whose topics broadly spanned philosophy, art, and cultural studies. Among them were *The New Negro*, as well as *Negro Art: Past and Present* and *The Negro and His Music* (both 1936). He also edited *The Negro in Art: A Pictorial Record of the Negro Artist and of the Negro Theme in Art* (1940). In 1942 he published a pioneering social sciences anthology, *When Peoples Meet: A Study in Race and Culture Contacts*, which he coedited with Bernhard Stern. Throughout the late 1940s and early 1950s he was in high demand as a visiting scholar until he retired in 1953—but not before he was able to secure a chapter of Phi Beta Kappa at Howard. After his retirement, he moved to New York City to finish what was to have been his major work, *The Negro in American Culture*. Unfortunately, the heart problems that had plagued him as a child recurred, and before he could finish the book, he died on June 9, 1954.

Explanation and Analysis of the Document

"Enter the New Negro" is a sophisticated, densely written analysis of the "New Negro," the African American who is shedding the cultural stereotypes and limitations of the past and asserting a new identity not just in the political and social spheres but in art and literature as well. It draws heavily on Locke's background as a student of both literature and philosophy. It was not in any sense a strident "call to arms" but rather a closely reasoned appeal to African Americans—and to white Americans—to recognize the fundamental change that was taking place in African American culture and in the psychology of the black community.

◆ **Paragraphs 1–6**

Locke begins by asserting that a change has taken place in the life of the American Negro. He refers to the sociologist, the philanthropist, and the race leader as the three "norns" who have traditionally examined issues surrounding blacks; the reference is to the three goddesses in Norse mythology who presided over human destiny. He argues that a transformation is taking place that the "norns" cannot account for. He then argues in paragraph 2 that the "New Negro" is not really new, that the "Old Negro" was more a creature of myth, a "historical fiction"—and that the Old Negro contributed to this myth by "social mimicry," or trying to fit in. He refers to the Old Negro as a "formula" who was regarded as someone to be defended, kept down, helped up, or kept in his place. Locke maintains that even the "thinking Negro" has fallen into the trap of this kind of stereotyping, which leads to "little true social or self-understanding." In paragraph 3 he notes that the focus of attention in race issues has been on the Civil War and Reconstruction; that focus on the North-South axis has blinded people to the East, with its implications of a new day dawning.

In the fourth paragraph, Locke cites the example of the Negro spiritual. He argues that formerly this form of music was limited by the "stereotypes of Wesleyan hymn harmony," a reference to John Wesley, the founder of Methodism in the eighteenth century. Now, though, Negro spirituals have come out of hiding and are regarded as folk music, a significant form of cultural expression. In the same way, African Americans have emerged from the "tyranny of social intimidation" and are undergoing "something like a spiritual emancipation" through self-understanding. Thus, says Locke, African American life is entering a "new dynamic phase." He alludes to the growing urbanization of the nation and with it the growth of the "Young Negro's" greater opportunities for art and self-expression. As an example he incorporates a quotation from "Youth," a poem by Langston Hughes whose imagery again suggests the dawn of a new day. Locke concludes this section by stating that the New Negro can no longer be seen through the "dusty spectacles" of past controversies—the black "mammy," the "Uncle Tom" of Harriet Beecher Stowe's novel *Uncle Tom's Cabin*, and "Sambo," a name that during the Civil War era became a racial slur. Locke maintains that it is time to put aside these and other stereotypes, to "scrap the fictions" and "garret the bogeys" (that is, to consign them to the attic), and face a new reality.

◆ **Paragraphs 7–14**

Locke next outlines some of the specific changes that have rendered old conceptions of African Americans obsolete. Again he refers to the Great Migration of blacks to the North and Midwest and their centers of industry, so the issues, he says, are no longer sectional. He suggests that the problems faced by blacks in their new surroundings are not entirely racial. Finally, he points to "class differentiation" in the black community, making it "ridiculous" to regard the black population "en masse," that is, as a homogeneous whole. In paragraph 8, Locke goes on to point out that "the Negro too, for his part, has idols of the tribe to smash," meaning that certain cherished views have to be cast aside. While it may be true, Locke says, that the white population denigrated blacks to excuse its treatment of them, blacks have too often excused themselves because of this treatment. The "intelligent Negro" does not use discrimination as an excuse for his shortcomings and wants to be seen as an equal, not an object of sentiment or "social discounts" or a victim of "self-pity." He refers to changes in attitude as a "bitter weaning" but one that will allow both black and white to see each other with "new mutual attitudes." In paragraph 10, Locke concedes that greater knowledge will not necessarily lead to greater liking or treatment, but an effort of will is needed on the part of the "more intelligent" people of both races, who, in Locke's view, are out of touch with one another.

Thus, in paragraph 10, Locke begins to argue that the notion that the lives of blacks and whites are separate is increasingly a fiction. In paragraph 11 he cites the example of interracial councils in the South— there were some eight hundred local councils under the auspices of the Commission on Interracial Cooperation based in Atlanta—yet he notes that in the North, black laborers have little "interplay" with their communities and the white business community. Locke calls for this to change but observes that it already is changing, that close cooperation is replacing "long-distance philanthropy," at least among "enlightened minorities of both race groups." In paragraph 12 he says that the New Negro is responding to this new democratic element in American culture and is no longer allowing discrimination in the social sphere to fetter him. Locke then specifically refers to New York as a center where intellectual contacts have been made, in large part through the "enrichment of American art and letters." In paragraph 13 he comments on the importance of this cultural contact as a way of offsetting the past. The conditions, he says, that are "moulding a New Negro are moulding a new American attitude." In the concluding paragraph of this section, Locke cautions that the new condition is "delicate" and runs the risk of engendering antagonism and prejudice. Now that the Negro has been "weaned," it is important for the public not to treat him paternalistically. Although the New Negro's outer life, where he participates in American institutions and democracy, is "well and finally formulated," his inner life and psychology are still undergoing formation.

◆ **Paragraphs 15–21**

Locke explores the psychology of the New Negro. At first that psychology was based on a "warped social perspective," but Locke believes that he is witnessing "the development of a more positive self-respect and self-

Flood waters fill the streets of Greenville, Mississippi, in April 1927. (AP/Wide World Photos)

reliance"—that is, a "race pride." His overall theme here is that African Americans are evolving past sentimental stereotypes and the need to be a "ward" of others. In paragraph 16, he expresses the hope that the prejudice of the past will convert from a handicap to an incentive. He notes that many African Americans, in adopting a newly militant posture, are turning leftward in their politics, that is, to Socialism and radicalism. In paragraph 17 he turns to the issue of separatism, such as that advocated by figures such as Marcus Garvey (sponsor of the Back to Africa movement), and characterizes such separatism as undesirable. He illustrates the tensions in African Americans' views of themselves through current poetry. Claude McKay's poem "To the Intrenched Classes" serves as an example of "defiant ironic challenge," referring to McKay's vision of a future of eroding possibilities. In contrast, he quotes from James Weldon Johnson's "O Southland!" as an example of "appeal" to the South to shed its historical limitations with regard to African Americans. Between these two extremes of "defiance and appeal" is Johnson's poem "To America." Locke's appeal is for African Americans to adopt this middle ground between "cynicism and hope."

◆ **Paragraphs 22–25**

Locke concludes his essay with an appeal to African American writers to follow "constructive channels." In paragraph 23 he urges these writers to serve as an "advance-guard" for Africa in its contact with the twentieth century and charges them with "rehabilitating the race." He goes on specifically to refer to the events taking place in Harlem, the home of African Americans' "Zionism." He uses this word as a figure of speech, comparing the African American's search for a home to that of the Jews. Later, in paragraph 24, he asserts that "the future development of Africa is one of the most constructive and universally helpful missions that any modern people can lay claim to." He notes some of the cultural developments taking place in Harlem and the neighborhood's ability to attract people from all over the world. All of these social and cultural achievements are creating a "group consciousness" that is healthy for the black community.

Paragraph 25 concludes the essay with a further appeal. He states that the black race can rehabilitate itself through its "artistic endowments and cultural contributions, past and prospective." He points out that African Americans have already made significant contributions to the nation's cultural life. He wants the African American to no longer be a "beneficiary and ward" and instead become a "conscious contributor." Locke expresses hope that the New Negro will in time "celebrate his full initiation into American democracy," but if he does not, he will at least take pride in his own "Coming of Age."

Essential Quotes

"The mind of the Negro seems suddenly to have slipped from under the tyranny of social intimidation and to be shaking off the psychology of imitation and implied inferiority. By shedding the old chrysalis of the Negro problem we are achieving something like a spiritual emancipation."
(Paragraph 4)

"The day of 'aunties,' 'uncles' and 'mammies' is equally gone. Uncle Tom and Sambo have passed on."
(Paragraph 6)

"The intelligent Negro of today is resolved not to make discrimination an extenuation for his shortcomings in performance, individual or collective; he is trying to hold himself at par, neither inflated by sentimental allowances nor depreciated by current social discounts."
(Paragraph 8)

"[The New Negro] resents being spoken for as a social ward or minor, even by his own, and to being regarded a chronic patient for the sociological clinic, the sick man of American Democracy."
(Paragraph 15)

"It must be increasingly recognized that the Negro has already made very substantial contributions, not only in his folk-art, music especially, which has always found appreciation, but in larger, though humbler and less acknowledged ways. For generations the Negro has been the peasant matrix of that section of America which has most undervalued him, and here he has contributed not only materially in labor and in social patience, but spiritually as well."
(Paragraph 25)

Audience

"Enter the New Negro" was published in a special issue of *Survey Graphic*. The nonprofit, mainstream journal was launched in 1921, and through 1932 it was the illustrated supplement to *The Survey*, the nation's premier social work journal. In 1933 it became a separate publication and survived until 1952. *Survey Graphic* published articles on a host of contemporary issues, including trade unionism, anti-Semitism, the rise of Fascism, poverty, and political and education reform. The roots of the journal were progressive, and it was never shy about taking on controversial issues. Its emphasis was on the role that government played in shaping the lives of individuals. Its audience, which was relatively small compared with that of other mainstream publications, consisted primarily of middle-class professionals who took an interest in issues pertaining to social welfare and who themselves were in a position to make decisions that affected the lives of all Americans. Later, during the 1930s, the journal played an important role in visually documenting the hardships of the Great Depression.

Impact

It is difficult to trace the immediate impact of a single article or book announcing the views of a movement such as the Harlem Renaissance. "Enter the New Negro" was part of a welter of books and articles examining the issue of race before, during, and after the 1920s. The climate for these publications was ripe. The nation had put aside the hardships and privations of World War I. In 1919 women were granted the right to vote, bringing the issue of civil rights to the national consciousness. But that year, too, numerous race riots plagued American cities; in some instances, blacks were attacked or lynched while still wearing their military uniforms. At the same time, the Progressive movement was still making its influence felt. Trade unionism, for example, was gaining more traction at a time when American workers were competing for jobs and there was considerable labor unrest. The 1920s, often called the Roaring Twenties, was a time of growing prosperity and seemingly endless possibilities. In this climate of growing freedom, of the casting off of old traditions and old ways of thinking, African American writers were determined to find a place in American culture and society.

Writers such as Alain Locke were showing them how, and why. His work helped launch the careers of writers such as Zora Neale Hurston, whose short story "Spunk" appeared in the anthology.

In a sense, Locke's work lit a fire under other African American writers. *Fire!!* was a black literary magazine launched in 1926 by a group of African American writers who defiantly called themselves the Niggerati (a play on the word *literati*): Wallace Thurman, Zora Neale Hurston, Aaron Douglas, John P. Davis, Richard Bruce Nugent, Gwendolyn Bennett, Countee Cullen, and Langston Hughes. Hughes explained the title by saying that it conveyed the desire to burn up old, conventional ideas and showcase the talent of younger writers. The magazine, which its founders said was inspired by Locke's work, lasted for only a single issue, and critical reaction to it exemplified differing views about the role of African American literature. While some critics applauded the magazine for its unique perspective, others, particularly some members of the black intelligentsia (Du Bois's "Talented Tenth") found some of its topics, such as homosexuality, vulgar and were troubled by what they regarded as the stereotyped use of southern vernacular. Despite differing views about the merits of any particular writer's work, in the years following the publication of Locke's essay, a tidal wave of fiction, poetry, and drama flowed from the pens of African American writers. No longer was American literature the sole province of New England's white middle and upper classes. African American literature was now part of the national cultural landscape.

See also Marcus Garvey: "The Principles of the Universal Negro Improvement Association" (1922); James Weldon Johnson's "Harlem: The Culture Capital" (1925).

Questions for Further Study

1. Describe the demographic trends in the United States that contributed to the Harlem Renaissance.

2. According to Locke, what is "the New Negro"? What does he mean by this term? What characteristics describe the African American community during this era?

3. Describe some of the racial stereotypes and racial attitudes that Locke believes have to be overcome.

4. Locke and W. E. B. Du Bois were arguably the two foremost African American intellectuals in the early decades of the twentieth century. Compare this document with Du Bois's *The Souls of Black Folk* (1903). Do they make any arguments that are similar? Do the two documents have different emphases? Explain.

5. Similarly, compare this document with James Weldon Johnson's "Harlem: The Culture Capital." Do the two writers express attitudes toward the Harlem Renaissance that are fundamentally the same or different? Explain.

6. Just three years earlier, Marcus Garvey published "The Principles of the Universal Negro Improvement Association." What do you think Locke's reaction to those principles was?

Further Reading

■ Articles

Holmes, Eugene C. "Alain Leroy Locke: A Sketch." *Phylon Quarterly* 20, no. 1 (1959): 82–89.

———. "Alain Locke and the New Negro Movement." *Negro American Literature Forum* 2, no. 3 (1968): 60–68.

■ Books

Eze, Chielozona. *The Dilemma of Ethnic Identity: Alain Locke's Vision of Transcultural Societies*. Lewiston, N.Y.: Edwin Mellen Press, 2005.

Grossman, James R. *Land of Hope: Chicago, Black Southerners, and the Great Migration*. Chicago: University of Chicago Press, 1991.

Harris, Leonard, and Charles Molesworth. *Alain Locke: Biography of a Philosopher*. Chicago: University of Chicago Press, 2008.

Huggins, Nathan. *Harlem Renaissance*. New York: Oxford University Press, 1973.

Lemann, Nicholas. *The Promised Land: The Great Black Migration and How It Changed America*. New York: Vintage, 1991.

Linnemann, Russell J., ed. *Alain Locke: Reflections on a Modern Renaissance Man*. Baton Rouge: Louisiana State University Press, 1982.

Washington, Johnny. *Alain Locke and Philosophy: A Quest for Cultural Pluralism*. Westport, Conn.: Greenwood Press, 1986.

———. *A Journey into the Philosophy of Alain Locke*. Westport, Conn.: Greenwood Press, 1994.

Watson, Steven. *The Harlem Renaissance: Hub of African-American Culture, 1920–1930*. New York: Pantheon, 1995.

Wintz, Cary D. *Black Culture and the Harlem Renaissance*. Houston, Tex.: Rice University Press, 1988.

———. *Harlem Speaks: A Living History of the Harlem Renaissance*. Naperville, Ill.: Sourcebooks, 2007.

■ Web Sites

"The *Survey Graphic* Harlem Number." University of Virginia Library Electronic Text Center Web site.
http://etext.virginia.edu/harlem/contents.html.

—Michael J. O'Neal

Alain Locke's "Enter the New Negro"

In the last decade something beyond the watch and guard of statistics has happened in the life of the American Negro and the three norns who have traditionally presided over the Negro problem have a changeling in their laps. The Sociologist, The Philanthropist, the Race-leader are not unaware of the New Negro but they are at a loss to account for him. He simply cannot be swathed in their formulae. For the younger generation is vibrant with a new psychology; the new spirit is awake in the masses, and under the very eyes of the professional observers is transforming what has been a perennial problem into the progressive phases of contemporary Negro life.

Could such a metamorphosis have taken place as suddenly as it has appeared to? The answer is no; not because the New Negro is not here, but because the Old Negro had long become more of a myth than a man. The Old Negro, we must remember, was a creature of moral debate and historical controversy. His has been a stock figure perpetuated as an historical fiction partly in innocent sentimentalism, partly in deliberate reactionism. The Negro himself has contributed his share to this through a sort of protective social mimicry forced upon him by the adverse circumstances of dependence. So for generations in the mind of America, the Negro has been more of a formula than a human being—a something to be argued about, condemned or defended, to be "kept down," or "in his place," or "helped up," to be worried with or worried over, harassed or patronized, a social bogey or a social burden. The thinking Negro even has been induced to share this same general attitude, to focus his attention on controversial issues, to see himself in the distorted perspective of a social problem. His shadow, so to speak, has been more real to him than his personality. Through having had to appeal from the unjust stereotypes of his oppressors and traducers to those of his liberators, friends and benefactors he has subscribed to the traditional positions from which his case has been viewed. Little true social or self-understanding has or could come from such a situation.

We have not been watching in the right direction; set North and South on a sectional axis, we have not noticed the East till the sun has us blinking.

Recall how suddenly the Negro spirituals revealed themselves; suppressed for generations under the stereotypes of Wesleyan hymn harmony, secretive, half-ashamed, until the courage of being natural brought them out—and behold, there was folk-music. Similarly the mind of the Negro seems suddenly to have slipped from under the tyranny of social intimidation and to be shaking off the psychology of imitation and implied inferiority. By shedding the old chrysalis of the Negro problem we are achieving something like a spiritual emancipation. Until recently, lacking self-understanding, we have been almost as much of a problem to ourselves as we still are to others. But the decade that found us with a problem has left us with only a task. The multitude perhaps feels as yet only a strange relief and a new vague urge, but the thinking few know that in the reaction the vital inner grip of prejudice has been broken.

With this renewed self-respect and self-dependence, the life of the Negro community is bound to enter a new dynamic phase, the buoyancy from within compensating for whatever pressure there may be of conditions from without. The migrant masses, shifting from countryside to city, hurdle several generations of experience at a leap, but more important, the same thing happens spiritually in the life-attitudes and self-expression of the Young Negro, in his poetry, his art, his education and his new outlook, with the additional advantage, of course, of the poise and greater certainty of knowing what it is all about. From this comes the promise and warrant of a new leadership. As one of them has discerningly put it:

> We have tomorrow
> Bright before us
> Like a flame.
> Yesterday, a night-gone thing
> A sun-down name.
> And dawn today
> Broad arch above the road we came.
> We march!

This is what, even more than any "most creditable record of fifty years of freedom," requires that the Negro of today be seen through other than the dusty spectacles of past controversy. The day of "aunties," "uncles" and "mammies" is equally gone. Uncle Tom and Sambo have passed on, and even the "Colonel" and "George" play barnstorm roles from which they escape with relief when the public spotlight is off. The popular melodrama has about played itself out, and it is time to scrap the fictions, garret the bogeys and settle down to a realistic facing of facts.

First we must observe some of the changes which since the traditional lines of opinion were drawn have rendered these quite obsolete. A main change has been, of course, that shifting of the Negro population which has made the Negro problem no longer exclusively or even predominantly Southern. Why should our minds remain sectionalized, when the problem itself no longer is? Then the trend of migration has not only been toward the North and the Central Midwest, but city-ward and to the great centers of industry—the problems of adjustment are new, practical, local and not peculiarly racial. Rather they are an integral part of the large industrial and social problems of our present-day democracy. And finally, with the Negro rapidly in process of class differentiation, if it ever was warrantable to regard and treat the Negro en masse it is becoming with every day less possible, more unjust and more ridiculous.

The Negro too, for his part, has idols of the tribe to smash. If on the one hand the white man has erred in making the Negro appear to be that which would excuse or extenuate his treatment of him, the Negro, in turn, has too often unnecessarily excused himself because of the way he has been treated. The intelligent Negro of today is resolved not to make discrimination an extenuation for his shortcomings in performance, individual or collective; he is trying to hold himself at par, neither inflated by sentimental allowances nor depreciated by current social discounts. For this he must know himself and be known for precisely what he is, and for that reason he welcomes the new scientific rather than the old sentimental interest. Sentimental interest in the Negro has ebbed. We used to lament this as the falling off of our friends; now we rejoice and pray to be delivered both from self-pity and condescension. The mind of each racial group has had a bitter weaning, apathy or hatred on one side matching disillusionment or resentment on the other; but they face each other today with the possibility at least of entirely new mutual attitudes.

It does not follow that if the Negro were better known, he would be better liked or better treated. But mutual understanding is basic for any subsequent cooperation and adjustment. The effort toward this will at least have the effect of remedying in large part what has been the most unsatisfactory feature of our present stage of race relationships in America, namely the fact that the more intelligent and representative elements of the two race groups have at so many points got quite out of vital touch with one another.

The fiction is that the life of the races is separate and increasingly so. The fact is that they have touched too closely at the unfavorable and too lightly at the favorable levels.

While inter-racial councils have sprung up in the South, drawing on forward elements of both races, in the Northern cities manual laborers may brush elbows in their everyday work, but the community and business leaders have experienced no such interplay or far too little of it. These segments must achieve contact or the race situation in America becomes desperate. Fortunately this is happening. There is a growing realization that in social effort the cooperative basis must supplant long-distance philanthropy, and that the only safeguard for mass relations in the future must be provided in the carefully maintained contacts of the enlightened minorities of both race groups. In the intellectual realm a renewed and keen curiosity is replacing the recent apathy; the Negro is being carefully studied, not just talked about and discussed. In art and letters, instead of being wholly caricatured, he is being seriously portrayed and painted.

To all of this the New Negro is keenly responsive as an augury of a new democracy in American culture. He is contributing his share to the new social understanding. But the desire to be understood would never in itself have been sufficient to have opened so completely the protectively closed portals of the thinking Negro's mind. There is still too much possibility of being snubbed or patronized for that. It was rather the necessity for fuller, truer, self-expression, the realization of the unwisdom of allowing social discrimination to segregate him mentally, and a counter-attitude to cramp and fetter his own living—and so the "spite-wall" that the intellectuals built over the "color-line" has happily been taken down. Much of this reopening of intellectual contacts has entered in New York and has been richly fruitful not merely in the enlarging of personal experience, but in the definite enrichment of American art and letters and in the clarifying of our common vision of the social tasks ahead.

The particular significance in the reestablishment of contact between the more advanced and representative classes is that it promises to offset some of the unfavorable reactions of the past, or at least to resurface race contacts somewhat for the future. Subtly the conditions that are moulding a New Negro are moulding a new American attitude.

However, this new phase of things is delicate; it will call for less charity but more justice; less help, but infinitely closer understanding. This is indeed a critical stage of race relationships because of the likelihood, if the new temper is not understood, of engendering sharp group antagonism and a second crop of more calculated prejudice. In some quarters, it has already done so. Having weaned the Negro, public opinion cannot continue to paternalize. The Negro today is inevitably moving forward under the control largely of his own objectives. What are these objectives? Those of his outer life are happily already well and finally formulated, for they are none other than the ideals of American institutions and democracy. Those of his inner life are yet in process of formation, for the new psychology at present is more of a consensus of feeling than of opinion, of attitude rather than of program. Still some points seem to have crystallized.

Up to the present one may adequately describe the Negro's "inner objectives" as an attempt to repair a damaged group psychology and reshape a warped social perspective. Their realization has required a new mentality for the American Negro. And as it matures we begin to see its effects; at first, negative, iconoclastic, and then positive and constructive. In this new group psychology we note the lapse of sentimental appeal, then the development of a more positive self-respect and self-reliance; the repudiation of social dependence, and then the gradual recovery from hyper-sensitiveness and "touchy" nerves, the repudiation of the double standard of judgment with its special philanthropic allowances and then the sturdier desire for objective and scientific appraisal; and finally the rise from social disillusionment to race pride, from the sense of social debt to the responsibilities of social contribution, and offsetting the necessary working and commonsense acceptance of restricted conditions, the belief in ultimate esteem and recognition. Therefore the Negro today wishes to be known for what he is, even in his faults and shortcomings, and scorns a craven and precarious survival at the price of seeming to be what he is not. He resents being spoken for as a social ward or minor, even by his own, and to being regarded a chronic patient for the sociological clinic, the sick man of American Democracy. For the same reasons he himself is through with those social nostrums and panaceas, the so-called "solutions" of his "problem," with which he and the country have been so liberally dosed in the past. Religion, freedom, education, money—in turn, he has ardently hoped for and peculiarly trusted these things; he still believes in them, but not in blind trust that they alone will solve his life-problem.

Each generation, however, will have its creed and that of the present is the belief in the efficacy of collective efforts in race cooperation. This deep feeling of race is at present the mainspring of Negro life. It seems to be the outcome of the reaction to proscription and prejudice; an attempt, fairly successful on the whole, to convert a defensive into an offensive position, a handicap into an incentive. It is radical in tone, but not in purpose and only the most stupid forms of opposition, misunderstanding or persecution could make it otherwise. Of course, the thinking Negro has shifted a little toward the left with the world-trend, and there is an increasing group who affiliate with radical and liberal movements. But fundamentally for the present the Negro is radical on race matters, conservative on others, in other words, a "forced radical," a social protestant rather than a genuine radical. Yet under further pressure and injustice iconoclastic thought and motives will inevitably increase. Harlem's quixotic radicalisms call for their ounce of democracy today lest tomorrow they be beyond cure.

The Negro mind reaches out as yet to nothing but American wants, American ideas. But this forced attempt to build his Americanism on race values is a unique social experiment, and its ultimate success is impossible except through the fullest sharing of American culture and institutions. There should be no delusion about this. American nerves in sections unstrung with race hysteria are often fed the opiate that the trend of Negro advance is wholly separatist, and that the effect of its operation will be to encyst the Negro as a benign foreign body in the body politic. This cannot be—even if it were desirable. The racialism of the Negro is no limitation or reservation with respect to American life; it is only a constructive effort to build the obstructions in the stream of his progress into an efficient dam of social energy and power. Democracy itself is obstructed and stagnated to the extent that any of its channels are closed. Indeed they cannot be selectively closed. So the choice is not between one way for the Negro and another way for the rest, but between American institutions frustrated on the one hand and American ideals progressively fulfilled and realized on the other.

There is, of course, a warrantably comfortable feeling in being on the right side of the country's professed ideals. We realize that we cannot be undone without America's undoing. It is within the gamut of this attitude that the thinking Negro faces America, but the variations of mood in connection with it are if anything more significant than the attitude itself. Sometimes we have it taken with the defiant ironic challenge of McKay:

> Mine is the future grinding down today
> Like a great landslip moving to the sea,
> Bearing its freight of debris far away
> Where the green hungry waters restlessly
> Heave mammoth pyramids and break and roar
> Their eerie challenge to the crumbling shore.

Sometimes, perhaps more frequently as yet, in the fervent and almost filial appeal and counsel of Weldon Johnson's:

> O Southland, dear Southland!
> Then why do you still cling
> To an idle age and a musty page,
> To a dead and useless thing.

But between defiance and appeal, midway almost between cynicism and hope, the prevailing mind stands in the mood of the same author's To America, an attitude of sober query and stoical challenge:

> How would you have us, as we are?
> Or sinking heath the load we bear,
> Our eyes fixed forward on a star,
> Or gazing empty at despair?
> Rising or falling? Men or things?
> With dragging pace or footsteps fleet?
> Strong, willing sinews in your wings,
> Or tightening chains about your feet?

More and more, however, an intelligent realization of the great discrepancy between the American social creed and the American social practice forces upon the Negro the taking of the moral advantage that is his. Only the steadying and sobering effect of a truly characteristic gentleness of spirit prevents the rapid rise of a definite cynicism and counter-hate and a defiant superiority feeling. Human as this reaction would be, the majority still deprecate its advent, and would gladly see it forestalled by the speedy amelioration of its causes. We wish our race pride to be a healthier, more positive achievement than a feeling based upon a realization of the shortcomings of others. But all paths toward the attainment of a sound social attitude have been difficult; only a relatively few enlightened minds have been able as the phrase puts it "to rise above" prejudice. The ordinary man has had until recently only a hard choice between the alternatives of supine and humiliating submission and stimulating but hurtful counter-prejudice. Fortunately from some inner, desperate resourcefulness has recently sprung up the simple expedient of fighting prejudice by mental passive resistance, in other words by trying to ignore it. For the few, this manna may perhaps be effective, but the masses cannot thrive on it.

Fortunately there are constructive channels opening out into which the balked social feelings of the American Negro can flow freely.

Without them there would be much more pressure and danger than there is. These compensating interests are racial but in a new and enlarged way. One is the consciousness of acting as the advance-guard of the African peoples in their contact with Twentieth Century civilization; the other, the sense of a mission of rehabilitating the race in world esteem from that loss of prestige for which the fate and conditions of slavery have so largely been responsible. Harlem, as we shall see, is the center of both these movements; she is the home of the Negro's "Zionism." The pulse of the Negro world has begun to beat in Harlem. A Negro newspaper carrying news material in English, French and Spanish, gathered from all quarters of America, the West Indies and Africa has maintained itself in Harlem for over five years. Two important magazines, both edited from New York, maintain their news and circulation consistently on a cosmopolitan scale. Under American auspices and backing, three pan-African congresses have been held abroad for the discussion of common interests, colonial questions and the future cooperative development of Africa. In terms of the race question as a world problem, the Negro mind has leapt, so to speak, upon the parapets of prejudice and extended its cramped horizons. In so doing it has linked up with the growing group consciousness of the dark-peoples and is gradually learning their common interests. As one of our writers has recently put it: "It is imperative that we understand the white world in its relations to the nonwhite world." As with the Jew, persecution is making the Negro international.

As a world phenomenon this wider race consciousness is a different thing from the much asserted rising tide of color. Its inevitable causes are not of our making. The consequences are not necessarily

Document Text

damaging to the best interests of civilization. Whether it actually brings into being new Armadas of conflict or argosies of cultural exchange and enlightenment can only be decided by the attitude of the dominant races in an era of critical change. With the American Negro his new internationalism is primarily an effort to recapture contact with the scattered peoples of African derivation. Garveyism may be a transient, if spectacular, phenomenon, but the possible role of the American Negro in the future development of Africa is one of the most constructive and universally helpful missions that any modern people can lay claim to.

Constructive participation in such causes cannot help giving the Negro valuable group incentives, as well as increased prestige at home and abroad. Our greatest rehabilitation may possibly come through such channels, but for the present, more immediate hope rests in the revaluation by white and black alike of the Negro in terms of his artistic endowments and cultural contributions, past and prospective. It must be increasingly recognized that the Negro has already made very substantial contributions, not only in his folk-art, music especially, which has always found appreciation, but in larger, though humbler and less acknowledged ways. For generations the Negro has been the peasant matrix of that section of America which has most undervalued him, and here he has contributed not only materially in labor and in social patience, but spiritually as well. The South has unconsciously absorbed the gift of his folk-temperament. In less than half a generation it will be easier to recognize this, but the fact remains that a leaven of humor, sentiment, imagination and tropic nonchalance has gone into the making of the South from a humble, unacknowledged source. A second crop of the Negro's gifts promises still more largely. He now becomes a conscious contributor and lays aside the

Glossary

argosies	fleets of merchant ships
Armadas	fleets of naval ships
changeling	a child secretly exchanged for another in infancy
chrysalis	the pupa of a butterfly enclosed in a cocoon
Garveyism	a reference to the views of Marcus Garvey, the founder of the Universal Negro Improvement Association
"How would you have us …"	from James Weldon Johnson's poem "To America"
idols of the tribe	a figure of speech, coined by Sir Francis Bacon, referring to deceptive beliefs
"Mine is the future …"	from Claude McKay's poem "To the Intrenched Classes"
norns	goddesses in Norse mythology that preside over human destiny
"O Southland, dear Southland! …"	from James Weldon Johnson's poem "O Southland"
Sambo	a commonly used racial slur in the nineteenth century
Uncle Tom	a character in Harriet Beecher Stowe's *Uncle Tom's Cabin*; often used disparagingly to refer to a black person who submits to whites
"We have tomorrow …"	from the poem "Youth" by Langston Hughes
Wesleyan	a reference to John Wesley, the eighteenth-century founder of the Methodist denomination
Zionism	a reference to the movement among Jews to create a homeland in Palestine

Document Text

status of a beneficiary and ward for that of a collaborator and participant in American civilization. The great social gain in this is the releasing of our talented group from the arid fields of controversy and debate to the productive fields of creative expression. The especially cultural recognition they win should in turn prove the key to that revaluation of the Negro which must precede or accompany any considerable further betterment of race relationships. But whatever the general effect, the present generation will have added the motives of self-expression and spiritual development to the old and still unfinished task of making material headway and progress. No one who understandingly faces the situation with its substantial accomplishment or views the new scene with its still more abundant promise can be entirely without hope. And certainly, if in our lifetime the Negro should not be able to celebrate his full initiation into American democracy, he can at least, on the warrant of these things, celebrate the attainment of a significant and satisfying new phase of group development, and with it a spiritual Coming of Age.

James Weldon Johnson's "Harlem: The Culture Capital"

"Harlem is more than a Negro community; it is a large scale laboratory experiment in the race problem."

Overview

The 1920s witnessed a virtual explosion of African American artistic expression of all kinds, which centered in Harlem on New York's Upper West Side. More popularly known as the Harlem Renaissance, this cultural movement attracted many of the most accomplished black writers, artists, actors, and musicians of the early twentieth century. James Weldon Johnson was one of the movement's most respected contributors and, in the eyes of many, its godfather and most illustrious statesman. Like thousands of other black Americans who moved to Harlem from the South during the three decades prior to the Great Depression, Johnson was optimistic that "Black Manhattan" would offer economic, cultural, and racial liberation for himself and others. Indeed, Johnson viewed Harlem as a model for black advancement that could be achieved with unprecedented speed and with a minimum of racial tension. His essay "Harlem: The Culture Capital" was included in Professor Alain Locke's famous 1925 anthology, *The New Negro*, which served to introduce some young black authors but also featured the work of older and better-known writers like Johnson. An illustrated draft of Johnson's essay had also appeared in the limited circulation magazine *Survey Graphic* earlier that year. In 1930 he completed his much-anticipated book on the full history of African Americans in New York, called *Black Manhattan*, which was built around both versions of this article.

Context

The migration of hundreds of thousands of African Americans from the mostly rural South to northern industrial centers in the two decades before World War I helped change in dramatic ways the black experience in American life. It began as early as the 1890s, with a trickle of black families seeking better economic conditions, and reached flood tide with World War I and the subsequent restrictions on immigration, which would create job opportunities in unprecedented numbers. Some families simply relocated to cities in the South, but many, especially those from the Southeast, chose to move northward to Philadelphia, New York, and Boston. Those further west, in states like Arkansas and Tennessee, were more likely to find new homes in Chicago, Detroit, or Cleveland. But the most spectacular growth in black urban populations occurred in New York City in Harlem. By 1905 there were already sixty thousand African Americans in the city, and most of them were in the crowded neighborhoods of San Juan Hill and the Tenderloin in west-central Manhattan. Five years later, they were the majority in the once solidly middle-class white Harlem, north of 130th Street. Just before the outbreak of World War I, the black population of Harlem alone had surpassed fifty thousand.

In the 1920s, thousands more southern blacks and significant numbers from the West Indies would eventually extend black Harlem from 115th Street north to 155th Street, between the Harlem River and Amsterdam Avenue. Just before the beginning of the Great Depression, Harlem's black population was almost one hundred seventy thousand, making it, in James Weldon Johnson's words, "the most important black city in the world."

Population growth in Harlem was only part of the story. Black restaurants, speakeasies, jazz clubs, cabarets, stores, and churches quickly followed. The Harlem branch of the New York Public Library had a black staff, and the Harlem Young Men's Christian Association was one of the few branches that catered to African Americans. Even many police officers walking their beats were black. The newly formed National Association for the Advancement of Colored People (NAACP) established its headquarters nearby in lower Manhattan, and so did the National Urban League. Harlem was also the home of the most influential black labor union, the Brotherhood of Sleeping Car Porters, led by the young Socialist A. Philip Randolph. The black nationalist and Pan-Africanist Marcus Garvey relocated his United Negro Improvement Association from Jamaica to Harlem, where it startled everyone with its appeal to working class blacks.

In little more than a decade, Harlem had clearly become the showcase for the "new Negro." The young Langston Hughes spoke for many new arrivals in Harlem when he expressed amazement at just how black Harlem was when he first emerged from the subway station at 135th Street and Lenox Avenue in 1921. As Hughes soon learned, how-

Time Line

1871
- **June 17**
  James Weldon Johnson is born in Jacksonville, Florida.

1900
- Johnson writes the lyrics to "Lift Every Voice and Sing," to music composed by his brother J. Rosamond Johnson.
- **August 15 and 16**
  Riots in the San Juan Hill District and the Tenderloin ghetto of Manhattan's West Side help push many African Americans seeking better living conditions north toward Harlem.

1902
- **Summer**
  Johnson and his brother Rosamond publish their first big hit song, "Under the Bamboo Tree."

1909
- **February 12**
  The National Association for the Advancement of Colored People (NAACP) is founded in New York City.

1910
- **September 29**
  The Committee on Urban Conditions among Negroes, a forerunner of the National Urban League, is founded in New York to assist the thousands of blacks recently arrived from the South.

1912
- Johnson publishes his only novel, *The Autobiography of an Ex-Colored Man*; a second edition would appear to great critical acclaim in the 1920s, at the height of the Harlem Renaissance.

1916
- **May**
  A year after the death of Booker T. Washington, whom he admired greatly, Johnson is elected vice president of the New York chapter of the NAACP, with national offices in Manhattan.

---

ever, whites still owned the most important stores and shops, and most of the clerks who worked in them were white as well. Even more disappointing was that some of the jazz clubs were white owned and catered to segregated audiences composed of whites who were eager to sample the mysteries of Harlem life. Still, it was a heady experience for Hughes and other recent arrivals to find for the first time a city of black people within a city controlled by whites.

Hughes was only one of many young black writers and artists attracted to the cultural excitement of Harlem. Between World War I and the Great Depression, Claude McKay, Zora Neale Hurston, Aaron Douglas, Wallace Thurman, Duke Ellington, and others added to the artistic flowering that came to be known as the Harlem Renaissance. Johnson was older than all of them, and his ties to Harlem were much deeper.

By the time Langston Hughes arrived in Harlem, it had been the city of residence for James Weldon Johnson for several years. Almost a generation older than Hughes, Johnson had visited New York from his native Florida as early as 1884, but his adult association with the city began in the late 1890s as a fledgling musician who, with his brother, hoped to establish himself as a songwriter. Johnson became a full-time resident in 1902. As a poet, journalist, and civil rights activist, he emerged as a dapper, sophisticated, and popular member of Harlem's intellectual elite.

Thus, it was altogether fitting, and perhaps strategically astute, that Alain Locke included Johnson's essay in *The New Negro*. In fact, "Harlem: The Culture Capital" helped set the tone of literary legitimacy for a group of younger black writers who had not yet established their own careers. Johnson was always willing to encourage young artists personally. He also used his influence as the executive secretary of the NAACP in the 1920s to advance the cause of the black artistic community generally.

About the Author

James Weldon Johnson, poet, novelist, essayist, anthologist, lyricist, diplomat, civil rights activist, and educator, was born in Jacksonville, Florida, in 1871 to Helen Louise Diller, a native of the Bahamas, and James Johnson. He was educated in the segregated public schools of Jacksonville and graduated from Georgia's Atlanta University in 1894 with a degree in music. At age twenty-three he became the principal of his former school in Jacksonville, while he simultaneously pursued careers as a journalist and lawyer. He was the first African American admitted to the Florida bar.

But his first love proved to be songwriting, often in collaboration with his brother Rosamond. Together the Johnson brothers visited New York several times in the late 1890s in an effort to market their songs and musical productions. They enjoyed modest commercial successes (as when their "Under the Bamboo Tree" sold four hundred thousand copies), but they are perhaps best remembered for the lyrics (by James) and the music (by Rosamond) of the Negro national anthem, "Lift Every Voice and Sing," which they wrote for a school celebration of Abraham Lincoln's birthday.

Johnson's musical career inevitably led him to become a permanent resident of New York City, where he stayed for the next thirty years, except for a brief stint as a U.S. consul, first in Venezuela and then in Nicaragua, from 1906 through 1912. While on diplomatic assignment he also wrote his only novel, *The Autobiography of an Ex-Colored Man*, which received mostly positive reviews. In 1910, while on leave in New York from the consular service, he married Grace Nail, the daughter of John B. Nail, a pioneering African American entrepreneur in Manhattan, whose son, John E. Nail, would be among the first black investors in Harlem real estate. In 1912, Johnson took an official leave from his consular post, to which he never returned. Johnson and his wife split time between New York and Jacksonville, Florida, during 1913, finally settling in Harlem in 1914. During this time, he wrote tightly reasoned editorials—often on racial issues—for the black newspaper the *New York Age* and dabbled in local Republican politics. But Johnson was also an accomplished poet whose work had been published several times and appeared most dramatically on the *New York Times* editorial page in 1913 on the fiftieth anniversary of the Emancipation Proclamation, in the form of a forty-one-stanza poem, "Fifty Years," that garnered rave reviews from, among others, the African American novelist Charles Chesnutt. Johnson would later author several volumes of his own poetry and edit a handful of others.

Johnson, whose career had often been identified with Booker T. Washington, surprised some by joining the NAACP in 1916 and was shortly thereafter elected the president of the New York City chapter. His association with this organization brought him into close contact with such civil rights luminaries as the mercurial W. E. B. Du Bois and the obstinate Oswald Villard, who eventually helped persuade Johnson to be the NAACP's field secretary. In 1920 he was chosen the organization's first black executive secretary, a post that he held for the next decade. Johnson proved to be a brilliantly effective administrator who instinctively understood how to deal with an organization full of strong-willed personalities and to reach an institutional consensus among competing strategies and agendas. Nowhere were his administrative and diplomatic talents more evident than in using the NAACP to encourage young African American writers and artists whose maverick personalities sometimes made them difficult to deal with. A 1924 banquet at the integrated Civic Club in Manhattan brought together black writers and white publishers in an event that was legendary in the history of the Harlem Renaissance and inspired the publication of Alain Locke's anthology of black poetry and prose, *The New Negro*, in 1925. Johnson's essay on Harlem appeared in that anthology.

Johnson's tenure at the NAACP came at a crucial moment in the civil rights movement. He took an active role in its unsuccessful initiative to pressure Congress into passing an antilynching bill and was also an outspoken crit-

Time Line

1916
- **December** Johnson is named field secretary in the national offices of the NAACP.

1917
- The black nationalist Marcus Garvey founds the first American branch of his United Negro Improvement Association in Harlem. The association has impressive popular appeal to working-class African Americans but is almost universally rejected by the black intelligentsia of Harlem, including Johnson.

1920
- Johnson becomes the first black executive secretary of the NAACP, and its membership soars.
- Harlem's population of black residents exceeds seventy thousand for the first time.

1921
- "Shuffle Along," the first musical produced, written, and acted by African Americans in Manhattan, becomes a blockbuster hit that sets the tone, content, and pace for other Harlem productions in the 1920s.

1924
- Charles Johnson of the National Urban League organizes the famous Civic Club banquet where Professor Alain Locke, acting as master of ceremonies, introduces many African American writers to white publishers and the public.

1925
- Locke edits *The New Negro*, a groundbreaking anthology of poetry and prose by black writers, most of whom are identified with the Harlem Renaissance. Johnson's essay "Harlem: The Culture Capital" is included in the volume.

Time Line

1930
- Johnson resigns his NAACP post and completes his *Black Manhattan*, a history of African Americans in New York City. He accepts the post of professor of creative literature at Fisk University in Nashville, Tennessee.

1935
- Destructive Harlem riots and the debilitating effects of the Great Depression help erode the image of Harlem as a model black community and weaken its reputation as the cultural capital of African Americans.

1938
- **June 26** James Weldon Johnson dies in a tragic automobile crash while on vacation in Maine.

ic of racial violence and prejudice of all kinds. On his watch, the NAACP expanded its chapter base into the South and West and became the premier civil rights advocacy group in the world. Johnson resigned from the NAACP in 1930 to become a professor of literature at Fisk University in Nashville, Tennessee, but found opportunities to return to his beloved New York on many occasions. He died as a result of injuries sustained in an automobile accident while on vacation in Maine in 1938.

Explanation and Analysis of the Document

In "Harlem: The Culture Capital," Johnson describes the past, present, and what he envisions as the future of the New York City neighborhood that black intellectuals considered the black capital. His observations chronicle the transitions in the ethnic makeup of Harlem and the migration of blacks from other parts of the city, in search of economic opportunity and financial security. Johnson closes with an optimistic vision of Harlem's prospects for ongoing prosperity and stability.

◆ **Paragraphs 1 and 2**

In the first two paragraphs of his essay, Johnson sounds a glowingly optimistic note about the brief past and promising future of black Harlem, which he describes as the "great Mecca" for the curious and enterprising who have in a very short period of time come from all parts of the United States and even from Africa and the Caribbean Islands. He points out at some length that although Harlem is heavily populated by blacks, it is not a ghetto or a slum but rather a "city within a city," where the quality of housing and high levels of commercial activity are virtually identical to the districts—mostly white—that lie immediately to its south and north. For Johnson, this curious circumstance of a neighborhood that is identified only by the skin color of its residents and not by the condition of its streets or the appearance of its buildings makes Harlem a unique experiment in racial uplift.

Johnson is careful to set Harlem apart in at least two ways from other neighborhoods in New York and elsewhere where blacks may live but where there is less potential for racial advancement. First, because blacks moved into Harlem while it was still thoroughly middle class, there was no inherited legacy of poverty, squalor, or urban decay. Second, unlike other urban black districts, Harlem had an unusually large critical mass of blacks who sought the same goals and had the same ambitions as other racial and ethnic groups. Johnson's upbeat appraisal of Harlem has not been supported by recent scholarship. Most historians today would point out that statistical evidence—some of which would not have been readily available to Johnson in the 1920s—suggests that if Harlem was not a ghetto in 1920 or even 1925, it was getting dangerously close by 1930 and beyond. Johnson's glowing account was, however, not necessarily the product of undiluted racial boosterism but more likely a reflection of his conviction that racial progress was inevitable and well under way in the Harlem he describes here.

◆ **Paragraphs 3 and 4**

The third and fourth paragraphs offer a brief and informative history of black residential patterns on Manhattan's West Side in the pre-Harlem years of the very late nineteenth century, a history in which Johnson himself had participated as a young aspiring musician and lyricist. It is important to note that in this and other sections of his essay Johnson is both historian and autobiographer, a chronicler of important developments but also a participant in the events he describes. Johnson accurately points out that the move northward by black residents of Manhattan was slow but inexorable. By 1890 the center of the black district on Manhattan's West Side had moved as far north as 30th Street; by 1900—roughly when Johnson first came to New York—the northward migration had reached 53rd Street, and there were already obvious stirrings of black culture, especially in music and theater. Johnson himself regularly patronized the Marshall Hotel on 53rd Street and was among the regular celebrity figures there. (His reference to Cole and Johnson, for example, is to himself and Bob Cole, with whom he teamed to write songs.) At least in terms of popular stage and music, it is clear that there was a significant artistic movement under way in midtown Manhattan twenty years before the center of Negro culture moved to Harlem.

◆ **Paragraphs 5–7**

In the next three paragraphs, Johnson accurately, though without much detail, describes the initial move-

Harlem River, which separates the Bronx from Manhattan, in the first decade of the twentieth century (Library of

ment of black people from the midtown Manhattan on the West Side to Harlem. He is correct in asserting that the initial wave of blacks to Harlem in the first decade of the twentieth century was in response to cheaper and better housing that was available in upper Harlem because that district had been hopelessly overbuilt by real estate investors hoping to sell to middle-class white residents. Not mentioned in Johnson's account (but discussed briefly in his autobiography) was the influence of the 1900 riots in midtown Manhattan, which also encouraged African Americans to look elsewhere for housing. Black real estate entrepreneurs (his example being Philip Payton, an aggressive investor) were important brokers in helping to find black tenants for available rental properties near 135th Street, east of Lenox Avenue (today known as Malcolm X Boulevard), an arrangement that initially created very little attention. But the eventual spread of the black migration west of Lenox Avenue and ultimately farther south and north encountered intermittent white resistance, mostly through property owners' associations that attempted to block the proliferation of black residential growth through evictions and collusion with lending institutions. For their part, black investors formed their own associations to facilitate the purchase and rental of Harlem property; Johnson's in-laws, his wife's father (J. B. Nail) and brother (J. E. Nail), were early investors in Harlem real estate.

◆ **Paragraphs 8 and 9**

For Johnson, the real stimulus for black interest in Harlem came as a result of the labor shortage created by World War I and the subsequent decline in immigration. In his account, government and private labor contractors descended on the South in search of willing workers to replace those displaced by military service. Newspaper editorials and advertisements in black northern newspapers like the *Chicago Defender* are not mentioned in Johnson's account but were also influential in stimulating interest in this steady northern migration of southern blacks, known as the Great Migration. Johnson's description of this phenomenon is predictably optimistic, almost charming at times, as he portrays the migrants, laden with baggage and full of hope for a better life. He compares them to immigrants from Europe, who also sought the promise of a better life in New York. Johnson, however, virtually ignores the large numbers of blacks who came from the South but wound up in other cities, like Chicago, Pittsburgh, Cleveland, and Detroit, which many scholars are beginning to discover had their own versions of Harlem. Johnson is also careful to point out that Harlem-bound black migrants found well-paying jobs in abundance and used their newfound affluence to buy property in unprecedented numbers. His account of "Pig Foot Mary," who sold soul food on Lenox Avenue and saved enough money to buy a five-story apartment house on 137th Street, is legendary in Harlem lore.

◆ **Paragraphs 10 and 11**

Johnson's argument in these two paragraphs is not simply that Harlem offered jobs and economic progress to thousands but also that it helped create a nascent black middle class that embraced the American dream of property ownership and financial security. His assertion that "today Negro Harlem is practically owned by Negroes" is only partially cor-

Essential Quotes

> "In the make-up of New York, Harlem is not merely a Negro colony or community, it is a city within a city, the greatest Negro city in the world."
> (Paragraph 2)

> "Fifteen years ago barely a half dozen colored men owned real property in all Manhattan. And down to ten years ago the amount that had been acquired in Harlem was comparatively negligible. Today, Negro Harlem is practically owned by Negroes."
> (Paragraph 11)

> "To my mind, Harlem is more than a Negro community; it is a large scale laboratory experiment in the race problem."
> (Paragraph 17)

rect, however. His statistics about black property ownership are accurate enough, but most modern historians would be skeptical about his suggestion that Harlem blacks owned Harlem, especially in the 1920s and 1930s. The Harlem riots of 1935, which Johnson would not have known about or anticipated in 1925, are a telling reminder of just how fragile economic prosperity could be for many African Americans in Harlem and elsewhere. The riots, which began as protests over charges of police brutality and were fueled by frustrations about widespread unemployment in Harlem, quickly turned violent and helped focus public attention on the deteriorating economy of the entire area.

◆ **Paragraphs 12–15**

These four paragraphs are devoted to the future of Harlem, which, in Johnson's mind at least, is bright indeed. He turns first to the question of whether "Negroes are going to be able to hold Harlem." His answer is succinct and optimistic: It is unlikely, he believes, that there would be a large-scale black migration from such a prosperous area. But if blacks were to leave Harlem, it would be because their property became so valuable that they could sell at a profit and not because they were forced out as undesirable residents or because their property had lost its value. In short, property in Harlem, often purchased by Negroes at discounted prices, would be a springboard for prosperity even if they left. Such a circumstance, Johnson argues, would actually mean that black property owners had reached the happy position of owning land "so valuable they can no longer afford to live on it." But, he asks rhetorically, is it likely that Harlem property owners could, in an economic downturn, be unable to keep the property he thinks is vital to their long-term security? With equal conviction he insists that Harlem blacks, thanks to their diversified and entrepreneurial economy, are much better protected from catastrophic loss than are African Americans in other urban areas. In fact, Johnson maintains, Harlem's unique makeup of cultural, financial, and religious institutions makes it the most stable black community in the world. For Johnson, Harlem is not another ethnic quarter whose ties to the larger metropolitan center are vague and weak; rather, Harlem "is not alien… ; it is not Italian or Yiddish; it is English. Harlem talks American, reads American, thinks American."

◆ **Paragraphs 16–18**

Johnson's last three paragraphs are devoted to his conclusion that Harlem is best seen not as a Negro residential area but rather as a "large scale laboratory experiment in the race problem." In his mind, there is very little chance that Harlem will be a source of racial tension because whites and blacks have learned to live and work together in ways that do not exist elsewhere in New York or anywhere in the United States, for that matter. The old friction between white residents and Negro intruders is a thing of the past for Johnson. Moreover, he insists that the record of crime in Harlem is the lowest of virtually any area in New York. Put simply, Johnson is convinced that "the Negro's advantages and opportunities are greater in Harlem than in any other place in the country."

Part of Johnson's optimism about Harlem stems from his upbeat personality and his own background of personal success. As one of the most accomplished African Americans of his time—in many ways more talented and certainly more versatile than the great Du Bois himself—it was simply not in his nature to be skeptical about the progress of his race. He was a modern man to be sure, but he was also of the old school of civil rights advocates who believed that once black people had demonstrated that they were the intellectual, artistic, commercial, and athletic equal of whites, their day in the sun would quickly follow. In 1925, when he wrote "Harlem: The Culture Capital," he thought that African Americans were very close to achieving that goal and that Harlem would be the crucible of their final and most glorious achievement. For him Harlem was his beloved home, but more important, he hoped it would be the birthplace of the "new Negro."

Audience

James Weldon Johnson's essay was written originally for a special edition of a limited-circulation artistic magazine, *Survey Graphic*, in 1925, but it was revised for publication in the famous and influential anthology of black literature entitled *The New Negro* later that same year. Some of Johnson's audience was undoubtedly black, but *The New Negro* was also intended to convince white readers (and publishers) that the rumors of black literary talent (and black progress generally) centered in Harlem were based on fact. Johnson had cultivated white audiences of various kinds for years; he knew how to reach them, and he understood what many of them wanted to hear. As a longtime resident of Harlem and as a leader of its intellectual elite, he also believed every word he wrote. He was only one of the contributors to *The New Negro*, but he may have been its most reassuring voice.

Impact

Johnson was one of the most respected black leaders of his time and arguably the most universally talented. The fact that his essay was included in the *Survey Graphic* issue as well as in *The New Negro* is testimony to his influence and skill as an author and a civil rights activist. It also sent a clear message to younger authors that he was a reliable source of aid and encouragement. Johnson had an impressive ability to find common ground among diverse constituencies. He was among the few who could maintain cordial relationships between such adversaries as Booker T. Washington and W. E. B. Du Bois, and he saw no contradiction in advancing his own optimistic views of black progress while encouraging more skeptical writers like Claude McKay and Langston Hughes to find their literary voices. His accomplishments were prodigious, and his faith that others could do the same was lifelong. Today, against the backdrop of modern historical scholarship, he is easily read as naive in his hope for black progress and unrealistic in his conviction that it could be achieved in the same way that other ethnic groups had won respect. Almost a century later, it is clear that Harlem never really came close to Johnson's ideal, but in the 1920s his positive and disarming message was comforting to many. For that reason, his essay was widely read and admired, as was his longer history of blacks in New York, entitled *Black Manhattan*, published in 1930.

See also Alain Locke's "Enter the New Negro" (1925).

Further Reading

- **Books**

Johnson, James Weldon. *James Weldon Johnson: Writings*. New York: Library of America, 2004.

Questions for Further Study

1. Johnson's essay invites comparison with Alain Locke's essay "Enter the New Negro" and, in fact, was published in Locke's 1925 anthology, *The New Negro*. What different perspectives do the two writers take on the Harlem Renaissance?

2. Describe the social and economic factors that gave rise to the Harlem Renaissance.

3. In Johnson's view, what distinguished Harlem from other neighborhoods in which African Americans lived? Why were these differences important?

4. Why, in Johnson's view, was Harlem a "large scale laboratory experiment in the race problem"? What did he mean by this expression? In your opinion, was he correct?

5. In your opinion, was Johnson perhaps naive and unrealistic about the future of the black community? Why or why not?

Levy, Eugene. *James Weldon Johnson: Black Leader, Black Voice.* Chicago: University of Chicago Press, 1972.

Lewis, David Levering. *When Harlem Was in Vogue.* New York: Penguin Books, 1997.

Osofsky, Gilbert. *Harlem: The Making of a Ghetto: Negro New York, 1890–1930.* Chicago: Ivan R. Dee Publishers, 1996.

■ Web Sites

"Modern American Poetry: James Weldon Johnson (1871–1938)." University of Illinois Web site.
http://www.english.illinois.edu/Maps/poets/g_l/johnson/johnson.htm.

—Orson Cook

James Weldon Johnson's "Harlem: The Culture Capital"

In the history of New York, the significance of the name Harlem has changed from Dutch to Irish to Jewish to Negro. Of these changes, the last has come most swiftly, throughout colored America, from Massachusetts to Mississippi, and across the continent to Los Angeles and Seattle, its name, which as late as fifteen years ago had scarcely been heard, now stands for the Negro metropolis. Harlem is indeed the great Mecca for the sight-seer, the pleasure-seeker, the curious, the adventurous, the enterprising, the ambitious and the talented of the whole Negro world; for the lure of it has reached down to every island of the Carib Sea and has penetrated even into Africa.

In the make-up of New York, Harlem is not merely a Negro colony or community, it is a city within a city, the greatest Negro city in the world. It is not a slum or a fringe, it is located in the heart of Manhattan and occupies one of the most beautiful and healthful sections of the city. It is not a "quarter" of dilapidated tenements, but is made up of new-law apartments and handsome dwellings, with well-paved and well-lighted streets. It has its own churches, social and civic centers, shops, theaters and other places of amusement. And it contains more Negroes to the square mile than any other spot on earth. A stranger who rides up magnificent Seventh Avenue on a bus or in an automobile must be struck with surprise at the transformation which takes place after he crosses One Hundred and Twenty-fifth Street. Beginning there, the population suddenly darkens and he rides through twenty-five solid blocks where the passers-by, the shoppers, those sitting in restaurants, coming out of theaters, standing in doorways and looking out of windows are practically all Negroes: and then he emerges where the population as suddenly becomes white again. There is nothing just like it in any other city in the country, for there is no preparation for it; no change in the character of the houses and streets: no change, indeed, in the appearance of the people, except their color.

Negro Harlem is practically a development of the past decade, but the story behind it goes back a long way. There have always been colored people in New York. In the middle of the last century they lived in the vicinity of Lispenard, Broome and Spring Streets. When Washington Square and lower Fifth Avenue were the center of aristocratic life, the colored people, whose chief occupation was domestic service in the homes of the rich, lived in a fringe and were scattered in nests to the south, east and west of the square. As late as the 80's the major part of the colored population lived in Sullivan, Thompson, Bleecker, Grove, Minetta Lane and adjacent streets. It is curious to note that some of these nests still persist. In a number of the blocks of Greenwich Village and Little Italy may be found small groups of Negroes who have never lived in any other section of the city. By about 1890 the center of colored population had shifted to the upper Twenties and lower Thirties west of Sixth Avenue. Ten years later another considerable shift northward had been made to West Fifty-third Street.

The West Fifty-third Street settlement deserves some special mention because it ushered in a new phase of life among colored New Yorkers. Three rather well appointed hotels were opened in the street and they quickly became the centers of a sort of fashionable life that hitherto had not existed. On Sunday evenings these hotels served dinner to music and attracted crowds of well dressed diners. One of these hotels, the Marshall, became famous as the headquarters of Negro talent. There gathered the actors, the musicians, the composers, the writers, the singers, dancers and vaudevillians. There one went to get a close up of Williams and Walker, Cole and Johnson, Ernest Hogan, Will Marion Cook, Jim Europe, Alda Overton, and of others equally and less known. Paul Laurence Dunbar was frequently there whenever he was in New York. Numbers of those who love to shine by the light reflected from celebrities were always to be found. The first modern jazz band ever heard in New York, or perhaps anywhere, was organized at the Marshall. It was a playing-singing-dancing orchestra, making the first dominant use of banjos, saxophones, clarinets and trap drums in combination, and was called the Memphis Students. Jim Europe was a member of that band, and out of it grew the famous Clef Club, of which he was the noted leader, and which for a long time monopolized the business of "entertaining" private parties and furnishing music for the new dance craze. Also in the Clef Club was "Buddy" Gilmore, who originated trap drumming as it is now practiced, and set hundreds of white men to juggling their sticks and doing acrobatic stunts while they manipulated a dozen other noise making devices aside from their drums. A good many well-known white performers frequented the Marshall and for seven or eight years the place was one of the sights of New York.

The move to Fifty-third Street was the result of the opportunity to get into newer and better houses. About 1900 the move to Harlem began, and for the same reason. Harlem had been overbuilt with large, new law apartment houses, but rapid transportation to that section was very inadequate—the Lenox Avenue Subway had not yet been built—and landlords were finding difficulty in keeping houses on the east side of the section filled. Residents along and near Seventh Avenue were fairly well served by the Eighth Avenue Elevated. A colored man in the real estate business at this time, Philip A. Payton, approached several of these landlords with the proposition that he would fill their empty or partially empty houses with steady colored tenants. The suggestion was accepted, and one or two houses on One Hundred and Thirty-fourth Street east of Lenox Avenue were taken over. Gradually other houses were filled. The whites paid little attention to the movement until it began to spread west of Lenox Avenue; they then took steps to check it. They proposed through a financial organization, the Hudson Realty Company, to buy all properties occupied by colored people and evict the tenants. The Negroes countered by similar methods. Payton formed the Afro-American Realty Company, a Negro corporation organized for the purpose of buying and leasing houses for occupancy by colored people. Under this counter stroke the opposition subsided for several years.

But the continually increasing pressure of colored people in the west over the Lenox Avenue dead line caused the opposition to break out again, but in a new and more menacing form. Several white men undertook to organize all the white people of the community for the purpose of inducing financial institutions not to lend money or renew mortgages on properties occupied by colored people. In this effort they had considerable success, and created a situation which has not yet been completely overcome, a situation which is one of the hardest and most unjustifiable the Negro property owner in Harlem has to contend with. The Afro-American Realty Company was now defunct, but two or three colored men of means stepped into the breach. Philip A. Payton and J. C Thomas bought two five-story apartments, dispossessed the white tenants and put in colored. J. B. Nail bought a row of five apartments and did the same thing. St. Philip's Church bought a row of thirteen apartment houses on One Hundred and Thirty-fifth Street, running from Seventh Avenue almost to Lenox.

The situation now resolved itself into an actual contest. Negroes not only continued to occupy available apartment houses, but began to purchase private dwellings between Lenox and Seventh Avenues. Then the whole movement, in the eyes of the whites, took on the aspect of an "Invasion"; they became panic-stricken and began fleeing as from a plague. The presence of one colored family in a block, no matter how well bred and orderly, was sufficient to precipitate a flight. House after house and block after block was actually deserted. It was a great demonstration of human beings running amuck. None of them stopped to reason why they were doing it or what would happen if they didn't. The banks and lending companies holding mortgages on these deserted houses were compelled to take them over. For some time they held these houses vacant, preferring to do that and carry the charges than to rent or sell them to colored people. But values dropped and continued to drop until at the outbreak of the war in Europe[;] property in the northern part of Harlem had reached the nadir.

In the meantime the Negro colony was becoming more stable; the churches were being moved from the lower part of the city; social and civic centers were being formed, and gradually a community was being evolved. Following the outbreak of the war in Europe, Negro Harlem received a new and tremendous impetus. Because of the war thousands of aliens in the United States rushed back to their native lands to join the colors and immigration practically ceased. The result was a critical shortage in labor. This shortage was rapidly increased as the United States went more and more largely into the business of furnishing munitions and supplies to the warring countries. To help meet this shortage of common labor, Negroes were brought up from the South. The government itself took the first steps, following the practice in vogue in Germany of shifting labor according to the supply and demand in various parts of the country. The example of the government was promptly taken up by the big industrial concerns, which sent hundreds, perhaps thousands, of labor agents into the South, who recruited Negroes by wholesale. I was in Jacksonville, Fla., for a while at that time, and I sat one day and watched the stream of migrants passing to take the train. For hours they passed steadily, carrying flimsy suit cases, new and shiny, rusty old ones, bursting at the seams, boxes and bundles and impedimenta of all sorts, including banjos, guitars, birds in cages and what not. Similar scenes were being enacted in cities and towns all over that region. The first wave of the great exodus of Negroes from the South was on. Great numbers of these migrants headed for New York or eventually got there, and naturally the majority went up into Harlem. But the Negro population of Harlem was not swollen by migrants from the South alone; the opportunity for Negro labor exerted its pull upon the Negroes of the West Indies, and those islanders in the course of time poured into Harlem to the number of twenty-five thousand or more.

These new-comers did not have to look for work; work looked for them, and at wages of which they had never even dreamed. And here is where the unlooked for, the unprecedented, the miraculous happened. According to all preconceived notions, these Negroes suddenly earning large sums of money for the first time in their lives should have had their heads turned; they should have squandered it in the most silly and absurd manners imaginable. Later, after the United States had entered the war and even Negroes in the South were making money fast, many stories in accord with the tradition came out of that section. There was the one about the colored man who went into a general store and on hearing a phonograph for the first time promptly ordered six of them, one for each child in the house. I shall not stop to discuss whether Negroes in the South did that sort of thing or not, but I do know that those who got to New York didn't. The Negroes of Harlem, for the greater part, worked and saved their money. Nobody knew how much they had saved until congestion made expansion necessary for tenants and ownership profitable for landlords, and they began to buy property. Persons who would never be suspected of having money bought property. The Rev. W. W. Brown, pastor of the Metropolitan Baptist Church, repeatedly made "Buy Property" the text of his sermons. A large part of his congregation carried out the injunction. The church itself set an example by purchasing a magnificent brownstone church building on Seventh Avenue from a white congregation. Buying property became a fever. At the height of this activity, that is, 1920–21, it was not an uncommon thing for a colored washerwoman or cook to go into a real estate office and lay down from one thousand to five thousand dollars on a house. "Pig Foot Mary" is a character in Harlem. Everybody who knows the corner of Lenox Avenue and One Hundred and Thirty-fifth Street knows "Mary" and her stand, and has been tempted by the smell of her pigsfeet, fried chicken and hot corn, even if he has not been a customer. "Mary," whose real name is Mrs. Mary Dean, bought the five-story apartment house at the corner of Seventh Avenue and One Hundred and Thirty-seventh Street at a price of $42,000. Later she sold it to the Y.W.C.A. for dormitory purposes. The Y.W.C.A. sold it recently to Adolph Howell, a leading colored undertaker, the price given being $72,000. Often companies of a half dozen men combined to buy a house—these combinations were and still are generally made up of West Indians—and would produce five or ten thousand dollars to put through the deal.

When the buying activity began to make itself felt, the lending companies that had been holding vacant the handsome dwellings on and abutting Seventh Avenue decided to put them on the market. The values on these houses had dropped to the lowest mark possible and they were put up at astonishingly low prices. Houses that had been bought at from $15,000 to $20,000 were sold at one third those figures. They were quickly gobbled up. The Equitable Life Assurance Company held 106 model private houses that were designed by Stanford White. They are built with courts running straight through the block and closed off by wrought iron gates. Every one of these houses was sold within eleven months at an aggregate price of about two million dollars. Today they are probably worth about 100 per cent more. And not only have private dwellings and similar apartments been bought but big elevator apartments have been taken over. Corporations have been organized for this purpose. Two of these, the Antillian Realty Company, composed of West Indian Negroes, and the Sphinx Securities Company, composed of American and West Indian Negroes, represent holdings amounting to approximately $750,000. Individual Negroes and companies in the South have invested in Harlem real estate. About two years ago a Negro institution of Savannah, Ga., bought a parcel for $115,000 which it sold a month or so ago at a profit of $110,000.

I am informed by John E. Nail, a successful colored real estate dealer of Harlem and a reliable authority, that the total value of property in Harlem owned and controlled by colored people would at a conservative estimate amount to more than sixty million dollars. These figures are amazing, especially when we take into account the short time in which they have been piled up. Twenty years ago Negroes were begging for the privilege of renting a flat in Harlem. Fifteen years ago barely a half dozen colored men owned real property in all Manhattan. And down to ten years ago the amount that had been acquired in Harlem was comparatively negligible. Today Negro Harlem is practically owned by Negroes.

The question naturally arises, "Are the Negroes going to be able to hold Harlem?" If they have been steadily driven northward for the past hundred years and out of less desirable sections, can they hold this choice bit of Manhattan Island? It is hardly probable that Negroes will hold Harlem indefinitely, but when they are forced out it will not be for the same reasons that forced them out of former quarters in New York City. The situation is entirely different and without precedent. When colored people do leave Harlem, their homes, their churches, their investments and their businesses, it will be because the land has become so valuable they can no longer afford to live on it. But the date of another move northward is very far in the future. What will Harlem be and become in the meantime? Is there danger that the Negro may lose his economic status in New York and be unable to hold his property? Will Harlem become merely a famous ghetto, or will it be a center of intellectual, cultural and economic forces exerting an influence throughout the world, especially upon Negro peoples? Will it become a point of friction between the races in New York?

I think there is less danger to the Negroes of New York of losing out economically and industrially than to the Negroes of any large city in the North. In most of the big industrial centers Negroes are engaged in gang labor. They are employed by thousands in the stockyards in Chicago, by thousands in the automobile plants in Detroit, and in those cities they are likely to be the first to be let go, and in thousands, with every business depression. In New York there is hardly such a thing as gang labor among Negroes, except among the longshoremen, and it is in the longshoremen's unions, above all others, that Negroes stand on an equal footing. Employment among Negroes in New York is highly diversified: in the main they are employed more as individuals than as nonintegral parts of a gang. Furthermore, Harlem is gradually becoming more and more a self-supporting community. Negroes there are steadily branching out into new businesses and enterprises in which Negroes are employed. So the danger of great numbers of Negroes being thrown out of work at once, with a resulting economic crisis among them, is less in New York than in most of the large cities of the North to which Southern migrants have come.

These facts have an effect which goes beyond the economic and industrial situation. They have a direct bearing on the future character of Harlem and on the question as to whether Harlem will be a point of friction between the races in New York. It is true that Harlem is a Negro community, well defined and stable; anchored to its fixed homes, churches, institutions, business and amusement places; basing its own working, business and professional classes. It is experiencing a constant growth of group consciousness and community feeling. Harlem is, therefore, in many respects, typically Negro. It has many unique characteristics. It has movement, color, gayety, singing, dancing, boisterous laughter and loud talk. One of its outstanding features is brass band parades. Hardly a Sunday passes but that there are several of these parades of which many are gorgeous with regalia and insignia. Almost any excuse will do—the death of an humble member of the Elks, the laying of a cornerstone, the "turning out" of the order of this or that. In many of these characteristics it is similar to the Italian colony. But withal, Harlem grows more metropolitan and more a part of New York all the while, why is it then that its tendency is not to become a mere "quarter"?

I shall give three reasons that seem to me to be important in their order. First, the language of Harlem is not alien; it is not Italian or Yiddish; it is English. Harlem talks American, reads American, thinks American, Second, Harlem is not physically a "quarter." It is not a section cut off. It is merely a zone through which four main arteries of the city run. Third, the fact that there is little or no gang labor gives Harlem Negroes the opportunity for individual expansion and individual contacts with the life and spirit of New York. A thousand Negroes from Mississippi put to work as a gang in a Pittsburgh steel mill will for a long time remain a thousand Negroes from Mississippi. Under the conditions that prevail in New York they would all within six months become New Yorkers. The rapidity with which Negroes become good New Yorkers is one of the marvels to observers.

These three reasons form a single reason why there is small probability that Harlem will ever be a point of race friction between the races in New York. One of the principal factors in the race riot in Chicago in 1919 was the fact that at that time there were 12,000 Negroes employed in gangs in the stockyards. There was considerable race feeling in Harlem at the time of the hegira of white residents due to the "invasion," but that feeling, of course, is no more. Indeed, a number of the old white residents who didn't go or

Document Text

could not get away before the housing shortage struck New York are now living peacefully side by side with colored residents. In fact, in some cases white and colored tenants occupy apartments in the same house. Many white merchants still do business in thickest Harlem. On the whole, I know of no place in the country where the feeling between the races is so cordial and at the same time so matter-of-fact and taken for granted. One of the surest safeguards against an outbreak in New York such as took place in so many Northern cities in the summer of 1919 is the large proportion of Negro police on duty in Harlem.

To my mind, Harlem is more than a Negro community; it is a large scale laboratory experiment in the race problem. The statement has often been made that if Negroes were transported to the North in large numbers the race problem with all or its acuteness and with new aspects would be transferred with them. Well, 175,000 Negroes live closely together in Harlem, in the heart of New York—75,000 more than live in any Southern city— and do so without any race friction. Nor is there any unusual record of crime. I once heard a captain of the 38th Police Precinct (the Harlem precinct) say that on the whole it was the most law abiding precinct in the city. New York guarantees its Negro citizens the fundamental rights of American citizenship and protects them in the exercise of those rights. In return the Negro loves New York and is proud of it, and contributes in his way to its greatness. He still meets with discriminations, but possessing the basic rights, he knows that these discriminations will be abolished.

I believe that the Negro's advantages and opportunities are greater in Harlem than in any other place in the country, and that Harlem will become the intellectual, the cultural and financial center for Negroes of the United States, and will exert a vital influence upon all Negro peoples.

Glossary

Cole and Johnson	Bob Cole and Billy Johnson, theatrical impresarios who produced the first-ever all-black musical play, *A Trip to Coontown*, and other musical plays
Elevated	an above-ground commuter train
Elks	a fraternal organization
hegira	an exodus of people, referring specifically to Muhammad's flight from Mecca to Medina in 622, marking the start of the Islamic calendar
Mecca	a city in Saudi Arabia, the holiest site of Islam; often used as a figure of speech for a place that draws people to it
new-law apartments	a reference to apartments built according to stricter construction standards under New York City's Tenement House Act of 1901
Paul Laurence Dunbar	a seminal African American poet of the late nineteenth and early twentieth centuries
war in Europe	World War I
West Indies	the islands in the Caribbean Sea
Williams and Walker	the vaudeville musical comedy team of Bert Williams and George Walker
Y.W.C.A.	the Young Women's Christian Association, a support organization for women; the first African American YWCA was formed in Dayton, Ohio, in 1889

Alice Moore Dunbar-Nelson: "The Negro Woman and the Ballot"

1927

"When she got the ballot she slipped quietly ... into the political party of her male relatives."

Overview

In 1927 the writer, educator, and activist Alice Moore Dunbar-Nelson published an article titled "The Negro Woman and the Ballot" in the African American magazine *The Messenger*, in which she posed the question What have black women done with their vote? Dunbar-Nelson believed that black women had accomplished not nearly enough as a result of their enfranchisement in 1920, and she encouraged them to start exercising their power as voters without bowing to pressure from their male peers or loyalty to the Republican Party. She noted that African American women had already demonstrated their power as a group in the congressional elections of 1922, in which their votes had helped oust Republican legislators in Delaware, New Jersey, and Michigan who had failed to support the antilynching legislation known as the Dyer bill. Dunbar-Nelson concluded her article by positing that when black women have realized that their children's futures could be helped or hindered by the way they voted, perhaps they would set aside allegiance to the Republican Party and use their ballot power to better the condition of all African Americans.

Context

Women in the United States had been agitating for the right to vote since the early nineteenth century. By mid-century, Lucretia Mott, Elizabeth Cady Stanton, Susan B. Anthony, and others had emerged as leading advocates for women's suffrage. In their nationwide movement, suffragists marched and picketed, gave lectures, published articles, submitted petitions, faced verbal and physical abuse, and sometimes even went to prison. In 1870 the Fifteenth Amendment to the Constitution extended the right to vote to African American men but not to women of any race. Women would still have to wait and work toward their enfranchisement. And work they did, although different factions went about it in different ways. Some worked for state voting rights, while others pressed for a national constitutional amendment. By 1918, fifteen states, most of them in the West, had granted women full suffrage (the right to vote in all elections), and women had limited voting rights in about two dozen other states. However, by this time most national women's suffrage organizations had become united behind the push for a constitutional amendment that would grant full suffrage to women.

When President Woodrow Wilson changed his stance and announced his support of the women's suffrage amendment in early 1918, the political atmosphere began to shift. In 1919 Congress passed the Nineteenth Amendment, which granted full suffrage to women. In August 1920 Tennessee became the thirty-sixth and final state needed to ratify the amendment. On August 26, Secretary of State Bainbridge Colby certified the amendment's adoption. Finally, women had been granted the right to vote in all elections nationwide.

In the congressional elections of 1922, women were given the opportunity to make a broad-based statement in support of the Dyer bill, the first piece of antilynching legislation ever to have reached the Senate for a vote. After the Civil War, white supremacists had sought ways to infringe upon the newly won rights of African Americans. Lynching had existed since the days of British rule, and its victims had included many white people and Native Americans. In the South during the late nineteenth and early twentieth centuries, lynching became one of the cruelest and more frequent forms of violence practiced against African Americans, who comprised the majority of its victims. In April 1918, Leonidas C. Dyer, a Republican congressman from Missouri, introduced a bill in the House of Representatives that would prohibit lynching and make it a federal offense. He was motivated by the horrible riots—including lynching and other violent acts—that took place in July of 1917 in East St. Louis, Illinois—directly across the Mississippi River from Dyer's district in St. Louis. The Dyer bill was sponsored by the National Association for the Advancement of Colored People (NAACP). Despite bitter opposition, the House passed a somewhat modified form of the Dyer bill by a substantial majority on January 26, 1922, and it moved on to the Senate for consideration.

A women's organization called the Anti-Lynching Crusaders was founded in the late spring of 1922, and that summer it launched a national campaign that pressed for passage of the Dyer bill in the Senate. The Anti-Lynching

Time Line

1918
- **April**
  Congressman Leonidas C. Dyer, a Republican representative from Missouri, introduces his antilynching bill, known as the Dyer bill, in the House of Representatives.

1920
- **August 26**
  The Nineteenth Amendment to the U.S. Constitution is adopted, giving all adult female citizens of the United States the right to vote.

1922
- **January 26**
  The Dyer bill passes the House of Representatives by a vote of 230 to 119.
- **Summer**
  The Anti-Lynching Crusaders organizes its political consciousness-raising and fund-raising program, which will last through the end of the year.
- **November**
  The Dyer bill is tabled because of a filibuster by Senator Oscar W. Underwood of Alabama, the Democratic Senate minority leader.

1922–1923
- Alice Dunbar-Nelson breaks with her long-standing allegiance to the Republican Party and joins the Democratic Party after Republican senators show a lack of support for the Dyer bill.

1927
- **April**
  "The Negro Woman and the Ballot" appears in the magazine *The Messenger*.

1928
- Dunbar-Nelson delivers speeches urging voters to cast their ballots for the Democratic presidential candidate Alfred E. Smith.

Crusaders set forth to raise money for its parent organization, the NAACP, and to educate the American public about the horrific practice of lynching. The campaign was to be completed on or before January 1, 1923. The organization was headed by the president of the National Association of Colored Women, Mary B. Talbert (referred to as "Mrs. Mary B. Talbot" in "The Negro Woman and the Ballot"). Although the Anti-Lynching Crusaders consisted largely of African American women, white women were encouraged to join, and some worked for the cause. At the end of a five-month campaign, all funds were turned over to the NAACP.

Because of the inaction of Republican senators and a filibuster by Democratic Senate minority leader Oscar W. Underwood of Alabama, the Senate did not vote on the Dyer bill in 1922. Congressman Dyer reintroduced the bill in the House of Representatives in 1923 and again in every succeeding congressional session in the 1920s but failed to gain congressional support. Further interest in antilynching legislation had to wait until the 1930s. But the Republican failure to secure passage of the Dyer bill in the Senate had not come without a political price.

In the early 1920s, most African American voters still were members of the Republican Party, the party of Abraham Lincoln, who had issued the Emancipation Proclamation in 1863. Because Lincoln, the first Republican president, had taken up the cause of emancipation, many African Americans felt they owed allegiance to his party. During Reconstruction some black Republicans were voted into Congress. The Republican Party also kept blacks' allegiance because Republicans seemed to be the only ones who cared anything for African American issues or helping to secure their rights, especially through the Civil Rights Act of 1875. However, the seeming indifference of Republican politicians toward the fate of the Dyer bill in the Senate disheartened many African Americans. The filibuster by a southern Democrat had not been surprising, since many politicians from the Deep South touted white-supremacist views.

Many African American women, as Dunbar-Nelson noted in "The Negro Woman and the Ballot," made their disappointment known in the congressional elections of 1922, especially in Delaware, New Jersey, and Michigan, by voting down those Republican legislators who had let the Dyer bill fade away. Indeed, Republican apathy about the Dyer bill caused many African Americans, a good number of them women, to switch their support to the Democratic Party, which at the national level had begun to embrace progressive values regardless of the views of some reactionary Democrats, mostly from the South. Dunbar-Nelson freely admitted that her own disappointment in her Republican congressional representatives had caused her to become a Democrat.

Women, both white and black, had worked tirelessly for the right to vote, and black women in particular had urged the passage of antilynching legislation. After the failure of the Dyer bill in the Senate, women proved that their vote counted when those legislators seen as careless with the power vested in them by their constituents were sent home.

Several years later in "The Negro Woman and the Ballot," Dunbar-Nelson examined what she thought it would take for African American women to build upon their display of political strength in 1922.

About the Author

Alice Moore Dunbar-Nelson was born Alice Ruth Moore, on July 19, 1875, in New Orleans, Louisiana. Her father, Joseph Moore, was a seaman who had some white ancestry. Her mother, Patricia Wright, a former slave turned seamstress, had Native American and African American blood. In Creole society, the light skin and reddish hair that Alice had inherited helped her socially and allowed her sometimes to pass for white when she desired to partake of the activities of high culture limited to whites.

After Dunbar-Nelson graduated from a two-year teaching program at Straight College (now Dillard University) in 1892, she taught at a New Orleans elementary school. In 1895, when she was just twenty, she published her first book, a collection of poetry, short stories, reviews, and essays titled *Violets and Other Tales*. Poetry from this book, along with her picture, was featured in the *Boston Monthly Review*, a literary magazine, and attracted the attention of the prominent African American poet Paul Laurence Dunbar. At first the two maintained an epistolary relationship, but they finally met in person in 1897. They were wed in March 1898 in New York City.

The Dunbars moved to Washington, D.C., where they became a celebrated literary couple. In 1899, Dunbar-Nelson published another collection of short fiction, *The Goodness of St. Rocque and Other Stories*, as the companion volume to her husband's *Poems of Cabin and Field*. In 1902 the couple separated after four tumultuous years. Because Paul Dunbar suffered from medically induced alcoholism and drug addiction, he occasionally flew into rages during which he physically abused his wife. That Dunbar-Nelson sometimes critiqued her husband's poetry written in African American dialect hardly eased tensions between the two. Four years after his separation from his wife, Dunbar died of tuberculosis. While Dunbar-Nelson's relationship with her husband at his death was not amicable, she would be honored for the rest of her life as the widow of Paul Dunbar.

After Dunbar-Nelson separated from her husband, she moved to Wilmington, Delaware, where she was joined by her mother, sister, and her sister's children. She started teaching at Howard High School, and in addition to teaching and administrative duties there, she studied at Cornell University, Columbia University, and the University of Pennsylvania. She edited two works, *Masterpieces of Negro Eloquence* (1914) and *The Dunbar Speaker and Entertainer* (1920). During these years, Dunbar-Nelson was involved in several relationships, including one with the principal of Howard High School, Edwina B. Kruse, and a secret marriage to fellow teacher Henry Arthur Callis on January 19, 1910. Callis was younger than Dunbar-Nelson by twelve years, and the marriage did not last long.

In 1916 Dunbar-Nelson married the journalist Robert J. Nelson. This union would last for the rest of her life, even though she would continue to have romantic affairs with both women and men. Dunbar-Nelson became even more of a political and social activist after she married Nelson. She participated in the movement for women's suffrage and World War I relief efforts. Together, the couple published the *Wilmington Advocate*, a liberal black newspaper, from 1920 to 1922. During this period, Dunbar-Nelson was also a member of the State Republican Committee of Delaware, and she chaired the Delaware branch of the Anti-Lynching Crusaders. She also became active in the Federation of Colored Women's Clubs. After the demise of the Dyer bill in the Senate, Dunbar-Nelson switched her allegiance to the Democratic Party and encouraged other African Americans to do the same. Beginning in 1924, she started to organize Democratic black women voters.

Dunbar-Nelson cofounded the Industrial School for Colored Girls in Marshallton, Delaware, where from 1924 to 1928 she served on the staff. From 1926 to 1930 she wrote columns regularly for various newspapers. Instead of the society gossip typical of female columnists of that time, Dunbar-Nelson wrote incisive pieces that addressed politics and cultural issues. She also traveled extensively as a public speaker, in part because of her position as executive secretary from 1928 to 1931 of the American Friends Inter-Racial Peace Committee.

In 1928 Dunbar-Nelson, along with many other middle-class African American women who previously had been Republicans, worked for the nomination of Alfred E. Smith as the Democratic presidential candidate. She gave speeches in support of Smith, whom she saw as the best presidential candidate for African Americans. One can only wonder how she must have viewed the victory of the Republican candidate Herbert Hoover that November.

In 1921 and again from 1926 to 1931, Dunbar-Nelson kept a diary in which she expressed her frustration with her literary career and other matters. She continued to write poetry and short fiction and completed two novels, and she was welcomed into the circle of Harlem Renaissance writers; however, she never found the success as an author that she had achieved as a journalist. In her diary she also gave voice to her concerns about personal financial instability. In 1932 Robert Nelson obtained a political appointment to the Pennsylvania Athletic Commission, a position that offered him a more steady income. The couple moved to Pennsylvania, where Dunbar-Nelson, finally living comfortably, continued to be active socially and politically. Her health, however, began to fail, and she died of a heart condition on September 18, 1935, at the University of Pennsylvania Hospital.

Explanation and Analysis of the Document

In late August 1920, the Nineteenth Amendment to the Constitution, which gave women the right to vote, was ratified. In the first paragraph of "The Negro Woman and the

Suffragists march on Pennsylvania Avenue in Washington, D.C., in March 1913. (Library of Congress)

Ballot," Dunbar-Nelson puts forth the question that "friend and foe alike are asking": What has the African American woman done with her right to vote in the six years she has had it? Dunbar-Nelson's aim in posing this question was to encourage African American women not to waste this right by being "just another vote" for the Republicans without evaluating issues and candidates for themselves. Blind Republican faith, according to her, was not the way to go.

In paragraph 2, Dunbar-Nelson acknowledges that "six years is a very short time in which to ask for results from any measure or condition, no matter how simple." She gives the examples of how at six a human being is still a mere child and how structures meant to last centuries could rarely be finished within six years. Likewise, she notes that most trees would not reach anything approaching their potential size in six years and that a nation only six years old stands for "but the beginnings of an idea." Was it fair, then, Dunbar-Nelson asks, to expect much of the African American woman in the six years she has been able to vote? Regardless of the question's fairness, people have persisted in asking it, and Dunbar-Nelson therefore offers an answer.

Before proceeding to her answer, Dunbar-Nelson in paragraph 4 asks what African American women who worked to gain the vote thought would be achieved by having this right. Dunbar-Nelson says that for these women "it seemed as if the ballot would be the great objective of life." All their social, economic, and racial troubles—stemming from political decisions made for them by men—would be overcome by gaining the right to vote. They would "step into the dominant place, politically, of the race" and rectify the injustices that African American men had allowed to stand. According to Dunbar-Nelson, African American men had given up their political power in return for "cheap political office and little political preferment," while the "great issues affecting the race" had taken a backseat. Women, it would seem, would not let this happen if they got the vote.

In paragraph 6, Dunbar-Nelson observes that as a rule black men had not wanted black women to have the vote. Although she is unsure exactly why, she accuses the black man of having hidden "behind the grandiloquent platitude of his white political boss." If black men had been thinking about the progress of African Americans, surely they would not have kept half of their race from voting. This was not the point, though, says Dunbar-Nelson. The point was that women, both white and black, had been given the franchise. Here she revisits a facet of her original question: How has the African American woman exercised her right to vote such that she has made an "appreciable difference" in bettering the situation of all African Americans? In paragraph 7, Dunbar-Nelson recalls that ideally the African American woman, when she got the vote, should not have been swayed in ways that the black man had been. She would be "independent," since she had come "into the political game with a clean slate." She would not allow Republican political pressure to influence her vote, since gratitude to Abraham Lincoln did not require "blind G.O.P. allegiance." Unquestioning loyalty to the Republican Party, according to Dunbar-Nelson, was what had made African American men's votes "a joke" instead of a bastion of political strength and had led everyone to believe all black men were Republicans by default.

Nevertheless, many African American women, like their male peers, became Republicans. As Dunbar-Nelson eloquently puts it in paragraph 8, they "slipped quietly, safely, easily, and conservatively into the political party of [their] male relatives." In the next paragraph, Dunbar-Nelson names only black women in New York City and "a sporadic break here and there" by voters elsewhere as exceptions. However, she notes that the flavor of Republicanism of many black women was often not particularly conservative. Dunbar-Nelson uses the word *conservative* to mean "restrained." Rather than restrained, these women were often "zealous," "virulent," and even "vituperative" when they expressed their political views. Some even might have forsaken a friendship over a difference of political opinion. These observations notwithstanding, Dunbar-Nelson states in paragraph 10 that the answer to her opening question as to what African American women have done with their right to vote must be that thus far their voting record has "by and large been a disappointment." Their votes in accordance with the Republican Party's policies may even have contributed to the problems facing their communities.

Still, Dunbar-Nelson maintains that there was room for hope in the form of "two bright lights." One of them, the brightest by far, was the ballot power demonstrated by African American women during the congressional elections of 1922. Dunbar-Nelson claims that their votes helped decide the outcome of elections in New Jersey, Delaware, and Michigan, in which legislators who had not actively supported the Dyer bill failed to be reelected. The other "bright light" Dunbar-Nelson characterizes as dim in comparison with the show of strength in the 1922 congressional elections—support for school bond measures. In elections involving school bond measures, many African American women had voted for what was best for their communities and had not allowed party pressure to sway them. However, Dunbar-Nelson observes, "the ripple" resulting from these elections was "so slight" that it barely stirred up discontent with the Republican Party.

In paragraph 13, Dunbar-Nelson laments that all too often young voters have submitted to the political status quo in exchange for preferred places in their communities and "easy social relations." Quite pointedly, she observes that "we still persecute socially those who disagree with us politically." Dunbar-Nelson views this as having been as true of women as of men and hardly limited to African

Alfred E. Smith and his wife voting in 1928 (Library of Congress)

Americans. As she notes, young women living with fathers, brothers, and uncles tended to defer to their political preferences. In the following paragraph, she adds that women's deference to men's political views was often true for older voters as well, judging by her encounters with hundreds of women across the United States. She blames men for having repeatedly mocked women's ideas, hopes, and "high ideals."

Essential Quotes

"It has been six years since the franchise as a national measure has been granted to women. The Negro woman has had the ballot in conjunction with her white sister, and friend and foe alike are asking the question, What has she done with it?"
(Paragraph 1)

"To those colored women who worked, fought, spoke, sacrificed, traveled, pleaded, wept, cajoled, all but died for the right of suffrage for themselves and their peers, it seemed as if the ballot would be the great objective of life.... That with the granting of the ballot the women would step into the dominant place, politically, of the race. That all the mistakes which men had made would be rectified."
(Paragraph 4)

"The Negro woman was going to be independent.... The name of Abraham Lincoln was not synonymous with ... blind G.O.P. allegiance.... She would break up the tradition that one could tell a black man's politics by the color of his skin."
(Paragraph 7)

"And when she got the ballot she slipped quietly, safely, easily, and conservatively into the political party of her male relatives. Which is to say, that with the exception of New York City, and a sporadic break here and there, she became a Republican."
(Paragraphs 8 and 9)

"When the Negro woman finds that the future of her children lies in her own hands—if she can be made to see this—she will strike off the political shackles she has allowed to be hung upon her, and win the economic freedom of her race. Perhaps some Joan of Arc will lead the way."
(Paragraphs 15 and 16)

Nevertheless, Dunbar-Nelson in paragraph 15 expresses hope that African American women might break out of the confines of party allegiance and male influence and vote for what they believe, particularly if something "near and dear" to them were to be threatened. Blind party allegiance could not help African Americans, and the ballot was one of the few instruments by which they could assert their power: "Whatever the Negro may hope to gain ...

must be won at the ballot box." Dunbar-Nelson states that once black women have realized that with their votes they might control the future of their children, they would cast votes in the best interest of their families and communities.

In her concluding paragraph, Dunbar-Nelson calls for "some Joan of Arc" to "lead the way." In other words, she was hoping for a leader like the "Maid of Orléans"—the peasant girl Joan of Arc, who, in the early fifteenth century, led the French army to several important victories during the Hundred Years' War, thus contributing to the coronation of Charles VII. Perhaps a woman of courage and divine inspiration would come forth to lead African American women in their struggle for economic freedom and political empowerment.

Audience

Dunbar-Nelson's article primarily targeted African American women. The magazine in which it was published, *The Messenger*, supported writers of the Harlem Renaissance and published literature, articles on political issues, and commentary on black theater. Although *The Messenger* was not as widely read as some African American periodicals of the 1920s, it had a national circulation and featured pieces by famous poets and writers as well as those new literary voices.

The issues that Dunbar-Nelson brought up in "The Negro Woman and the Ballot" without doubt reflected the content of the speeches she delivered when she campaigned for Alfred E. Smith, the Democratic Party's presidential candidate in 1928. Certainly, she would have spoken to her audiences about supporting "men and measures, not parties" and how important it was for a young woman not to allow a "father, sweetheart, brother, or uncle" to influence her vote. The ideas that Dunbar-Nelson expressed in her article in *The Messenger* found a wider audience through her speeches on behalf of Smith's campaign.

Impact

Dunbar-Nelson's work, although popular among African American publishers at the time, did not attract the attention of white publishers. Nonetheless, Dunbar-Nelson became one of the older and more traditional voices of the Harlem Renaissance of the 1920s and 1930s. She also is considered one of the founders of the African American short-story tradition. Her contributions to literature and journalism as well as education, politics, and social activism continue to attest to the varied abilities and achievements of educated African American women and men during the late nineteenth and early twentieth centuries.

See also Emancipation Proclamation (1863); Fifteenth Amendment to the U.S. Constitution (1870).

Further Reading

■ Books

Dray, Philip. *At the Hands of Persons Unknown: The Lynching of Black America.* New York: Random House, 2002.

Dunbar-Nelson, Alice. *Give Us Each Day: The Diary of Alice Dunbar-Nelson*, ed. Gloria T. Hull. New York: W. W. Norton, 1984.

Gordon, Ann D., et al., eds. *African American Women and the Vote, 1837–1965.* Amherst: University of Massachusetts Press, 1997.

Questions for Further Study

1. According to Dunbar-Nelson, "what have Negro women done with the vote?"

2. What impact did the fate of the Dyer bill, proposed to combat lynching, have on the voting patterns of women and on the Republican Party?

3. What was Dunbar-Nelson's attitude toward the Republican Party? Was she opposed to the party? Explain her views on party allegiance.

4. Dunbar-Nelson was concerned not only with suffrage issues but gender issues as well. What can we learn from this essay about her views on gender relations? Do you think that her personal life contributed in any way to her views on gender?

5. In the 2008 presidential election, the voter turnout rate among eligible black women was 68.8 percent, up from 63.7 percent in 2004 (according to Pew Research). Additionally, this turnout rate in 2008 was the highest of any demographic group. What do you think Dunbar-Nelson's reaction to these statistics, in both years, would have been?

Marable, Manning, and Leith Mullings, eds. *Let Nobody Turn Us Around: An African American Anthology.* Lanham, Md: Rowman & Littlefield, 2009.

■ **Web Sites**

Hull, Gloria T. "Alice Dunbar-Nelson (1875–1935)." Cengage Learning Web site.
http://college.cengage.com/english/lauter/heath/4e/students/author_pages/late_nineteenth/dunbarnelson_al.html.

Johnson, Wilma J. "Dunbar-Nelson, Alice Ruth Moore (1875–1935)." BlackPast.org Web site.
http://blackpast.com/?q=aah/dunbar-nelson-alice-ruth-moore-1875-1935.

Mungarro, Angelica, et al. "How Did Black Women in the NAACP Promote the Dyer Anti-Lynching Bill, 1918–1923?" Women and Social Movements in the United States, 1600–2000, Web site.
http://womhist.alexanderstreet.com/lynch/intro.htm.

—Angela M. Alexander

Alice Moore Dunbar-Nelson: "The Negro Woman and the Ballot"

It has been six years since the franchise as a national measure has been granted women. The Negro woman has had the ballot in conjunction with her white sister, and friend and foe alike are asking the question, What has she done with it?

Six years is a very short time in which to ask for results from any measure or condition, no matter how simple. In six years a human being is barely able to make itself intelligible to listeners; is a feeble, puny thing at best, with undeveloped understanding, no power of reasoning, with a slight contributory value to the human race, except in a sentimental fashion. Nations in six years are but the beginnings of an idea. It is barely possible to erect a structure of any permanent value in six years, and only the most ephemeral trees have reached any size in six years.

So perhaps it is hardly fair to ask with a cynic's sneer, What has the Negro woman done with the ballot since she has had it? But, since the question continues to be hurled at the woman, she must needs be nettled into reply.

To those colored women who worked, fought, spoke, sacrificed, traveled, pleaded, wept, cajoled, all but died for the right of suffrage for themselves and their peers, it seemed as if the ballot would be the great objective of life. That with its granting, all the economic, political, and social problems to which the race had been subject would be solved. They did not hesitate to say—those militantly gentle workers for the vote—that with the granting of the ballot the women would step into the dominant place, politically, of the race. That all the mistakes which the men had made would be rectified. The men have sold their birthright for a mess of pottage, said the women. Cheap political office and little political preferment had dazzled their eyes so that they could not see the great issues affecting the race. They had been fooled by specious lies, fair promises and large-sounding words. Pre-election promises had inflated their chests, so that they could not see the post-election failures at their feet.

And thus on and on during all the bitter campaign of votes for women.

One of the strange phases of the situation was the rather violent objection of the Negro man to the Negro woman's having the vote. Just what his objection racially was, he did not say, preferring to hide behind the grandiloquent platitude of his white political boss. He had probably not thought the matter through; if he had, remembering how precious the ballot was to the race, he would have hesitated at withholding its privilege from another one of his own people.

But all that is neither here nor there. The Negro woman got the vote along with some tens of million other women in the country. And has it made any appreciable difference in the status of the race? ... The Negro woman was going to be independent, she had averred. She came into the political game with a clean slate. No Civil War memories for her, and no deadening sense of gratitude to influence her vote. She would vote men and measures, not parties. She could scan each candidate's record and give him her support according to how he had stood in the past on the question of race. She owed no party allegiance. The name of Abraham Lincoln was not synonymous with her for blind G.O.P. allegiance. She would show the Negro man how to make his vote a power, and not a joke. She would break up the tradition that one could tell a black man's politics by the color of his skin.

And when she got the ballot she slipped quietly, safely, easily, and conservatively into the political party of her male relatives.

Which is to say, that with the exception of New York City, and a sporadic break here and there, she became a Republican. Not a conservative one, however. She was virulent and zealous. Prone to stop speaking to her friends who might disagree with her findings on the political issue, and vituperative in campaigns.

In other words the Negro woman has by and large been a disappointment in her handling of the ballot. She has added to the overhead charges of the political machinery, without solving racial problems.

One of two bright lights in the story hearten the reader. In the congressional campaign of 1922 the Negro woman cut adrift from party allegiance and took up the cudgel (if one may mix metaphors) for the cause of the Dyer Bill. The Anti-Lynching Crusaders, led by Mrs. Mary B. Talbot, found in several states—New Jersey, Delaware, and Michigan particularly—that its cause was involved in the congres-

Document Text

sional election. Sundry gentlemen had voted against the Dyer Bill in the House and had come up for re-election. They were properly castigated by being kept at home. The women's votes unquestionably had the deciding influence in the three states mentioned and the campaign conducted by them was of a most commendable kind.

School bond issues here and there have been decided by the colored woman's votes—but so slight is the ripple on the smooth surface of conservatism that it has attracted no attention from the deadly monotony of the blind faith in the "Party of Massa Linkun."

As the younger generation becomes of age it is apt to be independent in thought and in act. But it is soon whipped into line by the elders, and by the promise of plums of preferment or of an amicable position in the community or of easy social relations—for we still persecute socially those who disagree with us politically. What is true of the men is true of the women. The very young is apt to let father, sweetheart, brother, or uncle decide her vote....

Whether women have been influenced and corrupted by their male relatives and friends is a moot question. Were I to judge by my personal experience I would say unquestionably so, I mean a personal experience with some hundreds of women in the North Atlantic, Middle Atlantic, and Middle Western States. High ideals are laughed at, and women confess with drooping wings how they have been scoffed at for working for nothing, for voting for nothing, for supporting a candidate before having first been "seen." In the face of this sinister influence it is difficult to see how the Negro woman could have been anything else but "just another vote."

All this is rather a gloomy presentment of a well-known situation. But it is not altogether hopeless. The fact that the Negro woman CAN be roused when something near and dear to her is touched and threatened is cheering. Then she throws off the influence of her male companion and strikes out for herself. Whatever the Negro may hope to gain for himself must be won at the ballot box, and quiet "going along" will never gain his end. When the Negro woman finds that the future of her children lies in her own hands—if she can be made to see this—she will strike off the political shackles she has allowed to be hung upon her, and win the economic freedom of her race.

Perhaps some Joan of Arc will lead the way.

Glossary

Anti-Lynching Crusaders	a women's group organized to stop lynching
Dyer Bill	a bill first introduced in the U.S. House of Representatives, aimed at making lynching a federal offense
G.O.P.	"Grand Old Party," the nickname of the Republican Party
Joan of Arc	a French peasant girl who, in the early fifteenth century, led the French army to several important victories during the Hundred Years' War
Massa Linkun	mimicking southern black dialect, a reference to President Abraham Lincoln
"sold their birthright for a mess of pottage"	exchanged something of value for immediate gain, a reference to the story of Jacob and Esau in Genesis 25:29–34

President Franklin D. Roosevelt appeals to American industry for cooperation as he addresses several thousand members of the National Recovery Administration's code authorities at Constitution Hall, Washington, D.C., in March 1934. (AP/Wide World Photos)

John P. Davis: "A Black Inventory of the New Deal"

1935

"On every hand the New Deal has used slogans for the same raw deal."

Overview

John Preston Davis's essay "A Black Inventory of the New Deal" is a scathing indictment of President Franklin Delano Roosevelt's early programs to combat the economic woes of the Great Depression. Published in May of 1935 in *The Crisis*, the magazine of the National Association for the Advancement of Colored People (NAACP), this essay challenged African Americans to create their own solutions to their dire economic situation rather than relying on a government that had systematically failed to come through for them.

Davis's essay was published at the time of a conference held at Howard University in Washington, D.C., titled "The Position of the Negro in Our National Economic Crisis." The conference was organized by Davis and Ralph Bunche, who was a professor of political science at Howard University and would later become a key architect of the United Nations. Like Davis, most of the participants in the conference were highly critical of Roosevelt's New Deal, noting that the government programs had severely negative impacts on African Americans. "A Black Inventory of the New Deal" serves as a reminder that oft-celebrated historical achievements have not always included all Americans.

Context

In November 1932 Americans elected Franklin Delano Roosevelt as their new president. The nation was in the grip of the Great Depression, and former President Herbert Hoover's strategy for turning the economy around seemed one of complete failure. As America anxiously watched the new administration form its own ideas for bringing the nation back to financial health, most felt a renewed sense of optimism.

Living in a segregated society in the Jim Crow South and many places in the North, African Americans suffered immensely during the depression. Black tenant farmers in the South languished as crop prices fell, and black workers in the industrial North were the first to be let go as the unemployment rate climbed. Although most black voters had supported the Republican Party in the 1932 election, Roosevelt's Democratic administration showed signs of promise for the plight of African Americans. In the summer of 1933, Roosevelt created a position for a special adviser on "the economic status of negroes" to serve under the secretary of the Department of the Interior, Harold Ickes. Roosevelt would go on in later years to create what became known as the "Black Cabinet," an advisory group of prominent African American community leaders who counseled his administration regarding the concerns of black Americans. In a more direct show of support, for the first time, the government initiated programs to provide direct relief to the public. Two of these important programs were initiated, respectively, by the Agricultural Adjustment Act (AAA) and the National Industrial Recovery Act (NIRA), both passed in 1933. These sweeping initiatives were intended to help farmers and industrial workers through government intervention.

Not long after their creation, however, it became apparent that these two programs had considerable flaws. One component of the NIRA was to develop industry-specific standards that would govern competition, pricing, wages, and work hours in each industry. The idea was to promote efficiency and fairness in practices and to provide workers with a minimum wage and maximum work period for every given job category. However, as business leaders worked with government representatives to develop these industrial codes, it became clear that African Americans were being systematically discriminated against, especially in the South. Black workers in Atlanta, Georgia, protested against the industrial codes in August of 1933, but, despite such protests, southern business interests won concessions from the government that perpetuated racial discrimination.

Similarly, the AAA resulted in appalling consequences for black farmers, because many did not own their land but farmed as tenants, or sharecroppers. In order to increase farmers' income, the government paid farmers incentives to leave land fallow. Unfortunately, southern landowners fired their black tenant farmers first, as fewer crops grown meant fewer farmers needed. Just as black workers in the North protested against the NIRA, tenant farmers in the South, black and white, joined together to form the Southern Tenant Farmers Union in 1934, bringing the plight of African American farmers to the public's attention.

Time Line

1932
- **November 8** Franklin Delano Roosevelt is elected to his first term as president of the United States.

1933
- **May 12** Congress approves the Agricultural Adjustment Act (AAA).
- **May 18** Roosevelt signs the Tennessee Valley Authority Act.
- **June 16** Congress approves the National Industrial Recovery Act (NIRA).
- **June** John P. Davis creates the Negro Industrial League in order to represent black workers at National Recovery Administration hearings in Washington, D.C.
- **Fall** Davis organizes the Joint Committee on Negro Affairs, a coalition of African American organizations, to address racial discrimination in New Deal programs.

1934
- **July** The Southern Tenant Farmers Union forms in Arkansas.

1935
- **January** Congress begins discussion of the Social Security program.
- **May** Davis publishes "A Black Inventory of the New Deal" in *The Crisis* magazine.
- **May 18–20** Davis and Ralph Bunche hold a conference at Howard University titled "The Position of the Negro in Our National Economic Crisis," during which most participants criticize Roosevelt's New Deal programs.

In 1935 economic recovery in the United States seemed nowhere in sight. Unemployment was a staggering 20 percent, and the promises of the Roosevelt administration appeared unfulfilled. Still, African Americans remained loyal to the Democratic Party; in the 1934 midterm elections, Democrats won formerly Republican seats largely because of the increase in black voters. In Chicago, Arthur W. Mitchell became the first black Democrat ever elected to Congress. Nevertheless, while African Americans might have supported Roosevelt and his party, many were growing more and more disillusioned with the administration's unproductive policies. John P. Davis's "A Black Inventory of the New Deal" gave voice to the increasingly urgent demand from the black community for tangible strides to be made in America's move toward racial equality.

About the Author

John Preston Davis was born on January 19, 1905, and grew up in Washington, D.C., where his father worked in the office of the secretary of war during the administration of the Democratic president Woodrow Wilson, who served as chief executive from 1913 to 1921. Young Davis attended Paul Laurence Dunbar High School, a prestigious school for blacks, and graduated from Bates College in Maine in 1926, where he was nominated for a Rhodes Scholarship. Davis participated in the artistic and literary movement known as the Harlem Renaissance, replacing W. E. B. Du Bois as editor of *The Crisis* magazine. Along with Langston Hughes, Zora Neale Hurston, and Wallace Thurman, the leading black authors living in New York City at the time, he produced *Fire!!*, a publication dedicated to showcasing the works of young African American writers. Davis received a master's degree in journalism from Harvard University in 1927 and served as Fisk University's director of publicity until 1928. He went on to earn a law degree from Harvard in 1933.

Davis and several of his peers at Harvard, including Robert Weaver, grew increasingly concerned with the U.S. government's response to the deepening economic crisis that was the Great Depression. In the summer of 1933 Davis and Weaver traveled back to their hometown of Washington, D.C., in order to give voice to the plight of African Americans. The two men created the Negro Industrial League to call attention to the need for equitable treatment of black Americans in New Deal programs. Davis and Weaver's example led many civil rights organizations to form the Joint Committee on National Recovery, an organization dedicated to exposing racial injustice in the implementation of federal programs. In 1934 the NAACP sent Davis to the South to interview black farmers, an experience that exposed Davis to the inequalities of the New Deal program that resulted from the AAA.

In 1935, Davis became executive secretary of the National Negro Congress, which he had helped found. The organization sought to unite African Americans across class lines and involved the support of the Communist Party.

This affiliation became a political liability following the Nazi-Soviet Nonaggression Pact of 1939, and more conservative organizations withdrew from the National Negro Congress. Davis remained its executive secretary until 1942. The next year he filed the first lawsuit in Washington, D.C., to challenge the district's segregated school system. Davis sued on behalf of his five year-old son, Michael, who was refused admittance by Noyes Elementary School. In response to the suit, Congress appropriated funds to build a new black school across the street from Davis's house. Later in life, Davis turned to the literary world once again, founding *Our World*—a magazine dedicated to the African American community—in 1946, and publishing *The American Negro Reference Book* in 1964. He died on September 11, 1973.

Time Line

1935
- **May 27** In its ruling in *Schechter Poultry Corp. v. United States*, the U.S. Supreme Court invalidates the National Recovery Administration, judging it an overextension of legislative power.

1936
- **February** The National Negro Congress holds its first meeting in Chicago, Illinois.

Explanation and Analysis of the Document

Davis was an outspoken critic of the New Deal programs put forward by Franklin Roosevelt to ameliorate the effects of the Great Depression. In his article "A Black Inventory of the New Deal," he surveys two years of New Deal efforts and their effects on black Americans.

◆ **Paragraphs 1–4**

Davis sets the tone in the very first paragraph, stating clearly that his goal is to assess the impact that the Roosevelt administration's early New Deal policies have had on African Americans. He then systematically evaluates key measures enacted by the government, showing how, in fact, they have had mostly negative effects on black Americans. Davis next cites government statistics demonstrating that the number of black families receiving aid increased during Roosevelt's time in office. He argues that this is evidence that the administration's policies have created more poverty among African Americans. The increase in the number of people receiving public assistance is not, in Davis's eyes, a sign of growing government concern for the poor but rather the direct result of failed policy, particularly those programs aimed at relief for the rural poor.

Davis then turns to a lengthy discussion of the National Recovery Administration. The NIRA generated a wide range of programs aimed at providing direct relief to the public and stimulating the economy. The legislation had the support of many industrial leaders, including Gerard Swope, the president of General Electric, who helped to draft it. The National Recovery Administration, an administrative body created by the NIRA, monitored each industry's development of standardized codes for wage rates, prices, and work hours. The idea behind the codes was that workers would achieve better wages and job security, while manufacturers within each industry would be able to compete fairly against each other.

Davis states in paragraphs 3 and 4 that the National Recovery Administration as yet failed to live up to its promises. He specifically mentions problems with the "code-making process." During the 1933 code hearings in Washington, D.C., which Davis attended, it became clear that companies in the South were excluding black workers from the protective features of the labor codes. Southern manufacturers relied upon a racially based wage system, where black workers were paid less than white laborers for comparable work. Therefore, they vigorously fought the idea of national wage standards. As Davis points out, southern companies employed a variety of tactics to evade the codes. One early argument was for the existence of "occupational and geographical differentials"; southern interests used a vast array of statistics and figures to "prove" that black workers were less efficient than whites and that equal wages would result in massive layoffs and plant closures. Sometimes employers changed the job categories of black workers so that they were not covered by the codes. As Davis points out, these maneuvers were effective; the National Recovery Administration approved regional wage differentials in the codes, and because enforcement occurred at the local level, code violators often went unpunished even when they were caught. Thus, while the federal intent behind the codes was to eliminate racial bias in wages and hours for each industry, its implementation resulted in the continuation of "the inferior status of the Negro."

The problem was not just with the implementation of the law, however. Davis notes that even with an increased wage rate, African American workers were still disproportionately affected by layoffs or the reduction of work hours. He cites the case of longshoremen, who might earn a high hourly wage but work very infrequently. Davis also comments on the problem of the rising cost of living; one of the by-products of the codes was that the prices for food and other necessities were set above market value. This increase in the cost of living disproportionately affected poor Americans, including African Americans. Davis also comments in paragraph 4 on the practices of "speed-up and stretch-out" in assembly-line manufacturing. Speeding up the line involved increasing the rate at which parts moved past a worker (forcing the individual to work more quickly), while stretching out called for assigning more tasks or machines to a given worker, thus adding to his responsibilities (and thus his output) while keeping his pay the same. Because both "speed-up" and "stretch-out" increased the productivity of workers, they reduced the number of workers needed; as Davis notes, African American employees were always the first to be let go. Thus the promises of gains for workers under the NIRA went unfulfilled for black Americans.

◆ **Paragraphs 5–7**

Davis next turns his attention to the Agricultural Adjustment Administration, another government agency created during Roosevelt's early New Deal legislation. Just as the NIRA created a new government entity, the National Recovery Administration, the AAA created the Agricultural Adjustment Administration to implement the policies outlined in the legislation. The act gave the government substantial authority over agricultural production and prices. For example, it allowed the secretary of agriculture to reduce the production of a given commodity or to remove acreage from production altogether, through the use of incentives. The goal of the program was to prop up the prices of agricultural products and thus help raise the income and buying power of farmers.

The vast majority of black farmers were sharecroppers, or tenant farmers who did not own their land but rather paid rent to the landowner. Sharecroppers would pay their rent either with proceeds from the sale of the crops they raised or with crop liens—loans against the value of future crops. The Great Depression brought sharply lower prices for most commodities, which translated into drastically lower income for these farmers, many of whom could no longer meet their rent obligations. As Davis points out, although the Agricultural Adjustment Administration's goal was to improve the lot of farmers, it actually worsened their plight. The crop reduction program was a particular problem. Under the administration, the government paid incentives to farmers to keep part of their land idle. As Davis remarks in paragraph 5, "Although the contract with the government provided that the land owner[s] should not reduce [their] number of … tenants" under this program, many of them did. Uncultivated land meant fewer farmers were needed to tend to crops, and black sharecroppers were the first to be turned out.

Just as there were problems with local enforcement of the National Recovery Administration codes, corruption was rampant in the South in terms of implementing AAA policies. The government mandated that landowners pay a portion of the government incentive for crop reduction to its tenants, but many landowners simply kept all of the money for themselves. Local authorities refused to enforce the law, as Davis explains. This widespread abuse was one of the primary motivators behind the creation of the Southern Tenant Farmers Union, an organization of sharecroppers in Arkansas that sought to change government policies and step up enforcement. Davis uses an old frontier-era phrase, "root hog or die," which means, in essence, that one must either work or starve.

◆ **Paragraphs 8–14**

Davis then takes up the Public Works Administration (PWA), which was also created by the NIRA. The PWA was a job-creation program designed to put people to work building roads, dams, bridges, and other infrastructure. The program was headed by the secretary of the Department of the Interior, Harold Ickes, an advocate of racial equality. Ickes ordered that all PWA contracts include a nondiscrimination clause. However, just as was the case with the codes, southern interests found ways to circumvent the contractual language. Robert C. Weaver, one of Davis's peers at Harvard and a member of Ickes's staff, developed a quota system to aid in enforcement. PWA contract recipients would be required to hire a minimum percentage of black skilled workers based on the proportion of such workers in the local population. Davis notes several problems with this idea, including the tensions placed on unions. This was a significant problem; blacks were excluded from many of the skilled trade unions, and the government had to negotiate with local unions as well as individual contractors who employed black workers.

The PWA and other New Deal programs also funded public housing. Unfortunately, most of these housing projects were segregated, upholding the status quo of racial inequality in America. Davis criticizes two specific programs: the Subsistence Homestead projects and the Tennessee Valley Authority model towns. Part of the NIRA, the Subsistence Homesteads were designed to be communities based on the older American idea of the family subsistence farm, where families grew enough to sustain themselves but not to bring cash crops to market. Roosevelt's version, however, located these communities near urban centers, so that homesteaders of the 1930s could hold a part-time job in the city while living in a modern home in a rural environment. Aimed at poor rural families, the homestead project had much to offer African Americans. However, the earliest communities were designated for whites only, angering many black activists. In particular, the Arthurdale project in West Virginia, mentioned by Davis in paragraph 11, aroused virulent protest from civil rights activists. Under pressure from Ickes and others, the administration developed several black homestead projects. Thus, as Davis notes, the Subsistence Homestead program perpetuated the Jim Crow segregation of the South.

Similarly, the Tennessee Valley Authority (TVA) built segregated communities, including the model towns of Norris, Tennessee, and Dayton, Ohio. Roosevelt created the TVA to devise a regional development program for flood control and power supply in the Tennessee River basin. Part of the TVA's development program included the creation of housing in planned communities based on a social vision similar to that of the Subsistence Homestead program. The TVA model communities were to be examples of self-contained, self-sustaining rural towns tied to cooperative industries. Norris, Tennessee, was one such community. As Davis notes, Norris functioned more as a "company town" for workers building the Norris Dam; the government supplied housing and power, ran the town store, and controlled all aspects of town life, not to mention providing the monthly paycheck. While the all-black Dayton communities were "ghettoes," Norris was "lily-white," designated as a whites-only town. To make

White and black sharecroppers attend a convention of the Southern Tenant Farmers Union in Memphis, Tennessee, in September 1937. (AP/Wide World Photos)

matters worse, Davis remarks, the TVA hired relatively few blacks and had no plan for ameliorating the conditions of African Americans in the region. The TVA's planned communities, to Davis, were examples of "utter planlessness."

◆ **Paragraphs 15–18**

In early 1935 Congress began to consider various options for a federal program of unemployment insurance and old-age pension, which would eventually become the Social Security Act of 1935. Davis refers to this debate, commenting that members of the Roosevelt administration proposed to exempt domestic and agricultural workers from the program. Treasury secretary Henry Morgenthau suggested excluding these workers in order to prevent the Social Security program from being underfunded. Because Roosevelt had insisted that the plan finance itself, this provision was included in the initial Social Security Act. As a result, vast numbers of African Americans were excluded from one of the most sweeping reforms in American history.

Following his dissection of the impact of New Deal programs on black Americans, Davis discusses how the black community has responded to this litany of injustice. In paragraph 16, he references the "Don't Buy Where You Can't Work" campaigns, which began in Chicago in 1929 but spread to many cities by the mid-1930s. These campaigns encouraged African Americans to boycott establishments that refused to hire blacks and generated public protests on the streets of many cities. The Garvey Movement, as embodied in the Universal Negro Improvement Association, had been around since World War I. One of the first organizations involved in black rights, the Universal Negro Improvement Association emphasized pride in African heritage and roots under the leadership of the Jamaican immigrant and activist Marcus Garvey. By the depression, Garvey's organization had lost much of its popularity, but its message of racial pride found receptive ears in the mid-1930s. The National Movement for Establishment of a 49th State was a movement to create a separate, black state within the United States. Davis brings up these examples to show that African Americans were exerting their power and becoming increasingly intolerant of discrimination.

> **Essential Quotes**
>
> *"A worker cannot eat a wage rate."*
> (Paragraph 4)
>
> *"The fairest summary that can be made of T.V.A. is that for a year or so it has furnished bread to a few thousand Negro workers. Beyond that everything is conjecture which is most unpleasant because of the utter planlessness of those in charge of the project."*
> (Paragraph 14)
>
> *"On every hand the New Deal has used slogans for the same raw deal."*
> (Paragraph 15)
>
> *"On the problem of relief of Negroes from poverty there is little room for disagreement. The important thing is that throughout America as never before Negroes awake to the need for a unity of action on vital economic problems which perplex us."*
> (Paragraph 21)
>
> *"One thing is certain: the Negro may stand still but the depression will not. And unless there is concerted action of Negroes throughout the nation the next two years will bring even greater misery to the millions of underprivileged Negro toilers in the nation."*
> (Paragraph 22)

Having emphasized black separatism in paragraph 16, Davis goes on to highlight interracial protests. As the depression deepened in the 1930s, the Communist Party organized the growing masses of jobless Americans into Unemployed Councils, radical groups that employed a variety of tactics to demand relief. Bread riots, street demonstrations, and rent strikes were commonplace in cities such as New York and Detroit. These protestors were of various ethnicities, including Jewish immigrants as well as black Americans. Davis mentions the sharecroppers unions, specifically the Southern Tenant Farmers Union, an interracial group that had thirty thousand members by 1937. He also notes the interracial nature of labor activism. In the years leading up to the publication of "A Black Inventory of the New Deal," labor unrest had been increasing. In 1934 alone, two men were killed in the Electric Auto-Lite strike in Toledo, Ohio, a massive strike that left three dead, and the West Coast Longshoremen's strike resulted in the killing of four strikers. As Davis points out, many of these struggles involved black and white workers fighting on the same side.

◆ **Paragraphs 19–22**

At the end of his essay, Davis points to the future. He comments on the upcoming (May 18–20, 1935) conference at Howard University but indicates that the conference cannot act by itself. One can see the seeds of the National Negro Congress in Davis's call for existing organizations from a variety of sectors ("church, civic, fraternal, professional and trade union") to come together as a "mighty arm of protest." He uses the All India Congress as an example of such an organization. The All India Congress Committee arose out of nineteenth-century calls for home rule in India and the later nonviolent protests and Indian independence movement led by the activist Mahatma Gandhi. Divided by caste and religious differences, India overcame such differences to achieve independence and serve as a model for other repressed groups. Davis pointedly states that African Americans are responsible for overcoming their own divisions and must take responsibility for solving the economic and social problems that face them.

Audience

Davis's piece was published in *The Crisis*, the magazine of the NAACP. Founded in 1910, *The Crisis* was one of the oldest publications dedicated to advancing the cause of black civil rights in America. At the time of Davis's article, the magazine had recently experienced a change in editorial oversight. W. E. B. Du Bois, founder of *The Crisis*, had resigned over differences of opinion with the NAACP's vision for the black rights movement; Du Bois advocated a separatist position, while the NAACP favored integration. The new editors, George Streator and Roy Wilkins, gave more editorial room to young authors such as Davis. However, *The Crisis* continued to be read widely by both white and black audiences interested in issues of racial justice. The publication's circulation vastly exceeded the NAACP's membership.

Although segregation was ingrained in American society during the depression years, there was a vibrant and active movement comprising liberal progressive whites and activist African Americans dedicated to moving the nation forward in terms of racial justice. Organizations such as the National Urban League aimed at aiding the status of black Americans, and the Commission on Interracial Cooperation in Atlanta sought to bring black and white community leaders together in dialogue. By the 1930s, there was a growing cadre of educated, progressive-minded black and white people who were eager to address the myriad problems facing the African American community. These people would likely have read Davis's article, as well as similar pieces in magazines such as *Opportunity*, published by the Urban League, and *The Journal of Negro Life*.

Impact

Davis's critique of Roosevelt's New Deal programs gained him increased recognition as a black activist and leader. It also positioned him at odds with the more conservative African American figures who sought to work within the Roosevelt administration to effect change, such as Robert C. Weaver. Davis and Bunche, along with A. Philip Randolph, head of the Brotherhood of Sleeping Car Porters union, formed the National Negro Congress based on the vision Davis outlined in his essay. The congress hoped to forge a union that crossed boundaries of class and partisanship. Its increasingly leftist bent alienated many of its more moderate members, and cold war politics led to its demise in 1947.

Davis's position outside the political mainstream translated into his having little direct impact on the electoral landscape in his time. Despite the very real deficiencies of Roosevelt's policies, African American voters overwhelmingly supported the president in the 1936 election. In 1932 a majority of blacks had voted for the Republican candidate, Herbert Hoover, but four years later the Democratic Party could claim the allegiance of most black voters. Despite the racial inequities of the New Deal, African Americans saw in Roosevelt a president who cared about them.

It is with historical hindsight that Davis's essay has become important for a wider American audience. This

Questions for Further Study

1. What impact did the Great Depression have on African Americans? How did that impact differ in kind or degree from the impact felt by white Americans?

2. Did the New Deal of President Franklin Roosevelt alleviate the plight of African Americans? Why or why not?

3. Davis discusses the concept of self-help for African Americans. In what way was this message similar to that advocated by, for example, John S. Rock in "Whenever the Colored Man Is Elevated, It Will Be by His Own Exertions" (1858)?

4. In what sense did Davis's report prefigure that arguments made in A. Philip Randolph's "Call to Negro America to March on Washington" (1941)?

5. Discuss the history of trade unionism as it affected African Americans in the pre–World War II era.

document catalogs what are now well-established negative effects of New Deal programs on the African American community, effects that were minimized by many in the government and the public in 1935. One of the lasting impacts of this essay is its reminder to modern audiences that even the most well intentioned of public policies can sometimes have negative consequences for some citizens.

See also Robert Clifton Weaver: "The New Deal and the Negro: A Look at the Facts" (1935).

Further Reading

- **Articles**

Fishel, Leslie H., Jr. "The Negro in the New Deal Era." *Wisconsin Magazine of History* 8, no. 2 (Winter 1964–1965): 111–126.

Hamilton, Donna Cooper. "The National Association for the Advancement of Colored People and New Deal Reform Legislation: A Dual Agenda." *Social Service Review* 68, no. 4 (December 1994): 488–502.

- **Books**

Sitkoff, Harvard. *A New Deal for Blacks: The Emergence of Civil Rights as a National Issue: The Depression Decade.* New York: Oxford University Press, 1981.

Sullivan, Patricia. *Days of Hope: Race and Democracy in the New Deal Era.* Chapel Hill: University of North Carolina Press, 1996.

—Karen Linkletter

John P. Davis: "A Black Inventory of the New Deal"

It is highly important for the Negro citizen of America to take inventory of the gains and losses which have come to him under the "New Deal." The Roosevelt administration has now had two years in which to unfold itself. Its portents are reasonably clear to anyone who seriously studies the varied activities of its recovery program. We can now state with reasonable certainty what the "New Deal" means for the Negro.

At once the most striking and irrefutable indication of the effect of the New Deal on the Negro can be gleaned from relief figures furnished by the government itself. In October, 1933, six months after the present administration took office, 2,117,000 Negroes were in families receiving relief in the United States. These represented 17.8 per cent of the total Negro population as of the 1930 census. In January, 1935, after nearly two years of *recovery measures*, 3,500,000 Negroes were in families receiving relief, or 29 per cent of our 1930 population. Certainly only a slight portion of the large increase in the number of impoverished Negro families can be explained away by the charitable, on the grounds that relief administration has become more humane. As a matter of fact federal relief officials themselves admit that grave abuses exist in the administration of rural relief to Negroes. And this is reliably borne out by the disproportionate increase in the number of urban Negro families on relief to the number of rural Negro families on relief. Thus the increase in the number of Negroes in relief families is an accurate indication of the deepening of the economic crisis for black America.

The promise of N.R.A. to bring higher wages and increased employment to industrial workers has glimmered away, In the code-making process occupational and geographical differentials at first were used as devices to exclude from the operation of minimum wages and maximum hours the bulk of the Negro workers. Later, clauses basing code wage rates on the previously existing wage differential between Negro and white workers tended to continue the inferior status of the Negro. For the particular firms, for whom none of these devices served as an effective means of keeping down Negro wages, there is an easy way out through the securing of an exemption specifically relating to the *Negro* worker in the plant. Such exemptions are becoming more numerous as time goes on. Thus from the beginning relatively few Negro workers were even theoretically covered by N.R.A. labor provisions.

But employers did not have to rely on the code-making process. The Negro worker not already discriminated against through code provisions had many other gauntlets to run. The question of importance to him as to all workers was, "as a result of all of N.R.A.'s maneuvers will I be able to buy more?" The answer has been "No." A worker cannot eat a wage rate. To determine what this wage rate means to him we must determine a number of other factors. Thus rates for longshoremen seem relatively high. But when we realize that the average amount of work a longshoreman receives during the year is from ten to fifteen weeks, the wage rate loses much of its significance. When we add to that fact the increase in the cost of living—as high as 40 per cent in many cases—the wage rate becomes even more chimerical. For other groups of industrial workers increases in cost of living, coupled with the part time and irregular nature of the work, make the results of N.R.A. negligible. In highly mechanized industries speed-up and stretch-out nullify the promised result of N.R.A. to bring increased employment through shorter hours. For the workers are now producing more in their shorter work periods than in the longer periods before N.R.A. There is less employment. The first sufferer from fewer jobs is the Negro worker. Finally the complete break-down of compliance machinery in the South has cancelled the last minute advantage to Negro workers which N.R.A.'s enthusiasts may have claimed.

The Agricultural Adjustment Administration has used cruder methods in enforcing poverty on the Negro farm population. It has made violations of the rights of tenants under crop reduction contracts easy; it has rendered enforcement of these rights impossible. The reduction of the acreage under cultivation through the government rental agreement rendered unnecessary large numbers of tenants and farm laborers. Although the contract with the government provided that the land owner should not reduce the number of his tenants, he did so. The federal courts have now refused to allow tenants to enjoin such evictions. Faced with this Dred Scott decision against farm tenants, the A.A.A. has remained discreetly silent. Farm laborers are now jobless by the hundreds of thousands, the conservative government estimate of the decline in agricultural employment for the year 1934 alone being a quarter of a million. The larger portion of these are unskilled Negro agricultural workers—now without income and unable to secure work or relief.

But the unemployment and tenant evictions occasioned by the crop reduction policies of the A.A.A. is not all. For the tenants and sharecroppers who were retained on the plantations the government's agricultural program meant reduced income. Wholesale fraud on tenants in the payment of parity checks occurred. Tenants complaining to the Department of Agriculture in Washington have their letters referred back to the locality in which they live and trouble of serious nature often results. Even when this does not happen, the tenant fails to get his check. The remainder of the land he tills on shares with his landlord brings him only the most meagre necessities during the crop season varying from three to five months. The rest of the period for him and his family is one of "root hog or die."

The past year has seen an extension of poverty even to the small percentage (a little more than 20 per cent) of Negro farmers who own their own land. For them compulsory reduction of acreage for cotton and tobacco crops, with the quantum of such reduction controlled and regulated by local boards on which they have no representation, has meant drastic reduction of their already low income. Wholesale confiscation of the income of the Negro cotton and tobacco farmer is being made by prejudiced local boards in the South under the very nose of the federal government. In the wake of such confiscation has come a tremendous increase in land tenantry as a result of foreclosures on Negro-owned farm properties.

Nor has the vast public works program, designed to give increased employment to workers in the building trades, been free from prejudice. State officials in the South are in many cases in open rebellion against the ruling of P.W.A. that the same wage scales must be paid to Negro and white labor. Compliance with this paper ruling is enforced in only rare cases. The majority of the instances of violation of this rule are unremedied. Only unskilled work is given Negroes on public works projects in most instances. And even here discrimination in employment is notorious. Such is bound to be the case when we realize that there are only a handful of investigators available to seek enforcement.

Recently a move has been made by Negro officials in the administration to effect larger employment of Negro skilled and unskilled workers on public works projects by specifying that failure of a contractor to pay a certain percentage of his payroll to Negro artisans will be evidence of racial discrimination. Without doubting the good intentions of the sponsors of this ingenious scheme, it must nevertheless be pointed out that it fails to meet the problem in a number of vital particulars. It has yet to face a test in the courts, even if one is willing to suppose that P.W.A. high officials will bring it to a test. Percentages thus far experimented with are far too low and the number of such experiments far too few to make an effective dent in the unemployment conditions of Negro construction industry workers. Moreover the scheme gives aid and comfort to employer-advocates of strike-breaking and the open shop; and, while offering, perhaps, some temporary relief to a few hundred Negro workers, it establishes a dangerous precedent which throws back the labor movement and the organization of Negro workers to a considerable degree. The scheme, whatever its Negro sponsors may hope to contrary, becomes therefore only another excuse for their white superiors maintaining a "do-nothing" policy with regard to discrimination against Negroes in the Public Works Administration.

The Negro has no pleasanter outlook in the long term social planning ventures of the new administration. Planning for subsistence homesteads for industrially stranded workers has been muddled enough even without consideration of the problem of integrating Negroes into such plans. Subsistence Homesteads projects are overburdened with profiteering prices for the homesteads and foredoomed to failure by the lack of planning for adequate and permanent incomes for prospective homesteaders.

In callous disregard of the interdiction in the constitution of the United States against use of federal funds for projects which discriminate against applicants solely on the ground of color, subsistence homesteads have been planned on a strictly "lily-white" basis. The more than 200 Negro applicants for the first project at Arthurdale, West Virginia were not even considered, Mr. Bushrod Grimes (then in charge of the project) announcing that the project was to be open only to "native white stock." As far north as Dayton, Ohio, where state laws prohibit any type of segregation against Negroes, the federal government has extended its "lily-white" policy. Recently it has established two Jim-Crow projects for Negroes. Thus the new administration seeks in its program of social planning to perpetuate ghettoes of Negroes for fifty years to come.

An even more blatant example of this policy of "lily-white" reconstruction is apparent in the planning of the model town of Norris, Tennessee, by the Tennessee Valley Authority. This town of 450 model homes is intended for the permanent workers on Norris Dam. The homes are rented by the federal government, which at all times maintains title to the land and dwellings and has complete control of the town management. Yet officials at T.V.A. openly admit that no Negroes are allowed at Norris.

T.V.A. has other objectionable features. While Negro employment now approaches an equitable proportion of total employment, the payroll of Negro workers remains disproportionately lower than that of whites. While the government has maintained a trade school to train workers on the project, no Negro trainees have been admitted. Nor have any meaningful plans matured for the future of the several thousand Negro workers who in another year or so will be left without employment, following completion of work on the dams being built by T.V.A.

None of the officials of T.V.A. seems to have the remotest idea of how Negroes in the Tennessee Valley will be able to buy the cheap electricity which T.V.A. is designed to produce. They admit that standards of living of the Negro population are low, that the introduction of industry into the Valley is at present only a nebulous dream, that even if this eventuates there is no assurance that Negro employment will result. The fairest summary that can be made of T.V.A. is that for a year or so it has furnished bread to a few thousand Negro workers. Beyond that everything is conjecture which is most unpleasant because of the utter planlessness of those in charge of the project.

Recovery legislation of the present session of Congress reveals the same fatal flaws which have been noted in the operation of previous recovery ventures. Thus, for example, instead of genuine unemployment insurance we have the leaders of the administration proposing to exclude from their plans domestic and agricultural workers, in which classes are to be found 15 out of every 23 Negro workers. On every hand the New Deal has used slogans for the same raw deal.

The sharpening of the crisis for Negroes has not found them unresponsive. Two years of increasing hardship has seen strange movement among the masses. In Chicago, New York, Washington and Baltimore the struggle for jobs has given rise to action on the part of a number of groups seeking to boycott white employers who refuse to employ Negroes. "Don't Buy Where You Can't Work" campaigns are springing up everywhere. The crisis has furnished renewed vigor to the Garvey Movement. And proposals for a 49th State are being seriously considered by various groups.

In sharp contrast with these strictly racial approaches to the problem, have been a number of interracial approaches. Increasing numbers of unemployed groups have been organized under radical leadership and have picketed relief stations for bread. Sharecroppers unions, under Socialist leadership in Arkansas, have shaken America into a consciousness of the growing resentment of southern farm tenants and the joint determination of the Negro and white tenants to do something about their intolerable condition.

In every major strike in this country Negro union members have fought with their white fellow workers in a struggle for economic survival. The bodies of ten Negro strikers killed in such strike struggles offer mute testimony to this fact. Even the vicious policies of the leaders of the A. F. of L. in discrimination against Negro workers is breaking down under the pressure for solidarity from the ranks of whites.

This heightening of spirit among all elements of black America and the seriousness of the crisis for them make doubly necessary the consideration of the social and economic condition of the Negro at this time. It was a realization of these conditions which gave rise to the proposal to hold a national conference on the economic status of Negroes under the New Deal at Howard University in Washington, D.C., on May 18, 19 and 20. At this conference, sponsored by the Social Science Division of Howard University and the Joint Committee on National Recovery, a candid and intelligent survey of the social and economic condition of the Negro will be made. Unlike most conference it will not be a talk-rest. For months nationally known economists and other technicians have been working on papers to be presented. Unlike other conferences it will not be a one-sided affair. Ample opportunity will be afforded for high government officials to present their views of the "New Deal." Others not connected with the government, including representatives of radical political parties, will also appear to present their conclusions. Not the least important phase will be the appearance on the platform of Negro workers and farmers themselves to offer their own experience under the New Deal. Out of such a conference can and will come a clear-cut analysis of the problems faced by Negroes and the nation.

But a word of caution ought to be expressed with regard to this significant conference. In the final

Document Text

analysis it cannot and does not claim to be representative of the mass opinion of Negro citizen[s] in America. All it can claim for itself is that it will bring together on a non-representative basis well informed Negro and white technicians to discuss the momentous problem it has chosen as its topic. It can furnish a base for action for any organization which chooses to avail itself of the information developed by it. It cannot act itself.

Thus looking beyond such a conference one cannot fail to hope that it will furnish impetus to a national expression of black America demanding a tolerable solution to the economic evils which it suffers. Perhaps it is not too much to hope that public opinion may be moulded by this conference to such an extent that already existing church, civic, fraternal, professional and trade union organizations will see the necessity for concerted effort in forging a mighty arm of protest against injustice suffered by the Negro. It is not necessary that such organizations agree on every issue. On the problem of relief of Negroes from poverty there is little room for disagreement. The important thing is that throughout America as never before Negroes awake to the need for a unity of action on vital economic problems which perplex us.

Such a hope is not lacking in foundation upon solid ground. Such an instance as the All India Congress of British India furnishes an example of what repressed groups can do to better their social and economic status. Perhaps a *"National Negro Congress"* of delegates from thousands of Negro organizations (and white organizations willing to recognize their unity of interest) will furnish a vehicle for channeling public opinion of black America. One thing is certain: the Negro may stand still but the depression will not. And unless there is concerted action of Negroes throughout the nation the next two years will bring even greater misery to the millions of underprivileged Negro toilers in the nation.

Glossary

A. F. of L.	the American Federation of Labor, an umbrella organization for labor unions
Agricultural Adjustment Administration	a federal agency created by the Agricultural Adjustment Act that paid farmers to reduce crop production to raise prices
All India Congress of British India	the All India Congress Committee, which led the struggle for Indian independence from British rule
code-making process	a reference to Title I, Section 3, of the National Industrial Recovery Act, which permitted trade or industrial associations to seek presidential approval of codes of fair competition
Dred Scott decision	a reference to the 1858 U.S. Supreme Court decision in *Dred Scott v. Sandford*, which denied citizenship rights to African Americans
Garvey Movement	a reference to the black nationalism of Marcus Garvey, the founder of the United Negro Improvement Association
homestead	land acquired from U.S. public lands by filing a record and living on and cultivating it
New Deal	the name given to the legislative programs of the Franklin Roosevelt administration to alleviate the effects of the Great Depression
N.R.A.	the National Recovery Administration, created by the National Industrial Recovery Act; enacted changes in the American economy but was declared unconstitutional in 1935
open shop	place of employment where the employee is not required to join or pay dues to a labor union as a condition of hiring or continued employment
P.W.A.	Public Works Administration: a New Deal agency created to provide funds for public-works projects to increase employment during the Great Depression
relief	welfare payments

Robert Clifton Weaver (AP/Wide World Photos)

Robert Clifton Weaver: "The New Deal and the Negro: A Look at the Facts"

"The present economic position of the colored citizen was not created by recent legislation alone."

Overview

Robert Clifton Weaver's article "The New Deal and the Negro: A Look at the Facts" is a spirited defense of President Franklin Delano Roosevelt's New Deal programs in the face of mounting criticism from the African American community. Published in the July 1935 issue of *Opportunity Journal*, the oldest official magazine of the National Urban League, Weaver's essay acknowledged problems of discrimination in some of the Great Depression–era relief efforts, yet argued that these efforts had, in fact, greatly alleviated the economic woes facing the black community.

As a member of the Roosevelt administration, Weaver sought to improve the status of African Americans through government programs rather than by more radical means. Not everyone in the black community agreed, however; by 1935 the deepening problems of unemployment, racial tensions evidenced by a riot in Harlem in March, and growing rural poverty in the South led many black leaders to conclude that the U.S. government was incapable of coming to the aid of African Americans. "The New Deal and the Negro: A Look at the Facts" is a statistics-filled plea to logic in an emotional era.

Context

When U.S. president Franklin Delano Roosevelt took the oath of office in 1933, the nation was in the depths of the Great Depression. Unemployment figures were staggering, reaching nearly 50 percent in urban areas such as Chicago, Illinois, and Detroit, Michigan, and as high as 90 percent in Gary, Indiana. In the South, farmers faced continued crop price deterioration; following the stock market crash of 1929, cotton prices slipped from eighteen to six cents per pound. While all Americans were affected by the depression, African Americans suffered substantially for a variety of reasons. Employed primarily as domestic and agricultural workers, blacks were the first to be laid off when jobs were cut, as these positions were either temporary or expendable in a weak economy. White workers crowded out black workers for increasingly scarce jobs. By 1932 urban black unemployment was over 50 percent, and tenant farmers in the South found themselves increasingly without any means of earning a living.

At the same time, the black intellectual class spawned by the Harlem Renaissance movement began to exert its influence in the political sphere in new ways. The National Association for the Advancement of Colored People (NAACP), a prominent civil rights organization, began to turn its focus from fighting for rights within the court system to working with the federal government for more direct intervention to help the public. The incoming Roosevelt administration signaled that it was interested in addressing the concerns of the African American community. In 1933 Roosevelt began to bring in a series of black advisers to his cabinet to provide him with guidance regarding the status of African Americans. Robert Weaver was one such adviser, hired to serve as a member of the Department of the Interior's staff. These and other key appointments, later known as Roosevelt's "Black Cabinet," led many observers to believe that this administration would not forget the plight of the African American.

In the early years of his presidency, Roosevelt enacted a wide range of relief programs aimed at countering the effects of the Great Depression. These included direct relief payments to the public through federal grants to states, work programs designed to create jobs, farm subsidies and land-use reforms, rural development and housing projects, and plans for industrial organization and control to instill order on wages, prices, and competitive practices. Many of these programs held out particular promise for African Americans locked in rural poverty, unemployed owing to patterns of segregation and exclusion from certain job categories, or suffering from wage discrimination if employed.

The increasing prominence of black intellectuals and like-minded white progressives turned the public spotlight on Roosevelt's New Deal programs. The black community itself was involved in a very heated debate over the direction of the civil rights movement, notably the issue of segregation. African American journals such as *The Crisis* and *Opportunity* carried numerous articles about segregation. The black scholar, editor, and civil rights activist W. E. B. Du Bois of the NAACP advocated a position of voluntary segregation for blacks, stating that desegregation would not become a reality for a long time. In the meantime, argued

Time Line

1933

- **March 4**
  Franklin Delano Roosevelt takes the oath of office as president of the United States.

- **May 12**
  Congress approves the Agricultural Adjustment Act and the Federal Emergency Relief Act.

- **May 18**
  President Roosevelt signs the Tennessee Valley Authority Act.

- **June 16**
  Congress approves the National Industrial Recovery Act, creating the National Recovery Administration.

- **June**
  Weaver and John P. Davis attend National Recovery Administration hearings in Washington, D.C., to represent black workers.

- **Summer**
  President Roosevelt creates a new position in the Department of the Interior—special adviser on the economic status of Negroes—and Weaver is brought on board as an assistant.

1934

- The Federal Emergency Relief Administration creates the Submarginal Land Purchase Program.

1935

- **March**
  Congress passes the Emergency Relief Appropriations Act.

- **March 19**
  Rioting in Harlem injures fifty-seven residents and seven police officers.

- **May 18–20**
  John P. Davis and Ralph Bunche hold a conference at Howard University titled "The Position of the Negro in Our National Economic Crisis," during which most participants criticize Roosevelt's New Deal programs.

- **July**
  Weaver publishes his essay "The New Deal and the Negro: A Look at the Facts."

Du Bois, blacks should gain the resources they needed in order to unite and have power in the present. Others in the NAACP, including Walter White, took the opposite position, stating that succumbing to segregation was a mistake that only perpetuated the legacy of Jim Crow "separate but equal" discrimination in the South as well as continued segregation in areas of the North.

As African Americans within the Roosevelt administration and in outside organizations evaluated the impacts of various New Deal programs, it became apparent that there were some glaring problems with the implementation and, in some cases, design, of the recovery efforts. African Americans were excluded from certain relief programs entirely, prevented from legitimately claiming benefits in certain cases, and actually grew worse off because of the ways in which various New Deal programs were implemented. Some black intellectuals became increasingly disaffected with the Roosevelt administration. In May 1935 black activists held a conference at Howard University in Washington, D.C., during which most presenters attacked New Deal programs for their negative impacts on African Americans. For instance, Weaver's longtime friend and fellow Harvard graduate John P. Davis—a black activist, lawyer, and founding member of the National Negro Congress—had penned a sharp condemnation of the Roosevelt administration's representation of blacks in New Deal recovery programs. Titled "A Black Inventory of the New Deal," Davis's article, which was published in the May 1935 issue of *The Crisis*, argued that the relief efforts under President Roosevelt had actually worsened the plight of the African American community. In addition, frustrated blacks in Harlem had rioted in March of the same year, signaling the growing dissatisfaction with government's ability to deal with the problem of African American poverty. In this tension-filled environment, Robert C. Weaver served as a public spokesperson for the White House, writing articles such as "The New Deal and the Negro: A Look at the Facts" to both champion and reveal the inadequacies of the New Deal programs with which he was personally involved.

About the Author

Robert Clifton Weaver was born December 29, 1907, and raised in Washington, D.C., where his father worked for the U.S. Postal Service. He attended the prestigious Paul Laurence Dunbar High School, an elite black school in the nation's segregated capital. Weaver went on to Harvard University, completing his PhD in economics in 1934. In 1933 he joined the incoming Roosevelt administration as part of the Department of the Interior, where he worked on Secretary Harold Ickes's staff. In that capacity, Weaver was instrumental in ensuring that blacks were placed in supervisory roles in the Civilian Conservation Corps, a New Deal program that provided job training and relief for unemployed workers. Weaver also developed an antidiscrimination policy for the Public Works Administration (PWA), which required a minimum number of skilled black workers on federal projects overseen by this agency. In 1938 Weaver became special assistant in charge of race relations to Nathan Straus, the director of the U.S. Housing Authority. He continued to fight discrimination against African Americans, securing language prohibiting discrimination on the basis of race in PWA housing contracts.

As an increasingly prominent member of the Roosevelt administration, Weaver functioned as a leader in the president's "Black Cabinet." This group of African American advisers gained much publicity (both negative and positive) during the New Deal years, and by the beginning of World War II, Weaver and the other black intellectuals working in Washington had become well known. In 1940, as the United States began to inch its way toward involvement in the war, Weaver was named special administrative assistant on race relations to the Labor Division of the National Defense Advisory Commission, where he worked on the integration of black workers into the war effort. One of the by-products of segregation was the inferior education and job training afforded African Americans, a problem that made it difficult to integrate blacks into the military. On April 11, 1941, Weaver was named chief of the Negro Employment and Training Branch of the Labor Division in order to begin redressing this issue. From 1942 to 1944, he served as chief of the Minority Groups Service in the War Manpower Commission. Weaver retired from federal service on May 1, 1944.

After World War II, Weaver taught at several institutions and was New York's rent commissioner from 1955 to 1959. By 1960 he was a nationally recognized expert in public housing. The following year President John F. Kennedy appointed him administrator of the Housing and Home Finance Agency. Weaver became the first black member of a presidential cabinet when President Lyndon B. Johnson, Kennedy's successor, named him secretary of the newly created Department of Housing and Urban Development in 1966. Weaver retired from government service in 1968 and later served as president of Bernard Baruch College and professor of urban affairs at Hunter College, both in New York City. He died on July 17, 1997.

Explanation and Analysis of the Document

Weaver opens "The New Deal and the Negro: A Look at the Facts" by stating that an intelligent assessment of the New Deal is impossible without considering conditions that existed before its programs were implemented. If, as some argued, the New Deal made matters worse for black Americans, that would require showing that they were better off before the government initiated its relief efforts.

In paragraphs 2–4, Weaver addresses his first subject: unemployment. One of the complaints against Roosevelt's direct relief program, the Federal Emergency Relief Agency (FERA), was that it created a huge mass of black Americans who were barely surviving on government assistance. FERA was established in May 1933, disbursing federal funds to the states for food, child care, blankets, and other

Time Line

1936

■ **November**
Roosevelt receives overwhelming support from African Americans in the presidential election, winning his bid for a second term in office.

forms of direct relief. With so many African Americans receiving this public assistance, some black leaders worried that government policies were contributing to the development of a permanent black underclass. Weaver argues that the chronic unemployment problem among African Americans was not the result of government policy but of demographic factors. Long-standing practices of segregation and discrimination meant that blacks were primarily employed in farming or domestic service (janitorial work for men and housekeeping for women). Once the economy began to deteriorate, workers in these industries were among the first to be idled, as Weaver notes. Worse yet, recovery in domestic service jobs typically lagged behind other types of work, as employers waited to rehire workers until they were certain of their own financial status.

Weaver shows how government policies have helped and would continue to help black Americans who were disproportionately affected by the depression. Although he states that a general recovery will eventually result in increased demand for domestic workers, he places more emphasis— in paragraph 5—on the "creation of direct employment opportunities" for those on relief, which includes agricultural and other workers. FERA included a federal jobs program; Harry Hopkins, head of FERA, was adamant that the government not merely hand out money to those in need but allow Americans to feel that they were earning their government assistance. This philosophy of maintaining the spirit of a work ethic dominated most New Deal programs. Weaver's comments reflect this sentiment as well; using labor union statistics in paragraph 6, he emphasizes the successful reduction in the unemployment rate that federal relief provided, illustrating that many Americans found gainful employment as a result of government programs. Direct aid to the large numbers of blacks on assistance, he says, is a necessary by-product of the economic situation.

In paragraph 7, Weaver acknowledges the existence of "many abuses under the relief set-up." Because FERA gave the states the authority to distribute funds, many states in the segregated South funneled aid only to white recipients. One program, in particular, discriminated against African Americans when it was implemented: the National Recovery Administration (NRA). Created in June 1933, the NRA sought to bring government and industry together to develop guidelines for American manufacturers. The goal was to ensure protection for workers in the form of minimum wages and maximum hours as well as to create conditions that would favor fair competition within industries. Although the majority of black Americans worked in agricultural and

Police round up suspects attempting to flee during the March 1935 Harlem riot. (AP/Wide World Photos)

domestic jobs, which were excluded from the NRA, some two million black workers stood to benefit from the provisions of the NRA. Unfortunately, as southern manufacturers participated in the hearings to develop wage codes and production standards, many of them argued that the NRA codes should allow for regional differences, such as the lower cost of living in their area. In effect, this allowed southern manufacturers to exempt black workers from the codes even though this was not explicitly stated in racial terms. Weaver and fellow Harvard graduate John P. Davis attended many of the NRA hearings in Washington to testify on behalf of black workers. The NAACP and other black rights organizations soon after joined to protect the interests of African Americans in the implementation of the NRA.

In paragraph 8, Weaver points out that the plight of African Americans in the South is particularly troublesome. He notes that just as there were structural problems with respect to domestic workers before the depression, there were inherent problems with the agricultural system in the South before the beginning of the New Deal. Tenant farming, or sharecropping, was a long-standing institution in the rural South. Sharecroppers would rent land from the owner, making payments by using the proceeds from whatever crop they grew or from liens against future crop sales. As agricultural prices fell in the 1920s, sharecroppers either could not make enough money from their crop sales or were simply told by the landowner not to grow anything and leave. As Weaver points out, tenant farmers in the South were already in trouble before the depression.

Although Weaver acknowledges that the problems faced by black farmers in the South arose before the New Deal, he states in paragraph 9 that certain elements of the administration's policies have exacerbated these problems. Specifically, Weaver mentions the crop-reduction programs that were part of the Agricultural Adjustment Administration (AAA). In an effort to boost sagging crop prices and thus help farmers, the Roosevelt administration paid farmers *not* to grow crops on part of their land. The resulting reduction in the supply of a given crop would, it was hoped, raise the price, allowing farmers to earn more money per acre of crop produced. The problem was that tenant farmers suffered immensely: White landowners simply fired them in order to reduce their crop production. Furthermore, although landowners were required by AAA policy to share their incentive payments with their tenant farmers, few white landowners did so, keeping the money for themselves instead. Weaver remarks that these kinds of abuses were indicative of a resistance "as old as the system," a resistance that reflects the history of slavery and Jim Crow segregation in the South. He uses another example of abuse of a federal assistance program: Following a massive flood of the Mississippi River in 1927, the government provided federal loans to southern farmers to purchase feed, seed, and fertilizer in order to get back on their feet. According to Weaver, similar violations of the law existed then, reflecting a larger problem than the AAA itself.

Weaver argues in paragraph 10 that the solution to the problems facing black tenant farmers in the South lies in changing the sharecropping system itself by providing African Americans with broader opportunities for land ownership. Until the cycle of dependency was broken, Weaver states, government aid programs would not be successful. He mentions "the new program for land utilization, rural rehabilitation, and spreading land ownership" as a possible first step in the right direction. The Roosevelt administration initiated a number of programs aimed at reforming land use and ownership. The National Industrial Recovery Act of 1933 set aside twenty-five million dollars for developing "subsistence homesteads," which were family farms located near urban centers. Specifically designed not to compete with commercial agricultural enterprises, these homesteads were intended to allow workers to produce enough to feed themselves and their families while finding part-time employment in a nearby industrial center. The subsistence homestead was one New Deal approach to ending the cycle of rural poverty in the South.

In 1934 FERA created its Submarginal Land Purchase Program. Under this aid program, the federal government would help farmers who were living on poor-quality land to relocate, allowing the government to retire land that was no longer productive for agricultural purposes. Another program was the Tennessee Valley Authority, created to bring a number of improvements to the Tennessee River valley area, including flood control and electrical power for the region. In addition to these infrastructure projects, the Tennessee Valley Authority set aside funds for building planned communities that were envisioned as being self-sustaining through a mix of agricultural and industrial production.

The "new program" to which Weaver refers is the Emergency Relief Appropriations Act, passed in March 1935. This law created the Resettlement Administration, a new agency that took over the Subsistence Homestead program, FERA's and AAA's land use functions, and other programs related to rural rehabilitation and land distribution. Weaver comments that these programs would help African Americans only if they could sidestep the kind of systemic patterns of discrimination historically experienced by other such reforms. In fact, the Resettlement Administration became highly controversial by 1936, as charges of government efforts to socialize land distribution led the agency to abandon many of its more ambitious efforts to change patterns of land ownership in the South.

Weaver then states in paragraph 11 that the New Deal benefited African Americans in three key areas: housing, employment, and education. The first agency he singles out as an example of success is the PWA, created in 1933 as part of the National Industrial Recovery Act. The PWA invested federal funds in infrastructure projects, such as road and bridge building, in order to create jobs for unemployed urban Americans. Another important component of the program was its development of public housing. As Weaver notes in paragraphs 12 and 13, several of these housing developments were targeted for poor urban black communities. Weaver's statements regarding the planned projects illustrate the segregated nature of American society during the 1930s. The first federal housing projects in the nation were developed in Atlanta. The University project, located near Spelman and Morehouse colleges, was designated for black residents only. At this point in the article, Weaver does not mention Techwood, which was a whites-only project built at the same time. Thurman Street was another blacks-only project located in Alabama. Some black activists, notably John P. Davis, criticized the PWA for perpetuating segregation in the South through these kinds of housing projects.

As a Department of the Interior employee, Weaver was actively involved in devising policies related to the implementation of PWA programs. Largely as a result of his efforts, PWA housing contracts were modified to include the clause he describes in paragraph 14, which required that these contracts employ a certain percentage of black skilled workers. The percentage for each contract was based on the percentage of African Americans who belonged to a given occupational category in the 1930 census. Weaver and his staff calculated the required quota for each contract based on the census data for a given community and monitored contractors to ensure compliance. Weaver's efforts were highly successful, allowing African Americans to have access to union jobs that had formerly remained closed to them. Here, he uses the Techwood development, the all-white housing project in Atlanta, as a case study. Even though the project employed a significant number of black workers, it failed to mirror the actual proportion of skilled black workers in the area. Still, Weaver remains positive in his assessment of his efforts to promote what later became known as affirmative action.

Beginning with paragraph 15, Weaver addresses the second of the key benefits of New Deal programs for African Americans: education. FERA included funding for an Emergency Education Program aimed at helping unemployed teachers. Like many New Deal benefits, this program sought to provide alternative work opportunities rather than direct financial aid. The program reemployed teachers in a number of areas, including literacy education, vocational training, and general education courses for adults in a wide variety of subjects that might help them develop outside interests or new skills. Some of the funds, however, were used as direct aid in the form of emergency salaries to particularly impoverished rural communities. These communities were predominantly populated by African Americans. Weaver notes that government spend-

Essential Quotes

> "The present economic position of the colored citizen was not created by recent legislation alone. Rather, it is the result of the impact of a new program upon an economic and social situation."
>
> (Paragraph 1)

> "Although it is regrettable that the economic depression has led to the unemployment of so many Negroes and has threatened the creation of a large segment of the Negro population as a chronic relief load, one is forced to admit that Federal relief has been a godsend to the unemployed."
>
> (Paragraph 6)

> "We can admit that we have gained from the relief program and still fight to receive greater and more equitable benefits from it."
>
> (Paragraph 7)

> "In the execution of some phases of the Recovery Program, there have been difficulties, and the maximum results have not been received by the Negroes. But, given the economic situation of 1932, the New Deal has been more helpful than harmful to Negroes."
>
> (Paragraph 17)

ing on emergency aid in these rural southern areas breaks the trend seen in other New Deal programs, where the "status quo," the result of the legacies of slavery and Jim Crow segregation, led to abuse and discrimination. The fact that the South spent proportionately more on this type of assistance than the percentage of blacks in the population shows Weaver that, at least in the area of education, southern states saw the need for overcoming these legacies.

In paragraph 16, Weaver mentions the FERA college scholarship program, which made funds available to employ some 10 percent of students part time at public universities. These funds were administered by each university's administration and allowed many students who could otherwise not afford to attend college to do so. He states that black and white students appear to have benefited equally from this particular program.

Last, Weaver turns to New Deal programs designed to spur employment. In paragraph 17, he reiterates many of his earlier arguments, returning to his case for structural forces causing the economic woes facing African Americans; in his words, "the New Deal has been more helpful than harmful to Negroes." Weaver changes the tenor of his argument in the latter part of his essay; he states that African Americans have found jobs within the Roosevelt administration, making the point that the New Deal programs themselves have created new and lucrative positions for African Americans like himself. He notes the fifteen jobs created by his own Department of the Interior and the PWA and then extends his evidence to include the various staffers and clerical workers in the White House. Weaver was also concerned with providing benefits to black professionals through his role with the Department of the Interior and the PWA. He comments that federal housing projects have included the services of black architects and technicians, arguing that the New Deal programs have increased employment opportunities for professional blacks. Weaver closes with a claim of the promises of the New Deal to help African Americans and calls for an "intelligent appraisal" of the facts in order to accurately assess the recovery plan's efficacy as well as the areas for improvement.

Audience

Weaver's essay was published in the July 1935 issue of *Opportunity*, the journal of the National Urban League. The magazine was one of several mainstream publications targeting black readers, but white liberals interested in fighting discrimination also read it. *Opportunity* and the other journals, including *The Crisis*, had published a number of articles critical of President Roosevelt's New Deal programs. Weaver wrote his essay in part to counter these negative portrayals of the administration's policies.

Weaver's audience was educated, politically progressive, and reform minded. The fact-driven nature of his essay reflects his understanding of this audience; Weaver assumed that readers of *Opportunity* would want to see detailed evidence supporting his assertions that government programs were, in fact, helping to alleviate the problems facing black Americans. He also acknowledges that an "intelligent appraisal" of these programs would improve their implementation in many respects. This type of measured assessment, which draws on evidence rather than emotional appeal, would have appealed to the journal's readers.

Impact

Weaver wrote numerous articles that were published in prominent black magazines such as *The Crisis* and *Opportunity*, as well as pieces for scholarly publications such as the *Journal of Education*. As an insider in the Roosevelt administration, he wrote as an advocate of the president's New Deal programs, but he also pointed out their flaws. In this essay and others, Weaver was careful not only to demonstrate the positive attributes of recovery initiatives but also to indicate where improvements were already being made and could be made in the future.

Weaver's essay provided an effective counter to the more critical articles on the New Deal appearing in black periodicals during the 1930s. African Americans shifted their electoral support to the Democratic Party in 1936, voting overwhelmingly for Roosevelt in that year's presidential election, despite having voted primarily Republican just four years earlier. Many historians believe that even with the criticisms of Roosevelt's New Deal in *The Crisis* and *Opportunity*, African Americans believed, for the most part, that the recovery programs had helped them. Articles such as Weaver's, showing the tangible benefits of New Deal programs as well as the reality of their flaws and limitations, helped to maintain Roosevelt's overwhelmingly positive image in the black community.

See also John P. Davis: "A Black Inventory of the New Deal" (1935).

Further Reading

- **Articles**

Hill, Walter B., Jr. "Finding a Place for the Negro: Robert C. Weaver and the Groundwork for the Civil Rights Movement." *Prologue* 37, no. 1 (Spring 2005): 42–51.

Questions for Further Study

1. Summarize the events and economic developments that gave rise to Weaver's "The New Deal and the Negro: A Look at the Facts."

2. In the 1930s a number of observers referred to the New Deal as a "raw deal" for African Americans. On what basis did they make that judgment? How and why did the Great Depression disproportionately affect African Americans?

3. Compare this document with John P. Davis's "A Black Inventory of the New Deal," written the same year. To what extent do the two writers' positions differ? Are their arguments similar in any significant ways? Explain.

4. In the modern era, African Americans have tended to heavily support Democrats for high office, particularly the presidency. Why did African American allegiance shift from the Republican Party ("the party of Lincoln") to the Democrats during the 1930s?

5. Using this document and the events surrounding it alongside Davis's "A Black Inventory of the New Deal" and A. Philip Randolph's "Call to Negro America to March on Washington for Jobs and Equal Participation in National Defense" (1941), prepare a time line of key economic events that affected African Americans (and all Americans) throughout the 1930s and 1940s.

■ Books

Kirby, John B. *Black Americans in the Roosevelt Era: Liberalism and Race*. Knoxville: University of Tennessee Press, 1980.

Pritchett, Wendell E. *Robert C. Weaver and the American City: The Life and Times of an Urban Reformer*. Chicago, Ill.: University of Chicago Press, 2008.

Sullivan, Patricia. *Days of Hope: Race and Democracy in the New Deal Era*. Chapel Hill: University of North Carolina Press, 1996.

■ Web Sites

"African Americans." New Deal Network Web site.
http://newdeal.feri.org/texts/browse.cfm?MainCatID=40.

"'Please Help Us Mr. President': Black Americans Write to FDR." History Matters Web site.
http://historymatters.gmu.edu/d/137/.

—Karen Linkletter

Robert Clifton Weaver: "The New Deal and the Negro: A Look at the Facts"

It is impossible to discuss intelligently the New Deal and the Negro without considering the status of the Negro prior to the advent of the Recovery Program. The present economic position of the colored citizen was not created by recent legislation alone. Rather, it is the result of the impact of a new program upon an economic and social situation.

Much has been said recently about the occupational distribution of Negroes. Over a half of the gainfully employed colored Americans are concentrated in domestic service and farming. The workers in these two pursuits are the most casual and unstable in the modern economic world. This follows from the fact that neither of them requires any great capital outlay to buy necessary equipment. Thus, when there is a decline in trade, the unemployment of workers in these fields does not necessitate idle plants, large depreciation costs, or mounting overhead charges. In such a situation, the employer has every incentive to dismiss his workers; thus, these two classes are fired early in a depression.

The domestic worker has loomed large among the unemployed since the beginning of the current trade decline. This situation has persisted throughout the depression and is reflected in the relief figures for urban communities where 20 per cent of the employables on relief were formerly attached to personal and domestic service. Among Negroes the relative number of domestics and servants on relief is even greater....

In ... [a sample of 30 American] cities, 43.4 per cent of the Negroes on relief May 1, 1934, were usually employed as domestics. The demand for servants is a derived one; it is dependent upon the income and employment of other persons in the community. Thus, domestics are among the last rehired in a period of recovery.

The new work program of the Federal Government will attack this problem of the domestic worker from two angles. Insofar as it accelerates recovery by restoring incomes, it will tend to increase the demand for servants. More important, however, will be its creation of direct employment opportunities for all occupational classes of those on relief.

Although it is regrettable that the economic depression has led to the unemployment of so many Negroes and has threatened the creation of a large segment of the Negro population as a chronic relief load, one is forced to admit that Federal relief has been a godsend to the unemployed. The number of unemployed in this country was growing in 1933. According to the statistics of the American Federation of Labor, the number of unemployed increased from 3,216,000 in January, 1930, to 13,689,000 in March, 1933. In November, 1934, the number was about 10,500,000, and although there are no comparable current data available, estimates indicate that current unemployment is less than that of last November. Local relief monies were shrinking; and need and starvation were facing those unable to find an opportunity to work. A Federal relief program was the only possible aid in this situation. Insofar as the Negro was greatly victimized by the economic developments, he was in a position to benefit from a program which provided adequate funds for relief.

It is admitted that there were many abuses under the relief set-up. Such situations should be brought to light and fought. In the case of Negroes, these abuses undoubtedly existed and do exist. We should extend every effort to uncover and correct them. We can admit that we have gained from the relief program and still fight to receive greater and more equitable benefits from it....

The recent depression has been extremely severe in its effects upon the South. The rural Negro—poor before the period of trade decline—was rendered even more needy after 1929. Many tenants found it impossible to obtain a contract for a crop, and scores of Negro farm owners lost their properties. The displacement of Negro tenants (as was the case for whites) began before, and grew throughout the depression. Thus, at the time of the announcement of the New Deal, there were many families without arrangements for a crop—an appreciable number without shelter....

The problems facing the Negro farmer of the South are not new. They have been accentuated by the crop reduction program. They are, for the most part, problems of a system, and their resistance to reform is as old as the system. This was well illustrated by the abuses in the administration of the Federal feed, seed, and fertilizer laws in 1928–1929. These abuses were of the same nature as those which confront the A.A.A. [the Agricultural Adjustment Administration] in its dealings with Negro tenants.

The southern farm tenant is in such a position that he cannot receive any appreciable gains from a program until steps are taken to change his position of absolute economic dependence upon the landlord. Until some effective measure for rehabilitating him is discovered, there is no hope. The new program for land utilization, rural rehabilitation, and spreading land ownership may be able to effect such a change. Insofar as it takes a step in that direction, it will be advantageous to the Negro farmer. The degree to which it aids him will depend upon the temper of its administration and the extent to which it is able to break away from the *status quo*.

In listing some of the gains which have accrued to Negroes under the New Deal, there will be a discussion of three lines of activity: housing, employment, and emergency education. These are chosen for discussion because each is significant in itself, and all represent a definite break from the *status quo* in governmental activity, method, and policy. They do not give a complete picture; but rather, supply interesting examples of what is, and can be, done for Negroes.

The Housing Division of the Federal Emergency Administration of Public Works has planned 60 Federal housing projects to be under construction by December 31, 1935. Of these, 28 are to be developed in Negro slum areas and will be tenanted predominantly or wholly by Negroes. Eight additional projects will provide for an appreciable degree of Negro occupancy. These 36 projects will afford approximately 74,664 rooms and should offer accommodations for about 23,000 low income colored families. The estimated total cost of these housing developments will be $64,428,000, and they represent about 29 per cent of the funds devoted to Federal slum clearance developments under the present allotments.

Projects in Negro areas have been announced in seven cities: Atlanta, Cleveland, Detroit, Indianapolis, Montgomery, Chicago, and Nashville. These will cost about $33,232,000, and will contain about 20,000 rooms. Two of these projects, the University development at Atlanta and the Thurman Street development in Montgomery, are under construction. These are among the earliest Federal housing projects to be initiated by the P.W.A.

After a series of conferences and a period of experience under the P.W.A., it was decided to include a clause in P.W.A. housing contracts requiring the payment to Negro mechanics of a given percentage of the payroll going to skilled workers. The first project to be affected by such a contractual clause was the Techwood development in Atlanta, Georgia. On this project, most of the labor employed on demolition was composed of unskilled Negro workers. About 90 per cent of the unskilled workers employed laying the foundation for the Techwood project were Negroes, and, for the first two-month construction period, February and March, 12.7 per cent of the wages paid [to] skilled workers was earned by Negro artisans....

Under the educational program of the F.E.R.A., out of a total of 17,879 teachers employed in 13 southern states, 5,476 or 30.6 per cent were Negro. Out of a total of 570,794 enrolled in emergency classes, 217,000 or 38 per cent were Negro. Out of a total of $886,300 expended in a month (either February or March, 1935) for the program, Negroes received $231,320 or 26.1 per cent. These southern states in which 26.1 per cent of all emergency salaries were paid to Negro teachers, ordinarily allot only 11.7 per cent of all public school salaries to Negro teachers. The situation may be summarized as follows: Six of the 13 states are spending for Negro salaries a proportion of their emergency education funds larger than the percentage of Negroes in those states. The area as a whole is spending for Negro salaries a proportion of its funds slightly in excess of the percentage of Negroes in the population. This development is an example of Government activity breaking away from the *status quo* in race relations.

There is one Government expenditure in education in reference to which there has been general agreement that equity has been established. That is the F.E.R.A. college scholarship program. Each college or university not operated for profit, received $20 monthly per student as aid for 12 per cent of its college enrollment. Negro and white institutions have benefited alike under this program.

In the execution of some phases of the Recovery Program, there have been difficulties, and the maximum results have not been received by the Negroes. But, given the economic situation of 1932, the New Deal has been more helpful than harmful to Negroes. We had unemployment in 1932. Jobs were being lost by Negroes, and they were in need. Many would have starved had there been no Federal relief program. As undesirable as is the large relief load among Negroes, the F.E.R.A. has meant much to them. In most of the New Deal set-ups, there has been some Negro representation by competent Negroes. The Department of the Interior and the P.W.A. have appointed some fifteen Negroes to jobs of responsibility which pay good salaries. These per-

Document Text

sons have secretarial and clerical staffs attached to their offices. In addition to these new jobs, there are the colored messengers, who number around 100, and the elevator operators for the Government buildings, of whom there are several hundred. This is not, of course, adequate representation; but it represents a step in the desired direction and is greater recognition than has been given Negroes in the Federal Government during the last 20 years. Or again, in the Nashville housing project, a Negro architectural firm is a consultant; for the Southwest side housing project in Chicago, a Negro is an associate architect. One of the proposed projects will have two Negro principal architects, a Negro consultant architect, and a technical staff of about six Negro technicians. In other cities competent colored architects will be used to design housing projects.

This analysis is intended to indicate some advantages accruing to the Negro under the Recovery Program, and to point out that the New Deal, insofar as it represents an extension of governmental activity into the economic sphere, is a departure which can do much to reach the Negro citizens. In many instances it has availed itself of these opportunities. An intelligent appraisal of its operation is necessary to assure greater benefits to colored citizens.

Glossary

American Federation of Labor	an umbrella organization for a number of labor unions
crop reduction program	a federal program that paid farmers not to raise crops as a way of boosting crop prices by decreasing supply
F.E.R.A.	the Federal Emergency Relief Administration, a New Deal government agency whose goal was to provide relief to unemployed workers and their families
New Deal	the name given to the legislative initiatives of the Roosevelt administration to alleviate the effects of the Great Depression
P.W.A.	the Public Works Administration, a New Deal government agency whose goal was to increase employment by funding public works projects

Charles Hamilton Houston's "Educational Inequalities Must Go!"

"The ultimate objective of the association is the abolition of all forms of segregation in public education."

Overview

In October 1935 Charles Hamilton Houston published "Educational Inequalities Must Go!" in *The Crisis*, the official publication of the National Association for the Advancement of Colored People (NAACP). His purpose was to announce the long-range, carefully orchestrated legal strategy that would culminate with the U.S. Supreme Court's 1954 ruling in *Brown v. Board of Education of Topeka*, which held that segregation in public education was unconstitutional. The NAACP had been established in 1909 to fight for equal rights for African Americans. During the first twenty-five years of its operations, it relied on lobbying, demonstrations, and public education to promote its objectives. Litigation was deployed on a case-by-case basis, and some significant victories were won.

In the early 1930s, the NAACP embarked on a dramatic change in direction. The organization's leaders decided to launch a legal campaign in which court cases would be used systematically to attack segregation. The organization hired Houston, who was then the dean of Howard University's law school, to lead the campaign in 1935. In "Educational Inequalities Must Go!" Houston announced the beginning of the legal campaign.

Context

In 1896 the U.S. Supreme Court ruled in *Plessy v. Ferguson* that laws requiring segregation in public transportation did not violate the Fourteenth Amendment to the U.S. Constitution as long as the separate facilities provided for blacks were equal to those available to whites. By the 1930s segregation was firmly entrenched, especially in the South, where schools, restaurants, hotels, theaters, and public transportation were segregated. Elevators, parks, public restrooms, hospitals, drinking fountains, prisons, and places of worship were also segregated. Whites and blacks were born in separate hospitals, educated in separate schools, and buried in segregated graveyards.

Segregation was codified in state and local laws, and lynching and other forms of racial violence were routine. There were, in effect, two criminal justice systems: one for whites and another for blacks. In the North, African Americans resided in segregated neighborhoods that were perpetuated by "redlining" (the practice of drawing a red line on a map around black neighborhoods) and racially restrictive covenants that prohibited white homeowners from selling their homes to blacks. There were "black jobs" and "white jobs," with African Americans confined to the lowest-paying and least desirable occupations.

In 1922 Charles Garland, the son of a Boston millionaire, donated $800,000 to establish a fund to support radical causes. The Garland Fund, as it became known, was administered by a group of liberal activists that included James Weldon Johnson, the executive secretary of the NAACP, and Roger Baldwin, the founder of the American Civil Liberties Union, as well as the civil liberties lawyer and free speech advocate Morris Ernest, the *New York Herald* columnist Lewis Gannett, and the Socialist Party leader Norman Thomas. Garland turned over his inheritance with a request that it be given away as quickly as possible to unpopular causes, without regard to race, creed, or color. A Committee on Negro Work was formed, and it recommended that the fund award a grant of $100,000 to the NAACP to carry out a large-scale legal campaign to secure the constitutional rights of southern blacks. The grant was announced with an explanation that it would be used to defend civil liberties and assist in campaigns against specific handicaps facing African Americans, including the unequal apportionment of school funds, the barring of blacks from juries, Jim Crow laws, racially restrictive covenants, and disenfranchisement. The NAACP indicated that it would find a lawyer to review the relevant legal authorities, develop an overall strategy, and supervise the handling of the cases that would be filed.

The NAACP hired a recent Harvard graduate, Nathan Margold, to survey the laws requiring segregation and to recommend how a legal challenge might be mounted. The Margold Report, as it became known, contained a comprehensive analysis of laws and applicable legal precedents beginning with *Plessy v. Ferguson*. After analyzing the post-*Plessy* decisions, the report worked its way through the laws governing segregation up to the 1930s. Despite the weight of legal precedent supporting segregation, Margold suggested a means by which the legal obstacles might be

Time Line

1895
- September 3
  Charles Hamilton Houston is born in Washington, D.C.

1896
- May 18
  The U.S. Supreme Court rules in *Plessy v. Ferguson* that laws requiring segregated facilities do not violate the U.S. Constitution.

1919
- Houston enrolls in Harvard Law School.

1923
- After graduating from Harvard Law School, Houston earns a doctor of juridical science degree from Harvard and wins a fellowship to study in Spain at the University of Madrid, where he earns a doctor of civil law degree.

1924
- Houston is admitted to the bar of the District of Columbia.

1929
- July 1
  Houston is appointed vice dean of the Howard University School of Law.

1935
- Houston joins the National Association for the Advancement of Colored People (NAACP) as special counsel.
- October
  Houston publishes "Educational Inequalities Must Go!" in *The Crisis*.

1936
- January 15
  In *Pearson v. Murray* the Maryland Court of Appeals upholds a lower court ruling that the University of Maryland must admit African Americans to its law school if there is no other law school available to them.

---

overcome. He concluded that the "separate but equal" doctrine as practiced was unconstitutional. In the case of public schools, for example, conspicuous inequalities existed in the resources allocated to white schools compared with those provided to schools that served black students. However, there were Supreme Court decisions holding that absolute equality in funding was not required as long as some provision was made for both races. Margold's main conclusion was that segregation as practiced was unconstitutional under the rationale in *Plessy*. The system was, in reality, separation *and* discrimination, for the facilities provided for blacks were always separate but never equal. Margold contended that segregation coupled with discrimination resulting from governmental actions was as much a denial of equal protection of the laws as was segregation coupled with discrimination required by an explicit statutory enactment.

Margold took a job with the U.S. Department of the Interior in 1933, so the NAACP began searching for a full-time attorney to conduct the campaign. After considering several candidates, Walter White, the NAACP's executive director, chose Charles Houston as the ideal candidate for the position. Houston concluded that Margold's legal analysis was sound, but the 1930s courts were not prepared to respond favorably to a direct challenge to *Plessy*; consequently, a different legal strategy was devised, one that would be far more gradual and methodical than the direct challenge Margold proposed. Thus, the strategy that was adopted was not to ask the courts to overturn *Plessy* but to insist that blacks be treated equally with whites.

A few months before he joined the NAACP, Houston prepared a memorandum for the Garland Fund and the NAACP in which he outlined the equalization strategy. By this time, it was known that only $10,000 of the original $100,000 grant would be forthcoming, based on losses that had occurred during the Great Depression. With this tiny budget, Houston set out to transform the foundations of the American legal system.

Because of the diminished grant funds, the NAACP lowered its sights to legal challenges against discrimination in education and public transportation. After considering what the legal campaign would entail, however, Houston recommended an even narrower focus. He noted in a memorandum that a budget of $10,000 would make it exceedingly difficult to execute an effective program on a national scale on both issues. Although resources would be severely limited, Houston predicted that carefully targeted suits would stimulate public interest and encourage the affected communities of African Americans to continue the fight for equal rights after the NAACP led the way with test cases.

Houston presented two separate budget proposals. One was based on an assumption that the entire effort would focus on education cases. The second proposed an equal division of the funds between education and transportation litigation. Houston believed that education was the more important goal because of the immediate benefits the black community would receive. He thus recommended a two-pronged attack: The first involved the unequal apportionment of school funds. The second focused on disparities in teacher salaries. Houston explained that his goal was to work out model procedures that the local communities could apply to similar cases in the future.

About the Author

Charles Hamilton Houston was born in Washington, D.C., on September 3, 1895. His father, William Houston, was a lawyer who had obtained a law degree from Howard University, while his mother, Mary Houston, was a hairdresser. Houston attended segregated public schools in Washington before enrolling at Amherst College in Massachusetts in 1911. He was elected to Phi Beta Kappa during his senior year, and he delivered one of the commencement addresses. After graduating in 1915, Houston returned to Washington without any specific plans for a career. When the United States entered World War I, Houston decided to join the military. He enlisted in the segregated officers training corps that was established in Fort Des Moines, Iowa. In October 1917, Houston was among the 440 African Americans who received commissions as officers in the U.S. Army. At Fort Meade, Houston and the other black officers were harassed, humiliated, and subjected to the army's institutionalized racism, which continued after they were shipped to France.

Houston was almost lynched in France when he and a companion stumbled upon a heated dispute between a black serviceman and a group of white American soldiers. Houston and his companion found themselves surrounded by an angry mob of soldiers who shouted racial epithets and threats. The hostilities ended only after a military policeman intervened and restored order. Houston never forgot the incident and pledged at that point never to be caught again without knowing his rights. He would study law and fight for the rights of African Americans.

After his tour of duty, Houston enrolled in Harvard Law School in 1919. During his first year he joined the staff of the prestigious *Harvard Law Review*, an honor accorded to a limited number of students who receive the highest grades. Houston's performance on the *Law Review* staff resulted in his election to the editorial board, making him the first African American student to serve in that capacity.

In 1922 Houston graduated cum laude. The following fall he became a candidate for the advanced degree of doctor of juridical science. He received that degree in 1923 and was awarded a Sheldon Traveling Fellowship, which he used to study law at the University of Madrid in Spain through 1924. In addition to studying international law, Houston used the time abroad to travel in Europe and North Africa. He returned to Washington, was admitted to practice in the District of Columbia, and joined his father's law firm as well as the faculty at Howard Law School.

Houston was appointed resident vice dean in charge of the law school on July 1, 1929. He began almost immediately to upgrade the facility's quality of instruction. By late 1930 the law school employed four full-time professors and

Time Line

1938
- **November 12**
  In *Missouri ex rel. Gaines v. Canada*, the U.S. Supreme Court rules that Missouri must educate African American law students within its state borders.

1948
- **January 12**
  In *Sipuel v. Board of Regents of Oklahoma*, the U.S. Supreme Court rules that if a state does not have a law school for black students, it must admit them to its white law school.

1950
- **April 22**
  Houston dies in Washington, D.C.
- **June 5**
  In *McLaurin v. Board of Regents of Oklahoma*, the U.S. Supreme Court rules that students in graduate schools of education must be treated equally. That same day, in the case of *Sweatt v. Painter*, the Court rules that a separate law school in Texas for black students is not equal and that African Americans must be admitted to the white law school.

1954
- **May 17**
  The Supreme Court rules in *Brown v. Board of Education* that the "separate but equal" doctrine violates the Fourteenth Amendment guarantee of equal protection.

one full-time librarian, had developed a library of ten thousand volumes, and was fully accredited by the American Bar Association. In 1931 the school was elected to membership by the American Association of Law Schools. Houston's plans went beyond improving legal education for African American students. He intended to train a generation of black lawyers who would serve on the front lines in the war against discrimination. He urged his students to become highly skilled social engineers with a strong commitment to social justice and to use the Constitution as an engine of progress. Under Houston's leadership, the Howard Law School became the West Point of the civil rights movement.

Norman Thomas, Socialist Party leader and one of the board members of the Garland Fund (Library of Congress)

Houston applied for a leave of absence from Howard and moved to New York in 1935 to join the NAACP, where he developed the legal strategy that would be used to attack the "separate but equal" doctrine in higher education. In this position, he was intimately involved with several landmark cases that chipped away at the doctrine. He died on April 22, 1950, before his efforts could bear full fruit in the Supreme Court decision in *Brown v. Board of Education*.

Explanation and Analysis of the Document

In this 1935 article published in *The Crisis*, Houston announces what would become the NAACP's legal strategy. The approach was carried out over several years in hundreds of cases and ultimately resulted in the reversal of the *Plessy* doctrine and the end of formal segregation. Focusing on inequalities in education, Houston proposes that a series of suits be filed demanding that states comply with the letter of *Plessy* by providing equal allocations of financial and other resources for black students in segregated schools.

Houston's essay is relative simple and uncomplicated. In the opening sentence, he vigorously announces the NAACP's intention: "The National Association for the Advancement of Colored People is launching an active campaign against race discrimination in public education." He explains that the NAACP's campaign would encompass all levels of education, from elementary school to graduate school, and he notes that the organization had already begun legal action to have African American students admitted to graduate schools in Maryland and Virginia—efforts that would culminate in such cases as *Pearson v. Murray* in 1936. The goal was to end segregation in education but, failing that, to ensure that black schools were made equal to those attended by white students in terms of facilities, funding, and faculty. This was what was meant by the equalization strategy—using the "separate but equal" doctrine of the *Plessy* case against itself by demanding the "equal" part of "separate but equal."

◆ **"Linked to Other Objectives"**

In this section, Houston notes that the NAACP's campaign was one component of a wider effort to dismantle the Jim Crow system—the formal and informal system of segregation and discrimination that had been in place since the late nineteenth century. He states, "It ties in with the antilynching fight because there is no use educating boys and girls if their function in life is to be the playthings of murderous mobs." Houston continues by pointing out that educational improvements had to be part of a broader effort to improve all aspects of blacks' lives, and he regrets the impact of the Great Depression of the 1930s on skilled black workers, who often lost their jobs first because they had been the ones most recently hired.

◆ **"Specific Objectives"**

In this section, Houston specifies the NAACP's plan of attack, including the objective of equality in school terms, payment of teachers, transportation of students, buildings and equipment, per capita spending for students, and graduate and professional training. He goes on to explain that inequalities existed in both segregated and nonsegregated schools. Even in those schools that were integrated, African American teachers encountered professional obstacles, and black students were often, for example, denied access to extracurricular activities. At the graduate school level, segregation was largely confined to the South. He concludes this section of the article by arguing that the U.S. Supreme Court had supported this uneven system in ruling that "separate but equal" schools did not violate the equal protection clause of the Fourteenth Amendment, citing indirectly the 1896 case of *Plessy v. Ferguson*. In the decades that followed, this landmark case played a key role in maintaining the Jim Crow system that reduced African Americans to second-class status.

◆ **"Inequalities Glaring"**

In "Inequalities Glaring," Houston cites examples of educational inequities, often by referring to the findings of other researchers. He notes in particular the "glaring" imbalance in funding for white and black schools. The disparities were bad enough in 1900, but by the time Houston was writing, they had worsened sometimes by a factor of twenty. In the

Federal employees waiting for treatment at a Public Health Service dispensary with clearly marked waiting rooms for blacks and whites (Library of Congress)

mid-1930s, as many as 230 U.S. counties made no provision for educating African American students of high school age.

◆ **"No Graduate Training"**

In "No Graduate Training," Houston observes that in seventeen southern states, black students had no opportunities for professional or graduate study, though some states did provide scholarship funds, often inadequate, to send black students to other states willing to admit them. This problem, in Houston's view, was easy to attack from a legal perspective. In the South, certain states provided separate elementary schools, high schools, and colleges for black and white students, but difficulties arose in comparing the extent to which facilities were or were not truly equal. When a state funded white graduate students but provided no funding for black students, the inequality was clear and easier to confront. For this reason, the NAACP's immediate focus would be on graduate education.

◆ **"Unwise Attempt"**

In this section, Houston describes one such case, that involving a young black woman trying to gain admission to graduate school at the University of Virginia. He quotes Virginia newspapers that conceded that the student had an "abstract" right to attend the university, but they questioned why she would want to attend school where she was "not wanted." Houston asserts that because the university was a public institution, this question was irrelevant. Further, he responds to the notion that attending a school where they were not wanted could damage black students' "self-respect," noting that students could retain their self-respect by asserting their constitutional rights. They might have to endure "snubs and insults," but they had to do so in other settings throughout the South all the time. Houston concludes this section by leveling criticism at white southern "liberals" who paid "lip service" to equal rights; these same southerners expressed concern that the NAACP's actions would disturb "amicable race relations" and thus took no action to ensure that "amicable" relations are based on equal rights.

◆ **"Cannot Surrender Rights"**

The final section of Houston's article picks up the theme of "amicable race relations" by suggesting that the goal of the NAACP was to ensure that everyone be treated equally under the law and enjoy equality of opportunity. He says that the issue was not whether blacks and whites could get along when blacks are subordinated but rather whether they could get along when blacks "insist on sharing with whites the rights and advantages to which they are lawfully entitled." Amicable race relations have to be founded on "dignity and self-respect," not on the surrender of constitutional rights. Houston concludes by reassuring readers that the NAACP was not a "special pleader" in the long fight ahead; it was merely insisting that the Supreme Court enforce the Constitution.

Audience

The Crisis magazine was delivered each month to members of the NAACP and circulated widely in African American communities throughout the nation. The audience for "Educational Inequalities Must Go!" included members of the NAACP and their supporters. It was directed to a lay audience, written in a straightforward manner, and did not include any legal jargon.

Impact

As a result of Houston's article, the NAACP and its supporters were girded for battle. Not long after Houston joined the NAACP, one of his most significant cases began to unfold in Baltimore, Maryland. Donald Gaines Murray applied for admission to the law school at the University of Maryland in 1935, but fifteen years earlier Maryland had approved legislation that required racially segregated schools. Thus, he was rejected because of his race. The facilities provided for Maryland's black students were far below the standards of those provided for white students. University officials suggested that Murray apply to the all-black Princess Anne Academy, but it had limited facilities for college training and no facilities of any sort for graduate training.

One of Houston's former students, Thurgood Marshall, had established a law practice in Baltimore. After he became aware of efforts to desegregate the University of Maryland campus, Marshall wrote to Houston and asked whether the NAACP would be interested in the case. Donald Murray, the prospective black law student, was the ideal candidate to bring a legal case, for he was articulate and had strong educational credentials. Houston decided to take the case.

Houston filed a civil action in Baltimore City Court against the University of Maryland. Houston and Marshall handled the trial. At the conclusion of the proceedings, the judge held that Maryland had a legal obligation to provide the same educational opportunities for black students as those available to white students. Because the state had failed to comply with its constitutional obligation, the judge issued an order compelling the University of Maryland to admit Murray. The decision was affirmed by the Maryland Court of Appeals in *Murray v. Pearson* in 1936.

A similar case, *Missouri ex rel. Gaines v. Canada*, was filed in Missouri. Initially, at the state court level, Houston lost; the court held that Missouri's out-of-state scholarships for black students satisfied its obligation under *Plessy*. On appeal, though, the U.S. Supreme Court held in 1938 that the scholarships did not meet the state's constitutional obligation and ordered the admission of the black student.

With the U.S. entry into World War II in 1941, the NAACP's attention was diverted to other matters, including teacher salary cases and the defense of African Americans serving in the military. When the war ended in 1945, the focus returned to education. By this time, Thurgood Marshall had succeeded Houston at the NAACP. Houston was practicing law in Washington, but he handled several civil rights cases and continued to provide guidance and direction to Marshall. In 1946 the NAACP filed suit against the University of Oklahoma. In 1948 in *Sipuel v. Board of Regents*, the U.S. Supreme Court held that Oklahoma, which did not have a law school for black students, was obligated to provide legal instruction to them. A similar case, *Sweatt v. Painter*, was filed in Texas, and another case, *McLaurin v. Board of Regents*, was brought in Oklahoma in response to the treatment black students endured after *Sipuel*. The Supreme Court issued decisions in both cases on the same day in 1950.

In *McLaurin*, the Court ruled that separate seating in classrooms and separate libraries and other facilities violated the Fourteenth Amendment because these arrangements "handicapped" black students in their efforts to pursue their studies. In *Sweatt v. Painter*, the Court held that a separate law school established in Houston for black students was not equal to the University of Texas Law School in Austin. Intangible features such as reputation of the school and interactions of students could not be replicated in a separate school, so the Court ordered the admission of Heman M. Sweatt, the African American applicant named as the plaintiff in the case. As the NAACP lawyers hoped, these opinions acknowledged the stigmatic and other intangible injuries that segregation caused, but they stopped short of reversing *Plessy*.

After the rulings in *Sweatt* and *McLaurin*, the NAACP lawyers decided that an adequate foundation for a direct challenge to *Plessy* had been established and that it was time to abandon the "equalization" approach. Six cases were filed in five jurisdictions: *Brown v. Board of Education* in Topeka, Kansas; *Briggs v. Elliott* in South Carolina; *Davis v. County School Board of Prince Edward County* in Virginia; *Bolling v. Sharpe* in the District of Columbia; and *Gebhart v. Belton*, which had been consolidated with *Bulah v. Gebhart*, both in Delaware. Houston initially handled *Bolling v. Sharpe*, but ill health prevented him from completing the case before his death in 1950.

Four of the six cases were consolidated as *Brown v. Board of Education* in the U.S. Supreme Court and argued in December 1952. The case was held over and reargued in December 1953. The decision in *Brown* was announced on

Essential Quotes

> "The National Association for the Advancement of Colored People is launching an active campaign against race discrimination in public education. The campaign will reach all levels of public education from the nursery school through the university. The ultimate objective of the association is the abolition of all forms of segregation in public education."
>
> (Introduction)

> "This campaign for equality of educational opportunity is indissolubly linked with all the other major activities of the association. It ties in with the antilynching fight because there is no use educating boys and girls if their function in life is to be the playthings of murderous mobs."
>
> ("Linked to Other Objectives")

> "The test of 'amicable race relations' is not whether whites and Negroes can remain friends while the Negro is at the little end of the horn, but whether they can remain friends when Negroes insist on sharing with whites the rights and advantages to which they are lawfully entitled and which the whites have illegally appropriated to themselves all these years."
>
> ("Cannot Surrender Rights")

May 17, 1954, with Chief Justice Earl Warren reading the unanimous opinion. After emphasizing the importance of education to a democratic society, the Court held that "separate educational facilities are inherently unequal" and violate the equal protection clause of the Fourteen Amendment.

In the early 1930s, Houston had predicted that successful lawsuits would stimulate public interest and encourage the affected communities to continue the fight for equality after the NAACP lawyers led the way with test cases. This finally happened with *Brown*, which sparked an era of unprecedented civil rights activism, including the Montgomery bus boycott in Alabama; the emergence of Martin Luther King, Jr., as the nation's preeminent civil rights leader; and the student sit-ins in Greensboro, North Carolina. Mass marches, boycotts, and other forms of protests were held in cities and towns across the South. The 1963 March on Washington was organized by a group of civil rights, labor, and religious organizations. On August 28, 1963, approximately 250,000 protestors conducted a day of peaceful demonstration that began at the Washington Monument and ended at the Lincoln Memorial. King delivered his "I Have a Dream" speech at this event. These activities spurred the enactment of the Civil Rights Act of 1964, the Voting Rights Act of 1965, and the Fair Housing Act of 1968—laws that ended the era of state-sponsored segregation and discrimination in the United States. Such victories would not have occurred without the litigation campaign Charles H. Houston announced in "Educational Inequalities Must Go!"

See also Fourteenth Amendment to the U.S. Constitution (1868); *Plessy v. Ferguson* (1896); *Sweatt v. Painter* (1950); *Brown v. Board of Education* (1954); Martin Luther King, Jr.: "I Have a Dream" (1963); Civil Rights Act of 1964.

Further Reading

- **Books**

James, Rawn, Jr. *Root and Branch: Charles Hamilton Houston, Thurgood Marshall, and the Struggle to End Segregation.* New York: Bloomsbury Press, 2010.

Kluger, Richard. *Simple Justice: The History of Brown v. Board of Education and Black America's Struggle for Equality.* New York: Knopf, 2004.

McNeil, Genna Rae. *Groundwork: Charles Hamilton Houston and the Struggle for Civil Rights*. Philadelphia: University of Pennsylvania Press, 1983.

Samson, Gloria. *The American Fund for Public Service: Charles Garland and Radical Philanthropy, 1922–1941*. Westport, Conn.: Greenwood Press, 1996.

Tushnet, Mark V. *The NAACP's Legal Strategy against Segregated Education, 1925–1950*. 2nd ed. Chapel Hill: University of North Carolina Press, 2005.

■ **Web Sites**

"Charles Hamilton Houston." NAACP Web site.
http://www.naacp.org/about/history/chhouston/index.htm.

"Charles Hamilton Houston: The Man Who Killed Jim Crow." America.gov Web site.
http://www.america.gov/st/peopleplace-english/2008/December/20090105175532jmnamdeirf0.3197138.html.

—Leland Ware and Michael J. O'Neal

Questions for Further Study

1. What was the legal strategy of the NAACP for breaking down segregation during this period? Why did the organization adopt this strategy? What role did the Great Depression play in motivating this strategy?

2. Using this document in conjunction with the circumstances surrounding *Sweatt v. Painter* and *Brown v. Board of Education*, prepare a time line of the key events in the history of desegregation from 1935 to 1954. Be prepared to explain why each event was important.

3. What were some of the common inequalities in black and white schools during this era? What types of specific changes in the educational system did Houston propose?

4. Houston saw educational inequalities as bound up with other inequalities. What were these inequalities, and what bearing did they have on the issue of education?

5. Much of the NAACP's attention was focused on graduate school education, including, for example, law schools. Why do you think the organization made this segment of the education system its focus.

Charles Hamilton Houston's "Educational Inequalities Must Go!"

The National Association for the Advancement of Colored People is launching an active campaign against race discrimination in public education. The campaign will reach all levels of public education from the nursery school through the university. The ultimate objective of the association is the abolition of all forms of segregation in public education, whether in the admission or activities of students, the appointment or advancement of teachers, or administrative control. The association will resist any attempt to extend segregated schools. Where possible it will attack segregation in schools. Where segregation is so firmly entrenched by law that a frontal attack cannot be made, the association will throw its immediate force toward bringing Negro schools up to an absolute equality with white schools. If the white South insists upon its separate schools, it must not squeeze the Negro schools to pay for them.

It is not the purpose or the function of the national office of the N.A.A.C.P. to force a school fight upon any community. Its function is primarily to expose the rotten conditions of segregation, to point out the evil consequences of discrimination and injustice to both Negroes and whites, and to map out ways and means by which these evils may be corrected. The decision for action rests with the local community itself. If the local community decides to act and asks the N.A.A.C.P. for aid, the N.A.A.C.P. stands ready with advice and assistance.

The N.A.A.C.P. proposes to use every legitimate means at its disposal to accomplish actual equality of educational opportunity for Negroes. A legislative program is being formulated. Court action has already begun in Maryland to compel the University of Maryland to admit a qualified Negro boy to the law school of the university. Court action is imminent in Virginia to compel the University of Virginia to admit a qualified Negro girl in the graduate department of that university. Activity in politics will be fostered due to the political set-up of and control over public school systems. The press and the public forum will be enlisted to explain to the public the issues involved and to make both whites and Negroes realize the blight which inferior education throws over them, their children and their communities.

Linked to Other Objectives

This campaign for equality of educational opportunity is indissolubly linked with all the other major activities of the association. It ties in with the anti-lynching fight because there is no use educating boys and girls if their function in life is to be the playthings of murderous mobs. It connects up with the association's new economic program because Negro boys and girls must be provided with work opportunities commensurate with their education when they leave school. One of the greatest tragedies of the depression has been the humiliation and suffering which public authorities have inflicted upon trained Negroes, denying them employment at their trades on public works and forcing them to accept menial low-pay jobs as an alternative to starvation. Civil rights, including the right of suffrage, free speech, jury service, and equal facilities of transportation, are directly involved. The N.A.A.C.P. recognizes the fact that the discriminations which the Negro suffers in education are merely part of the general pattern of race prejudice in American life, and it knows that no attack on discrimination in education can have any far reaching effect unless it is bound to a general attack on discrimination and segregation in all phases of American life.

Specific Objectives

At the present time the N.A.A.C.P. educational program has six specific objectives for its immediate efforts:

(a) equality of school terms;
(b) equality of pay for Negro teachers having the same qualifications and doing the same work as white teachers;
(c) equality of transportation for Negro school children at public expense;
(d) equality of buildings and equipment;
(e) equality of *per capita* expenditure for education of Negroes:
(f) equality in graduate and professional training.

The first five objectives relate to segregated and separate school systems. Equality of educational opportunity in separate school systems is the greatest immediate educational problem of the Negro masses. But the problem of Negro education would not stand completely solved even if segregated schools were suddenly abolished. There would still be the question of the Negro's position in the unified system. At the present time Negro children and white children attend the same schools in the North, but Negroes suffer bitterly from prejudice in many northern schools. Negro students are frequently excluded from extra-curricular activities; they are kept out of class offices; cases are known where the white teacher has actively tried to discourage the Negro pupils from even attending the school. It is difficult for a Negro teacher to obtain placement in a nonsegregated school system; more difficult for a Negro teacher to rise to an administrative position in such a system; and apparently impossible for a Negro, regardless of merit, to become head of any public school system segregated or nonsegregated. The N.A.A.C.P. expects to fight race prejudice in nonsegregated school systems just as hard as it fights for equality in separate school systems.

The sixth objective: equality in graduate and professional training, is essentially a problem of the South. In the North Negroes are freely admitted to the state universities for graduate and professional training, except in some instances in medicine. The established policy of the South is segregated schools. The United States supreme court has endorsed this policy to the extent of saying that segregated schools do not violate the guaranties of equal protection of the law under the Constitution of the United States *provided* equal facilities are offered to each race in the segregated system.

Inequalities Glaring

The South has never even made a serious effort to obey the mandate of the supreme court that the schools may be separate but they *must* be equal. The Commission on Interracial Cooperation in the fourth edition of its *Recent Trends in Race Relations* (revised May, 1935) states:

"In his excellent study, 'Financing Schools in the South in 1930,' Prof. Fred McCuistion shows that in the eleven Southern States in which separate records are kept, the public school outlay averaged $44.31 for the white and $12.57 for the colored child enrolled, or nearly four to one against the group most completely dependent upon public funds for its educational opportunity. In South Carolina the respective figures were $56.06 and $7.84; in Mississippi they were $45.34 and $5.45.

"But even these figures do not tell the worst. Within these averages there are unbelievable extremes. In Alabama, for example, where the averages for the State were $36.43 for the white child and $10.09 for the colored, there is one county in which the figures were found to be $75.50 for the white child and $1.82 for the Negro. In hundreds of counties in many of the states the proportion runs as high as ten to one, or twenty to one, in favor of the white child."

The Journal of Negro Education published by Howard University (4th Yearbook Number, July, 1935, p. 290) shows that

"in 1900 the discrimination in per capita expenditure for white and Negro children was 60 per cent in favor of the white; by 1930, this discrimination had increased to 253 per cent. Again, despite the fact that the training of Negro teachers, today, more nearly approximates that of the white teachers, the discrimination in salaries of white and Negro teachers increased from 52.8 per cent in 1900 to 113 per cent in 1930."

Ambrose Caliver, Senior Specialist in the Education of Negroes, the United States Office of Education, reports in the *National Survey of Secondary Education* that

"in the 15 states comprising this investigation, 230 counties, with a Negro population of 12½ per cent or more of the total, are without high-school facilities for colored children. These counties contain 1,397,304 colored people, 158,939 of whom are 15 to 19 years of age. These young people represent 16.5 per cent of all Negroes between the ages of 15 and 19 in the 15 Southern States represented."

Yet every one of the 230 counties provided high school facilities for its white children.

No Graduate Training

Although the southern states provide a measure of undergraduate instruction for Negroes on the college level, not one of them provides any graduate or professional training for Negroes. *The Journal of Negro Education* above cited found that

"... there is not a single state-supported institution of higher learning in any one of 17 of the 19 states which require separation by law, to which a Negro may go to pursue graduate and professional education. On the other hand in 1930, some 11,037 white students were enrolled in publicly-supported higher institutions in 15 of these states, pursuing graduate and professional training."

West Virginia, Missouri, and this year Maryland provide certain scholarship money for their respective Negro students who desire graduate and professional training, toward their tuition fees in universities outside the state which will enroll them as students. But these scholarship grants do not include the differential in travel expense between the fare from the student's home to the state university which will not admit him, and his fare to the university outside the state which will. They do not include any differential in case of increased living expenses outside the state, and are frequently subject to conditions and restrictions not imposed upon white students taking the same work in the state university. In Maryland there was not even enough money to pay tuition fees for all the qualified Negro students who applied for scholarships.

For purely technical reasons the first problem the association attacked in court was the exclusion of qualified Negroes from graduate or professional training in state-supported universities, solely on account of race or color. The legal problem was simpler; and since much of its educational program will involve pioneer work the association began with the simpler problem first. As regards primary, secondary and collegiate education in the South, there is a system, albeit inadequate, of separate primary and secondary schools and colleges for Negroes supported from public funds. A challenge to the inadequacies of these primary, secondary schools and colleges would raise the question whether the facilities offered by them are equal to the facilities offered in similar schools to whites. This would involve complex problems of comparative budget analyses, faculty qualifications, and other facts. But in the case of the graduate or professional training there are no facilities whatsoever provided for Negroes by the state, and the question narrows down to a simple proposition of law: whether the state can appropriate public money for graduate and professional education for white students exclusively. The Baltimore City Court in the case of Donald Gaines Murray vs. Raymond A. Pearson, president of the University of Maryland, et al., has answered that this could not be done, and on June 25, 1935, issued its writ of mandamus commanding the officers of the university to admit Murray into the first year class of the law school. The university has appealed, and the case will be argued before the Court of Appeals of Maryland early this fall.

Investigations are in progress covering the exclusion of qualified Negro students from the universities of Missouri, Virginia, North Carolina and other southern states. A qualified Negro girl has applied for admission to the graduate department of the University of Virginia, and her application is now pending before the Rector and Board of Visitors of the university.

Unwise Attempt

The reactions of the white press of Virginia to this heretical attempt of a Negro girl to enter the graduate department of the University of Virginia are indicative of the opposition which the N.A.A.C.P. will face when its general educational program gets well under way. The editors admit the young woman has the *legal right* to attend the university, but urge her and the N.A.A.C.P. not to force the issue. Sample editorials state "it is inexpedient, ill-advised, and heavily charged with potential injury to the cause which the Association is designed to advance" (Norfolk *Ledger-Dispatch*). "The question here, it seems to us, is not what the Negro has an abstract right to do, but what it is wise to attempt" (Richmond *Times-Dispatch*). "Law bears on the question from one side; custom from another" (Newport *News Daily Press*). "The question instantly arises why any educated person should wish to impose his or her presence upon an institution where they are not wanted and where they could not possibly remain in justice to their own self-respect or to their hope of achievement" (*Northern Virginia Daily*).

White Virginians evidently cannot bring themselves to admit that the University of Virginia is a public institution, and not their own private property. It *is* a public institution, so the question put by the *Northern Virginia Daily* as to whether a Negro student "is wanted" at the university is beside the point. A Negro student can preserve her self-respect much more by standing up for her constitutional rights and facing the snubs and insults of the white students with calm and dignity than by supinely yielding up her constitutional rights. Unless the white students offer her actual physical violence, they cannot snub or insult her any worse than the white men students snubbed and insulted the first white woman student who dared enter the University of Virginia.

Insults and snubs will not deter Negro students from insisting on their right to graduate and professional study. Since the daily portion of Negroes in American life is snubs and insults, regardless how submissive they are, Negro students can afford to face a few more snubs and insults temporarily in defense of their constitutional rights to equal educational opportunities, until the white students and white authorities become reconciled to allowing them to pursue their education in peace. As a matter of fact, the voting southern white students have not been heard from; but there are indications that there is a growing sentiment among them for recognition of the Negro as a real human being and citizen entitled to all the legal rights and public benefits as such.

Another point that the older white Virginians make is that any attempt to force the university issue will disturb "amicable race relations" in Virginia. It seems strange that white people always use "amicable race relations" as an excuse to discourage the Negro from insisting on his rights. The slaveholders told the abolitionists the same thing before the Civil War. If the "liberal" white Virginians would just manifest a little courage, and take a few chances with their own comfort and social position in a firm stand for real equality of opportunity between the races, there would be no occasion for "amicable race relations" to be disturbed. The difficulty is that white southern liberals give lip-service to equality before the law; but except in rare instances their qualms of conscience do not spur them into action.

Cannot Surrender Rights

It may be that the white Virginians and the N.A.A.C.P. mean different things by "amicable race relations." To the N.A.A.C.P. "amicable race relations" means mutual helpfulness in promoting the common welfare allowing to everybody concerned the full benefit of the law and equality of opportunity. The test of "amicable race relations" is not whether whites and Negroes can remain friends while the Negro is at the little end of the horn, but whether they can remain friends when Negroes insist on sharing with whites the rights and advantages to which they are lawfully entitled and which the whites have illegally appropriated to themselves all these years.

The N.A.A.C.P. and all Negroes desire to live at peace with their white fellow citizens. They crave amicable race relations, but they want them founded on dignity and self-respect. Real amicable race relations cannot be purchased by the surrender of fundamental constitutional rights.

The N.A.A.C.P. appreciates the magnitude of the task ahead of it. but it has its duty to its constituency and to the America of the future. It conceives that in equalizing educational opportunities for Negroes it raises the whole standard of American citizenship, and stimulates white Americans as well as black. Fundamentally the N.A.A.C.P. is not a special pleader; it merely insists that the United States respect its own Constitution and its own laws.

Glossary

Board of Visitors	the governing board, or trustees, of a university, often today called the board of regents
Commission on Interracial Cooperation	an organization formed in the South following the widespread race riots of 1919 to prevent lynching, mob violence, and other forms of racial abuse
Rector	the highest academic official at a university
writ of mandamus	from the Latin for "we command," a court order compelling an official to do something or refrain from doing something

Walter White (far right), walking with Eleanor Roosevelt and President Harry Truman (AP/Wide World Photos)

Walter F. White's "U.S. Department of (White) Justice"

"The attorney general continues his offensive against crime — except crimes involving the deprivation of life and liberty and citizenship to Negroes."

Overview

During the 1920s and 1930s, Walter White published dozens of essays to rally public opposition to lynching, including the 1935 article "U.S. Department of (White) Justice." As the executive secretary of the National Association for the Advancement of Colored People (NAACP), White called on the federal government to enact laws to prevent mob violence and punish its perpetrators. Published in *The Crisis*, the NAACP's monthly journal, this particular essay focused on the reluctance of federal law enforcement officials to intervene in southern lynching cases.

The antilynching movement was one of the first civil rights causes to emerge on the national political scene. Walter White and the NAACP spearheaded a diverse alliance of churchwomen, labor unions, progressive activists, and southern liberals united in their opposition to lynching. Their crusade forced a showdown with southern politicians, who resisted any effort by the federal government to intervene in their affairs. While the national crusade against mob violence failed to enact federal antilynching laws, White's efforts to publicize the horrors of lynching were a crucial step in the emergence of civil rights as a national issue.

Context

By the 1930s American lynch mobs had murdered nearly five thousand documented victims since the end of Reconstruction. Lynchings had occurred across the country during the late nineteenth century, claiming men and women of various racial and ethnic backgrounds. Yet as mob violence peaked at the turn of the century, lynching became an increasingly regional and racial phenomenon. From 1890 to 1910, southern legislatures enacted laws to segregate African Americans and strip them of their civil rights. Mob violence was an instrumental component of these white supremacy campaigns. White supremacists condoned or explicitly endorsed vigilante violence as a means of discouraging black political participation and resisting any semblance of racial equality. By the early twentieth century, the vast majority of lynchings occurred in the South, and nearly all the victims were black. While lynching is often associated with hanging, vigilantes frequently shot, stabbed, burned, and tortured their victims as well.

After an upsurge in mob violence during and immediately after World War I, the number of lynchings declined steadily throughout the 1920s. But as the United States sunk into the Great Depression at the end of the decade, racial tension and mob violence erupted across the South. There had been an average of ten lynchings per year in the late 1920s, yet thirty occurred in the first nine months of 1930 alone. Civil rights activists like Walter White blamed the resurgence on the economic crisis, arguing that southern whites had resorted to desperate measures to control black labor.

As lynchings surged in the early 1930s, the antilynching movement gained momentum. The NAACP had led the charge in this fight since its founding in 1909. During World War I the organization spearheaded a protest parade down Fifth Avenue in New York City. As many as ten thousand African Americans marched silently to the beat of muffled drums, carrying banners reading "Thou Shalt Not Kill" and "Give Us a Chance to Live." Behind the scenes, the organization lobbied congressmen to enact federal protections against mob violence. In 1918 Republican congressman Leonidas Dyer sponsored the first antilynching bill in American history. Four years later, the House of Representatives passed the Dyer bill despite the nearly unanimous opposition of its southern members.

That antilynching bill made it through the House, but it could not survive a Senate filibuster. After southern senators blocked the passage of the Dyer bill in 1922, Congress did not take up antilynching legislation again until 1934. While some African American activists hoped that the 1932 election of Franklin Delano Roosevelt as president signaled a new era for civil rights, the new president was reluctant to endorse the antilynching crusade. In a 1934 meeting at the White House, Roosevelt informed Walter White that he could not endorse any legislation that would alienate southern Democrats. "If I come out for the anti-lynching bill now," Roosevelt admitted, as recalled by White in *A Man Called White*, "they will block every bill I ask Congress to pass to keep America from collapsing. I just can't take that risk."

Roosevelt's unwillingness to publicly support antilynching legislation encouraged widespread apathy toward mob violence within the federal government. With Roosevelt

Time Line

1909
- **February 12**
  The National Association for the Advancement of Colored People (NAACP) is formed in New York City.

1917
- **July 28**
  In New York City, an estimated ten thousand African Americans march in a silent antilynching parade organized by the NAACP.

1918
- **January 31**
  Walter White reports for his first day as an NAACP staff member.

1922
- **January 26**
  The House of Representatives passes the Dyer antilynching bill. Southern Democrats later block its passage in the Senate.

1931
- **January**
  White is promoted from acting secretary to secretary of the NAACP.

1933
- **August 12**
  Three black teenagers, A. T. Hardin, Dan Pippen, and Elmore Clark, are lynched near Tuscaloosa, Alabama, for the alleged rape and murder of a white woman.

1934
- **January–February**
  Democratic senators Edward Costigan of Colorado and Robert Wagner of New York introduce an antilynching bill. The Senate Judiciary subcommittee holds hearings on lynchings, but the bill is eventually defeated by a southern filibuster.

- **October 26**
  A mob tortures and lynches Claude Neal near Marianna, Florida, for the alleged rape and murder of a white woman. Members of a crowd of three thousand mutilate the body before it is dragged into town and hung from a tree.

---

reluctant to offend his southern white supporters, federal agencies took no steps to intervene in southern lynching cases. Civil rights laws passed during Reconstruction ostensibly protected southern African Americans from racial violence, but the Department of Justice made no attempts to prevent lynchings or prosecute mob members. The department's chief law-enforcement agency, the Federal Bureau of Investigation (FBI), did not assist in a single lynching investigation during the 1930s.

Despite White's and others' mounting frustration with the federal government, the antilynching movement was gaining momentum by 1935, as the NAACP was working alongside civil rights groups, organized labor, and white southern women to rally public opposition to lynching. In early 1935 the organization sponsored "An Art Commentary on Lynching" at a New York City gallery. Gruesome exposés and scholarly studies of lynching fed public indignation. Contemporary polls revealed that even a significant percentage of white southerners favored legislation to stamp out lynching. But such promising shifts in public attitudes were meaningless without government action. By publishing articles like "U.S. Department of (White) Justice," Walter White hoped to spotlight governmental apathy and pressure federal authorities to stamp out lynching once and for all.

About the Author

Walter White was an influential journalist and civil rights activist who led the NAACP from 1929 until his death in 1955. Born on July 1, 1893, to a light-skinned Atlanta mail collector and his equally fair-complexioned wife, White enjoyed a relatively privileged upbringing among the city's black middle class. But this did not shield White from the racial violence that swept Atlanta in 1906. During the three-day race riot, White watched as marauding whites assaulted hundreds of African Americans and destroyed black property.

White never forgot that mob. After graduating from Atlanta University in 1916, the young insurance salesman threw himself into a local campaign to increase funding for black schools. Later that year, White wrote directly to the national headquarters of the NAACP, asking for its help in organizing an Atlanta chapter. Impressed by the young leader's energy and organizing skills, the NAACP executive secretary James Weldon Johnson invited White to join the national staff.

Thanks to his blond hair, blue eyes, and remarkable courage, White became the NAACP's secret weapon in its antilynching campaign. Less than two weeks after moving to New York to work at the national headquarters, White traveled south to investigate a lynching firsthand. Posing as a traveling salesman, White gathered gruesome details from local whites who had no idea they were speaking with a man of African ancestry. Over the next decade, White investigated dozens of lynchings and race riots at great personal risk. By the late 1920s he was one of the country's foremost authorities on lynching. He recounted his investigations in northern newspapers and national magazines. An active figure in the Harlem Renaissance, White published a novel, *The Fire in the Flint* (1924), and a nonfiction book, *Rope and Faggot* (1929), both based on his firsthand investigations of southern lynchings.

When Johnson retired from the NAACP in 1929, White assumed leadership of the organization as acting secretary. Two years later the NAACP made White's promotion permanent. During his long tenure as executive secretary, White enlisted powerful allies in NAACP campaigns against racial violence, discrimination, and segregation. The antilynching campaign was always close to White's heart, and he spent much of the 1930s lobbying Congress and federal officials to take action against mob violence. White died on March 21, 1955, after leading the NAACP for nearly three decades.

Explanation and Analysis of the Document

White opens "U.S. Department of (White) Justice" by stating that the Department of Justice has absolutely failed to protect African Americans from violence and discrimination. He argues that this negligence is not confined to lynching cases but is a much broader pattern of disregard for the plight of African Americans. White briefly mentions the refusal of the Department of Justice to intervene on behalf of southern blacks who could not vote because of discriminatory laws and intimidation tactics. During the 1930s southern blacks faced numerous obstacles at the ballot box, including literacy tests, understanding clauses, and poll taxes. White contends that federal agencies are moving slowly on civil rights because the Roosevelt administration is unwilling to do anything that would offend its white southern supporters. While White sees disfranchisement and segregation as part of the NAACP's broader civil rights campaign, he contends that the federal government has shown a particularly lax attitude toward mob violence in the South.

In the second paragraph, White reveals his journalistic skill and his experience as a lynching investigator. There was probably no one in the country more familiar with the patterns of mob violence in the South than Walter White. He believed that one of the most valuable weapons in the fight against lynching was to expose the harsh reality of southern lynchings. By revealing the gruesome details, the motives behind the murders, and the generally callous attitude of local authorities toward the killings, White hoped to convince the American public and federal officials that outside intervention was necessary to eliminate lynching.

The Tuscaloosa case that White describes reveals that local law enforcement officials played a part, perhaps knowingly, in the lynching. Typically, in the wake of a lynching, southern policemen would claim that they had done everything they could to prevent mob violence. They usually reported that the lynch mob had overpowered them, stolen the prisoners, and then left them tied up and blindfolded. But White points out that the police officers in Tuscaloosa showed callous disregard for the safety of the prisoner and

Time Line

1934
- **December 13** NAACP members picket the National Crime Conference, sponsored by the Department of Justice, for refusing to place lynching on the agenda.

1935
- **February 15** NAACP sponsors "An Art Commentary on Lynching" exhibit at a New York City gallery; the exhibit runs to March 2.
- **March 12** A mob abducts Ab Young in southwestern Tennessee and lynches him in Slayden, Mississippi.
- **October** *The Crisis*, the NAACP's official monthly magazine, publishes Walter White's "U.S. Department of (White) Justice."

1938
- **February 21** Southern senators end a thirty-day filibuster of the Wagner–Van Nuys anti-lynching bill after its supporters agree to shelve the bill. It is the longest filibuster since 1893.

1939
- **January** The new attorney general, Frank Murphy, establishes a Civil Liberties Unit within the U.S. Department of Justice. Two years later it is renamed the Civil Rights Section.

1942
- **February 10** For the first time ever, the U.S. attorney general dispatches FBI agents and Civil Rights Section attorneys to investigate a lynching, that of Cleo Wright in Sikeston, Missouri.

played right into the hands of the waiting mob. The federal antilynching legislation that White and his allies demanded would have imposed stiff penalties on local law enforcement and government officials who failed to adequately protect prisoners from mobs. Therefore, it was very important that White point out instances where local authorities demonstrated negligence or even complicity in a lynching.

In paragraphs 3 and 4, White reveals that he and fellow activists have repeatedly lobbied the Department of Justice to investigate lynchings. By the 1930s White was the most recognizable black activist in Washington, D.C. He had enlisted the support of numerous congressmen and government officials in the antilynching campaign, but he had less success at the Department of Justice. Although federal statutes already existed that allowed the attorney general to prosecute the Tuscaloosa sheriff, White could not persuade a Justice Department official to meet with his delegation. Undeterred, White and his colleagues refused to leave the building until officials escorted them to see the attorney general in person. Yet they left with no commitment and waited months to hear back from the Department of Justice about their demands.

The fifth paragraph reveals the ingenuity and persistence of antilynching activists in using the legal system to their advantage. With no antilynching legislation on the books, the only way to justify federal prosecution of mob violence was to cite other laws that lynch mobs had violated. White had hoped that a revised version of a federal interstate kidnapping law would be broad enough to cover lynchings in which a mob carried a victim across state lines. This federal kidnapping law was named after the infant son of the aviator Charles Lindbergh, who had been kidnapped and murdered in early 1932. In paragraphs 6–10, White reveals that the same attorney general who had refused to investigate the Tuscaloosa lynching had agreed in principle to broader laws against interstate kidnapping. But when civil rights activists cited this revised law to urge the Department of Justice to investigate lynchings, the attorney general once again refused to take action.

White's discussion of the Lindbergh kidnapping law reveals the importance of litigation in the NAACP's civil rights activism. Before, during, and after White's tenure as executive secretary, the organization pursued a strategy that was primarily legal, focusing on laws and litigation to force government action on civil rights. Through a succession of lawsuits in the 1930s and 1940s, the NAACP won a series of school segregation cases that led to *Brown v. Board of Education* in 1954. The NAACP also used this strategy to combat disfranchisement laws and other discriminatory practices. The organization's antilynching campaign employed legal strategies as well. By using test cases, like the Curtis James lynching described in paragraph 12, the NAACP hoped to force the federal government to apply existing laws to civil rights violations.

In paragraphs 11–14, White describes how the Department of Justice evaded the NAACP's claim that the James lynching violated the expanded language of the recently revised Lindbergh law. White uses the department's own words to highlight the lengths that federal authorities are willing to go to avoid any involvement in a southern lynching case. White argues that Department of Justice officials are willfully misrepresenting existing laws and making excuses to justify their inaction. He points out that the Department of Justice is asking the NAACP to perform the duties that should be the responsibility of its own Federal Bureau of Investigation—to gather facts in order to establish the basis for prosecution.

In paragraph 15, White mentions the lynching of Claude Neal. This particularly brutal incident made headlines across the country. The Neal lynching harked back to earlier decades, when local newspapers announced lynchings in advance and huge crowds turned out to watch. Local authorities had arrested Neal for raping and murdering a white woman and had carried him to an Alabama jail. A white mob abducted Neal and held him in an undisclosed location for two days, while newspapers in Alabama and Florida announced the upcoming lynching. On October 26, 1934, a crowd of three thousand gathered at a farm owned by the murdered woman's family. Much to their dismay, the mob killed Neal with a shotgun in a nearby forest after hours of torture. They then took Neal to the farm, where the gathered crowd defiled his body. Finally, the mob brought Neal's remains into Marianna and hung the body from a downtown tree.

This brutal and brazen incident made national headlines, and White saw an opportunity to rally public support for the antilynching campaign. But he also recognized that the Neal lynching was an ideal test case for the interstate kidnapping law. Authorities had apprehended the suspect in Florida and carried him to Alabama. The lynch mob had then kidnapped him and carried him back to the scene of his alleged crime in Florida. But before the NAACP could even request a federal investigation, the Department of Justice announced publicly that the Lindbergh law did not apply to lynching cases.

In paragraphs 16–22, White describes the NAACP's reaction to a highly publicized crime conference sponsored by the Department of Justice. Despite White's intensive lobbying and the upsurge in lynchings during the early 1930s, the Department of Justice refused to include mob violence on the agenda. Moreover, conference planners failed to invite representatives of any civil rights organizations to the conference to discuss their concerns. Even with the highly publicized lynching cases of recent years, conference participants seemed more concerned with gangsters and kidnappers.

Despite the cold shoulder from conference organizers, White notes a hopeful sign on the first night of the conference. In his keynote speech, President Roosevelt spoke out forcefully against lynching. Just a few months earlier, he had confided to White that he could not support antilynching legislation without offending his southern supporters. Faced with mounting pressure from antilynching activists, the president could not ignore lynching altogether. As Roosevelt rallied support for his New Deal programs, he walked a fine line between alienating his powerful southern allies and offending his growing number of African American supporters. His lynching statement at the crime conference was intended to reassure his black supporters without committing himself to any actions that would anger southern Democrats.

Despite the president's condemnation of lynching on the opening night of the conference, conference organizers continued to deny NAACP requests to put lynching on the agenda. White and his allies would not give up without a fight. When the Department of Justice denied repeated

The charred body of Cleo Wright, a black man who was burned by a mob after being taken from the custody of officers, is observed by a crowd in Sikeston, Missouri, on January 27, 1942. (AP/Wide World Photos)

requests to address the lynching problem, civil rights activists took to the streets. The local NAACP prepared signs and started a picket line outside the Justice building. Local police responded by arresting the picketers, but the protest yielded tangible results. The attorney general invited African American representatives to participate in the conference and suggested that they could bring up lynching during an informal discussion session. When the conference coordinators backed off this promise, the local NAACP resumed its protest outside of the conference.

The willingness of the NAACP to stage peaceful protests reveals another dimension to the antilynching campaign. Decades before nonviolent protests hit the television screens, civil rights activists employed nonviolent measures to publicize their cause. In the antilynching protests outside the 1934 crime conference, activists carefully planned a public action that would dramatize the lynching problem. Because policemen had arrested early picketers under sign and parade laws, the second round of protestors planned a perfectly legal public action. Standing silently with lynching ropes looped around their necks and small signs pinned to their chests, the protestors forced the conference delegates to confront the reality of lynching even if they refused to discuss it. The protest stumped the local police and department officials, who could find no grounds on which to arrest the sixty protestors standing outside the conference. The spectacle finally forced the conference participants to adopt a vague resolution that did not name lynching specifically but conceded that racial violence was illegal and wrong.

In the closing three paragraphs, White makes clear that the moral victory at the crime conference did little to ease the bitterness and frustration of the antilynching movement. Less than three months after the conference, another lynching occurred that involved an interstate abduction. Vigilantes in southwestern Tennessee abducted Ab Young for killing a white highway worker. After crossing the border into Mississippi, they hanged him from a tree and riddled his body with bullets. The lynch mob tipped off a Memphis newspaper, which dispatched a reporter and photographer to the scene. Despite the well-documented mob murder, local authorities ruled that Young had died by hanging yet named no suspects. One local attorney even claimed that Young had hanged himself.

Essential Quotes

"The Department of Justice in Washington may lay claim to a 100 per cent performance in at least one branch of its activities—the evasion of cases involving burning questions of Negro rights."

(Paragraph 1)

"The crime of lynching was not even within the range of the department's vision."

(Paragraph 15)

"The attorney general continues his offensive against crime—except crimes involving the deprivation of life and liberty and citizenship to Negroes."

(Paragraph 23)

The phrase "at the hands of parties unknown" was a common one in southern lynching cases. Most southern whites refused to incriminate fellow whites for participating in mob violence. Even if they opposed lynchings and took steps to prevent mob violence in their communities, local authorities stopped short of singling out their friends and neighbors for punishment. White worked for years to expose this culture of secrecy and complicity, but southern whites continued to close ranks when outsiders criticized their handling of lynching cases.

White responded to the latest lynching by firing off yet another investigation request to both the Department of Justice and the White House. The NAACP received no reply. Despite years of relentless pressure to publicize lynchings and force a response from the federal government, White concludes his article with the bitter admission that the Department of Justice remained reluctant to use its enforcement powers to protect African Americans from mob violence.

Audience

Walter White wrote this article for publication in *The Crisis*, the NAACP's official monthly magazine. His immediate audience was the membership and supporters of the NAACP, including northern white liberals and other progressive allies. While this particular article appeared in an African American publication, White knew that it would also be quoted or reprinted in other newspapers and magazines. Earlier in his career, many white publications had refused to publish White's articles on lynching. But by 1935 White had recruited influential white allies. Mainstream newspapers and magazines followed suit, publishing articles similar to this one.

Throughout his antilynching work, White firmly believed in the power of publicity and exposure. He hoped that his writing would rally African Americans to the antilynching crusade and shock the white majority out of its complacency. He also hoped that the article would cross the desks of government officials who, either out of embarrassment or goodwill, might take steps to force action on lynching.

Impact

White was clearly skeptical that the Department of Justice would suddenly reverse its stance on lynching, but he firmly believed that the campaign against mob violence depended on publicity and propaganda. Every piece of literature he produced was meant to turn up the heat on government officials by increasing the public outcry against lynching. By the end of the 1930s, this undeniable public indignation forced antilynching legislation onto the congressional agenda despite President Roosevelt's ambivalence and southern politicians' opposition. Yet while public attitudes toward lynching had changed dramatically, powerful opposition to federal legislation remained; despite the intensive antilynching campaign waged by the NAACP, southern senators remained opposed to a federal antilynching law. When the Democratic senators Frederick Van Nuys and Robert Wagner introduced a new bill in January 1938, southern senators filibustered for nearly seven weeks straight. Like every antilynching bill before and since, the Wagner–Van Nuys bill failed in the face of southern opposition.

While Congress never passed an antilynching bill, the spotlight that White and his allies fixed on the problem of mob violence yielded tangible results. In addition to mobilizing public sentiment against lynching, White's relentless pressure forced government officials to take their first halting steps toward combating racial violence. In 1939 the Department of Justice set up a Civil Liberties Unit, which was renamed the Civil Rights Section two years later. In 1942 the Federal Bureau of Investigation for the first time dispatched agents to the site of a lynching— that of Cleo Wright in Sikeston, Missouri. Roosevelt's successor, Harry Truman, believed that lynching was not only a moral outrage but also a diplomatic nightmare for the United States. Convinced that racial violence weakened the country's prestige and influence in the world, Truman made the elimination of lynching a cornerstone of his unprecedented civil rights program in 1948. Southern senators continued to thwart such legislation, but the isolated lynchings of the 1950s and 1960s drew global condemnation and even resulted in a few federally assisted criminal convictions. Walter White did more than any other activist to bring about this slow but significant transformation in public attitudes toward mob violence. No single person was more influential in making lynching a national political issue, and articles like "U.S. Department of (White) Justice" were a crucial part of White's crusade.

Further Reading

■ **Books**

Dray, Philip. *At the Hands of Persons Unknown: The Lynching of Black America*. New York: Random House, 2002.

Janken, Kenneth Robert. *Walter White: Mr. NAACP*. Chapel Hill: University of North Carolina Press, 2003.

Sitkoff, Harvard. *A New Deal for Blacks: The Emergence of Civil Rights as a National Issue during the Depression Decade*. New York: Oxford University Press, 1978.

White, Walter. *The Fire in the Flint*. New York: Knopf, 1924.

———. *Rope and Faggot: A Biography of Judge Lynch*. New York: Knopf, 1929.

———. *A Man Called White*. New York: Viking, 1948.

■ **Web Sites**

Without Sanctuary: Photographs and Postcards of Lynching in America Web site.
   http://www.withoutsanctuary.org/main.html.

"Jim Crow Stories: Walter White." PBS "The Rise and Fall of Jim Crow" Web site.
   http://www.pbs.org/wnet/jimcrow/stories_people_white.html.

"Walter White (1893–1955)." Eleanor Roosevelt National Historic Site Web site.
   http://www.nps.gov/archive/elro/glossary/white-walter.htm.

—Jason Morgan Ward

Questions for Further Study

1. Using this document in combination with John Edward Bruce's "Organized Resistance Is Our Best Remedy," Ida B. Wells-Barnett's "Lynch Law in America," and Haywood Patterson and Earl Conrad's *Scottsboro Boy*, summarize the history of lynching and other forms of violence against African Americans in the late nineteenth and early twentieth centuries.

2. What economic conditions factored into the upsurge in lynchings and violence against African Americans in the 1930s?

3. What political circumstances prevented President Franklin D. Roosevelt from lending his full support to an antilynching law?

4. If lynching is murder, why were laws against murder inadequate in dealing with the problem of lynching? Put differently, what specific tools would a federal antilynching law have put into the hands of law-enforcement officials?

5. In light of the fact that no federal antilynching bill was ever passed, do you believe that White's essay, along with similar documents by other writers, ultimately had an effect? Explain.

Walter F. White's "U.S. Department of (White) Justice"

The Department of Justice in Washington may lay claim to a 100 per cent performance in at least one branch of its activities—the evasion of cases involving burning questions of Negro rights. It sidestepped the issue of the exclusion of Negroes from southern elections on the ground that it was loaded with political dynamite. Other legalistic reasons were later added but the first orders to "Go Slow" were placed on purely political grounds. On the lynching issue the department has set a new record for its ability to dodge from one excuse to another.

On June 6, 1933, a white girl was murdered near Tuscaloosa, Alabama, and shortly thereafter three Negro boys were thrown in jail on suspicion of the murder. On August 12, 1933, the sheriff of Tuscaloosa county unlawfully under color of authority took it upon himself to order their removal from Tuscaloosa to Birmingham "for safekeeping." The sheriff's deputies started at night for Birmingham in two automobiles: two deputies and the boys in the leading car, and a car full of deputies trailing behind. The sheriff ordered the convoy to take a back road because, as the deputies later testified, he did not want to risk the convoy being overtaken by a mob on the highway. When the convoy reached the Tuscaloosa county line, the trailing car turned back, leaving the first car with the boys in it to make the rest of the journey alone. Two miles across the county line the car with the boys in it was *met*, not overtaken, by other cars full of masked men. The boys were taken out, riddled with bullets, and two of them killed. The Southern Association for the Prevention of Lynching made an investigation which found the sheriff culpable.

A delegation made up of representatives from several national organizations on August 24 called at the Department of Justice pursuant to [an] appointment made with William Stanley, executive assistant to Attorney General Homer S. Cummings, who had promised to receive it in the absence of the attorney general, to request the department to investigate the lynching and prosecute the offending sheriff under Revised Statutes 5510 which makes it a federal offense to deprive an inhabitant of any state of any rights, privileges or immunities secured or protected by the federal Constitution under color of law or custom. But although Stanley had made the appointment himself, when the delegation arrived at the department, Stanley was not present, had sent no excuse for his absence, and investigation disclosed that he had not even entered the appointment on his calendar pad.

The delegation was so indignant that the officials of the department four hours later carried them in to see the attorney general himself. The attorney general was suave; he would make no commitment; he called for a brief. Accordingly a thorough brief was filed with the department October 13, 1933, and Stanley stated that he would let the delegation know the decision of the department by November 1. Actually he kept the delegation in suspense until March 5, 1934, although months before both he and the attorney general had told Roger N. Baldwin of the American Civil Liberties Union that the department did not intend to take any action in the case.

In the meanwhile a bill amending the original Lindbergh kidnaping law of 1932 had been introduced in Congress. The 1932 act had made kidnaping a federal offense where the kidnaped person was knowingly transported in interstate or foreign commerce and "held for ransom or reward." The amendment to the 1932 act proposed to broaden the scope of federal jurisdiction and make kidnaping a federal offense when the person kidnaped was knowingly transported in interstate or foreign commerce and "held for ransom or reward *or otherwise*" (italics ours). It also proposed that there should be a prima facie presumption that the person kidnaped had been carried across the state line unless released within three days.

While the bill was before the Senate judiciary committee the attorney general submitted a memorandum to the committee in support of the amendment as follows:

"This amendment adds thereto (to the Lindbergh Act of 1932) the word 'otherwise'.... The object of the word 'otherwise' is to extend the jurisdiction of this act to persons who have been kidnaped and held, not only for reward *but for any other reason*.

"In addition this bill adds a proviso to the Lindbergh Act that in the absence of the return of the person kidnaped ... during a period of three days *the presumption arises* that such person has been transported in interstate or foreign commerce, but such presumption is not conclusive.

"I believe that this is a sound amendment which will clear up border line cases, justifying federal investigation in most of such cases and assuring the validity of federal prosecution in numerous instances in which such prosecution would be questionable under the present form of this act" (italics ours).

In other words, at this stage the attorney general placed the Department of Justice squarely behind the amendment, giving to its provisions the broadest possible interpretation. But as soon as questions of lynching were raised, the attorney general abandoned his broad construction and began hopping from one position to another to avoid taking jurisdiction.

The bill passed Congress and became enacted into law June 22, 1934, with all the provisions of the amendment adopted except that the time within which a kidnaped person had to be held for presumption of an interstate transportation to arise was increased from three days to seven; and certain other changes not here material.

On October 4, 1934, one Curtis James' house was broken into near Darien, Georgia, about fifty miles from the Florida line, and James, a Negro, shot and abducted by a mob. In spite of an intensive search he was not found. After waiting more than the seven days provided by the amended Lindbergh law, the National Association for the Advancement of Colored People on October 15 wrote the Department of Justice asking whether the abductors of James could not be prosecuted under the amended Lindbergh law. Under date of October 20 the department replied:

"... there is nothing to indicate that the person alleged to have been kidnaped was transported in interstate commerce and was held for ransom, reward or otherwise. In the absence of these facts establishing these elements it would seem that the matter would be one entirely for the authorities of the State of Georgia..."

It is interesting that in the James case the Department of Justice recognized that a lynching case might be covered under the words "or otherwise" of the amended Lindbergh act, but it dodged jurisdiction by repudiating the presumption. In short the department deliberately ignored the fact that not returning James within seven days created a presumption that there had been an interstate kidnaping, and thereby gave the federal government jurisdiction over the crime. It demanded that the N.A.A.C.P. substitute itself for the department's own Bureau of Investigation and produce the *facts* establishing an interstate kidnaping.

Then on October 26, 1934, a Negro named Claude Neal was kidnaped from the jail in Brewton, Alabama, by a mob which came to the scene in automobiles bearing Florida licenses. Neal was transported across the Alabama line into Florida, held for fifteen hours and then murdered after unspeakable barbarities near Marianna, Florida. The N.A.A.C.P. felt that at last it had a perfect case for federal prosecution, but before it could even get a letter to the Department of Justice requesting an investigation, the department had issued a public statement that the words "or otherwise" in the amended Lindbergh law did not cover the case of lynching. Faced by the indisputable fact of an interstate kidnaping, the department was forced to the position that the amend[ed] Lindbergh law covered kidnaping for purposes of gain, but not for purposes of murder.

With loud fan-fare and carefully staged publicity, on November 7, 1934, the attorney general announced to the country a National Crime Conference called by him in Washington, December 10-13, 1934, "to give broad and practical consideration to the problem of crime" including causes and prevention of crime; investigation; detection and apprehension of crime and criminals. A comprehensive and distinguished list of delegates, including bar associations, was invited; but no Negro associations. On November 9 the N.A.A.C.P. wrote the attorney general asking whether lynching would be placed on the conference agendum. On November 16 the department replied:

"... the program for the conference has not as yet been completed, obviously it will be impossible to cover all the phases of the crime problem in the short space of three days. No definite decision has been made with reference to the subject of lynching. I wish to thank you, however, for bringing this matter to our attention."

The crime of lynching was not even within the range of the department's vision.

No word came from the department concerning its decision whether to place lynching on the conference agendum, so on November 22 the N.A.A.C.P. wired the attorney general inquiring whether the decision had been made, and what. The department replied November 27 that "it was not probable that the subject of lynching will be given place on program of Crime Conference." Repeated efforts were made by local representatives of N.A.A.C.P. to see the Department of Justice in an attempt to obtain a reconsideration of the decision not to place lynching on the agendum, but the department remained unmoved.

Document Text

Finally on the opening night of the conference when President Roosevelt made his key-note speech and roundly denounced lynching as one of the major crimes confronting this country, another wire was sent the attorney general asking in view of the President's pronouncement whether he would not at that date place lynching on the agendum. No reply was received the following morning, so at 12:30 P. M. that day the District of Columbia branch of the N.A.A.C.P. began to picket the Crime Conference.

The pickets were arrested almost as soon as they appeared and charged with violation of the District of Columbia sign law and parading without a permit. But that afternoon at 2:25 P. M. the branch received a telegram from the attorney general stating that although there was no room for a discussion of lynching on the formal agendum of the conference, there was a discussion period after each session and that if a discussion period were free, he hoped that the subject of lynching would be taken up on the floor. He further invited a delegation consisting of representatives of the local colored bar association to membership in the conference.

In spite of this action by the attorney general however, the chairman of the conference announced that the discussion period would be limited to the papers read on the formal agendum at the particular session. Under the circumstances the District of Columbia branch of the N.A.A.C.P. decided to resume the picketing.

On the last day of the conference, December 13, just before the morning session adjourned, about sixty pickets suddenly appeared on the sidewalk in front of the convention hall, and silently took up pre-arranged stations about ten feet apart, stretching all the way from the entrance of the hall about three squares along the street the delegates had to use in leaving the conference. To avoid the sign law which prohibited signs twelve inches or over, the pickets carried signs across their breasts eleven inches wide. Ropes were looped around their necks to symbolize lynching. To avoid the charge of parading, each picket remained silent and stationary. The police were taken completely by surprise. To add to the confusion of the police the pickets were provided with a mimeographed sheet of instructions, one of which read that if anybody bothered them they were to call on the police for protection, as the police would not arrest them if they were not violating any law, since to do so would subject the police to an action for damages. The police fumed; an attorney for the Department of Justice hurriedly left to consult the law and find grounds for arresting the pickets, but never returned. That afternoon the conference, smoked out beyond the point of endurance, adopted a completely inane and harmless resolution condemning the use of illegal means in disposing of matters arousing racial antagonisms. The attorney general held both his peace and his hand.

Finally March 12, 1935, a Negro, Ab Young, was lynched near Slayden, Mississippi, allegedly for shooting a white man. Young had been seized in Tennessee, and taken across the line into Mississippi for the ceremonies. Memphis news reporters were on hand either by accident or previous notice.

The N.A.A.C.P. telegraphed both the attorney general and the President of the United States asking for investigation and prosecution under the amended Lindbergh law. To date it is still awaiting a reply. The coroner's jury returned a verdict that Young had died at the hands of parties unknown.

The attorney general continues his offensive against crime—except crimes involving the deprivation of life and liberty and citizenship to Negroes.

Glossary

color	as a legal term, pretense, as in "under color of authority, law, or custom"
Lindbergh kidnapping law	a law passed in 1932 in response to the highly publicized kidnapping and murder of the son of the aviation hero Charles Lindbergh in New Jersey
prima facie	a legal term from the Latin for "at first sight," referring to a fact presumed to be true unless rebutted by evidence

Mary McLeod Bethune (Library of Congress)

Mary McLeod Bethune's "What Does American Democracy Mean to Me?"

1939

"The democratic doors of equal opportunity have not been opened wide to Negroes."

Overview

On the evening of November 23, 1939, Mary McLeod Bethune was part of a panel discussion on *America's Town Meeting of the Air*, a weekly public affairs broadcast on NBC Radio—one of the nation's first "talk radio" programs—revolving around the title question "What Does American Democracy Mean to Me?" Bethune was eminently qualified to join the panel that evening. She was the founder of a school that evolved into the modern-day Bethune-Cookman University. She was a past president of the National Association of Colored Women and the founder of the National Council of Negro Women. She was also a key figure in the Black Cabinet, or, more formally, the Federal Council on Negro Affairs, an advisory group that kept the administration of President Franklin Roosevelt apprised of the concerns of the black community. She delivered her remarks during what would prove to be the tail end of the Great Depression, a time when African American workers faced enormous challenges. Looming on the horizon was American entry into World War II, which had started less than three months earlier with the German invasion of Poland. As Americans vigorously discussed issues involving the direction the country should take, both economically and militarily, the topic of the panel that evening was particularly timely.

Context

Two major historical developments formed the cultural backdrop for Bethune's speech (which was less a speech and more a sort of script for her remarks as part of the broadcast panel). One was the ongoing Great Depression; the other was the threat of American involvement in war, a threat that would materialize when the United States entered World War II after the bombing of the U.S. Navy base at Pearl Harbor, Hawaii, in December 1941.

The Great Depression began in 1929, marking the end of the Roaring Twenties, a decade of prosperity in the United States. Through the 1930s, the nation's income dropped by half, while unemployment was a major scourge: At the height of the depression, some 25 percent of the total labor force was unemployed, but among black Americans the figure was as high as 50 percent, particularly in urban areas. During the depression, it was almost impossible for black Americans to find work. Many southern blacks had been able to squeeze out a living as sharecroppers, but when the price of cotton dropped from eighteen cents per pound in the late 1920s to six cents per pound in 1933, many sharecroppers were forced off their land. Worse, mechanical cotton pickers were replacing black labor. Many displaced black agricultural workers took refuge in cities, where they faced animosity from the white labor forces and labor unions, which saw the influx of blacks as a threat to whatever few job opportunities existed.

African Americans were initially suspicious of President Franklin Roosevelt's New Deal, a package of legislation whose goal was to put Americans to work in an assortment of federal agencies. Indeed, provisions in these agencies perpetuated a pattern of discrimination against black workers, leading many to refer to Roosevelt's New Deal as a "raw deal." A good example of a measure that hurt African American interests was the 1933 Agricultural Adjustment Act. At the time, most black farmers did not own their land but farmed as tenants, or sharecroppers. As a way of increasing farm income, the government paid farmers incentives to leave land fallow, which would decrease crop supplies and presumably drive up prices. Accordingly, southern landowners fired their black tenant farmers, as fewer crops meant that fewer farmers were needed. These kinds of problems led John Preston Davis to write "A Black Inventory of the New Deal," a scathing indictment of Roosevelt's programs published in May 1935 in *The Crisis*, the magazine of the National Association for the Advancement of Colored People (NAACP). His essay called on African Americans to forge their own solutions to their economic condition rather than relying on a government that had failed to help them. That month, disaffected black intellectuals and activists held a conference at Howard University, in Washington, D.C., during which most presenters attacked New Deal programs for their adverse impacts on African Americans. Frustrated blacks in Harlem had rioted in March that year, indicating growing dissatisfaction with the government's ability to deal with African American poverty. In response to this sort of societal alarm, Robert Clifton Weaver, one of Bethune's colleagues on Roosevelt's

Time Line

1875
- July 10
Mary Jane McLeod is born near Mayesville, South Carolina.

1894
- McLeod graduates from Scotia Seminary in North Carolina.

1904
- Now married, Mary McLeod Bethune establishes the Educational and Industrial Training School for Negro Girls in Daytona Beach, Florida.

1917
- Bethune becomes president of the Florida chapter of the National Association of Colored Women, to serve until 1925.

1920
- Bethune becomes president of the Southeastern Federation of Colored Women's Clubs, serving until 1925.

1923
- Bethune's school, now called the Daytona Normal and Industrial Institute for Negro Girls, completes a merger with the Cookman Institute for Men to become a coeducational school, later accredited as Bethune-Cookman College.

1924
- Bethune is named national president of the National Association of Colored Women.

1935
- Bethune founds the National Council of Negro Women in New York City.

1936
- Bethune plays a key role in the formation of the Federal Council on Negro Affairs, commonly called the Black Cabinet.

Black Cabinet, published "The New Deal and the Negro: A Look at the Facts," a defense of the Roosevelt administration's efforts, in the black literary journal *Opportunity*.

By 1939, the year of Bethune's radio remarks, African Americans were beginning to benefit somewhat from New Deal programs. Their income from public sector employment, for example, was almost as large as their income in the private sector. Some of this modest growth in black income came at the hands of the union movement. The chief obstacle for black workers had been the American Federation of Labor, which had supported discriminatory practices in the labor unions that were part of the federation. In 1935 the American Federation of Labor did grant a charter to the Brotherhood of Sleeping Car Porters, a union made up almost entirely of blacks founded by A. Philip Randolph a decade earlier. But in 1936 a rival group, soon known as the Congress of Industrial Organizations, was formed, in part, to organize black as well as white workers. Aided by such organizations as the National Urban League and the NAACP, the Congress of Industrial Organizations organized new unions, such as the Packinghouse Workers Organizing Committee, the United Automobile Workers, and the Steel Workers Organizing Committee. Meanwhile, in 1937 the Brotherhood of Sleeping Car Porters reached a landmark agreement with the Pullman Company, which operated the railway coaches on which black porters and maids worked.

African American workers and civil rights organizations took additional steps to improve the plight of black workers. The Urban League and the NAACP, for example, played a key role in the formation of the Joint Committee on National Recovery in 1933. The committee's goal was to bring inequities in New Deal programs to the public's attention, for example, by spearheading "Don't Buy Where You Can't Work" campaigns to boycott businesses that operated in black communities but would not employ black workers in any but menial jobs. Pressure from the Citizens' League for Fair Play forced the New York City Chamber of Commerce and other citywide organizations to promote the hiring of blacks in higher-paying retail jobs. In the rural South, black workers were joining such organizations as the Southern Tenant Farmers Union, a Socialist group, and the Alabama Sharecroppers Union, a Communist one. In Birmingham, Alabama, black workers were drawn to the League of Struggle for Negro Rights.

On the political front, African Americans were changing party allegiance. Traditionally they had supported the Republican Party, the party of Abraham Lincoln and emancipation. But during the Great Depression, black political affiliation began to shift as the Democratic Roosevelt administration appointed dozens of blacks to New Deal agencies. Many of these people joined to create the Federal Council on Negro Affairs, known informally as the Black Cabinet. As a member of the Black Cabinet, Bethune, who herself had been a Republican, championed Roosevelt's programs. In 1935 hundreds of civil rights leaders joined to form the National Negro Congress with the goal of uniting some six hundred fraternal, civil rights, and church organizations under a single umbrella to improve the economic and social position of African Americans.

Despite some progress, the position of unemployed African American workers in the late 1930s remained tenuous. The nation was emerging from the depression, in part because of increased defense spending, which allowed white workers to return to full-time employment, but black workers were continuing to rely on public sector jobs and relief programs.

Equally important, though, were the war clouds gathering over the horizon. For several years Americans had been watching with unease certain developments in Europe as well as the Far East. One was the rise of Adolf Hitler, who seized power in 1933 as Germany's chancellor. In the months and years that followed, Hitler consolidated his power. The Reichstag Fire Decree curtailed civil liberties; the Law against the Establishment of Parties made Nazi Germany a one-party state. Hitler eliminated his rivals within the Nazi Party during the "Night of the Long Knives" at the end of June 1934. Through these years, Hitler and his supporters launched their persecution of Jews, Communists, trade unionists, and political opponents. In defiance of the Treaty of Versailles, which ended Germany's participation in World War I, Hitler remilitarized the nation. He formed alliances with the Soviet Union, led by Joseph Stalin; Fascist Italy, which invaded Ethiopia in 1935; and imperialist Japan, which was flexing its muscles in the Pacific and invaded China in 1937. China fought back against Japan with help from the United States and the Soviet Union, which in turn joined the Allies in the fight against Germany. Hitler, in the meantime, merged German-speaking Austria with Germany and grabbed the German-speaking Sudetenland region of Czechoslovakia. Few were surprised when he launched World War II in Europe with the invasion of Poland on September 1, 1939.

Americans vigorously debated the question of American participation in the war. Isolationists and antiwar activists argued that the war was Europe's war, and the United States had no business taking part. Others, including Roosevelt himself, knew that American entry into the war was inevitable. At the same time, Americans watched the rise of Communism in the Soviet Union. Many American intellectuals, disgusted with the apparent failures of capitalism that had led to the Great Depression, were drawn to the ideology of Communism and the Soviet Union. Prominent among them were black intellectuals such as W. E. B. Du Bois and Paul Robeson, who traveled to the Soviet Union and came to believe that the Communist state did not carry the same burden of racism that the United States did. Mainstream Americans, however, regarded Communism as an alien ideology and were growing to fear the might and influence of the Soviets.

Thus, when the panel of participants was formed to address the personal question "What does American democracy mean to me?" the overarching universal questions of American democracy—regarding its origins, its role in the world, its ideological underpinnings, its response to Fascism and Communism, and its future—were already topics of intense discussion throughout the nation. Mary McLeod Bethune articulated a response to this question from an African American perspective.

Time Line

1939
- **September 1** World War II begins in Europe with the German invasion of Poland.
- **November 23** As part of a panel discussion, Bethune gives her radio address "What Does American Democracy Mean to Me?"

1955
- **May 18** Bethune dies in Daytona Beach, Florida.

About the Author

Mary Jane McLeod was born near Mayesville, South Carolina, on July 10, 1875. She was the fifteenth of seventeen children born to Samuel and Patsy McLeod, both former slaves; most of her siblings had been born into slavery. Her mother worked for her former owner, while her father worked on a nearby cotton plantation. From an early age, Mary exhibited a desire to learn to read and go to school. One of her earliest formative experiences was an encounter with a white girl who commanded her, "Put down that book. You can't read." Determined to prove the girl wrong, she enrolled at the one-room Trinity Mission School, run by the Presbyterian Church, when it opened. At the urging of her teacher, she enrolled at Scotia Seminary (now Barber-Scotia College) in Concord, North Carolina, in 1888. After completing her degree in 1894, McLeod moved to Chicago to attend Dwight Moody's Institute for Home and Foreign Missions (now Moody Bible College). Her earliest goal was to become a missionary in Africa, but after being told that there was no call for black missionaries there, she decided to embark on a teaching career, which included stints at the school she had attended as a child; at the Haines Normal and Industrial Institute in Augusta, Georgia; and at the Kindell Institute in Sumter, South Carolina. In 1898 she married Albertus Bethune, who left her in 1907 and died in 1918.

In 1899 Bethune was persuaded to relocate to Florida to run a mission school. During this time she supplemented her income by selling life insurance. But in 1904 she launched efforts to establish her own school for girls. She rented a house (for ten dollars a month), gathered discarded and donated materials, built desks out of old packing crates, and formed the Educational and Industrial Training School for Negro Girls in Daytona Beach, initially with six students and cash on hand of one dollar and fifty cents. She continued to scrounge for donations, securing a substantial grant from the industrialist John D. Rockefeller, and she persuaded prominent white men in the bustling economic climate of Daytona Beach to sit on the school's board of directors. The school had over a hundred students by 1910 and more than three hundred by 1920. In 1923 the school, now called the Daytona Normal and Industrial Institute for Negro Girls, completed the process of merging with the Cookman Institute for Men of Jacksonville to become the Daytona-Cookman Collegiate Institute. In 1929 the coeducational institution was renamed Bethune-Cookman College. Bethune served as president of the college until 1942. As of the twenty-first century, the school, which achieved university status in 2007, has some four thousand students on a seventy-acre campus and an operating budget of $50 million.

Bethune's career continued to evolve after the establishment of Bethune-Cookman College. From 1917 to 1925 she served as the Florida chapter president of the National Association of Colored Women, using her position to register black voters. She also served as the president of the Southeastern Federation of Colored Women's Clubs from 1920 to 1925. With these positions on her résumé, she was named national president of the National Association of Colored Women in 1924. Then, in 1935, Bethune founded the National Council of Negro Women in New York City. The council brought together twenty-eight organizations to form a united voice that would work to improve the quality of life for women and their communities. In 1936 Bethune earned a position in the National Youth Administration, a New Deal agency in Franklin Roosevelt's administration whose goal was to increase educational and occupational opportunities for young people. Two years later, in 1938, she was appointed director of the administration's Division of Negro Affairs, making her the first black woman to head a federal agency. Also that year, Bethune's National Council of Negro Women played host to the White House Conference on Negro Women and Children. The goal of the conference was to highlight the democratic roles of black women, which would later include providing opportunities for black women as officers in the Women's Army Corps during World War II.

Bethune was a close friend to President Franklin Roosevelt and, particularly, First Lady Eleanor Roosevelt. This friendship gave her access to the White House, and she used that access to help form the Federal Council on Negro Affairs, commonly known as the Black Cabinet. This was an informal group made up primarily of a number of prominent African Americans who worked in various federal government agencies. The Black Cabinet's role was to function in an advisory capacity, keeping the administration informed about the concerns of black Americans while at the same time demonstrating to African American voters that the Roosevelt administration heard those concerns. Late in her life Bethune wrote weekly editorial columns for black newspapers such as the *Chicago Defender* and the *Pittsburgh Courier*.

Bethune was known almost as much for her personal manner as for her achievements. On the Black Cabinet she was referred to affectionately as "Ma Bethune." A matronly figure even in her thirties, she took to walking with a cane not because she needed it but because, she said, it gave her "swank." She was a teetotaler—one who does not consume alcohol—and often approached drunken men in the street to chastise them. Her peers said that she was able to assume a kind of feminine helplessness that concealed a ruthlessness about getting what she wanted. She also possessed an uncanny knack for bringing blacks and whites together. One noteworthy example was her investment in a stretch of private beach in Daytona Beach, where blacks—barred from other beaches—mingled with whites.

Bethune was the recipient of numerous honors, including the Spingarn Medal, an award given by the NAACP for outstanding achievement. She was the only black woman present at the founding of the United Nations in 1948, co-representing the NAACP. After her death on May 18, 1955, she was inducted into the National Women's Hall of Fame in 1973. Numerous schools throughout the United States are named in her honor.

Explanation and Analysis of the Document

At under six hundred words, Bethune's remarks were appropriately brief for a radio audience. She begins by saying that for the nation's twelve million blacks, democracy remained a goal, not something that had been fully achieved. (The total population then was just under 132 million.) She cites her Christian faith, which told her that African Americans were "rising out of the darkness of slavery into the light of freedom." She points out that progress has been made; dramatically more African Americans were literate, and significant numbers owned and operated their own farms. She notes that blacks had moved from being "chattels"—that is, property—to full contributors to American culture. In the second paragraph she cites some prominent African American artists and intellectuals, including Paul Laurence Dunbar, perhaps the first black American poet to achieve national recognition; Booker T. Washington, the founder of the Tuskegee Institute in Alabama; the singer Marian Anderson, who, with the backing of Eleanor Roosevelt, gave an open-air concert on the steps of the Lincoln Memorial in Washington, D.C., on Easter Sunday that year (having been refused access to Constitution Hall by the Daughters of the American Revolution); and George Washington Carver, a scientist and educator who was a model of the kind of frugality and humanitarianism that Bethune preached as an educator.

In the third paragraph, Bethune points to some of the inequalities that remained. She notes, for example, that in the South black youth lacked the same educational opportunities afforded to white youth. An examination of spending patterns of that era shows that per-student budgets for black schools were actually worse than Bethune indicates: as little as one-twentieth of those for white schools. She

A group of guests gather around the radio at the Hotel Hamilton in Washington, D.C., in the 1920s. (Library of Congress)

also points out that blacks were often barred from labor unions and forced to accept the most poorly paid menial work. Additionally, blacks continued to be denied civil rights, including the right to vote. They too often lived in squalid housing, and they continued to fear the lynch mob.

In paragraph 4, Bethune acknowledges that the black community had sometimes been slow to assume the burdens of civic responsibility, but she notes, too, that it had done so because it had been denied full equality. Perhaps making reference to the growing threat of war, she asserts that "we have always been loyal when the ideals of American democracy have been attacked." As an example she cites Crispus Attucks, a man of African and Native American descent who was slain in the Boston Massacre. And, in a reference to World War I, she comments that blacks had shed blood on the battlefields of France. Part of the fight, however, had been for civil liberties, particularly the right to vote. She alludes to the Declaration of Independence when she states, "We have fought to preserve one nation, conceived in liberty and dedicated to the proposition that all men are created equal." According to Bethune, America had imperfections, yet African Americans always fought for what they knew the nation could become. She stresses this point in the final paragraph, where she looks forward to a time when blacks and whites could work shoulder to shoulder for "a new birth of freedom" in the hope "that government of the people, for the people and by the people shall not perish from the earth"—words of Abraham Lincoln from the Gettysburg Address of 1863.

Audience

Bethune's address was aired live on NBC Radio, a broadcasting company that had emerged out of a complex set of business relationships—and a period of vigorous competition—involving the Radio Corporation of America (known as RCA), Westinghouse Electric, American Telephone & Telegraph, and various independent radio stations as well as other corporations. As early as the 1920s NBC Radio, originally seen as a marketing device for RCA's radio equipment, was attracting a huge listening audience with its serial programming, including the mass hit *Amos 'n' Andy*. The Great Depression boosted demand for radio,

Essential Quotes

> "Under God's guidance in this great democracy, we are rising out of the darkness of slavery into the light of freedom."
> (Paragraph 1)

> "The democratic doors of equal opportunity have not been opened wide to Negroes."
> (Paragraph 3)

> "We have always been loyal when the ideals of American democracy have been attacked."
> (Paragraph 4)

> "Perhaps the greatest battle is before us, the fight for a new America: fearless, free, united, morally re-armed, in which 12 million Negroes, shoulder to shoulder with their fellow Americans, will strive that this nation under God will have a new birth of freedom."
> (Paragraph 5)

which provided people with an inexpensive form of entertainment. NBC Radio emerged as the industry leader by compiling a lineup of highly popular performers, including Al Jolson, Jack Benny, Edgar Bergen, Fred Allen, and Bob Hope. NBC Radio also helped created the NBC Symphony Orchestra under the direction of the famed musician Arturo Toscanini. Popular programs during the depression era included *Fibber McGee and Molly*, *One Man's Family*, *Ma Perkins*, and *Death Valley Days*. Because NBC affiliate stations were often the most powerful in their markets, they reached broad audiences, particularly at night, when their signals traveled thousands of miles farther than they did during the day.

Thus, a program such as *America's Town Meeting of the Air*, on which Bethune delivered her remarks, reached a large coast-to-coast audience. That program, one of America's first talk-radio shows, had been launched on May 30, 1935; its topic that night was "Which Way America: Fascism, Communism, Socialism or Democracy?" The program's format was to assemble a group of experts to discuss a topic selected by the moderator George V. Denny, Jr., the executive director of the League for Political Education, which produced the program. The goal of the program was to use modern technology to recreate the feel of a town meeting for a scattered audience, in this way involving a variety of citizens from across the nation in discussion of important public issues. Always present in the studio for the program was a live audience, which alternately cheered or booed in reaction to the speakers. Audience members were also allowed to ask questions; many openly challenged the viewpoints of the panelists and even mocked them or called them names. By 1936 listeners were able to call into the show, and they, too, often responded to what they were hearing with great vigor, sometimes expressing highly inflammatory views.

Impact

One measure of the popularity of *America's Town Meeting of the Air* was the amount of fan mail its host, Denny, received—generally about two thousand to four thousand letters per week, a remarkable number for a political program at that time. Also, throughout the country, many people formed "listener clubs": People would gather to listen to the broadcast and then discuss the topic among themselves. Yet another measure of the show's popularity was civics teachers' interest in using the program's content in their classes; for this reason, Denny condensed what panelists said into pamphlet form and distributed the pamphlets to teachers. In sum, *America's Town Meeting of the Air* was a popular and widespread part of the nation's political discourse when Bethune delivered her remarks in 1939, and many thousands of people likely heard them.

To assess any particular impact borne by Bethune's remarks, of course, would be difficult. But her eloquent and inspired voice was part of a swelling chorus of African American voices in this era that were calling for a nationwide reappraisal of segregation and discrimination. Journalists and authors such as Walter White were documenting the often-oppressive circumstances of African Americans. Charles Hamilton Houston, as special counsel for the NAACP, was launching a legal campaign to end discrimination and inequity in the nation's schools. A. Philip Randolph, president of the National Negro Congress and head of the Brotherhood of Sleeping Car Porters labor union, was lobbying for access for African Americans to jobs in the growing defense industry. These and other prominent public figures were impressing on the Roosevelt administration the need to take steps to end segregation, and their efforts began to bear fruit. In 1941 Roosevelt issued Executive Order 8802, banning discrimination in hiring by the federal government and in the defense industries. His successor, President Harry S. Truman, ended segregation in the armed forces with Executive Order 9981, issued in 1948. The far-reaching educational and political efforts of Mary McLeod Bethune contributed significantly to the progress of African Americans through the World War II era and beyond.

See also John P. Davis: "A Black Inventory of the New Deal" (1935); Robert Clifton Weaver: "The New Deal and the Negro: A Look at the Facts" (1935); Charles Hamilton Houston's "Educational Inequalities Must Go!" (1935); Walter F. White's "U.S. Department of (White) Justice" (1935); A. Philip Randolph's "Call to Negro America to March on Washington" (1941); Executive Order 9981 (1948); Marian Anderson's *My Lord, What a Morning* (1956).

Further Reading

- **Articles**

Denny, George V., Jr. "Radio Builds Democracy." *Journal of Educational Sociology* 14, no. 6 (February 1941): 370–377.

Ross, B. Joyce. "Mary McLeod Bethune and the National Youth Administration: A Case Study of Power Relationships in the Black Cabinet of Franklin D. Roosevelt." *Journal of Negro History* 60 (January 1975): 1–28.

- **Books**

Bennett, Carolyn LaDelle. *An Annotated Bibliography of Mary McLeod Bethune's* Chicago Defender *Columns, 1948–1955.* Lewiston, N.Y.: Edwin Mellen Press, 2000.

Carruth, Ella K. *She Wanted to Read: The Story of Mary McLeod Bethune.* New York: Pocket Books, 1977.

Hanson, Joyce A. *Mary McLeod Bethune and Black Women's Political Activism.* Columbia: University of Missouri Press, 2003.

Questions for Further Study

1. What international events might have made the topic of Bethune's remarks of particular interest to her radio listeners?

2. What was the Black Cabinet? What role did it play in the administration of President Franklin Roosevelt?

3. Read this document in conjunction with Marian Anderson's *My Lord, What a Morning.* Imagine a discussion between Bethune and Anderson about the position and progress of African Americans in the 1930s. Would they have seen matters in the same way? How might their views have differed?

4. Imagine that Bethune was in a position to defend the viewpoints either of John P. Davis in "A Black Inventory of the New Deal" or of Robert Clifton Weaver in "The New Deal and the Negro: A Look at the Facts." Which side of the debate would she most likely have supported? Why?

5. Imagine that you attend a school where you are required to use desks made of old packing crates, similar to the kinds of facilities Bethune had when she formed the Educational and Industrial Training School for Negro Girls. What would your reaction be? What do you think the reaction of your parents or guardians would be? What lessons can be learned today about school funding as well as about the deep desire for education a century or more ago?

Holt, Rackham. *Mary McLeod Bethune: A Biography*. Garden City, N.Y.: Doubleday, 1964.

McCluskey, Audrey Thomas, and Elaine M. Smith, eds. *Mary McLeod Bethune: Building a Better World—Essays and Selected Documents*. Bloomington: Indiana University Press, 2002.

Okoye, Chiazam Ugo. *Mary McLeod Bethune: Words of Wisdom*. Bloomington, Ind.: AuthorHouse, 2008.

Poole, Bernice Anderson. *Mary McLeod Bethune: Educator*. Los Angeles: Melrose Square, 1994.

Sterne, Emma Gelders. *Mary McLeod Bethune*. New York: Random House, 1957.

■ **Web Sites**

"Mary McLeod Bethune, Educator." State Library and Archives of Florida "Florida Memory" Web site.
http://www.floridamemory.com/onlineclassroom/marybethune.

—Michael J. O'Neal

Mary McLeod Bethune's "What Does American Democracy Mean to Me?"

Democracy is for me, and for 12 million black Americans, a goal towards which our nation is marching. It is a dream and an ideal in whose ultimate realization we have a deep and abiding faith. For me, it is based on Christianity, in which we confidently entrust our destiny as a people. Under God's guidance in this great democracy, we are rising out of the darkness of slavery into the light of freedom. Here my race has been afforded [the] opportunity to advance from a people 80 percent illiterate to a people 80 percent literate; from abject poverty to the ownership and operation of a million farms and 750,000 homes; from total disfranchisement to participation in government; from the status of chattels to recognized contributors to the American culture.

As we have been extended a measure of democracy, we have brought to the nation rich gifts. We have helped to build America with our labor, strengthened it with our faith and enriched it with our song. We have given you Paul Laurence Dunbar, Booker T. Washington, Marian Anderson and George Washington Carver. But even these are only the first fruits of a rich harvest, which will be reaped when new and wider fields are opened to us.

The democratic doors of equal opportunity have not been opened wide to Negroes. In the Deep South, Negro youth is offered only one-fifteenth of the educational opportunity of the average American child. The great masses of Negro workers are depressed and unprotected in the lowest levels of agriculture and domestic service, while the black workers in industry are barred from certain unions and generally assigned to the more laborious and poorly paid work. Their housing and living conditions are sordid and unhealthy. They live too often in terror of the lynch mob; are deprived too often of the Constitutional right of suffrage; and are humiliated too often by the denial of civil liberties. We do not believe that justice and common decency will allow these conditions to continue.

Our faith in visions of fundamental change as mutual respect and understanding between our races come in the path of spiritual awakening. Certainly there have been times when we may have delayed this mutual understanding by being slow to assume a fuller share of our national responsibility because of the denial of full equality. And yet, we have always been loyal when the ideals of American democracy have been attacked. We have given our blood in its defense—from Crispus Attucks on Boston Commons to the battlefields of France. We have fought for the democratic principles of equality under the law, equality of opportunity, equality at the ballot box, for the guarantees of life, liberty and the pursuit of hap-

Glossary

battlefields of France	an allusion to World War I
Booker T. Washington	founder of the Tuskegee Institute in Alabama
Crispus Attucks	a man of African and Native American descent who was killed in the Boston Massacre prior to the Revolutionary War
George Washington Carver	a prominent black scientist and educator
Marian Anderson	a singer who gave an open-air concert on the steps of the Lincoln Memorial in Washington, D.C., on Easter Sunday 1939
Paul Laurence Dunbar	the first black poet to achieve national recognition

Document Text

piness. We have fought to preserve one nation, conceived in liberty and dedicated to the proposition that all men are created equal. Yes, we have fought for America with all her imperfections, not so much for what she is, but for what we know she can be.

Perhaps the greatest battle is before us, the fight for a new America: fearless, free, united, morally rearmed, in which 12 million Negroes, shoulder to shoulder with their fellow Americans, will strive that this nation under God will have a new birth of freedom, and that government of the people, for the people and by the people shall not perish from the earth. This dream, this idea, this aspiration, this is what American democracy means to me.

Pullman porter making up an upper berth aboard the "Capitol Limited," bound for Chicago, Illinois (Library of Congress)

A. Philip Randolph's "Call to Negro America to March on Washington"

1941

"If American democracy will not insure equality of opportunity, freedom and justice to its citizens, black and white, it is a hollow mockery."

Overview

In the May 1941 issue of *Black Worker*, A. Philip Randolph, a prominent civil rights leader in his capacity as president of the National Negro Congress and head of the Brotherhood of Sleeping Car Porters labor union, issued a call for African Americans to march on Washington, D.C., to demand an end to discrimination in the defense industry and in the military. His call, made in cooperation with the civil rights leaders Bayard Rustin and A. J. Muste, initiated the March on Washington Movement, which lasted until 1947. This movement influenced future civil rights leaders such as Martin Luther King, Jr., who joined with Randolph in 1963 to organize the historic March on Washington for Jobs and Freedom (where King made his famous "I Have a Dream" speech). Randolph's "call to Negro America" took place in the context of America's transition from the Great Depression of the 1930s to the wartime economy that would employ millions of industrial workers during World War II.

Ultimately, the march Randolph envisioned never took place. Under pressure from civil rights leaders and out of his recognition that the United States would need all the manpower it could muster in the coming years, President Franklin Delano Roosevelt issued an executive order banning racial discrimination in the defense industries and in the federal government. Accordingly, the number of African Americans employed in defense industries and government swelled, although the armed forces remained segregated throughout World War II. It would fall to Roosevelt's successor, President Harry S. Truman, to desegregate the military by executive order in 1948—in large part because of the efforts of the Committee against Jim Crow in Military Service and Training, which Randolph founded.

Context

The Great Depression, which began in 1929, marked the end of an era of prosperity in the United States. Throughout the 1930s, the nation's income dropped by half. At the height of the depression, an estimated 25 percent of the total labor force was unemployed, but among black Americans the figure was as high as 50 percent, especially in urban areas. For most of the decade, it was nearly impossible for black Americans to find work. In the South, where many African Americans had been able to scratch out a living as sharecroppers, the price of cotton dropped from eighteen cents a pound in the late 1920s to six cents a pound in 1933, forcing many sharecroppers off their land. Making matters worse was the introduction of mechanical cotton pickers, which replaced a significant segment of black labor. As displaced black agricultural workers took refuge in cities, they met with hostility from the white labor force and labor unions, both of which saw the influx of blacks as a threat to whatever few job opportunities existed.

African Americans were initially skeptical of President Franklin Roosevelt's "New Deal," a package of legislation designed to provide relief for suffering Americans by putting them to work in an assortment of federal agencies. Various provisions in these laws and the agencies they created continued a pattern of discrimination against African Americans, leading many to refer to Roosevelt's New Deal as a "raw deal." Over the course of the decade, though, some progress was made. By 1939 African Americans were beginning to benefit from New Deal programs, and their income from public sector employment was almost as large as their income in the private sector. Helping to spur this modest growth in black income was the union movement. For years, the American Federation of Labor had supported discriminatory practices in the labor unions that were part of the federation. But in 1935 the Congress of Industrial Organizations was formed with the goal, in part, of organizing black as well as white workers. With the help of such organizations as the Urban League and the National Association for the Advancement of Colored People, the Congress of Industrial Organizations organized new unions, including the Packinghouse Workers Organizing Committee, the United Automobile Workers, and the Steel Workers Organizing Committee. In the face of competition from the Congress of Industrial Organizations, in 1935 the American Federation of Labor granted a charter to the Brotherhood of Sleeping Car Porters, the union A. Philip Randolph had founded a decade earlier. In 1937 the union finally signed an agreement with the Pullman Company, which operated the railway coaches on which black porters and maids worked.

Time Line

1889
- **April 15**
  A. Philip Randolph is born in Crescent City, Florida.

1925
- **August 25**
  Randolph forms the Brotherhood of Sleeping Car Porters.

1935
- **June 1**
  The Brotherhood of Sleeping Car Porters is certified as the union representing porters working on rail cars operated by the Pullman Company.

1936
- **February 14**
  The first meeting of the National Negro Congress begins in Chicago, ending on February 15; Randolph is named the organization's first president.

1939
- **September 1**
  World War II begins in Europe with the invasion of Poland by Nazi Germany.

1941
- **March 11**
  The U.S. Congress passes the Lend-Lease Act to aid countries fighting Fascism.

- **May**
  Randolph publishes his "Call to Negro America to March on Washington for Jobs and Equal Participation in National Defense" in the journal *Black Worker*.

- **June 18**
  President Franklin Delano Roosevelt meets with Randolph to discuss the planned march on Washington.

- **June 25**
  Roosevelt issues Executive Order 8802, banning discrimination in hiring by the federal government and in the defense industries.

- **July 19**
  Roosevelt appoints the first members of the Fair Employment Practices Committee.

Black workers and civil rights organizations took additional steps to improve the plight of African American workers. In 1933, for example, the Urban League and the National Association for the Advancement of Colored People were instrumental in forming the Joint Committee on National Recovery. The organization's goal was to bring inequities in New Deal programs to the public's attention. The committee also spearheaded "Don't Buy Where You Can't Work" campaigns to boycott businesses that served black communities but refused to hire black workers in any but menial jobs. In New York City, pressure from the Citizens League for Fair Play forced the local chamber of commerce and other citywide organizations to promote the hiring of blacks in higher paying retail jobs. Meanwhile, in the rural South, black workers were joining such organizations as the Socialist Southern Tenant Farmers Union and the Communist Alabama Sharecroppers Union. In Birmingham, Alabama, black workers were drawn to the League of Struggle for Negro Rights.

Efforts were also made on the political front. Historically, African Americans had supported the Republican Party, the party of Abraham Lincoln and emancipation. Throughout the 1930s, though, black political affiliation began to shift as the Democratic Roosevelt administration appointed dozens of blacks to New Deal agencies, forming what came to be called Roosevelt's Black Cabinet. Among these politically powerful African Americans were Mary McLeod Bethune, the founder of Bethune-Cookman College, and Howard University professor Ralph Bunche. In 1936 hundreds of civil rights leaders came together to form the National Negro Congress, electing Randolph as the organization's first president. The goal of the congress was to unite some six hundred fraternal, civil rights, and church organizations under a single umbrella to improve the economic and social position of African Americans.

Despite some progress, the position of unemployed African American workers in the late 1930s remained dire. As the nation was emerging from the depression, white workers were able to return to full-time employment, but black workers continued to rely on relief programs and public sector jobs, primarily in construction and infrastructure building. However, war clouds were gathering over the horizon. On September 1, 1939, World War II began in Europe when Nazi Germany invaded Poland. In 1940, Belgium, Denmark, France, the Netherlands, and Norway fell to the Nazis. In preparation for the possibility of war, the United States instituted a peacetime draft, and under the Lend-Lease program, begun in 1941, the U.S. government began sending military supplies to England, China, Russia, and Brazil.

As the nation mobilized for the possibility of war, the unemployment rate fell below 10 percent for the first time since 1932. Industrial output was up, as exemplified by an increase in production in the shipbuilding industry: From 1930 to 1936, U.S. shipbuilders had produced only seventy-one ships; however, in 1936 a New Deal agency called the U.S. Maritime Commission was formed to revive the shipbuilding industry—with great success, as 106 new ships were built from 1938 to 1940, and in 1941 nearly as many more were produced. African Americans, however, were getting only a handful of the new jobs being created. Accordingly, on January 15, 1941, Randolph issued a press release in which he called on African Americans to protest this inequity by marching on Washington. His March on Washington Movement had previously announced its goals, among them:

> We demand, in the interest of national unity, the abrogation of every law which makes a distinction in treatment between citizens based on religion, creed, color, or national origin. This means an end to Jim Crow in education, in housing, in transportation and in every other social, economic, and political privilege. Especially, we demand, in the capital of the nation, an end to all segregation in public places and in public institutions.

The date of the proposed march was to be July 1, 1941. The Roosevelt administration, alarmed by the prospect of tens of thousands of protesters descending on the nation's capital, tried to dissuade Randolph from this course of action and call off the march. Randolph, however, remained steadfast, and in May of that year he redoubled his efforts with his "Call to Negro America to March on Washington for Jobs and Equal Participation in National Defense," published in the journal *Black Worker*.

About the Author

Asa Philip Randolph was born on April 15, 1889, in Crescent City, Florida, the son of a Methodist minister. After graduating as valedictorian of his high school class in 1907, he moved to New York City with the early goal of becoming an actor; in Harlem, he organized a Shakespearean society and performed the lead role in several of Shakespeare's plays. During the 1910s he became a Socialist and began his earliest involvement in trade unionism. Along with his close friend and collaborator, Chandler Owen, he founded and edited *The Messenger*, a radical journal that espoused Socialism and trade unionism and urged African Americans to resist the military draft after the United States entered World War I.

During the 1920s Randolph's involvement in trade unionism intensified, and in 1925 he organized the Brotherhood of Sleeping Car Porters, the first black trade union. By the mid-1930s the union had over seven thousand members. For a decade Randolph and the union carried on bitter negotiations with the Pullman Company, which operated the sleeping and dining railroad cars on which black porters and maids worked—often for low wages, with no overtime pay. Finally, in 1935, the Brotherhood of Sleeping Car Porters was certified as the union that would represent the Pullman employees. Two years later the union reached an agreement with Pullman that provided workers with significant wage increases, overtime pay, and a shorter work week. Meanwhile, in 1936, Randolph was named the first president of the National Negro Congress.

Time Line

1943
- **May 27** Roosevelt's Executive Order 9346 strengthens and reorganizes the Fair Employment Practices Committee.

1947
- Randolph, with other black leaders, establishes the Committee against Jim Crow in Military Service and Training.

1948
- **July 26** President Harry Truman issues Executive Order 9981, desegregating the U.S. military.

1979
- **May 16** Randolph dies in New York City.

In January 1941, as U.S. industrial output was increasing with the growing threat of American involvement in World War II, Randolph issued a call for a march on Washington, D.C., to demand equality of opportunity in the defense industries and in the U.S. military. He met with President Franklin Roosevelt in June of that year; as a result of that meeting, Roosevelt issued Executive Order 8802, which desegregated the defense industries and the federal government. After the war, Randolph, in concert with other black leaders, established the Committee against Jim Crow in Military Service and Training. In large part as a result of Randolph's efforts, in 1948 President Harry Truman issued Executive Order 9981, desegregating the military. In 1950 Randolph founded the Leadership Conference on Civil Rights, one of the nation's leading civil rights organizations. Later, in 1963, he was instrumental in organizing the March on Washington for Jobs and Freedom. With his velvety baritone voice, Randolph was often the voice of black America on television and the radio as the struggle for civil rights continued throughout the 1960s. History came full circle when Amtrak, the organization that operates the U.S. passenger rail system, named one of its deluxe sleeping cars in Randolph's honor. Randolph died at the age of ninety on May 16, 1979, in New York City.

Explanation and Analysis of the Document

Randolph's "Call to Negro America to March on Washington for Jobs and Equal Participation in National Defense" is a highly rhetorical document consisting of a large number of short paragraphs and sentences that make his purpose absolutely clear. He sweeps his reader along with repetition and exclamations ("What a dilemma! What a runaround! What a disgrace!") and such literary devices as alliteration ("deepest disappointments and direst defeats ... dreadful days of destruction and disaster to democracy")—all perhaps reflecting his early theatrical background. He announces his purpose in the opening paragraph of his address, where he says, "We call upon you to fight for jobs in National Defense. We call upon you to struggle for the integration of Negroes in the armed forces." He then condemns "Jim-Crowism," a reference to the pattern of discrimination and segregation that had existed since the nineteenth century and that kept African Americans in inferior social and economic positions; the phrase *Jim Crow* was taken from the name of a character in a popular nineteenth-century minstrel show.

Randolph stresses his view of the black employment situation as a "crisis," indeed, a "crisis of democracy." He goes on to note that African Americans are being systematically denied employment in the defense industries and that they are segregated in the U.S. military. Randolph was, of course, correct. In the early decades of the twentieth century, African Americans served primarily in menial and service jobs in the military. In the U.S. Navy and Marine Corps, for example, African Americans were pushed into the Steward's Branch, where they worked as cooks and waiters in officers' mess halls. During World War II they fought in segregated units; the few black officers commanded segregated African American units. Many military officers argued that integrating units, and thus having blacks and whites serve side by side, would result in conflict and low morale. Randolph then goes on to point out that African American workers were caught on the horns of a dilemma: They could not get jobs because there were not members of unions, and they could not gain union membership because they were without jobs.

Midway into the essay, Randolph begins to express hope that the situation can be remedied; he foresees black Americans rising from their current position to new heights of achievement in the "struggle for freedom and justice in Government, in industry, in labor unions, education, social service, religion, and culture." He then asserts that African Americans, through "their own power for self-liberation," can break down "barriers of discrimination" and slay the "deadly serpent of race hatred" in the military, government, labor unions, and industry. Here, Randolph calls for efforts to provide unskilled African American workers with job training that will enable them to make a contribution.

Randolph then makes explicit what he wants: not just an end to discrimination but, more specifically, an executive order from the president that will put an end to discrimination in the defense industry and the military. In the following brief paragraphs, he notes that efforts on the part of the black community to gain jobs will not be easy and will require money and sacrifice. He calls on African Americans to take action, urging them to "build a mammoth machine of mass action" and to "harness and hitch" their power. He then arrives at his key goal: the organization of a march on Washington to demand economic equality. Randolph asserts that such a march will "shake up white America" and "shake up official Washington." Further, the massing of thousands of black demonstrators will give encouragement not only to African Americans but also to "our white friends" who fight for justice by the side of African Americans.

Randolph next takes up a potential objection to the proposed march on Washington. Critics would argue that such a march at such a time, with war looming, might affect national unity. Randolph rejects this argument, arguing instead that "we believe in national unity which recognizes equal opportunity of black and white citizens." The paragraph goes on to reject all forms of dictatorship, including Fascism, Nazism, and Communism, and to emphasize that African Americans are "loyal, patriotic Americans all." Interestingly, early in his career, during World War I, Randolph had been arrested for breaking the 1917 Espionage Act because of the left-wing Socialist ideals he espoused in the journal he founded, *The Messenger*. By the late 1930s Randolph was muting his Socialist beliefs, and here he makes clear that he regards the Communist Soviet Union as a dictatorship.

In the final paragraphs Randolph sums up his views. He states that American democracy would be a "hollow mockery" if it failed to protect its protectors and to extend equality of opportunity to all citizens, black and white. He again calls on President Roosevelt to end "Jim-Crowism" in the military and in the defense industry and closes by stating that if the federal government is guilty of discrimination, it has forfeited the right to take industry and the labor unions to task for the same discrimination.

Audience

The audience for Randolph's "Call to Negro America to March on Washington for Jobs and Equal Participation in National Defense" was clear. The document was addressed to African Americans, in particular African American workers, urging them to participate in a march on Washington, D.C., to demand equality in the defense industries and in the military. Clearly, too, the audience for the document was the federal government, in particular, President Franklin Roosevelt, as part of a campaign to pressure him to take steps to end segregation in the defense industries and in the military. Roosevelt heard the message: Just a month after the document appeared in *Black Worker* (a journal Randolph founded and that was in essence a continuation of the earlier journal *The Messenger*), the president agreed to meet with Randolph to discuss the proposed march on Washington.

Impact

Randolph's "Call to Negro America to March on Washington for Jobs and Equal Participation in National Defense," in combination with the creation of March on Washington Movement committees formed in various cities to organize the proposed march, had a significant impact. President Roosevelt, with his wife, Eleanor Roosevelt, was

Essential Quotes

"While billions of the taxpayers' money are being spent for war weapons, Negro workers are finally being turned away from the gates of factories, mines and mills—being flatly told, 'Nothing Doing.'"

"With faith and confidence of the Negro people in their own power for self-liberation, Negroes can break down the barriers of discrimination against employment in National Defense."

"We propose that ten thousand Negroes MARCH ON WASHINGTON FOR JOBS IN NATIONAL DEFENSE AND EQUAL INTEGRATION IN THE FIGHTING FORCES OF THE UNITED STATES."

"But if American democracy will not defend its defenders; if American democracy will not protect its protectors; if American democracy will not give jobs to its toilers because of race or color; if American democracy will not insure equality of opportunity, freedom and justice to its citizens, black and white, it is a hollow mockery and belies the principles for which it is supposed to stand."

troubled by the prospect of large numbers of protesters descending on the capital, and they tried to persuade black leaders to cancel the event. Randolph, however, remained firm, so the president decided to meet with him.

The meeting took place on June 18, 1941, with the proposed march scheduled for July 1. Roosevelt was unable to persuade Randolph to back down and realized that the only way he could forestall the march was to issue an order that Randolph and the black leadership would find acceptable. Roosevelt had resisted such civil rights initiatives, including backing any bill against lynching, because he did not want to alienate southern Democrats, who formed a significant part of his political base. Motivated, perhaps, by a combination of the justice of the cause, the need for labor as the country prepared for war, and the fact that, having just been elected to a third term, he did not have to be concerned about appeasing his political base, Roosevelt acceded. On June 25, 1941, he issued Executive Order 8802, which stated: "As a prerequisite to the successful conduct of our national defense production effort, I do hereby reaffirm the policy of the United States that there shall be no discrimination in the employment of workers in defense industries or government because of race, creed, color, or national origin." To implement the order, Roosevelt created the Fair Employment Practices Commission (FEPC).

In response to Roosevelt's pledge to issue the order, Randolph and his associates did, in fact, cancel the march. Randolph was the target of considerable criticism for doing so, for the executive order failed to desegregate the military, so some black activists accused Randolph of selling out. Nonetheless, Randolph recognized that Roosevelt had taken a significant step, at potentially great political cost to himself, in civil rights. Accordingly, he saved the issue of desegregating the military for another day.

Still, the FEPC lacked teeth. Both the staff and the agency's annual budget were small, and the agency did not have the authority to subpoena, fine, or jail those who ignored its directives. Further, it could not regulate the hiring procedures of private employers or the membership practices of labor unions. To remedy these weaknesses, Roosevelt announced on July 30, 1942, that the War Manpower Commission would take over the administration of the FEPC. This move, however, made matters worse, for the commission's head, the former Indiana governor Paul V. McNutt, had little sympathy for the FEPC, cut its budget, and generally impeded its efforts. After the resignation of three key members of the FEPC's staff, the agency's future looked grim, prompting Randolph to revive the March on Washington Movement. President Roosevelt once again bowed to pressure and on May 27, 1943, issued Executive Order 9346, strengthening and reorganizing the FEPC and placing it under the direction of Monsignor Francis J. Hass, a Catholic priest. Within months, the agency had set up nine regional offices and three satellite offices.

Scholars continue to debate the question of whether the FEPC was effective. Some argue that whatever gains black workers made would have occurred without the FEPC, for the pressure of war created a manpower shortage in industry that would have provided jobs for African Americans. Others argue that were it not for the FEPC, gains would not have been made in such industries as utilities, shipbuilding, steel mills, and public transportation. The facts, though, are indisputable. Between 1941 and 1945, 1.5 million minority workers gained employment in the defense industries; after 1942 the share of African Americans who held jobs in the defense industries more than tripled and by 1944 had risen from 2.5 percent to 8.3 percent. Additionally, another two hundred thousand to three hundred thousand minorities were employed by the federal government.

The final item on Randolph's agenda was desegregation of the military. In 1947 Randolph founded the Committee against Jim Crow in Military Service and Training. He and other black American leaders threatened to urge black workers to go on strike, which would have exacerbated the economic disruptions caused by the nation's conversion to a peacetime economy. Moreover, the widespread destruction of World War II, with the denial of human rights by Nazi Germany and the expansionist Japanese empire, focused attention on human rights throughout the world. African American soldiers who continued to serve in Europe in the years after the war found greater acceptance there, and they demanded this same acceptance from white American society. In this climate, Roosevelt's successor, President Harry Truman, created the President's Commission on Civil Rights. In 1947 the commission issued its final report, *To Secure These Rights*, recommending specific ways to protect the civil rights of African Americans and other minority groups. Truman faced resistance, particularly from southern senators, so he took the issue of civil rights into his own hands. On July 26, 1948, he issued Executive Order 9981, which desegregated the U.S. military. Although the military services initially resisted his order (believing they were already in compliance with earlier directives), eventually they complied, and in 1954 the U.S. Department of Defense was able to announce that the last racially segregated armed forces unit had been abolished. The second major goal of Randolph's "Call to Negro America" was finally realized.

See also *To Secure These Rights* (1947); Executive Order 9981 (1948); Martin Luther King, Jr.: "I Have a Dream" (1963).

Further Reading

■ Articles
Barnhill, J. Herschel. "Civil Rights in the 1940s." *Negro History Bulletin* 45, no. 1 (January–March 1982): 21–22.

■ Books
Anderson, Jervis. *A. Philip Randolph: A Biographical Portrait*. Berkeley: University of California Press, 1986.

Garfinkel, Herbert. *When Negroes March: The March on Washington Movement in the Organizational Politics for FEPC*. New York: Atheneum, 1969.

Questions for Further Study

1. What impact did the advent of World War II have on the U.S. economy?

2. What impact, if any, did the labor union movement have on African Americans in the 1930s and early 1940s?

3. Randolph's march on Washington never took place. Does this mean that his "call" was unsuccessful? Why or why not?

4. Randolph's article is in no sense a sober, academic-sounding call to the African American community. What rhetorical devices did Randolph use to spur African Americans to action? To what extent do you believe that Randolph's early career as an actor may have contributed to his writing style?

5. Randolph wrote that "we believe in national unity which recognizes equal opportunity of black and white citizens." Compare this document with William Pickens's "The Kind of Democracy the Negro Expects" (1918). To what extent do the two writers make similar arguments, each in the context of world war?

Harris, William H. *The Harder We Run: Black Workers since the Civil War*. New York: Oxford University Press, 1982.

Kersten, Andrew E. *A. Philip Randolph: A Life in the Vanguard*. Lanham, Md.: Rowman and Littlefield, 2007.

Miller, Calvin Craig. *A. Philip Randolph and the African American Labor Movement*. Greensboro, N.C.: Morgan Reynolds, 2005.

Pfeffer, Paula F. *A. Philip Randolph, Pioneer of the Civil Rights Movement*. Baton Rouge: Louisiana State University Press, 1996.

Sternsher, Bernard, ed. *The Negro in Depression and War: Prelude to Revolution, 1930–1945*. Chicago, Ill.: Quadrangle Books, 1969.

Taylor, Cynthia. *A. Philip Randolph: The Religious Journey of an African American Labor Leader*. New York: New York University Press, 2006.

Wolters, Raymond. *Negroes and the Great Depression: The Problem of Economic Recovery*. Westport, Conn.: Greenwood Press, 1970.

Wright, Sarah E. *A. Philip Randolph: Integration in the Workplace*. Englewood Cliffs, N.J.: Silver Burdett Press, 1990.

■ Web Sites

Chenoweth, Karin. "Taking Jim Crow Out of Uniform: A. Philip Randolph and the Desegregation of the U.S. Military: Special Report: The Integrated Military—50 Years." *Black Issues in Higher Education* Web site.
http://findarticles.com/p/articles/mi_m0DXK/is_n13_v14/ai_20031732.

"Executive Order 8802." TeachingAmericanHistory.org.
http://teachingamericanhistory.org/library/index.asp?document=547.

Randolph, A. Philip. "'The March on Washington Movement': Address to the Policy Conference of the March on Washington Movement, Detroit, Michigan, September 26, 1942." University of Maryland Web site.
http://www.bsos.umd.edu/aasp/chateauvert/mowmcall.htm.

—Michael J. O'Neal

A. Philip Randolph's "Call to Negro America to March on Washington"

We call upon you to fight for jobs in National Defense.

We call upon you to struggle for the integration of Negroes in the armed forces....

We call upon you to demonstrate for the abolition of Jim-Crowism in all Government departments and defense employment.

This is an hour of crisis. It is a crisis of democracy. It is a crisis of minority groups. It is a crisis of Negro Americans.

What is this crisis?

To American Negroes, it is the denial of jobs in Government defense projects. It is racial discrimination in Government departments. It is widespread Jim-Crowism in the armed forces of the Nation.

While billions of the taxpayers' money are being spent for war weapons, Negro workers are finally being turned away from the gates of factories, mines and mills—being flatly told, "Nothing Doing." Some employers refuse to give Negroes jobs when they are without "union cards," and some unions refuse Negro workers union cards when they are "without jobs."

What shall we do?
What a dilemma!
What a runaround!
What a disgrace!
What a blow below the belt!

Though dark, doubtful and discouraging, all is not lost, all is not hopeless. Though battered and bruised, we are not beaten, broken, or bewildered.

Verily, the Negroes' deepest disappointments and direst defeats, their tragic trials and outrageous oppressions in these dreadful days of destruction and disaster to democracy and freedom, and the rights of minority peoples, and the dignity and independence of the human spirit, is the Negroes' greatest opportunity to rise to the highest heights of struggle for freedom and justice in Government, in industry, in labor unions, education, social service, religion, and culture.

With faith and confidence of the Negro people in their own power for self-liberation, Negroes can break down the barriers of discrimination against employment in National Defense. Negroes can kill the deadly serpent of race hatred in the Army, Navy, Air and Marine Corps, and smash through and blast the Government, business and labor-union red tape to win the right to equal opportunity in vocational training and re-training in defense employment.

Most important and vital of all, Negroes, by the mobilization and coordination of their mass power, can cause President Roosevelt to Issue an Executive Order Abolishing Discriminations in All Government Department, Army, Navy, Air Corps and National Defense Jobs.

Of course, the task is not easy. In very truth, it is big, tremendous and difficult.

It will cost money.

It will require sacrifice.

It will tax the Negroes' courage, determination and will to struggle. But we can, must and will triumph.

The Negroes' stake in national defense is big. It consists of jobs, thousands of jobs. It may represent millions, yes, hundreds of millions of dollars in wages. It consists of new industrial opportunities and hope. This is worth fighting for.

But to win our stakes, it will require an "all-out," bold and total effort and demonstration of colossal proportions.

Negroes can build a mammoth machine of mass action with a terrific and tremendous driving and striking power that can shatter and crush the evil fortress of race prejudice and hate, if they will only resolve to do so and never stop, until victory comes.

Dear fellow Negro Americans, be not dismayed by these terrible times. You possess power, great power. Our problem is to harness and hitch it up for action on the broadest, daring and most gigantic scale.

In this period of power politics, nothing counts but pressure, more pressure, and still more pressure, through the tactic and strategy of broad, organized, aggressive mass action behind the vital and important issues of the Negro. To this end, we propose that ten thousand Negroes MARCH ON WASHINGTON FOR JOBS IN NATIONAL DEFENSE AND EQUAL INTEGRATION IN THE FIGHTING FORCES OF THE UNITED STATES.

An "all-out" thundering march on Washington, ending in a monster and huge demonstration at Lincoln's Monument will shake up white America.

Document Text

It will shake up official Washington.

It will give encouragement to our white friends to fight all the harder by our side, with us, for our righteous cause.

It will gain respect for the Negro people.

It will create a new sense of self-respect among Negroes.

But what of national unity?

We believe in national unity which recognizes equal opportunity of black and white citizens to jobs in national defense and the armed forces, and in all other institutions and endeavors in America. We condemn all dictatorships, Fascist, Nazi and Communist. We are loyal, patriotic Americans all.

But if American democracy will not defend its defenders; if American democracy will not protect its protectors; if American democracy will not give jobs to its toilers because of race or color; if American democracy will not insure equality of opportunity, freedom and justice to its citizens, black and white, it is a hollow mockery and belies the principles for which it is supposed to stand....

Today we call on President Roosevelt, a great humanitarian and idealist, to ... free American Negro citizens of the stigma, humiliation and insult of discrimination and Jim-Crowism in Government departments and national defense.

The Federal Government cannot with clear conscience call upon private industry and labor unions to abolish discrimination based on race and color as long as it practices discrimination itself against Negro Americans.

Glossary

Fascist — a reference to right-wing authoritarian rule at the time in such places as Italy under Benito Mussolini

Jim-Crowism — from "Jim Crow," the term commonly used to refer to laws and social systems that kept African Americans in disadvantaged positions

Morris Ernst, a member of the Committee on Civil Rights (Library of Congress)

To Secure These Rights

"The only aristocracy that is consistent with the free way of life is an aristocracy of talent and achievement."

Overview

Drafted by President Harry S. Truman's Committee on Civil Rights in 1947, *To Secure These Rights* (subtitled "The Report of the President's Committee on Civil Rights") remains one of the most important federal civil rights reports in United States history. Issued on the heels of World War II, *To Secure These Rights* identified remarkable disparities in racial treatment in both the North and the South and called for a series of measures to improve race relations in the United States. Among them were police professionalization, federal protection of black voting rights, enforcement of antilynching laws, and an end to segregation in schools, housing, and public accommodations.

Although President Truman refrained from addressing many of the committee's recommendations, he did order the desegregation of the armed forces in 1948 with Executive Order 9981, signaling the beginning of the federal government's push for desegregation generally. Outraged at Truman's commitment to civil rights, southerners like then governor of South Carolina Strom Thurmond abandoned the Democratic Party, formed the Dixiecrats, and initiated a realignment of America's political landscape that is still discernible today. Long before the U.S. Supreme Court's desegregation decision in *Brown v. Board of Education* (1954) or the student sit-ins of the 1960s, *To Secure These Rights* introduced a blueprint for the civil rights movement.

Context

To Secure These Rights emerged out of the immediate political context of World War II. During the war, almost one million African Americans left the South for work in military-related industries in the North and West. Once there, African Americans formed powerful political blocs in urban areas important for both state and national elections, New York, Chicago, and Detroit among them. Yet African American voters did not completely abandon the Republican Party, many still remaining loyal to the legacy of Abraham Lincoln. Eager to continue his predecessor's success at winning over black voters, Harry S. Truman made civil rights an important component of his domestic platform.

Although the Supreme Court had indicated as early as 1937 that the federal government might be constitutionally authorized to protect civil rights abuses against the states, Truman was arguably the first federal official to truly embrace such a vision. His first statement to this effect occurred during his State of the Union address before Congress on January 6, 1947, when he invoked "the will to fight" crimes against blacks and lobbied to extend "the limit of federal power to protect the civil rights of the American people." Truman reiterated this interest during an organizational meeting of the Civil Rights Committee at the White House, requesting that the committee inform him of "exactly how far" his attorney general could go in enforcing civil rights at the state and local levels.

On December 5, 1946, Truman issued Executive Order 9808, establishing a committee to investigate civil rights abuses and recommend possible solutions. Issued on the heels of World War II, Truman's order drew a direct line between civil rights and World War II. "Freedom from Fear"—one of Franklin Delano Roosevelt's Four Freedoms as articulated in January 1941 at the outset of the war—had come "under attack," Truman declared in this order, by individuals willing to "take the law into their own hands" and target African American "ex-servicemen." Of particular concern to Truman were stories of white violence against black soldiers in the American South, including the murder of a black soldier and his wife in Georgia in July 1946 and the blinding of a black sergeant in South Carolina in February of that year. Truman confronted the fallout of such events personally when the National Association for the Advancement of Colored People picketed the White House in late July and sent a delegation to confront him directly in September 1946, prompting him to write Attorney General Tom Clark immediately to request that "some sort of policy" be implemented to prevent future violence.

That Truman ultimately decided to issue an executive order was not unprecedented. Truman's predecessor, Franklin Delano Roosevelt, had also responded to pressure from the National Association for the Advancement of Colored People by issuing an executive order favoring civil rights in 1941, ultimately leading to the creation of the Fair Employment Practices Commission. Yet Roosevelt's decision shared the support of organized labor, muting its potentially radical, racial effect.

Time Line

1939
- **September 1**
  Germany invades Poland.

1941
- **June 25**
  Executive Order 8802 prohibits racial discrimination in government contracts.

1945
- World War II ends, and the Nazi Holocaust is made public.

1946
- **December 5**
  Harry S. Truman establishes the federal Committee on Civil Rights.

1947
- **October 29**
  The Committee on Civil Rights issues the report *To Secure These Rights*.

1948
- **July 14**
  The Democratic National Convention adopts Truman's civil rights plank, and southern delegates walk out.
- **July 15**
  Truman accepts the Democratic nomination for the presidency.
- **July 17**
  The States' Rights Party, or "Dixiecrats," hold a separate convention in Birmingham, Alabama.
- **July 26**
  Truman issues Executive Order 9981, desegregating the armed forces.

1954
- **May 17**
  The U.S. Supreme Court decides the case *Brown v. Board of Education*.

1960
- **February 1**
  Sit-ins begin in Greensboro, North Carolina.

Truman faced more complex problems. Suffering low approval ratings in the polls, he risked losing even more support by coming out in favor of black rights, particularly among powerful southern contingents in the Senate and House of Representatives. However, he also confronted an embarrassing string of democratic losses in the congressional elections of 1946, alerting him to the possible abandonment of the Democratic Party by black voters in the North. Eager to assuage blacks without forcing an open confrontation with southern whites, Truman followed Roosevelt's use of the executive order, a move that could be funded out of his own discretionary accounts independent of congressional approval. To build public support for such an initiative, Truman warned of an impending wave of racial hysteria akin to that which followed World War I "when organized groups fanned hatred and intolerance," as he put it in his instructions to the civil rights committee. Incidentally, one such organized group, the Ku Klux Klan, had become particularly repugnant to Truman, smearing him as a Jew (which he was not) during his race for county judge in 1922.

Global concerns also haunted Truman's thoughts in late 1946, possibly pushing him to align America's domestic treatment of minorities with its foreign policy. For example, he expressed open support for his predecessor's emphasis on the Four Freedoms (freedom of speech and expression, freedom of religion, freedom from want, and freedom from fear) and embraced America's new role as leader of the free world. Indeed, Truman hosted former British Prime Minister Winston Churchill in Fulton, Missouri, on March 5, 1946, applauding as Churchill delivered a rousing alarm that the Soviet Union had erected an "iron curtain" across Europe threatening "freedom and democracy" the world over. Exactly one year later, Truman articulated his bold, interventionist policy of containment, the now famous Truman Doctrine. Although the Truman Doctrine did not have an overt tie to civil rights, Truman did realize that at least part of America's struggle against the Soviet Union and China was ideological and that glaring examples of persistent, state-sanctioned racism undermined America's cold war image. Truman also rankled at the irony of black soldiers being ordered to fight racism in Nazi Germany, only to then suffer domestic abuses once they returned home, an eventuality that pressed him to establish a federal committee dedicated to investigating civil rights.

About the Author

A committee of fifteen prominent citizens drafted *To Secure These Rights*. Hoping for balance, Truman appointed two women, two southerners, two business leaders, and two labor leaders. General Electric president Charles E. Wilson agreed to chair, while Rabbi Roland B. Gittelsohn, Catholic bishop Francis J. Haas, Episcopal bishop Henry Knox Sherrill, and Methodist official M. E. Tilley provided religious diversity. Labor's representatives included Boris Shishkin of the American Federation of Labor, and James B. Carey of the Congress of Industrial Organizations. University of North Carolina president Frank P. Graham and Dartmouth president John S. Dickey provided an academic aspect, while Morris L. Ernst, Francis P. Matthews, Franklin D. Roosevelt, Jr., and Dr. Channing H. Tobias represented the public and nonprofit sectors. Perhaps most notably, the civil rights lawyer Sadie Tanner Alexander was the committee's only African American.

Alexander wrote Truman on December 9, 1946, that the committee's work was "the greatest venture in the protection of civil liberty officially undertaken by the government since reconstruction." Holding a PhD in economics, Alexander had served on the board of directors of the National Urban League, worked with National Council of Negro Women president Mary McLeod Bethune, and practiced law in Philadelphia. Her presence went far toward establishing the committee's credibility in civil rights circles.

Explanation and Analysis of the Document

With Truman's blessing, the committee decided not simply to focus on the most "flagrant outrages" against minorities but to look more "broadly" at civil rights generally. To aid its inquiry, the fifteen-person group devised four baseline questions, each of which warranted its own, individual section in the body's final report. The questions were these: "What is the historic civil rights goal of the American people?" "In what ways does our present record fall short of the goal?" "What is government's responsibility for the achievement of the goal?" "What further steps does the nation now need to take to reach this goal?"

Conceding that the term *civil rights* "has with great wisdom been used flexibly in American history," the committee dedicated its first section to identifying which rights, precisely, needed to be secured. In so doing, it went a long way toward framing the civil rights debate for decades to come, drawing not simply from the Bill of Rights but also from the Declaration of Independence, President Roosevelt's Four Freedoms, and its own conceptions of what the federal government should protect. Out of this democratic assortment of legal and nonlegal sources, the committee identified four primary rights: "the right to safety and security of the person," "the right to citizenship and its privileges," "the right to freedom of conscience and expression," and, perhaps most notably, "the right to equality of opportunity."

On the first, the committee noted that freedom was meaningless so long as citizens were subject to "bondage, lawless violence, and arbitrary arrest and punishment," warranting the need for federal protection of the "due process of law" against any "threat of violence by private persons or mobs." At least part of this "security" right rested on firm legal footing, particularly the due process rights of the Fifth and Fourteenth amendments as well as the procedural protections of the Fourth, Sixth, and Eighth amendments—though they had yet to be incorporated to the states. However, the committee's concern for mob violence indicated a departure from written law, especially the Constitution's focus on state actors. Even the Fourteenth Amendment, for example, did not protect citizens from abuses by "private persons" and "mobs," a point made clear by the Supreme Court in *United States v. Cruikshank* in 1876. The committee's rejection of this opinion would be one of several remarkable innovations in the conception of rights that it devised.

The second innovation that the committee devised emerged in tandem with its second right: the "right to citizenship and its privileges." Clearly based on the Fourteenth Amendment, the right to citizenship adhered to "every mature and responsible person," who in turn deserved "an equal voice in his government." With an eye to disfranchisement in the South, the committee noted that participation in the political process could not be limited to individuals of a particular "race, color, creed, ... or national origin." Then, in a move that went decidedly off the Fourteenth Amendment, the committee included the right to military combat as a core civil right, noting that all citizens "must enjoy the right to serve the nation and the cause of freedom in time of war." Those who did not enjoy such a right, noted the committee in an allusion to the Supreme Court's infamous 1896 decision in *Plessy v. Ferguson*, suffered a "badge of inferiority." Precisely because *Plessy* sanctioned racial segregation, not combat service, the committee's invocation of a right to combat played fast and loose with legal doctrine, essentially creating a new civil right out of whole cloth. Even the most militia-friendly reading of the Second Amendment, which was arguably the only constitutional protection applicable to military service, did not indicate that citizens had the constitutional right to join a militia.

Third on the committee's list of vital rights was the "right to freedom of conscience and expression," perhaps the only right firmly grounded in legal doctrine. Paraphrasing the First Amendment, the committee denounced the suppression of private "arguments, viewpoints, or opinions" meanwhile recognizing Oliver Wendell Holmes's "clear and present danger" qualification as articulated in *Schenck v. United States* (1919). "Complete religious liberty" also struck the committee as a central right, except when "pleaded as an excuse for criminal or clearly anti-social conduct."

If the committee's third right was the most doctrinaire, then its final right proved to be its most unmoored. Abandoning both written and unwritten law, the committee called for federal protection of "the right to equality of opportunity." Observing that it was "not enough" that citizens were guaranteed political participation, the committee also judged the federal government responsible for providing citizens with the "right to enjoy the benefits of society." This included the right to "obtain useful employment" as well as the right to "have access to services in the fields of education, housing, health, recreation and transportation" independent of "race, color, creed, and national origin." While the eradication of racial and national animus anticipated the Supreme Court's equal protection jurisprudence in the 1950s, the committee's interest in equality of opportunity marked a relatively radical departure from anything mentioned in the Constitution or subsequent Supreme Court jurisprudence. Even *Plessy v. Ferguson*, which held that separate public accommodations like streetcars needed to be equal, did not provide any indication that such equality extended to opportunity. Nor did Thomas Jefferson's invocation of the right to "life, liberty, and the pursuit of happiness" in the Declaration of Independence necessarily mean that the government was obligated to provide equal access to private employment. Here, the committee's work truly forged new ground, setting the stage not only for the establishment of the Equal Employment Opportunity Commission in 1965 but also for the Age Discrimination in Employment Act of 1967, the Rehabilitation Act of 1973, and the Americans with Disabilities Act of 1990.

Prescient in scope, the committee also proved persuasive in fact, as illustrated in the second section of its report, titled "The Condition of Our Rights," which built the case for unprecedented federal intervention in state affairs by recounting a parade of shocking abuses at the local level, many in the South. Included in the first part of this section were shocking depictions of lynchings coupled with the observation that "communities in which lynchings occur tend to condone the crime." Also in this section are discussions of police brutality, "unwarranted arrests, unduly prolonged detention[s] before arraignment, and abuse[s] of the search and seizure power," all recognizable targets of the Warren Court over a decade later. Recognizing the close ties between police and local majorities, the committee identified one of the core issues that would come to plague police departments for the next half century, namely the plight of "unpopular racial or religious minorities" in the face of "prejudices of the region or of dominant local groups."

Perhaps even more problematic were lapses in the administration of justice. Again focusing on the South, the committee found shocking evidence of confessions resulting from torture; incompetent, even nonexistent counsel; and use of the "fee system" by which judges were paid based on the number of "fines levied." Exacerbating such travesties were even more alarming cases of forced labor, both against employees who owed debts and prisoners who endured false convictions only to be hired out by sheriffs to "local entrepreneurs."

As the committee unearthed clear infringements on the "right to security," so too did it uncover alarming violations of the right to citizenship, many leveled at Asian immigrants on the West Coast and African Americans in the South. In states like California, for example, natives of Japan and Korea were "forbidden an opportunity to attain citizenship status" and also barred from owning land. Meanwhile, blacks in the American South confronted myriad "qualifications" standards, among them requests to read and interpret the Constitution, pay exorbitant poll taxes, and even endure outright physical violence.

Convinced that combat duty was also a right of citizenship, the committee exposed numerous discrepancies in the treatment of white and black soldiers. Enrollment in officer candidate schools for all four branches was generally restricted to whites; meanwhile, "cooks, stewards, and steward's mates," tended overwhelmingly to be black. Further, the armed forces enjoyed relatively little success in eliminating discrimination from admission to the military academies, further ensuring that blacks did not occupy positions of rank in the armed forces.

As for the right to freedom of conscience and expression, the committee did not focus on race so much as political affiliation, particularly individuals suspected of being Communists. Conceding that Communists were "hostile to the American heritage of freedom and equality," the committee still opposed "any attempt to impose special limitations on the rights of these people to speak and assemble." Predicting the national backlash against Senator Joseph McCarthy (who led a Senate investigation of supposed Communist infiltration of government) almost a decade later, the committee observed that "public excitement about 'Communists'" exceeded both "good judgment" and "calmness."

Finally, the committee considered the right to equal opportunity in employment, schools, housing, and health care. Noting that World War II had actually triggered a "marked advance both in hiring policies and in the removal of on-the-job discriminatory practices," the committee still recognized that discrepancies remained. Particularly vulnerable were "minority group members," including African Americans, Mexicans, and Jews. To illustrate, the committee cited a 1946 survey of private employment agencies in over one hundred major cities, concluding that "89 percent" of the agencies polled "included questions covering religion on their registration forms." In Chicago alone, "60 percent of the executive jobs" and "50 percent of the sales executive jobs" were closed to Jews.

African Americans also tended to suffer considerable employment discrimination. A poll of government employees indicated that while whites tended to enjoy a promotion once every two years, African Americans could expect to be promoted once every fourteen years. Even greater obstacles existed to union membership as organized labor proved less willing to end discrimination than "private industry." Despite such disparities, however, only six states boasted "laws directed against discrimination in private employment."

Perhaps surprisingly, discrimination in schools occupied a relatively small portion of the committee's findings, even though it did focus those findings on the South. Stating that the South boasted only "one-fifth of the taxpaying wealth of the nation," the committee framed the region's decision to "maintain two sets of public schools, one for whites and one for Negroes," economic folly. Exacerbating this folly was the unconscionable "difference in quality" between schools for whites and schools for blacks, black schools suffering significantly lower rates of "expenditure per pupil, teachers' salaries, the number of pupils per teacher, transportation of students, adequacy of school buildings and educational equipment, length of school term," and "extent of curriculum." Yet, despite the region's "considerable progress in the last decade in narrowing the gap" between white and black schools, the committee doubted that the South could ever achieve true parity without "federal financial assistance."

Although the committee was dubious of southern commitment to funding black schools, it did not make the argument that the National Association for the Advancement of Colored People would eventually make in *Brown v. Board of Education*, namely, that segregated schools were inherently discriminatory because they negatively affected the psychological development of African American children. The absence of such a critique indicates that even as late as 1947 school integration was not viewed in quite the same way as it was in 1954 and may, in fact, have been less important than the problem of disparate funding.

By contrast, the committee successfully foreshadowed Supreme Court jurisprudence in the realm of housing, targeting the restrictive covenant as an impermissible means of discrimination against minorities, including "Armenians, Jews, Negroes, Mexicans, Syrians, Japanese, Chinese and Indians." Noting that such covenants were essentially private, the committee nevertheless documented their remarkable affect on America's urban landscape, noting that the "amount of land covered by racial restrictions in Chicago has been estimated at 80 percent." Identifying covenants as a handmaiden of the ghetto, the committee advanced what was at that point a relatively novel interpretation of state action, remarking that deed restrictions could be enforced only by "obtaining court orders," thereby making covenants a kind of state action precisely because they placed "the power of the state behind the enforcement of the private agreement." Knowing full well that recasting legally enforceable private agreements—essentially contracts—as state action boasted little precedent in American law, the committee cited a Canadian court ruling to defend its position, marking yet another innovative act of rights creation.

Perhaps the most stunning act of rights creation engaged in by the committee emerged in the realm of health care, where the committee identified a "right to health service." Well aware that no doctrinal support existed for such a right, the committee simply cited data indicating "discrepancies between the health of the majority and the minorities," caused by factors such as "crowded, dirty" living conditions; segregated health facilities; and a lack of minority health care professionals. "In 1937" alone, said the committee, "only 35 percent of southern Negro babies were delivered by doctors, as compared to 90 percent of northern babies of both races." Further, black life expectancies were considerably lower than those for whites, with black males and females expecting to live fifty-two and fifty-five years, respectively, while their white counterparts expected to live at least a decade longer. Part of the explanation for these disparities, continued the committee, was "the discriminatory policy of our medical schools in admitting minority students" as well as the "refusal of some medical societies to admit Negro physicians."

Audience

The primary audience for *To Secure These Rights* was the black community, particularly that portion of the community living in the urban North. There, African Americans found

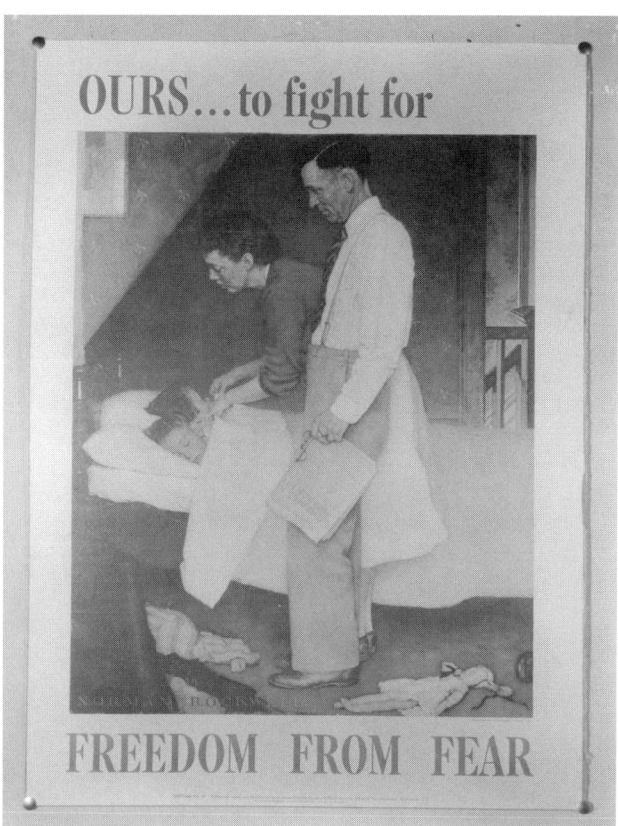

One of a set of posters of the Four Freedoms by Norman Rockwell: Freedom from Fear (Library of Congress)

themselves numerous enough to tip the scales in favor of Democrats or Republicans in state and national elections. Afraid that blacks might return to the Republican Party after supporting Democrats during the New Deal, Truman viewed his platform on civil rights to be vital to consolidating the Democratic Party's liberal, New Deal coalition.

Truman also recognized that America's racial politics possessed an international component. Acutely conscious of the need to cobble together a political rationale for containment, Truman continued President Woodrow Wilson's emphasis on ideals, even to the point of justifying the cold war as a struggle not simply for resources or territorial control but also for much more abstract concepts like liberty and democracy. White recriminations against African American soldiers returning home from the war shocked Truman, alerting him to the need for measures aimed at improving America's international reputation for democracy and freedom.

Impact

With a right to health care providing the best example, the committee's enumeration of what civil rights, precisely, needed to be secured amounted to nothing less than a dramatic act of rights prioritization, if not outright creation. Ignoring traditional rights like freedom of contract and

Essential Quotes

> "The only aristocracy that is consistent with the free way of life is an aristocracy of talent and achievement."
>
> ("The Ideal of Freedom and Equality")

> "It is not enough that full and equal membership in society entitles the individual to an equal voice in the control of his government; it must also give him the right to enjoy the benefits of society."
>
> ("The Ideal of Freedom and Equality")

> "Vital to the integrity of the individual and to the stability of a democratic society is the right of each individual to physical freedom, to security against illegal violence, and to fair, orderly legal process."
>
> ("The Ideal of Freedom and Equality")

---

property, the committee did much to set the agenda for the modern civil rights movement, establishing equality of access to the political process, equality of opportunity in employment, and procedural due process protections against police as central to America's post–World War II constitutional project. Further, the committee expanded the reach of the Constitution to protect citizens against discriminatory private actions, particularly in the housing context, prefiguring the Supreme Court's turn against restrictive covenants in *Shelley v. Kraemer* in 1948.

Perhaps the most interesting aspect of the committee's report was its treatment of racial segregation. Initially reluctant to claim that segregated schools harmed black children, the committee revisited the topic in a separate section, flagging Jim Crow as a "complex" system that attempted to recognize African Americans as "citizens" but ultimately branded them as inferior beings not fit to associate with white people. Although the report had little substantive impact on schools, it did the important work of publicly stating that segregation had, in fact, evolved into a complex structure of discrimination. Moreover, evidence that the abolition of such a system would not lead to interracial violence emerged in army units during World War II, where white soldiers who found themselves fighting side by side with blacks indicated that their feelings toward their black colleagues had changed after serving with them in combat. Such findings led Truman to desegregate the armed forces with confidence in 1948.

Based on its observations of the evils of Jim Crow, coupled with its discovery of rampant racial discrimination in the realms of health care, employment, voting, and criminal justice, the committee concluded that the "Government of the United States" needed to lead the effort of safeguarding the civil rights of all Americans, even those who were harmed by "private persons or groups." Traditional conceptions of states' rights factored negligibly, if at all, in the committee's solution, which counseled in favor of encouraging "the local community" to "set its own house in order." Animating such a move was a sense that isolated lynchings did not affect simply local norms but also the entire nation, potentially even echoing "from one end of the globe to the other." Indeed, America's foreign policy objectives could be jeopardized unless it brought racial transgressors to heel, since "an American diplomat cannot forcefully argue for free elections in foreign lands without meeting the challenge that in many sections of America qualified voters do not have free access to the polls." Here was a direct link between American foreign policy and domestic civil rights, almost a decade before *Brown*. Here, too, was an indication that despite its awareness that "the American people are loyal to the institutions of local government," foreign affairs warranted a larger role for the federal government in protecting citizens from both public and private abuses.

In the final section of its report, the committee set forth recommendations for how each of its enumerated rights might be secured, beginning with the overarching need to professionalize state and local law enforcement, expand the scope and reach of the Civil Rights Section of the Department of Justice, and establish a special unit within the Federal Bureau of Investigation to investigate civil rights abuses. Once such institutional needs were met, the committee went on to propose that the right to security be bolstered by the enactment of a congressional antilynching act, the right to citizenship be reinforced by legislation ending poll taxes, and the right to equality of opportunity be encouraged by the "elimination of segregation." Although other recommendations were issued as well, this last suggestion was perhaps the committee's boldest—one that included no precise directives on how Jim Crow was, in fact, to be abolished. Perhaps the only indication that the committee made of a possible solution was its mention of money, noting that "federal aid to the states for education, health, research, and other public benefits should be granted provided that the states do not discriminate." Rather than wait for courts to get involved, the committee recommended that "independent administrative commissions" be created to "consider complaints and hold hearings to review them."

Although federal commissions like the Equal Employment Opportunity Commission would not be created until 1965, the committee essentially identified all of the major fronts upon which the civil rights battles of the 1950s and 1960s would be fought. Indeed, it might even be said that even though few of the committee's recommendations were enacted into law immediately, the report nevertheless succeeded in framing the core issues of the civil rights movement. For black civil rights activists like Walter White, *To Secure These Rights* represented "the most courageous and specific document of its kind in American history."

Not surprisingly, the report triggered a backlash in the South. Newspapers protested, state officials balked, and angry letters poured into the White House, yet Truman remained undeterred. Inspired by his committee's findings, the president made it a point to emphasize the need for federal leadership on civil rights during his State of the Union Address on January 7, 1948. "Our first goal," announced Truman, "is to secure fully the essential human rights of our citizens." Less than a month later, Truman reiterated this point, remarking that "all men are created equal" and that "basic civil rights" were the "source and the support of our democracy." To support this point, he introduced into Congress a ten-point proposal that included the creation of a permanent Commission on Civil Rights, increased support for "existing civil rights statutes," "federal protection against lynching," and heightened protections of "the right to vote."

Enraged, southern delegates to the Democratic National Convention in July 1948 bolted from the party only two days after Truman won the Democratic nomination, forming their own "Dixiecrat" bloc. This schism would fundamentally alter the course of Democratic politics in America, robbing the Democrats of their most conservative element and ultimately leading many of their once loyal southerners into the hands of the Republican Party in protest in the 1970s and 1980s. In the meantime, Truman forged ahead, desegregating both the federal government and the armed forces and setting in motion forces of racial progress that would build through the end of the twentieth century. Although the report was often eclipsed by more sensational flashpoints like *Brown v. Board of Education* and the 1964 Civil Rights Act, *To Secure These Rights* not only set the tone for racial reform in the post–World War II era but also framed the terms upon which that reform would take place.

See also Fourteenth Amendment to the U.S. Constitution (1868); *United States v. Cruikshank* (1876); *Plessy v. Ferguson* (1896); Executive Order 9981 (1948); *Brown v. Board of Education* (1954); Civil Rights Act of 1964.

Questions for Further Study

1. In what ways can *To Secure These Rights* be considered a "blueprint" for the civil rights movement in the 1950s and 1960s?

2. What impact did the Great Depression, World War II, and the cold war have on the issue of civil rights during the 1940s and beyond?

3. Examine this document in light of the events surrounding A. Philip Randolph's "Call to Negro America to March on Washington" in 1941. To what extent did the later document embody views that Randolph and others expressed at that time?

4. Refer to the events surrounding the U.S. Supreme Court's decision in *Sweatt v. Painter*, issued in 1950. To what extent did the executive branch under President Harry Truman and the judicial branch led by the Supreme Court work hand in hand to dismantle segregation during this period?

5. What impact did *To Secure These Rights* have on the U.S. political landscape?

Further Reading

■ Articles

Billington, Monroe. "Civil Rights, President Truman and the South." *Journal of Negro History* 58, no. 2 (April 1973): 127–139.

Fredrickson, Kari. "'The Slowest State' and 'Most Backward Community': Racial Violence in South Carolina and Federal Civil-Rights Legislation, 1946–1948." *South Carolina History Magazine* 98, no. 2 (1997) 177–202.

■ Books

Gardner, Michael R. *Harry Truman and Civil Rights: Moral Courage and Political Risks.* Carbondale: Southern Illinois University Press, 2002.

McCullough, David. *Truman.* New York: Simon & Schuster, 1992.

Spalding, Elizabeth Edwards. *The First Cold Warrior: Harry Truman, Containment, and the Remaking of Liberal Internationalism.* Lexington: University Press of Kentucky, 2006.

■ Web Sites

"Truman and Civil Rights." Harry S. Truman Library and Museum Web site.
 http://www.trumanlibrary.org/military_deseg/civilrights.html.

—Anders Walker

TO SECURE THESE RIGHTS

The Report of the President's Committee on Civil Rights ...

Mr. President:

This is the report which we have prepared in accordance with the instructions which you gave to us in your statement and Executive Order on December 5, 1946: ...

The Committee's first task was the interpretation of its assignment. We were not asked to evaluate the extent to which civil rights have been achieved in our country. We did not, therefore, devote ourselves to the construction of a balance sheet which would properly assess the great progress which the nation has made, as well as the shortcomings in the record. Instead, we have almost exclusively focused our attention on the bad side of our record—on what might be called the civil rights frontier....

At an early point in our work we decided to define our task broadly, to go beyond the specific *flagrant* outrages to which the President referred in his statement to the Committee. We have done this because these individual instances are only reflections of deeper maladies. We believe we must cure the disease as well as treat its symptoms. Moreover, we are convinced that the term "civil rights" itself has with great *wisdom* been used flexibly in American history....

From all of this and our own discussions and deliberations we have sought answers to the following:

(1) What is the historic civil rights goal of the American people?

(2) In what ways does our present record fall short of the goal?

(3) What is government's responsibility for the achievement of the goal?

(4) What further steps does the nation now need to take to reach the goal?

Our report which follows is divided into four sections which provide our answers to these questions....

The Ideal of Freedom and Equality

The central theme of our American heritage is the importance of the individual person. From the earliest moment of our history we have believed that every human being has an essential dignity and integrity which must be respected and safeguarded. Moreover, we believe the welfare of the individual is the final goal of group life. Our American heritage further teaches that to be secure in the rights he wishes for himself, each man must be willing to respect the rights of other men. This is the conscious recognition of a basic moral principle: all men are created equal as well as free. Stemming from this principle is the obligation to build social institutions that will guarantee equality of opportunity to all men. Without this equality freedom becomes an illusion. Thus the only aristocracy that is consistent with the free way of life is an aristocracy of talent and achievement. The grounds on which our society accords respect, influence or reward to each of its citizens must be limited to the quality of his personal character and of his social contribution.

The Essential Rights

The rights essential to the citizen in a free society can be described in different words and in varying orders. The three great rights of the Declaration of Independence have just been mentioned. Another noble statement is made in the Bill of Rights of our Constitution. A more recent formulation is found in the Four Freedoms.

Four basic rights have seemed important to this Committee and have influenced its labors. We believe that each of these rights is essential to the well-being of the individual and to the progress of society.

1. The Right to Safety and Security of the Person. Freedom can exist only where the citizen is assured that his person is secure against *bondage*, lawless violence, and arbitrary arrest and punishment. Freedom from slavery in all its forms is clearly necessary if all men are to have equal opportunity to use their talents and to lead worthwhile lives. Moreover, to be free, men must be subject to discipline by society only for commission of offenses clearly defined by law and only after trial by due process of law. Where the administration of justice is discriminatory, no man can be sure of security. Where the threat of violence by private persons or mobs exists, a cruel inhibition of the sense of freedom of activity and security of the person inevitably results. Where a society permits private and arbitrary violence to be done to its members, its own integrity is inevitably corrupted. It cannot permit human beings to be imprisoned or killed in the absence of due process of law without degrading its entire fabric.

2. *The Right to Citizenship and its Privileges.* Since it is a purpose of government in a democracy to regulate the activity of each man in the interest of all men, it follows that every mature and responsible person must be able to enjoy full citizenship and have an equal voice in his government. Because the right to participate in the political process is customarily limited to citizens there can be no denial of access to citizenship based upon race, color, creed, … or national origin. Denial of citizenship for these reasons cheapens the personality of those who are confined to this inferior status and endangers the whole concept of a democratic society.

To deny qualified citizens the right to vote while others exercise it is to do violence to the principle of freedom and equality. Without the right to vote, the individual loses his voice in the group effort and is subjected to rule by a body from which he has been excluded. Likewise, the right of the individual to vote is important to the group itself. Democracy assumes that the majority is more likely as a general rule to make decisions which are wise and desirable from the point of view of the interests of the whole society than is any minority. Every time a qualified person is denied a voice in public affairs, one of the components of a potential majority is lost, and the formation of a sound public policy is endangered.

To the citizen in a democracy, freedom is a precious possession. Accordingly, all able-bodied citizens must enjoy the right to serve the nation and the *cause of freedom in time of war.* Any attempt to curb the right to fight in its defense can only lead the citizen to question the worth of the society in which he lives. A sense of frustration is created which is wholly alien to the normal emotions of a free man. In particular, any discrimination which, while imposing an obligation, prevents members of minority groups from rendering full military service in defense of their country is for them a peculiarly humiliating badge of *inferiority.* The nation also suffers a loss of manpower and is unable to marshal maximum strength at a moment when such strength is most needed.

3. *The Right to Freedom of Conscience and Expression.* In a free society there is faith in the ability of the people to make sound, rational judgments. But such judgments are possible only where the people have access to all relevant facts and to all prevailing interpretations of the facts. How can such judgments be formed on a sound basis if arguments, viewpoints, or opinions are arbitrarily suppressed? How can the concept of the marketplace of thought in which truth ultimately prevails retain its validity if the thought of certain individuals is denied the right of circulation? The Committee reaffirms our tradition that freedom of expression may be curbed by law only where the danger to the well-being of society is clear and present.

Our forefathers fought bloody wars and suffered torture and death for the right to worship God according to the varied dictates of conscience. Complete religious liberty has been accepted as an unquestioned personal freedom since our Bill of Rights was adopted. We have insisted only that religious freedom may not be pleaded as an excuse for criminal or clearly anti-social conduct.

4. *The Right to Equality of Opportunity.* It is not enough that full and equal membership in society entitles the individual to an equal voice in the control of his government; it must also give him *the right to enjoy the benefits of society* and to contribute to its progress. The opportunity of each individual to obtain useful employment, and to have access to services in the fields of education, housing, health, recreation and transportation, whether available free or at a price, must be provided with complete disregard for race, color, creed, and national origin. Without this equality of opportunity the individual is deprived of the chance to develop his potentialities and to share the fruits of society. The group also suffers through the loss of the contributions which might have been made by persons excluded from the main channels of social and economic activity.

The Condition of Our Rights

1. *The Right to Safety and Security of the Person.* Vital to the integrity of the individual and to the stability of a democratic society is the right of each individual to physical freedom, to security against illegal violence, and to fair, orderly legal process. Most Americans enjoy this right, but it is not yet secure for all. Too many of our people still live under the harrowing fear of violence or death at the hands of a mob or of brutal treatment by police officers. Many fear entanglement with the law because of the knowledge that the justice rendered in some courts

is not equal for all persons. In a few areas the freedom to move about and choose one's job is endangered by attempts to hold workers in peonage or other forms of involuntary servitude.

THE CRIME OF LYNCHING. In 1946 at least six persons in the United States were lynched by mobs. Three of them had not been charged, either by the police or anyone else, with an offense. Of the three that had been charged, one had been accused of stealing a saddle. (The real thieves were discovered after the lynching.) Another was said to have broken into a house. A third was charged with stabbing a man. All were Negroes. During the same year, mobs were prevented from lynching 22 persons, of whom 21 were Negroes, 1 white....

The communities in which lynchings occur tend to condone the crime. Punishment of lynchers is not accepted as the responsibility of state or local governments in these communities. Frequently, state officials participate in the crime, actively or passively. Federal efforts to punish the crime are resisted. Condemnation of lynching is indicated by the failure of some local law enforcement officials to make adequate efforts to break up a mob. It is further shown by failure in most cases to make any real effort to apprehend or try those guilty. If the federal government enters a case, local officials sometimes actively resist the federal investigation. Local citizens often combine to impede the effort to apprehend the criminals by convenient "loss of memory"; grand juries refuse to indict; trial juries acquit in the face of overwhelming proof of guilt....

POLICE BRUTALITY. We have reported the failure of some public officials to fulfill their most elementary duty—the protection of persons against mob violence. We must also report more widespread and varied forms of official misconduct. These include violent physical attacks by police officers on members of minority groups, the use of third degree methods to extort confessions, and brutality against prisoners. Civil rights violations of this kind are by no means universal and many law enforcement agencies have gone far in recent years toward stamping out these evils.

In various localities, scattered throughout the country, unprofessional or undisciplined police, while avoiding brutality, fail to recognize and to safeguard the civil rights of the citizenry. Insensitive to the necessary limits of police authority, untrained officers frequently overstep the bounds of their proper duties. At times this appears in unwarranted arrests, unduly prolonged detention before *arraignment*, and abuse of the search and seizure power.

Cases involving these breaches of civil rights constantly come before the courts. The frequency with which such cases arise is proof that improper police conduct is still widespread, for it must be assumed that there are many instances of the abuse of police power which do not reach the courts. Most of the victims of such abuses are ignorant, friendless persons, unaware of their rights, and without the means of challenging those who have violated those rights.

Where lawless police forces exist, their activities may impair the civil rights of any citizen. In one place the brunt of illegal police activity may fall on suspected vagrants, in another on union organizers, and in another on unpopular racial or religious minorities, such as Negroes, Mexicans, or Jehovah's Witnesses. But wherever unfettered police lawlessness exists, civil rights may be vulnerable to the prejudices of the region or of dominant local groups, and to the caprice of individual policemen. Unpopular, weak, or defenseless groups are most apt to suffer....

ADMINISTRATION OF JUSTICE. In addition to the treatment experienced by the weak and friendless person at the hands of police officers, he sometimes finds that the judicial process itself does not give him full and equal justice. This may appear in unfair and perfunctory trials, or in fines and prison sentences that are heavier than those imposed on other members of the community guilty of the same offenses.

In part, the inability of the Negro, Mexican, or Indian to obtain equal justice may be attributed to extrajudicial factors. The low income of a member of any one of these minorities may prevent him from securing *competent counsel* to defend his rights. It may prevent him from posting bail or bond to secure his release from jail during trial. It may predetermine his choice, upon conviction, of paying a fine or going to jail. But these facts should not obscure or condone the extent to which the judicial system itself is responsible for the less-than-equal justice meted out to members of certain minority groups.

The United States Supreme Court in a number of recent decisions has censured state courts for accepting evidence procured by third-degree methods, for failing to provide accused persons with adequate legal counsel, and for excluding Negroes from jury lists. For example, in one of these cases, Chambers v. Florida, the Supreme Court, in 1940, set aside the conviction by the state court of four young Negroes on the ground that it should have rejected confessions extorted from the accused by the use of third-degree methods. The Court referred to the basic principle that "all people must stand on an equality before the bar of justice in each American court." ...

The use of the fee system in many communities—where court officials are paid in whole or in part from the *fines* levied—also sometimes stimulates arbitrary arrests and encourages unjust convictions. It is the unpopular minorities again that suffer most from this system, since it is relatively easy for unscrupulous, fee-seeking officers to "railroad" such persons to jail. The existence of the fee system and the frontier conditions in certain areas of Alaska contribute to discrimination against Indians and Eskimos in the administration of justice there. The situation is such that federal officials are seriously considering a proposal made by the Governor of Alaska to appoint a public defender for those groups.

The different standards of justice which we have allowed to exist in our country have had further repercussions. In certain states, the white population can threaten and do violence to the minority member with little or no fear of legal reprisal. Minority groups are sometimes convinced that they cannot expect fair treatment from the legal machinery. Because of this belief they may harbor and protect any of their members accused of crime. Their experience does not lead them to look upon the courts as "havens of refuge" for the victims of prejudice and public excitement.

INVOLUNTARY SERVITUDE. Slavery was abolished in this country nearly a century ago, and in its traditional form has disappeared. But the temptation to force poor and defenseless persons, by one device or another, into a condition of virtual slavery, still exists. As recently as 1944, in the case of *Pollock v. Williams*, the Supreme Court struck down as a violation of the Thirteenth Amendment to the Constitution an Alabama statute which enabled employers to force employees, in debt on account of advanced wage payments, to continue to work for them under threat of criminal punishment. This is one of the more subtle devices for securing forced labor. More direct is the practice whereby sheriffs in some areas free prisoners into the custody of local *entrepreneurs* who pay fines or post bonds. The prisoners then work for their "benefactors" under threat of returning to jail. Sometimes the original charge against the prisoners is trumped up for the purpose of securing labor by this means. In still other instances persons have been held in peonage by sheer force or by threats of prosecution for debt.

2. The Right to Citizenship and Its Privileges. The status of citizenship is basic to the enjoyment of many of the rights discussed in this report. First of all one must be a citizen in order to participate fully in the political process of the United States. Only citizens of the United States are accorded the right to vote. Only citizens may hold public office....

In granting citizenship by naturalization, a democracy may establish reasonable tests of the individual alien's eligibility for citizenship. But some of the standards of eligibility in our naturalization laws have nothing to do with a person's fitness to become a citizen. These standards are based solely on race or national origins, and penalize some residents who may otherwise have all the attributes necessary for American citizenship. The largest group of American residents presently subject to this discrimination are those born in Japan. Residents of Korean origins, as well as persons born in certain other Asiatic countries and Pacific Island areas, are also denied citizenship status. Although many of these people have lived in this country for decades, will probably remain here until they die, have raised families of native-born American citizens, and are devoted to American principles, they are forbidden an opportunity to attain the citizenship status to which their children are born....

In addition to the disabilities suffered by ineligible aliens at the hands of private persons—in employment, housing, etc.—they are singled out for additional discrimination under the law. Arizona, California, Idaho, Kansas, Louisiana, Montana, New Mexico, and Oregon forbid or severely restrict land ownership by ineligible aliens....

THE RIGHT TO BEAR ARMS. Underlying the theory of compulsory wartime military service in a democratic state is the principle that every citizen, regardless of his station in life, must assist in the defense of the nation when its security is threatened. Despite the discrimination which they encounter in so many fields, minority group members have time and again met this responsibility. Moreover, since equality in military service assumes great importance as a symbol of democratic goals, minorities have regarded it not only as a duty but as a right.

Yet the record shows that the members of several minorities, fighting and dying for the survival of the nation in which they met bitter prejudice, found that there was discrimination against them even as they fell in battle. Prejudice in any area is an ugly, undemocratic phenomenon; in the armed services, where all men run the risk of death, it is particularly repugnant....

Within the services, studies made within the last year disclose that actual experience has been out of keeping with the declarations of policy on discrimination. In the Army, less than one Negro in 70 is commissioned, while there is one white officer for approximately every seven white enlisted men. In the Navy, there are only two Negro officers in a ratio of less than one to 10,000 Negro enlisted men; there are 58,571 white officers, or one for every seven enlisted whites. The Marine Corps has 7,798 officers, none of whom is a Negro, though there are 2,190 Negro enlisted men. Out of 2,981 Coast Guard officers, one is a Negro; there are 910 Negro enlisted men. The ratio of white Coast Guard commissioned to enlisted personnel is approximately one to six.

Similarly, in the enlisted grades, there is an exceedingly high concentration of Negroes in the lowest ratings, particularly in the Navy, Marine Corps, and Coast Guard. Almost 8o percent of the Negro sailors are serving as cooks, stewards, and steward's mates; less than two percent of the whites are assigned to duty in the same capacity. Almost 15 percent of all white enlisted marines are in the three highest grades; less than 2½ percent of the Negro marines fall in the same category. The disparities in the Coast Guard are similarly great. The difference in the Army is somewhat smaller, but still significant: Less than nine percent of the Negro personnel are in the first three grades, while almost 16 percent of the whites hold these ranks.

Many factors other than discrimination contribute to this result. However, it is clear that discrimination is one of the major elements which keeps the services from attaining the objectives which they have set for themselves....

3. *The Right to Freedom of Conscience and Expression* ... At the present time, in our opinion, the most immediate threat to the right to freedom of opinion and expression is indirect. It comes from efforts to deal with those few people in our midst who would destroy democracy. There are two groups whose refusal to accept and abide by the democratic process is all too clear. The first are the Communists whose counterparts in many countries have proved, by their treatment of those with whom they disagree, that their ideology does not include a belief in universal civil rights. The second are the native Fascists. Their statements and their actions—as well as those of their foreign counterparts—prove them to be equally hostile to the American heritage of freedom and equality.

It is natural and proper for good citizens to worry about the activities of these groups. Every member of this Committee shares that concern. Communists and Fascists may assert different objectives. This does not obscure the identity of the means which both are willing to use to further themselves. Both often use the words and symbols of democracy to mask their totalitarian tactics. But their concern for civil rights is always limited to themselves. Both are willing to lie about their political views when it is convenient. They feel no obligation to come before the public openly and say who they are and what they really want.

This Committee unqualifiedly opposes any attempt to impose special limitations on the rights of these people to speak and assemble. Our national past offers us two great touchstones to resolve the dilemma of maintaining the right to free expression and yet protecting our democracy against its enemies. One was offered by Jefferson in his first inaugural address: "If there be any among us who wish to dissolve the Union, or to change its republican form, let them stand undisturbed as monuments of the safety with which error of opinion may be tolerated where reason is left free to combat it." The second is the doctrine of "clear and present danger." This was laid down as a working principle by the Supreme Court in 1919 in *Schenck v. United States* in an opinion written by Justice *Holmes*. It says that no limitation of freedom of expression shall be made unless "the words are used in such circumstances and are of such a nature as to create a clear and present danger that they will bring about the substantive evils that Congress has a right to prevent." The next year in a dissenting opinion in *Schaefer v. United States* Justice Brandeis added this invaluable word of advice about the application of the doctrine: "Like many other rules for human conduct, it can be applied correctly only by the exercise of good judgment, and in the exercise of good judgment, calmness is, in time of deep feeling and on subjects which excite passion, as essential as fearlessness and honesty."

It is our feeling that the present threat to freedom of opinion grows out of the failure of some private and public persons to apply these standards. Specifically, public excitement about "Communists" has gone far beyond the dictates of the "good judgment" and "calmness" of which [justices] Holmes and Brandeis spoke. A state of near hysteria now threatens to inhibit the freedom of genuine democrats.

At the same time we are afraid that the "reason" upon which Jefferson relied to combat error is hampered by the successful effort of some totalitarians to conceal their true nature. To expect people to reject totalitarians, when we do not provide mechanisms to guarantee that essential information is available, is foolhardy. These two concerns go together. If we fall back upon hysteria and repression as our weapons against totalitarians, we will defeat ourselves. Communists want nothing more than to be lumped with freedom-loving non-Communists. This simply makes it easier for them to conceal their true nature and to allege that the term "Communist" is "meaningless." Irresponsible opportunists who make it a practice to attack every person or group with whom they disagree as "Communists" have thereby actually aided their supposed "enemies." At the same time we cannot let these abuses deter us from the legitimate exposing of real Communists and real Fascists. Moreover, the same zeal must be shown in defending our democracy against one group as against the other....

4. *The Right to Equality of Opportunity.*

THE RIGHT TO EMPLOYMENT. A man's right to an equal chance to utilize fully his skills and knowledge is essential. The meaning of a job goes far beyond the paycheck. Good workers have a pride in the organization for which they work and feel satisfaction in the jobs they are doing. A witness before a congressional committee has recently said:

> Discrimination in employment damages lives, both the bodies and the minds, of those discriminated against and those who discriminate. It blights and perverts that healthy ambition to improve one's standard of living which we like to say is peculiarly American. It generates insecurity, fear, resentment, division and tension in our society.

In private business, in government, and in labor unions, the war years saw a marked advance both in hiring policies and in the removal of on-the-job discriminatory practices. Several factors contributed to this progress. The short labor market, the sense of unity among the people, and the leadership provided by the government all helped bring about a lessening of unfair employment practices. Yet we did not eliminate discrimination in employment. The Final Report of the federal Fair Employment Practice Committee, established in 1941 by President Roosevelt to eliminate discrimination in both government and private employment related to the war effort, makes this clear.

Four out of five cases which arose during the life of the Committee, concerned Negroes. However, many other minorities have suffered from discriminatory employment practices. The FEPC reports show that eight percent of the Committee's docket involved complaints of discrimination because of creed, and 70 percent of these concerned Jews. It should be noted that FEPC jurisdiction did not extend to financial institutions and the professions, where discrimination against Jews is especially prevalent. Witnesses before this Committee, representing still other minority groups, testified as follows:

The Japanese Americans: "We know, too, what discrimination in employment is. We know what it means to be unacceptable to union membership; what it means to be the last hired and first fired; what it means to have to work harder and longer for less wages. We know these things because we have been forced to experience them."

The Mexican Americans: "We opened an employment bureau (to help Mexican Americans) in our office last year for San Antonio. We wrote to business firms throughout the city, most of whom didn't answer. We would call certain firms and say that we heard they had an opening for a person in a stock room or some other type of work; or I would go myself. But thinking I was the same in prejudice as they, they would say, 'You know we never hire Mexicans.'"

The American Indians: "As with the Negroes, Indians are employed readily when there is a shortage of labor and they can't get anyone else. When times get better, they are the first ones to be released."

Discriminatory hiring practices.—Discrimination is most acutely felt by minority group members in their inability to get a job suited to their qualifications. Exclusions of Negroes, Jews, or Mexicans in the process of hiring is effected in various ways—by newspaper advertisements requesting only whites or gentiles to apply, by registration or application blanks on which a space is reserved for "race" or "religion," by discriminatory job orders placed with employment agencies, or by the arbitrary policy of a company official in charge of hiring.

A survey conducted by the United States Employment Service and contained in the Final Report of the Fair Employment Practice Committee reveals that of the total job orders received by USES offices in 11 selected areas during the period of February 1–15, 1946, 24 percent of the orders were discriminatory. Of 38,195 orders received, 9,171 included specifications with regard to race, citizenship, religion, or some combination of these factors.

The National Community Relations Advisory Council has studied hiring practices since V-J Day. A 1946 survey of the practices of 134 private employment agencies in 10 cities (Boston, Chicago, Cincinnati, Cleveland, Detroit, Kansas City, Milwaukee, Philadelphia, St. Louis, and San Francisco) disclosed that 89 percent of these agencies included questions covering religion on their registration forms. In Chicago, a statistical count of discriminatory job orders was made by one of the largest commercial agencies in the city. This revealed that 60 percent of the executive jobs, 50 percent of the sales executive jobs, and 41 percent of the male clerical openings, and 24 percent of the female clerical openings were closed to Jews. Fully 83 percent of all orders placed with the agency carried discriminatory specifications. A companion study of help-wanted ads conducted in eight major cities during corresponding weeks in 1945 and 1946 showed that while the total volume of help-wanted advertising had declined, there was an over-all increase of 195 percent in discriminatory ads for 1946 over 1945.

The minority job seeker often finds that there are fields of employment where application is futile no matter how able or well-trained he is. Many northern business concerns have an unwritten rule against appointing Jews to executive positions; railroad management and unions discourage the employment of Negroes as engineers or conductors....

There are six states which have laws directed against discrimination in private employment. The New York, New Jersey, Massachusetts, and Connecticut statutes have strong enforcement provisions. In general, the statutes in these four states make it unlawful for employers to discriminate in hiring, firing, or conditions of employment, or for labor unions to exclude, expel, or discriminate, because of race, color, creed, or national origin. They also prohibit the use of discriminatory help wanted ads and job applications by employers and employment agencies. State commissions are empowered to investigate complaints, to hold hearings, to attempt to conciliate, to issue cease-and-desist orders, and finally, to seek court enforcement of these orders. Indiana and Wisconsin have antidiscrimination statutes without enforcement provisions. The commissions in these two states serve therefore as educational and advisory agencies....

THE RIGHT TO EDUCATION. The United States has made remarkable progress toward the goal of universal education for its people. The number and variety of its schools and colleges are greater than ever before. Student bodies have become increasingly representative of all the different peoples who make up our population. Yet we have not finally eliminated prejudice and discrimination from the operation of either our public or our private schools and colleges. Two inadequacies are extremely serious. We have failed to provide Negroes and, to a lesser extent, other minority group members with equality of educational opportunities in our public institutions, particularly at the elementary and secondary school levels. We have allowed discrimination in the operation of many of our private institutions of higher education, particularly in the North with respect to Jewish students.

Discrimination in public schools.—The failure to give Negroes equal educational opportunities is naturally most acute in the South, where approximately 10 million Negroes live. The South is one of the poorer sections of the country and has at best only limited funds to spend on its schools. With 34.5 percent of the country's population, 17 southern states and the District of Columbia have 39.4 percent of our school children. Yet the South has only one-fifth of the *taxpaying* wealth of the nation. Actually, on a percentage basis, the South spends a greater share of its income on education than do the wealthier states in other parts of the country. For example, Mississippi, which has the lowest expenditure per school child of any state, is ninth in percentage of income devoted to education. A recent study showed Mississippi spending 3.41 percent of its income for education as against New York's figure of only 2.61 percent. But this meant $400 per classroom unit in Mississippi, and $4,100 in New York. Negro and white school children both suffer because of the South's basic inability to match the level of educational opportunity provided in other sections of the nation.

But it is the South's segregated school system which most directly discriminates against the Negro. This segregation is found today in 17 southern states and the District of Columbia. Poverty-stricken though it was after the close of the Civil War, the South chose to maintain two sets of public schools, one for whites and one for Negroes. With respect to education, as well as to other public services, the Committee believes that the "separate but equal" rule has not been obeyed in practice. There is a marked difference in quality between the educational opportunities offered white children and Negro children in the separate schools. Whatever test is used—expenditure per pupil, teachers' salaries, the number of pupils per teacher, transportation of students, adequacy of school buildings and educational equipment, length of school term, extent of curriculum—Negro students are invariably at a disadvantage. Opportunities for Negroes in public institutions of higher education in the South—particularly at the professional graduate school level—are severely limited.

Statistics in support of these conclusions are available. Figures provided by the United States Office of Education for the school year, 1943–44, show that the average length of the school term in the areas having separate schools was 173.5 days for whites, and 164 for Negroes; the number of pupils per teacher was 28 for white and 34 for Negroes; and the average annual salary for Negro teachers was lower than that for white teachers in all but three of the 18 areas....

The South has made considerable progress in the last decade in narrowing the gap between educational opportunities afforded the white children and that afforded Negro children. For example, the gap between the length of the school year for whites and the shorter one for Negroes has been narrowed from 14.8 days in 1939–40 to 9.5 days in 1943–44. Similarly, the gap in student load per teacher in white and Negro schools has dropped from 8.5 students in 1939–40 to six students in 1943–44.

In spite of the improvement which is undoubtedly taking place, the Committee is convinced that the gap between white and Negro schools can never be completely eliminated by means of state funds alone. The cost of maintaining separate, but truly equal, school systems would seem to be utterly prohibitive in many of the southern states. It seems probable that the only means by which such a goal can finally be won will be through federal financial assistance. The extension of the federal grant-in-aid for educational purposes, already available to the land-grant colleges and, for vocational education, to the secondary school field, seems both imminent and desirable.

Whether the federal grant-in-aid should be used to support the maintenance of separate schools is an issue that the country must soon face.

In the North, segregation in education is not formal, and in some states is prohibited. Nevertheless, the existence of residential restrictions in many northern cities has had discriminatory effects on Negro education. In Chicago, for example, the schools which are most crowded and employ double shift schedules are practically all in Negro neighborhoods.

Other minorities encounter discrimination. Occasionally Indian children attending public schools in the western states are assigned to separate classrooms. Many Texas schools segregate Mexican American children in separate schools. In California segregation of Mexican American children was also practiced until recently. The combined effect of a federal court ruling, and legislative action repealing the statute under which school boards claimed authority to segregate, seems to have ended this pattern of discrimination in California schools....

THE RIGHT TO HOUSING. Equality of opportunity to rent or buy a home should exist for every American. Today, many of our citizens face a double barrier when they try to satisfy their housing needs. They first encounter a general housing shortage which makes it difficult for any family without a home to find one. They then encounter prejudice and discrimination based upon race, color, religion or national origin, which places them at a disadvantage in competing for the limited housing that is available. The fact that many of those who face this double barrier are war veterans only underlines the inadequacy of our housing record....

The restrictive covenant.—Under rulings of the Supreme Court, it is legally impossible to segregate housing on a racial or religious basis by zoning ordinance. Accordingly, the restrictive covenant has become the most effective modern method of accomplishing such segregation. Restrictive covenants generally take the form of agreements written into deeds of sale by which property owners mutually bind themselves not to sell or lease to an "undesirable." These agreements have thus far been enforceable by court action. Through these covenants large areas of land are barred against use by various classes of American citizens. Some are directed against only one minority group, others against a list of minorities. These have included *Armenians*, Jews, Negroes, Mexicans, Syrians, Japanese, Chinese and Indians.

While we do not know how much land in the country is subject to such restrictions, we do know that many areas, particularly large cities in the North and West, such as Chicago, Cleveland, Washington, D.C., and Los Angeles, are widely affected. The amount of land covered by racial restrictions in Chicago has been estimated at 80 percent. Students of the subject state that virtually all new subdivisions are blanketed by these covenants. Land immediately surrounding ghetto areas is frequently restricted in order to prevent any expansion in the ghetto....

The purpose of the restrictive covenant can only effectively be achieved in the final analysis by obtaining court orders putting the power of the state behind the enforcement of the private agreement. While our American courts thus far have permitted judicial power to be utilized for these ends, the Supreme Court of Ontario has recently refused to follow this course. The Ontario judge, calling attention to the policy of the United Nations against racial or religious discrimination, said:

> In my opinion, nothing could be more calculated to create or deepen divisions between existing religious and ethnic groups in this province than the sanction of a method of land transfer which would permit the segregation and confinement of particular groups to par-

ticular business or residential areas, or conversely, would exclude particular groups from particular business or residential areas.

There is eminent judicial and professional opinion in this country that our courts cannot constitutionally enforce racial restrictive covenants. In a recent California case a lower court judge held that the courts could not enforce such an agreement. And in a strong dissenting opinion in a recent covenant case, Justice Edgerton of the United States Court of Appeals for the District of Columbia, said:

> Suits like these, and the ghetto system they enforce are among our conspicuous failures to live together in peace. The question in these cases is not whether law should punish racial discrimination, or even whether law should try to prevent racial discrimination, or even whether law should interfere with it in any way. The question is whether law should affirmatively support and enforce racial discrimination....

THE RIGHT TO HEALTH SERVICE. Increased attention is being given throughout the United States to the health needs of our people. Minority groups are sharing in the improvements which are taking place. But there is serious discrimination in the availability of medical care, and many segments of our population do not measure up to the standards of health which have been attained by our people as a whole.

For example, the death rate from all causes for the entire country in 1945 was 10.5 per thousand of estimated population. The Chinese, however, had a rate of 12.8; the Negroes, 12.0; the Indians, 12.0; and the Japanese, 11.5. Similarly, many diseases strike minorities much harder than the majority groups. Tuberculosis accounts for the death of more than twice as many Negroes as whites. Among Indians in rural United States, the death rate from tuberculosis is more than 10 times as high as that for whites; in Alaska, the native deaths from this cause are over 30 times greater. In Texas, seven Latin Americans died of tuberculosis for every Anglo American. Infant deaths furnish another example of this pattern. On a nationwide basis, the infant mortality rate was more than half again as high for Negroes as for whites. In Texas, it was almost three times as high for Latin as for Anglo infants. Maternal deaths show like disproportions. In New York City, where the vast majority of the Puerto Ricans in this country are located, reports from social workers and city health authorities indicate that the frequency of illness among the Puerto Ricans is much higher than among other groups.

There are many factors which contribute to the discrepancies between the health of the *majority and the minorities*. As has already been noted, our minorities are seriously handicapped by their economic status. Frequently, because of poverty, they are unable to afford even the minimum of medical care or a diet adequate to build up resistance to disease. The depressed economic status of many of our minorities combined with restrictive covenants in housing prevents them from living in a sanitary, health-giving environment. Children who are not admitted to clean, healthful playgrounds must find their fun in the crowded, dirty areas in which they are allowed. Discrimination in education withholds from many people the basic information and knowledge so essential to good health.

A more direct cause of unequal opportunity in the field of health is the discriminatory pattern that prevails with respect to medical facilities and personnel. Many hospitals will not admit Negro patients. The United States Public Health Service estimates on the basis of a preliminary survey that only approximately 15,000 hospital beds out of a total of one and one-half million beds are presently available to Negroes. Thus, though Negroes constitute about ten percent of the population, only one percent of the hospital beds are open to them. In Chicago, a study by the Mayor's Commission on Human Relations in 1946 disclosed that "although most hospital officials denied the existence of a discriminatory admission policy, Negroes represented a negligible percentage of patients admitted."

The situation is further complicated by the shortage of medical personnel available for the treatment of patients from minority groups. This is particularly evident among the Negroes; in 1937, only 35 percent of southern Negro babies were delivered by doctors, as compared to 90 percent of northern babies of both races. There were in 1940 only 3,530 Negro physicians and surgeons; 7,192 trained and student Negro nurses; and 1,471 Negro dentists in a total Negro population of 13,000,000. The ratio of Negro physicians to the total Negro population was about one to 3,377, while that of the total number of physicians to the general population of the country was one to 750. Moreover, a high proportion of these were employed in the North. In the South, with a Negro population of almost 10,000,000, there were in 1940 about 2,000 Negro doctors, or only one to every 4,900 colored persons.

One important reason for this acute shortage of skilled medical men is the discriminatory policy of our medical schools in admitting minority students.

Document Text

Medical schools graduate approximately 5,000 students a year, but only about 145 of these are Negro. And of these 145, 130 are from two Negro schools; thus, only about fifteen Negroes are graduated from all the other medical schools of the country each year.

To these handicaps must be added the refusal of some medical societies and many hospitals to admit Negro physicians and interns for practice. Denied the facilities and training which are available to other doctors, Negro members of the profession are often unable to keep abreast of developments in medicine and to qualify as specialists. This discrimination contributes to the state of Negro health.

Though the expectation of life at birth is still lower for nonwhites than whites, the relative increase in life expectancy between 1930 and 1940 was nearly twice as great for nonwhites as whites. The life expectancy of Negro males in this period increased 9.9 percent; of Negro females, 11.5 per cent; of white males and females, 6.0 per cent and 7.0 percent respectively. However, the figure for white persons is still appreciably higher than for nonwhite persons; white males can expect to live sixty-three years as compared with fifty-two for Negro males, and white females sixty-seven years compared with fifty-five years for Negro females.

Progress has been made in reducing Negro deaths due to tuberculosis, diphtheria, whooping cough, diarrhea, enteritis, and syphilis. Among the Mexicans in Texas, vigorous programs have been undertaken by federal and local officials. Baby clinics, home nursing classes, family life courses, maternity clinics and other measures have been established. The Indian Service now operates 69 hospitals and sanatoria in the United States, 7 in Alaska; 14 school health centers; and 100 field dispensaries. Special efforts are being made to combat tuberculosis, a leading cause of illness and death among Indians. Another sign of progress is the decision of the American Nurses Association, in 1946, to accept all qualified applicants as members of the national organization, even when they cannot, for local reasons, enter county societies.

Glossary

all men are created equal	a quotation from the Declaration of Independence
arraignment	a legal proceeding in which the accused is formally charged with a crime
Four Freedoms	goals articulated by President Franklin Roosevelt in a 1941 speech, including freedom of speech and expression, freedom of religion, freedom from want, and freedom from fear
gentiles	non-Jews
Jehovah's Witnesses	an evangelical Christian sect
Justice Brandeis	U.S. Supreme Court justice Louis Brandeis, known for his articulation of the right to privacy and for his commitment to social justice
Justice Holmes	U.S. Supreme Court justice Oliver Wendell Holmes, Jr., widely know for his "clear and present danger" doctrine
land-grant colleges	colleges and universities established under the Morrill Act of 1862, which granted federally owned land to the states to establish institutions of higher education
"loss of memory"	a reference to a common expression found in police reports of lynchings supposedly carried out "by a person or persons unknown"
peonage	a system by which debtors' work off their debt through labor
"separate but equal"	the doctrine created by the 1896 U.S. Supreme Court case *Plessy v. Ferguson*
third degree	extreme or painful interrogation of criminals
V-J Day	Victory over Japan Day, August 14, 1945, marking the end of World War II

EXECUTIVE ORDER

ESTABLISHING THE PRESIDENT'S COMMITTEE ON EQUALITY OF TREATMENT AND OPPORTUNITY IN THE ARMED SERVICES

WHEREAS it is essential that there be maintained in the armed services of the United States the highest standards of democracy, with equality of treatment and opportunity for all those who serve in our country's defense:

NOW, THEREFORE, by virtue of the authority vested in me as President of the United States, by the Constitution and the statutes of the United States, and as Commander in Chief of the armed services, it is hereby ordered as follows:

1. It is hereby declared to be the policy of the President that there shall be equality of treatment and opportunity for all persons in the armed services without regard to race, color, religion or national origin. This policy shall be put into effect as rapidly as possible, having due regard to the time required to effectuate any necessary changes without impairing efficiency or morale.

2. There shall be created in the National Military Establishment an advisory committee to be known as the President's Committee on Equality of Treatment and Opportunity in the Armed Services, which shall be composed of seven members to be designated by the President.

3. The Committee is authorized on behalf of the President to examine into the rules, procedures and practices of the armed services in order to determine in what respect such rules, pro-

Executive Order 9981 (National Archives and Records Administration)

Executive Order 9981

1948

"There shall be equality of treatment and opportunity for all persons in the armed services without regard to race."

Overview

In 1948 racial divisions in the United States continued to run deep, but major changes in the social and legal climate were about to occur. During World War II, which the United States entered in 1941 and fought until the war's end in 1945, African Americans and other minorities, including Native Americans and Japanese Americans, fought with great distinction. On the home front, minority-group women made major contributions to the war effort. Nevertheless, segregation in nearly every facet of American life remained entrenched—nowhere more so than in the U.S. armed forces.

In response to growing pressure to remedy this state of affairs, President Harry S. Truman issued Executive Order 9981. Specifically, the executive order was written with the intent of "Establishing the President's Committee on Equality of Treatment and Opportunity in the Armed Forces." The purpose of the order then was twofold. One purpose was to declare that it would be the policy of the United States to provide equality of opportunity for members of the armed forces without regard to race, color, religion, or national origin. In this sense, armed forces desegregation could be said to have launched the civil rights movement that dominated the 1950s and 1960s. The second, more specific, purpose was to establish a seven-member advisory committee to study and recommend specific steps that the armed forces could take to implement the desegregation policy. The order granted the committee investigative authority and ordered the armed forces and other federal executive agencies to provide testimony and documents that the committee needed to carry out its mandate.

Context

Throughout American history, African Americans and members of other minority groups fought in the nation's wars with distinction. However, they did so generally in separate units that were segregated from all-white units. During the Civil War (1861–1865), for example, "colored" brigades were formed in the North, and even the Confederate States of America, starved for troops late in the war, formed brigades of black soldiers (although none ever fought).

In the decades following the Civil War, large numbers of African Americans, many of them former slaves, served in the U.S. Navy, but through the early decades of the twentieth century, they worked primarily in menial and service jobs. In the U.S. Navy and the Marine Corps, for example, many African Americans were pushed into the Steward's Branch, where they worked as cooks and served as waiters in the officers' mess halls. This state of affairs continued through World War II. During the war and its aftermath, minority groups fought in segregated units. There were few African American officers, and they all commanded African American units. The Marine Corps included few African Americans in its ranks, and the navy continued to limit the service of African Americans to such positions as cooks and stewards. Most military leaders believed that integrated units, where blacks and whites served side by side, would produce conflict and lower the morale of the troops.

President Franklin D. Roosevelt took an early step to remedy this situation in June 1941 when he issued Executive Order 8802. Arguing that the defense of the nation required the participation of all groups, he ordered that all defense contractors eliminate discrimination in employment. More specifically, he ordered that blacks be included in job-training programs at defense plants. He also ordered the formation of a Fair Employment Practices Committee. In 1942 Roosevelt took another step when he directed the navy to review its racial policies. The navy responded by allowing blacks to fill more positions in technical specialties, such as construction, supply, aviation, metalworking, and shore patrol. Later that year, as the military was rapidly increasing its manpower levels, Roosevelt issued a further executive order requiring that 10 percent of new draftees be black.

Roosevelt's executive orders had no impact on segregation in the military, but they did increase the number of African American troops. Although African Americans made up about 10 percent of the population and although about one million African Americans served during World War II, blacks continued to be assigned to segregated units. Opportunities for promotion were limited, black sailors were rarely allowed to serve at sea, and most blacks—even those trained for more specialized and technical positions—continued to fill service positions. Throughout this

Time Line

1945

- **October 1**
  After its appointment in September by U.S. Secretary of War Robert Patterson, the "Gillem Board," a three-member commission directed by Admiral Alvan Gillem, Jr., holds its first meeting to review army racial policies.

1946

- **February 27**
  The U.S. Navy, in Circular Letter 48-46, makes African American sailors eligible for all types of naval assignments.

- **April 10**
  U.S. War Department issues Circular 105, explicitly excluding "Negroes" from assignment to critically needed areas, though the circular was later revised to include all enlisted men.

- **April 27**
  War Department Circular 124 maintains racial segregation but makes integration the army's ultimate goal.

- **July 17**
  The U.S. secretary of war puts on hold black enlistments in the regular army.

- **September 19**
  President Harry Truman meets with a delegation from the National Emergency Committee against Mob Violence.

- **December 5**
  President Truman establishes the President's Committee on Civil Rights.

1947

- The Army Air Forces close the flight training school at Alabama's Tuskegee Airfield, the last segregated officer training program.

- The civil rights leader A. Philip Randolph, with other black leaders, establishes the Committee against Jim Crow in Military Service.

- **October 29**
  The President's Committee on Civil Rights issues its final report.

---

period, the navy took steps to integrate its officer corps by training twelve line officers and one warrant officer at a special training school in 1943. These officers, called the "Golden Thirteen," were the first black officers in the navy's history. Nevertheless, they were trained at a segregated school, and while some 160,000 African Americans served in the navy during World War II, just fifty-eight were officers. All of these were lower-ranking officers who served under the supervision of a white officer.

In the years immediately following the war, the U.S. Department of Defense faced a severe manpower shortage as those who had served in the war left for civilian employment. Nevertheless, the armed services continued to deter African Americans from serving. They tried to ensure that the proportion of African Americans remained no higher than 10 percent primarily by demanding that African Americans achieve higher scores on enlistment tests than their white counterparts. However, as the cold war with the Soviet Union deepened, it became apparent to President Truman and others that cutting off a valuable population of potential military recruits could hamper the nation's defense.

During these years, African American leaders were clamoring for changes in the nation's attitudes toward civil rights. One of the most outspoken leaders, A. Philip Randolph, formed the Committee against Jim Crow in Military Service; "Jim Crow" refers to the legal and social systems that segregated African Americans and kept them in inferior positions. Randolph and other African American leaders raised the possibility that black workers would go on strike, a situation that would have added to the economic turmoil caused by the nation's shift from a wartime to a peacetime economy. Additionally, the horrors of World War II, with the wholesale denial of human rights on the part of the German Nazi Party and the expansionist Japanese Empire, focused attention on human rights throughout the world. In 1948 the United Nations would issue its Universal Declaration of Human Rights, further drawing attention to the pressing issues of discrimination and civil rights. African American soldiers who served in Europe in the postwar years found greater acceptance and tolerance there, and they demanded this same level of acceptance from white American society.

Helping to improve the status of black military personnel was the appointment of James Forrestal as secretary of the navy. His predecessor, Frank Knox, had opposed integration, but Forrestal believed that integration might be a way to reduce racial tensions in the military. To that end, in 1944–1945 he ordered an experiment in which black personnel were placed on twenty-five ships at sea. The experiment proved successful, with few racial incidents reported.

It was in this climate that President Truman took on the issue of civil rights and desegregation in the years following World War II. In 1946 he created the President's Committee on Civil Rights. The committee recommended "more adequate and effective means and procedures for the protection of the civil rights of the people of the United States." In 1947 the committee issued its final report, *To Secure These Rights*, making specific recommendations for ways to ensure the civil rights of African Americans and other minority groups.

Truman urged Congress to enact the recommendations of the committee. However, he faced opposition from members of Congress, including southern senators who threatened to filibuster civil rights legislation. (The word *filibuster* refers to any delaying tactics, such as long, continuous speeches, to block action on proposed legislation.) Frustrated with Congress, Truman took matters into his own hands. He appointed an African American to a federal judgeship, he strengthened the civil rights division of the Department of Justice, and he appointed several African Americans to high-level administrative positions. Most important, he issued Executive Order 9981, calling for desegregation of the armed forces. Although the services resisted, they eventually implemented the president's order. By the end of the Korean War, segregation as a matter of military policy had largely ended.

About the Author

Harry S. Truman, the thirty-third president of the United States (1945–1953), was born in Lamar, Missouri, on May 8, 1884. (While it has become conventional to regard "S" as a middle initial, with a period, in fact the S does not stand for anything. It was his middle name, given to him by his parents to honor both of his grandfathers, whose names began with the letter S—a practice not uncommon among people of Scots-Irish descent.) Early in his life, Truman worked as a drugstore clerk before turning to farming. In the 1920s he was co-owner of a men's clothing store, leading to his reputation as the "haberdasher" who became president. He was the nation's last president to serve without benefit of a college degree. In 1905 he joined the Missouri National Guard, remaining a member until 1911. An early goal was to attend the United States Military Academy at West Point, but extremely poor eyesight rendered this goal impossible. After the outbreak of World War I, he rejoined the National Guard; it is believed that he passed the eye examination by memorizing the eye chart. He served as a captain of an infantry battery in France, often organizing and disciplining his men with firmness. His experience as a military officer brought out leadership qualities that enabled him to succeed in politics.

Truman began his political career in 1922, when he was elected to the position of judge of the county court, though the position was not judicial but administrative. In 1933 he was appointed head of Federal Reemployment for Missouri, part of President Franklin Roosevelt's New Deal to overcome the effects of the Great Depression. In 1934 he was elected to the U.S. Senate, and in 1940 he was reelected, despite numerous allegations of irregularities and favoritism in the federal reemployment program. In 1944 Roosevelt, running for a fourth term as president, selected Truman as his running mate. The two were elected, but after just eighty-two days as vice president, Truman ascended to the presidency on April 12, 1945, upon Roosevelt's death.

The nearly eight years of Truman's presidency were eventful. He authorized the atomic bombing of Japan to end World War II. He then dealt with the labor turmoil and economic upheavals of the postwar years. He presided over the formation of the United Nations and the Marshall Plan for the reconstruction of Europe, the formation of the state

Time Line

1948
- **May 28** Lieutenant John E. Rudder is the first African American to receive a regular Marine Corps commission as an officer.
- **July 26** President Truman issues Executive Order 9981.

1949
- **February 28** The Department of Defense's newly formed personnel policy board establishes uniform standards for the military draft and abolishes racial quotas.
- **May 11** Air Force Letter 35-3 ends segregation in the workplace and living quarters in the U.S. Air Force.

1950
- **January 16** The U.S. Army publishes Special Regulation 600-629-1, "Utilization of Negro Manpower in the Army." The new policy creates a list of vacancies to be filled without consideration of race.
- **August** During the Korean War, in the First Provisional Marine Brigade, African Americans are integrated in combat service for the first time in the nation's history.

1951
- **March** By this time the U.S. Army has integrated its nine training divisions.

1954
- **October 30** The U.S. secretary of defense announces the abolishment of the last racially segregated armed forces unit.

Harry S. Truman (Library of Congress)

of Israel, the Communist takeover of China, and increasing U.S. involvement in Indochina. The cold war with the Soviet Union deepened during the Berlin airlift of 1948–1949, the formation of the North Atlantic Treaty Organization in 1949, and the Korean War (1950–1952). During the war Truman seized control of the striking steel industry in the interest of national security. One of the most noteworthy incidents of his administration was his reelection in 1948. Until the end of the campaign he badly trailed his opponent, Thomas Dewey. A famous photograph shows Truman holding a newspaper with the headline "Dewey Defeats Truman," run because few people had given Truman any chance to win. Truman died on December 26, 1972. He remains one of the nation's most popular presidents, highly regarded for his pragmatism and blunt outspokenness.

Explanation and Analysis of the Document

Executive Order 9981, similar to most executive orders, is relatively brief and to the point. The purpose of such an order is not to deal with details and procedures but to outline a broad policy or directive that the president wants to give the force of law. The first two paragraphs of the order contain a broad justification of the new policy. The president states that it is "essential" for the armed forces to maintain "standards of democracy" and for military personnel to have equality of opportunity. In the second paragraph, the president reiterates his authority as president and commander in chief to issue such an order.

Following the two introductory paragraphs are six specific goals. In the first, the president states that U.S. policy will ensure that all military personnel are treated equally without regard to their race, color, religion, or national origin. Although the status of African Americans in the military is of primary concern, the new policy applies to all ethnic, racial, and religious groups. While the president calls for the new policy to be implemented as soon as possible, he recognizes that it will not happen overnight—that it has to happen in a way that maintains the efficiency and morale of the troops.

The second item creates a seven-member advisory committee called the President's Committee on Equality of Treatment and Opportunity in the Armed Forces. The president will appoint the members. The third item outlines the duties of the committee. These duties are to examine the policies and procedures of each of the armed forces with regard to racial segregation. The committee is to confer with and advise the secretaries of each of the military branches as well as the Department of Defense and to make recommendations to those branches and to the president.

The fourth item orders other agencies of the government's executive branch to cooperate with the committee as it gathers information, primarily by providing documents and the services of anyone who can help the committee. While the order does not say so, it was understood by all that the president, as the nation's chief executive officer, had the authority to compel cooperation only from the executive branch. The U.S. Constitution's separation of powers gives the president no authority over the legislative branch (Congress) or the judicial branch (the courts). Such agencies as the Department of Defense are part of the executive branch. The fifth item gives the committee the authority to compel testimony and to obtain documents from all federal executive departments in carrying out its work. The final item grants to the committee an indefinite life, noting that it will continue to exist until the president, through another executive order, terminates its existence.

Audience

The immediate audience for Executive Order 9981 was the Department of Defense and the commanders of the U.S. armed services, including the army, the army air forces (the precursor to today's air force, which is now a separate branch of the military), the coast guard, and the navy (including the Marine Corps). The U.S. Constitution identifies the president as the commander in chief of the nation's military, giving him the authority to order such a change in personnel policies. Through this executive order, the president instructed the various branches of the military to begin a program of desegregation.

A second, larger audience was the nation's population of African Americans and other groups defined in part by national origin, religion, and race. Although the executive order encompassed all such groups—including, for example, Asian Americans, Hispanics, and Native Americans—the reality was that the focus of the order was African

Essential Quotes

> "It is essential that there be maintained in the armed services of the United States the highest standards of democracy, with equality of treatment and opportunity for all those who serve in our country's defense."
>
> (Introductory Paragraph)

> "It is hereby declared to be the policy of the President that there shall be equality of treatment and opportunity for all persons in the armed services without regard to race, color, religion, or national origin."
>
> (Item 1)

Americans, who made up nearly 10 percent of the total U.S. population in the 1940s. By issuing this executive order, President Truman sought to assure African Americans that the federal government was making efforts to ensure racial equality. In this sense, the audience for Executive Order 9981 was the American population as a whole. The order was one of the first major steps on the part of the federal government to protect the rights of minorities. By issuing it, Truman sent a message to the American people that segregation was no longer to be tolerated.

A third audience was the U.S. Congress. In February 1948 the president spoke to Congress and urged the nation's senators and congressional representatives to address the problem of racial inequality. He pressed for the strengthening of civil rights laws, the establishment of a permanent commission on civil rights, protection against lynching, protection of the right to vote, the establishment of a fair employment commission, and other steps to promote civil rights. He believed, however, that Congress was not acting on these proposals as quickly and as forcefully as it should. In particular, he faced a filibuster (delaying tactics) by southern senators on civil rights legislation. By issuing Executive Order 9981, he was able to institute a major change without having to rely on Congress.

Impact

One of the essential problems that arose in connection with Executive Order 9981 and other documents bearing on racial matters in the military had to do with the definition of terms. Another problem concerned precisely how the president's policy might be implemented. Ultimately, the goal of the order was to have a completely integrated military, one in which no regard was given to race in the assignment of personnel to units, in their appointment to fill particular military jobs, and in the selection of officers. Many military commanders, however, believed that the forces under their command were "integrated" if there were units composed of African Americans attached to "parent" white units. Some military commanders, as well as legislators, believed that both blacks and whites should be allowed to serve in all-white or all-black units if they preferred to do so. Thus, for example, a battalion might have consisted of a number of all-white companies of soldiers and one all-black company, with the all-black company performing essentially the same job as the all-white companies. At bottom, the difficulty was distinguishing "segregation" from "discrimination." Some military commanders and legislators did not believe that a segregated military was discriminatory.

The result is that Truman's order did not have any immediate impact. Neither the army nor the navy altered its policies. The decision of these branches to maintain the status quo was based on their commanders' belief that they were already in compliance with the president's order because they were in compliance with such directives as Circular 124 and Circular Letter 48-46.

Through most of 1949, in the estimation of many historians, the armed services were slow in taking steps to implement the president's policy. Change, however, began to occur in late 1949. Both the navy and the air force significantly changed their racial policies, concluding that they needed to expand the pool of available sailors and airmen in a period when the size of the military was shrinking. The army was slower to respond, but finally, in 1950, the army issued Special Regulation 600-629-1, "Utilization of Negro Manpower in the Army," ordering that openings in critical specialties were to be filled without regard to race. The Marine Corps was slower still, but in 1951, during the Korean War, the corps ended its policy of segregation.

Other changes took place. Military recruiters no longer regarded the race of candidates for service. Training units were fully integrated. All-black units were gradually taken out of commission and replaced with fully integrated units.

Additional training was provided to ensure that African American enlistees could overcome the effects of poverty and poor schooling to succeed in the military. Finally, on October 30, 1954, the U.S. secretary of defense announced the abolishment of the last racially segregated unit in the military. In the decades that followed, the U.S. armed forces became a model for complete integration and for a culture in which race plays no role in determining a soldier's or a sailor's opportunities for advancement.

See also A. Philip Randolph's "Call to Negro America to March on Washington" (1941); *To Secure These Rights* (1947).

Further Reading

■ **Articles**

Barnhill, J. Herschel. "Civil Rights in the 1940's." *Negro History Bulletin* 45, no. 1 (January–March 1982): 21–22.

Chenoweth, Karin. "Taking Jim Crow Out of Uniform: A. Philip Randolph and the Desegregation of the U.S. Military: Special Report: The Integrated Military—50 Years." *Black Issues in Higher Education*, August 21, 1997.

■ **Books**

Bernstein, Barton J., ed. *Politics and Policies of the Truman Administration*. Chicago: Quadrangle Books, 1970.

Bogart, Leo, ed. *Social Research and the Desegregation of the U.S. Army*. Chicago: Markham Publishing, 1969.

Dalfiume, Richard M. *Desegregation of the U. S. Armed Forces: Fighting on Two Fronts, 1939–1953*. Columbia: University of Missouri Press, 1969.

Davis, Lenwood G., and George Hill, comps. *Blacks in the American Armed Forces 1776–1983: A Bibliography*. Westport, Conn.: Greenwood Press, 1985.

Questions for Further Study

1. President Truman ordered the desegregation of the armed forces three years after the end of World War II. Discuss the impact of the war on his decision. What effect did the events of the war have on the position of African Americans and other minorities in the military?

2. The U.S. armed forces remained segregated until roughly 1950. However, the United States had participated in a number of wars throughout its history, including the Revolutionary War, the War of 1812, the Civil War, the Spanish American War, World War I, and World War II. To what extent did African Americans and other minorities, including Native Americans, take part in those wars? How did their participation change over time, if at all?

3. By 1948 the United States was entering the cold war with the Soviet Union. One of the battlegrounds on which this war would be fought was Korea. What impact did the cold war have on Truman's goal of desegregating the armed forces?

4. Some historians believe that in ordering desegregation of the armed forces, President Truman was motivated less by a desire for fairness and equality than by a desire to avoid labor strikes and other forms of public protest by African Americans. Further, they argue that the timing of the order suggests that Truman was trying to appeal to black voters in the upcoming 1948 presidential election. What evidence supports the view that Truman may have been motivated by politics rather than by a sense of what was right? What evidence suggests that this view is incorrect?

5. In 1954 the U.S. Supreme Court ordered the desegregation of the nation's public schools. To what extent did the desegregation of the armed forces contribute to the climate of public opinion that led to this decision?

6. In the 1990s President Bill Clinton dealt with the issue of gays and lesbians serving in the armed forces. To what extent was that issue similar to the issues Truman faced in the 1940s? What arguments that applied to African Americans in the 1940s were also applied to gays fifty years later? What arguments against allowing gays to serve in the military were also used in the 1940s in opposition to armed forces desegregation?

Donaldson, Gary A. *The History of African-Americans in the Military: Double V*. Malabar, Fla.: Krieger Publishing, 1991.

Donovan, Robert J. *Conflict and Crisis: The Presidency of Harry Truman, 1945–1948*. New York: W. W. Norton, 1977.

Dornfeld, Margaret. *The Turning Tide, 1946–1958: From the Desegregation of the Armed Forces to the Montgomery Bus Boycott*. New York: Chelsea House 1995.

Foner, Jack. *Blacks and the Military in American History: A New Perspective*. New York: F. A. Praeger, 1974.

Freedom to Serve: Equality of Treatment and Opportunity in the Armed Services. A Report by the President's Committee on Civil Rights. Washington, D.C.: Government Printing Office, 1950.

Hamby, Alonzo L. *Man of the People: A Life of Harry S. Truman*. New York: Oxford University Press, 1995.

Hope, Richard O. *Racial Strife in the U.S. Military: Toward the Elimination of Discrimination*. New York: Praeger, 1979.

MacGregor, Morris J., Jr. *Integration of the Armed Forces, 1940–1965*. Washington, D.C.: Center for Military History, U.S. Army, 1981.

McGuire, Phillip, ed. *Taps for a Jim Crow Army: Letters from Black Soldiers in World War II*. Santa Barbara, Calif.: ABC-CLIO, 1983.

Mershon, Sherie, and Steven Schlossman. *Foxholes and Color Lines: Desegregating the U.S. Armed Forces*. Baltimore, Md.: Johns Hopkins University Press, 2002.

Motley, Mary P., ed. *The Invisible Soldier: The Experience of the Black Soldier, World War II*. Detroit: Wayne State University Press, 1975.

Nalty, Bernard C. *Strength for the Fight: A History of Black Americans in the Military*. New York: Free Press, 1986.

Nelson, Dennis D. *The Integration of the Negro into the U.S. Navy*. New York: Farrar, Straus, and Young, 1951.

■ **Web Sites**

"Desegregation of the Armed Forces." Harry S. Truman Library and Museum Web site.
http://www.trumanlibrary.org/whistlestop/study_collections/desegregation/large/.

"Harry S. Truman (1884–1972)." University of Virginia Miller Center of Public Affairs "American President: Online Reference Resource" Web site.
http://millercenter.org/academic/americanpresident/truman.

"Harry S. Truman Special Message to the Congress on Civil Rights. February 2, 1948." The Gilder Lerhman Center for the Study of Slavery, Resistance, and Abolition Web site.
http://www.yale.edu/glc/archive/972.htm.

"To Secure These Rights: The Report of the President's Committee on Civil Rights." Harry S. Truman Library and Museum Web site.
http://www.trumanlibrary.org/civilrights/srights1.htm.

—Michael J. O'Neal

Document Text

Executive Order 9981

Establishing the President's Committee on Equality of Treatment and Opportunity in the Armed Forces.

WHEREAS it is essential that there be maintained in the armed services of the United States the highest standards of democracy, with equality of treatment and opportunity for all those who serve in our country's defense:

NOW THEREFORE, by virtue of the authority vested in me as President of the United States, by the Constitution and the statutes of the United States, and as Commander in Chief of the armed services, it is hereby ordered as follows:

1. It is hereby declared to be the policy of the President that there shall be equality of treatment and opportunity for all persons in the armed services without regard to race, color, religion or national origin. This policy shall be put into effect as rapidly as possible, having due regard to the time required to effectuate any necessary changes without impairing efficiency or morale.

2. There shall be created in the National Military Establishment an advisory committee to be known as the President's Committee on Equality of Treatment and Opportunity in the Armed Services, which shall be composed of seven members to be designated by the President.

3. The Committee is authorized on behalf of the President to examine into the rules, procedures and practices of the Armed Services in order to determine in what respect such rules, procedures and practices may be altered or improved with a view to carrying out the policy of this order. The Committee shall confer and advise the Secretary of Defense, the Secretary of the Army, the Secretary of the Navy, and the Secretary of the Air Force, and shall make such recommendations to the President and to said Secretaries as in the judgment of the Committee will effectuate the policy hereof.

4. All executive departments and agencies of the Federal Government are authorized and directed to cooperate with the Committee in its work, and to furnish the Committee such information or the services of such persons as the Committee may require in the performance of its duties.

5. When requested by the Committee to do so, persons in the armed services or in any of the executive departments and agencies of the Federal Government shall testify before the Committee and shall make available for use of the Committee such documents and other information as the Committee may require.

6. The Committee shall continue to exist until such time as the President shall terminate its existence by Executive order.

Harry Truman
The White House, July 26, 1948

Glossary

Armed Forces	in the 1940s the army, the army air forces, the coast guard, and the navy (which included the Marine Corps)
Executive Order	a rule issued by the executive branch of government (the president) that has the force of law
hereof	of this

Ralph Bunche receives the Nobel Peace Prize in December 1950. (AP/Wide World Photos)

Ralph J. Bunche: "The Barriers of Race Can Be Surmounted"

1949

"The entire history of the Negro in this country has been a history of continuous, relentless progress over these barriers."

Overview

"The Barriers of Race Can Be Surmounted"—Ralph J. Bunche's commencement address to the graduating class at Fisk University in Nashville, Tennessee, on May 30, 1949— is perhaps the most personal speech this normally private man ever made. Weeks earlier, after eighty-one days of nonstop negotiations on the Greek island of Rhodes, Bunche, the chief United Nations mediator for Palestine, successfully secured armistice agreements from the state of Israel and the Arab states of Egypt, Lebanon, Jordan, and Syria, bringing an end to the 1948 Arab-Israeli War. The Palestine Accords, as these agreements were known, earned Bunche international acclaim for bringing peace to the Middle East. In the United States the accords were seen as yet another triumph for a highly respected national figure, an African American whose career as a scholar and public servant had made him, at age forty-five, one of the most distinguished Americans of his generation.

In recognition of his public service, Fisk University awarded Bunche an honorary degree, the second of seventy that would come to him from universities in the United States, Canada, and Europe. One of the first of the historic black colleges and universities, Fisk held its first classes in Nashville's former Union army barracks in January 1866. The university became internationally known in subsequent decades for the Fisk Jubilee Singers, who introduced audiences in America and Europe to Negro spirituals as a unique American art form. Fisk was the first historic black college to earn accreditation from the Southern Association of Colleges and Schools (1930) and approval from the Association of American Universities (1933). Booker T. Washington, the most powerful African American in the country at the end of the nineteenth century, was on Fisk's board of trustees. A prominent early graduate was W. E. B. (William Edward Burghardt) Du Bois, class of 1888, whose scholarly writings influenced generations of African American intellectuals, including Ralph Bunche.

Context

In 1903 Du Bois, a professor of economics and history at Atlanta University in Georgia, published *The Souls of Black Folk: Essays and Sketches*, a seminal study of post–Civil War African Americans. Its second chapter opens with the now famous sentence: "The problem of the twentieth century is the problem of the color-line—the relation of the darker to the lighter races of men in Asia and Africa, in America and the islands of the sea"—a stark assessment of race relations in 1900 that proved to be dead on the mark.

In 1900, 8.8 million African Americans lived in the United States. They experienced the problem of the color line on a daily basis, especially in the rural South, where an estimated 90 percent of them lived, the majority as sharecroppers renting their fields from white landowners. Their number had doubled from the 4.4 million in the census of 1860, when all but some four hundred and eighty thousand were chattel slaves. In the intervening years, slavery, of course, had been abolished, and constitutionally African Americans were free. In reality, however, their freedom throughout the southern states was substantially diminished by harsh Jim Crow laws that, since the end of Reconstruction in 1877, restricted or denied African Americans access to housing, medical care, public parks and pools, public transportation, and all levels of education because of their race. This segregation of blacks from whites was held to be constitutional by the U.S. Supreme Court in *Plessy v. Ferguson* in 1896, when the Court ruled that laws based on a "separate but equal" doctrine did not violate the Fourteenth Amendment's "equal protection" clause. In subsequent decisions well into the 1930s, the Court extended the reach of *Plessy* to almost every area of daily life in the South.

Efforts by African Americans to protest their status as second-class citizens often brought with them swift punishment by local police and courts or by lawless mobs that, according to statistics from the Tuskegee Institute, lynched 3,445 African American men, women, and children from 1882 to 1964. Few arrests were made, and when they were, all-white juries commonly set the accused killer or killers free. Sharecroppers who opposed Jim Crow laws often lost their leases and their lands; workers in towns were simply fired.

In consequence, as economic conditions worsened and racial violence increased after 1910, hundreds and then thousands of African Americans left the region for northern cities and the West in search of jobs, housing, and political

Time Line	
1887	Southern state legislatures begin enacting Jim Crow laws, denying African Americans access to a broad range of social services and civil rights; many of these laws remain in place until the 1950s.
1895	**September 18** Booker T. Washington delivers his Atlanta Exposition Address at the Cotton State and International Exposition in Atlanta, Georgia.
1896	**May 18** The U.S. Supreme Court makes Jim Crow laws separating the races constitutional in *Plessy v. Ferguson*.
1903	W. E. B. Du Bois publishes *The Souls of Black Folk: Essays and Sketches* and "The Talented Tenth." **August 7** Ralph Johnson Bunche is born in Detroit, Michigan.
1905	Du Bois and other African American critics of Booker T. Washington's policy of accommodation organize the Niagara Movement to actively seek civil rights for African Americans.
1909	**February 12** The National Association for the Advancement of Colored People (NAACP) is founded on the 100th anniversary of Abraham Lincoln's birth, "to secure for all people" their rights under the Thirteenth, Fourteenth, and Fifteenth Amendments to the Constitution.
1910	The Great Migration begins, drawing an estimated six million African Americans in two large waves from the South to the North, Midwest, and West Coast and reducing the proportion of African Americans in the South's population from 90 percent to 53 percent by 1970.

and civil rights. By the 1930s the first wave of this Great Migration had carried 1.6 million African Americans out of the South. The seven million who remained behind—with notable exceptions—did little to openly challenge the segregated world in which they lived.

That passive accommodation to Jim Crow was exactly what Booker T. Washington, the president of the Tuskegee Institute in Alabama, proposed in his Atlanta Exposition Address at the Cotton States and International Exposition in Atlanta, Georgia, in September 1895. Speaking to a largely white audience, Washington, a former slave, argued that "my race" should for the moment abandon its demands for political power, civil rights, and higher education for its young people to concentrate on vocational and industrial training so that they could earn their rightful place in American life. He counseled, "It is at the bottom of life we must begin, and not at the top." African Americans would prosper and gain acceptance "as we learn to dignify and glorify common labor, and put brains and skill into the common occupations of life." Agitating "questions of social equality," he warned, "is the extremist folly." He emphasized his view that the separation of the races was the way to racial harmony: "We can be as separate as the fingers, yet one as the hand in all things essential to mutual progress."

Washington's call for conciliation and gradualism was an instant success with the white world both north and south, as was his 1901 autobiography, *Up from Slavery*, which carried a similar message. In time, a majority of African Americans accepted his precepts as he gained a national reputation as the voice of black America. White industrial leaders and philanthropists underwrote Washington's efforts to build five thousand rural schoolhouses throughout the South in which to teach young black people the virtues of honest labor and civic responsibility. He was invited to the White House, and the philosopher William James asked for his criticism of a draft essay on race. Having earned the white world's respect, Washington came to hold great power: Almost all charitable funds earmarked for African Americans passed through his hands; he was consulted on personnel matters; and he controlled coverage of black news in African American newspapers, thereby suppressing, when necessary, opposition to his advocacy of vocational training and his continuing counsel of compromise. To the white world he was the Wizard of Tuskegee who had created racial peace.

The principal challenge to Washington came from the leading African American intellectual of his time, W. E. B. Du Bois, a native of Great Barrington, Massachusetts, who held degrees from Fisk and Harvard (where he was the first African American to earn a PhD) and had studied at the University of Berlin. A brilliant and unyielding polemicist, he argued in the third chapter of *The Souls of Black Folk* that the effect of Washington's approach to racial harmony had shifted the burden of the Negro problem to the Negro's shoulders, "when in fact the burden belongs to the nation."

The Atlanta Exposition Address, Du Bois wrote, was in reality "the Atlanta Compromise." Its program for racial peace had won the approval of the South and the admiration of the North not because it benefited African Americans but because it promised to end "decades of bitter complaint" that had unsettled both regions. Washington's program of "of industrial education, conciliation of the South, and submission and silence to civil and political rights" was a series of half-truths that over time would prove counterproductive to securing long-term racial equality. After more than a decade of "tendering the palm branch," Du Bois noted, African Americans had been disenfranchised, were given second-class status with all its "emasculating effects," and had seen financial aid for their higher education gradually withdrawn.

These problems would be resolved, Du Bois declared in *The Souls of Black Folk*, only through "ceaseless agitation and insistent demand for equality" and in "the use of force of every sort: moral suasion, propaganda, and where possible even physical resistance." He wrote in his 1903 essay "The Talented Tenth" that the way forward would require effective African American leaders: "The Negro race, like all races, is going to be saved by its exceptional men," that is, by "the talented tenth," who would be prepared for leadership through a rigorous higher education curriculum that would give them broad "knowledge of the world that was and is, and of the relation of men to it." There could be no compromise. As he declared in his 1906 address at the second annual meeting of the short-lived Niagara Movement—an organization of African American intellectuals—"We claim for ourselves every single right that belongs to a freeborn American." But as perceptive as Du Bois's assessments of "the Negro problem" were, they were not powerful enough to overcome Washington's policies of accommodation. The "ceaseless agitation and insistent demands" would have to wait for another time.

Forty-one years after Du Bois raised the issue of the color line as the central problem of the twentieth century, Gunnar Myrdal, a Swedish social scientist and economist, published *An American Dilemma: The Negro Problem and Modern Democracy* (1944), a two-volume report on African American life that essentially proved that Du Bois's statement was correct and that the issues he raised were largely unresolved. Initially commissioned by the Carnegie Corporation in 1938—its publication delayed by World War II—the report was based on a two-year field study by Myrdal and forty-eight researchers, who conducted interviews throughout the South and elsewhere. Ralph Bunche, then a professor of political science at Howard University, was Myrdal's chief assistant and a cowriter of the final report.

An American Dilemma documented an enlarging division between American values and the daily lives of African Americans. In every part of society, they were treated differently from whites: in education, employment, housing, transportation, and recreational facilities. This was especially true, Myrdal wrote, in the South, where the majority of African Americans lived and where they faced racial bias and unfair treatment as a direct result of the local authorities' failure to enforce the Constitution. Throughout the United States, discrimination regularly bred further discrimination.

Time Line

1927
- Ralph Bunche graduates with a bachelor of arts degree from the University of California, Los Angeles; his education continues with a master of arts degree (1928) and a Ph.D. (1934) in government and international relations from Harvard.

1928
- Bunche joins the faculty of Howard University, where he remains until 1941; there he establishes and chairs the department of political science.

1938
- Bunche becomes the chief assistant to the Swedish economist Gunnar Myrdal in the Carnegie Corporation's study of racism in America, a position he holds until 1940.

1944
- Gunnar Myrdal's two-volume landmark study, *An American Dilemma: The Negro Problem and Modern Democracy*, is published.

1945
- Bunche is a member of the U.S. delegation to the Constituent Assembly of the United Nations in San Francisco, where he drafts key provisions of the UN Charter.

1947
- Bunche is named director of the Trusteeship Department of the UN Secretariat, the start of a twenty-two year career with the United Nations.

1948
- **May 20** Count Folke Bernadotte of Sweden and Bunche are appointed by the United Nations to mediate the Palestinian conflict between Israel and the Arab states.
- **September 17** Bunche becomes head of the UN mission in Palestine, following the assassination of Bernadotte by Israeli terrorists in Jerusalem.

Time Line

1949

- **Spring**
  On the island of Rhodes, Bunche brings an end to the 1948 Arab-Israeli War, securing armistice agreements between Israel and Egypt, Lebanon, Jordan, and Syria.

- **May 30**
  Bunche speaks to the graduating class of 1949 at Fisk University in Nashville, Tennessee.

1950

- **December 10**
  Bunche receives the 1950 Nobel Peace Prize.

Despite the data he and his team assembled, Myrdal was optimistic about America's ability to close the racial divide, principally by returning the nation to its founding principles. He advocated institutional changes in education and job creation and urged government-supported acceleration of black emigration from the rural South to the industrial North and West. In the end, however, he placed his faith in American idealism and in the Constitution as the means by which America could transform and transcend the segregated world that had kept African Americans subordinated and marginalized for so long.

Bunche's contribution to *An American Dilemma* was substantial. Like other black intellectuals of his generation, he wanted to understand what it meant to be black in America, so he served enthusiastically as Myrdal's personal guide on several extended trips through the Jim Crow South. He researched and wrote four chapters for the book, in which he focused, among other topics, on the political status of Negroes under the New Deal and on the nature of black leadership. Although his analyses and conclusions reflect something of W. E. B. Du Bois's arguments on these subjects—particularly those in "The Talented Tenth"—Bunche's voice is more temperate. He deplores the damage segregation has done to his race, but unlike Du Bois he does not despair. Rather, he shares Myrdal's optimism that the fairness and justice embodied in American idealism can and will effect real change. That the barriers to racial equality could be surmounted was the message he would bring to Fisk University in 1949.

About the Author

Ralph Johnson Bunche, Nobel laureate, UN official, international mediator, university scholar, and arguably the most celebrated African American of his generation, was born in Detroit, Michigan, on August 7, 1903. His father, Fred Bunche, was a barber; his mother, Olive Agnes Bunche, fostered in him a love of learning. Following the birth of a daughter, Grace, in 1915, the family moved to Albuquerque, New Mexico, in the hope that the dry climate would aid Olive Bunche's health problems, but she died within months of their relocation. The father's death came three months later, and the two orphaned children were placed in the care of their maternal grandmother, Lucy Taylor Johnson.

Johnson took the children to Los Angeles, where they lived in a mixed-race but largely white neighborhood. A tiny woman with a fierce will, Johnson (always called "Nana" by Bunche) refused to let school authorities enroll her grandson in a commercial training program—a common fate of African American youngsters in a white school—because, she insisted, he was going to college. Valedictorian of the class of 1922 at Jefferson High School, he was nonetheless denied membership in the school's academic honor society because of his race. (In 1952, when Bunche was world famous and had been heaped with honors, the high school offered him belated admission to the society.)

Bunche won an academic scholarship to the University of California at Los Angeles, where he starred in football and basketball until he sustained a knee injury that would bother him throughout his life and make him ineligible for military service in World War II. He was elected to Phi Beta Kappa and earned a bachelor of arts degree in 1927. At Harvard he earned a master of arts (1928) and a doctorate in international relations (1934), and he completed postdoctoral studies at Northwestern University, the London School of Economics, and the University of Cape Town, South Africa. Despite that résumé, he, like other African American scholars at the time, was not recruited by any white university and instead earned tenure at Howard University, a historically black college in Washington, D.C., where he founded and led the political science department.

In the early years of his teaching, Bunche was considered a radical in his political philosophy and in faculty politics. He was active on behalf of the NAACP in a number of demonstrations against segregation in Washington, but like other activists of the period he found little support from the local authorities. As a scholar, he developed an expertise on African colonialism and wrote a number of articles on racism in America that influenced the civil rights movement in the 1960s. In 1938 he was named chief associate to Gunnar Myrdal for the Carnegie Corporation's two-year study of African American life in America and accompanied Myrdal through the South to conduct interviews and gather data. On one occasion he and Myrdal drove all night across two states to elude a lynch mob that took exception to the kinds of questions the two were asking. Bunche wrote four chapters of the finished report, which was published in 1944 as *An American Dilemma*.

During World War II, Bunche worked in the War Department as an African and Far Eastern specialist and in the State Department, where, in 1944, he joined the team that helped to design the United Nations. A delegate to the San Francisco Conference in 1945, he wrote the two chapters of the UN Charter on colonial territories and trusteeships. In 1947 he joined the UN Secretariat as director of its Trusteeship Department, overseeing decolonization in Africa and Asia. In his twenty-two-year career with the United Nations, Bunche secured an armistice in the first Arab-Israeli War of 1948, for which he was awarded the Nobel Peace Prize in 1950 (the first black man so honored). He directed UN peacekeeping efforts at the Suez Canal (1956), in the Congo (1960), and in Cyprus (1964).

Bunche cared deeply about civil rights and was on occasion a blunt spokesman on their behalf, but most often, in keeping with his sensitive position at the United Natons, he worked out of the public eye. He served on the board of the NAACP for twenty-two years and in 1965 joined Martin Luther King, Jr., at marches in Selma and Montgomery, Alabama. Ill health forced him to retire in June 1971. At the time he was completing his fifteenth year as undersecretary for Special Political Affairs and principal adviser to the UN secretary-general. Bunche died on December 9, 1971.

Explanation and Analysis of the Document

Bunche's speech "The Barriers of Race Can Be Surmounted" was delivered within a few weeks of the peace agreements he had negotiated in the spring of 1949, bringing an end to an Arab-Israeli conflict in Palestine. Although he had been interviewed in the weeks following the peace talks and would shortly present his report on the Palestinian Accords to the United Nations, Bunche's appearance at Fisk University was an opportunity for him to reflect on his long career of teaching and public service, which had made him arguably the most visible and respected African American in the country. His speech, just over 2,200 words, is in many ways autobiographical; in it he deals with his fame and grapples with the question that W. E. B. Du Bois had first raised in *The Souls of Black Folk* nearly a half-century before: What does it mean to be a Negro in America?

It was appropriate for Bunche to raise that question at Fisk, a historically black school that had long been in the forefront of African American education. He spoke as the African American population nationally was approaching fifteen million, but only 13.7 percent of blacks had a high school diploma and only three hundred thousand held college degrees. The black population was again moving out of the South into the urban centers of the North, Midwest, and California in the second Great Migration, but whether in the rural South or the other regions of the country, most African Americans faced racial discrimination in its various forms and many saw themselves as second-class citizens.

Bunche speaks to these matters throughout using "Negro" rather than "African American," a term not current in his lifetime, to describe himself, his subject, and his audience. According to his biographer (who was also his friend and colleague at the United Nations), Brian Urquhart, Bunche almost always used that word because, he said, "It is an ethnic term with no objectionable connotation at all. It describes my ethnic roots, and I have always had a deep pride in those roots." On occasion he used "Black American."

Bunche notes at the outset that his remarks will be brief. (An experienced and fluent speaker, he probably spoke for fifteen minutes or less.) The introductory section in paragraphs 1–3 begins on a humorous note with Bunche's playful remarks about the traditional rituals that surround graduation day: the academic gowns and tasseled mortarboard hats; the entry of the graduates to the strains of a triumphal march; an audience of proud parents, families, and friends. He concludes, again humorously, that it is likely the graduates' celebrations actually preceded the day's ceremony.

Paragraphs 4 and 5 introduce Bunche's main theme: that the graduates before him are at once Americans, American citizens, and Negroes and that each of these identities carries with it a certain poignancy and a measure of responsibility. In paragraph 6, Bunche attempts to sketch briefly what it means to be American, emphasizing, as Myrdal had done in *An American Dilemma*, the idealism underlying the founding principles on which the nation is based. He speaks of inalienable rights and the dignity of man as the basis for "a great and virile democracy."

In paragraph 7, Bunche says it is the fundamental responsibility of every American citizen to preserve "a free and dignified existence" for all Americans. This leads him, in paragraphs 8 and 9, to examine briefly the irony of being a Negro in America. He is echoing here the dilemma that Du Bois introduced in his 1903 book, *The Souls of Black Folk*: that because of the color line African Americans must live behind the veil of race with a "double-consciousness," that is, with "a sense of always looking at one's self through the eyes of others." Negroes are Americans by birth, but because of their color, white Americans see them and treat them as a race apart, outsiders who are not really American.

In paragraphs 10 and 11, Bunche attacks the color line, asserting that the Fisk graduates, like Negroes everywhere, are "one hundred per cent American," and their goal is to enter the mainstream of American life. He dismisses the labels and stereotypes that keep them subordinate to white Americans. But he warns in paragraph 12 that it would be folly for him to tell them that their goal of attaining full citizenship is easily reached: To say that racism no longer endangers them "would be criminally misleading."

In paragraph 13, much like Myrdal in *An American Dilemma*, Bunche holds out hope that Negroes will secure their birthright as Americans because of the Constitution and the endorsement of the UN Charter, which he helped to write. Support for the Negroes' cause is building, he says, and time is on their side. But again, in a self-referential aside in paragraph 14, Bunche warns that the success of individual Negroes in crossing the color line is a rarity, so rare that it becomes front-page news. What lies behind this comment, of course, is his experience: Every triumph was shadowed by a racist setback. Bunche does not mention it here, but like other African American scholars of his generation who had earned doctorates from such schools as Harvard and Columbia, he was unable to find a teaching position at any white college or university. He had escaped lynch mobs in the South in 1938 while working with Gunnar Myrdal, and in 1948 he had rejected Presi-

Essential Quotes

> *"For who are they these graduates? They are Americans, they are American citizens, and they are Negroes. And unless they have led remarkably sheltered lives, they undoubtedly have a poignant realization of the significance of at least the latter."*
>
> (Paragraph 4)

> *"I am an American and I like the American way of life. I like freedom, and equality, and respect for the dignity of the individual. I believe that these graduates like them too. They like them so well that they bitterly resent being denied them because of an accident of birth."*
>
> (Paragraph 8)

> *"The barriers of race are formidable, but they can be surmounted. Indeed, the entire history of the Negro in this country has been a history of continuous, relentless progress over these barriers."*
>
> (Paragraph 18)

---

dent Truman's offer of an appointment as undersecretary of state because he would have had to move to Washington from New York and submit to the Jim Crow laws that kept the capital city as segregated as any state in the South.

In paragraphs 15 through 18, Bunche lays out what the Fisk graduates and Negroes in general must do if they hope to enter the mainstream of American life. It is a capsule history of his own life, from his graduation as valedictorian of his high school class to his successes at Harvard graduate school to his rapid rise in the War Department and State Department during World War II and his recent triumphs with the United Nations. Although Bunche was too private and modest to name these successes outright, it is certain his listeners knew exactly what he was saying and whose progress had been described.

In paragraphs 19 through 22, Bunche pays a moving tribute to his maternal grandmother, Lucy Taylor Johnson, who helped him develop a sense of self-worth and self-confidence, to set goals and strive to reach them despite all obstacles the world might put in his way, to defend and remain true to the principles he had embraced, and to be proud of his heritage.

Bunche concludes his remarks in paragraphs 23 and 24 with brief affirmation of his faith in the goals of the United Nations: to create a world of peace, tolerance, freedom, and equality. These are among the principles that have undergirded his actions as a member of the UN Secretariat, that have made possible his achievements, and that have helped him overcome the color barrier these graduates will also face and can, like him, transcend.

Audience

The commencement audience comprised the graduates in the Fisk University class of 1949, their family and friends, and the Fisk faculty, including the university's first African American president, Charles Spurgeon Johnson. A reporter from the Associated Press, who was present, filed a brief account that appeared in newspapers across the country; it was published in the *New York Times* on May 31 under the headline: "Bunche Says Negro Will Win Equality."

Impact

Within a month "The Barriers of Race Can Be Surmounted" was printed in its entirety in the July 1, 1949, edition of *Vital Speeches*, a semimonthly magazine (at that time published in New York). The editor of the *Negro Digest* revised Bunche's words without his permission and published a shortened version (1949) with a new title: "Nothing Is Impossible for the Negro." Several key points of the speech—those concerning the important role of Bunche's maternal grandmother as well as Bunche's perception of how the barriers of race could be overcome—found their way into the 1950 Nobel Peace Prize presentation speech, given by Gunnar Jahn, chairman of the Nobel Committee. Bunche's full speech was included in Willard Hayes Yeager's *Effective Speaking for Every Occasion*, published by Prentice-Hall in 1951.

As it turned out, the temperate voice of the UN mediator, so evident in Bunche's speech at Fisk, was not heard in the tumultuous years of the 1960s. What linked him to the civil rights movement was his work with Myrdal on *An American Dilemma*, the predictive wisdom of which was tested by time. In November 1971, Myrdal would acknowledge that *An American Dilemma* had underestimated the level of bias outside the South. It erroneously predicted that American labor unions would support racial equality, and he and his researchers had not foreseen the postwar white flight to the suburbs that led to the decay of the nation's inner cities, nor did they anticipate the civil rights movement of the 1960s. Still, *An American Dilemma* played a major role in *Brown v. Board of Education*, the 1954 U.S. Supreme Court decision that ordered an end to segregation in the nation's public schools. In asserting that the long-standing "separate but equal" doctrine was, in fact, a cause of inequality and feelings of inferiority, the Court succinctly cited Myrdal's book as proof. Following the *Brown* decision, textbook publishers regularly included parts of Bunche's speech in middle and high school social studies texts until well into the 1970s.

See also Booker T. Washington's Atlanta Exposition Address (1895); *Plessy v. Ferguson* (1896); W. E. B. Du Bois: *The Souls of Black Folk* (1903); Niagara Movement Declaration of Principles (1905); *Brown v. Board of Education* (1954).

Further Reading

- **Articles**

McFadden, Robert D. "Dr. Bunche of U.N., Nobel Winner, Dies." *New York Times*, December 10, 1971. Available online at www.nytimes.com/learning/general/onthisday/bday/0807.html.

- **Books**

Bunche, Ralph J. *The Political Status of the Negro in the Age of FDR*, ed. Dewey W. Grantham. Chicago: University of Chicago Press, 1973.

———. *A Brief and Tentative Analysis of Negro Leadership*, ed. Jonathan Scott Holloway. New York: New York University Press, 2005.

Du Bois, W. E. B. *The Souls of Black Folk*. New York: Oxford University Press, 2007.

Henry, Charles P., ed. *Ralph Bunche: Selected Speeches and Writings*. Ann Arbor: University of Michigan Press, 1995.

———. *Ralph Bunche: Model Negro or American Other?* New York: New York University Press, 1999.

Urquhart, Brian. *Ralph Bunche: An American Life*. New York: W. W. Norton, 1993.

Questions for Further Study

1. Compare this document with Alain Locke's "Enter the New Negro." What impact did Locke's views have on Bunche? How did the views of the two men differ?

2. What impact did Gunnar Myrdal's *An American Dilemma* have on the examination of race relations in the United States in the mid-twentieth century?

3. How did Bunche's address represent a reversal of the views expressed in Booker T. Washington's Atlanta Exposition Address (1895)?

4. Bunche places a great deal of emphasis on entering the "mainstream" of American life. Many black activists have disagreed, calling for separate black organizations and black nationalism. Which view do you believe has emerged as the dominant one in the African American community generally? Why?

5. Compare this document with *To Secure These Rights*, a report drafted by President Harry S. Truman's Committee on Civil Rights just two years before, in 1947. Discuss the extent to which the report, coupled with views such as those expressed by Bunche, began to represent a turning point in the issue of civil rights at midcentury.

Washington, Booker T. *Up from Slavery*. New York: Signet Classics, 2010.

■ **Web Sites**

"A Century of Segregation." PBS's "The Rise and Fall of Jim Crow" Web site.
http://www.pbs.org/wnet/jimcrow/segregation.html.

Du Bois, W. E. B. "The Talented Tenth." Gilder Lehrman Center for the Study of Slavery, Resistance, and Abolition Web site.
http://www.yale.edu/glc/archive/1148.htm.

Jahn, Gunnar. "The Nobel Peace Prize 1950: Presentation Speech." Nobel Prize Web site.
http://nobelprize.org/nobel_prizes/peace/laureates/1950/press.html.

"The Niagara Movement." Circle Association's "African American History of Western New York State, 1900 to 1935" Web site.
http://www.math.buffalo.edu/~sww/0history/hwny-niagara-movement.html.

—Allan L. Damon

Ralph J. Bunche: "The Barriers of Race Can Be Surmounted"

In the brief remarks I will make you will understand that today I think exclusively of these young Negro men and women who are graduating, and of the great number like them who will be graduating from other institutions of higher learning in the coming two or three weeks. I have been puzzled no little about what to say to them on this great day in their lives, this milestone along their road of progress in life.

This is, or certainly should be, a joyous occasion, an occasion so joyous, indeed, that all the participants must wear black robes and somber hats to leaven the joy, to keep it from effervescing excessively and to afford at least a semblance of solemnity, academic dignity and sobriety. Despite the black crepe and the mournful facade this is pure ritual a cultural lag one is tempted to be light hearted, and gay and poetic, to play with words and music, and preserve the fanciful mood. But in this age time is short even for the young. The sands run fast. And in any case, my poetry would be doggerel and my music discordant. A wise man always sticks to his last.

Unless young graduates have changed radically since the day twenty-two years ago when I first donned the academic gown, they have a number of things on their minds as they sit here. First, they are thinking of how they are going to celebrate when this final ritual is over or rather, continue the celebration, for unless I miss my guess, they began to celebrate as soon as it was certified that they would be sitting here today. And since there are undoubtedly timid souls amongst us, it would probably be tactful not to elaborate on the varied and even ingenious forms which such celebration may take. But I daresay there are also some very sober thoughts lurking in the recesses of the minds of these graduates.

For who are they these graduates? They are Americans, they are American citizens, and they are Negroes. And unless they have led remarkably sheltered lives, they undoubtedly have a poignant realization of the significance of at least the latter.

I would like to explore with them just what, at this very moment in this great nation, it means to be an American, a citizen, and a Negro. I cannot imagine that any question could be of more vital import to these young people on the threshold of a new adventure. Nor do I have any illusions that I can give them all the answers they must seek.

We Americans are part of a vast and powerful and dynamic nation, a great power whose responsibilities and influence in the modern world are frightening in their scope. The origin, traditions and creed of this nation are an inspiration to all freedom loving peoples. Our country's history is brave. Americans fought and died for their freedom and liberty. Having won by their blood the right to maintain an independent existence, our founding fathers established the nation on the cardinal principles of individual liberty and the equality of man. They spoke of inalienable rights, of the incontestable fact that all men are born free and equal, of the dignity of man. These were the essential virtues. In my view they still are. The founding fathers charted the way for the development of a great and virile democracy. They immortalized these concepts in our Constitution.

The American citizen is at once the benefactor and protector of this great American legacy. The privileges and rights of the American citizen—of all American citizens—are writ large in our Constitution, in our traditions, in what has been called the American creed. I need not detail them. But they guarantee to every citizen of this great nation all of the essential attributes of a free and dignified existence. In return, they require of the citizen that he meet his obligations to the State and to his fellow man in order that the American way of life may be preserved and perpetuated.

I am an American and I like the American way of life. I like freedom, and equality, and respect for the dignity of the individual. I believe that these graduates like them too. They like them so well that they bitterly resent being denied them because of an accident of birth.

There is a certain irony in the situation with which we are faced here. These Negro graduates of Fisk University today are better Americans than they are Negroes. They are Negroes primarily in a negative sense—they reject that sort of treatment that deprives them of their birthright as Americans. Remove that treatment and their identification as Negroes in the American society would become meaningless, at least as meaningless as it is to be of English, or French, or German or Italian ancestry.

These graduates are one hundred per cent Americans. Who, indeed, is a better American, a better protector of the American heritage, of the American way, than he who demands the fullest measure of respect for those cardinal principles which are the pillars of our society?

If we could probe deeply into the minds of these graduates we would discover, I am sure, that the basic longing, the aspiration of every one of them, is to be an American in full. Not a semi-American. Not a Negro American. Not an Afro-American. Not a "Colored Gentleman." Not "one of our Colored Brethren." Just an American with no qualifications, no ifs or buts, no apologies, condescension or patronization. Just Americans, with a fair and equal opportunity as individuals to make or break their futures on the basis of their individual abilities without the un-American handicap of race. Can it be doubted that these young men and women must even now be calculating their chances to make their way into the mainstream of American life? And can it be doubted that they must be greatly tormented at the prospect that because of their race they may be kept out of the mainstream and shunted into the bayous and creeks and backwashes of American life?

And what may be told to them? That as Americans and citizens of this great democracy they are as entitled as the next man to negotiate the waters of the mainstream could be disputed only by racial bigots. But to encourage them to believe that their course is charted and the shoals of racialism no longer endanger them would be criminally misleading.

This, it seems to me, is what they should know. The democratic framework of our society is their great hope. The American Negro suffers cruel disabilities because of race which are in most flagrant violation of the constitutional tenets and ideals of the American democracy. But the saving grace for the Negro is the democratic warp and woof of the society which permits the Negro to carry on his incessant and heroic struggle to come into his own, to win those rights, that dignity and respect for the Negro, individually and collectively, which are his birthright as an American. And, fortunately, the American, white and black alike, has a conscience. The Negro American daily wins increasing support for his struggle from all those other Americans who aspire toward a democratic, not a semi-democratic America; who wish a four fourths, not a three fourths democracy. Moreover, the sympathy of the world is with him. The Charter of the United Nations endorses his aspirations.

This also, these graduates should know well and underscore. It is true that on occasion, an individual Negro may, by tremendous effort, successfully negotiate the racial rapids and find himself in the mainstream. But that this is a rarity and his group is far behind, is abundantly testified to by the fact that this very presence in the mainstream is front page news. The status of the individual, in the long view, can be no more secure than the status of his group.

We Negroes must be great realists: The road over which we must travel is clear, though the prospect may not be pleasant We suffer crippling disadvantages because of our origin. But we are Americans, in a basically democratic American society. That society is a competitive society. The going is hard even for white Americans. It is harder for us. To make his way, the Negro must have firm resolve, persistence, tenacity. He must gear himself to hard work all the way. He can never let up. He can never have too much preparation and training. He must be a strong competitor. He must adhere staunchly to the basic principle that anything less than full equality is not enough. If he ever compromises on that principle his soul is dead. He must realize that he and his group have not attained the goal until it is no longer necessary to make reference to the fact that "X" was the "first Negro" to do this or that, and until accomplishment by a Negro is taken by the public at large as a matter of fact.

This may have a harsh ring, but it is the gospel truth. The road of Negro progress is no road for weaklings. Those who cannot summon up the courage, the resolve and the stamina to travel along it can find refuge in a handy alibi: the disadvantages of race. And they can find ample documentation to support their plea. But a community of people cannot adopt an alibi, however credible, as its philosophy of life.

My own philosophy on such matters is quite simple: whatever is worthwhile is worth working, striving, sacrificing, and struggling for.

There is no substitute for hard work as the key to success in the American society. This is true for white Americans. It is even more true for black Americans. Few Americans of any color or creed can ever find easy the climb up the ladder.

But while nothing is easy for the Negro in America, neither is anything impossible. The barriers of race are formidable, but they can be surmounted. Indeed, the entire history of the Negro in this country has been a history of continuous, relentless progress over these barriers. Like "Old Man River," the Negro keeps "movin' along," and if I know my people, the Negro will keep on moving resolutely along until his goal of complete and unequivocal equality is attained.

If I may be pardoned for a personal reference, I should like to say that in my own struggle against the barriers of race, I have from early age been strongly fortified by the philosophy taught me by my maternal grandmother, and it may be of interest to you.

She was a tiny woman, but a personality of indomitable will and invincible moral and spiritual strength. "Nana" we all called her, and she was the ruler of our family "clan." She had come from Texas, married in Indian territory, and on the premature death of my grandfather, was left with five young children.

Nana had traveled the troubled road. But she had never flinched or complained. Her indoctrination of the youngsters of the "clan" began at an early age. The philosophy she handed down to us was as simple as it has proved invaluable. Your color, she counseled, has nothing to do with your worth. You are potentially as good as anyone. How good you may prove to be will have no relation to your color, but with what is in your heart and your head. That is something which each individual, by his own effort, can control. The right to be treated as an equal by all other men, she said, is man's birthright. Never permit any one to treat you otherwise. For nothing is as important as maintaining your dignity and self respect. She told us that there would be many and great obstacles in our paths and that this was the way of life. But only weaklings give up in the face of obstacles. Set a goal for yourself and determine to reach it despite all obstacles. Be honest and frank with yourself and the world at all times. Never compromise what you know to be the right. Never pick a fight, but never run from one if your principles are at stake. Never be content with any effort you make until you are certain you have given it the best you have in you. Go out into the world with your head high and keep it high at all times.

Nana's advice and philosophy is as good today for these graduates as it was when she gave it to me in my childhood. I certainly cannot improve upon it, nor would I try to do so. For me it has been a priceless heritage from a truly noble woman.

In conclusion, I may say only that I have great faith that the kind of world we all long for can and will be achieved. It is the kind of world the United Nations is working incessantly to bring about: a world at peace; a world in which people practice tolerance and live together in peace with one another as good neighbors; a world in which there is full respect for human rights and fundamental freedom for all without distinction as to race, sex, language, or religion; a world in which all men shall walk together as equals and with dignity.

I trust that among these graduates there are many who will consecrate their lives to the struggle to achieve that kind of world.

Fred M. Vinson, in the year of his appointment to the U.S. Court of Appeals (Library of Congress)

Sweatt v. Painter

1950

"The Fourteenth Amendment requires that petitioner be admitted to the University of Texas Law School."

Overview

On June 5, 1950, the U.S. Supreme Court rendered its decision in the case *Sweatt v. Painter*. In 1946 an African American, Heman Marion Sweatt, applied for admission to the law school at the University of Texas in Austin; at the time, the president of the university was Theophilus Painter. The Texas constitution, however, prohibited integrated education; therefore, Sweatt was denied admission because of his race. He filed suit, but a Texas trial court delayed the case for six months to give the state time to establish a "separate but equal" law school for blacks in Houston; that law school would eventually evolve into Texas Southern University. Sweatt challenged this step in the Texas Court of Civil Appeals, which affirmed the trial court's ruling. After the Texas Supreme Court refused to hear the case on appeal, Sweatt, represented by William J. Durham and Thurgood Marshall (the future U.S. Supreme Court justice), appealed to the U.S. Supreme Court. The fundamental legal question the case presented was whether the University of Texas admissions policy violated the equal protection clause of the Fourteenth Amendment to the U.S. Constitution. The Court unanimously held that it did and ruled that Sweatt be admitted to the University of Texas Law School. In its ruling, written by Chief Justice Frederick Moore (Fred M.) Vinson, the Court stated that the law school for "Negroes," which had begun operation in 1947, was not equal to the University of Texas Law School in such matters as course selection, faculty, the library, and prestige. Further, the Court found that the proposed law school's separation from the University of Texas Law School would make it difficult for its graduates to compete in the legal profession.

Context

The backdrop for *Sweatt v. Painter* was the landmark case *Plessy v. Ferguson*, on which the U.S. Supreme Court ruled in 1896. After the Civil War, the Thirteenth Amendment to the Constitution outlawed slavery in the United States. The Fourteenth Amendment was adopted on July 9, 1868, in large part to secure the civil liberties of newly freed slaves. The key section of the Fourteenth Amendment is Section 1, which states:

> All persons born or naturalized in the United States and subject to the jurisdiction thereof, are citizens of the United States and of the State wherein they reside. No State shall make or enforce any law which shall abridge the privileges or immunities of citizens of the United States; nor shall any State deprive any person of life, liberty, or property, without due process of law; nor deny to any person within its jurisdiction the equal protection of the laws.

Thus, the Fourteenth Amendment extends "equal protection of the laws" to all citizens.

In 1883 the Supreme Court heard a set of cases that had been consolidated into what are called the Civil Rights Cases. The Court's ruling in the Civil Rights Cases was a setback for African Americans, for it held that the Fourteenth Amendment applied only to the actions of government. Thus, segregation on the part of government was unconstitutional, but segregation on the part of private parties, including businesses, was not. Worse, the Court ruled that the Civil Rights Act of 1875 was unconstitutional. That act had said that

> all persons within the jurisdiction of the United States shall be entitled to the full and equal enjoyment of the accommodations, advantages, facilities, and privileges of inns, public conveyances on land or water, theaters, and other places of public amusement; subject only to the conditions and limitations established by law, and applicable alike to citizens of every race and color, regardless of any previous condition of servitude.

In the wake of the Civil Rights Cases decision, numerous states and municipalities, particularly (but not exclusively) in the South, passed so-called Jim Crow laws that segregated African Americans and kept them in subservient positions. One well-known law was Act 111, also known as the Separate Car Act, which the state of Louisiana passed in 1890 and required separate accommodations for blacks

Time Line

1868
- **July 9**
  The Fourteenth Amendment to the U.S. Constitution is adopted.

1875
- **March 1**
  President Ulysses S. Grant signs the Civil Rights Act of 1875 into law.

1883
- **October 15**
  In the Civil Rights Cases decision, the U.S. Supreme Court declares the Civil Rights Act of 1875 unconstitutional.

1890
- **January 22**
  Frederick Moore Vinson is born in Louisa, Kentucky.

1896
- **May 18**
  The Supreme Court upholds the separate-but-equal doctrine in public accommodations in its *Plessy v. Ferguson* ruling.

1936
- **January 15**
  In its ruling on *Murray v. Maryland*, a case argued by the future Supreme Court justice Thurgood Marshall, the Maryland Court of Appeals orders the University of Maryland to integrate its student body.

1938
- **December 12**
  In *Missouri ex rel. Gaines v. Canada*, the Supreme Court rules that states with a school for white students must provide in-state education to blacks, either by allowing blacks and whites to attend the same school or by creating a second school for blacks.

1946
- Heman Sweatt attempts to enroll at the University of Texas Law School but is denied admission because of his race.

---

and whites on railroad cars. To challenge the law, the Citizens' Committee to Test the Separate Car Act enlisted Homer Plessy, who was one-eighth black (and thus black according to Louisiana law), to ride in a railroad car reserved for whites. While he was on the train, Plessy announced that he was black and submitted to arrest for violating the act. The committee had ensured that a detective was in the car to make the arrest.

Plessy's case wound its way to the Supreme Court, which in an eight-to-one decision held that the separate accommodations called for in the Louisiana law did not violate the equal protection clause of the Fourteenth Amendment. Writing for the majority, Justice Henry Billings Brown stated:

> We consider the underlying fallacy of the plaintiff's argument to consist in the assumption that the enforced separation of the two races stamps the colored race with a badge of inferiority. If this be so, it is not by reason of anything found in the act, but solely because the colored race chooses to put that construction upon it.

The lone dissenter was Justice John Marshall Harlan, who famously wrote:

> But in view of the Constitution, in the eye of the law, there is in this country no superior, dominant, ruling class of citizens. There is no caste here. Our Constitution is color-blind, and neither knows nor tolerates classes among citizens. In respect of civil rights, all citizens are equal before the law.

Harlan's view would ultimately gain acceptance, but for the next half century the Court's decision in *Plessy v. Ferguson* upheld the doctrine of "separate but equal." Determined to attack it was the National Association for the Advancement of Colored People (NAACP) and its Legal Defense and Education Fund. Under the leadership of Charles Hamilton Houston and, later, Thurgood Marshall, the NAACP made the decision to launch an assault on Jim Crow in the courts by focusing on education.

One of the first cracks in the separate-but-equal doctrine appeared in the mid-1930s with the *Murray v. Maryland* case (sometimes referred to as *Pearson et al. v. Murray*). It was argued by Marshall, who himself had been denied admission to the University of Maryland Law School because he was black. Marshall's argument before the Baltimore City Circuit Court was that because the "white" and "black" law schools in Maryland were unequal, the only remedy was to allow the plaintiff, Donald Gaines Murray, to enroll in the University of Maryland Law School. The Maryland Court of Appeals agreed, ruling in January 1936 that "the state has undertaken the function of education in the law, but has omitted students of one race from the only adequate provision made for it, and omitted them solely because of their color," and Murray was admitted. The crack widened in 1938 with the

Supreme Court's decision in *Missouri ex rel. Gaines v. Canada*. (*Ex rel.* is an abbreviation of *ex relatione*, a Latin expression used in the law to mean "on behalf of.") The Court ruled that states with a school for white students must provide in-state education to blacks, either by allowing blacks and whites to attend the same school or by creating a second school for blacks. The problem with this ruling, of course, was that any such educational institution hurriedly thrown together solely for blacks was unlikely to be equal to all-white institutions in facilities, faculty, and prestige, but at least the Court was beginning to chip away at the denial of higher education to African Americans by all-white institutions.

During World War II, issues involving national security preoccupied the Court. After the war, however, civil rights began to dominate the Court's docket, and wider fissures opened in the separate-but-equal doctrine. The time for change was ripe. During the war, President Franklin Roosevelt had desegregated the defense industries and federal government hiring. After the war, the public was growing more aware of the atrocities that had been committed by Nazi Germany, including the wholesale denial of civil rights to Jews and other groups. On July 26, 1948, President Harry S. Truman issued Executive Order 9981, desegregating the military, and that year the United Nations passed the Universal Declaration of Human Rights. In this climate, other key Supreme Court cases challenged the separate-but-equal doctrine. In 1948 the Court ruled in *Sipuel v. Board of Regents of the University of Oklahoma* that Oklahoma was required to admit qualified African Americans to the previously all-white University of Oklahoma Law School. This was only a partial victory, for when Ada Lois Sipuel was finally admitted, she was compelled to sit in a raised chair apart from other students behind a sign that read "colored." She was also required to use a separate entrance to the law school and eat alone in the cafeteria. Later that year, the Court struck down restrictive racial covenants in housing in *Shelley v. Kraemer*. (A covenant is an agreement, in this case an agreement by a property owner not to sell his or her property to non-Caucasians.) On the same day that the Court issued its decision in *Sweatt v. Painter*, it also issued its decision in *McLaurin v. Oklahoma State Regents*, ruling that African Americans admitted to a state university had to be granted full access to the school's facilities.

Heman Sweatt was born in 1912 in Houston, Texas. He graduated from college in 1934 and worked as a schoolteacher before entering the University of Michigan Medical School. He soon returned to Houston, however, and found work as a postal clerk. In the 1940s he became active in the civil rights movement; he attended meetings of the Houston branch of the NAACP and worked on voter-registration drives. During his efforts to end discrimination among postal workers, he became interested in the law and decided to pursue a law degree. His suit against the University of Texas Law School was a test case. The Houston NAACP had wanted to find an African American who would apply to the law school and, after that person inevitably had been rejected because of race, file suit. Sweatt volunteered to assume that role. As

Time Line

1947
- **March 3** A law school for African Americans is opened in Houston, Texas; the school will become Texas Southern University.

1948
- **January 12** In *Sipuel v. Board of Regents of the University of Oklahoma*, the Supreme Court rules that Oklahoma is required to admit qualified African Americans to the previously all-white University of Oklahoma Law School.
- **May 3** In *Shelley v. Kraemer*, the Supreme Court strikes down restrictive racial covenants in housing.

1950
- **June 5** In *McLaurin v. Oklahoma State Regents*, the Supreme Court rules that African Americans admitted to a state university have to be granted full access to its facilities.
- **June 5** The U.S. Supreme Court issues its decision in *Sweatt v. Painter*.

1954
- **May 17** The U.S. Supreme Court issues its landmark decision in *Brown v. Board of Education*.

the case wound its way through the court system, Sweatt gave public presentations at NAACP fund-raising events; he was also subjected to threats and harassment. Finally, the Supreme Court heard oral arguments on the case on April 4, 1950, and issued its decision on June 5.

About the Author

Frederick Moore Vinson was the only member of the Supreme Court to have served in all three branches of government. He was born in Louisa, Kentucky, on January 22, 1890, and from an early age displayed a remarkable intellect, graduating at the top of his class from Kentucky Normal College in 1908. In 1911 he graduated from Centre College Law School with the highest scores in the school's history. A talented baseball player, he played semiprofessional ball in the Kentucky Blue Grass League and tried out for the Cincinnati Reds. But he returned to Louisa, where he became a small-town lawyer. He won his first elective office in 1921 as commonwealth attorney for the Thirty-second Judicial District of Kentucky. Three years later, Vinson won a special election to complete an unexpired term in the U.S. House of Representatives, where he served until 1938, except for the years from 1929 to 1931. For his support of New Deal programs, President Franklin Roosevelt appointed him to the U.S. Court of Appeals for the District of Columbia, where he took his seat on the bench in 1938.

Vinson's service in the executive branch of government began in 1943, when he resigned from the court and became director of the Office of Economic Stabilization. There his chief task was controlling inflation during the war by fighting off requests from businesses for price increases and from organized labor for wage increases. Other posts in the executive branch soon followed. In March 1945 he became administrator of the Federal Loan Agency. One month later, he was appointed director of the Office of War Mobilization and Reconversion, the purpose of which was to ensure the smooth conversion from a wartime to a peacetime economy. President Truman recognized Vinson's skills as a fiscal manager and in July 1945 appointed him secretary of the Treasury. In this post he played a major role in creating the International Bank for Reconstruction and Development and the International Monetary Fund.

In April 1946, Chief Justice Harlan Fiske Stone died. To replace him, Truman turned to Vinson, who took his seat on the High Court as chief justice on June 24, 1946, a position he held until his death. His tenure as chief justice coincided with the early years of the cold war and the nation's fear of Communism. Vinson supported the right of the federal government to legislate against groups that advocated the overthrow of the American system. Throughout his judicial career, he was deferential to executive and legislative authority. He upheld, for example, President Truman's emergency seizure of the coal mines following a nationwide strike in 1946, and in 1952 he dissented from a Court ruling that Truman had exceeded his authority by interceding in the steelworkers' strike during the Korean War and forcing a labor settlement, claiming wartime executive power. Truman held Vinson in high regard and mentioned his name as a possible successor as president. Vinson died of a heart attack in his apartment in Washington, D.C., on September 8, 1953. He had devoted nearly his entire career to public service and left behind an estate worth less than $1,000.

Explanation and Analysis of the Document

The written decision in *Sweatt v. Painter* begins with a number of legalities typically found in a Supreme Court written decision. Usually, these introductory remarks are prepared by the justice's clerk (often a recent law school graduate who does research for the justice). The opening paragraph, called the syllabus, is a brief description of the case. It identifies the petitioner (Sweatt) and the respondent (nominally Painter but in reality the University of Texas Law School) and summarizes the basis of the Court's ruling and the ruling itself. A person can read the syllabus and get the essence of the case without having to read the entire decision. The word *Reversed* indicates that the Court has reversed the decision of the lower court, in this instance the Texas Court of Civic Appeals. What follows is a brief description of the case's history, noting that it had begun in a Texas trial court, was appealed to the Texas Court of Civic Appeals, was returned to the trial court, and then was appealed to the Texas Supreme Court. The document states that the trial court "denied mandamus to compel [Sweatt's] admission to the University of Texas Law School." *Mandamus* is Latin for "we command" and is commonly used in law to refer to a court order requiring a lower court or a government official to perform a duty or to refrain from doing something. In this instance, the trial court refused to require the university law school to admit Sweatt, thus giving the state of Texas time to cobble together a law school for African Americans.

Further legalities follow. The document identifies the attorneys who argued the case for both the petitioner and the respondent. It then notes that amici curiae briefs were filed for both the plaintiff and the defendant. *Amici curiae* is a Latin expression meaning "friends of the court" and refers to briefs submitted by outside parties in support of one position or the other. In complex litigation, particularly a case with broad implications, it is common for individuals and organizations to attempt to sway the Court with analyses of the case and additional information that the Court might find useful. Typically, in a brief filed by one who appeals a case, in this instance Sweatt, the emphasis must be on legal errors that the lower courts made; the brief does not reargue the facts of the case or anything outside of the law. Amici curiae briefs often range widely in discussing the broader implications of the issues at hand.

With preliminaries disposed of, Vinson outlines the Court's decision. In the first paragraph, he presents the legal question the case raises: "To what extent does the Equal Protection Clause of the Fourteenth Amendment limit the power of a state to distinguish between students of different races in professional and graduate education in a state university?" He goes on to note that "broader issues have been urged for our consideration," likely a reference to the content of the amici curiae briefs, but Vinson indicates that he is going to rule on the case strictly in conformity with the law as he sees it. This is an indication that the Court was not going to reexamine *Plessy v. Ferguson*.

Paragraphs 2 and 3 summarize the facts of the case and refer again to its history, from the trial court through the Texas Supreme Court. Vinson notes that mandamus was denied, which gave the state time to establish a law school for African Americans. Sweatt, though, refused to enroll in the new law school. The Texas Court of Civic Appeals then returned the case to the trial court "without prejudice," meaning that none of the rights or privileges of the persons involved was waived or lost. In other words, the court said that essentially the case was to begin again. In paragraph 4, Vinson notes that when the case was remanded, or sent back to the trial court, the court ruled that the new law school for African Americans was "substantially equivalent" to the University of Texas Law School. The Texas Court of Civic Appeals affirmed the ruling of the trial court, and the Texas Supreme Court refused to hear Sweatt's appeal of this ruling. Accordingly, Sweatt appealed to the U.S. Supreme Court, which "granted certiorari," a legal term that means the Court has required the lower court to turn over the trial records; it also indicates that the Court has agreed to hear the case.

With paragraphs 5 and 6, Vinson begins his analysis of the case. He notes that the facilities at the two institutions were markedly different. At the University of Texas, the faculty was larger, and the law library contained considerably more materials. In contrast, the law school for African Americans was not accredited, though Vinson points out in paragraph 7 that the school, three years after its formation, was on its way toward accreditation. He also mentions that the new law school lacked the prestige of the University of Texas; for example, the new law school did not have an Order of the Coif, a prestigious national scholastic society whose members have an inside track to the best jobs as attorneys. In paragraph 8, Vinson concludes that the University of Texas Law School was clearly superior in the opportunities it afforded students. He also notes that the University of Texas was superior in intangible features: "reputation of the faculty, experience of the administration, position and influence of the alumni, standing in the community, traditions and prestige." Paragraph 10 goes on to point out another disadvantage that the African American students would face at a separate law school: They would be isolated from the 85 percent of the state's population, including judges, other attorneys, officials, and others who were part of the environment in which a person would practice law.

Paragraph 10 responds to the state's claim that excluding blacks from the University of Texas would be no different from excluding whites from the new law school. Vinson dismisses this argument by saying that as a practical matter, no University of Texas student would want to attend the new law school, given its obvious inferiority. Notice that Vinson cites *Shelley v. Kraemer*: "Equal protection of the laws is not achieved through indiscriminate imposition of inequalities." In paragraph 11, Vinson cites other precedents, including *Sipuel v. Board of Regents of the University of Oklahoma* and *Missouri ex rel. Gaines v. Canada*, to emphasize that the equal protection clause of the Fourteenth Amendment requires states to provide equal opportunities in legal education for their citizens. Bowing to these precedents, Vinson concludes in paragraph 12 that the "petitioner may claim his full constitutional right: legal education equivalent to that offered by the State to students of other races." Vinson rejects the view that *Plessy v. Ferguson* allowed the state to provide a pretense of equivalency. At the same time, he rejects the view that the Court should reexamine *Plessy*. Paragraph 13 concludes the decision: "We hold that the Equal Protection Clause of the Fourteenth Amendment requires that petitioner be admitted to the University of Texas Law School."

Audience

The immediate audience for Vinson's decision in *Sweatt v. Painter* was, of course, the parties to the suit: Sweatt and the University of Texas in the person of its president, Theophilus Painter. A broader audience was the entire higher education community. This case, in combination with *McLaurin v. Oklahoma State Regents* decided on the same day, sent a message to state colleges and universities throughout Texas and the nation that the separate-but-equal doctrine would no longer stand in the provision of higher education for African Americans. A third audience consisted of members of the NAACP and those who sympathized with the organization's goals. *Sweatt v. Painter* was a test case, specifically engineered by the NAACP to challenge the separate-but-equal doctrine in the state of Texas. Although the ruling in the case did not specifically overturn the ruling in *Plessy v. Ferguson*, it represented a significant victory in the effort to render that case impotent and to dismantle the Jim Crow system.

Impact

One specific impact of the case was the establishment of what is today Texas Southern University in Houston, with an enrollment of more than nine thousand undergraduates and more than two thousand graduate students. The university was established on March 3, 1947, in response to Sweatt's lawsuit. At the time, the Houston College for Negroes was part of the Houston public school district. The state assumed control of the college, which then formed the core of what was originally called Texas State University for Negroes. The law school is now called the Thurgood Marshall School of Law.

The chief goal of the NAACP in the 1930s and 1940s was to overturn *Plessy v. Ferguson*. Thurgood Marshall and the NAACP had hoped that *Sweatt v. Painter* would have given the Supreme Court that opportunity. They were disappointed. The Court, under the leadership of Chief Justice Vinson, was essentially conservative, and Vinson himself was reluctant to overturn earlier Supreme Court decisions. He said as much in his decision in this case when he wrote: "Because of this traditional reluctance to extend constitutional interpretations to situations or facts which are not before the Court, much of the excellent research and detailed argument presented in these cases is unnecessary to their disposition." Near the end of his decision he stated explicitly that *Plessy* would not be reexamined. Put simply, the Court declined specifically to overturn *Plessy v. Ferguson*.

Matters did not end there, however. Civil rights advocates in 1950 recognized that *Sweatt v. Painter*, along with

Essential Quotes

> *"Whether the University of Texas Law School is compared with the original or the new law school for Negroes, we cannot find substantial equality in the educational opportunities offered white and Negro law students by the State."*
>
> (Paragraph 8)

> *"Petitioner may claim his full constitutional right: legal education equivalent to that offered by the State to students of other races. Such education is not available to him in a separate law school as offered by the State."*
>
> (Paragraph 12)

> *"We hold that the Equal Protection Clause of the Fourteenth Amendment requires that petitioner be admitted to the University of Texas Law School."*
>
> (Paragraph 13)

McLaurin v. Oklahoma State Regents and earlier cases with a bearing on equal protection in the realm of higher education, had undermined the separate-but-equal doctrine and that it was only a matter of time before the doctrine would collapse. That time arrived four years later with the watershed case *Brown v. Board of Education*, which Marshall argued before the Court. In a unanimous decision, the Court, under Chief Justice Earl Warren, held that "separate educational facilities are inherently unequal" and that racial segregation in public schools—then mandated by law in the District of Columbia and seventeen states in the South and Midwest—violated the equal protection clause of the Fourteenth Amendment. (It should be noted that sixteen states in the Northeast, Midwest, and West specifically outlawed racial segregation in schools, and another eleven states had no laws on the matter.) This decision finally drove a stake through the heart of the separate-but-equal doctrine.

Sweatt enrolled at the University of Texas Law School in 1950. The case had taken a toll on his physical and emotional health, however, and he withdrew from the school in 1952. He then received a scholarship from the School of Social Work at Atlanta University and completed a master's degree there in 1954. In the ensuing years he worked for the NAACP in Cleveland, Ohio; returned to Atlanta as the assistant director of the city's chapter of the Urban League; and taught at Atlanta University. In 1987 the University of Texas Law School inaugurated the annual Heman Sweatt Symposium in Civil Rights and offers an annual scholarship in his name.

See also Thirteenth Amendment to the U.S. Constitution (1865); Fourteenth Amendment to the U.S. Constitution (1868); Civil Rights Cases (1883); *Plessy v. Ferguson* (1896); Executive Order 9981 (1948); *Brown v. Board of Education* (1954).

Further Reading

■ Articles

Kirk, W. Aston, and John T. Q. King. "Desegregation of Higher Education in Texas." *Journal of Negro Education* 27, no. 3 (Summer 1958): 318–323.

Levy, David W. "Before Brown: The Racial Integration of American Higher Education." *Journal of Supreme Court History* 24, no. 3 (1999): 298–313.

■ Books

Browne-Marshall, Gloria J. *Race, Law, and American Society: 1607–Present*. New York: Routledge, 2007.

Davis, Abraham L., and Barbara Luck Graham. *The Supreme Court, Race, and Civil Rights: From Marshall to Rehnquist*. Thousand Oaks, Calif.: Sage Publications, 1995.

Greenberg, Jack. *Crusaders in the Courts: How a Dedicated Band of Lawyers Fought for the Civil Rights Revolution*. New York: Basic Books, 1994.

Harrison, Maureen, and Steve Gilbert, eds. *Civil Rights Decisions of the U.S. Supreme Court: 20th Century.* San Diego, Calif.: Excellent Books, 1994.

Howard, John R. *The Shifting Wind: The Supreme Court and Civil Rights from Reconstruction to Brown.* Albany: State University of New York Press, 1999.

Klarman, Michael J. *From Jim Crow to Civil Rights: The Supreme Court and the Struggle for Racial Equality.* New York: Oxford University Press, 2004.

Tsesis, Alexander. *We Shall Overcome: A History of Civil Rights and the Law.* New Haven, Conn.: Yale University Press, 2008.

Woodward, C. Vann. *The Strange Career of Jim Crow*, 3rd rev. ed. New York: Oxford University Press, 1974.

■ Web Sites

Burns, Richard Allen. "Heman Marion Sweatt." Handbook of Texas Online.
http://www.tshaonline.org/handbook/online//articles/SS/fsw23.html.

—Michael J. O'Neal

Questions for Further Study

1. What was the "separate-but-equal" doctrine? Where and how did it originate? What impact did the doctrine have on African Americans?

2. Read this document in conjunction with Charles Hamilton Houston's "Educational Inequalities Must Go!" (1935). How was *Sweatt v. Painter* part of an overall strategy designed to challenge the separate-but-equal doctrine?

3. What other developments in the 1940s perhaps contributed to a climate of opinion that led to the Court's ruling in *Sweatt v. Painter*?

4. How did *Sweatt v. Painter* (and other Court cases) pave the way for the Court's landmark ruling in *Brown v. Board of Education*?

5. What is the meaning of the equal protection clause of the Fourteenth Amendment? Why was this clause at the center of the Court's ruling in *Sweatt v. Painter* and other cases?

Sweatt v. Painter

Petitioner was denied admission to the state-supported University of Texas Law School, solely because he is a Negro and state law forbids the admission of Negroes to that Law School. He was offered, but he refused, enrollment in a separate law school newly established by the State for Negroes. The University of Texas Law School has 16 full-time and three part-time professors, 850 students, a library of 65,000 volumes, a law review, moot court facilities, scholarship funds, an Order of the Coif affiliation, many distinguished alumni, and much tradition and prestige. The separate law school for Negroes has five full-time professors, 23 students, a library of 16,500 volumes, a practice court, a legal aid association and one alumnus admitted to the Texas Bar; but it excludes from its student body members of racial groups which number 85% of the population of the State and which include most of the lawyers, witnesses, jurors, judges, and other officials with whom petitioner would deal as a member of the Texas Bar. Held: The legal education offered petitioner is not substantially equal to that which he would receive if admitted to the University of Texas Law School; and the Equal Protection Clause of the Fourteenth Amendment requires that he be admitted to the University of Texas Law School.

Reversed.

A Texas trial court found that a newly-established state law school for Negroes offered petitioner "privileges, advantages, and opportunities for the study of law substantially equivalent to those offered by the State to white students at the University of Texas" and denied mandamus to compel his admission to the University of Texas Law School. The Court of Civil Appeals affirmed.... The Texas Supreme Court denied writ of error. This Court granted certiorari.... Reversed....

W. J. Durham and Thurgood Marshall argued the cause for petitioner. With them on the brief were Robert L. Carter, William R. Ming, Jr., James M. Nabrit and Franklin H. Williams.

Price Daniel, Attorney General of Texas, and Joe R. Greenhill, First Assistant Attorney General, argued the cause for respondents. With them on the brief was E. Jacobson, Assistant Attorney General.

Briefs of amici curiae, supporting petitioner, were filed by Solicitor General Perlman and Philip Elman for the United States; Paul G. Annes for the American Federation of Teachers; Thomas I. Emerson, Erwin N. Griswold, Robert Hale, Harold Havighurst and Edward Levi for the Committee of Law Teachers Against Segregation in Legal Education; Phineas Indritz for the American Veterans Committee, Inc.; and Marcus Cohn and Jacob Grumet for the American Jewish Committee et al.

An amici curiae brief in support of respondents was filed on behalf of the States of Arkansas, by Ike Murray, Attorney General; Florida, by Richard W. Ervin, Attorney General, and Frank J. Heintz, Assistant Attorney General; Georgia, by Eugene Cook, Attorney General, and M. H. Blackshear, Jr., Assistant Attorney General; Kentucky, by A. E. Funk, Attorney General, and M. B. Holifield, Assistant Attorney General; Louisiana, by Bolivar E. Kemp, Jr., Attorney General; Mississippi, by Greek L. Rice, Attorney General, and George H. Ethridge, Acting Attorney General; North Carolina, by Harry McMullan, Attorney General, and Ralph Moody, Assistant Attorney General; Oklahoma, by Mac Q. Williamson, Attorney General; South Carolina, by John M. Daniel, Attorney General; Tennessee, by Roy H. Beeler, Attorney General, and William F. Barry, Solicitor General; and Virginia, by J. Lindsay Almond, Jr., Attorney General, and Walter E. Rogers, Assistant Attorney General....

Mr. Chief Justice Vinson delivered the opinion of the Court.

This case and McLaurin v. Oklahoma State Regents, post, present different aspects of this general question: To what extent does the Equal Protection Clause of the Fourteenth Amendment limit the power of a state to distinguish between students of different races in professional and graduate education in a state university? Broader issues have been urged for our consideration, but we adhere to the principle of deciding constitutional questions only in the context of the particular case before the Court. We have frequently reiterated that this Court will decide constitutional questions only when necessary to the disposition of the case at hand, and that such decisions will be drawn as narrowly as possible. *Rescue Army v. Municipal Court*, ... (1947), and cases cited therein. Because of this traditional reluctance to extend constitutional interpretations to situations or facts which are not before the Court, much of the excellent research and detailed argument presented in these cases is unnecessary to their disposition.

In the instant case, petitioner filed an application for admission to the University of Texas Law School for the February, 1946 term. His application was rejected solely because he is a Negro. Petitioner thereupon brought this suit for mandamus against the appropriate school officials, respondents here, to compel his admission. At that time, there was no law school in Texas which admitted Negroes.

The state trial court recognized that the action of the State in denying petitioner the opportunity to gain a legal education while granting it to others deprived him of the equal protection of the laws guaranteed by the Fourteenth Amendment. The court did not grant the relief requested, however, but continued the case for six months to allow the State to supply substantially equal facilities. At the expiration of the six months, in December, 1946, the court denied the writ on the showing that the authorized university officials had adopted an order calling for the opening of a law school for Negroes the following February. While petitioner's appeal was pending, such a school was made available, but petitioner refused to register therein. The Texas Court of Civil Appeals set aside the trial court's judgment and ordered the cause "remanded generally to the trial court for further proceedings without prejudice to the rights of any party to this suit."

On remand, a hearing was held on the issue of the equality of the educational facilities at the newly established school as compared with the University of Texas Law School. Finding that the new school offered petitioner "privileges, advantages, and opportunities for the study of law substantially equivalent to those offered by the State to white students at the University of Texas," the trial court denied mandamus. The Court of Civil Appeals affirmed ... (1948). Petitioner's application for a writ of error was denied by the Texas Supreme Court. We granted certiorari ... (1949), because of the manifest importance of the constitutional issues involved.

The University of Texas Law School, from which petitioner was excluded, was staffed by a faculty of sixteen full-time and three part-time professors, some of whom are nationally recognized authorities in their field. Its student body numbered 850. The library contained over 65,000 volumes. Among the other facilities available to the students were a law review, moot court facilities, ... scholarship funds, and Order of the Coif affiliation. The school's alumni occupy the most distinguished positions in the private practice of the law and in the public life of the State. It may properly be considered one of the nation's ranking law schools.

The law school for Negroes which was to have opened in February, 1947, would have had no independent faculty or library. The teaching was to be carried on by four members of the University of Texas Law School faculty, who were to maintain their offices at the University of Texas while teaching at both institutions. Few of the 10,000 volumes ordered for the library had arrived; nor was there any full-time librarian. The school lacked accreditation.

Since the trial of this case, respondents report the opening of a law school at the Texas State University for Negroes. It is apparently on the road to full accreditation. It has a faculty of five full-time professors; a student body of 23; a library of some 16,500 volumes serviced by a full-time staff; a practice court and legal aid association; and one alumnus who has become a member of the Texas Bar.

Whether the University of Texas Law School is compared with the original or the new law school for Negroes, we cannot find substantial equality in the educational opportunities offered white and Negro law students by the State. In terms of number of the faculty, variety of courses and opportunity for specialization, size of the student body, scope of the library, availability of law ... review and similar activities, the University of Texas Law School is superior. What is more important, the University of Texas Law School possesses to a far greater degree those qualities which are incapable of objective measurement but which make for greatness in a law school. Such qualities, to name but a few, include reputation of the faculty, experience of the administration, position and influence of the alumni, standing in the community, traditions and prestige. It is difficult to believe that one who had a free choice between these law schools would consider the question close.

Moreover, although the law is a highly learned profession, we are well aware that it is an intensely practical one. The law school, the proving ground for legal learning and practice, cannot be effective in isolation from the individuals and institutions with which the law interacts. Few students and no one who has practiced law would choose to study in an academic vacuum, removed from the interplay of ideas and the exchange of views with which the law is concerned. The law school to which Texas is willing to admit petitioner excludes from its student

Document Text

body members of the racial groups which number 85% of the population of the State and include most of the lawyers, witnesses, jurors, judges and other officials with whom petitioner will inevitably be dealing when he becomes a member of the Texas Bar. With such a substantial and significant segment of society excluded, we cannot conclude that the education offered petitioner is substantially equal to that which he would receive if admitted to the University of Texas Law School.

It may be argued that excluding petitioner from that school is no different from excluding white students from the new law school. This contention overlooks realities. It is unlikely that a member of a group so decisively in the majority, attending a school with rich traditions ... prestige which only a history of consistently maintained excellence could command, would claim that the opportunities afforded him for legal education were unequal to those held open to petitioner. That such a claim, if made, would be dishonored by the State, is no answer. "Equal protection of the laws is not achieved through indiscriminate imposition of inequalities." *Shelley v. Kraemer* ... (1948).

It is fundamental that these cases concern rights which are personal and present. This Court has stated unanimously that "The State must provide [legal education] for [petitioner] in conformity with the equal protection clause of the Fourteenth Amendment and provide it as soon as it does for applicants of any other group." *Sipuel v. Board of Regents* ... (1948). That case "did not present the issue whether a state might not satisfy the equal protection clause of the Fourteenth Amendment by establishing a separate law school for Negroes." *Fisher v. Hurst* ... (1948). In *Missouri ex rel. Gaines v. Canada* ... (1938), the Court, speaking through Chief Justice Hughes, declared that "petitioner's right was a personal one. It was as an individual that he was entitled to the equal protection of the laws, and the State was bound to furnish him within its borders facilities for legal education substantially equal to those which the State there afforded for persons of the white race, whether or not other negroes sought the same opportunity." These are the only cases in this Court which present the issue of the constitutional validity of race distinctions in state-supported graduate and professional education.

In accordance with these cases, petitioner may claim his full constitutional right: legal education equivalent to that offered by the State to students of other races. Such education is not available to him in a separate law school as offered by the State. We cannot, therefore, ... agree with respondents that the doctrine of *Plessy v. Ferguson* ... (1896), requires affirmance of the judgment below. Nor need we

Glossary

Amici curiae	Latin for "friends of the court," referring to outside parties who submit briefs to the court in support of one position or the other
certiorari	a writ by an appeals court commanding a lower court to produce the records of a case; "granting certiorari" means that the higher court has agreed to hear the case.
Chief Justice Hughes	Charles Evans Hughes, whose tenure as chief justice coincided with the years of the Great Depression
ex relatione	a Latin expression used in the law to mean "on behalf of"
mandamus	Latin for "we command," used in law to refer to a court order requiring a lower court or a government official to perform a duty or to refrain from doing something
Order of the Coif	a prestigious national scholastic society for law students
remand	the act of a higher court sending a case back to a lower court for action
Reversed	an indication that a higher court has reversed the ruling of a lower court in the case at hand
writ of error	a judicial writ from an appellate court ordering the court of record to produce the records of trial; an appeal

reach petitioner's contention that *Plessy v. Ferguson* should be reexamined in the light of contemporary knowledge respecting the purposes of the Fourteenth Amendment and the effects of racial segregation....

We hold that the Equal Protection Clause of the Fourteenth Amendment requires that petitioner be admitted to the University of Texas Law School. The judgment is reversed and the cause is remanded for proceedings not inconsistent with this opinion.

Reversed.

Haywood Patterson, shown sitting in jail on July 25, 1937, in Decatur, Alabama (AP/Wide World Photos)

Haywood Patterson and Earl Conrad's Scottsboro Boy

1950

"In the South most poor whites feel they are better than Negroes and a black man has few rights."

Overview

Haywood Patterson, with the assistance of Earl Conrad, wrote *Scottsboro Boy* more than a decade after he was tried four times in one of the most notorious and racially controversial cases of the early twentieth century. Nine African American youths were charged with raping two white women while all of them were riding on a train. All but one were quickly sentenced to death, and the case attracted international attention. Both the Communists and the National Association for the Advancement of Colored People wanted to defend the boys, but ultimately the Communists took the case, through their legal arm, International Labor Defense.

After several trials (with Patterson convicted four times and sentenced to death three times) and two appeals to the U.S. Supreme Court (with the Supreme Court refusing to hear a third case), all nine youths were eventually freed. Patterson escaped from prison in 1948, and in 1950, nineteen years after the case was first brought against him and at the dawn of the civil rights movement in America, he wrote *Scottsboro Boy*. In his book, published in June of that year, Patterson details his experiences during the trial and what he faced in the years of his imprisonment.

Context

The Scottsboro case began in many ways during Reconstruction, which preceded it by about sixty years. After the American Civil War, the United States promised to give equal rights, including the right to vote, to African Americans. To this end, the Fourteenth Amendment, guaranteeing equal protection of the laws and the right to due process, and the Fifteenth Amendment, requiring that the vote not be restricted on the basis of race, were passed. However, these guarantees were only as strong as the people enforcing them, and interest in equal rights for African Americans, both in the North and in the South, waned quickly. Americans disputed the outcome of the election of 1876 between the Republican Rutherford B. Hayes and the Democrat Samuel Tilden, and the resulting Compromise of 1877 gave concessions to the Democrats in return for their accepting Hayes's election. With that compromise, federal troops were withdrawn from the South, and southern whites were given free rein to treat blacks as they chose.

Most southern states limited opportunities for African Americans. Around 1900, Jim Crow laws sprang up in the South, segregating facilities and removing nearly all blacks from the voting rolls. The overall legal restrictions on blacks throughout the South were extensive. Separate schools, water fountains, bathrooms, and even separate Bibles in courtrooms existed—and the separate facilities were not at all equal. Extralegal measures such as lynchings were also used against African Americans; it has been estimated that between 1865 and 1930 more than four thousand lynchings took place in the United States, most in the South and with most victims being black. The alleged offenses that brought about lynchings of blacks could be anything from making an improper advance to a white woman to failing to step aside when a white approached. The most publicized cause (though it factored in only a small percentage of cases) was accusations of rape, almost always by a white woman against a black man. This was the accusation made against the Scottsboro boys, and it almost resulted in their lynchings.

The Scottsboro boys' cases were also a product of the Great Depression. Besides causing millions to lose their jobs, the depression prompted huge numbers of people to migrate in search of work. While the most famous were the Okies, depicted in John Steinbeck's novel *The Grapes of Wrath*, millions of others, both black and white, migrated as well. Three groups of migrants played a role in the Scottsboro incident: a group of white youths, a group of black youths (the Scottsboro boys), and two white girls.

In March of 1931, the nine Scottsboro boys, ranging in age from twelve to nineteen (Clarence Norris, Charles Weems, Haywood Patterson, Olen Montgomery, Ozie Powell, Willie Roberson, Eugene Williams, Roy Wright, and Andy Wright) were riding a freight train from Chattanooga to Memphis, Tennessee—four of them looking for work. (The youths were not all traveling together and did not all know each other.) Also traveling as hobos on the train was a group of white youths and two women. A few

Time Line

1929
- The Great Depression starts, leading many in the country to ride the railways to look for work.

1931
- **March 25**
  The Scottsboro boys are arrested in Paint Rock, Alabama, initially on assault charges, but charges of rape are later added.
- **March 26**
  The Scottsboro boys are almost lynched when a crowd of a hundred whites gather outside the prison where they are being held.
- **April 6**
  The trials of all nine boys begin before Judge A. E. Hawkins.
- **April 7**
  All nine are convicted, with eight sentenced to death.

1932
- **January**
  One of the two girls admits that she was not raped; the other would maintain that she was raped throughout the trials and for the rest of her life.
- **March**
  The Alabama Supreme Court upholds the death sentences of seven of the youths. The eighth, as a juvenile, is spared the death penalty.
- **November**
  The U.S. Supreme Court reverses the convictions.

1933
- **January**
  The International Labor Defense, a Communist group, hires Samuel Liebowitz to defend the Scottsboro boys.
- **April**
  Haywood Patterson is tried again, convicted, and sentenced to death.
- **June**
  Patterson's conviction is set aside.

---

of the black youths got into a fight with the white youths and pushed some of the whites off the train. The white youths complained to the station master at Stevenson, Alabama, and the train was held at the next stop and searched by a deputized posse of fifty men. The nine African American youths, some of whom were in different parts of the train from where the fight occurred, were all arrested for assault. The two white girls, Ruby Bates and Victoria Price, who were prostitutes, were found on the train as well. Bates and Price, fearing that they would be arrested, accused the blacks of raping them. The nine blacks were taken to Scottsboro, Alabama, and jailed for trial, giving the case its name.

The youths were indicted for rape (a capital offense) on March 30. None of them was represented by an attorney. Most of them were illiterate, and none had any knowledge of criminal law or court procedure. The judge had ordered the Alabama bar to find attorneys for the defense, but when the trial started on April 6, no attorney had come forward. Finally, the youths' parents found two attorneys: a Chattanooga real estate lawyer, Stephen Roddy, and Milo Moody, a lawyer who had not defended a case at trial in decades. This was an inauspicious start to a complicated process that played out in the courts over the course of four trials and nineteen years. By 1950, all the Scottsboro boys had been released.

The Scottsboro boys' case was unique in a number of ways. It was the first to focus long-term international attention on African Americans in the South. The Scottsboro cases were also the first that the U.S. Supreme Court heard twice, and they resulted in two landmark rulings. The first was *Powell v. Alabama* (1932), in which the Supreme Court reversed the convictions of the youths sentenced to death by the Alabama courts on the ground that they had lacked effective counsel and had not received a fair trial as mandated by the due process clause of the Fourteenth Amendment. In the second case, *Norris v. Alabama* (1935), the Court ruled that blacks had to be included on the voting rolls—and thus in the jury pool—in order to have a fair trial. African Americans had been systematically excluded from the grand jury that indicted Clarence Norris and from the trial jury that convicted him, and so his conviction was overturned.

These cases were some of the longest in American history, even though no physical evidence suggested that any rape had occurred. They also were among the first in nearly sixty years, since perhaps the end of Reconstruction, in which blatant racism received front-page coverage not just in African American newspapers but in many mainstream white newspapers as well. In addition to the racism of the trials, racism and chicanery became evident at the Supreme Court hearings. To attempt to answer the defense's argument that there were no African Americans on the jury rolls, someone in the local government added the names of black voters at the end of the rolls before sending them to the Supreme Court. It was an inept and obvious forgery, and when the rolls were produced at the Supreme Court the justices were outraged.

In some ways, the cases also demonstrated progress toward civil rights. They showed that the national and international communities would pay attention to a case in the South and would put pressure upon the South to ensure that justice was done, even if it took nineteen years. They likewise showed progress, sadly enough, in that there was a trial at all. A lynch mob of nearly a hundred people gathered right after the nine were arrested, but this mob was unable to take any action. The state was also unable to carry out its own legal lynching, even though it tried to do so on several occasions, in that death sentences were often imposed simply on the word of one accuser. The fact that the National Association for the Advancement of Colored People and the Communist International Labor Defense were willing to spend the time and money to defend the boys also suggests a kind of progress. Before the 1930s such a case in the South might very well have been swept under the rug. That the cases went to the U.S. Supreme Court twice was unprecedented; before the 1930s the Supreme Court largely ignored race relations when it could. Progress is also evident in the Supreme Court's willingness to twice rule in favor of the Scottsboro boys; before the 1930s most legal rulings disadvantaged blacks. No defense attorneys were required at all for anyone when the trial started, and prison officials were allowed to listen in on conversations between defense counsel and their clients at the time of the case. Such practices are no longer allowed.

About the Author

Haywood Patterson, one of the leading defendants in the Scottsboro case, was born in Elberton, Georgia, in 1913 and then moved to Tennessee. He quit school after the third grade and took to riding the railways in the early years of the Great Depression, in search of work. He was viewed as the most violent and strong-willed of the defendants. For his alleged role in the Scottsboro affair, he was tried for rape four times and was sentenced to death three times. Two of the sentences were overturned, and a third was set aside. The fourth time, Patterson was sentenced to seventy-five years in jail, but he escaped from prison in 1948, ending up in Detroit.

While in Detroit, he wrote his memoir, *Scottsboro Boy*, which was published in June of 1950. Soon after its publication, he was arrested by the FBI. Alabama sought his extradition in order to return him to prison, but a large outcry and letter-writing effort persuaded the governor of Michigan not to extradite him. Later that year he was arrested after a barroom brawl in which a man died. Patterson was charged with murder and convicted of manslaughter in his third trial on the counts. He served about a year in prison, dying in 1952 from cancer at the age of thirty-nine.

Earl Conrad was born in 1912 in New York and worked primarily as a journalist. He also authored more than twenty books of history and criticism and ghostwrote several biographies, including one of the actor Errol Flynn. Several of his works focus on African Americans, including *Harriet Tubman: Negro Soldier and Abolitionist* (1942). Conrad died in 1986.

Time Line

1933
- **December** Patterson and another defendant, Clarence Norris, are tried again for rape in front of a different judge and sentenced to death.

1934
- **June** The Alabama Supreme Court upholds the convictions.

1935
- **April** The U.S. Supreme Court reverses the convictions on the ground that African Americans were systematically excluded from the jury pool.

1936
- **January** Patterson is tried a fourth time, convicted, and sentenced to seventy-five years in prison.

1937
- **July** Four of the other youths are tried on rape and related charges, and all are sentenced to long prison terms, with Norris being sentenced to death. The remaining four are released when all charges are dropped.

1938
- **July** Governor Bibb Graves reduces Norris's death sentence to life in prison. Later the same year Graves rejects pardon applications for all five still in prison.

1943
- The first of the Scottsboro boys is paroled; two more are paroled three years later, leaving only Patterson and one other in prison.

1948
- Patterson escapes from prison.

1950
- The last of the Scottsboro boys is released from prison. Patterson writes *Scottsboro Boy*.

Time Line

1951
- Patterson is convicted of manslaughter for his role in another man's death.

1952
- **August 24**
  Patterson dies in prison.

Explanation and Analysis of the Document

Scottsboro Boy covers Patterson's interaction with the Alabama prison system during his trial and years of incarceration. After telling of the trial and his convictions, Patterson discusses his life over his seventeen years in various Alabama prisons. The eleven-chapter book ends with his escape from prison in 1948. Four chapters are excerpted here.

◆ **Chapter 1**

The book begins with Patterson's recounting of the train journey that led to the black youths' arrests and trials. He assumes that everyone knows about riding the railways and does not explain why they were riding. Patterson then replays the interchange between himself and the white boys that led to the fight and explains why and how he resisted, noting how southern whites frequently felt that African Americans had no rights. He notes, too, that it is often forgotten that there were quite a few other African Americans on the train who were not arrested along with the Scottsboro boys. After the blacks had won a fight with some of the whites and forced them off the train, the whites complained to a station agent. The agent phoned ahead to the next stop, and the boys were arrested in the small town of Paint Rock, Alabama. Given the racial politics of the time, the word of the whites was accepted over any presumed innocence of the blacks. Further, the station agent failed to ask whether the whites were also fighting and to perhaps arrest them for illegally riding on the train. Patterson then describes the boys and points out that not all of those involved in the fight were arrested and that some were arrested solely for being black. After being taken to Scottsboro, they were accused of rape. Patterson describes the scene at night with the mob outside yelling for the chance to lynch the boys. He remarks that the lynchings might have happened if it were not for the opposition of the sheriff and his wife and the fact that the sheriff called for National Guard troops to protect them.

◆ **Chapter 2**

Patterson then discusses the trial. The boys were moved to Gadsden, Alabama, where they were protected and quickly tried. None of them saw a lawyer before the trial, he says, and they did not even know whether their parents were aware of their predicament, for they were not allowed to make phone calls. Of course, the concept of the "rights" of defendants was still decades in the future. So-called Miranda warnings, for example, were not mandated until 1966.

Patterson includes much description of small-town culture. He describes a large throng gathered for the trial and explains it as a combination of interest in seeing a lynching and local custom. As gruesome as it may sound, lynchings typically drew huge crowds in this period, and sometimes picture postcards were even sold. The local custom that drew the crowd on April 6—the day the trial started—was Scottsboro's fair day. Fair day took place on the first Monday of the month. In many small towns, people gathered on certain days to buy, sell, and trade and generally to meet and discuss things. For Scottsboro, this was the day when area farmers came to town to sell their produce and buy supplies. Patterson also notes how weak his defense team was, in the persons of a local lawyer who was actually opposed to the boys and an attorney from Chattanooga who had little interest in defending them. The account never explains how the lawyer from Chattanooga became connected with the case.

The decisions collectively took only two days to be handed down; thus the juries reached their conclusions in less than sixteen hours of work. According to Patterson, the same jury heard all three cases. He comments that "that was one jury that got exercise," referring to how many times the jury had to walk in and out of the jury room (twelve times). In actuality there were three different juries. Patterson's trial took only three hours. He had seen the girls he was accused of raping only twice before the trial, once when they were arrested and a second time in the jail. He observes that the women were much more presentable in court, wearing dresses rather than the overalls in which they had been traveling.

Patterson also discusses the racial hostility in the packed courtroom. One of the more extended bits of the trial he recounts is the prosecution's closing argument to the jury, stating that the jury members should do their duty as men and quickly condemn the defendants. Patterson notes that there were very few African Americans in Scottsboro at the time of the trial and that the spectators in the courtroom cheered when the sentence was pronounced. Still, Patterson managed to keep his spirits up and told the prosecutor that he did not believe that the state would execute him quickly.

Patterson then launches into his own rebuttal of the charge of rape against him. He first notes that he prefers to be with African Americans and that he has always loved his own kind. He then argues that only a "fool or a crazy man" would attempt to rape a white woman, as all African Americans knew that death would result. Patterson adds that he did not ever have a desire to rape anyone, as plenty of women wanted him; he did not have to force himself on them. But he also says that his parents taught him to respect people, and so he would not have raped anyone. Patterson closes by saying that he is stating his views in this book for the first time. "No Alabama judge or jury in the four trials I had ever asked me for my views," he notes ironically. "Those Alabama people, they didn't believe I had any, nor the right to any."

◆ **Chapter 3**

The Scottsboro boys were taken back to the jail in Gadsden to await transfer to Kilby Prison in Montgomery, Alabama. There they started protesting, in large part because they knew that they were facing execution. "We didn't like nothing at all about the place; we didn't like our death sentence; and we decided to put on a kick." The main thing they protested directly was the food; even after they received the pork chops they had asked for, they still were not satisfied and continued to protest. The National Guard was sent in to take control, and the boys were beaten and handcuffed together so that they could not move. The guards left them there that day and the next without food, Patterson says, before transferring them to the city jail.

There the boys were separated and jailed with other inmates. Patterson was threatened until the other inmates discovered that he was one of the Scottsboro boys. At that point, he says they were all treated better, at least by the inmates. They were directly threatened, though, by the guards. Patterson recounts how they were all gathered together to be fingerprinted and how the jailers beat Charlie Weems when he did not spit out his gum fast enough. As a deterrent, the jailer also showed the boys the various punishments used against recalcitrant prisoners, including where they hung inmates by the fingers above the ground. Horrific punishments were quite common for those in jail in the South. Many spent their time in brutal convict labor camps, where the death rates were high. Even so, Patterson does not describe being afraid.

Patterson then moves on to the start of their successful defense, noting the arrival of two Jewish lawyers from the International Labor Defense. He did not have a problem with that, he says, as he had dealt with Jews in Chattanooga and they had treated him fairly. In some ways, Patterson is stereotyping in the same way as whites did in the South—by assuming that all people of one race or one religion would act the same. The lawyers told the boys about the interest that their case was drawing. The jailer, Dick Barnes, came into the meeting and listened; this practice is illegal today, but "attorney-client privilege" was a right not granted for another thirty years. During the visit, the attorneys asked about the availability of medical care. As Patterson describes it, "The prison was very filthy. It was making me sick, making us all sick." When Patterson asked to see an outside doctor, Barnes insisted that the prison doctor was fine. Patterson argued that he needed medicine for lice, as the lice had "stole his cap" the night before. All that gained him, though, was a threat from Barnes.

Patterson then goes on to explain the rush of mail that arrived, along with money to buy items such as cigarettes, which had long served as currency inside many prisons. The boys were emboldened by the attention and began to demand more. The increased demand in reality brought only more attention from the jailer, and so they were eventually transferred to Kilby Prison in Montgomery, which also housed death row. Patterson notes that Kilby Prison was more substantially built than the ones in which the boys had previously been held. "It was a bitter thing to see the door of Kilby Prison.... Those walls looked so high and hard to get over. They were concrete." The boys were then moved to death row, but they could not see the execution chamber—only "a dozen cells facing each other, six to a side, and a thirteenth cell for toilet work."

◆ **Chapter 4**

Patterson tells of meeting a man called Gunboat at Kilby, who immediately asks him, "Do you want a Bible to make your soul right? ... You going to die tonight, you know. You Scottsboros better get busy with the Lord." And so Patterson took up reading the Bible. "You see, a man in the death cell, he clings to anything that gives him a little hope," he says. He notes that he had little formal education before being imprisoned and that he could hardly read; he found himself "stumbling through the small printed words." Two Scottsboro boys were imprisoned in each cell, which was big enough for only a single cot or a bunk bed. Patterson ends the chapter saying that he "dreamed bad dreams, with freight trains, guards' faces, and courtrooms mixed up with the look of the sky at night.

Audience

Scottsboro Boy was aimed primarily at the supporters of civil rights and the Scottsboro boys throughout their struggle, giving this group a firsthand account of what happened. Secondarily, the book addressed all those who were simply interested in learning more about the case. There also was a third audience, in Patterson's view—anyone interested in paying for the book. This is not to suggest that Patterson was more mercenary than other people who sell their life stories but just that he had spent the better part of two decades behind bars and had very few marketable skills. The only tangible asset he had was his story, and he needed to sell it to live.

Impact

The short-term impact of this publication was relatively small. The basic details of the Scottsboro case were already known, and all of the Scottsboro boys were out of prison when the book was published; the resulting publicity thus changed little. The aim of the book was to help Patterson, but it did not accomplish that goal either. Soon after its publication, Patterson was arrested and convicted of manslaughter for his role in a man's death in a barroom fight. He was sentenced to at least six years in prison but died behind bars in 1952.

The real impact of this book is upon the historical record of the experience of the Scottsboro boys. Even if all of the legal details are known, the experience of the defendants cannot be fully understood without reading such a firsthand account. Such an account also contributes to an understanding of the legal processes of the time and the role racial prejudice played in court cases. Likewise, it gives a stark portrayal of prison conditions and the life of black inmates. This biography demonstrates that firsthand accounts are necessary to an understanding of how African Americans were

Essential Quotes

"But it happens in the South most poor whites feel they are better than Negroes and a black man has few rights."
(Chapter 1)

"Round about dusk hundreds of people gathered around the jail-house. 'Let these niggers out,' they yelled. We could hear it coming in the window. 'If you don't, we're coming in after them.' White people were running around like mad ants, white ants, sore that someone had stepped on their hill. We heard them yelling like crazy about how they were coming in after us and what ought to be done with us."
(Chapter 1)

"When Bailey [the prosecutor] finished with me he said to the jury: 'Gentlemen of the jury, I don't say give that nigger the chair. I'm not going to tell you to give him the electric chair. You know your duty. I'm not going to tell you to give the nigger a life sentence. All I can say is, hide him. Get him out of our sight.'"
(Chapter 2)

"It was never in me to rape, not a black and not a white woman. Only a Negro who is a fool or a crazy man, he would chance his life for anything like that. A Negro with sound judgment and common sense is not going to do it. They are going to take his life away from him if he does. Every Negro man in the South knows that."
(Chapter 2)

"I could hardly make out the words in the book. The little training in reading I had had I never much followed up. Never read no papers, no books, nothing. I did not know how to pronounce things, could not even say 'Alabama' so you could understand me.... But the Bible felt solid in my hands."
(Chapter 4)

treated in the South during the early twentieth century. White officials and participants in events like this often did not fully and accurately record them, and personal accounts help to paint a truthful picture and to demonstrate the underpinnings of the civil rights movement.

See also Fourteenth Amendment to the U.S. Constitution (1868); Fifteenth Amendment to the U.S. Constitution (1870).

Further Reading

Books

Carter, Dan T. *Scottsboro: A Tragedy of the American South*. Baton Rouge: Louisiana State University Press, 2007.

Goodman, James E. *Stories of Scottsboro*. New York: Vintage, 1995.

Howard, Walter T., ed. *Black Communists Speak on Scottsboro: A Documentary History*. Philadelphia: Temple University Press, 2008.

Miller, James A. *Remembering Scottsboro: The Legacy of an Infamous Trial*. Princeton, N.J.: Princeton University Press, 2009.

Web Sites

"Scottsboro: An American Tragedy." PBS's "American Experience" Web site.
http://www.pbs.org/wgbh/amex/scottsboro.

"The 'Scottsboro Boys' Trials: 1931–1937." Famous American Trials Web site.
http://www.law.umkc.edu/faculty/projects/FTrials/scottsboro/scottsb.htm.

—Scott A. Merriman

Questions for Further Study

1. In what ways was the Scottsboro boys case similar to the events surrounding the 1921 race riot in Tulsa, Oklahoma, detailed in Walter F. White's "The Eruption of Tulsa"?

2. In what sense was the Scottsboro boys case a product of the Great Depression? What impact did economics have on the events surrounding the case?

3. The Scottsboro boys case had at least one important judicial outcome that improved the criminal justice system for African Americans. What was that outcome, and why was it important?

4. *Scottsboro Boy* is a firsthand account of one man's encounter with a criminal justice system that was stacked against him. In what sense was his account a twentieth-century version of a slave narrative published in the nineteenth century? Consider the document in connection with, for example, *The Narrative of the Life of Henry Box Brown, Written by Himself* or *Twelve Years a Slave: Narrative of Solomon Northup*.

5. *Scottsboro Boy* was published on the eve of the civil rights movement in the United States. In what ways might the publication of this book have helped fuel the civil rights movement?

Haywood Patterson and Earl Conrad's *Scottsboro Boy*

Chapter 1

The freight train leaving out of Chattanooga, going around the mountain curves and hills of Tennessee into Alabama, it went so slow anyone could get off and back on.

That gave the white boys the idea they could jump off the train and pick up rocks, carry them back on, and chunk them at us Negro boys.

The trouble began when three or four white boys crossed over the oil tanker that four of us colored fellows from Chattanooga were in. One of the white boys, he stepped on my hand and liked to have knocked me off the train. I didn't say anything then, but the same guy, he brushed by me again and liked to have pushed me off the car. I caught hold of the side of the tanker to keep from falling off.

I made a complaint about it and the white boy talked back— mean, serious, white folks Southern talk.

That is how the Scottsboro case began ... with a white foot on my black hand.

"The next time you want by," I said, "just tell me you want by and I let you by."

"Nigger, I don't ask you when I want by. What you doing on this train anyway?"

"Look, I just tell you the next time you want by you just tell me you want by and I let you by."

"Nigger bastard, this a white man's train. You better get off. All you black bastards better get off!"

I felt we had as much business stealing a ride on this train as those white boys hoboing from one place to another looking for work like us. But it happens in the South most poor whites feel they are better than Negroes and a black man has few rights. It was wrong talk from the white fellow and I felt I should sense it into him and his friends we were human beings with rights too. I didn't want that my companions, Roy and Andy Wright, Eugene Williams and myself, should get off that train for anybody unless it was a fireman or engineer or railroad dick who told us to get off.

"You white sons of bitches, we got as much right here as you!"

"Why, you goddamn nigger, I think we better just put you off!"

"Okay, you just try. You just try to put us off!"

Three or four white boys, they were facing us four black boys now, and all cussing each other on both sides. But no fighting yet.

The white boys went on up the train further.

We had just come out of a tunnel underneath Lookout Mountain when the argument started. The train, the name of it was the Alabama Great Southern, it was going uphill now, slow. A couple of the white boys, they hopped off, picked up rocks, threw them at us. The stones landed around us and some hit us. Then the white fellows, they hopped back on the train two or three cars below us. We were going toward Stevenson, Alabama, when the rocks came at us. We got very mad.

When the train stopped at Stevenson, I think maybe to get water or fuel, we got out of the car and walked along the tracks. We met up with some other young Negroes from another car. We told them what happened. They agreed to come in with us when the train started again.

Soon as the train started the four of us Chattanooga boys that was in the oil tanker got back in there—and the white boys started throwing more rocks. The other colored guys, they came over the top of the train and met us four guys. We decided we would go and settle with these white boys. We went toward their car to fight it out. There must have been ten or twelve or thirteen of us colored when we came on a gang of six or seven white boys.

I don't argue with people. I show them. And I started to show those white boys. The other colored guys, they pitched in on these rock throwers too. Pretty quick the white boys began to lose in the fist fighting. We outmanned them in hand-to-hand scuffling. Some of them jumped off and some we put off. The train, picking up a little speed, that helped us do the job. A few wanted to put up a fight but they didn't have a chance. We had color anger on our side.

The train was picking up speed and I could see a few Negro boys trying to put off one white guy. I went down by them and told them not to throw this boy off because the train was going too fast. This fellow, his name was Orville Gilley. Me and one of the Wright boys pulled him back up.

After the Gilley boy was back on the train the fight was over. The four of us, Andy and Roy Wright, Eugene Williams and myself, we went back to the tanker and sat the same way we were riding when the train left Chattanooga.

The white fellows got plenty sore at the whupping we gave them. They ran back to Stevenson to complain that they were jumped on and thrown off—and to have us pulled off the train.

The Stevenson depot man, he called up ahead to Paint Rock and told the folks in that little through-road place to turn out in a posse and snatch us off the train.

It was two or three o'clock in the afternoon, Wednesday, March 25, 1931, when we were taken off at Paint Rock....

A mob of white farmers was waiting when the train rolled in. They closed in on the boxcars. Their pistols and shotguns pointed at us. They took everything black off the train. They even threw off some lumps of coal, could be because of its color. Us nine black ones they took off from different cars. Some of these Negroes I had not seen before the fight and a couple I was looking at now for the first time. They were rounding up the whites too, about a half dozen of them. I noticed among them two girls dressed in men's overalls and looking about like the white fellows.

I asked a guy who had hold of me, "What's it all about?"

"Assault and attempt to murder."

I didn't know then there was going to be a different kind of a charge after we got to the Jackson County seat, Scottsboro.

They marched us up a short road. We stopped in front of a little general store and post office. They took our names. They roped us up, all us Negroes together. The rope stretched from one to another of us. The white folks, they looked mighty serious. Everybody had guns. The guy who ran the store spoke up for us:

"Don't let those boys go to jail. Don't anybody harm them."

But that passed quick, because we were being put into trucks. I kind of remember this man's face, him moving around there in the storm of mad white folks, talking for us. There are some good white people down South but you don't find them very fast, them that will get up in arms for a Negro. If they come up for a Negro accused of something, the white people go against him and his business goes bad.

After we were shoved into the truck I saw for the first time all us to become known as "The Scottsboro Boys." There were nine of us. Some had not even been in the fight on the train. A few in the fight got away so the posse never picked them up.

There were the four from Chattanooga, Roy Wright, about fourteen; his brother, Andy Wright, nineteen; Eugene Williams, who was only thirteen; and myself. I was eighteen. I knew the Wright boys very well. I had spent many nights at their home and Mrs. Wright treated me as if I were her own son. The other five boys, they were Olen Montgomery, he was half blind; Willie Roberson, he was so sick with the venereal he could barely move around; a fellow from Atlanta named Clarence Norris, nineteen years old; Charlie Weems, the oldest one among us, he was twenty; and a fourteen-year-old boy from Georgia, Ozie Powell. I was one of the tallest, but Norris was taller than me.

All nine of us were riding the freight for the same reason, to go somewhere and find work. It was 1931. Depression was all over the country. Our families were hard pushed. The only ones here I knew were the other three from Chattanooga. Our fathers couldn't hardly support us, and we wanted to help out, or at least put food in our own bellies by ourselves. We were freight-hiking to Memphis when the fight happened.

Looking over this crowd, I figured that the white boys got sore at the whupping we gave them, and were out to make us see it the bad way.

We got to Scottsboro in a half hour. Right away we were huddled into a cage, all of us together. It was a little two-story jimcrow jail. There were flat bars, checkerboard style, around the windows, and a little hallway outside our cell.

We got panicky and some of the kids cried. The deputies were rough. They kept coming in and out of our cells. They kept asking questions, kept pushing us and shoving, trying to make us talk. Kept cussing, saying we tried to kill off the white boys on the train. Stomped and raved at us and flashed their guns and badges.

We could look out the window and see a mob of folks gathering. They were excited and noisy. We were hot and sweaty, all of us, and pretty scared. I laughed at a couple of the guys who were crying. I didn't feel like crying. I couldn't figure what exactly, but didn't have no weak feeling.

After a while a guy walked into our cell, with him a couple of young women.

"Do you know these girls?"

They were the two gals dressed like men rounded up at Paint Rock along with the rest of us brought off the train. We had seen them being hauled in. They looked like the others, like the white hobo fellows, to me. I paid them no mind. I didn't know them. None of us from Chattanooga, the Wrights, Williams, and

Document Text

myself, ever saw them before Paint Rock. Far as I knew none of the nine of us pulled off different gondolas and tankers ever saw them.

"No," everybody said.

"No," I said.

"No? You damn-liar niggers! You raped these girls!"

Round about dusk hundreds of people gathered about the jail-house. "Let these niggers out," they yelled. We could hear it coming in the window. "If you don't, we're coming in after them." White folks were running around like mad ants, white ants, sore that somebody had stepped on their hill. We heard them yelling like crazy how they were coming in after us and what ought to be done with us. "Give 'em to us," they kept screaming, till some of the guys, they cried like they were seven or eight years old. Olen Montgomery, he was seventeen and came from Monroe, Georgia, he could make the ugliest face when he cried. I stepped back and laughed at him.

As evening came on the crowd got to be to about five hundred, most of them with guns. Mothers had kids in their arms. Autos, bicycles, and wagons were parked around the place. People in and about them.

Two or three deputies, they came into our cell and said, "All right, let's go." They wanted to take us out to the crowd. They handcuffed us each separately. Locked both our hands together. Wanted to rush us outside into the hands of that mob. We fellows hung close, didn't want for them to put those irons on. You could see the look in those deputies' faces, already taking some funny kind of credit for turning us over.

High Sheriff Warren—he was on our side—rushed in at those deputies and said, "Where you taking these boys?"

"Taking them to another place, maybe Gadsden or some other jail."

"*You can't take those boys out there!* You'll be overpowered and they'll take the boys away from you."

The deputies asked for their handcuffs back and beat it out.

That was when the high sheriff slipped out the back way himself and put in a call to Montgomery for the National Guards.

He came back to our cell a few minutes later and said, "I don't believe that story the girls told."

His wife didn't believe it either. She got busy right then and went to the girls' cell not far from ours. We all kept quiet and listened while Mrs. Warren accused them of putting down a lie on us. "You know you lied," she said, so that we heard it and so did the white boys in their cell room. The girls stuck to their story; but us black boys saw we had some friends.

It had been a fair day, a small wind blowing while we rode on the freight. Now, toward evening, it was cool, and the crowd down there was stomping around to keep warm and wanting to make it real hot. When it was coming dark flashlights went on, and headlights from a few Fords lit up the jail. The noise was mainly from the white folks still calling for a lynching party. Every now and then one of them would yell, for us to hear, "Where's the rope. Bill?" or "Got enough rope, Hank?" They were trying to find something to help them to break into jail, begging all the while to turn us fellows over to them.

Round four o'clock in the morning we heard a heavy shooting coming into the town. It was the National Guards. They were firing to let the crowd know they were coming, they meant business, and we weren't to be burned or hung. The mob got scared and fussed off and away while the state soldiers' trucks came through.

I was young, didn't know what it was all about. I believed the National Guard was some part of the lynching bee. When they came into my cell I figured like the others—that we were as good as long gone now.

First guard to walk in, he was full of fun. He asked some of the boys, "Where you want your body to go to?"

Willie Roberson, he had earlier told one of the deputies he was from Ohio, but now he took this guard serious. He said, "Send my body to my aunt at 992 Michigan Avenue, Atlanta." His aunt owned the place at that address. Others told false names, like people do at first when they're arrested.

Charlie Weems, he had a lot of guts. He understood it was a gag. He said, "Just bury me like you do a cat. Dig a hole and throw me in it." He understood the guard was funning, but the others didn't. I didn't very well understand it myself.

After the National Guards told us they were for us, I believed them. I told them right away where I came from, "Just over the state line, Chattanooga, Tennessee."

I don't tell people stories, I tell the truth.

I told the truth about my name and where I came from. I knew that was all right with my people, they would wade through blood for me.

And which they did.

Early the next morning we had breakfast. Then the National Guards led us out of the jail. We were going to Gadsden, Alabama, where it was supposed to be safer. Soon as we filed out of the jail-house another mob was there screaming the same stuff at us and talking mean to the National Guards. "We're going to kill you niggers!"

"You ain't going to do a goddamned thing," I yelled back at them. That made them wild.

They sat us down among other colored prisoners at the Gadsden jail. It was the same kind of a little old jimcrow lockup as the one at Scottsboro. White guys, they were in cells a little way down the hall. We talked back and forth with them.

We waited to see what the Jackson County law was going to do with us. The Scottsboro paper had something to say about us. In big headlines, editorials and everything, they said they had us nine fiends in jail for raping two of their girls. The editor had come rummaging around the jail himself.

Then we heard that on March 31 we were indicted at Scottsboro. A trial was set for April 6, only a week away. Down around that way they'll hoe potatoes kind of slow sometimes but comes to trying Negroes on a rape charge they work fast. We had no lawyers. Saw no lawyers. We had no contact with the outside. Our folks, as far as we knew, didn't know the jam we were in. I remember the bunch of us packed in the cell room, some crying, some mad. That was a thinking time, and I thought of my mother, Jannie Patterson, and my father, Claude Patterson. I thought of my sisters and brothers and wondered if they had read about us by now.

What little we heard was going on about us we got from the white inmates. Some were pretty good guys. They saw the papers, read them to us, and the guards talked with them. These fellows, they told us the story had got around all over Alabama and maybe outside the state. They told us, "If you ever see a good chance, you better run. They said they're going to give every one of you the death seat."

I couldn't believe that. I am an unbelieving sort.

Chapter 2

Came trial time, the National Guards took us to Scottsboro. We had to go down through the country from Gadsden to the county seat. We went in a truck. There were guards in front, at the side and behind. I never trusted these guards too much. They were white folks, Alabama folks at that, and I felt they could as lief knock us off as anyone else. State and federal and county law didn't make much difference to us down there. It was all law, and it was all against us, the way we figured.

Got to Scottsboro and there was just about the same crowd as when we left—only much bigger. For two blocks either way they were thick as bees, bees with a bad sting and going to sting us pretty quick now.

The sixty or seventy National Guards, they got orders to make a lane through the crowd so we could get through. They had rifles, looked smart in their uniform. They could handle the crowd. When the guards formed a tunnel for us to walk through we heard the mob roaring what I heard a thousand times if I heard once:

"We going to kill you niggers!"

Later I found out why the crowd was so big. A "nigger lynching" might be enough to bring out a big crowd anyway, but this day was what they called "First Monday" or "horse-swapping day." First day of each month the Jackson County farmers came down from the hills into Scottsboro to swap horses and mules and talk. They'd bring in their families and have a time of it. It happened our trial opened on the same day so the mountain people living around here had two good reasons to come to town—and there were thousands out. They were gathered around the courthouse square while we colored boys went into the courthouse. Near the courthouse was a brass band getting ready to celebrate either our burning or hanging, whichever it was going to be.

We boys sat there in court and watched how Judge E. A. Hawkins had a talk with a man named Stephen Roddy. Roddy said he was a lawyer sent in from Chattanooga to help us fellows. I had a hunch when I heard he was from Chattanooga that my folks and the Wrights had got wind of our jam and hired him. But I saw right away he wasn't much for us. Hawkins said to him, "You defending these boys?" Roddy answered, "Not exactly. I'm here to join up with any lawyers you name to defend them. Sort of help out." The judge asked, "Well, you defending them or aren't you?" Words about like that. So Roddy said, "Well, I'm not defending them, but I wouldn't want to be sent off the case. I'm not being paid or anything. Just been sent here to sort of take part." Then the judge, he said, "Oh, I wouldn't want to see you out of the case. You can stay."

Now that was the kind of defense we Scottsboro boys had when we first went on trial.

Right after that Judge Hawkins put a local guy named Milo Moody, an oldish lawyer, to represent us. But he didn't do anything for us. Not a damned thing. He got up and said a few words now and then: but he was against us.

Document Text

After Moody was set up to be our lawyer, the trials went on. The courtroom was packed. Jammed in, the people were. Standing up in back and along the sides. Not enough seats there. Weems and Norris were tried together. I was tried separate. The rest were tried together. The trials and convictions went on for about two days. The jury kept going in and out of the jury room and coming back with convictions.

That was one jury that got exercise.

I was tried on April 7, the second day of the trials. Solicitor H. G. Bailey, the prosecutor, he talked excited to the jurymen. They were backwoods farmers. Some didn't even have the education I had. I had only two short little periods of reading lessons. But these men passed a decision on my life....

The girls I and the others were accused of raping I saw for the third time in court. The first I saw them was at Paint Rock when we were all picked up. The second was in Scottsboro jail when they were brought to our cell. And now in court. This time they were not wearing men's overalls, but dresses. Victoria Price, the older girl, she was to me a plain-looking woman. Ruby Bates was more presentable.

Solicitor Bailey, he asked me questions. The way he handled me was the same way he handled all of us. Like this:

"You ravished that girl sitting there."

"I ravished nobody. I saw no girl."

"You held a knife to her head while the others ravished her."

"I had no knife. I saw no knife. I saw no girl."

"You saw this defendant here ravish that girl there."

"I saw nobody ravish nobody. I was in a fight. That's all. Just a fight with white boys."

"You raped that girl. You did rape that girl, didn't you?"

"I saw no girl. I raped nobody."

Bailey, he kept firing that story at me just like that. He kept pounding the rape charge against me, against all of us. We all kept saying no, we saw no girls, we raped nobody, all we knew of was a fight.

The girls got up and kept on lying. There was only one thing the people in the courtroom wanted to hear. Bailey would ask, "Did the niggers rape you?"

"Yes," the girls would answer.

That's all the people in that court wanted to hear, wanted to hear "yes" from the girls' mouths.

When Bailey finished with me he said to the jury:

"Gentlemen of the jury, I don't say give that nigger the chair. I'm not going to tell you to give him the electric chair.

"*You know your duty.*

"I'm not going to tell you to give the nigger a life sentence. All I can say is, *hide him. Get him out of our sight.*

"Hide them. Get them out of our sight.

"They're not our niggers. Look at their eyes, look at their hair, gentlemen. They look like something just broke out of the zoo.

"*Guilty or not guilty, let's get rid of these niggers.*"

I went on trial about nine o'clock in the morning. Within two hours the jury had come back with a conviction. I was convicted in their minds before I went on trial. I had no lawyers, no witnesses for me. All that spoke for me on that witness stand was my black skin—which didn't do so good. Judge Hawkins asked the jurymen: "Have you reached a verdict?"

"Yes."

"Have the clerk read it."

The clerk read it off: "We, the jurymen, find the defendant guilty as charged and fix his punishment as death."

If I recollect right the verdicts against us all were in in two days. All of us got the death sentence except Roy Wright. He looked so small and pitiful on the stand that one juryman held out for life imprisonment. They declared a mistrial for Roy.

No Negroes were allowed in Scottsboro during the entire time. I didn't see a Negro face except two farmers in jail for selling corn. One of the National Guards, he fired a shot through the courtroom window about noon of the day I was convicted. Later he said that was an accident.

On the night of the first day's trials we could hear a brass band outside. It played, "There'll Be a Hot Time in the Old Town Tonight" and "Dixie."

It was April 9 when eight of us—all but Roy Wright—were stood up before Judge Hawkins for sentencing. He asked us if we had anything to say before he gave sentence. I said:

"Yes, I have something to say. I'm not guilty of this charge."

He said, "The jury has found you guilty and it is up to me to pass sentence. I set the date for your execution July 10, 1931 at Kilby Prison. May the Lord have mercy on your soul."

The people in the court cheered and clapped after the judge gave out with that. I didn't like it, people feeling good because I was going to die, and I got ruffed.

I motioned to Solicitor Bailey with my finger.

He came over. I asked him if he knew when I was going to die.

Document Text

He mentioned the date, like the judge gave it, and I said, "You're wrong. I'm going to die when you and those girls die for lying about me."

He asked me how I knew and I said that that was how I felt.

I looked around. That courtroom was one big smiling white face.

All my life I always loved my own people. I like my kind best because I understand them best. When I was a young man in Chattanooga, before the train ride that ended at Paint Rock, I knew and loved Negro girls, Negro people. My friends were of black color. I knew them as fellow human beings, as good as all others, and needing as good a chance. It was never in me to rape, not a black and not a white woman. Only a Negro who is a fool or a crazy man, he would chance his life for anything like that. A Negro with sound judgment and common sense is not going to do it. They are going to take his life away from him if he does. Every Negro man in the South knows that. No, most Negroes run away from that sort of thing, fear in their hearts. And nine of us boys, most unbeknownst to each other, a couple sick, all looking for work and a chance to live, and rounded up on a freight train like lost black sheep, we did not do such a thing and could not.

I wouldn't make advances on any woman that didn't want me. Too many women from my boyhood on have shown a desire for me so that I don't have to press myself on anyone not wanting me.

My mother and father, they lived together as husband and wife for thirty-seven years, honest working people. They had many children and they taught us to respect the human being and the human form.

I was also taught to demand respect from others.

Now it is a strange thing that what I have just said I never had a chance to say in an Alabama court. No Alabama judge or jury in the four trials I had ever asked me for my views. Nobody asked about my feelings. Those Alabama people, they didn't believe I had any, nor the right to any.

Chapter 3

Back in Gadsden jail we could look outside and see where an old gallows was rigged up. Must have gone back to the slavey days. We didn't like nothing at all about the place; we didn't like our death sentence; and we decided to put on a kick. I said to the man who brought me a prison meal, "I don't want that stuff. Bring me some pork chops."

"Huh, pork chops?"

"Yes, pork chops. You got to get it. We're going to die and we can have anything we want."

All the fellows laid down a yell, "Pork chops!"

We crowded up to the bars. We put our hands out and shook fingers at him. We hollered, "Pork chops. Nothing else."

This guy, he went down someplace and got the pork chops. He brought it to us. Just the food I wanted. I always liked pork meats. After we ate, still we weren't satisfied.

The deputies and guards, they were scared of us now like we would make a jailbreak. Our heads were up against those checkerboard bars and we talked sharp.

The sheriff spoke to me because I was raising the most dust. He said. "Look here, nigger. See that gallows. If you don't quieten down I'll take you around to that gallows and hang you myself."

I had a broom in my hand and maybe he wondered what it was or where I got it. He came up to the bars to take a look at what it was. I jiggled the broom in his face. The fellows laughed.

That was the last that sheriff could take by himself. He beat it downstairs to call Governor B. M. Miller to send in some National Guards.

They came in serious. The cell door banged open. They beat on us with their fists. They pushed us against the walls. They kicked and tramped about on our legs and feet. They beat up most of the fellows, but Eugene Williams and me backed up in the dark of the cell and escaped the worst part of it.

The state soldiers handcuffed us in twos. They had a big rope. They fastened the rope in between the handcuffs and bound us all together.

We laid up against the walls and against each other like that till night. We were in a quiet misery, unable to move around. When it was night we tried to sleep like that but we couldn't. Morning came and we were still trussed to each other and tired. Day went on, no food, just laying there moaning atop each other; until it was seven o'clock in the evening.

The National Guards came up again. This time they had more rope. I said to the sheriff, "What you going to do, hang us?"

"I'd like to, goddamn your souls," he said.

They roped us together tighter, then chain-gang marched us outside to a big state patrol truck they called the dog wagon. They tied us to the sides so we couldn't make any break, so we couldn't even move. One of the guards asked, "What you guys raise so much hell for?"

"We just don't like that death sentence," I told him.

The kid I was handcuffed to, he slept rough, and by the time we got to the city jail those handcuffs had swollen my wrists.

They couldn't get the handcuffs off. They had to call in a blacksmith to get them loose.

They split up us Scottsboro boys so we couldn't raise any more sand like we had at Gadsden. They put us in with other prisoners two or three to a cell.

About the middle of the night I was stashed into a cell with two other guys. One was called Box Car. He had burgled a boxcar and had a fifteen-year sentence. The other was a lifer. I was played out and fell on the bunk. One of the guys woke me. "Get up."

I raised up and I looked at him.

"Did you bring my money?"

"What money?"

"Jail feed."

I knew what this was, kangaroo business. I had a pair of shears under the mattress. I had brought it from the Gadsden jail. I just rested my hands on the shears and said, "I got nothing."

This guy, he just kept insisting. Told me to get up. He wanted to see me. "If you don't pay us kangaroo money you know what it means."

"No, what it means?"

"It means we going to whup you."

They asked for twenty-five cents. If I wouldn't pay, it meant I would get twenty-five licks.

I raised up a little more and I said, "You can see me. In the morning you can see me."

"Hey, where you say you from?"

"Scottsboro."

"You one of them Scottsboro boys?"

When I told him yes he just gave right over, got tender. He felt sorry for me, brought me food and tried to give it to me. I was tired and I didn't accept it. I laid down to sleep, thinking how the word "Scottsboro" touched them. That was when I first learned that this word would mean special favors in prison—and special torture.

Next day we were together again, all except Roy Wright, while they fingerprinted us.

Charlie Weems was chewing gum. The jailer, Dick Barnes, told Weems to spit the gum out. He refused to do it.

Barnes gave Weems a lick across the side of the head for that. Weems went down. When he got up he stood his distance from the jailer, a little quieter. Dick Barnes turned on me:

"You like ham and eggs?"

"I don't like nothing." I knew he was talking about the fuss we made at the other jail over pork chops.

"Patterson, I heard about you up in Gadsden ordering ham and eggs. You can get it here any time you want it. You love ham and eggs, don't you?"

"I don't love nothing." He wanted me to say something so he could beat on me, but I didn't give him the chance.

He changed tone, got serious. His voice dropped like from the high end of a piano to the low end, and he said, "We got your waters on to you here. Any time you fellows get funky we got your waters on here."

Right away he showed us what he meant. Took us all down in the basement where they gave punishment. He looked at me and said, "Nigger, keep quiet. If you don't behave …" He showed where you hang up by two fingers with your feet not touching the ground. There was a time limit they would hold you up that way.

It was supposed to frighten us and maybe it did scare some. I didn't like it either. But I always protested when I didn't like things. Down South I always talked like I wanted: before Scottsboro, during it, and since.

A few minutes afterward Barnes told a Negro trusty, "I sure like to be there when they execute these guys. You'll smell flesh burning a mile."

I asked the trusty, "How do you know they're going to kill me?"

"That chair sure going to get you," the trusty said.

I didn't believe nothing like that. Two days later there was the first sign Barnes and the trusty might be wrong—and I might be right.…

Two guys from New York, head men from the International Labor Defense, brought us pops and candy and gave them to us boys in the visiting room. They were Jewish. Which was okay with me. I worked for Jews in Chattanooga. Did porter and delivery work and such for them and always got along well. They told us the people were up in arms over our case in New York and if they had our say-so they would like to appeal our case.

These were the first people to call on us, to show any feelings for our lives, and we were glad, We hadn't even heard from our own families; they weren't allowed to see us. But these lawyers got in.

About us nine boys unfairly sentenced, they said their organization was doing all it could to wake up the people in this country and Europe.

Jailer Dick Barnes, he came in and listened when these lawyers asked us whether we got the right medical treatment. They suggested to Barnes a doctor should be sent in. Barnes is the kind of a guy, if you are a Negro, you can read hate in his face and his voice. He said, "We got a doctor here. These boys don't need any treatment."

I wanted a doctor and I didn't want the prison doctor. The prison was very filthy. It was making me sick, making us all sick. It was an old jail. The bed lice would get all over you; they would come up close to you to warm up. I said, "Yes, I want a doctor."

Barnes said, "What do you want a doctor? We got any medicine you can name."

"You have any medicine for these lice?" I asked. "One of them stole my cap last night."

The lawyers and the fellows laughed.

After the visitors went Barnes said, "Nigger, you're too smart. If you want to get along with me you just keep your mouth."

Now we knew why we had been getting mail from white folks. The I.L.D., or the Labor Defense, as we got to call them, had been causing around the country. They had told people at meetings and in newspapers to send us letters and cigarettes to make it easier for us in jail. Mail from white people was confusing to me. All my life I was untrusting of them. Now their kind words and presents was more light than we got through the bars of the windows. The next few days the mail got heavier; and the prison officials were upset what to do. We had the money to get whatever we could buy at the jail commissary, and this outside pressure gave us guts. Me, at least. My guts went up so I could demand a bath which Jailer Dick Barnes promised but didn't let me have. "You'll get it Saturday," he said. Saturday came and he put me off. "I haven't got time to fool with you." I got tight with him. "I got to have a bath!" That jacked up the other Scottsboro fellows and all together we raised hell for a bath. Barnes, he came back and let us out three at a time for showers.

Prisoners told me registered mail wasn't supposed to be opened. I found out mine was being opened and even kept from me. I told the guards I wanted to have some words with somebody about it. A little old man named Ervin, he came around. "I got to okay your mail," he said. "I have to look in the mail of all you Scottsboro niggers."

That got me sore. "Now listen, don't you open no letter of mine. If you do I'll see what I can do about it."

Ervin beat it off, and one of my cellmates said, "You can't talk to him like that. He's a chief warden."

"I don't care if he's President Hoover."

From then on, whenever mail came to me, Ervin, he would bring it himself. I opened it, Ervin saw me take out the money, then he'd read the letter.

It went on like that for many days until Barnes got to hate me. I kept after him; he kept after me. I had my own fight in me to begin with and now I had white folks fronting for me. One day he came up to my door and shook his finger at me and said, "I'll have you sent to Kilby tomorrow."

Sure enough, the next day, April 23, Barnes banged on the cell door and said, "Okay, sonofabitch, you and the other niggers get ready. You going to the death row in Kilby. You can't take nothing with you either.... I hope they burn that black dick off of you first before they burn the rest of you."

My cigarettes I gave away. Then I walked out the cell.

Outside the jail I was put in a private car, handcuffed to Willie Roberson. Guards were on each side and in the front seat.

That ride I can remember. It was my last good feeling of the outdoors. It was a fast ride for several hours, with the day getting warmer, the sun hotter. There was no talk, even between Willie and me. My eyes took in everything along the roadsides. It was spring, my favorite time of year. I was a tight guy who would not show people tears, but I felt the water behind my lids.

Willie and myself were the first to reach Kilby.

It was a bitter thing to see the door of Kilby Prison, what the free people of Alabama call "the little green gate." Those walls looked so high and hard to get over. They were concrete. We could see guards in the shacks along the wall tops next to their machine guns. Barbed wire stretched on top of the walls all around. They took us in through steel gates.

Then, death row opened to us ... a dozen cells facing each other, six to a side, and a thirteenth cell for toilet work.

Right off a guy in the cell opposite, he said, "So you're from Scottsboro. Been reading about you guys. The papers in New York making a big fuss about it. The governor will insist you go now."

"Go where?"

"To the chair ... it's right there."

I tried twisting my neck and eyes out the front of the cell to see the death room: but it was just out of my sight.

Chapter 4

That guy opposite, they called him Gunboat, he kept talking. "Do you want a Bible to make your soul right?" He was holding up a little red book in his hands for us to see. "You going to die tonight, you know. You Scottsboros better get busy with the Lord."

Willie Roberson, he was leaning up against the door with me listening, and he put a frown on. Willie got scared and excited and started talking about things. "You sure we going to die tonight?" he asked. We were both afraid. We didn't know. Sometimes other prisoners, they heard about things before we did.

Another guy in a cell next to Gunboat's was shaking his head from side to side like we should pay no mind to him. This fellow, name of Ricketts, called Gunboat a liar and said, "You fellows ain't going to die tonight. Gunboat don't know nothing about your case."

Gunboat yelled out, "Them guys going to die tonight! Here, take this here Bible!"

Ricketts waved his hands and said, "Keep away from that thing. That Bible never did us niggers any good!"

I never had really read the Bible. Couldn't read much anyway. But I was upset and leaned toward what Gunboat said....

"You better take to the Bible. You got souls and you better clean 'em."

Ricketts put it different. "You ain't got good lawyers, then you're done for. You ain't got white folks to front for you, then you're done for. *But leave that thing alone!*"

"What you heard about us getting the chair tonight?" Willie Roberson asked Gunboat.

"I know. Don't ask how I know."

"You heard something?"

"The Lord tell me so."

"Get that Bible across to me," I said to Gunboat.

"Don't take it!" Ricketts made a last try.

Gunboat, he tied a piece of wood to the end of a string and threw it over in front of my cell door. The Bible was on the other end and I started dragging it across to me.

Just then a tall, rawbony guard named L. J. Burrs saw Gunboat telegraphing the Bible to me. He stopped before our cell and said to Willie and me, "Pray, you goddamned black bastards. You'll still burn anyway."

"Hand me the book, will you?" I said to the guard.

"Q-o-h, you goddamned black sonofabitch. What you mean talking like that to me? Don't you know to call me *Captain*, call me *Boss*?"

"I don't call no one Captain. I don't call no one Boss."

"You nigger, you better get right with me before you get right with your Lord. You call me Captain when you talk to me."

He made to open the cell door, like he might come in to beat on me, then he changed his mind. Instead he kicked the Bible under my door and said, "I fix you, Patterson. You the ringleader of all these Scottsboro bastards. We got your record. You going to reckon with me." He walked down by the toilet.

I could hardly make out the words in the book. The little training in reading I had had I never much followed up. Never read no papers, no books, nothing. I did not know how to pronounce things, could not even say "Alabama" so you could understand me. I had to ask prisoners to tell me, and I would try and repeat it. Negroes called this way of speaking "flat talk."

But the Bible felt solid in my hands. I found myself stumbling through the small printed words.

Pretty soon the other fellows came in. They put Weems and Andy Wright in one cell, Powell and Norris together, and Eugene Williams and Olen Montgomery in another cell.

Right off Gunboat, he started to work on all of them, telling them the juice was going on tonight, and to get right with the Lord.

Charlie Weems wasn't easy to fool and he answered, "Aw, I know better than that. Our date set for July 10. They ain't going to do it before. You're a damned liar."

The religious stuff got going, all up and down the death row, them that was there trying to convert those of us just arrived. You see, a man in the death cell, he clings to anything that gives him a little hope.

That kind of talk mixed with the guessing about whether we would die tonight or in July. It went all up and down the twelve cells. My cell number was 222. I told the others my cell number and they told me theirs. Cell number 231 was right next to the chair room and none of us Tennessee and Georgia boys in the Scottsboro case had that one.

Each cell was just big enough for a single cot. Sometimes, when it was crowded in the death row, like now, they would put up a double-deck bed. Then you couldn't move around. One fellow would have to lay up on the bunk while the other could take about three steps forward and turn and take three steps back—if he was nervous and needed to walk.

White and black were in the death row, but mostly Negroes. Around us were desperate men who tried to question us about the Scottsboro case. They were killers, stoolies, and crazy guys. Some hoped to hear something they could carry to the warden so as to

Document Text

escape punishment for their crimes. They got nothing out of us. There was nothing to get out of us anyway. We just kept quiet about the case, all of us.

Night pushed into death row. I knew there were stars outside. The face of the sky I could see and remember clearly because I had looked at it at night all my life. I laid on the top bunk, in a way still feeling I was on a moving freight. Nothing was standing still. I was busy living from minute to minute. Everything was rumbling. I dreamed bad dreams, with freight trains, guards' faces, and courtrooms mixed up with the look of the sky at night.

Glossary

gondolas	low, flat-bottomed freight cars with fixed sides but no roof
jimcrow	Jim Crow (adj.), that is, segregated
President Hoover	Herbert Hoover, the thirty-first U.S. president, in office at the start of the Great Depression
stoolies	a stool pigeon, or informer
trusty	a convict who is considered trustworthy and granted special privileges
venereal	venereal disease, possibly syphilis or gonorrhea

SUPREME COURT OF THE UNITED STATES

Nos. 1, 2, 4 AND 10.—OCTOBER TERM, 1953.

1	Oliver Brown, et al., Appellants, *v.* Board of Education of Topeka, Shawnee County, Kansas, et al.	On Appeal From the United States District Court for the District of Kansas.
2	Harry Briggs, Jr., et al., Appellants, *v.* R. W. Elliott, et al.	On Appeal From the United States District Court for the Eastern District of South Carolina.
4	Dorothy E. Davis, et al., Appellants, *v.* County School Board of Prince Edward County, Virginia, et al.	On Appeal From the United States District Court for the Eastern District of Virginia.
10	Francis B. Gebhart, et al., Petitioners, *v.* Ethel Louise Belton, et al.	On Writ of Certiorari to the Supreme Court of Delaware.

[May 17, 1954.]

Mr. Chief Justice Warren delivered the opinion of the Court.

These cases come to us from the States of Kansas, South Carolina, Virginia, and Delaware. They are premised on different facts and different local conditions,

Brown v. Board of Education (National Archives and Records Administration)

Brown v. Board of Education

1954

"In the field of public education, the doctrine of 'separate but equal' has no place."

Overview

Brown v. Board of Education of Topeka was the 1954 Supreme Court decision that declared that legally mandated segregation in public schools was unconstitutional under the Fourteenth Amendment's equal protection clause. The landmark case was actually a combination of five cases that challenged school segregation in Delaware, South Carolina, Virginia, and Topeka, Kansas. In a companion case, *Bolling v. Sharpe*, segregation in the District of Columbia's public schools was declared unconstitutional under the due process clause of the Fifth Amendment. *Brown* was a pivotal case in the history of the Supreme Court. Although *Brown* did not explicitly reverse the Court's earlier ruling in the 1896 case *Plessy v. Ferguson*, which permitted states to provide "separate but equal" facilities for people of different races, it was clearly the beginning of the end of the Supreme Court's willingness to give constitutional sanction to state-sponsored segregation. *Brown* was the first decision authored by the recently appointed Chief Justice Earl Warren and was a harbinger of the new, more activist role that the Court would take in protecting civil rights and civil liberties under his leadership.

Brown should be seen against the broader background of segregation in American history. By the end of the nineteenth century, southern states and, indeed, quite a few states outside the South were developing an American system of apartheid through what were often called Jim Crow laws. This system of segregation mandated the separation of blacks and whites in almost every observable facet of public life. Separate water fountains, park benches, railroad cars, and other facilities were common. All of the southern states and a number of border states also maintained separate school facilities for blacks and whites. Although the Supreme Court's decision in *Plessy* had declared that blacks could be required to use separate facilities if those facilities were equal to those provided for whites, states that maintained racially separate schools provided schools for African Americans that were usually greatly inferior in resources and programs to those provided for whites. Glaring inequalities in educational facilities prompted the National Association for the Advancement of Colored People (NAACP) to begin a decades-long litigation campaign to challenge segregation in public education. That campaign would eventually result in the decision in *Brown*.

Context

The NAACP began to develop its strategy to attack segregation in state schools in the 1930s. The organization began cautiously enough by attacking segregation in professional schools, principally law schools, of state universities. Law schools were selected because state university systems usually had only one law school each, and it would be relatively easy to make the case that providing a state law school for white students while providing none for blacks violated the principle that a state had to provide equal facilities. The NAACP also believed that litigation designed to force states to permit black students to attend state law schools would provoke less adverse political reaction than lawsuits designed to integrate public primary and secondary schools. The architect of the NAACP's litigation strategy, Charles Hamilton Houston, would achieve success before World War II with his victory in the 1938 case *Missouri ex rel. Gaines v. Canada*. In that case the Supreme Court held that Missouri's exclusion of African Americans from the state's law school was unconstitutional even though Missouri was willing to pay tuition for black students to attend law school out of state. The NAACP met with success in similar litigation in other states.

While the NAACP had some success with litigation designed to desegregate professional schools before World War II, the changes in racial attitudes brought about by the war played a key role in paving the way for the decision in *Brown*. In particular, the war brought about a new assertiveness on the part of African Americans, as many blacks left the rural South and traditional patterns of racial domination for the armed forces and the industrial cities of the North and West. With these changes came a new willingness to struggle for equal rights. The fight against Nazi racism also caused many white Americans to question traditional racial attitudes. Furthermore, the social sciences were increasingly calling established racial prejudices into question. The publication in 1944 of the Swedish social scientist Gunnar Myrdal's book *An American Dilemma:*

Time Line

1896
- **May 18**
  In *Plessy v. Ferguson*, the Supreme Court declares the "separate but equal" doctrine, permitting segregation in government-run facilities.

1909
- **February 12**
  A group to later be known as the National Association for the Advancement of Colored People (NAACP) is formed to fight segregation.

1929
- Charles Hamilton Houston is appointed vice-dean of Howard University Law School. Houston would transform the law school into a vehicle for training civil rights lawyers, including Thurgood Marshall, the principal lawyer for the NAACP in the *Brown* case.

1938
- **December 12**
  In *Missouri ex rel. Gaines v. Canada*, the Supreme Court holds that the state of Missouri must admit black students to the state law school.

1948
- **May 3**
  In *Shelley v. Kraemer*, the Supreme Court bars the judicial enforcement of restrictive covenants used to prevent home owners from selling their homes to members of minority groups.

- **July 26**
  President Harry Truman issues Executive Order 9981, requiring equality of opportunity in and the desegregation of the armed forces.

1950
- **June 5**
  In *Sweatt v. Painter*, the Court orders that black students be admitted to the University of Texas School of Law, declaring that the separate law school established for black students did not provide equal treatment.

The Negro Problem and Modern Democracy also had a significant impact, causing many university-educated people to question the practice of segregation.

The changes in the racial atmosphere in postwar America spurred the NAACP to confront legally mandated segregation. While the organization achieved significant victories in its fight against segregated professional education, other important victories came in the legal struggle against general discrimination. The 1948 case *Shelley v. Kraemer*, in which the Supreme Court declared that courts could not enforce restrictive covenants barring minorities from buying homes in white neighborhoods, was an indication of the Court's willingness to give the Fourteenth Amendment a broader reading than it had in the past. Following this decision, many in the NAACP believed that the time was right for a frontal assault on segregated education.

Between 1950 and 1952 the NAACP, under the leadership of Thurgood Marshall and his associates, began preparing the cases that would come to be known as *Brown v. Board of Education*. The case by which the litigation is known arose in Topeka, Kansas—a state that, unlike those in the South, did not have statewide segregation. Instead, the state gave localities the option to have segregated schools. The elementary schools in Topeka were indeed segregated, and Oliver Brown, a black resident of the city, filed suit so that his daughter might attend a school reserved for whites. That school was nearer to the Brown home and had better facilities.

In 1952 the Supreme Court consolidated the different desegregation cases. The first set of oral arguments were heard by the Court in December of that year; in June 1953, the Court asked for a second set of oral arguments designed to specifically address the issue of whether or not the Fourteenth Amendment was intended to mandate school desegregation. As that issue was being researched, Chief Justice Frederick M. Vinson died in September 1953. He was replaced by Earl Warren. Most observers agree that the new chief justice made a critical difference to the outcome of the case.

About the Author

Earl Warren was born in Los Angeles, California, in 1891. He was a graduate of the University of California at Berkeley and of that university's law school. Warren served in the U.S. Army during World War I as an officer in charge of training troops deploying to France. He began his legal career in California in 1920 as a prosecutor with the Alameda County district attorney's office. In 1925 he was appointed district attorney to fill a vacancy. Elected district attorney in his own right the following year, he would remain in that office until his election as California's attorney general in 1938.

Warren was a product of the California Republican politics of the Progressive Era. As district attorney and as attorney general he was generally supportive of reforms in the criminal justice system, such as with his willingness to extend due process rights and legal representation to defendants in criminal cases. These were generally not required at the time by the federal courts, which by and large were not applying most of the criminal defendants' rights provisions of the Fourth, Fifth, and Sixth amendments to the states. Warren was also somewhat ahead of the times in his attitudes toward African Americans. He considered appointing a black attorney to the attorney general's staff in 1938.

Ironically enough, anti-Asian bias probably helped propel Warren to the national stage. Warren shared the anti-Asian sentiments that were common among whites on the West Coast in the early part of the twentieth century. Near the beginning of his career he was a member of an anti-Asian group, Native Sons of the Golden West. As attorney general in the winter and spring of 1942, Warren was a leading advocate of Japanese internment, at first advocating internment only for Japanese aliens but later supporting the internment of Japanese Americans as well. His support for Japanese internment doubtless aided Warren in his gaining election as governor of California in 1942. Warren would run for vice president on the Republican ticket with Governor Thomas Dewey of New York in 1948.

Warren was appointed chief justice by President Dwight David Eisenhower in 1953 to replace Chief Justice Frederick M. Vinson, who had died in office. Warren's entire tenure as chief justice was marked by controversy, beginning with the decision in *Brown* and continuing until his retirement from the Supreme Court in 1969. Under Warren, the Court dealt with some of the most contentious issues in postwar American life, including school desegregation, reapportionment, the rights of criminal defendants, birth control, and the right to privacy, among others. Warren's critics charged that he extended the reach of the Court into areas unauthorized and unintended by the Constitution's framers and that he and his allies on the Court often employed dubious legal reasoning. Warren's supporters responded by noting that the Court under his direction was a vital force in making equal protection and the Bill of Rights living principles for millions of Americans. Later on as chief justice, at the direction of Lyndon B. Johnson, Warren would head the President's Commission on the Assassination of President Kennedy, often referred to as the Warren Commission. Warren died in 1974.

Explanation and Analysis of the Document

Brown v. Board of Education of Topeka is a Supreme Court case and as such begins with a syllabus presenting basic information about the case. This information includes the parties, the lower court whose decision is being appealed, and the dates that the case was argued before the Supreme Court. The case was taken on appeal from a decision by the District Court for the District of Kansas. An asterisked footnote relates that *Brown* is being consolidated with other school segregation cases from South Carolina, Virginia, and Delaware. The syllabus also

Time Line

1954
- **May 17** The Supreme Court issues its decision in *Brown v. Board of Education*, declaring segregation in public schools unconstitutional.

1955
- **May 31** The Court issues its decision in the second *Brown v. Board of Education* case, calling for the implementation of the first decision with "all deliberate speed."

1957
- **September 24** President Dwight D. Eisenhower sends federal troops to Little Rock, Arkansas, to enforce a federal district court school desegregation order; the order had produced large-scale mob resistance by opponents of integration.

1960
- **November 8** In response to a federal district court order calling for the desegregation of New Orleans schools, the Louisiana state legislature passes an "interposition statute" declaring that the legislature did not recognize the authority of the ruling in *Brown*.

1962
- **September** President John F. Kennedy sends federal marshals and federal troops to Oxford, Mississippi, to assist in the enrollment of the African American student James Meredith in the University of Mississippi; Meredith's enrollment had been ordered by the U.S. Court of Appeals for the Fifth Circuit but was obstructed by state officials, including Governor Ross Barnett.

1971
- **April 20** Supreme Court approves of busing as a means of achieving school desegregation.

Time Line

1974

- **July 25**
  In *Milliken v. Bradley*, the Court declares that the constitutional requirement to desegregate does not require desegregation across municipal lines. The decision means that lower federal courts cannot require the integration of urban and suburban school districts across municipal lines.

gives a summary of the decision and lists the attorneys who made oral arguments before the Court on behalf of the parties in *Brown* and the companion cases. In addition, it lists briefs filed by amici curiae ("friends of the court," persons or organizations not party to a case who file a brief in support of a party or to inform the court with respect to a legal or policy issue) in *Brown* and the companion cases. Of special interest is the fact that the assistant attorney general J. Lee Rankin argued for the United States in support of desegregation.

♦ **Chief Justice Earl Warren's Majority Opinion**

Warren begins with a straightforward presentation of the issues. His first paragraph notes that the desegregation cases have come from different states—Kansas, South Carolina, Virginia, and Delaware—and that while each state presents somewhat different issues with respect to local laws and local conditions, the clear principal issue of legal segregation is common to all of the cases.

Stylistically, Warren's opinion makes extensive use of footnotes not only to cite relevant authorities but also to carry the burden of informing the reader of major legal and factual arguments. As had become common in twentieth-century legal writing, footnotes served to supply a judicial decision with a kind of supplemental narrative, augmenting the main points being made in the body of the opinion. This style of judicial writing was doubtless encouraged, perhaps mandated, by the practice of parties and amici curiae filing extensive briefs in major cases. The increasing use of "Brandeis briefs"—briefs providing wide-ranging amounts of information to the Court from the social and physical sciences, as modeled after that filed by Louis Brandeis in *Muller v. Oregon* (1908)—probably also hastened the development of the lengthy use of footnotes in judicial opinions.

The first footnote here discusses how *Brown* and the companion cases had fared in the U.S. district courts. Included in this discussion are the legal and factual findings of these courts. With respect to *Brown*, a three-judge panel of the District Court for the District of Kansas found that segregated public education indeed had a detrimental effect on black students, but that court nonetheless upheld segregated education because the facilities for blacks and whites were held to be equal with respect to buildings, transportation, curricula, and the educational qualifications of the teachers. The district court in South Carolina found that the facilities available to black students were inferior to those of whites, but that court nonetheless upheld segregation on the ground that South Carolina officials were making efforts to equalize facilities. In Virginia, the district court ordered officials to make efforts to equalize the schools. In Delaware, the state courts had ordered desegregation, and state officials were appealing that order.

Warren moves in the second and third paragraphs to presenting the central claims of the NAACP and of the parents who were bringing suit. He zeroes in on the crux of these claims in the third paragraph, noting, "The plaintiffs contend that segregated public schools are not 'equal' and cannot be made 'equal,' and that hence they are deprived of the equal protection of the laws." Warren's opinion spends relatively little time examining the history of this argument, but it is a claim with a long history, one that predates *Brown* by at least a century. In particular, the NAACP argued that segregation was inherently stigmatizing, an argument that was older than the Fourteenth Amendment (ratified in 1868) and its equal protection clause, under which *Brown* and the other cases were brought. This argument made its first judicial appearance in the antebellum Massachusetts school desegregation case *Roberts v. City of Boston* (1850). In that case, African American parents argued that Boston's system of school segregation essentially stigmatized black children by setting up a caste system dividing black and white. The Massachusetts supreme judicial court rejected the argument, in effect establishing the "separate but equal" doctrine, a point Warren notes in footnote 6. The argument that segregation stigmatized African Americans and hence violated the Fourteenth Amendment's guarantee of equal protection under the law would later be heard and rejected by the Supreme Court in *Plessy v. Ferguson* (1896), with the Supreme Court making the "separate but equal" doctrine a part of federal constitutional law.

Part of the NAACP's aim in *Brown* was to have segregated schools declared unconstitutional on the ground that the system of school segregation forced black children into schools that were vastly inferior to those reserved for white students. The systems of school segregation that prevailed in the southern states usually featured vast inequalities in the levels of education provided to black and white children. Black schools were typically funded at a fraction of the level of white schools. In many districts, blacks were confined to one-room schoolhouses in which all grades were to be educated, while whites had separate elementary and secondary schools. Black schools were usually separate and decidedly unequal with respect to the qualifications and pay for black teachers and the physical facilities in which black schools were housed. Correcting all of this was part of the NAACP's aim in litigating against school segregation. In addition, the civil rights organization shared the view held by its nineteenth-century predecessors that the very act of segregating, of singling out blacks for separate treatment, was inherently stigmatizing and more appropriate to a caste system than to the practices of American democracy. The NAACP advocate Thurgood Marshall, in his oral argument before Earl Warren and other members of the Court on December 8, 1953, presented the issue starkly: "Why of all the multitudinous groups in this country, you have to single out the Negroes and give them this separate treatment?"

This was clearly an issue involving the Fourteenth Amendment's equal protection clause, and in the fourth and fifth paragraphs the new chief justice begins addressing the Fourteenth Amendment and what it mandated in these circumstances. Here, Warren begins moving into territory that would forever make *Brown* an object of controversy among constitutional commentators. He argues that the history of the Fourteenth Amendment is inconclusive regarding what it had to say with respect to school segregation. In fact, Warren frames *Brown* as a case pitting modern realities against inconclusive history. In the fifth paragraph he focuses on the history of public education at the time of the enactment of the Fourteenth Amendment, noting that public education had not yet taken hold in the South and that practically all southern blacks at the time were illiterate. He juxtaposes that situation with modern circumstances: "Today, in contrast, many Negroes have achieved outstanding success in the arts and sciences, as well as in the business and professional world." Warren uses this contrast between the relative lack of importance of public education at the time of the enactment of the Fourteenth Amendment and its much greater importance at the time of the *Brown* decision to set up what will be his principal argument in paragraphs 8 and 9, namely, that the question of segregated education and its constitutionality under the Fourteenth Amendment had to be considered in light of the importance of public education in modern—that is, post–World War II—American society and not in light of its relative unimportance at the beginning of the Reconstruction era.

In the sixth paragraph Warren takes on the "separate but equal" doctrine, seeking to show that it is less than the solid precedent that its champions claimed. Indeed, the argument for the constitutionality of segregated schools rested on the "separate but equal" precedent provided in *Plessy*. The former solicitor general John W. Davis, representing South Carolina in an oral argument before the Supreme Court, emphasized the importance of *Plessy*, highlighting the fact that the lower federal courts and the Supreme Court had repeatedly reaffirmed the "separate but equal" doctrine and asserting that the Court should follow precedent and apply the doctrine in the case of school segregation. Davis's arguments were echoed by other supporters of school segregation.

Warren notes that the Court's earliest interpretations of the Fourteenth Amendment stressed that the amendment was designed to prohibit state-imposed racial discrimination; the "separate but equal" doctrine did not become part of the Supreme Court's jurisprudence until 1896—more than a generation after the enactment of the amendment. He also notes that *Plessy* involved transportation, not education. Warren further states that since *Plessy*, the Supreme Court had only heard six cases involving the "separate but equal" doctrine, with none reviewing the essential validity of

Earl Warren (Library of Congress)

the doctrine. He next cites the decisions involving segregation in graduate and professional schools. Warren's aims in this discussion are clear. While not directly challenging the *Plessy* precedent, he effectively isolates it as a decision that was not consistent with judicial interpretations made close to the enactment of the Fourteenth Amendment. He also gives *Plessy* a narrow reading so that it might be seen as a precedent that at most applies to the field of transportation. That case, according to Warren, was one that had not been thoroughly examined by the Court and in any event was made problematic, particularly in the field of education, by the graduate-school segregation cases.

Paragraphs 7–9 are used to frame the issues before the Court. Warren largely frames these issues in the way that the NAACP and the plaintiffs had presented them. The primary issue is segregation, and it is an issue that goes beyond tangible factors to encompass philosophical ones as well as the subtle reality of stigmatization. In paragraph 7 Warren uses footnote 9 to relate that the district court in Kansas had actually found substantial equality in the black and white schools. Warren indicates that regardless of this finding, segregation itself and its effect on public education remain of paramount concern.

Paragraph 8 is where Warren stakes out a clear claim as a proponent—indeed, one of the earliest explicit proponents—of the notion of a "living constitution," the idea that jurists should go beyond the concerns and assumptions of the framers of constitutional provisions and

Essential Quotes

> "In approaching this problem, we cannot turn the clock back to 1868, when the Amendment was adopted, or even to 1896, when Plessy v. Ferguson was written."
>
> (Chief Justice Earl Warren, Majority Opinion)

> "Today, education is perhaps the most important function of state and local governments."
>
> (Chief Justice Earl Warren, Majority Opinion)

> "Such an opportunity, where the state has undertaken to provide it, is a right which must be made available to all on equal terms."
>
> (Chief Justice Earl Warren, Majority Opinion)

> "To separate them from others of similar age and qualifications solely because of their race generates a feeling of inferiority as to their status in the community that may affect their hearts and minds in a way unlikely ever to be undone."
>
> (Chief Justice Earl Warren, Majority Opinion)

> "Whatever may have been the extent of psychological knowledge at the time of Plessy v. Ferguson, this finding is amply supported by modern authority."
>
> (Chief Justice Earl Warren, Majority Opinion)

> "We conclude that, in the field of public education, the doctrine of 'separate but equal' has no place. Separate educational facilities are inherently unequal."
>
> (Chief Justice Earl Warren, Majority Opinion)

instead look at and reevaluate the Constitution in light of modern circumstances. He starts the paragraph, "In approaching this problem, we cannot turn the clock back to 1868, when the Amendment was adopted, or even to 1896, when *Plessy v. Ferguson* was written. We must consider public education in the light of its full development and its present place in American life throughout the Nation." In paragraphs 9–11 Warren goes on to outline the importance of education in modern American life and to conclude that segregated schools deprive members of minority groups of equal educational opportunities even when the tangible resources are equal.

Paragraph 12 lays a psychological basis for the opinion—one that would leave the *Brown* decision with a lingering controversy that persists to the present day. Warren cites the works of a number of psychologists—including, most prominently, the black psychologist Kenneth Clark—on the effects of segregation on the self-esteem of black children. These citations would lead many critics to charge that the chief justice was engaging in sociology rather than jurisprudence. Even many critics sympathetic to the outcome in *Brown* later expressed some discomfort with the use of psychological evidence, claiming that it gave the decision less of a firm footing, such that it could potentially be undone by shifts in findings in the social sciences. Clearly, Warren was examining the plaintiffs' arguments that segregation stigmatized black students by comparing those claims to the findings of the psychological experts of the day.

Paragraph 14 provides the Court's conclusion that "in the field of public education, the doctrine of 'separate but equal' has no place." Paragraph 15 provides a hint about some of the behind-the-scenes negotiations that Warren and the other justices went through in order to secure a unanimous decision in *Brown*. Here, Warren calls for the reargument of the cases to allow the Court to consider remedies for school segregation. Warren recognized the importance of establishing the constitutional principle that segregated public schools violated the equal protection clause of the Fourteenth Amendment. As such, he was greatly concerned with getting a unanimous Court to agree to that constitutional principle—an achievement that had been very much in doubt during judicial conferences. Thus, as part of the strategy to obtain a unanimous opinion, Warren agreed to have *Brown* initially decide only the principle that segregated schools were unconstitutional, deferring the question of how the decision would be implemented for another day. Paragraph 14, the last paragraph, lays the groundwork for the second case, commonly known as *Brown II*, which would be heard the following year, and the more than two decades of desegregation litigation that would follow.

Audience

Brown v. Board of Education was first and foremost a Supreme Court decision designed to settle the constitutional question of whether or not segregated public schools were prohibited by the Fourteenth Amendment. Warren wrote the opinion to resolve that constitutional controversy and to inform states that they could no longer maintain segregated school systems. It was also written to inform African American parents that they had a legal right to send their children to nonsegregated schools.

Warren clearly also had a broader, national audience in mind while writing the decision. An experienced politician, the chief justice knew that the decision would be controversial and, indeed, hotly contested. He sought to write the decision in such a way as to present the policy case to the American public at large. His controversial use of psychological evidence to buttress the case against segregated schools was an attempt to appeal to the public by showing that children were being harmed by the policy of segregation. Warren's discussion of Negro accomplishments in education, business, and science can also be seen as an attempt to counter strong prejudices against African Americans, thus fortifying the case for school integration.

Impact

It is probably no exaggeration to say that *Brown* was the most significant case decided by the Supreme Court in its history. While the decision would take decades to implement, *Brown* was critical as a harbinger of the federal government's return to the civil rights arena, an arena from which it had been largely absent since Reconstruction. *Brown* would also provide a tremendous boost to the civil rights movement of the 1950s and 1960s. The knowledge that the Court was now going to interpret the Constitution as prohibiting the kind of caste-like distinctions that had been a feature of black life in the United States from the very beginning helped encourage a greater assertiveness on the part of African Americans, who proceeded to successfully protest the formal segregation of Jim Crow laws in the South and, later, more subtle forms of discrimination throughout the nation.

Brown's impact in the courts was a little more complicated. The case commonly known as *Brown v. Board of Education* led to a successor case of the same name, known as *Brown II*, in 1955. That case resulted in a ruling that required the desegregation of separate school systems with "all deliberate speed." This order, in turn, led to protracted battles in federal district courts over the precise details and timing of school desegregation plans, which lasted decades. Nonetheless, the decision in *Brown* effectively led to the death of the "separate but equal" doctrine as well as to the negation of the idea that governmental bodies could practice the kind of formal discrimination against members of minority groups that had been common before *Brown*.

See also *Roberts v. City of Boston* (1850); Fourteenth Amendment (1868); *Plessy v. Ferguson* (1896); Charles Hamilton Houston's "Educational Inequalities Must Go!" (1935).

Further Reading

■ Books

Cottrol, Robert J., et al. *Brown v. Board of Education: Caste, Culture, and the Constitution*. Lawrence: University Press of Kansas, 2003.

Kluger, Richard. *Simple Justice: The History of* Brown v. Board of Education *and Black America's Struggle for Equality*. New York: Knopf, 2004.

Myrdal, Gunnar. *An American Dilemma: The Negro Problem and Modern Democracy*. New York: Harper & Brothers, 1944.

Patterson, James T. Brown v. Board of Education: *A Civil Rights Milestone and Its Troubled Legacy*. New York: Oxford University Press, 2001.

Tushnet, Mark. *The NAACP's Legal Strategy against Segregated Education, 1925–1950*. Chapel Hill: University of North Carolina Press, 1987.

White, G. Edward. *Earl Warren: A Public Life*. New York: Oxford University Press, 1982.

- **Web Sites**

"Brown v. Board of Education: Digital Archive." University of Michigan Library Web site.
 http://www.lib.umich.edu/exhibits/brownarchive/.

"Teaching with Documents: Documents Related to *Brown v. Board of Education*." National Archives "Educators and Students" Web site.
 http://www.archives.gov/education/lessons/brown-v-board/.

—Robert Cottroll

Questions for Further Study

1. Compare and contrast Chief Justice Earl Warren's opinion in *Brown* with Justice John Marshall Harlan's dissent in *Plessy v. Ferguson*. Although both opinions argue against the "separate but equal" doctrine, they do so in different ways. Which opinion do you believe is stronger and why?

2. Many have criticized Warren's opinion for ignoring the original intent of the Fourteenth Amendment. How important should the intentions of the framers be considered in modern constitutional interpretation?

3. In light of the continued existence of de facto school segregation in many communities, should *Brown* be judged a failure?

4. Some critics fault Warren for writing a weak decision that would take very long to implement. Other students of the case argue that if Warren had not written a cautious decision, he would have had difficulty getting a unanimous Court to agree with the decision, which would have brought about more resistance to *Brown*. Which argument do you find more persuasive?

5. Should Warren have included psychological evidence in his decision or should he have based his decision solely on legal sources?

BROWN V. BOARD OF EDUCATION

Syllabus

Segregation of white and Negro children in the public schools of a State solely on the basis of race, pursuant to state laws permitting or requiring such segregation, denies to Negro children the equal protection of the laws guaranteed by the Fourteenth Amendment—even though the physical facilities and other "tangible" factors of white and Negro schools may be equal.

(a) The history of the Fourteenth Amendment is inconclusive as to its intended effect on public education.

(b) The question presented in these cases must be determined not on the basis of conditions existing when the Fourteenth Amendment was adopted, but in the light of the full development of public education and its present place in American life throughout the Nation.

(c) Where a State has undertaken to provide an opportunity for an education in its public schools, such an opportunity is a right which must be made available to all on equal terms.

(d) Segregation of children in public schools solely on the basis of race deprives children of the minority group of equal educational opportunities, even though the physical facilities and other "tangible" factors may be equal.

(e) The "separate but equal" doctrine adopted in *Plessy v. Ferguson*, 163 U.S. 537, has no place in the field of public education.

(f) The cases are restored to the docket for further argument on specified questions relating to the forms of the decrees.

Opinion

◆ Mr. Chief Justice Warren Delivered the Opinion of the Court

These cases come to us from the States of Kansas, South Carolina, Virginia, and Delaware. They are premised on different facts and different local conditions, but a common legal question justifies their consideration together in this consolidated opinion.

In each of the cases, minors of the Negro race, through their legal representatives, seek the aid of the courts in obtaining admission to the public schools of their community on a nonsegregated basis. In each instance, they had been denied admission to schools attended by white children under laws requiring or permitting segregation according to race. This segregation was alleged to deprive the plaintiffs of the equal protection of the laws under the Fourteenth Amendment. In each of the cases other than the Delaware case, a three-judge federal district court denied relief to the plaintiffs on the so-called "separate but equal" doctrine announced by this Court in *Plessy v. Ferguson*, 163 U.S. 537. Under that doctrine, equality of treatment is accorded when the races are provided substantially equal facilities, even though these facilities be separate. In the Delaware case, the Supreme Court of Delaware adhered to that doctrine, but ordered that the plaintiffs be admitted to the white schools because of their superiority to the Negro schools.

The plaintiffs contend that segregated public schools are not "equal" and cannot be made "equal," and that hence they are deprived of the equal protection of the laws. Because of the obvious importance of the question presented, the Court took jurisdiction. Argument was heard in the 1952 Term, and reargument was heard this Term on certain questions propounded by the Court.

Reargument was largely devoted to the circumstances surrounding the adoption of the Fourteenth Amendment in 1868. It covered exhaustively consideration of the Amendment in Congress, ratification by the states, then-existing practices in racial segregation, and the views of proponents and opponents of the Amendment. This discussion and our own investigation convince us that, although these sources cast some light, it is not enough to resolve the problem with which we are faced. At best, they are inconclusive. The most avid proponents of the post-War Amendments undoubtedly intended them to remove all legal distinctions among "all persons born or naturalized in the United States." Their opponents, just as certainly, were antagonistic to both the letter and the spirit of the Amendments and wished them to have the most limited effect. What others in Congress and the state legislatures had in mind cannot be determined with any degree of certainty.

Document Text

An additional reason for the inconclusive nature of the Amendment's history with respect to segregated schools is the status of public education at that time. In the South, the movement toward free common schools, supported by general taxation, had not yet taken hold. Education of white children was largely in the hands of private groups. Education of Negroes was almost nonexistent, and practically all of the race were illiterate. In fact, any education of Negroes was forbidden by law in some states. Today, in contrast, many Negroes have achieved outstanding success in the arts and sciences, as well as in the business and professional world. It is true that public school education at the time of the Amendment had advanced further in the North, but the effect of the Amendment on Northern States was generally ignored in the congressional debates. Even in the North, the conditions of public education did not approximate those existing today. The curriculum was usually rudimentary; ungraded schools were common in rural areas; the school term was but three months a year in many states, and compulsory school attendance was virtually unknown. As a consequence, it is not surprising that there should be so little in the history of the Fourteenth Amendment relating to its intended effect on public education.

In the first cases in this Court construing the Fourteenth Amendment, decided shortly after its adoption, the Court interpreted it as proscribing all state-imposed discriminations against the Negro race. The doctrine of "separate but equal" did not make its appearance in this Court until 1896 in the case of *Plessy v. Ferguson*, supra, involving not education but transportation. American courts have since labored with the doctrine for over half a century. In this Court, there have been six cases involving the "separate but equal" doctrine in the field of public education. In *Cumming v. County Board of Education*, 175 U.S. 528, and *Gong Lum v. Rice*, 275 U.S. 78, the validity of the doctrine itself was not challenged. In more recent cases, all on the graduate school level, inequality was found in that specific benefits enjoyed by white students were denied to Negro students of the same educational qualifications. *Missouri ex rel. Gaines v. Canada*, 305 U.S. 337; *Sipuel v. Oklahoma*, 332 U.S. 631; *Sweatt v. Painter*, 339 U.S. 629; *McLaurin v. Oklahoma State Regents*, 339 U.S. 637. In none of these cases was it necessary to reexamine the doctrine to grant relief to the Negro plaintiff. And in *Sweatt v. Painter*, supra, the Court expressly reserved decision on the question whether *Plessy v. Ferguson* should be held inapplicable to public education.

In the instant cases, that question is directly presented. Here, unlike *Sweatt v. Painter*, there are findings below that the Negro and white schools involved have been equalized, or are being equalized, with respect to buildings, curricula, qualifications and salaries of teachers, and other "tangible" factors. Our decision, therefore, cannot turn on merely a comparison of these tangible factors in the Negro and white schools involved in each of the cases. We must look instead to the effect of segregation itself on public education.

In approaching this problem, we cannot turn the clock back to 1868, when the Amendment was adopted, or even to 1896, when *Plessy v. Ferguson* was written. We must consider public education in the light of its full development and its present place in American life throughout the Nation. Only in this way can it be determined if segregation in public schools deprives these plaintiffs of the equal protection of the laws.

Today, education is perhaps the most important function of state and local governments. Compulsory school attendance laws and the great expenditures for education both demonstrate our recognition of the importance of education to our democratic society. It is required in the performance of our most basic public responsibilities, even service in the armed forces. It is the very foundation of good citizenship. Today it is a principal instrument in awakening the child to cultural values, in preparing him for later professional training, and in helping him to adjust normally to his environment. In these days, it is doubtful that any child may reasonably be expected to succeed in life if he is denied the opportunity of an education. Such an opportunity, where the state has undertaken to provide it, is a right which must be made available to all on equal terms.

We come then to the question presented: Does segregation of children in public schools solely on the basis of race, even though the physical facilities and other "tangible" factors may be equal, deprive the children of the minority group of equal educational opportunities? We believe that it does.

In *Sweatt v. Painter*, supra, in finding that a segregated law school for Negroes could not provide them equal educational opportunities, this Court relied in large part on "those qualities which are incapable of objective measurement but which make for greatness in a law school." In *McLaurin v. Oklahoma State Regents*, supra, the Court, in requiring that a Negro admitted to a white graduate school be treated like all other students, again resorted to intangible considerations: "… his ability to study, to engage in discussions and exchange views with other students, and, in general, to learn his profession." Such considerations apply with added force to children in grade and high schools. To separate them from others of similar age and qualifications solely because of their race generates a feeling of inferiority as to their status in the community that may affect their hearts and minds in a way unlikely ever to be undone. The effect of this separation on their educational opportunities was well stated by a finding in the Kansas case by a court which nevertheless felt compelled to rule against the Negro plaintiffs:

> Segregation of white and colored children in public schools has a detrimental effect upon the colored children. The impact is greater when it has the sanction of the law, for the policy of separating the races is usually interpreted as denoting the inferiority of the negro group. A sense of inferiority affects the motivation of a child to learn. Segregation with the sanction of law, therefore, has a tendency to [retard] the educational and mental development of negro children and to deprive them of some of the benefits they would receive in a racial[ly] integrated school system.

Whatever may have been the extent of psychological knowledge at the time of *Plessy v. Ferguson*, this finding is amply supported by modern authority. Any language in *Plessy v. Ferguson* contrary to this finding is rejected.

We conclude that, in the field of public education, the doctrine of "separate but equal" has no place. Separate educational facilities are inherently unequal. Therefore, we hold that the plaintiffs and others similarly situated for whom the actions have been brought are, by reason of the segregation complained of, deprived of the equal protection of the laws guaranteed by the Fourteenth Amendment. This disposition makes unnecessary any discussion whether such segregation also violates the Due Process Clause of the Fourteenth Amendment.

Because these are class actions, because of the wide applicability of this decision, and because of the great variety of local conditions, the formulation of decrees in these cases presents problems of considerable complexity. On reargument, the consideration of appropriate relief was necessarily subordinated to the primary question—the constitutionality of segregation in public education. We have now announced that such segregation is a denial of the equal protection of the laws. In order that we may have the full assistance of the parties in formulating decrees, the cases will be restored to the docket, and the parties are requested to present further argument on Questions 4 and 5 previously propounded by the Court for the reargument this Term. The Attorney General of the United States is again invited to participate. The Attorneys General of the states requiring or permitting segregation in public education will also be permitted to appear as amici curiae upon request to do so by September 15, 1954, and submission of briefs by October 1, 1954.

It is so ordered.

Glossary

amici curiae	persons or organizations not party to a case who file a brief in support of a party or to inform the court with respect to a legal or policy issue
class actions	suits where representatives of a class of persons may sue on behalf of themselves and similarly situated individuals
common schools	public schools (as used in the nineteenth century)
disposition	settlement; resolution
sanction	approval

An estimated seventy-five thousand people of all races massed before the Lincoln Memorial to hear Marian Anderson sing on Easter Sunday 1939. (Library of Congress)

Marian Anderson's *My Lord, What a Morning*

1956

"I had become, whether I liked it or not, a symbol, representing my people."

Overview

"Easter Sunday," an excerpt from Marian Anderson's autobiography, *My Lord, What a Morning* (1956) details the world-renowned contralto's recollections of her most famous performance. A landmark in African American history and a prelude to the civil rights movement of the 1950s and 1960s, Anderson's 1939 Easter Sunday concert at the Lincoln Memorial in Washington, D.C., developed when the Daughters of the American Revolution (DAR) denied her the opportunity to perform at Constitution Hall because of her race. Led by Walter White, executive secretary of the National Association for the Advancement of Colored People (NAACP), an interracial coalition of influential individuals and organizations turned Anderson's plight into a national cause célèbre.

The mobilization of liberal outrage began in January 1939 and took on new life in late February after First Lady Eleanor Roosevelt publicly resigned from the DAR as a result of their snubbing of Anderson. In the weeks that followed, White; Roosevelt; the NAACP legal activist Charles Hamilton Houston; Secretary of the Interior Harold Ickes; Anderson's promotional agent, Sol Hurok; and many others worked behind the scenes to find some way of countering the DAR's decision. Eventually, with President Franklin Roosevelt's enthusiastic approval, they fastened upon the idea of inviting Anderson to sing at the Lincoln Memorial, a hallowed site fraught with democratic symbolism. At Hurok's urging, Anderson accepted the invitation, though neither she nor anyone else knew exactly what to expect. Anderson's "Easter Sunday" memoir provides a glimpse into the events leading up to her historic performance, her trepidations about performing at such a momentous event, and her reactions to the emotional experience.

Context

On Easter Sunday (April 9) 1939, seventy-five thousand Americans gathered at the Lincoln Memorial in Washington to hear the sound of freedom. Young and old, black and white, they braved the elements on an unseasonably cold April afternoon to listen to the soulful voice of Marian Anderson, a forty-three-year-old African American from Philadelphia who had been denied the right to sing at Constitution Hall because she was black.

One of the world's most popular classical performers, Anderson had established her reputation in Europe during the early 1930s before returning to the United States in December 1935. Following a recital in Salzburg, Austria, in September 1935, the Italian maestro Arturo Toscanini exclaimed that Anderson's contralto was a voice that "one is privileged to hear only once in a hundred years." Many American concertgoers and critics came to hold her in similarly high regard, and in February 1936, Anderson interrupted a string of sold-out performances to sing at the White House, where she charmed President and Mrs. Roosevelt. None of this, however, seemed to carry any weight with the national leadership of the DAR, the venerable all-white heritage organization that owned and managed Constitution Hall, near the White House. Racial discrimination had long been a fact of life in the nation's capital, and DAR leaders claimed that they were simply following tradition when they turned Anderson away. But this time the discrimination did not go unchallenged.

In mid-February 1939, several dozen progressive organizations in the Washington area formed the Marian Anderson Citizens Committee, a broad-based civil rights coalition determined to overturn the DAR's decision. Spurred by the public's growing outrage, First Lady Eleanor Roosevelt resigned from the DAR on February 27, ensuring an ever-widening controversy and provoking a national press debate on the compatibility of democracy and racial discrimination. For several weeks, the Marian Anderson Citizens Committee, working in close collaboration with NAACP leaders, Sol Hurok, and a number of black intellectuals and activists associated with Howard University, pressured the DAR to end the "white artists only" policy at Constitution Hall. But they were eventually forced to seek an alternative venue for Anderson's performance. After an unsuccessful attempt to book the auditorium of Central High School, a segregated institution that had occasionally opened its doors to black groups on a limited basis, the committee and its allies reluctantly concluded that the only viable option was an outdoor concert.

By mid-March, Walter White had seized upon the idea of the Lincoln Memorial as "the most logical place" for

Time Line

1897
- **February 27**
  Marian Anderson is born in Philadelphia.

1931
- **January**
  Two years after the opening of Constitution Hall, an incident involving the noted black tenor Roland Hayes prompts the DAR to institute a "white artists only" policy.

1933
- **September**
  Anderson's European tour earns great acclaim, especially in Scandinavia, leading to a contract with Sol Hurok Productions.

1935
- **December**
  Anderson returns to the United States to begin her first major American concert tour.

1938
- **June**
  Anderson receives an honorary degree from Howard University and accepts Howard's invitation to sing in Washington on Easter Sunday 1939.

1939
- **January 6**
  Charles Cohen, the director of the Howard concert series, tries to book Constitution Hall but is rebuffed by the hall manager, Fred Hand.

- **February 1**
  The national board of the Daughters of the American Revolution supports Hand and confirms their "white artists only" policy, provoking widespread outrage and public criticism.

- **February 26**
  The Marian Anderson Citizens Committee, with the NAACP attorney Charles Hamilton Houston as chairman, holds its first mass meeting.

Anderson's concert. The logic of holding a gathering at the seventeen-year-old Memorial was not as obvious in 1939 as it would become later. Over the coming decades, the Memorial would host literally hundreds of mass meetings, including the August 1963 March on Washington for Jobs and Freedom, which drew a quarter of a million people to the west end of the National Mall. But the notion of holding a rally, a concert, or any other mass assemblage at the site was both novel and daring in 1939. The federal agencies in charge of the site, the National Park Service and the Department of the Interior, had never granted a permit for a large gathering at the Memorial, and the only black organization of any size to use the site was the African Methodist Episcopal Zion Church, which had held a religious service there for two thousand people in 1926.

The choice of the Lincoln Memorial as the backdrop was a calculated gamble. The organizers could not be certain how the American public would respond to the juxtaposition of a black concert singer and a white Republican president from Illinois. Physically and aesthetically, the Memorial and the adjacent rectangular reflecting pool stretching eastward toward the Washington Monument represented a stunning site. But the political and cultural implications of staging a controversial concert on sacred ground were complex and potentially dangerous. The situation called for careful planning and just the right touches to ensure that the event communicated the right messages to the right people. With help from Secretary Ickes, who secured the president's approval, the organizers announced to the world on March 30 that Marian Anderson would sing at the Lincoln Memorial on Easter Sunday, April 9.

The organizers went to great lengths to ensure that the free, open-air concert would attract a large audience and that a number of dignitaries would be on hand to underscore the significance of the occasion. When Anderson arrived at the Memorial, she was stunned to learn that the platform from which she would sing contained two hundred seats reserved for Supreme Court justices, congressional leaders, cabinet officials, and other political and cultural luminaries. Even more shocking was the size of the crowd, the largest gathering since the Memorial's opening in 1922.

As soon as Anderson, a solitary figure wrapped in a fur coat to block the cold wind and drizzle, strode to the bank of microphones and began to sing the words to "America," it was obvious that an extraordinary event was unfolding. No one could have missed the symbolic irony of the opening lyrics: "My country 'tis of thee, / Sweet land of liberty." The Reverend Martin Luther King, Jr., speaking to an even-larger gathering at the Lincoln Memorial a quarter-century later, would turn to the same anthem in his "I Have a Dream" speech. For him, as for Anderson, the closing words of the opening stanza—"Let freedom ring"—paid tribute to an unrealized ideal, engaging the audience in an aspiring celebration of democratic nationalism.

With the throng standing in rapt attention, Anderson went on to sing Franz Schubert's "Ave Maria" and several spirituals, culminating with "Nobody Knows the Troubles I've Seen." Following a thunderous final ovation, she tried to return the crowd's affection: "I am overwhelmed.... I just can't talk." she explained. "I can't tell you what you've done for me today. I thank you from the bottom of my heart." Moments later she had to be rushed from the stage as thousands of well-wishers pressed forward to congratulate her. Taken into the recesses of the Memorial by security guards, she stood for a few minutes under Daniel Chester French's towering sculpture of Lincoln before joining her mother and sisters in a rented limousine that whisked them to the private home where they would spend the night. That no hotel in the rigidly segregated capital city was willing to lift its color bar to accommodate the Andersons underscored the bittersweet character of the occasion.

The entire program, including a short intermission, lasted a mere half hour. In that brief space of time, Marian Anderson became an iconic figure, gaining a new life and identity. Already renowned as a singer, she became forever after a symbol of racial pride and democratic promise. "No one present at that moving performance ever forgot it," the historian Constance McLaughlin Green wrote in 1967. One suspects that Anderson's performance was only slightly less moving for those who listened to the live broadcast of the concert on the NBC radio network. In the days and weeks following the concert, millions more read about it in newspapers and magazines or watched the newsreel footage in movie houses. Most of the news coverage stressed Anderson's humility and dignity as well as the restraint and respectability of the crowd that had gathered to hear her sing. Not everyone welcomed her rising fame, especially in the white South, where Jim Crow segregation was not only a hallowed folkway but also the law of the land. Still, for many Americans, Anderson had become a model of African American achievement. Among black Americans her image took on heroic proportions, while for many northern whites her perceived mode of striving became an attractive alternative to the exploits of more menacing figures such as the boxer Joe Louis, the actor Paul Robeson, and the labor leader A. Philip Randolph. Occupying the moral high ground in her struggle with the DAR and Jim Crow, she helped to reawaken the nation's conscience and its commitment to the American creed of "liberty and justice for all."

About the Author

Born in Philadelphia in 1897, Marian Anderson grew up in a predominantly black neighborhood that exemplified both the strengths and the weaknesses of inner-city life. While her childhood was marked by poverty and the early death of her father, she enjoyed the benefits of being raised in a close-knit extended family that nurtured her personal and musical development. Both sides of her family had migrated to Pennsylvania from Virginia in the early 1890s.

All four of Anderson's grandparents had lived as slaves, but in Philadelphia her parents and grandparents found a measure of freedom and stability anchored in religious faith. Followed closely by two talented younger sisters, Anderson joined the Union Baptist Church junior choir at

Time Line

1939
- **February 27**
  In her nationally syndicated *My Day* newspaper column, Eleanor Roosevelt announces her resignation from the DAR, triggering a national debate.
- **March 30**
  After consulting with President Franklin Roosevelt, Secretary of the Interior Harold Ickes announces that Anderson will sing at the Lincoln Memorial.
- **April 9**
  Anderson sings before seventy-five thousand people at the Lincoln Memorial.

1943
- **January 7**
  Anderson sings at Constitution Hall for the first time; the occasion is a war bond rally, and the audience is racially integrated.

1955
- **January 7**
  Anderson becomes the first black singer to perform with the Metropolitan Opera Company in New York.
- **August**
  Howard Taubman begins taping a series of interviews with Anderson for the memoir *My Lord, What a Morning*.

1963
- **August 28**
  Marian Anderson returns to the Lincoln Memorial to participate in the March on Washington.

1993
- **April 8**
  Marian Anderson dies in Portland, Oregon, at the age of ninety-six.

2009
- **April 12**
  The Abraham Lincoln Bicentennial Committee sponsors a seventieth-anniversary commemorative concert at the Lincoln Memorial.

Marian Anderson performs on the steps of the Lincoln Memorial in April 1939. (Library of Congress)

the age of six and eventually became the pride of the congregation. As an adolescent, she became the leading soloist of the People's Chorus, a revered institution among black Philadelphians. By the time she had reached the age of eighteen, Union Baptist and the surrounding community were raising funds for her musical education. The funds raised were modest, and Anderson was shunned by the first vocal school that she unwittingly tried to desegregate. But by 1917 her prospects for a professional career were brightening, and she had reason to hope that someday she would be able to share her talent with the wider world.

Anderson took her first trip to the South in December 1917, when at the age of twenty she sang before a mixed but segregated audience in Savannah, Georgia. During the mid-1920s, annual southern tours took her to as many as nine states and as far away as Florida. Over time she developed a loyal following among southern whites as well as blacks, but her growing popularity did not protect her from the humiliations of Jim Crow travel and segregated concert halls.

In late 1927, Anderson found a temporary refuge in London, joining the growing number of other black musicians studying and performing in Europe. She returned to the United States in October 1928, but in June 1930 a Rosenwald Fellowship funded an extended visit to Berlin, where she honed her skills as a classical singer of German lieder. By 1931, the escalating tensions of Weimar Germany had driven her to Scandinavia, where she remained for nearly three years. A wildly successful concert tour in 1933–1934 made her a celebrity throughout Scandinavia, and during the following year her fame spread to France, England, Austria, and beyond—especially after she signed a contract with the legendary promotional agent Sol Hurok in the fall of 1934.

In 1935 Anderson returned to the United States, where she confronted the ambiguous realities of a depression-ravaged nation that had found a measure of hope in New Deal reforms. These ambiguities were especially apparent in matters of race, and nowhere was this more evident than in the nation's capital, where a rigid color line coexisted with the iconography of democracy and freedom. In mid-February 1936, Anderson sang before a mixed audience in the auditorium of an all-black Washington high school, and a few days later she entertained Franklin and Eleanor Roosevelt at the White House. Over the next three years, Anderson performed all across the nation to considerable acclaim, but her manager, Sol Hurok, had great difficulty arranging appropriate venues in the Jim Crow South and in Washington. In January 1939, Hurok's unsuccessful attempt to book an Anderson concert in Constitution Hall, the city's only large auditorium, provoked a national controversy that highlighted the racist conservatism of both the DAR and the nation's capital.

From 1939 until her death, Anderson maintained an active role in the civil rights movement. Beginning with her Easter Sunday concert, a series of events and honors reinforced her visibility as a symbol of democratic and racial promise. In July of 1939, at the NAACP's annual convention, Eleanor Roosevelt presented her with the organization's prestigious Spingarn Medal for outstanding achievement. In January of 1943, a mural commemorating her Lincoln Memorial concert was installed at the Department of the Interior. Later that year, she finally appeared at Constitution Hall at a war-relief benefit concert, and in March of 1953 she sang once more at Constitution Hall, this time to an integrated audience. Her celebrated appearance as Ulrica in the Metropolitan Opera's 1955 performance of Verdi's *Un ballo in maschera* broke the Met's long-standing color bar. In 1958 Anderson was appointed as an American delegate to the United Nations Human Rights Committee, and in 1961 she was invited to sing at the inauguration of President John F. Kennedy. Kennedy's successor, Lyndon B. Johnson, awarded her the Presidential Medal of Freedom in 1963. Her farewell tour began at Constitution Hall in October 1964, three months after the signing of the Civil Rights Act, and ended at Carnegie Hall on Easter Sunday 1965, three weeks after the Selma-to-Montgomery voting rights march.

In her twenty-five years of retirement, Anderson made only sporadic stage appearances, but she remained in the public eye as a philanthropist and as an enduring symbol of dignity and courage. When she died in 1993, at the age of ninety-six, there was an outpouring of tribute and affection as Americans of all races and political persuasions lamented the passing of a woman of unrivaled talent and character.

Explanation and Analysis of the Document

Although it is titled "Easter Sunday," Anderson's account actually provides relatively few details about the 1939 Lincoln Memorial Concert or the series of events that led up to it. She remarks that upon finding out that she had been denied access to Constitution Hall, "I was saddened, but as it is my belief that right will win I assumed that a way would be found." Indeed, Anderson appears almost entirely disengaged from the planning of the event, leaving the arrangements to her manager, Sal Hurok, and his staff. She mentions Eleanor Roosevelt's resignation from the DAR only briefly. Although it was a pivotal event in Washington and a large-scale scandal for the DAR, Anderson refers to it as a fleeting headline that caught her attention in passing a newsstand.

Rather, in the lead-up to her arrival in Washington, Anderson's energy was focused on the sudden illness of her accompanist Kosti Vehanen. "Here was a crisis of immediate concern to me," she said and concentrated her attention on preparing her new accompanist, Franz Rupp. However, as Easter Sunday approached, Anderson could not avoid the uproar ongoing in Washington. Friends, fans, and reporters were clamoring to find out what she had to say about Washington. But, as she recalls, "I did not want to talk, and I particularly did not want to say anything about the D.A.R." Even nearly twenty years later in her autobiography, Anderson seems to hold back from being overly emotional about the facts. She admits that she "was saddened and ashamed" and describes the situation as mere "unpleasantness."

It is unclear how much she was holding back about her feelings. Anderson was a private person by nature and did not wish to reveal too much to the public. Her autobiography itself was an exercise in reconciling her private and public personae. She was initially opposed to the idea of releasing an autobiography at all, but Hurok persuaded her to allow the *New York Times* music critic Howard Taubman to ghostwrite the project. As Allan Keiler outlines in his biography of Anderson, Taubman spent several months interviewing and tape-recording his conversations with Anderson in order to compile the book. But he encountered difficulties in getting Anderson to open up about her experiences:

> Taubman found her unable to be frank about the difficulties of her childhood, or to talk easily about the prejudice and discrimination she faced. Whenever a subject arose that gave her any discomfort—the music school that turned her away, the need to criticize others, the Lincoln Memorial incident—she more often than not turned the tape recorder off before she was willing to go on.

Despite the difficulties in eliciting Anderson's memories about the Lincoln Memorial concert, the pages of "Easter Sunday" underscore Anderson's grace under pressure. She struggled with her role in a controversial and embarrassing situation but overcame her discomfort for the greater good. In discussing her decision to approve the concert plan, she admits that she hesitated, but ultimately said yes. She recalls, "I could see that my significance as an individual was small in this affair. I had become, whether I liked it or not, a symbol, representing my people. I had to appear."

Anderson's descriptions of the concert itself do not dwell on the symbolic nature of her performance or on her status as a burgeoning civil rights icon. Instead, she comments on nervousness about performing in front of such a crowd and how she is unsure how she even mustered the ability to sing. She is unfailingly modest about her role in the Lincoln Memorial concert. She avoids any characterizations of herself as a civil rights pioneer, giving herself no credit for influencing the DAR racial policies. She matter-

Eleanor Roosevelt (Library of Congress)

of-factly states, "In time the policy at Constitution Hall changed." Nor does she espouse any sense of triumph at her first Constitution Hall recital: "I had no feeling different from what I have in other halls.... I felt that it was a beautiful concert hall, and I was happy to sing in it."

She ends the chapter remembering the bond she formed with Eleanor Roosevelt in the years following her Easter Sunday concert. The first lady's understated role in the DAR controversy and her quiet support for Anderson throughout her career created a lasting relationship between them. Drawn together by mutual admiration and common purpose, these two remarkable women from radically different backgrounds overcame barriers of race and class to bring about a pivotal moment in the history of the American freedom struggle.

Audience

By the 1950s Marian Anderson had become one of the most recognizable women in the world. Her soulful voice had attracted millions of followers from around the globe, and her role in the early civil rights movement had inspired generations. Anderson and Taubman's collaborative autobiography of 1956 was designed and marketed both as a resource for music lovers and as a book that would appeal to Anderson fans, black and white, who were curious about her views and reflections on topics related to her musical career, her personal life, and her experiences as a public figure.

Impact

Although it lasted for only a half-hour, the 1939 Lincoln Memorial concert had profound and lasting consequences, for Marian Anderson and for the nation. First, on a personal level it established Anderson as a civil rights icon, uniquely identified with the Lincoln Memorial, the Lincoln legacy, and the ongoing struggle for black rights and racial equality. For the remainder of her life, an eventful fifty-four years punctuated with civil rights milestones and public service, she enjoyed an eminence that transcended the world of music.

Second, the 1939 concert initiated a long tradition of civil rights protest and pageantry associated with the Lincoln Memorial. In the years since the original Anderson concert, the Memorial has served as the designated backdrop and ceremonial site for scores of social and political protest rallies, including the epochal August 1963 March for Jobs and Freedom. In 2009 the Memorial was the scene of a memorable pre-inauguration concert celebrating the election of the nation's first African American president, Barack Obama. And four days later, at the actual inauguration ceremony, the great soul singer Aretha Franklin evoked memories of the Easter Sunday concert when she sang "America," the same song that had opened Anderson's history-making performance seventy years earlier.

The third and most important consequence of the 1939 Lincoln Memorial Concert resides in its connection to the broad course of the civil rights movement. For the movement to gain strength and ultimately succeed, several changes had to occur, including the recognition that racial discrimination is a national, not just a sectional, problem—that violations of the American creed of "liberty and justice for all" undermine national honor and the prospects for national greatness.

The "rediscovery" of racial discrimination as a national problem began during the mid-1930s, as the rising tide of totalitarianism in Europe brought attention to the dark side of racialist ideology and practice. This rediscovery hinged on a series of public events, of which the Lincoln Memorial concert was one of the most significant. The others included the 1936 Berlin Olympics, when the victorious African American track star Jesse Owens was snubbed by Adolf Hitler; the world heavyweight championship match of 1938, when the "Brown Bomber" Joe Louis defeated the German Max Schmeling at Yankee Stadium; A. Philip Randolph's threatened March on Washington in 1941; the controversy surrounding Jackie Robinson's desegregation of Major League baseball in 1947; and the desegregation of the American armed forces during the Truman Administration.

Each of these episodes helped to push the nation toward recognition of a long-neglected national problem, but the Easter 1939 concert was especially important in this regard. The concert help set the stage for later developments, and the "symbolic geography" of the controversy—a segregated national capital, the Lincoln Memorial, and Constitution Hall, in the shadow of the White House—magnified the episode's impact. The Washington backdrop—a distinctively southern city that served as the

Essential Quotes

> "I could see that my significance as an individual was small in this affair. I had become, whether I liked it or not, a symbol, representing my people. I had to appear."

> "All I knew then as I stepped forward was the over-whelming impact of that vast multitude. There seemed to be people as far as the eye could see. The crowd stretched in a great semicircle from the Lincoln Memorial around the reflecting pool on to the shaft of the Washington Monument. I had a feeling that a great wave of good will poured out from these people, almost engulfing me."

> "The essential point about wanting to appear in the hall was that I wanted to do so because I felt I had that right as an artist."

seat of national government, a community that tolerated and fostered a paradoxical mix of cradle-to-grave segregation and democratic pretense—carried special significance for the cause of civil rights. Add to this the national scope and prominence of the DAR, and it made a dramatic conflict that could not help but disturb the complacency of many Americans.

The Anderson-DAR controversy made it difficult to dismiss racial discrimination as a mere sectional problem. For the remainder of her career, Anderson's almost unparalleled celebrity served as a reminder that the national commitment to equal opportunity requires eternal vigilance. By the mid-1950s, public opinion polls identified Anderson as one of the most admired women in the world, yet many

Questions for Further Study

1. Why was the Lincoln Memorial chosen as the site of Anderson's concert after she was refused access to Constitution Hall?

2. What role did First Lady Eleanor Roosevelt play in the debate surrounding Anderson's concert?

3. How would you describe Anderson's tone and attitude with regard to the controversy surrounding her concert? How do you think you would have reacted had you been in her position?

4. What national and international events played a role in the growing civil rights movement of the 1930s? Why were they important?

5. Discuss the following proposition: Marian Anderson's concert was more important for its symbolism than for its music.

Americans could not listen to her voice without recalling both the shameful prejudice that barred her from Constitution Hall and the glorious sound of freedom that enveloped the Lincoln Memorial on Easter Sunday 1939.

See also A. Philip Randolph's "Call to Negro America to March on Washington" (1941); Executive Order 9981 (1948); Civil Rights Act of 1964; Jesse Owen's *Blackthink* (1970); Jackie Robinson's *I Never Had It Made* (1972).

Further Reading

- **Articles**

Black, Allida M. "Championing a Champion: Eleanor Roosevelt and the Marian Anderson 'Freedom Concert.'" *Presidential Studies Quarterly* 20 (1990): 719–736.

Sandage, Scott A. "A Marble House Divided: The Lincoln Memorial, the Civil Rights Movement, and the Politics of Memory, 1939–1963." *Journal of American History* 80 (June 1993): 135–167.

- **Books**

Anderson, Peggy. *The Daughters: An Unconventional Look at America's Fan Club—the DAR*. New York: St. Martin's Press, 1974.

Arsenault, Raymond. *The Sound of Freedom: Marian Anderson, the Lincoln Memorial, and the Concert That Awakened America*. New York: Bloomsbury Press, 2009.

Green, Constance McLaughlin. *The Secret City: A History of Race Relations in the Nation's Capital*. Princeton, N.J.: Princeton University Press, 1967.

Hurok, Sol, with Ruth Goode. *Impresario: A Memoir*. New York: Random House, 1946.

Keiler, Allan. *Marian Anderson: A Singer's Journey*. New York: Scribner, 2000.

Robinson, Harlow. *The Last Impresario: The Life, Times, and Legacy of Sol Hurok*. New York: Viking Press, 1994.

Taubman, Howard. *The Pleasure of Their Company: A Reminiscence*. Portland, Ore.: Amadeus, 1994.

Vehanen, Kosti. *Marian Anderson: A Portrait*. New York: McGraw-Hill, 1941.

—Raymond Arsenault

Marian Anderson's *My Lord, What a Morning*

"Easter Sunday"

The division between time spent in Europe and in the United States changed gradually. In my second season under Mr. Hurok's management there was already more to do at home, and less time was devoted to Europe. Soon there were so many concerts to do in the cities of the United States that a trip abroad for concerts had to be squeezed in. There is no doubt that my work was drawing the attention of larger circles of people in wider areas of our country. Fees went up, and I hope that I was making a return in greater service.

Mr. Hurok's aim was to have me accepted as an artist worthy to stand with the finest serious ones, and he sought appearances for me in all the places where the best performers were expected and taken for granted. The nation's capital was such a place. I had sung in Washington years before—in schools and churches. It was time to appear on the city's foremost concert platform—Constitution Hall.

As it turned out, the decision to arrange an appearance in Constitution Hall proved to be momentous. I left bookings entirely to the management. When this one was being made I did not give it much thought. Negotiations for the renting of the hall were begun while I was touring, and I recall that the first intimation I had that there were difficulties came by accident. Even then I did not find out exactly what was going on; all I knew was the something was amiss. It was only a few weeks before the scheduled date for Washington that I discovered the full truth—that the Daughters of the American Revolution, owners of the hall, had decreed that it could not be used by one of my race. I was saddened, but as it is my belief that right will win I assumed that a way would be found. I had no inkling that the thing would become a cause célèbre.

I was in San Francisco, I recall, when I passed a newsstand, and my eye caught a headline: Mrs. Roosevelt Takes Stand. Under this was another line, in bold print just a bit smaller: resigns from D.A.R., etc. I was on my way to the concert hall for my performance and could not stop to buy a paper. I did not get one until after the concert, and I honestly could not conceive that things had gone so far.

As we worked our way back East, continuing with our regular schedule, newspaper people made efforts to obtain some comment from me, but I had nothing to say. I really did not know precisely what the Hurok office was doing about the situation and, since I had no useful opinions to offer, did not discuss it. I trusted the management. I knew it must be working on every possible angle, and somehow I felt I would sing in Washington.

Kosti became ill in St. Louis and could not continue on tour. Here was a crisis of immediate concern to me. I was worried about Kosti's well-being and we had to find a substitute in a hurry. Kosti had had symptoms of this illness some time before and had gone to see a physician in Washington, who had recommended special treatment. It was decided now that Kosti should be taken to Washington and hospitalized there.

Franz Rupp, a young man I had never met before, was rushed out to St. Louis by the management to be the accompanist. I had a piano in my hotel room, and as soon as Franz, who is now my accompanist, arrived, we went over the program. I was impressed by the ease with which he handled the situation. He could transpose a song at sight, and he could play many of my numbers entirely from memory. I found out later that he had had a huge backlog of experience playing for instrumentalists and singers. He assured me that I had seen and heard him in Philadelphia when I had attended a concert by Sigrid Onegin years before, as he had been her accompanist.

Mr. Rupp and I gave the St. Louis concert, and then we filled two other engagements as we headed East. Our objective was Washington. We knew by this time that the date in Constitution Hall would not be filled, but we planned to stop in Washington to visit Kosti. I did not realize that my arrival in Washington would in itself be a cause for a commotion, but I was prepared in advance when Gerald Goode, the public-relations man on Mr. Hurok's staff, came down to Annapolis to board our train and ride into the capital with us.

Mr. Goode is another person who made a contribution to my career the value of which I can scarcely estimate. He was with Mr. Hurok when I joined the roster, and I am sure that he labored devotedly and effectively from the moment of my return from Europe for that first Hurok season in America. His publicity efforts were always constructive, and they took account of my aversion to things flamboyant. Everything he did was tasteful and helpful. And in the Washington affair he was a tower of strength.

Mr. Goode filled me in on developments as we rode into Washington, and he tried to prepare me for what he knew would happen—a barrage of questions from the newspaper people. They were waiting for us in the Washington station. Questions flew at me, and some of them I could not answer because they involved things I did not know about. I tried to get away; I wanted to go straight to the hospital to see Kosti. There was a car waiting for me, and the reporters followed us in another car. I had some difficulty getting into the hospital without several reporters following me. They waited until I had finished my visit, and they questioned me again—about Kosti's progress and his opinion of the Washington situation. Finally we got away and traveled on to New York.

The excitement over the denial of Constitution Hall to me did not die down. It seemed to increase and to follow me wherever I went. I felt about the affair as about an election campaign; whatever the outcome, there is bound to be unpleasantness and embarrassment. I could not escape it, of course. My friends wanted to discuss it, and even strangers went out of their way to express their strong feelings of sympathy and support.

What were my own feelings? I was saddened and ashamed. I was sorry for the people who had precipitated the affair. I felt that their behavior stemmed from a lack of understanding. They were not persecuting me personally or as a representative of my people so much as they were doing something that was neither sensible nor good. Could I have erased the bitterness, I would have done so gladly. I do not mean that I would have been prepared to say that I was not entitled to appear in Constitution Hall as might any other performer. But the unpleasantness disturbed me, and if it had been up to me alone I would have sought a way to wipe it out. I cannot say that such a way out suggested itself to me at the time, or that I thought of one after the event. But I have been in this world long enough to know that there are all kinds of people, all suited by their own natures for different tasks. It would be fooling myself to think that I was meant to be a fearless fighter; I was not, just as I was not meant to be a soprano instead of a contralto.

Then the time came when it was decided that I would sing in Washington on Easter Sunday. The invitation to appear in the open, singing from the Lincoln Memorial before as many people as would care to come, without charge, was made formally by Harold L. Ickes, Secretary of the Interior. It was duly reported, and the weight of the Washington affair bore in on me.

Easter Sunday in 1939 was April 9, and I had other concert dates to fill before it came. Wherever we went I was met by reporters and photographers. The inevitable question was, "What about Washington?" My answer was that I knew too little to tell an intelligent story about it. There were occasions, of course, when I knew more than I said. I did not want to talk, and I particularly did not want to say anything about the D.A.R. As I have made clear, I did not feel that I was designed for hand-to-hand combat, and I did not wish to make statements that I would later regret. The management was taking action. That was enough.

It was comforting to have concrete expressions of support for an essential principle. It was touching to hear from a local manager in a Texas city that a block of two hundred tickets had been purchased by the community's D.A.R. people. It was also heartening; it confirmed my conviction that a whole group should not be condemned because an individual or section of the group does a thing that is not right.

I was informed of the plan for the outdoor concert before the news was published. Indeed, I was asked whether I approved. I said yes, but the yes did not come easily or quickly. I don't like a lot of show, and one could not tell in advance what direction the affair would take. I studied my conscience. In principle the idea was sound, but it could not be comfortable to me as an individual. As I thought further, I could see that my significance as an individual was small in this affair. I had become, whether I liked it or not, a symbol, representing my people. I had to appear.

I discussed the problem with Mother, of course. Her comment was characteristic: "It is an important decision to make. You are in this work. You intend to stay in it. You know what your aspirations are. I think you should make your own decision."

Mother knew what the decision would be. In my heart I also knew. I could not run away from this situation. If I had anything to offer, I would have to do so now. It would be misleading, however, to say that once the decision was made I was without doubts.

We reached Washington early that Easter morning and went to the home of Gifford Pinchot, who had been Governor of Pennsylvania. The Pinchots had been kind enough to offer their hospitality, and it was needed because the hotels would not take us.

Then we drove over to the Lincoln Memorial. Kosti was well enough to play, and we tried out the piano and examined the public-address system, which had six microphones, meant not only for the people who were present but also for a radio audience.

When we returned that afternoon I had sensations unlike any I had experienced before. The only comparable emotion I could recall was the feeling I had had when Maestro Toscanini had appeared in the artist's room in Salzburg. My heart leaped wildly, and I could not talk. I even wondered whether I would be able to sing.

The murmur of the vast assemblage quickened my pulse beat. There were policemen waiting at the car, and they led us through a passageway that other officers kept open in the throng. We entered the monument and were taken to a small room. We were introduced to Mr. Ickes, whom we had not met before. He outlined the program. Then came the signal to go out before the public.

If I did not consult contemporary reports I could not recall who was there. My head and heart were in such turmoil that I looked and hardly saw, I listened and hardly heard. I was led to the platform by Representative Caroline O'Day of New York, who had been born in Georgia, and Oscar Chapman, Assistant Secretary of the Interior, who was a Virginian. On the platform behind me sat Secretary Ickes, Secretary of the Treasury Morgenthau, Supreme Court Justice Black, Senators Wagner, Mead, Barkley, Clark, Guffey, and Capper, and many Representatives, including Representative Arthur W. Mitchell of Illinois, a Negro. Mother was there, as were people from Howard University and from churches in Washington and other cities. So was Walter White, then secretary of the National Association for the Advancement of Colored People. It was Mr. White who at one point stepped to the microphone and appealed to the crowd, probably averting serious accidents when my own people tried to reach me.

I report these things now because I have looked them up. All I knew then as I stepped forward was the over-whelming impact of that vast multitude. There seemed to be people as far as the eye could see. The crowd stretched in a great semicircle from the Lincoln Memorial around the reflecting pool on to the shaft of the Washington Monument. I had a feeling that a great wave of good will poured out from these people, almost engulfing me. And when I stood up to sing our National Anthem I felt for a moment as though I were choking. For a desperate second I thought that the words, well as I know them, would not come.

I sang, I don't know how. There must have been the help of professionalism I had accumulated over the years. Without it I could not have gone through the program. I sang—and again I know because I consulted a newspaper clipping—"America," the aria "O mio Fernando," Schubert's "Ave Maria," and three spirituals—"Gospel Train," "Trampin'," and "My Soul Is Anchored in the Lord."

I regret that a fixed rule was broken, another thing about which I found out later. Photographs were taken from within the Memorial, where the great statue of Lincoln stands, although there was a tradition that no pictures could be taken from within the sanctum.

It seems also that at the end, when the tumult of the crowd's shouting would not die down, I spoke a few words. I read the clipping now and cannot believe that I could have uttered another sound after I had finished singing. "I am overwhelmed," I said. "I just can't talk. I can't tell you what you have done for me today. I thank you from the bottom of my heart again and again."

It was the simple truth. But did I really say it?

There were many in the gathering who were stirred by their own emotions. Perhaps I did not grasp all that was happening, but at the end great numbers of people bore down on me. They were friendly; all they wished to do was to offer their congratulations and good wishes. The police felt that such a concentration of people was a danger, and they escorted me back into the Memorial. Finally we returned to the Pinchot home.

I cannot forget that demonstration of public emotion or my own strong feelings. In the years that have passed I have had constant reminders of that Easter Sunday. It is not at all uncommon to have people come backstage after a concert even now and remark, "You know, I was at that Easter concert." In my travels abroad I have met countless people who heard and remembered about that Easter Sunday.

In time the policy at Constitution Hall changed. I appeared there first in a concert for the benefit of China Relief. The second appearance in the hall, I believe, was also under charitable auspices. Then, at last, I appeared in the hall as does any other musical performer, presented by a concert manager, and I have been appearing in it regularly. The hall is open to other performers of my group. There is no longer an issue, and that is good.

It may be said that my concerts at Constitution Hall are usually sold out. I hope that people come because they expect to hear a fine program in a first-class performance. If they came for any other reason I would be disappointed. The essential point about wanting to appear in the hall was that I wanted to do so because I felt I had that right as an artist.

I wish I could have thanked personally all the people who stood beside me then. There were musicians who canceled their own scheduled appearances at Constitution Hall out of conviction and principle. Some of these people I did not know personally. I appreciate the stand they took.

May I say that when I finally walked into Constitution Hall and sang from its stage I had no feeling different from what I have in other halls. There was no sense of triumph. I felt that it was a beautiful concert hall, and I was happy to sing in it.

The story of that Easter Sunday had several sequels. A mural was painted in the Department of Interior Building in Washington, commemorating the event, and I was invited down for the unveiling. I met Mr. Ickes again, and as we talked and as I studied the immense mural the impact of it all was unmistakable. More recently I was in Kansas City for a concert, and a young man phoned me and asked whether he could come to see me. He had competed as a painter in the mural contest, and had won second prize. The purpose of his visit was to offer me the painting for the mural that he submitted in the contest. It was a huge picture and, like the prize-winning work, contained a message. I could not find space for so large a painting in my home, and I sent it to the Countee Cullen Foundation in Atlanta. Countee Cullen was a gifted American Negro poet who died prematurely.

I do not recall meeting Mrs. Franklin D. Roosevelt on that Easter Sunday. Some weeks later in 1939 I had the high privilege of making her acquaintance. It was on the occasion of the visit to this country of King George VI and his Queen, and I was one of those honored with an invitation to perform for the royal guests.

While waiting to sing I was in Mrs. Roosevelt's room in the White House. There was a traveling bag on a chair, and the tab on it indicated that she would soon be off again. I can still see it plainly.

Knowing that I would be introduced to the President, I tried to prepare a little speech suitable for such an occasion. When I met him, he spoke first. "You look just like your photographs, don't you?" he said, and my pretty speech flew right out of my head. All I could say was, "Good evening, Mr. President."

After the concert for the visitors was over, we were told that we would be presented to the King and Queen. I had returned to Mrs. Roosevelt's room to prepare myself. It occurred to me that it might be the right thing to curtsy. I had seen people curtsy in the movies, and it looked like the simplest thing in the world. I practiced a few curtsies in Mrs. Roosevelt's room. An aide came to call me, and I happened to be the first woman in line to meet Their Majesties. I remember that I was looking into the queen's eyes as I started my curtsy, and when I had completed it and was upright again I had turned a quarter- or half-circle and no longer faced the queen. I don't know how I managed it so inelegantly, but I never tried one again, not even for the king.

As I approached the center of the receiving line, there stood Mrs. Roosevelt, and at her right His Majesty the King. Mrs. Roosevelt put out her hand and said, "How do you do?"

I met Mrs. Roosevelt a number of times in the ensuing years, in New York, at Hyde Park, in Tokyo, and in Tel-Aviv. When I was in Japan several years ago I heard that Mrs. Roosevelt was about to arrive. I knew from my own experience with the Japanese that an extensive program would be arranged for her and that there would be an abundance of flowers waiting for her everywhere. I thought that an orchid might be the thing to get for her, so I went down to the lobby of the Imperial Hotel, intent on obtaining the orchid. But Mrs. Roosevelt arrived ahead of schedule, entered the hotel, and walked up several steps to where I had been caught standing before I could complete my errand. She stared at me. "Well, how long have you been here?" she asked.

I told her, adding that I was making a tour in Japan.

"When are you singing in Tokyo?" she asked.

"Tonight," I replied.

She turned to the people who were escorting her. "May I hear Marian Anderson tonight?"

I hesitate to think how her hosts had to rearrange their plans for her that evening, but she was at the concert. I know how crowded her schedule must have been, and I am sure that she did not have many minutes to herself. I shall never forget that she took the time to come and listen again.

When I was in Israel, more recently, Mrs. Roosevelt was there too. She was staying at the same hotel in Tel-Aviv, and she had left word at the desk that when I arrived she would like to be informed. We managed to have a brief visit, and soon she was on her way again.

She is one of the most admirable human beings I have ever met. She likes to have first-hand information about the things she talks about and deals with. Her bags seem to be ready for travel at any moment. Wherever she goes there is praise for her and what she stands for. I suspect that she has done a great deal for people that has never been divulged publicly. I know what she did for me.

Once when I was occupying the artist's room of a hall the stage manager told me with great enthusiasm that Mrs. Roosevelt would occupy the same room two days later. And so on the large mirror I left a greeting, written with soap.

Glossary

China Relief	aid to China in the wake of the Japanese invasion of 1937
contralto	a singer whose voice is in the deepest pitch range of female voices
D.A.R.	Daughters of the American Revolution
Daughters of the American Revolution	a heritage organization based on lineage founded in the 1890s
Hurok	Sol Hurok, Anderson's promotional agent
Kosti	Kosti Vehanen, Anderson's accompanist
Maestro Toscanini	"Master" Arturo Toscanini, a famed orchestral conductor
Salzburg	a city in Austria, the birthplace of Mozart and an important musical center
Sigrid Onegin	a noted German contralto singer
soprano	a singer whose voice is in the highest pitch ranges
Tel-Aviv	a city in modern-day Israel

Roy Wilkins (Library of Congress)

Roy Wilkins: "The Clock Will Not Be Turned Back"

"[Little Rock] dealt a stab in the back to American prestige as the leader of the free world."

Overview

"The Clock Will Not Be Turned Back" was a speech given by Roy Wilkins as head of the National Association for the Advancement of Colored People (NAACP), the oldest and largest civil rights organization in the United States. The speech was delivered in San Francisco at the Commonwealth Club of California on November 1, 1957, just over a month after the end of the school desegregation crisis in Little Rock, Arkansas. Founded in 1903 by a group of leading Californians—including the *San Francisco Chronicle* editorial writer Edward F. Adams and Frederick Burk, president of what would become San Francisco State University—the Commonwealth Club is the nation's oldest public affairs forum, providing an arena where prominent figures can discuss issues of local, national, and international importance. Previous speakers had included former president Theodore Roosevelt, the film director Cecil B. DeMille, and the philosopher (and founder of the Aspen Institute) Mortimer J. Adler. Until 1971 membership in the club was restricted to men.

In his speech, Wilkins addressed directly the problem of racial discrimination in general and the issue of school segregation in particular. The civil rights leader's aim was to make clear that black Americans were entitled to first-class citizenship in all areas of American life, including education. Wilkins also used his speech to argue that civil rights was not simply a moral and legal issue but also a matter of critical importance to America's international prestige and leadership of the free world in the cold war struggle against Communism.

Context

In 1892 Homer Plessy was arrested for traveling in a "whites only" railroad car in his native state of Louisiana. In an effort to strike down segregation laws, Plessy, who was classified as seven-eighths white ("octoroon" in the idiom of his day), might have traveled without notice. As part of a preplanned strategy, however, he bought a first-class ticket and sat down in a "whites only" car. When confronted by the conductor, he refused to move and was arrested. A group of black professionals then challenged the constitutionality of the state's segregation law by appealing Plessy's conviction. In 1896 the case of *Plessy v. Ferguson* reached the U.S. Supreme Court, where, in an eight-to-one decision, the constitutionality of the segregation law was upheld. The decision in *Plessy* provided the legal foundation ("separate but equal") for the broader system of enforced racial segregation that came to characterize the America South.

The 1954 decision in *Brown v. Board of Education of Topeka, Kansas,* in which the U.S. Supreme Court declared that segregated schooling was inherently unequal and thus unconstitutional, marked the crowning achievement of the NAACP's use of litigation to bring change to the South's racial order. Beginning in the 1930s the NAACP filed lawsuits that led to equal rates of pay for black and white teachers and opened up graduate schools to African American students, before launching an all-out assault on the Supreme Court's 1896 decision that the "separate but equal" system was constitutional. The *Brown* ruling actually involved five separate challenges to school segregation (from Delaware, the District of Columbia, Kansas, South Carolina, and Virginia) and numerous plaintiffs. The cases were consolidated as *Brown v. Board of Education of Topeka* (the Brown in question being Oliver Brown, an African American who wanted his daughter, Linda, to attend her local all-white school).

Those who hoped that the *Brown* decision might lead to the rapid demise of segregation were to be disappointed. Encouraged by President Dwight D. Eisenhower's lukewarm reaction to the ruling (in that he refused to state publicly whether he agreed with the justices) and by the court's rather weak enforcement decree in 1955 (*Brown II*) and alarmed by the NAACP's determination to press actively for speedy desegregation, white southerners mobilized to maintain the racial status quo. White Citizens' Councils, white supremacist organizations that sprang up across the South in the wake of the *Brown* decision, lobbied politicians, supported candidates for office who promised to resist desegregation, published alarmist tracts, and used intimidation in an effort to cement white opposition to civil rights. Many of the region's leading politicians began to play the race card for political gain—pledging defiance of the *Brown* ruling and championing segregation. On March 12, 1956, all but three

Time Line

1954
- **May 17**
  The U.S. Supreme Court rules in *Brown v. Board of Education* that segregated schools are unconstitutional.

1955
- **May 31**
  In its enforcement ruling, known as *Brown II*, the Supreme Court declares that desegregation should be undertaken "with all deliberate speed."

1956
- **March 12**
  Nineteen southern senators and seventy-seven southern congressmen sign the "Southern Manifesto,' which denounces *Brown* as an abuse of judicial power and pledges to use "all lawful means" to reverse it.

1957
- **May–August**
  The Little Rock School Board prepares a desegregation plan.

- **September 2**
  Arkansas Governor Orval Faubus orders the National Guard to surround Little Rock's Central High School and block any attempt by black students to enter, claiming that this is necessary in order to preserve peace and maintain order.

- **September 4**
  Nine black students attempt to enter Central High School but are turned away by the National Guard.

- **September 20**
  A federal court rules that Faubus was seeking to prevent integration and orders the removal of the National Guard. Faubus complies and then leaves for Georgia.

- **September 23**
  The nine black students enter the school but leave when a one-thousand-strong mob outside becomes unruly.

---

of the South's senators, along with the overwhelming majority of its congressional representatives, signed the "Southern Manifesto," which denounced the *Brown* ruling as an act of judicial tyranny, upheld the right of the states to govern their internal affairs, and pledged to use all lawful means to reverse the decision. Partly as a result of Massive Resistance, the policy declared by U.S. senator Harry Byrd, Sr., in 1956 to unite the white South in opposition to integration, progress on school desegregation proved painfully slow, and as late as 1963–1964 little more than 1 percent of black children in the South were attending school with whites.

Little Rock was not the only place where a southern governor sought to prevent school desegregation. (Texas governor Allan Shivers had used state troopers to prevent integration in Mansfield in August 1956.) Still, Little Rock was certainly the most famous. On September 2, 1957, Arkansas governor Orval Faubus ordered National Guard troops to Little Rock's Central High School to prevent nine black schoolchildren from attending classes. Faubus justified his actions—and his defiance of the federal court ruling that had ordered the school's desegregation—on the ground that he was preserving domestic order. On September 4 the black children attempted to attend class but were turned away by the National Guard troops as a hostile mob shoved and jostled the students and shouted abuse. One of the nine black children, Elizabeth Eckford, who had arrived at Central High before the others, had actually been pursued by angry whites who threatened to lynch her, before being spirited away by a sympathetic white woman, Grace Lorch. A subsequent series of tense negotiations involving Faubus, the U.S. Justice Department, and President Eisenhower failed to resolve the crisis, leaving the matter in the hands of the courts.

On September 20 a federal judge granted an injunction preventing any further interference with the desegregation of Central High, and Faubus ordered that the National Guard be withdrawn. He then flew to Georgia for a meeting of southern governors knowing that by having stoked racial tensions the withdrawal of the troops would likely lead to a breakdown of law and order. On September 23 a mob of angry whites surrounded Central High, and at 11 AM the black children were removed from the school for their own safety. The following morning white segregationists again assembled to prevent integration—and with the local police unwilling to intervene and the situation deteriorating, Little Rock's mayor, Woodrow Wilson Mann, sent a telegram to the White House requesting that federal troops be deployed as a matter of urgency. That evening, Eisenhower announced that he would send one thousand paratroopers serving with the 101st Airborne Division to Little Rock to enforce federal law; he also placed the Arkansas National Guard under the control of the federal government. On September 25 federal troops escorted the nine black children to classes in Central High. The school desegregation crisis made Faubus, who had previously been a racial moderate, something of a hero to white segregationists. He easily won reelection in 1958 and eventually left the governor's mansion, undefeated, in 1967.

In his television and radio address to the nation explaining his decision to send federal troops to Little Rock, President Eisenhower emphasized the importance of upholding the federal court ruling and maintaining the rule of law. However, he also drew attention to the international repercussions of the crisis, arguing that Little Rock had implications for America's efforts to lead the "free world" in the cold war struggle against international Communism. The respective global positioning of the Soviet Union and United States would come to the forefront of the public consciousness when the Soviets launched *Sputnik*, the world's first man-made satellite, less than two weeks later, on October 4, 1957. In his address, the president noted that America's enemies had been "gloating" over the Little Rock incident, using it to discredit U.S. claims to support democracy and freedom, and the resulting damage done to America's standing in the world was considerable. Indeed, the American government was well aware that its domestic record on race relations was an issue of international significance, particularly because the Soviet Union used the persistence of racial discrimination to try to undermine America's democratic credibility. Moreover, civil rights leaders were eager to exploit this vulnerability to create pressure for meaningful civil rights reform at home; Wilkins's speech to the Commonwealth Club, delivered a month after the Little Rock crisis, demonstrates as much.

About the Author

Roy Wilkins dedicated more than fifty years of his life to the cause of civil rights for black Americans. Born in 1901 in St. Louis, Missouri, he was raised in St. Paul, Minnesota, by an aunt and uncle after his mother died of tuberculosis when Wilkins was four years old. In an early display of his love of journalism, Wilkins edited the student newspaper while he was a pupil at the integrated Mechanic Arts High School. At the University of Minnesota, where he majored in sociology and minored in journalism, Wilkins took a number of jobs (including slaughterhouse worker and Pullman car waiter) to support his studies, but he also made time to write for the university newspaper, the *Minnesota Daily*; edit the *St. Paul Appeal*, a black weekly; and join the local branch of the NAACP. After graduating in 1924, Wilkins moved to Kansas City to work for the *Kansas City Call*, an influential black newspaper. Rising quickly to the position of managing editor, Wilkins was something of a crusading journalist, using the pages of his paper to urge blacks to mobilize their voting strength to defeat racist politicians. In 1931 Walter White, the NAACP's executive secretary, appointed Wilkins as his assistant. Three years later Wilkins succeeded the legendary W. E. B. Du Bois as editor of the NAACP's magazine, *The Crisis*. In 1955, following Walter White's death, Wilkins became head of the NAACP (the position was later renamed executive director); he would lead the organization until his retirement in July 1977.

Throughout his career Wilkins remained firmly committed to the goal of integration, and he sought equal rights for black Americans within the framework of America's constitutional system. Indeed, Wilkins was a proud patriot who argued that blacks were entitled, as Americans, to life, liberty, and the pursuit of happiness and the equal protection of the laws. Uncomfortable with the civil rights movement's enthusiastic embrace of direct action during the early 1960s, Wilkins chose to emphasize the importance of litigation, court rulings, and legislative victories in winning black freedom. Not renowned as a public speaker, and not a little jealous of the fame and plaudits that came the way of the Reverend Martin Luther King, Jr., Wilkins was most effective when working behind the scenes—negotiating with presidents and politicians, testifying before congressional committees, and lobbying for change. In 1950 he helped to found the Leadership Conference on Civil Rights, a coalition of organizations that coordinated national efforts to produce civil rights legislation. During the mid-1960s Wilkins worked particularly closely with the presidential administration of Lyndon B. Johnson—and it was Johnson who awarded the Presidential Medal of Freedom, the nation's highest civilian honor, to the NAACP chief in 1969. Often accused of exerting excessive control over the NAACP (as when he sought to eliminate any hint of Communism or racial separatism among the member-

Time Line

1957

- **September 24**
  A mob again prevents integration, and President Dwight D. Eisenhower announces that he is sending one thousand members of the U.S. Army's 101st Airborne Division to Little Rock to maintain order and enforce integration. He also federalizes the Arkansas National Guard.

- **September 25**
  The Little Rock Nine are escorted into Central High by federal troops.

- **November 1**
  The NAACP leader Roy Wilkins delivers his speech "The Clock Will Not Be Turned Back" at the Commonwealth Club of California.

1958

- **September 12**
  Governor Faubus orders the closure of Little Rock's three high schools for the entire school year.

- **November**
  Faubus wins reelection as governor in a landslide.

ship), Wilkins was succeeded by Benjamin Hooks in July 1977. Admitted to the New York University Medical Center in August 1981 suffering from heart trouble, Wilkins died from kidney failure, aged eighty, on September 8, 1981.

Explanation and Analysis of the Document

Unsurprisingly, during the fall of 1957 the crisis at Central High occupied a good deal of Wilkins's time and energy. Speaking in Georgia on September 23, for example, the NAACP chief condemned Faubus's actions and the "shameful spectacle" that had occurred in Little Rock. On October 11, in a keynote speech to the North Carolina NAACP state convention, Wilkins spoke at length on the Little Rock crisis, highlighting themes to which he would return in his Commonwealth Club speech, and on November 3 he addressed two thousand five hundred civil rights supporters at a New York City rally held to show support for the Little Rock Nine. Interestingly, Wilkins was not the first speaker to address the Commonwealth Club on the Little Rock crisis. On October 4, Mississippi judge Tom P. Brady, a staunch segregationist and leader of the Citizens' Council movement, had delivered a speech to the club in which he defended segregated schooling and denounced the *Brown* decision.

At the outset of his own speech, Wilkins seeks to create a sense of drama by arguing that white southerners' defiance of the U.S. Supreme Court over the question of school desegregation constitutes the gravest of crises. He then goes on to describe how in Little Rock angry mobs had assailed young black children—beating, kicking, and spitting at them—simply because they were attempting to attend school. Wilkins claims that the media coverage of these events had brought home to millions of Americans the "ugly" reality of what was happening in the South. But Wilkins was also keen to emphasize that Little Rock was not simply a domestic issue but, indeed, an international crisis—one that imperiled America's prestige and standing abroad.

During the late 1940s and early 1950s the United States and the Soviet Union became embroiled in the cold war. Adopting the role of "leader of the free world," America and its allies sought to contain Soviet influence, resist the expansion of Communism, and promote democracy. The American government was particularly keen to win over countries in Africa and Asia that were emerging from European colonialism. Yet, as Wilkins points out, the existence of segregation in the American South was an international embarrassment for the United States and an obstacle to its cold war mission. Indeed, incidents such as the violence at Little Rock were seized upon by the Soviet Union as evidence of America's hypocrisy and made it more difficult for the United States to win the support of newly independent nonwhite nations. Desegregation was not simply a moral or legal issue, then—it was also a matter of national security. And Wilkins is uncompromising in his use of language—he accuses white segregationists of undermining America's international leadership by stabbing the nation in the back and thus weakening the forces of democracy. Wilkins was not alone in seeking to place the struggle for black rights within the wider international context. Numerous civil rights leaders, including Martin Luther King, Jr., claimed that segregation and the denial of black voting rights in the South undermined America's cold war leadership and argued that government action on civil rights would strengthen the nation's democratic credentials.

Wilkins is also keen to point out that education itself is of vital national importance; he argues that America needs all of its citizens, black as well as white, to achieve their full potential to help defeat the Communist threat. Segregation is, says Wilkins, a source of division that saps the nation's strength and leaves it vulnerable in the face of Soviet advances in science and technology. Indeed, Wilkins speaks of the shadow cast by *Sputnik*, the world's first satellite. When it was launched by the USSR in early October 1957, it had shocked the U.S. public, sparking alarm that the nation was falling behind the Russians. The NAACP chief again raises the stakes, claiming that an intelligent, informed, and educated citizenry is vital to the struggle against international Communism; the provision of equal educational opportunities could, says Wilkins, "mean the difference between democratic life and totalitarian death."

With white southerners seeking to hold the line against the civil rights movement and prevent meaningful change to the racial order, Wilkins makes clear that black Americans are not about to give up. The clock, in his words, is not going to be turned back, and he reminds his audience that the North won the Civil War (with the South's surrender at Appomattox) and that white southerners, despite their efforts, would not be able to overturn this defeat. Wilkins invokes African Americans' positive contribution to national life—including their service in the U.S. military—to justify the demand for equality, and he argues that white violence and obstruction has not shaken blacks' belief that they are entitled—as Americans—to first-class citizenship. Indeed, he uses the bravery and dignity of the Little Rock Nine, who maintained their composure in the face of enormous provocation, as proof that black Americans remained resolute in their commitment to achieving equal rights. But Wilkins has a message for northerners too—that they must not sit back and simply observe the civil rights fight from afar, viewing it as a regional problem. Instead, they must make a collective decision to support decisive action on civil rights on the basis that it is in the interests not just of black Americans, but the nation as a whole.

Wilkins ends his speech on an optimistic and patriotic note, arguing that the virtues of America's founding values and the strength of her political institutions will help deliver a just solution to the racial problem. While the road to equality might not always run smooth, says Wilkins, it will ultimately lead to the establishment of the "kingdom of righteousness"—a society in which all Americans, black as well as white, are able to enjoy justice, equality, dignity, and respect. Here, the NAACP leader goes as far as to claim that God is on the side of civil rights protesters. Like other black leaders, most notably Martin Luther King, Jr., Wilkins views the civil rights movement as being inspired,

Essential Quotes

> "[Little Rock] dealt a stab in the back to American prestige as the leader of the free world and presented our totalitarian enemies with made-to-order propaganda."
> (Paragraph 2)

> "The Negro citizens of our common country, a country they have sweated to build and died to defend, are determined that the verdict at Appomattox will not be renounced, that the clock will not be turned back, that they shall enjoy what is justly theirs."
> (Paragraph 4)

> "Can we afford to deny to any boy or girl the maximum of education, that education which may mean the difference between democratic life and totalitarian death?"
> (Paragraph 8)

> "To deny our ability to achieve a just solution within the framework of our Declaration of Independence and our Bill of Rights is to deny the genius of Americans."
> (Paragraph 9)

in part, by Christian teaching and as enjoying divine sanction. His speech thus helps illustrate the importance of religion to the civil rights movement.

Audience

Wilkins's speech was delivered before an audience at the Commonwealth Club in San Francisco, California. Doubtless many, if not all, of the educated, civic-minded members of the audience were appalled by the recent violence in Little Rock and generally supportive of Wilkins's remarks. But Wilkins's words were also directed at the broader public in the North, whose support was needed to push forward the civil rights agenda, and his speech was carried on numerous radio stations. In emphasizing the negative impact that segregation had on America's cold war foreign policy, Wilkins was also seeking to increase the pressure on the federal government. Finally, Wilkins's remarks, particularly his emphasis on black dignity, pride, and African Americans' historic contribution to the nation's development, including service in its armed forces, were also intended to boost the morale and the resolve of the wider black community, particularly in the South, where the fight against white supremacy was being fought.

Impact

Wilkins's remarks are important because they reveal how the civil rights movement's leaders sought to invoke the nation's founding ideals of equality and liberty and use the cold war context as leverage in their efforts to secure meaningful change for African Americans. This tactic was particularly astute, given the fact that segregationists sought to portray the civil rights movement as part of an un-American Communist-orchestrated conspiracy. Attempts to use the cold war as leverage worked particularly effectively during the presidency of John F. Kennedy (1961–1963); Kennedy understood that his desire to strengthen America's position vis-à-vis the Soviet Union was threatened by high-profile incidents of discrimination against black

Americans and the failure to make significant progress on civil rights. Ultimately, civil rights leaders' ability to portray their movement as firmly within the mainstream of American democracy and committed to patriotic values (rather than as a radical or subversive threat to them), along with the use of nonviolent protests rooted in Christian teaching, contributed to making the civil rights movement "respectable," thereby helping it win a significant measure of public (and political) support in the North.

In the short term, Faubus's opposition to school desegregation and his defiant stand against the federal government proved fruitful. Indeed, in August 1958, a year after the initial crisis, the governor persuaded a special session of the state legislature to grant him the power to close any school that had been ordered to integrate by the federal authorities. After he ordered that all of Little Rock's schools be shut down, voters in the affected school district endorsed his decision in a referendum by 19,470 votes to 7,561. Faubus's hard-line policy on segregation contributed to his election victory that November, making him only the second governor in the state's history to win a third consecutive term in office.

In the longer term, however, such tactics played into the hands of the civil rights movement. The failure of the *Brown* decision to lead quickly to comprehensive desegregation and the strength of Massive Resistance helped convince civil rights leaders and organizations that new tactics were required to complement litigation (which often proved both expensive and time-consuming). By the early 1960s, nonviolent direct action—including sit-ins by blacks demanding service at segregated restaurants and other public facilities, mass marches, and voter registration drives—became increasingly prominent. The proliferation of direct action and the stubborn and violent response of many white southerners (encouraged by political leaders who were pledged to Massive Resistance) helped to pressure the federal government to take decisive action. The Civil Rights Act of 1964, which outlawed Jim Crow segregation, and the Voting Rights Act of 1965, which led to the enfranchisement of millions of African Americans, resulted from civil rights campaigns (in Birmingham and Selma, respectively) in which black southerners and their allies took to the streets to demand equal rights, only to be met with violence by the white authorities. As for school desegregation, it would not be until the late 1960s—following a series of assertive Supreme Court rulings and threats by the Department of Health, Education, and Welfare to withhold federal funding from segregated school districts—that meaningful integration took place in the South.

See also *Plessy v. Ferguson* (1896); *Brown v. Board of Education* (1954); Civil Rights Act of 1964.

Further Reading

- **Articles**

Arnold, Martin. "There Is No Rest for Roy Wilkins." *New York Times*, September 28, 1969.

Questions for Further Study

1. The Supreme Court case *Brown v. Board of Education* was and still is regarded as a major victory in the quest for equal rights. However, at the time, the consequences of *Brown* were disappointing. What subsequent events dramatically illustrated that *Brown* did not resolve the issue of civil rights?

2. In 2002, the majority leader in the U.S. Senate, Republican Trent Lott from Mississippi, was essentially driven out of office by remarks he made that were regarded as racially insensitive about events that had taken place over a half century earlier. Yet Democratic senator Robert Byrd of West Virginia remains in office as the longest-serving member of Congress in history after having been a member of the Ku Klux Klan in the 1940s and after leading the Senate filibuster of the 1964 Civil Rights Act. Do you see any inconsistency in the public reaction to these figures?

3. What impact did the events in Little Rock, Arkansas, have on the civil rights movement? How is this impact reflected in Wilkins's speech?

4. What role did the cold war between the United States and its allies and the Soviet Union and its satellite states have on the civil rights movement of the 1950s?

5. The focus of the civil rights movement from the mid-1930s through the 1950s was education. Using this document in conjunction with Charles Houston's "Educational Inequalities Must Go!", *Sweatt v. Painter*, and *Brown v. Board of Education*, prepare a time line of important cases in the effort to integrate education.

Krebs, Alan. "Roy Wilkins, 50-Year Veteran of Civil Rights Fight, Is Dead." *New York Times*, September 9, 1981.

Layton, Azza Salama. "International Pressure and the U.S. Government's Response to Little Rock." *Arkansas Historical Quarterly* 56, no 3 (Autumn 1997): 257–272.

■ Books

Cook, Robert. *Sweet Land of Liberty? The African-American Struggle for Civil Rights in the Twentieth Century*. New York: Longman, 1998.

Dudziak, Mary L. *Cold War Civil Rights: Race and the Image of American Democracy*. Princeton, N.J.: Princeton University Press, 2000.

Kirk, John A. *Redefining the Color Line: Black Activism in Little Rock, Arkansas, 1940–1970*. Gainesville: University Press of Florida, 2002.

Ling, Peter J. *Martin Luther King, Jr.* New York: Routledge, 2002.

Ryan, Yvonne. "Leading from the Back: Roy Wilkins's Leadership of the NAACP." In *Long Is the Way and Hard: One Hundred Years of the National Association for the Advancement of Colored People*, ed. Kevern Verney and Lee Sartain. Fayetteville: University of Arkansas Press, 2009.

Sitkoff, Harvard. *The Struggle for Black Equality, 1954–1992*. New York: Hill and Wang, 1993.

Wilkins, Roy. "Integration Crisis in the South." In *In Search of Democracy: The NAACP Writings of James Weldon Johnson, Walter White, and Roy Wilkins (1920–1977)*, ed. Sondra Kathryn Wilson. New York: Oxford University Press, 1999.

Wilkins Roy, with Tom Matthews. *Standing Fast: The Autobiography of Roy Wilkins*. New York: De Capo Press, 1994.

■ Web Sites

"Civil Rights: The Little Rock School Integration Crisis." Eisenhower Presidential Library and Museum Web site.
   http://www.eisenhower.archives.gov/Research/Digital_Documents/LittleRock/littlerockdocuments.html.

"History of the Little Rock Nine and *Brown v. Board of Education*." Arkansas Department of Parks and Tourism Web site.
   http://www.arkansas.com/central-high/history/.

"Roy Wilkins." The NAACP Web site.
   http://naacp.org/about/history/wilkins/index.htm.

—Simon Hall

Roy Wilkins: "The Clock Will Not Be Turned Back"

It is no exaggeration, I think, to state that the situation presented by the resistance to the 1954 decision of the United States Supreme Court in the public school segregation cases is fully as grave as any which have come under the scrutiny and study of the Commonwealth Club....

Little Rock brought the desegregation crisis sharply to the attention of the American people and the world. Here at home, it awakened many citizens for the first time to the ugly realities of a challenge to the very unity of our nation. Abroad, it dealt a stab in the back to American prestige as the leader of the free world and presented our totalitarian enemies with made-to-order propaganda for use among the very nations and peoples we need and must have on the side of democracy....

The world cannot understand nor long respect a nation in which a governor calls out troops to bar little children from school in defiance of the Supreme Court of the land, a nation in which mobs beat and kick and stone and spit upon those who happen not to be white. It asks: "Is this the vaunted democracy? Is this freedom, human dignity and equality of opportunity? Is this fair play? Is this better than Communism?" No, the assertion that Little Rock has damaged America abroad does not call for sneers. Our national security might well hang in the balance....

The Negro citizens of our common country, a country they have sweated to build and died to defend, are determined that the verdict at Appomattox will not be renounced, that the clock will not be turned back, that they shall enjoy what is justly theirs....

Their little children, begotten of parents of faith and courage, have shown by their fearlessness and their dignity that a people will not be denied their heritage. Complex as the problem is and hostile as the climate of opinion may be in certain areas, Negro Americans are determined to press for not only a beginning, but a middle and a final solution, in good faith and with American democratic speed.

The Negro position is clear. Three years of intimidation on the meanest and most brutal of levels have not broken their ranks or shaken their conviction.

What of the rest of our nation? It must make a decision for morality and legality and move in support of it, not merely for the good of the Negroes, but for the destiny of the nation itself.

Already I have indicated that this is a new and dangerous world. This cold war is a test of survival for the West. The Soviet *Sputnik*, now silent and barely visible, casts a shadow not lightly to be brushed aside. Can we meet the challenge of Moscow in the sciences and in war with a country divided upon race and color? Can we afford to deny to any boy or girl the maximum of education, that education which mean the difference between democratic life and totalitarian death?

To deny our ability to achieve a just solution within the framework of our Declaration of Independence and our Bill of Rights is to deny the genius of Americans. To reject our moral precepts is to renounce our partnership with God in bringing the kingdom of righteousness into being here on earth.

We may falter and stumble, but we cannot fail.

Alabama Governor George Wallace makes his stand against desegregation at the schoolhouse door of the University of Alabama in Tuscaloosa in 1963. (AP/Wide World Photos)

George Wallace's Inaugural Address as Governor

"From this Cradle of the Confederacy ... we sound the drum for freedom as have our generations of forebears before us done."

Overview

George Wallace's inaugural address as governor of Alabama, delivered on January 14, 1963, served in many ways both to launch him into national politics and to symbolize the last futile public resistance of the American South in the 1960s to segregation. During the height of the civil rights movement, Wallace proclaimed in the opening of his inaugural address, "I say ... segregation today ... segregation tomorrow ... segregation forever." The Deep South had long been the worst place for African Americans to live, and the white attitudes that brought about this treatment are well evidenced in this speech. However, within six months of Wallace's address, the University of Alabama was integrated, if just in a token manner. Wallace would nonetheless show the resiliency and pliability of politicians by winning office again in the 1970s and even the 1980s, with a majority of the black vote in his last election. He was a national force as well, running in the presidential primaries of 1964, 1972, and 1976 and in the presidential election of 1968, when during his best national showing he won 13.5 percent of the popular vote and five Deep South states with forty-six electoral votes, even though he ran as an independent candidate.

Context

In losing the Civil War, the South was forced to free all African American slaves. However, the South did not decide to treat the former slaves on an equal basis with whites. The North created Reconstruction and the Reconstruction Amendments, including the Fourteenth Amendment (1868), which broadened the definition of citizenship and required equal treatment of all citizens, and the Fifteenth Amendment (1870), which guaranteed male citizens the right to vote regardless of race. The Democratic Party, however, won back political power in the mid-1870s and vowed to reverse the moves toward equality that had occurred under Reconstruction.

Segregation was imposed, generally starting in the early 1890s, in all areas of life, ranging from separate street cars to separate Bibles to swear on in court. While the facilities provided to African Americans were not equal, the dubious "separate but equal" formula was approved by the Supreme Court in the infamous *Plessy v. Ferguson* case in 1896. Constitutions adopted throughout the South made segregation legal. These documents also generally disenfranchised African Americans through some combination of poll taxes, grandfather clauses (which created restrictions on voting except for those whose ancestors had the right to vote at the time of or shortly after the Civil War), and literacy tests.

African Americans protested at the time but accomplished little. Throughout the early twentieth century, the National Association for the Advancement of Colored People fought discrimination in the courts, and this effort accelerated after World War II, resulting in the Supreme Court decision in *Brown v. Board of Education* (1954), which declared segregation in education unconstitutional. The administration of President Dwight D. Eisenhower, however, preferred to ignore or delay implementation of that ruling. In the early 1960s, the administration of President John F. Kennedy started haltingly to enforce desegregation in higher education. For residents of Alabama, this was most notable through actions taken nearby, at the University of Mississippi, in 1962. Federal troops were called in to escort James Meredith, the first African American student to attend that university, throughout the year, after unarmed federal marshals had come under attack when they earlier had tried to calmly and unobtrusively shepherd Meredith through the campus. A riot had ensued, resulting in two deaths and hundreds of injuries, including soldiers and federal marshals wounded by gunfire. Northerners viewed this national tragedy as the result of the South's refusal to follow the law, while many southerners intrepreted the federal presence as an imposition of northern values reminiscent of the Reconstruction era.

Thus, at the time of Wallace's speech, many were wondering how long it would take for the Kennedy administration to finally act and enforce all of the civil rights laws and court rulings across the South. But those who favored civil rights were not the target of Wallace's address; rather, his speech was aimed at winning the loyalty of those citizens who opposed civil rights. The divisiveness of the speech was heightened by the city in which he gave it: Montgomery, the state's capital. It was there that the modern civil rights movement was started with Rosa Parks' defiant stand that

Time Line

1901
- Fourteen years after the end of Reconstruction, Alabama's new constitution formally puts segregation into law in almost all areas and makes change nearly impossible.

1919
- George Wallace is born in Clio, Alabama.

1946
- **May**
  Wallace wins election to the Alabama House of Representatives from Barbour County.

1954
- **May 17**
  The U.S. Supreme Court announces the *Brown v. Board of Education* decision, desegregating public schools. This decision is widely denounced and obstructed by whites in the South.

1955
- **December 1**
  Rosa Parks is arrested in Montgomery, Alabama, an event that touches off the Montgomery bus boycott.

1958
- **May 6**
  Running as a moderate, Wallace is defeated in the Democratic gubernatorial primary by hard-core segregationist John Patterson, who is endorsed by the Ku Klux Klan. This is Wallace's only electoral defeat in Alabama.

1962
- **November**
  Advocating hard-line segregation and "states' rights," Wallace is elected governor of Alabama.

1963
- **January 14**
  Wallace delivers his inaugural address as governor.
- **June 11**
  Wallace temporarily blocks admission of two African Americans into the University of Alabama.

resulted in the Montgomery bus boycott, and it was there that Dr. Martin Luther King, Jr., first came to national attention. Alabama remained one of the two most segregated states of the South, so it was an important battleground.

Wallace's own political history played into the content of his speech. He was first elected as a legislator after World War II and had his eye on higher office much of his life. He positioned himself to be a candidate for governor in 1958 but lost in the Democratic primary to John Patterson. Patterson was a more hard-core segregationist than Wallace, and Wallace vowed never to get outmaneuvered on the segregation issue again. He believed that hard-core segregation was the way to win political favor in the 1960s, and, aiming for national political prominence, that was what he endorsed in his inaugural address.

About the Author

Born in Clio, Alabama, in 1919, Wallace got his first taste of politics as a legislative page in his teens, and he became enraptured. He matriculated at the University of Alabama Law School at age eighteen, graduating in 1942. Wallace then entered the U.S. Army Air Forces and served for three years during World War II. In a show of political ambition, he decided to remain an enlisted man rather than becoming an officer, reasoning that there were more enlisted men than officers in the voting pool, and so remaining an enlisted man would help his political aspirations. In 1946 he won election to the Alabama House of Representatives and, in 1953, was elected a circuit judge. Throughout this period he was known as a moderate on racial issues and, most famously, refused to walk out of the 1948 Democratic National Convention when a strong civil rights plank was added to the Democratic platform. In 1949 Wallace was appointed as a trustee of Tuskegee Institute—a private black university that had once been headed by the former slave Booker T. Washington. Wallace then ran for governor of Alabama in 1958, losing in the primaries. He ran as a progressive moderate and was even endorsed by the National Association for the Advancement of Colored People, while his successful opponent was endorsed by the Ku Klux Klan. Wallace then moved to the right and successfully ran for governor in 1962 as a hard-core segregationist.

Through his inaugural speech and initial performance as Alabama's governor, Wallace burst onto the national stage. He ran for president in 1964, winning one-third of the vote in primaries in Wisconsin, Maryland, and Indiana. Prevented by state law from running again for governor in 1966, he nominated his wife, who won and thus allowed Wallace to retain political influence until her death in 1968. Wallace then ran for president in the 1968 campaign on the American Independent Party ticket. He would also run in the 1972 and 1976 presidential primaries, but his best national showing was in the 1968 general election, where he won five states. Wallace was reelected Alabama's governor in 1970, 1974, and 1982. By 1982 he had experienced a change of heart, claiming that his earlier stance on segregation was a mistake, and in that election he courted the black vote and won handily. On May 15, 1972, Wallace was shot in an assassination attempt while campaigning for the Democratic nomination for president. He remained paralyzed for the rest of his life. At the end of his final stint as governor, Wallace retired from politics, his health in decline. He died in Montgomery on September 13, 1998.

Explanation and Analysis of the Document

Wallace begins his speech by offering his thanks to his hometown and others around the state (many named individually) for electing him and citing the "dear little old lady" and the "mountain man" by way of personalizing his message. His special thanks are reserved for his wife and particularly his mother: "I want my mother to know that I realize my debt to her."

◆ Duty

Wallace then embarks on a discussion of duty, or his version of duty, saying that his focus will be on "honesty and economy in our state government." He says that he will run the liquor agents out of town, returning the money to the people of the state. This was in reference to Alabama's state-controlled system of liquor sales, which supported an extensive patronage and kickbacks system whose beneficiaries were legislators and the governor. Wallace remarks that he is "filling orders for several hundred one-way tickets ... out of Alabama" for these agents. In enumerating his duties, he pledges not to forget the senior citizen, the farmer, the laboring man, and children. Wallace next turns to the heart of his speech, a challenge thrown down to the rest of the country.

◆ Cradle of the Confederacy

Wallace invokes the name of the president of the Confederacy, noting that he stood to take his oath of office on the same spot where Jefferson Davis stood more than one hundred years before and that as Davis defended the southern way of life against the North's tyranny, Wallace would defend the South in similar fashion. He links segregation with freedom and argues that the only way to have freedom is to have segregation. It is here that he issues the famous words "In the name of the greatest people that have ever trod this earth, I draw the line in the dust and toss the gauntlet before the feet of tyranny ... and I say ... segregation today ... segregation tomorrow ... segregation forever."

Wallace defends the South by pointing out the difficulties that the North was having. He argues that the federal government, rather than desegregating the South, should be policing Washington, D.C. Wallace then suggests that the South will fight the efforts to change its lifestyle and will resist the "heel of tyranny," which was crushing it, in his estimation. The fact that not much of the South's lifestyle had actually changed and that, as of January 1963, no African Americans attended the University of Alabama made no difference to Wallace. The challenge came not in results for Wallace, but in the very idea that segregation should end.

Time Line

1964
- **July 2** Congress passes the Civil Rights Act.

1965
- **August 6** Congress passes the Voting Rights Act.

1968
- Wallace runs for president as the American Independent Party candidate, winning five southern states and 14 percent of the vote.

1970
- **November 3** Wallace wins election as governor of Alabama.

1974
- **November 5** Wallace wins election for a third term as governor of Alabama.

1982
- **November 2** Wallace is reelected governor, winning a majority of the black vote. During his term he announces that his past support of segregation was wrong.

1998
- **September 13** Wallace dies in Montgomery, Alabama.

Wallace then turns and urges the rest of the nation to support him. He posits that all who have left the South should rally to its defense. The speech also tries to enlist the support of those living beyond the South, arguing that all who love freedom should unite with it: "You are Southerners too and brothers with us in our fight." Freedom, of course, applied only to whites and, more specifically, white males. Wallace's speech was clearly not addressed to those who believed in the notion of freedom for all citizens.

◆ Alabama Blessed by God

Ending his call for whites to defend Alabama and the South, Wallace moves on, proudly referencing Alabama's blessings, her unparalleled natural resources: waterways, minerals, forestry, grasslands. He looks to a future that will see Alabama become a center for meatpacking and prepared foods. And he notes that Alabama is a tourist destination and is growing in importance in the space industry with the development of a "rocket center" in the Tennessee Valley. This reference is to the National Aeronautics and Space Administration's first field center, the Marshall Space Flight Center in Huntsville, set up in 1961.

Wallace also notes Alabama's shipping industry, citing the port of Mobile as the "gateway" to South America and trade. He cites the rise of manufacturing and, with it, the expansion of settlement. He envisions the "trickle" of workers, growing to a "stream of enterprise and endeavor, capital and expansion." Throughout, Wallace argues that the federal government "encourages our fears" to increase its own power by creating crises and then demanding muscle to fix them. He asserts that Alabama should stand strong against such increased governmental authority. He ignores the negative impacts of segregation and racism while noting that the influx of capital derives from the North and that most of the profits leave the state.

Circling back, the governor then notes how freedom is required to build Alabama and how the federal government, in his estimation, is restricting the freedom of the state. As the government "must increase its expenditures of bounties, then this government must assume more and more police powers." Wallace predicts that if the federal concentration is not stopped, it will become a new god, replacing the Christian God. He heavily emphasizes religion and argues that religion should be at the core, not government. As he puts it, "we find we are become government-fearing people—not God-fearing people."

Hand in hand with this, Wallace argues that individual rights—and by implication the right to segregate and discriminate—should be the main rights protected, rather than "human rights." He then offers up a defense of Alabama's practice of not allowing African Americans to vote, suggesting that voting rights should be given only to those who have the "spiritual responsibility of preserving freedom." Wallace never asserts directly that African Americans are not defenders of freedom. At the time of Wallace's address, African Americans were serving with distinction in the U.S. military and had fought recently in World War II and the Korean War.

Wallace returns to the subject of God and argues that the Ten Commandments were being challenged by progressive ideas. Although he does not mention President Franklin Delano Roosevelt directly by name, Wallace refers to him when he asserts that some politicians thought that the Constitution was written for "horse and buggy days." (Roosevelt had made that claim when the Supreme Court struck down much of his New Deal legislation.) Wallace disagrees with this assessment, adding sarcastically that the Ten Commandments were also "written for 'horse and buggy' days." His implication is that if the Constitution can be updated for progressives, then perhaps the Ten Commandments are also suspect.

◆ **International White Minority**

Wallace finds historical comparisons to what he believed was occurring in America. Adolph Hitler's Germany and the Roman Empire both had fallen because these societies had "rotted the souls of the builders," and he argues that the United States would be next if it continued on its present course. Turning civil rights on its head, he argues that the whites of Mississippi, who were unjustly wronged when the University of Mississippi was integrated, were a minority being persecuted by the majority: "As the *national* racism of Hitler's Germany persecuted a *national* minority to the whim of a *national* majority, so the *international* racism of the liberals seeks to persecute the *international* white minority to the whim of the *international* colored majority."

Continuing his attack on civil rights, Wallace denigrates the *Brown v. Board of Education* decision, even while never naming it. He combines anti–civil rights rhetoric with anti-Communism by noting that many of the scholars cited by the Court in that decision belonged to "communist-front organizations" and continued to attack the Supreme Court, arguing that it was removing prayer from the schools and "In God We Trust" from the currency. Wallace distorts history when he states that the Founding Fathers added "In God We Trust" to the U.S. currency, when in, in fact, this change occurred only in the 1950s as part of the federal government's anti-Communist agenda. He attacks President Kennedy for issuing an executive order banning housing discrimination, claiming that it restricted the freedom of people to sell to those whom they chose, and he castigates Kennedy further for integrating the University of Mississippi, pointing out that the troops would be better defending Berlin against the Communists.

◆ **Defying the Supreme Court**

Not content to rely on God and anti-Communism, Wallace tries to seize the progressive label for himself. He contends that the real progressives were the Founding Fathers, who, in Wallace's interpretation of history, formed a government based on faith, hard work, and charity, not a fear of government. Wallace makes no mention of the First Amendment, with its emphasis on freedom from government establishment of religion and freedom of religion, and he neglects to comment on major changes since 1776, including the end of slavery.

Wallace directly challenges the authority of the Supreme Court. He notes Alabama's defiance in having set up a sign stating "In God We Trust" in the capitol, and he challenges the Court to "let them make the most of it." Here he is drawing a comparison between himself and Patrick Henry. In 1765, Henry rose in the Virginia House of Burgesses to present resolutions in a debate concerning the newly enacted Stamp Act. In his speech, he criticizes the British Parliament and King George III, allegedly saying that "Caesar had his Brutus and Charles the First his Cromwell" (references to assassinations of leaders) and that George III might "profit by their example." Henry went on to state that if his words were treason, the people of Virginia who were listening should "make the most of it" and rebel. Here Wallace was at least rhetorically calling for a new revolution, or so it would seem.

◆ **Unit of One, United of the Many**

The governor defends the existence of the states and argues that they should be free to go their own way—what might be called states' rights. He also argues that all religious groups, racial groups, and political parties should respect freedom. It is a sign of Alabama at the time that he lists, as examples of religions, "Baptist, Methodist, Presbyterian, Church of Christ" and for political parties "Republican, Democrat, Prohibition." In his discussion of racial groups he proposes that all races have "separate stations" and that those who want to eliminate racial distinctions are Communists. That amalgamation will cause the United States to become "a mongrel unit of one under a single all powerful government," standing "for everything and for nothing."

Wallace then turns and extends a questionable hand of brotherhood to African Americans, offering to let them grow, as long as they stay in their "separate racial station." He refutes the "liberals' theory" that argued that racism and its effects—namely, "poverty, discrimination, and lack of opportunity"—needed to be addressed because it would lead to Communism. He posits that if such a theory were true, the whole South would have turned to Communism after it was destroyed by the North, with its "vulturous carpetbagger" and the "bayonets" of federal troops. Wallace makes no mention of how rich southerners had disenfranchised African Americans and most poor whites, thus denying them their desires for change. Wallace trumpets that "there are not enough native communists in the South to fill up a telephone booth, and THAT is a matter of public FBI record."

◆ **Southland's Fathers**

Wallace ends his address with a defense of the South, citing the region's contributions to the founding of America. He praises Patrick Henry, James Madison, George Washington, and others as leading Founding Fathers. Freedom—for whites—is a key element of his address, and he urges all Alabamians to defend it across America. He mentions the divine inspiration for freedom and argues that it is Alabama's destiny to protect freedom, particularly freedom from fear of government. Finally, Wallace states that he will "Stand Up for Alabama" and wants his listeners to do the same. He concludes his remarks with a prayer, seemingly at odds with the civil rights reforms that he has just stridently denounced: "And my prayer is that the Father who reigns above us will bless all the people of this great sovereign State and nation, both white and black."

Audience

Wallace had two main audiences for his speech. The first was the people who watched, listened to, or read a transcript of the speech, including most Alabamians of the time. Wallace wanted to start out his administration with a bang, and he probably achieved this goal with his speech. Those who favored segregation would have gotten a big boost from the speech. The second audience was composed of those people across the nation who opposed

Jefferson Davis addresses the citizens of Montgomery, Alabama, as president-elect of the Confederacy. (Library of Congress)

desegregation or big government—or both. Wallace used the speech as vehicle to move himself onto a larger stage, and in this respect he clearly spoke to a national audience.

Impact

In his inaugural address, Wallace was directly throwing down the gauntlet and challenging those who wanted desegregation. As such, the speech clearly demonstrated that nearly ten years after the *Brown* Supreme Court decision, the South was not willing to accept even the slow progress toward desegregation that had been made during the presidential administrations of Dwight D. Eisenhower and John F. Kennedy. In fact, many court rulings and civil rights laws remained far from enforced after Wallace took office. In 1964, less than 1 percent of schoolchildren in the former Confederate states attended integrated schools. Thus, the Kennedy administration had been able to accomplish token change in the universities, but not elsewhere. The speech, and Wallace's national campaigns in the years that followed, also rallied further opposition to segregation and shifted the political landscape in the South. Wallace's efforts made it difficult for Kennedy to accomplish anything in civil rights, but he and other southern politicians were unable to stop Lyndon Johnson's juggernaut, which pushed through the civil rights legislation in 1964 and 1965. Wallace's campaigning and rhetoric also helped to push the South toward a political shift that resulted in Republican Party dominance in the area. In that it effec-

Essential Quotes

"Today I have stood, where once Jefferson Davis stood, and took an oath to my people. It is very appropriate then that from this Cradle of the Confederacy, this very Heart of the Great Anglo-Saxon Southland, that today we sound the drum for freedom as have our generations of forebears before us done, time and time again through history."

"Hear me, Southerners! You sons and daughters who have moved north and west throughout this nation.… We call on you from your native soil to join with us in national support and vote."

"But the strong, simple faith and sane reasoning of our founding fathers has long since been forgotten as the so-called 'progressives' tell us that our Constitution was written for 'horse and buggy' days. So were the Ten Commandments."

"We intend, quite simply, to practice the free heritage as bequeathed to us as sons of free fathers. We intend to re-vitalize the truly new and progressive form of government that is less than two hundred years old, a government first founded in this nation simply and purely on faith that there is a personal God who rewards good and punishes evil, that hard work will receive its just desserts."

"We invite the negro citizens of Alabama to work with us from his separate racial station, as we will work with him, to develop, to grow in individual freedom and enrichment. We want jobs and a good future for BOTH races, the tubercular and the infirm. This is the basic heritage of my religion, of which I make full practice, for we are all the handiwork of God."

"My pledge to you—to "Stand up for Alabama"—is a stronger pledge today than it was the first day I made that pledge. I shall "Stand up for Alabama," as Governor of our State. You stand with me, and we, together, can give courageous leadership to millions of people throughout this nation who look to the South for their hope in this fight to win and preserve our freedoms and liberties."

tively represented the enduring resistance of the South, Wallace's inaugural gubernatorial address catapulted him to national prominence. Those who opposed liberalism, integration, and social progress had no better spokesman throughout the 1960s.

From a modern perspective, historians today view Wallace's inaugural address both as a brilliant political document, in that it greatly improved Wallace's political standing, and as the last gasp of political support for public segregation. After Wallace's failed stance of the mid-1960s, and after President Johnson pushed through legislation that gave millions more African Americans the vote in the South, it was impossible to argue politically for segregation. Those who opposed civil rights for African Americans or who wanted to pander to those southern whites who opposed civil rights instead used terms like "law and order" and argued for limiting or eliminating such social programs as welfare. These politicians also allowed schools and areas to resegregate. These approaches, taken by politicians like Richard Nixon, were more successful than Wallace's bluntly segregationist efforts.

See also Fourteenth Amendment to the U.S. Constitution (1868); Fifteenth Amendment to the U.S. Constitution (1870); *Plessy v. Ferguson* (1896); *Brown v. Board of Education* (1954); Civil Rights Act of 1964.

Further Reading

■ Books

Carter, Dan T. *The Politics of Rage: George Wallace, the Origins of the New Conservatism, and the Transformation of American Politics.* 2nd ed. Baton Rouge: Louisiana State University Press, 2000.

Clark, E. Culpepper. *The Schoolhouse Door: Segregation's Last Stand at the University of Alabama.* New York: Oxford University Press, 1993.

Frederick, Jeff. *Stand Up for Alabama: Governor George Wallace.* Tuscaloosa: University of Alabama Press, 2007.

Kazin, Michael. *The Populist Persuasion: An American History.* Rev. ed. Ithaca, N.Y.: Cornell University Press, 1998.

■ Web Sites

"George Wallace: Settin' the Woods on Fire." PBS's "American Experience" Web site.
  http://www.pbs.org/wgbh/amex/wallace/.

"Oral History Interview with George Wallace." Documenting the American South Web site.
  http://docsouth.unc.edu/sohp/A-0024/menu.html.

—Scott Merriman

Questions for Further Study

1. Do you believe Wallace's segregationist views were the result of political calculation or of deeply held personal convictions?

2. Many people would be surprised to learn that the National Association for the Advancement of Colored People endorsed Wallace's candidacy for governor in 1958 and that in 1982 he won the majority of the black vote in his race for reelection as governor. Why do you think that a man known for his segregationist views would be able to successfully court the black vote?

3. How did Wallace's inaugural speech reflect the ongoing tension in the United States between the power and authority of the federal government and the rights of individual states?

4. Wallace's address was not only a document with implications for the civil rights movement but also a document in the history of America's response to Communism during the cold war. How so?

5. What role did party politics play in the slow pace of integration during the late 1950s and early 1960s? How was Wallace able to exploit the hesitancy of leaders such as presidents Dwight Eisenhower and John Kennedy?

George Wallace's Inaugural Address as Governor

Before I begin my talk with you, I want to ask you for a few minutes patience while I say something that is on my heart: I want to thank those home folks of my county who first gave an anxious country boy his opportunity to serve in state politics. I shall always owe a lot to those who gave me that *first* opportunity to serve.

I will never forget the warm support and close loyalty at the folks of Suttons, Haigler's Mill, Eufaula, Beat 6 and Beat 14, Richards Cross Roads and Gammage Beat; at Baker Hill, Beat 8 and Comer, Spring Hill, Adams Chapel and Mount Andrew, White Oak, Baxter's Station, Clayton, Louisville and Cunnigham Place, Horns Crossroads, Texasville and Blue Springs, where the vote was 304 for Wallace and 1 for the opposition. And the dear little lady whom I heard had made that one vote against me, by mistake, because she couldn't see too well and she had pulled the wrong lever. Bless her heart. At Clio, my birthplace, and Elamville. I shall never forget them. May God bless them.

And I shall forever remember that election day morning as I waited, and suddenly at ten o'clock that morning the first return of a box was flashed over this state: it carried the message "Wallace 15, opposition zero," and it came from the Hamrick Beat at Putman's Mountain where live the great hill people of our state. May God bless the mountain man; his loyalty is unshakeable, he'll do to walk down the road with.

I hope you'll forgive me these few moments of remembering, but I wanted them—and you—to know, that I shall never forget.

And I wish I could shake hands and thank all of you in this state who voted for me and those of you who did not, for I know you voted your honest convictions, and now, we must stand together and move the great State of Alabama forward.

I would be remiss, this day, if I did not thank my wonderful wife and fine family for their patience, support and loyalty. And there is no man living who does not owe more to his mother than he can ever repay, and I want my mother to know that I realize my debt to her.

This is the day of my Inauguration as Governor of the State of Alabama. And on this day I feel a deep obligation to renew my pledges, my covenants with you, the people of this great state.

General Robert E. Lee said that "duty" is the sublimest word in the English language and I have come, increasingly, to realize what he meant. I SHALL do my duty to you, God helping, to every man, to every woman, yes, to every child in this state. I shall fulfill my duty toward honesty and economy in our state government so that no man shall have a part of his livelihood cheated and no child shall have a bit of his future stolen away.

I have said to you that I would eliminate the liquor agents in this state and that the money saved would be returned to our citizens. I am happy to report to you that I am now filling orders for several hundred one-way tickets and stamped on them are these words "for liquor agents—destination: out of Alabama." I am happy to report to you that the big-wheeling cocktail-party boys have gotten the word that their free whiskey and boat rides are over, that the farmer in the field, the worker in the factory, the businessman in his office, the housewife in her home, have decided that the money can be better spent to help our children's education and our older citizens, and they have put a man in office to see that it is done. It shall be done. Let me say one more time: no more liquor drinking in your governor's mansion.

I shall fulfill my duty in working hard to bring industry into our state, not only by maintaining an honest, sober and free-enterprise climate of government in which industry can have confidence but in going out and getting it, so that our people can have industrial jobs in Alabama and provide a better life for their children.

I shall not forget my duty to our senior citizens, so that their lives can be lived in dignity and enrichment of the golden years, nor to our sick, both mental and physical, and they will know we have not forsaken them. I want the farmer to feel confident that in this state government he has a partner who will work with him in raising his income and increasing his markets. And I want the laboring man to know he has a friend who is sincerely striving to better his field of endeavor.

I want to assure every child that this State government is not afraid to invest in their future through education, so that they will not be handicapped on every threshold of their lives.

Today I have stood, where once Jefferson Davis stood, and took an oath to my people. It is very appropriate then that from this Cradle of the Confederacy, this very Heart of the Great Anglo-Saxon Southland, that today we sound the drum for freedom as have our generations of forebears before us done, time and time again through history. Let us rise to the call of freedom-loving blood that is in us and send our answer to the tyranny that clanks its chains upon the South. In the name of the greatest people that have ever trod this earth, I draw the line in the dust and toss the gauntlet before the feet of tyranny, and I say ... segregation today ... segregation tomorrow ... segregation forever.

The Washington, D.C., school riot report is disgusting and revealing. We will not sacrifice our children to any such type school system—and you can write that down. The federal troops in Mississippi could be better used guarding the safety of the citizens of Washington, D.C., where it is even unsafe to walk or go to a ballgame—and that is the nation's capitol. I was safer in a B-29 bomber over Japan during the war in an air raid than the people of Washington are walking to the White House neighborhood. A closer example is Atlanta. The city officials fawn for political reasons over school integration and THEN build barricades to stop residential integration—what hypocrisy!

Let us send this message back to Washington by our representatives who are with us today, that from this day we are standing up, and the heel of tyranny does not fit the neck of an upright man. That we intend to take the offensive and carry our fight for freedom across the nation, wielding the balance of power we know we possess in the Southland. That WE, not the insipid bloc of voters of some sections will determine in the next election who shall sit in the White House of these United States. That from this day, from this hour, from this minute, we give the word of a race of honor that we will tolerate their boot in our face no longer. And let those certain judges put *that* in their opium pipes of power and smoke it for what it is worth.

Hear me, Southerners! You sons and daughters who have moved north and west throughout this nation. We call on you from your native soil to join with us in national support and vote, and we know, wherever you are—away from the hearths of the Southland—that you will respond, for though you may live in the farthest reaches of this vast country, your heart has never left Dixieland.

And you native sons and daughters of old New England's rock-ribbed patriotism, and you sturdy natives of the great Midwest, and you descendants of the far West flaming spirit of pioneer freedom: We invite you to come and be with us, for you are of the Southern spirit and the Southern philosophy. You are Southerners too and brothers with us in our fight.

What I have said about segregation goes double this day, and what I have said to or about some federal judges goes TRIPLE this day.

Alabama has been blessed by God as few states in this Union have been blessed. Our state owns ten percent of all the natural resources of all the states in our country. Our inland waterway system is second to none and has the potential of being the greatest waterway transport system in the entire world. We possess over thirty minerals in usable quantities, and our soil is rich and varied, suited to a wide variety of plants. Our native pine and forestry system produces timber faster than we can cut it, and yet we have only pricked the surface of the great lumber and pulp potential.

With ample rainfall and rich grasslands, our livestock industry is in the infancy of a giant future that can make us a center of the big and growing meat-packing and prepared foods marketing. We have the favorable climate, streams, woodlands, beaches, and natural beauty to make us a recreational mecca in the booming tourist and vacation industry. Nestled in the great Tennessee Valley, we possess the rocket center of the world and the keys to the space frontier.

While the trade with a developing Europe built the great port cities of the East Coast, our own fast-developing port of Mobile faces as a magnetic gateway to the great continent of South America, well over twice as large and hundreds of times richer in resources, even now awakening to the growing probes of enterprising capital with a potential of growth and wealth beyond any present dream for our port development and corresponding results throughout the connecting waterways that thread our state.

And while the manufacturing industries of free enterprise have been coming to our state in increasing numbers, attracted by our bountiful natural resources, our growing numbers of skilled workers and our favorable conditions, their present rate of settlement here can be increased from the trickle they now represent to a stream of enterprise and endeavor, capital and expansion that can join us in our work of development and enrichment of the educational futures of our children, the opportunities of our citizens and the fulfillment of our talents as God has given them to us. To realize our ambitions and to bring to fruition our dreams, we as Alabamians must

Document Text

take cognizance of the world about us. We must redefine our heritage, re-school our thoughts in the lessons our forefathers knew so well, firsthand, in order to function and to grow and to prosper. We can no longer hide our head in the sand and tell ourselves that the ideology of our free fathers is not being attacked and is not being threatened by another idea, for it is. We are faced with an idea that if a centralized government assumes enough authority, enough power over its people, that it can provide a utopian life. That if given the power to dictate, to forbid, to require, to demand, to distribute, to edict and to judge what is best and enforce that will of judgment upon its citizens, it will produce only "good," and it shall be our father and our God. It is an idea of government that encourages our fears and destroys our faith, for where there is faith, there is no fear, and where there is fear, there is no faith. In encouraging our fears of economic insecurity it demands we place that economic management and control with government; in encouraging our fear of educational development it demands we place that education and the minds of our children under management and control of government, and even in feeding our fears of physical infirmities and declining years, it offers and demands to father us through it all and even into the grave. It is a government that claims to us that it is bountiful as it buys its power from us with the fruits of its rapaciousness of the wealth that free men before it have produced and builds on crumbling credit without responsibilities to the debtors, our children. It is an ideology of government erected on the encouragement of fear and fails to recognize the basic law of our fathers that governments do not produce wealth. People produce wealth—free people, and those people become less free as they learn there is little reward for ambition; that it requires faith to risk, and they have none. As the government must restrict and penalize and tax incentive and endeavor and must increase its expenditures of bounties, then this government must assume more and more police powers, and we find we are become government-fearing people—not God-fearing people. We find we have replaced faith with fear, and though we may give lip service to the Almighty, in reality, government has become our god. It is, therefore, a basically ungodly government and its appeal to the pseudo-intellectual and the politician is to change their status from servant of the people to master of the people, to play at being God without faith in God and without the wisdom of God. It is a system that is the very opposite of Christ, for it feeds and encourages everything degenerate and base in our people as it assumes the responsibilities that we ourselves should assume. Its pseudo-liberal spokesmen and some Harvard advocates have never examined the logic of its substitution of what it calls "human rights" for individual rights, for its propaganda play on words has appeal for the unthinking. Its logic is totally material and irresponsible as it runs the full gamut of human desires, including the theory that everyone has voting rights without the spiritual responsibility of preserving freedom. Our founding fathers recognized those rights, but only within the framework of those spiritual responsibilities. But the strong, simple faith and sane reasoning of our founding fathers has long since been forgotten as the so-called "progressives" tell us that our Constitution was written for "horse and buggy" days. So were the Ten Commandments.

Not so long ago men stood in marvel and awe at the cities, the buildings, the schools, the autobahns that the government of Hitler's Germany had built, just as centuries before they stood in wonder of Rome's building. But it could not stand, for the system that built it had rotted the souls of the builders and in turn rotted the foundation of what God meant that men should be. Today that same system on an international scale is sweeping the world. It is the "changing world" of which we are told; it is called "new" and "liberal." It is as old as the oldest dictator. It is degenerate and decadent. As the *national* racism of Hitler's Germany persecuted a *national* minority to the whim of a *national* majority, so the *international* racism of the liberals seeks to persecute the *international* white minority to the whim of the *international* colored majority—so that we are footballed about according to the favor of the Afro-Asian bloc. But the Belgian survivors of the Congo cannot present their case to a war crimes commission, nor the Portuguese of Angola, nor the survivors of Castro, nor the citizens of Oxford, Mississippi.

It is this theory of international power politic that led a group of men on the Supreme Court for the first time in American history to issue an edict, based not on legal precedent, but upon a volume, the editor of which said our Constitution is outdated and must be changed and the writers of which, some had admittedly belonged to as many as half a hundred communist-front organizations. It is this theory that led this same group of men to briefly bare the ungodly core of that philosophy in forbidding little schoolchildren to say a prayer. And we find the evidence of that ungodliness even in the removal of the words "in God we trust"

Document Text

from some of our dollars, which was placed there as like evidence by our founding fathers as the faith upon which this system of government was built. It is the spirit of power thirst that caused a President in Washington to take up Caesar's pen and with one stroke of it make a law. A law which the law-making body of Congress refused to pass. A law that tells us that we can or cannot buy or sell our very homes, except by his conditions and except at HIS discretion. It is the spirit of power thirst that led the same President to launch a full offensive of twenty-five thousand troops against a university, of all places, in his own country and against his own people, when this nation maintains only six thousand troops in the beleaguered city of Berlin. We have witnessed such acts of "might makes right" over the world as men yielded to the temptation to play God, but we have never before witnessed it in America. We reject such acts as free men. We do not defy, for there is nothing to defy, since as free men we do not recognize any government right to give freedom or deny freedom. No government erected by man has that right. As Thomas Jefferson said, "The God who gave us life, gave us liberty at the same time; no King holds the right of liberty in his hands." Nor does any ruler in American government.

We intend, quite simply, to practice the free heritage as bequeathed to us as sons of free fathers. We intend to re-vitalize the truly new and progressive form of government that is less than two hundred years old, a government first founded in this nation simply and purely on faith that there is a personal God who rewards good and punishes evil, that hard work will receive its just desserts, that ambition and ingenuity and incentiveness … are admirable traits and goals that the individual is encouraged in his spiritual growth and from that growth arrives at a character that enhances his charity toward others and from that character and that charity so is influenced business and labor and farmer and government. We intend to renew our faith as God-fearing men, *not* government-fearing men nor any other kind of fearing-men. We intend to roll up our sleeves and pitch in to develop this full bounty God has given us, to live full and useful lives and in absolute freedom from all fear. Then can we enjoy the full richness of the Great American Dream.

We have placed this sign, "In God We Trust," upon our State Capitol on this Inauguration Day as physical evidence of determination to renew the faith of our fathers and to practice the free heritage they bequeathed to us. We do this with the clear and solemn knowledge that such physical evidence is evidently a direct violation of the logic of that Supreme Court in Washington, D.C., and if they or their spokesmen in this state wish to term this defiance, I say, then let them make the most of it.

This nation was never meant to be a unit of one but a united of the many. That is the exact reason our freedom-loving forefathers established the states, so as to divide the rights and powers among the states, insuring that no central power could gain master government control.

In united effort we were meant to live under this government, whether Baptist, Methodist, Presbyterian, Church of Christ, or whatever one's denomination or religious belief—each respecting the others right to a separate denomination; each, by working to develop his own, enriching the total of all our lives through united effort. And so it was meant in our political lives, whether Republican, Democrat, Prohibition, or whatever political party—each striving from his separate political station, [each] respecting the rights of others to be separate and work from within their political framework, and each separate political station making its contribution to our lives.

And so it was meant in our racial lives—each race, within its own framework has the freedom to teach, to instruct, to develop, to ask for and receive deserved help from others of separate racial stations. This is the great freedom of our American founding fathers. But if we amalgamate into the one unit as advocated by the communist philosophers, then the enrichment of our lives, the freedom for our development, is gone forever. We become, therefore, a mongrel unit of one under a single all powerful government, and we stand for everything and for nothing.

The true brotherhood of America, of respecting the separateness of others and uniting in effort, has been so twisted and distorted from its original concept that there is a small wonder that communism is winning the world.

We invite the negro citizens of Alabama to work with us from his separate racial station, as we will work with him, to develop, to grow in individual freedom and enrichment. We want jobs and a good future for BOTH races, the tubercular and the infirm. This is the basic heritage of my religion, of which I make full practice, for we are all the handiwork of God.

But we warn those, of any group, who would follow the false doctrine of communistic amalgamation that we will not surrender our system of government, our freedom of race and religion. That freedom was won at a hard price, and if it requires a hard price to retain it, we are able and quite willing to pay it.

Document Text

The liberals' theory that poverty, discrimination and lack of opportunity is the cause of communism is a false theory. If it were true, the South would have been the biggest single communist bloc in the western hemisphere long ago. For after the great War between the States, our people faced a desolate land of burned universities, destroyed crops and homes, with manpower depleted and crippled, and even the mule, which was required to work the land, was so scarce that whole communities shared one animal to make the spring plowing. There were no government handouts, no Marshall Plan aid, no coddling to make sure that *our* people would not suffer; instead, the South was set upon by the vulturous carpetbagger and federal troops, all loyal Southerners were denied the vote at the point of bayonet, so that the infamous, illegal 14th Amendment might be passed. There was no money, no food and no hope of either. But our grandfathers bent their knee only in church and bowed their head only to God.

Not for a single instant did they ever consider the easy way of federal dictatorship and amalgamation in return for fat bellies. They fought. They dug sweet roots from the ground with their bare hands and boiled them in iron pots. They gathered poke salad from the woods and acorns from the ground. They fought. They followed no false doctrine. They knew what they wanted, and they fought for freedom! They came up from their knees in the greatest display of sheer nerve, grit and guts that has ever been set

Glossary

Anglo-Saxon	a reference to the Germanic tribes that invaded much of northern Europe early in the medieval period; often used loosely to refer to white northern Europeans
autobahns	the highway system of Germany, similar to the U.S. interstate highway system
Beat	a precinct
Berlin	the largest city in Germany, which, at the time, was surrounded by Communist East Germany and was itself divided into democratic West Berlin and Communist East Berlin
Caesar	Julius Caesar, an ancient Roman emperor whose name is often used as a figure of speech for a temporal ruler
carpetbagger	northerners who traveled to the South (often with their belongings packed in a type of suitcase called a carpetbag) seeking political or economic advantage
Dixieland	the American South, especially the Confederacy during the Civil War; the origins of the nickname are obscure
General Robert E. Lee	the commander of Confederate forces during the Civil War
"The God who gave us life …"	quotation from Thomas Jefferson's "A Summary View of the Rights of British America"
Jefferson Davis	the president of the Confederate States of America during the Civil War
Marshall Plan	a program that provided economic aid to the nations of Europe to rebuild after World War II
poke salad	a food made from boiled pokeweed leaves
Prohibition	a reference to the Prohibition Party, a minor political party whose sole goal was elimination of the consumption of alcohol
Rudyard Kipling	a British author and poet of the late nineteenth and early twentieth centuries
War between the States	the U.S. Civil War

down in the pages of written history, and they won! The great writer Rudyard Kipling wrote of them that: "There in the Southland of the United States of America, lives the greatest fighting breed of man … in all the world!"

And that is why today, I stand ashamed of the fat, well-fed whimperers who say that it is inevitable that our cause is lost. I am ashamed *of* them, and I am ashamed *for* them. They do not represent the people of the Southland.

And may we take note of one other fact, with all the trouble with communists that some sections of this country have—there are not enough native communists in the South to fill up a telephone booth, and THAT is a matter of public FBI record.

We remind all within hearing of this Southland that a *Southerner*, Peyton Randolph, presided over the Continental Congress in our nation's beginning … that a *Southerner*, Thomas Jefferson, wrote the Declaration of Independence, that a *Southerner*, George Washington, is the Father of our country … that a *Southerner*, James Madison, authored our Constitution, that a *Southerner*, George Mason, authored the Bill of Rights and it was a Southerner who said, "Give me liberty, or give me death," Patrick Henry.

Southerners played a most magnificent part in erecting this great divinely inspired system of freedom, and as God is our witnesses, Southerners will save it.

Let us, as Alabamians, grasp the hand of destiny and walk out of the shadow of fear and fill our divine destination. Let us not simply defend, but let us assume the leadership of the fight and carry our leadership across this nation. God has placed us here in this crisis. Let us not fail in this, our most historical moment.

You are here today, present in this audience, and to you over this great state, wherever you are in sound of my voice, I want to humbly and with all sincerity, thank you for your faith in me.

I promise you that I will try to make you a good governor. I promise you that, as God gives me the wisdom and the strength, I will be sincere with you. I will be honest with you.

I will apply the old sound rule of our fathers, that anything worthy of our defense is worthy of one hundred percent of our defense. I have been taught that freedom meant freedom from any threat or fear of government. I was born in that freedom. I was raised in that freedom. I intend to live in that freedom. And God willing, when I die, I shall leave that freedom to my children, as my father left it to me.

My pledge to you—to "Stand up for Alabama"—is a stronger pledge today than it was the first day I made that pledge. I shall "Stand up for Alabama," as Governor of our State. You stand with me, and we, together, can give courageous leadership to millions of people throughout this nation who look to the South for their hope in this fight to win and preserve our freedoms and liberties.

So help me God.

And my prayer is that the Father who reigns above us will bless all the people of this great sovereign State and nation, both white and black.

I thank you.

Martin Luther King, Jr. (Library of Congress)

Martin Luther King, Jr.: "Letter from Birmingham Jail"

1963

"Injustice anywhere is a threat to justice everywhere."

Overview

In his "Letter from Birmingham Jail," Martin Luther King, Jr., delivered an important statement on civil rights and civil disobedience. The 1963 racial crisis in Birmingham, Alabama, was a critical turning point in the struggle for African American civil rights. Nonviolent protestors led by King faced determined opposition from hard-core segregationists. King and his organization, the Southern Christian Leadership Conference (SCLC), needed a victory to sustain the momentum of their movement. The integration of downtown stores and lunch counters was the primary focus of SCLC's "Project C"—the "C" stood for *confrontation*. Demonstrations began one day after a new city government was elected. Many observers criticized King for protesting at a time when Birmingham's race relations appeared to be moving in a more positive direction. These critics included eight prominent white clergymen who published a statement characterizing these protests as "unwise and untimely" and asking African Americans to withdraw their support from King's efforts.

The SCLC timed its campaign to coincide with the Easter shopping season. Its strategy involved using economic pressure to force white businesses to remove segregated facilities, extend more courteous treatment to African American customers, and hire black salespeople. King was arrested on Good Friday in 1963 and remained imprisoned for eight days. He used his jail time to compose a response to the clergymen. In his "Letter from Birmingham Jail," King articulated a moral and philosophical defense of his tactics and delivered a stinging rebuke to those who counseled caution on civil rights. Although King's letter was not published until after the Birmingham crisis was resolved, it is widely regarded as the most important written document of the modern civil rights movement and a classic text on civil disobedience.

Context

Birmingham had long had a reputation as one of the most racist and violent cities in the South. Starting in 1947 a series of bombings targeted the homes of African Americans who had moved into previously all-white neighborhoods. The Ku Klux Klan operated openly and was widely believed to be responsible for these attacks. When the outspoken black minister the Reverend Fred Shuttlesworth formed the Alabama Christian Movement for Human Rights to press for civil rights, the terrorists struck his home and church. Because no one was apprehended for any of the more than fifty explosions, Birmingham blacks concluded that the police were in league with the bombers. Public Safety Commissioner Eugene "Bull" Connor, an outspoken segregationist, used all resources at his disposal to preserve the Jim Crow system of laws and social practices that segregated and discriminated against African Americans.

Connor's heavy-handed methods aroused the ire of more temperate civic leaders, who hoped to create a more favorable image for their city. These leaders spearheaded an effort to oust Connor by shifting the form of city government from three commissioners to a mayor and a city council. On April 2, 1963, Birmingham voters rejected Connor and elected Albert Boutwell, a moderate segregationist, as their mayor. The losers immediately sued to prevent the new administration from taking office. For a time Birmingham had two competing city governments.

In January 1963 the SCLC decided to make Birmingham the site of its next major civil rights drive. The SCLC had suffered a serious setback the previous year in Albany, Georgia, where, despite months of nonviolent struggle and hundreds of arrests, African Americans were unable to wrest any concessions from an intransigent city government. Shuttlesworth, the most prominent Birmingham civil rights activist, assured the SCLC board that his city would be different; Connor could be counted on to react in his usual heavy-handed fashion. King also had a larger objective in mind: He hoped that by creating a crisis in Birmingham, he could force President John F. Kennedy to take much-needed action on civil rights.

After a delay in demonstrations until the Boutwell-Connor runoff election was resolved, protests began on April 3 with sit-ins and picketing at downtown department stores. On April 10, Judge W. A. Jenkins issued an injunction prohibiting King and other civil rights leaders from participating in or encouraging any civil disobedience. King decided to defy the court order, and on Good Friday

Time Line

1963

- **January 10**
  The Southern Christian Leadership Conference targets Birmingham for civil rights demonstrations during the pre-Easter shopping season.

- **April 2**
  Albert Boutwell defeats Eugene "Bull" Connor in a runoff election for mayor of Birmingham.

- **April 3**
  Birmingham demonstrations begin.

- **April 12**
  Martin Luther King, Jr., is arrested, refuses bail, and is placed in solitary confinement; "A Call for Unity" by eight Birmingham clergymen appears in the *Birmingham News*.

- **April 16**
  The text of "Letter from Birmingham Jail" is smuggled out of jail.

- **April 20**
  King is released from jail.

- **May 3**
  Connor orders fire hoses and police dogs to be turned on young demonstrators. Television coverage creates a groundswell of support for King's movement.

- **May 9**
  King announces an agreement with Birmingham business leaders to desegregate their establishments, ending the demonstrations.

- **May 28**
  "Letter from Birmingham Jail" is published by the American Friends Service Committee.

- **June 11**
  President John F. Kennedy proposes a comprehensive civil rights bill.

- **August 28**
  King delivers his "I Have a Dream" Speech at the March on Washington for Jobs and Freedom.

(April 12) he, the Reverend Ralph Abernathy, and more than fifty other demonstrators were arrested. They were taken to the Birmingham City Jail, where King was placed in solitary confinement.

On April 12 a statement by eight white clergymen—a rabbi, a Catholic bishop, and six prominent Protestant leaders—appeared in the *Birmingham News* under the title "A Call for Unity." They characterized the demonstrations as "unwise and untimely" and claimed that the protests were likely to "incite to hatred and violence." The authors praised the Birmingham media and police for the "calm manner" in which they handled the civil rights forces and urged blacks to withdraw their support from King's efforts. They implied that King should return to Atlanta and allow local residents to resolve their differences without outside interference.

King probably read the churchmen's declaration in a newspaper smuggled into his cell. Taylor Branch, author of *Parting the Waters: America in the King Years, 1954–63*, credits Harvey Shapiro, an editor for the *New York Times Magazine*, for planting the idea that King write a letter from prison during the Albany campaign. That message never materialized, but now King realized the time was right. Almost immediately he began formulating a response. When King's lawyer, Clarence Jones, visited him on April 16, the jailed civil rights leader handed Jones the newspaper with his notes scribbled in the margins. S. Jonathan Bass, author of *Blessed Are the Peacemakers: Martin Luther King, Jr., Eight White Religious Leaders, and the "Letter from Birmingham Jail,"* describes what happened next. The Reverend Wyatt T. Walker, SCLC executive director, deciphered King's "chicken scratch" handwriting and dictated to his secretary, Willie Pearl Mackey, who typed the first rough copy. Lawyers returned the draft to King, who continued writing on scraps of paper provided by a black jail trustee. When he was released from jail on April 20, the bulk of the letter was composed, but King, according to Bass, "continued writing, editing, and revising drafts several days after the date on the manuscript."

The SCLC sent the letter to national media in early May, but there was little immediate reaction. The *New York Post* printed excerpts in its May 19 edition. The American Friends Service Committee published the full text of the letter as a pamphlet on May 28. It subsequently appeared in *Christian Century*, the *New Leader*, *Atlantic Monthly*, and *Ebony*. A slightly revised version was included in King's 1964 book *Why We Can't Wait*.

About the Author

Martin Luther King, Jr., was the preeminent leader of the modern civil rights movement. His philosophy of nonviolent direct action and inspirational oratory helped overthrow the Jim Crow system of racial segregation and win greater rights for African Americans.

King was born in Atlanta, Georgia, on January 15, 1929, the son, grandson, and great-grandson of Baptist ministers. He was educated at Morehouse College and Crozier Theological Seminary. He studied philosophy at Boston University, receiving his doctorate in 1955.

In 1953 he married Coretta Scott, and together they had four children. Also in 1953 he accepted the pastorate of Dexter Avenue Baptist Church in Montgomery, Alabama. After Rosa Parks was arrested on December 1, 1955, for refusing to give up her bus seat to a white passenger, King was persuaded to head the Montgomery Improvement Association, an organization formed to coordinate the 381-day boycott of city buses. King's successful leadership of the boycott and his application of Gandhian nonviolence to civil rights issues thrust him into national prominence.

King and other African American ministers formed the SCLC in 1957 to expand the struggle against racial segregation in the South. In 1962 King and the SCLC suffered a major defeat in Albany, Georgia, where months of demonstrations had failed to desegregate any public facilities. Mass protests in Birmingham produced a more successful outcome. In response to growing pressure for legislative action, President John F. Kennedy introduced a comprehensive civil rights bill. On August 28, 1963, King delivered his "I Have a Dream" Speech before two hundred and fifty thousand people assembled for the March on Washington. He was named *Time* magazine's "Man of the Year" for 1963 and was awarded the Nobel Peace Prize in 1964.

King and the SCLC focused on voting rights in 1965. Selma, Alabama, was targeted for demonstrations because of white authorities' determined opposition to African American voter registration. A vicious attack by Alabama state troopers on nonviolent protesters drew national attention. King then led marchers from Selma to Montgomery to press for national voting rights legislation. President Lyndon B. Johnson responded by sponsoring the Voting Rights Act, which became law that summer. In subsequent years King extended his crusade beyond the South, tackling slum housing in Chicago in 1966, declaring his opposition to the Vietnam War in 1967, and calling for a Poor People's Campaign for economic justice in 1968. King was assassinated in Memphis, Tennessee, on April 4, 1968, while supporting a strike by sanitation workers. In 1983 Congress declared King's birthday a national holiday.

Explanation and Analysis of the Document

King establishes a tone of rational dialogue as he begins his letter to the eight clergymen. He explains that he rarely responds to critics, but since they are "men of genuine good will" who are sincere in their criticism, he is making an exception. He hopes that they will find his remarks "patient and reasonable." Because they had questioned his presence in Birmingham, he relates that he was invited to their city by the Alabama Christian Movement for Human Rights. A more compelling reason, however, was the pervasive racial oppression in Birmingham. King compares himself to the apostle Paul, who spread the Christian faith among the Gentiles. Paul traveled more widely than any of

Time Line

1963
- **September 15**
  Birmingham's 16th Street Baptist Church is bombed, killing four young girls attending Sunday school.

1964
- **July 2**
  President Lyndon B. Johnson signs the Civil Rights Act of 1964.
- **December 10**
  King is awarded the Nobel Peace Prize in Oslo, Norway.

1968
- **April 4**
  King is assassinated in Memphis, Tennessee.

1983
- **November 2**
  King's birthday is declared a national holiday.

the early Christian missionaries, preaching and establishing churches throughout Greece and Asia Minor. The "Macedonian call" mentioned in the third paragraph refers to Acts 16:9, in which a man appears to Paul in a dream, asking him to "come over into Macedonia, and help us." During his journeys Paul was persecuted for spreading unpopular beliefs and spent more than four years in prison before being executed by Roman authorities. Three of his famous epistles were written from jail. King justifies his arrest by invoking Paul's sufferings—an example that the Christian ministers could appreciate. He further defends his presence in Alabama by citing the "interrelatedness of all communities." King asserts that people living outside Alabama cannot ignore blatant racism in Birmingham. Every citizen has an obligation to act against injustice wherever it may be found, King explains. Those who consider him an "outside agitator" reveal their own "narrow, provincial" outlook.

King takes the clergymen to task for their statement deploring the Birmingham demonstrations. Instead of worrying about threats to public order, they should be concerned about racism and inequality in their city—the "underlying causes" that gave rise to the African American protests. Because the white leadership had been unresponsive to repeated appeals to dismantle the Jim Crow system, King contends that black citizens of Birmingham had "no alternative" other than to take to the streets.

King goes on to outline the stages of his nonviolent crusade. Fact finding was the first phase. Among the damaging information uncovered were Birmingham's long history of unpunished attacks on its black citizens and the failure of city fathers to negotiate in good faith with civil rights advocates. King reminds the clergymen that Birmingham merchants had not honored an earlier agreement to remove Jim Crow signs from their stores. African American activists also were mindful of the need to defeat Connor and thus delayed their demonstrations until the conclusion of the runoff election. Now the merchants must deal with the economic consequences of protests timed to coincide with the Easter shopping season. These actions were not irresponsible, King insists. Rather, black leaders exercised great restraint in the face of numerous provocations.

The second stage was negotiation. The clergymen had criticized King for resorting to confrontation instead of negotiating to achieve his goals. King claims that he, too, desires negotiation but explains that sometimes pressure must be applied to bring reluctant parties to the bargaining table. Rather than avoiding conflict and tension, he freely admits his intention to create a crisis in order to expose the evils of segregation. In support of his position, he cites Socrates, who maintained that mental tension stimulates intellectual growth.

The eight Birmingham clerics had claimed that the Birmingham demonstrations were "untimely." They were not the only observers voicing this objection. Attorney General Robert Kennedy and the *Washington Post*, among others, had complained that the new Boutwell administration should be given a chance to show that it was more open to change than the outgoing Connor regime. King rejects this reasoning. He maintains that those in positions of power cannot be expected to surrender their privileges voluntarily; they must be persuaded forcefully to do the right thing. In this assertion, he echoes the words of the great abolitionist Frederick Douglass, who said, "Power concedes nothing without a demand. It never did and it never will." He also cites the Protestant theologian Reinhold Niebuhr to support his contention that change is more difficult for groups than for individuals.

King points out that any action disrupting the status quo is likely to be considered poorly timed by those who are comfortable with existing arrangements. For those suffering from oppression, however, change cannot come soon enough. He then launches into an eloquent defense of his movement by concentrating on the word *wait*. Whites who counsel patience in the quest for civil rights, he asserts, have not personally experienced the harsh sting of discrimination. King explains why he and other African Americans are unwilling to slow the pace of their crusade. He quotes the nineteenth-century British jurist and prime minister William Gladstone, saying that "'justice … delayed is justice denied.'" To drive home the devastating impact of segregation, he recites a weary litany of potent examples of the injuries inflicted by racism. These range from lynch mobs to whites' refusal to use courtesy titles when addressing African Americans. Perhaps the most poignant is the plight of a black father who must explain to his young daughter why she cannot attend the amusement park she has seen advertised on television. One wonders whether this girl is one of King's own children.

At the conclusion of this powerful passage, he pleads with the clergymen to understand the "legitimate and unavoidable impatience" felt by African Americans.

King next addresses the most difficult question raised by the Birmingham clergymen: How can he encourage his followers to violate some laws and at the same time urge whites to observe such legal decisions as *Brown v. Board of Education*? Here he draws on the concept of "natural law" developed by Saint Thomas Aquinas and other Catholic philosophers. A man-made law is just if it accords with the divinely established code to uplift the human spirit. All such laws should be obeyed. King cites the Jewish philosopher Martin Buber and the Protestant theologian Paul Tillich to give ecumenical sanction to his contention that segregation laws are immoral and therefore should not be obeyed. Other examples of unjust laws are those applied to one group (African Americans) but not another (whites) and laws adopted by legislatures, such as Alabama's, that exclude participation by large numbers of their citizens. Laws also may be unjust if used to deprive citizens of their constitutionally guaranteed rights.

King maintains that those who advocate civil disobedience do not contribute to anarchy. In the tradition of Henry David Thoreau and Mahatma Gandhi, he asserts that those who violate unjust laws must do so "openly, lovingly, and with a willingness to accept the penalty." Rather than expressing defiance, the protestor shows respect for the law by acting to remove injustice from a community. King cites several well-known examples of civil disobedience of which the eight clergymen would most certainly approve. These include the biblical story from the book of Daniel in which Shadrach, Meshach, and Abednego are cast into a fiery furnace for refusing to worship the golden idol erected by the Babylonian king Nebuchadnezzar. King contends that in the modern era religious people have a moral duty to confront Hitler's anti-Semitic codes and the atheistic decrees of Communist regimes.

The longest section of the letter addresses the role of the white moderate in the struggle for civil rights. King hits hard at the clergymen who objected to the Birmingham demonstrations, expressing his frustration with liberals who claimed to support the goal of equal rights while objecting to the methods of the movement. He accuses them of being almost as harmful as members of the Ku Klux Klan or the White Citizens' Council, a supremacist organization. The main reason for King's impatience is the moderates' frequently expressed insistence that change must be peaceful and orderly. These critics of the movement fail to understand the true source of the conflicts that surface during civil rights protests. These conflicts are not caused by those participating in civil disobedience; rather, the demonstrations bring to the surface long-standing community tensions. If they are to be resolved, they must first be exposed to public scrutiny.

Many detractors also denounced civil rights activists for precipitating violence from those opposed to integration. King has no patience with this line of reasoning. Accusing nonviolent demonstrators of causing violence is a classic

Two robed ministers lead a line of protesters in a racial demonstration in Birmingham, Alabama, April 14, 1963.
(AP/Wide World Photos)

example of blaming the victim. According to King, these critics suffer from distorted vision; they should defend those being attacked and condemn their attackers.

White moderates frequently argued that civil rights advocates like King were pressing too hard to transform southern society. If only African Americans could be more patient, they insisted, change would come in time. King forcefully rebuts this argument. Time is neutral, King insists; it can be used for good or evil. There is nothing inevitable about progress; the passage of time does not guarantee the solution of social problems. People of goodwill cannot afford to be silent in the face of injustice; they must "use time creatively" to realize "the promise of democracy."

The eight clergymen had described the Birmingham protestors as extremists. King at first repudiates this label.

Rather than viewing himself as an extremist, he claims that he is a moderate caught between Uncle Toms who have acquiesced to segregation and the Black Muslims who charge that the white man is "the devil." In this context, the true extremists are those advocating separation from American society. Believers in nonviolent, direct action seek inclusion in the larger community, not its destruction. To call them extremists is an error. King even argues that demonstrations against segregation have therapeutic value. They allow African Americans to release their many "pent-up resentments and latent frustrations." Whites should not see them as a threat to the status quo but as a creative alternative to mass violence.

After considering the extremist label, however, King reverses course and embraces it. "Was not Jesus an extremist?" he asks. He then recites a long list of heroic figures who could be considered extremists: the Old Testament prophet Amos; the New Testament evangelist Paul; the Christian reformer Martin Luther; the English preacher and writer John Bunyan; Abraham Lincoln, who ended slavery; and Thomas Jefferson, author of the Declaration of Independence. All of these men were seen as extremists in their time. King implies that the United States needs more visionaries of this sort.

Although King harshly criticizes those moderates who had failed to defend the civil rights movement, he praises a handful of southern whites who risked persecution and ostracism by their public support of the movement. These people include the Atlanta editor Ralph McGill, the Georgia novelist Lillian Smith, the North Carolina writer Harry Golden, the South Carolina author James McBride Dabbs, the Alabama journalist Anne Braden, and Sarah Patton Boyle, who advocated racial integration in Virginia schools.

King then launches a sustained critique of established religion in the South. He acknowledges a few instances of courageous action by white churches, but these are "notable exceptions." During the Montgomery bus boycott, for example, the leaders of white congregations remained silent or actively opposed the protest. The same was true in Birmingham, where King's organization reached out to white denominations but was consistently rebuffed. King scorns the view that religion should focus solely on the hereafter and avoid involvement in social issues. He squarely embraces the Social Gospel tradition that calls upon Christians to work for the welfare of their fellow humans. The South was known for its strong religious institutions, yet King notes the ironic correlation of high rates of church membership and the popularity of racist governors, like Mississippi's Ross Barnett and Alabama's George Wallace. As the scion of a long line of Baptist ministers, King confesses his love of the church and, at the same time, his deep disappointment in it. He calls upon his white brethren to emulate early Christians who were not afraid to become "disturbers of the peace" while following their divine calling. A few members of the clergy had joined the movement in confronting segregation in the South, but not nearly enough. Nevertheless, despite the opposition of organized religion, King expresses confidence that the movement he leads eventually will be victorious because both the principles of American democracy and the "eternal will of God" require it.

King's final paragraphs dwell on the clergymen's ironic praise of the Birmingham police force for keeping order during the demonstrations. Three weeks after their statement was published, Connor ordered his men to turn police dogs and fire hoses on peaceful demonstrators, revealing to the world the lengths to which Alabama segregationists were willing to go in defense of the Jim Crow system. King points out that the police may have been restrained in public but were harsh in their treatment of jailed activists. He faults the ministers for not praising the discipline and courage of the African American protestors, who remained nonviolent in the face of great provocation. King's clerical critics reveal their one-sided perspective when they defend the white guardians of racial privilege and consistently find fault with those who seek to change this oppressive system.

King closes his letter on a brotherly note, apologizing for the length of his missive and asking for understanding. He expresses the hope that one day they may be able to meet person to person without the antagonism and misunderstanding that currently surround them.

Audience

Although the "Letter from Birmingham Jail" was nominally addressed to the eight white clergymen who had publicly urged African Americans to curtail their Birmingham demonstrations, King had a much wider audience in mind; his letter was produced for national consumption. Specifically, his letter was intended to answer his critics, especially white liberals who questioned the timing of his decision to initiate sit-ins, pickets, and marches following the electoral defeat of Connor. More generally, King hoped to explain the religious and philosophical foundations of nonviolent, direct action to all who shared his Judeo-Christian beliefs.

Impact

King's "Letter from Birmingham Jail" had no direct effect on his Birmingham campaign, since most issues were resolved prior to its publication. The eight white clergymen felt that King had singled them out unfairly. For the rest of their lives they would be known as the men who publicly chastised King. As the letter reached a larger audience, support for civil rights legislation began to swell. Liberal white religious organizations, especially the National Council of Churches, responded by unequivocally endorsing the movement's goals. Religious groups played a critical role in lobbying Congress on behalf of the 1964 Civil Rights Act. When King called upon church leaders to join him for the 1965 march from Selma to Montgomery, hundreds of ministers, rabbis, priests, and nuns came to Alabama to participate in the protest. Their consciences no doubt had been pricked by King's letter.

King's "Letter from Birmingham Jail" has been hailed as the most important written document of the modern civil rights struggle. In it King set forth in prophetic language the aspirations of African Americans to be accepted as human beings entitled to the same respect and rights as other Americans. He articulated the objectives of his movement and offered an eloquent defense of civil disobedience and nonviolent, direct action. His letter has been included in anthologies alongside the classic works of Thoreau and Gandhi. King's words and example have inspired people fighting for freedom around the world, from workers in Poland's Solidarity movement to Chinese students in Beijing's Tiananmen Square.

See also Martin Luther King, Jr.: "I Have a Dream" (1963); John F. Kennedy's Civil Rights Address (1963).

Essential Quotes

"Injustice anywhere is a threat to justice everywhere. We are caught in an inescapable network of mutuality, tied in a single garment of destiny. Whatever affects one directly, affects all indirectly."

(Paragraph 4)

"Nonviolent direct action seeks to create such a crisis and foster such a tension that a community that has constantly refused to negotiate is forced to confront the issue. It seeks to so dramatize the issue that it can no longer be ignored."

(Paragraph 10)

"We have not made a single gain in civil rights without determined legal and nonviolent pressure. Lamentably, it is an historical fact that privileged groups seldom give up their privileges voluntarily."

(Paragraph 12)

"We know through painful experience that freedom is never voluntarily given by the oppressor; it must be demanded by the oppressed. Frankly, I have yet to engage in a direct-action campaign that was 'well timed' in the view of those who have not suffered unduly from the disease of segregation. For years now I have heard the word 'Wait!' It rings in the ear of every Negro with piercing familiarity. This 'Wait' has almost always meant 'Never.'"

(Paragraph 13)

"One who breaks an unjust law must do so openly, lovingly, and with a willingness to accept the penalty. I submit that an individual who breaks a law that conscience tells him is unjust, and who willingly accepts the penalty of imprisonment in order to arouse the conscience of the community over its injustice, is in reality expressing the highest respect for law."

(Paragraph 20)

"I must confess that over the past few years I have been gravely disappointed with the white moderate ... who is more devoted to 'order' than to justice."

(Paragraph 23)

Further Reading

■ Articles

Colaiaco, James A. "The American Dream Unfulfilled: Martin Luther King, Jr., and the 'Letter from Birmingham Jail.'" *Phylon* 45 (1984): 1–18.

Mott, Wesley T. "The Rhetoric of Martin Luther King, Jr.: Letter from Birmingham Jail." *Phylon* 36 (1975): 411–421.

■ Books

Bass, S. Jonathan. *Blessed Are the Peacemakers: Martin Luther King, Jr., Eight White Clergymen, and the "Letter from Birmingham Jail."* Baton Rouge: Louisiana State University Press, 2001.

Branch, Taylor. *Parting the Waters: America in the King Years, 1954–63.* New York: Simon & Schuster, 1988.

Durham, Michael S. *Powerful Days: The Civil Rights Photography of Charles Moore.* New York: Stewart, Tabori & Chang, 1991.

Eskew, Glenn T. *But for Birmingham: The Local and National Movements in the Civil Rights Struggle.* Chapel Hill: University of North Carolina Press, 1997.

Garrow, David J. *Bearing the Cross: Martin Luther King, Jr., and the Southern Christian Leadership Conference, 1955–1968.* New York: William Morrow, 1986.

———, ed. *Birmingham, Alabama, 1956–1963: The Black Struggle for Civil Rights.* New York: Carlson Publishing, 1989.

King, Martin Luther, Jr. *Why We Can't Wait.* New York: Signet Books, 1964.

Manis, Andrew M. *A Fire You Can't Put Out: The Civil Rights Life of Birmingham's Reverend Fred Shuttlesworth.* Tuscaloosa: University of Alabama Press, 1999.

McWhorter, Diane. *Carry Me Home: Birmingham, Alabama—The Climactic Battle of the Civil Rights Revolution.* New York: Simon & Schuster, 2001.

Washington, James M., ed. *A Testament of Hope: The Essential Writings of Martin Luther King, Jr..* San Francisco: Harper & Row, 1986.

■ Web Sites

Douglass, Frederick. "The Significance of Emancipation." The International Endowment for Democracy Web site.
http://www.iefd.org/manifestos/significance_of_emancipation.php

"Statement by Alabama Clergymen." The Martin Luther King, Jr., Research and Education Institute Web site.
http://www.stanford.edu/group/King/frequentdocs/clergy.pdf.

Thoreau, Henry David. "On Civil Disobedience." The Thoreau Reader Web site.
http://thoreau.eserver.org/civil.html.

—Paul T. Murray

Questions for Further Study

1. King argues that a person is justified in breaking unjust laws, but how does one distinguish between just and unjust laws? What are some examples of unjust laws in contemporary society?

2. In Birmingham nonviolent demonstrators repeatedly confronted the police, who eventually responded with police dogs and fire hoses. In this case, were the demonstrators guilty of provoking the police? To what extent, if any, were the demonstrators responsible for this violence?

3. King's critics often said that he pushed too hard for change and that he should have allowed his opponents more time to adjust to the social changes he advocated. Why did King reject these arguments? In his opinion, who should determine the timetable for social change? Why?

4. King often was accused of being an "extremist." Is this charge accurate? Why did King both reject and embrace this label?

5. In his letter, King takes white churches to task for not openly denouncing the evil of segregation, yet many ministers maintain that religious organizations should not take sides in partisan political issues. What is the proper role of the church in social issues? Should churches become involved in movements for social change? Why or why not?

Martin Luther King, Jr.: "Letter from Birmingham Jail"

My Dear Fellow Clergymen:

While confined here in the Birmingham city jail, I came across your recent statement calling my present activities "unwise and untimely." Seldom do I pause to answer criticism of my work and ideas. If I sought to answer all the criticisms that cross my desk, my secretaries would have little time for anything other than such correspondence in the course of the day, and I would have no time for constructive work. But since I feel that you are men of genuine good will and that your criticisms are sincerely set forth, I want to try to answer your statements in what I hope will be patient and reasonable terms.

I think I should indicate why I am here In Birmingham, since you have been influenced by the view which argues against "outsiders coming in." I have the honor of serving as president of the Southern Christian Leadership Conference, an organization operating in every southern state, with headquarters in Atlanta, Georgia. We have some eighty-five affiliated organizations across the South, and one of them is the Alabama Christian Movement for Human Rights. Frequently we share staff, educational and financial resources with our affiliates. Several months ago the affiliate here in Birmingham asked us to be on call to engage in a nonviolent direct-action program if such were deemed necessary. We readily consented, and when the hour came we lived up to our promise. So I, along with several members of my staff, am here because I was invited here. I am here because I have organizational ties here.

But more basically, I am in Birmingham because injustice is here. Just as the prophets of the eighth century B.C. left their villages and carried their "thus saith the Lord" far beyond the boundaries of their home towns, and just as the Apostle Paul left his village of Tarsus and carried the gospel of Jesus Christ to the far corners of the Greco-Roman world, so am I compelled to carry the gospel of freedom beyond my own home town. Like Paul, I must constantly respond to the Macedonian call for aid.

Moreover, I am cognizant of the interrelatedness of all communities and states. I cannot sit idly by in Atlanta and not be concerned about what happens in Birmingham. Injustice anywhere is a threat to justice everywhere. We are caught in an inescapable network of mutuality, tied in a single garment of destiny. Whatever affects one directly, affects all indirectly. Never again can we afford to live with the narrow, provincial "outside agitator" idea. Anyone who lives inside the United States can never be considered an outsider anywhere within its bounds.

You deplore the demonstrations taking place in Birmingham. But your statement, I am sorry to say, fails to express a similar concern for the conditions that brought about the demonstrations. I am sure that none of you would want to rest content with the superficial kind of social analysis that deals merely with effects and does not grapple with underlying causes. It is unfortunate that demonstrations are taking place in Birmingham, but it is even more unfortunate that the city's white power structure left the Negro community with no alternative.

In any nonviolent campaign there are four basic steps: collection of the facts to determine whether injustices exist; negotiation; self-purification; and direct action. We have gone through all these steps in Birmingham. There can be no gainsaying the fact that racial injustice engulfs this community. Birmingham is probably the most thoroughly segregated city in the United States. Its ugly record of brutality is widely known. Negroes have experienced grossly unjust treatment in the courts. There have been more unsolved bombings of Negro homes and churches in Birmingham than in any other city in the nation. These are the hard, brutal facts of the case. On the basis of these conditions, Negro leaders sought to negotiate with the city fathers. But the latter consistently refused to engage in good-faith negotiation

Then, last September, came the opportunity to talk with leaders of Birmingham's economic community. In the course of the negotiations, certain promises were made by the merchants—for example, to remove the stores' humiliating racial signs. On the basis of these promises, the Reverend Fred Shuttlesworth and the leaders of the Alabama Christian Movement for Human Rights agreed to a moratorium on all demonstrations. As the weeks and months went by, we realized that we were the victims of a broken promise. A few signs, briefly removed, returned; the others remained.

Document Text

As in so many past experiences, our hopes had been blasted, and the shadow of deep disappointment settled upon us. We had no alternative except to prepare for direct action, whereby we would present our very bodies as a means of laying our case before the conscience of the local and the national community. Mindful of the difficulties involved, we decided to undertake a process of self-purification. We began a series of workshops on nonviolence, and we repeatedly asked ourselves: "Are you able to accept blows without retaliating?" "Are you able to endure the ordeal of jail?" We decided to schedule our direct-action program for the Easter season, realizing that except for Christmas, this is the main shopping period of the year. Knowing that a strong economic withdrawal program would be the by-product of direct action, we felt that this would be the best time to bring pressure to bear on the merchants for the needed change.

Then it occurred to us that Birmingham's mayoralty election was coming up in March, and we speedily decided to postpone action until after election day. When we discovered that the Commissioner of Public Safety, Eugene "Bull" Connor, had piled up enough votes to be in the run-off, we decided again to postpone action until the day after the run-off so that the demonstrations could not be used to cloud the issues. Like many others, we waited to see Mr. Connor defeated, and to this end we endured postponement after postponement. Having aided in this community need, we felt that our direct-action program could be delayed no longer.

You may well ask: "Why direct action? Why sit-ins, marches and so forth? Isn't negotiation a better path?" You are quite right in calling for negotiation. Indeed, this is the very purpose of direct action. Nonviolent direct action seeks to create such a crisis and foster such a tension that a community which has constantly refused to negotiate is forced to confront the issue. It seeks so to dramatize the issue that it can no longer be ignored. My citing the creation of tension as part of the work of the nonviolent-resister may sound rather shocking. But I must confess that I am not afraid of the word "tension." I have earnestly opposed violent tension, but there is a type of constructive, nonviolent tension which is necessary for growth. Just as Socrates felt that it was necessary to create a tension in the mind so that individuals could rise from the bondage of myths and half-truths to the unfettered realm of creative analysis and objective appraisal, so must we see the need for nonviolent gadflies to create the kind of tension in society that will help men rise from the dark depths of prejudice and racism to the majestic heights of understanding and brotherhood.

The purpose of our direct-action program is to create a situation so crisis-packed that it will inevitably open the door to negotiation. I therefore concur with you in your call for negotiation. Too long has our beloved Southland been bogged down in a tragic effort to live in monologue rather than dialogue.

One of the basic points in your statement is that the action that I and my associates have taken in Birmingham is untimely. Some have asked: "Why didn't you give the new city administration time to act?" The only answer that I can give to this query is that the new Birmingham administration must be prodded about as much as the outgoing one, before it will act. We are sadly mistaken if we feel that the election of Albert Boutwell as mayor will bring the millennium to Birmingham. While Mr. Boutwell is a much more gentle person than Mr. Connor, they are both segregationists, dedicated to maintenance of the status quo. I have hope that Mr. Boutwell will be reasonable enough to see the futility of massive resistance to desegregation. But he will not see this without pressure from devotees of civil rights. My friends, I must say to you that we have not made a single gain in civil rights without determined legal and nonviolent pressure. Lamentably, it is an historical fact that privileged groups seldom give up their privileges voluntarily. Individuals may see the moral light and voluntarily give up their unjust posture; but, as Reinhold Niebuhr has reminded us, groups tend to be more immoral than individuals.

We know through painful experience that freedom is never voluntarily given by the oppressor; it must be demanded by the oppressed. Frankly, I have yet to engage in a direct-action campaign that was "well timed" in the view of those who have not suffered unduly from the disease of segregation. For years now I have heard the word "Wait!" It rings in the ear of every Negro with piercing familiarity. This "Wait" has almost always meant "Never." We must come to see, with one of our distinguished jurists, that "justice too long delayed is justice denied."

We have waited for more than 340 years for our constitutional and God-given rights. The nations of Asia and Africa are moving with jetlike speed toward gaining political independence, but we still creep at horse-and-buggy pace toward gaining a cup of coffee at a lunch counter. Perhaps it is easy for those who have never felt the stinging darts of segregation to say, "Wait." But when you have seen vicious mobs lynch your mothers and fathers at will and drown your sisters and brothers at whim; when you have seen hate-filled policemen curse, kick and even kill your black brothers and sisters; when you see the vast majority of your twenty million Negro brothers smothering in an airtight cage of poverty in the midst of an affluent society; when you suddenly find your tongue twisted and your speech stammering as you seek to explain to your six-year-old daughter why she can't go to the public amusement park that has just been advertised on television, and see tears welling up in her eyes when she is told that Funtown is closed to colored children, and see ominous clouds of inferiority beginning to form in her little mental sky, and see her beginning to distort her personality by developing an unconscious bitterness toward white people; when you have to concoct an answer for a five-year-old son who is asking: "Daddy, why do white people treat colored people so mean?"; when you take a cross-county drive and find it necessary to sleep night after night in the uncomfortable corners of your automobile because no motel will accept you; when you are humiliated day in and day out by nagging signs reading "white" and "colored"; when your first name becomes "nigger," your middle name becomes "boy" (however old you are) and your last name becomes "John," and your wife and mother are never given the respected title "Mrs."; when you are harried by day and haunted by night by the fact that you are a Negro, living constantly at tiptoe stance, never quite knowing what to expect next, and are plagued with inner fears and outer resentments; when you are forever fighting a degenerating sense of "nobodiness"—then you will understand why we find it difficult to wait. There comes a time when the cup of endurance runs over, and men are no longer willing to be plunged into the abyss of despair. I hope, sirs, you can understand our legitimate and unavoidable impatience.

You express a great deal of anxiety over our willingness to break laws. This is certainly a legitimate concern. Since we so diligently urge people to obey the Supreme Court's decision of 1954 outlawing segregation in the public schools, at first glance it may seem rather paradoxical for us consciously to break laws. One may well ask: "How can you advocate breaking some laws and obeying others?" The answer lies in the fact that there are two types of laws: just and unjust. I would be the first to advocate obeying just laws. One has not only a legal but a moral responsibility to obey just laws. Conversely, one has a moral responsibility to disobey unjust laws. I would agree with St. Augustine that "an unjust law is no law at all."

Now, what is the difference between the two? How does one determine whether a law is just or unjust? A just law is a man-made code that squares with the moral law or the law of God. An unjust law is a code that is out of harmony with the moral law. To put it in the terms of St. Thomas Aquinas: An unjust law is a human law that is not rooted in eternal law and natural law. Any law that uplifts human personality is just. Any law that degrades human personality is unjust. All segregation statutes are unjust because segregation distorts the soul and damages the personality. It gives the segregator a false sense of superiority and the segregated a false sense of inferiority. Segregation, to use the terminology of the Jewish philosopher Martin Buber, substitutes an "I-it" relationship for an "I-thou" relationship and ends up relegating persons to the status of things. Hence segregation is not only politically, economically and sociologically unsound, it is morally wrong and sinful. Paul Tillich has said that sin is separation. Is not segregation an existential expression of man's tragic separation, his awful estrangement, his terrible sinfulness? Thus it is that I can urge men to obey the 1954 decision of the Supreme Court, for it is morally right; and I can urge them to disobey segregation ordinances, for they are morally wrong.

Let us consider a more concrete example of just and unjust laws. An unjust law is a code that a numerical or power majority group compels a minority group to obey but does not make binding on itself. This is *difference* made legal. By the same token, a just law is a code that a majority compels a minority to follow and that it is willing to follow itself. This is *sameness* made legal.

Let me give another explanation. A law is unjust if it is inflicted on a minority that, as a result of being denied the right to vote, had no part in enacting or devising the law. Who can say that the legislature of Alabama which set up that state's segregation laws was democratically elected? Throughout Alabama all sorts of devious methods are used to prevent Negroes from becoming registered voters, and there are some counties in which, even though Negroes constitute a majority of the population, not a single Negro is registered. Can any law enacted under such circumstances be considered democratically structured?

Sometimes a law is just on its face and unjust in its application. For instance, I have been arrested on a charge of parading without a permit. Now, there is nothing wrong in having an ordinance which requires a permit for a parade. But such an ordinance becomes unjust when it is used to maintain segregation and to deny citizens the First-Amendment privilege of peaceful assembly and protest.

I hope you are able to see the distinction I am trying to point out. In no sense do I advocate evading or defying the law, as would the rabid segregationist. That would lead to anarchy. One who breaks an unjust law must do so openly, lovingly, and with a willingness to accept the penalty. I submit that an individual who breaks a law that conscience tells him is unjust, and who willingly accepts the penalty of imprisonment in order to arouse the conscience of the community over its injustice, is in reality expressing the highest respect for law.

Of course, there is nothing new about this kind of civil disobedience. It was evidenced sublimely in the refusal of Shadrach, Meshach and Abednego to obey the laws of Nebuchadnezzar, on the ground that a higher moral law was at stake. It was practiced superbly by the early Christians, who were willing to face hungry lions and the excruciating pain of chopping blocks rather than submit to certain unjust laws of the Roman Empire. To a degree, academic freedom is a reality today because Socrates practiced civil disobedience. In our own nation, the Boston Tea Party represented a massive act of civil disobedience.

We should never forget that everything Adolf Hitler did in Germany was "legal" and everything the Hungarian freedom fighters did in Hungary was "illegal." It was "illegal" to aid and comfort a Jew in Hitler's Germany. Even so, I am sure that, had I lived in Germany at the time, I would have aided and comforted my Jewish brothers. If today I lived in a Communist country where certain principles dear to the Christian faith are suppressed, I would openly advocate disobeying that country's antireligious laws.

I must make two honest confessions to you, my Christian and Jewish brothers. First, I must confess that over the past few years I have been gravely disappointed with the white moderate. I have almost reached the regrettable conclusion that the Negro's great stumbling block in his stride toward freedom is not the White Citizens Counciler or the Ku Klux Klanner, but the white moderate, who is more devoted to "order" than to justice; who prefers a negative peace which is the absence of tension to a positive peace which is the presence of justice; who constantly says: "I agree with you in the goal you seek, but I cannot agree with your methods of direct action"; who paternalistically believes he can set the timetable for another man's freedom; who lives by a mythical concept of time and who constantly advises the Negro to wait for a "more convenient season."

Shallow understanding from people of good will is more frustrating than absolute misunderstanding from people of ill will. Lukewarm acceptance is much more bewildering than outright rejection.

I had hoped that the white moderate would understand that law and order exist for the purpose of establishing justice and that when they fail in this purpose they become the dangerously structured dams that block the flow of social progress. I had hoped that the white moderate would understand that the present tension in the South is a necessary phase of the transition from an obnoxious negative peace, in which the Negro passively accepted his unjust plight, to a substantive and positive peace, in which all men will respect the dignity and worth of human personality Actually, we who engage in nonviolent direct action are not the creators of tension. We merely bring to the surface the hidden tension that is already alive. We bring it out in the open, where it can be seen and dealt with. Like a boil that can never be cured so long as it is covered up but must be opened with all its ugliness to the natural medicines of air and light, injustice must be exposed, with all the tension its exposure creates, to the light of human conscience and the air of national opinion before it can be cured.

In your statement you assert that our actions, even though peaceful, must be condemned because they precipitate violence. But is this a logical assertion? Isn't this like condemning a robbed man because his possession of money precipitated the evil act of robbery? Isn't this like condemning Socrates because his unswerving commitment to truth and his philosophical inquiries precipitated the act by the misguided populace in which they made him drink hemlock? Isn't this like condemning Jesus because his unique God-consciousness and never-ceasing devotion to God's will precipitated the evil act of crucifixion? We must come to see that, as the federal courts have consistently affirmed, it is wrong to urge an individual to cease his efforts to gain his basic constitutional rights because the quest may precipitate violence. Society must protect the robbed and punish the robber.

I had also hoped that the white moderate would reject the myth concerning time in relation to the struggle for freedom. I have just received a letter from a white brother in Texas. He writes: "All Christians know that the colored people will receive equal rights eventually, but it is possible that you are in too great a religious hurry. It has taken Christianity almost two thousand years to accomplish what it has. The teachings of Christ take time to come to earth." Such an attitude stems from a tragic misconception of time, from the strangely irrational notion that there is something in the very flow of time that will inevitably cure all ills. Actually, time itself is neutral; it can be used either destructively or constructively. More and more I feel that the people of ill will have used time much more effectively than have the people of good will. We will have to repent in this generation not merely for the hateful words and actions of the bad people but for the appalling silence of the good people. Human progress never rolls in on wheels of inevitability; it comes through the tireless efforts of men willing to be co-workers with God, and without this hard work, time itself becomes an ally of the forces of social stagnation. We must use time creatively, in the knowledge that the time is always ripe to do right. Now is the time to make real the promise of democracy and transform our pending national elegy into a creative psalm of brotherhood. Now is the time to lift our national policy from the quicksand of racial injustice to the solid rock of human dignity.

You speak of our activity in Birmingham as extreme At first I was rather disappointed that fellow clergymen would see my nonviolent efforts as those of an extremist. I began thinking about the fact that I stand in the middle of two opposing forces in the Negro community. One is a force of complacency, made up in part of Negroes who, as a result of long years of oppression, are so drained of self-respect and a sense of "somebodiness" that they have adjusted to segregation; and in part of a few middle-class Negroes who, because of a degree of academic and economic security and because in some ways they profit by segregation, have become insensitive to the problems of the masses. The other force is one of bitterness and hatred, and it comes perilously close to advocating violence. It is expressed in the various black nationalist groups that are springing up across the nation, the largest and best-known being Elijah Muhammad's Muslim movement. Nourished by the Negro's frustration over the continued existence of racial discrimination, this movement is made up of people who have lost faith in America, who have absolutely repudiated Christianity, and who have concluded that the white man is an incorrigible "devil."

I have tried to stand between these two forces, saying that we need emulate neither the "do-nothingism" of the complacent nor the hatred and despair of the black nationalist. For there is the more excellent way of love and nonviolent protest I am grateful to God that, through the influence of the Negro church, the way of nonviolence became an integral part of our struggle.

If this philosophy had not emerged, by now many streets of the South would, I am convinced, be flowing with blood. And I am further convinced that if our white brothers dismiss as "rabble-rousers" and "outside agitators" those of us who employ nonviolent direct action, and if they refuse to support our nonviolent efforts, millions of Negroes will, out of frustration and despair, seek solace and security in black-nationalist ideologies—a development that would inevitably lead to a frightening racial nightmare.

Oppressed people cannot remain oppressed forever. The yearning for freedom eventually manifests itself, and that is what has happened to the American Negro. Something within has reminded him of his birthright of freedom, and something without has reminded him that it can be gained. Consciously or unconsciously, he has been caught up by the Zeitgeist and with his black brothers of Africa and his brown and yellow brothers of Asia, South America and the Caribbean, the United States Negro is moving with a sense of great urgency toward the promised land of racial justice. If one recognizes this vital urge that has engulfed the Negro community, one should readily understand why public demonstrations are taking place. The Negro has many pent-up resentments and latent frustrations, and he must release them. So let him march; let him make prayer pilgrimages to the city hall; let him go on freedom rides—and try to understand why he must do so. If his repressed emotions are not released in nonviolent ways, they will seek expression through violence; this is not a threat but a fact of history. So I have not said to my people: "Get rid of your discontent." Rather, I have tried to say that this normal and healthy discontent can be channeled into the creative outlet of nonviolent direct action. And now this approach is being termed extremist.

But though I was initially disappointed at being categorized as an extremist, as I continued to think about the matter I gradually gained a measure of satisfaction from the label. Was not Jesus an extremist for love: "Love your enemies, bless them that curse you, do good to them that hate you, and pray for them which despitefully use you, and persecute you." Was not Amos an extremist for justice: "Let justice roll down like waters and righteousness like an ever-flowing stream." Was not Paul an extremist for the Christian gospel: "I bear in my body the marks of the Lord Jesus." Was not Martin Luther an extremist: "Here I stand; I cannot do otherwise, so help me God." And John Bunyan: "I will stay in jail to the end of my days before I make a butchery of my conscience." And Abraham Lincoln: "This nation cannot survive half slave and half free." And Thomas Jefferson: "We hold these truths to be self-evident, that all men are created equal…" So the question is not whether we will be extremists, but what kind of extremists we will be. Will we be extremists for hate or for love? Will we be extremist for the preservation of injustice or for the extension of justice? In that dramatic scene on Calvary's hill three men were crucified. We must never forget that all three were crucified for the same crime—the crime of extremism. Two were extremists for immorality, and thus fell below their environment. The other, Jesus Christ, was an extremist for love, truth and goodness, and thereby rose above his environment. Perhaps the South, the nation and the world are in dire need of creative extremists.

I had hoped that the white moderate would see this need. Perhaps I was too optimistic; perhaps I expected too much. I suppose I should have realized that few members of the oppressor race can understand the deep groans and passionate yearnings of the oppressed race, and still fewer have the vision to see that injustice must be rooted out by strong, persistent and determined action. I am thankful, however, that some of our white brothers in the South have grasped the meaning of this social revolution and committed themselves to it. They are still too few in quantity, but they are big in quality. Some—such as Ralph McGill, Lillian Smith, Harry Golden, James McBride Dabbs, Ann Braden and Sarah Patton Boyle—have written about our struggle in eloquent and prophetic terms. Others have marched with us down nameless streets of the South. They have languished in filthy, roach-infested jails, suffering the abuse and brutality of policemen who view them as "dirty nigger-lovers" Unlike so many of their moderate brothers and sisters, they have recognized the urgency of the moment and sensed the need for powerful "action" antidotes to combat the disease of segregation.

Let me take note of my other major disappointment. I have been so greatly disappointed with the white church and its leadership. Of course, there are some notable exceptions. I am not unmindful of the fact that each of you has taken some significant stands on this issue. I commend you, Reverend Stallings, for your Christian stand on this past Sunday, in welcoming Negroes to your worship service on a nonsegregated basis. I commend the Catholic leaders of this state for integrating Spring Hill College several years ago.

But despite these notable exceptions, I must honestly reiterate that I have been disappointed with the church. I do not say this as one of those negative critics who can always find something wrong with the church. I say this as a minister of the gospel, who loves the church; who was nurtured in its bosom; who has been sustained by its spiritual blessings and who will remain true to it as long as the cord of life shall lengthen.

When I was suddenly catapulted into the leadership of the bus protest in Montgomery, Alabama, a few years ago, I felt we would be supported by the white church. I felt that the white ministers, priests and rabbis of the South would be among our strongest allies. Instead, some have been outright opponents, refusing to understand the freedom movement and misrepresenting its leaders; all too many others have been more cautious than courageous and have remained silent behind the anesthetizing security of stained-glass windows.

In spite of my shattered dreams, I came to Birmingham with the hope that the white religious leadership of this community would see the justice of our cause and, with deep moral concern, would serve as the channel through which our just grievances could reach the power structure. I had hoped that each of you would understand. But again I have been disappointed.

I have heard numerous southern religious leaders admonish their worshipers to comply with a desegregation decision because it is the law, but I have longed to hear white ministers declare: "Follow this decree because integration is morally right and because the Negro is your brother." In the midst of blatant injustices inflicted upon the Negro, I have watched white churchmen stand on the sideline and mouth pious irrelevancies and sanctimonious trivialities. In the midst of a mighty struggle to rid our nation of racial and economic injustice, I have heard many ministers say: "Those are social issues, with which the gospel has no real concern." And I have watched many churches commit themselves to a completely other-worldly religion which makes a strange, un-Biblical distinction between body and soul, between the sacred and the secular.

I have traveled the length and breadth of Alabama, Mississippi and all the other southern states. On sweltering summer days and crisp autumn mornings I have looked at the South's beautiful churches with their lofty spires pointing heavenward. I have beheld the impressive outlines of her massive religious-education buildings. Over and over I have found myself asking: "What kind of people worship here? Who is their God? Where were their voices when the lips of Governor Barnett dripped with words of interposition and nullification? Where were they when Governor Wallace gave a clarion call for defiance and hatred? Where were their voices of support when bruised and weary Negro men and women decided to rise from the dark dungeons of complacency to the bright hills of creative protest?"

Yes these questions are still in my mind. In deep disappointment I have wept over the laxity of the church. But be assured that my tears have been tears of love. There can be no deep disappointment where there is not deep love. Yes, I love the church. How could I do otherwise? I am in the rather unique position of being the son, the grandson and the great-grandson of preachers. Yes, I see the church as the body of Christ. But oh! How we have blemished and scarred that body through social neglect and through fear of being nonconformists.

There was a time when the church was very powerful—in the time when the early Christians rejoiced at being deemed worthy to suffer for what they believed. In those days the church was not merely a thermometer that recorded the ideas and principles of popular opinion; it was a thermostat that transformed the mores of society. Whenever the early Christians entered a town, the people in power became disturbed and immediately sought to convict the Christians for being "disturbers of the peace" and "outside agitators'" But the Christians pressed on, in the conviction that they were "a colony of heaven," called to obey God rather than man. Small in number, they were big in commitment. They were too God-intoxicated to be "astronomically intimidated." By their effort and example they brought an end to such ancient evils as infanticide and gladiatorial contests.

Things are different now. So often the contemporary church is a weak, ineffectual voice with an uncertain sound. So often it is an archdefender of the status quo. Far from being disturbed by the presence of the church, the power structure of the average community is consoled by the church's silent—and often even vocal—sanction of things as they are.

But the judgment of God is upon the church as never before. If today's church does not recapture the sacrificial spirit of the early church, it will lose its authenticity, forfeit the loyalty of millions, and be dismissed as an irrelevant social club with no meaning for the twentieth century. Every day I meet young people whose disappointment with the church has turned into outright disgust.

Perhaps I have once again been too optimistic. Is organized religion too inextricably bound to the status quo to save our nation and the world? Perhaps I must turn my faith to the inner spiritual church, the church within the church, as the true *ekklesia* and the hope of the world. But again I am thankful to God that some noble souls from the ranks of organized religion have broken loose from the paralyzing chains of conformity and joined us as active partners in the struggle for freedom. They have left their secure congregations and walked the streets of Albany, Georgia, with us. They have gone down the highways of the South on tortuous rides for freedom. Yes, they have gone to jail with us. Some have been dismissed from their churches, have lost the support of their bishops and fellow ministers. But they have acted in the faith that right defeated is stronger than evil triumphant. Their witness has been the spiritual salt that has preserved the true meaning of the gospel in these troubled times. They have carved a tunnel of hope through the dark mountain of disappointment.

I hope the church as a whole will meet the challenge of this decisive hour. But even if the church does not come to the aid of justice, I have no despair about the future. I have no fear about the outcome of our struggle in Birmingham, even if our motives are at present misunderstood. We will reach the goal of freedom in Birmingham and all over the nation, because the goal of America is freedom. Abused and scorned though we may be, our destiny is tied up with America's destiny. Before the pilgrims landed at Plymouth, we were here. Before the pen of Jefferson etched the majestic words of the Declaration of Independence across the pages of history, we were here. For more than two centuries our forebears labored in this country without wages; they made cotton king; they built the homes of their masters while suffering gross injustice and shameful humiliation—and yet out of a bottomless vitality they continued to thrive and develop. If the inexpressible cruelties of slavery could not stop us, the opposition we now face will surely fail. We will win our freedom because the sacred heritage of our nation and the eternal will of God are embodied in our echoing demands.

Before closing I feel impelled to mention one other point in your statement that has troubled me profoundly. You warmly commended the Birmingham police force for keeping "order" and "preventing violence." I doubt that you would have so warmly commended the police force if you had seen its dogs sinking their teeth into unarmed, nonviolent Negroes. I doubt that you would so quickly com-

Document Text

mend the policemen if you were to observe their ugly and inhumane treatment of Negroes here in the city jail; if you were to watch them push and curse old Negro women and young Negro girls; if you were to see them slap and kick old Negro men and young boys; if you were to observe them, as they did on two occasions, refuse to give us food because we wanted to sing our grace together. I cannot join you in your praise of the Birmingham police department.

It is true that the police have exercised a degree of discipline in handling the demonstrators. In this sense they have conducted themselves rather "nonviolently" in public. But for what purpose? To preserve the evil system of segregation. Over the past few years I have consistently preached that nonviolence demands that the means we use must be as pure as the ends we seek. I have tried to make clear that it is wrong to use immoral means to attain moral ends. But now I must affirm that it is just as wrong, or perhaps even more so, to use moral means to preserve immoral ends. Perhaps Mr. Connor and his policemen have been rather nonviolent in public, as was Chief Pritchett in Albany, Georgia, but they have used the moral means of nonviolence to maintain the immoral end of racial injustice. As T. S. Eliot has said: "The last temptation is the greatest treason: To do the right deed for the wrong reason."

I wish you had commended the Negro sit-inners and demonstrators of Birmingham for their sublime courage, their willingness to suffer and their amazing discipline in the midst of great provocation. One day the South will recognize its real heroes. They will be the James Merediths, with the noble sense of purpose that enables them to face jeering, and hostile mobs, and with the agonizing loneliness that characterizes the life of the pioneer. They will be old, oppressed, battered Negro women, symbolized in a seventy-two-year-old woman in Montgomery, Alabama, who rose up with a sense of dignity and with her people decided not to ride segregated buses, and who responded with ungrammatical profundity to one who inquired about her weariness: "My feets is tired, but my soul is at rest." They will be the young high school and college students, the young ministers of the gospel and a host of their elders, courageously and nonviolently sitting in at lunch counters and willingly going to jail for conscience' sake. One day the South will know that when these disinherited children of God sat down at lunch counters, they were in reality standing up for what is best in the American dream and for the most sacred values in our Judaeo-Christian heritage, thereby bringing our nation back to those great wells of democracy which were dug deep by the founding fathers in their formulation of the Constitution and the Declaration of Independence.

Never before have I written so long a letter. I'm afraid it is much too long to take your precious time. I can assure you that it would have been much shorter if I had been writing from a comfortable desk, but what else can one do when he is alone in a narrow jail cell, other than write long letters, think long thoughts and pray long prayers?

If I have said anything in this letter that overstates the truth and indicates an unreasonable impatience, I beg you to forgive me. If I have said anything that understates the truth and indicates my having a patience that allows me to settle for anything less than brotherhood, I beg God to forgive me.

I hope this letter finds you strong in the faith. I also hope that circumstances will soon make it possible for me to meet each of you, not as an integrationist or a civil rights leader but as a fellow clergyman and a Christian brother. Let us all hope that the dark clouds of racial prejudice will soon pass away and the deep fog of misunderstanding will be lifted

Glossary

black nationalism	the belief that blacks should live separately from whites
ekklesia	Greek term for a congregation of believers
gainsaying	contradicting
paternalistically	in a fatherly manner exercised authoritatively
sanctimonious	pretending to be pious or righteous
Zeitgeist	German term for "spirit of the times"

Document Text

from our fear-drenched communities, and in some not too distant tomorrow the radiant stars of love and brotherhood will shine over our great nation with all their scintillating beauty.

 Yours for the cause of Peace and Brotherhood,
 Martin Luther King, Jr.

John F. Kennedy (Library of Congress)

John F. Kennedy's Civil Rights Address

"We are confronted primarily with a moral issue."

Overview

The modern American civil rights movement, which began with the Montgomery bus boycott in 1955, was aimed at regaining the ground that had been achieved in the aftermath of the Civil War, such as through the enactment of the Fourteenth and Fifteenth amendments to the U.S. Constitution and of civil rights laws in 1866 and 1875, and moving toward the complete elimination of racial inequality in all its forms. Civil rights organizations pursued a variety of tactics, including lawsuits, boycotts, lobbying, sit-ins, freedom rides, street demonstrations, and marches, in attempts to demand freedom, equality, jobs, dignity, and an end to racial segregation, disfranchisement, and second-class citizenship.

President John F. Kennedy's Civil Rights Address, delivered to the nation by radio and television, marked the first time that a president called on Americans to recognize civil rights as a lofty moral cause to which all persons should contribute, so that the nation might fully end discrimination against and provide equal treatment to African Americans. In 1963, the centennial year of President Abraham Lincoln's Emancipation Proclamation, to which Kennedy alludes in his speech, the movement led by African Americans and their allies for civil rights reached the center stage of American politics. Although Kennedy had hesitated to seek progress with regard to civil rights during his first two years in the White House because of the strength of southern Democratic opponents in Congress, he now added the moral weight of the presidency to the demand for civil rights, and he emerged as an ally of the movement. Kennedy explained the economic, educational, and moral dimensions of racial discrimination and announced that he would be submitting legislation to ensure equal access to public accommodations and to address other aspects of ongoing discrimination. On July 2, 1964, seven months after Kennedy was assassinated, the Civil Rights Act of 1964, abolishing discrimination in public accommodations, employment, and federally funded programs, became law.

Context

Two sets of events in Alabama in the spring of 1963 brought the civil rights movement a new level of public attention. Television viewers witnessed the Birmingham sheriff Eugene "Bull" Connor's use of water hoses and dogs against demonstrators as young as nine years old who were seeking equal access to public accommodations as well as Governor George Wallace's campaign pledge to "stand in the schoolhouse door" to prevent the integration of any Alabama school. On June 11, 1963, President Kennedy ended Wallace's resistance by federalizing the Alabama National Guard to support the court-mandated entry of Vivian J. Malone and James A. Hood to the University of Alabama. The determination of civil rights demonstrators, the violent and repressive actions of Alabama authorities, the solidarity protests galvanized by national civil rights organizations, and widespread public sympathy for the cause led Kennedy to take dramatic action to support civil rights.

In taking to the television and radio airwaves later that same day (June 11, 1963) to support the civil rights cause, Kennedy abandoned his previous go-slow approach to the issue. Moreover, he departed radically from the silence held by the Republican president Dwight D. Eisenhower when the Supreme Court handed down the historic 1954 *Brown v. Board of Education* decision, overturning the *Plessy v. Ferguson* separate-but-equal precedent of 1896. Kennedy's speech was momentous because he called on the nation to support civil rights as a moral cause.

About the Author

John Fitzgerald Kennedy was born in Massachusetts in 1917, the second of nine children of Joseph P. and Rose Fitzgerald Kennedy. John Kennedy's maternal grandfather had served as mayor of Boston, while his father was a successful businessperson and had served President Franklin Roosevelt as head of the Securities and Exchange Commission and then as ambassador to Great Britain. Kennedy's childhood was shaped by his family's great wealth, his parents' aloofness, attendance at boarding schools beginning in the seventh grade, and frequent illnesses. Kennedy would contend with physical pain and a variety of illnesses throughout his life.

Rose Kennedy's focus on caring for her mentally retarded daughter, Rosemary, who was one year younger than

Time Line

1954
- **May 17**
  Supreme Court decision in *Brown v. Board of Education* overturns the *Plessy v. Ferguson* separate-but-equal ruling and renews the protection of civil rights under the Fourteenth Amendment.

1955
- **December 1**
  The Montgomery bus boycott begins when Rosa Parks, an African American woman, is arrested for refusing to surrender her seat on a bus to a white person; the campaign of protest lasts until December 20, 1956.

1957
- The Southern Christian Leadership Conference, headed by Martin Luther King, Jr., is founded.

1960
- **February 1**
  The first civil rights sit-in demonstration takes place in Greensboro, North Carolina.
- **April 15–17**
  The Student Nonviolent Coordinating Committee is founded at Shaw University, in Raleigh, North Carolina.
- **December 5**
  The Supreme Court decision in *Boynton v. Virginia* bars discrimination against interstate bus passengers in station restaurants.

1961
- The Congress of Racial Equality renews Freedom Rides, a tactic previously used in 1947; Freedom Riders set out to challenge racial segregation by riding various forms of public transportation in the South to challenge local laws or customs that enforced segregation.

1962
- **November 20**
  President John F. Kennedy signs Executive Order 11063, providing for the desegregation of new federal housing.

John, led all the children to emulate their mother's example of caring. Kennedy graduated from Harvard College in 1940. Thanks to his father's prominence and the assistance of the *New York Times* columnist Arthur Krock, Kennedy succeeded in having his senior thesis published as a book, *Why England Slept*.

Kennedy and his older brother, Joseph Kennedy, Jr., both served in World War II, John as a PT boat commander; only John returned home safely. Their father had been grooming Joseph, Jr., for a political career that might culminate in the presidency. When John Kennedy decided to enter politics after a brief stint as a journalist, he received his father's financial and political backing. Kennedy was elected to the U.S. House of Representatives in 1946 and served as a member of the Committee on Education and Labor. His principal interests were foreign and defense policies. He was strongly anti-Communist and critical of the administration of Harry Truman for being insufficiently aggressive. In 1952 he won election to the U.S. Senate.

Kennedy married Jacqueline Bouvier in 1953. The couple had three children, one of whom died in infancy. Kennedy had been promiscuous prior to his marriage, and this behavior continued during the marriage and during his presidency, but in this era the press customarily declined to focus on the private lives of officeholders.

Kennedy's stance on domestic economic issues was liberal, but he failed to join in the 1954 Senate vote to censure Senator Joseph McCarthy for his tactics in pursuing what McCarthy claimed were Communist subversion and sympathizers in the U.S. government. In 1956 Kennedy gained national attention with his unsuccessful bid to win the Democratic nomination for vice president. Kennedy's second book, *Profiles in Courage*, was awarded a Pulitzer Prize in 1957. The book highlights the careers of members of Congress who took principled stands, often in opposition to what was politically prudent. In the Senate, Kennedy served on a special committee on labor and on the Foreign Relations Committee. He was elected to a second term in the Senate in 1958, won the Democratic nomination for president in 1960, and claimed a narrow victory over the Republican candidate, Vice President Richard Nixon, in the general election later that year. Civil rights became a key issue in the campaign when Martin Luther King, Jr., was sentenced to four months of hard labor on a misdemeanor traffic charge, leading some civil rights leaders to fear that King would be killed in prison. Kennedy called Coretta King, King's wife, to express his sympathy, and his brother Robert called the judge and persuaded him to release King on bail. Kennedy won 70 percent of the black vote, 30 percent higher than the Democratic percentage in the 1956 election.

As president, Kennedy initially disappointed civil rights partisans by proceeding slowly with civil rights initiatives and appointing segregationist judges in the South. Kennedy had criticized the Eisenhower administration for failing to ban discrimination in federal housing via an executive order but then delayed the issuance of his own limited executive order addressing the matter until November

1962. Kennedy thought that an assertive approach to civil rights would hurt his chances for spurring legislative action on medical insurance, federal aid to education, and other initiatives, but he failed to achieve gains in these areas even with his go-slow approach to civil rights. His main focus was on an aggressive cold war foreign policy. The failure of the Bay of Pigs invasion in Cuba (in an attempt to overthrow the Communist regime of Fidel Castro) in 1961 and the October 1962 crisis with the Soviet Union over the placement of nuclear missiles in Cuba were key events in his presidency. He was also involved in increasing the number of U.S. military advisers in South Vietnam, where the U.S.-backed government was increasingly unpopular.

In the third and last year of his presidency, Kennedy moved toward rethinking the cold war and affirmative leadership on civil rights. He negotiated the Nuclear Test Ban Treaty with the Soviet Union and Great Britain, spoke out forcefully for civil rights, and submitted a major civil rights proposal to Congress. Kennedy was a popular president, and his assassination on November 22, 1963, shocked the nation. President Lyndon B. Johnson was able to carry to fruition Kennedy's domestic civil rights program.

Explanation and Analysis of the Document

After an initial greeting to his "fellow citizens"—marking the familiar tone the president adopted throughout the address—Kennedy reports on the day's events at the University of Alabama, where he had acted to enforce a U.S. district court decision for the admission of two African American students, Vivian Malone and James Hood. By federalizing the Alabama National Guard, the president overcame the resistance of Governor George Wallace and ended Alabama's status as the only remaining state with state universities closed to African Americans. In contrast to the president's similar experience with the desegregation of the University of Mississippi the previous year, no violence occurred. The president takes note of this fact and praises students at the University of Alabama "who met their responsibilities in a constructive way." In highlighting the good behavior of students, the president introduces one of the important themes of the address, the need for individual citizens to contribute to the solution of the civil rights crisis.

In the third paragraph the president begins to emphasize the key theme of the address, the morality of the civil rights cause, which he links to the responsibility of each American to act in accord with the nation's values and the principle of basic fairness. In an allusion to President Abraham Lincoln's Gettysburg Address, Kennedy notes that the nation was "founded on the principle that all men are created equal." He implicitly criticizes racist concepts regarding the nation's origins when he affirms that "this Nation was founded by men of many nations and backgrounds." In asserting that "the rights of every man are diminished when the rights of one man are threatened," the president alludes to a long-standing labor movement slogan, "An injury to

Time Line

1963

- **June 11**
  Kennedy federalizes the Alabama National Guard to prevent Alabama governor George Wallace's interference with the admission of Vivian Malone and James Hood to the University of Alabama. Kennedy later addresses the nation regarding civil rights on television and radio.

- **June 12**
  Medgar Evers, leader of the National Association for the Advancement of Colored People, in Mississippi, is assassinated.

- **June 19**
  Kennedy submits a civil rights bill to Congress.

1964

- **June 21**
  During the Freedom Summer voting campaign, organized by the Student Nonviolent Coordinating Committee, the civil rights workers Michael Schwerner, Andrew Goodman, and James Chaney are murdered.

- **July 2**
  President Lyndon Johnson signs the Civil Rights Act of 1964.

one is the concern of all." Organized labor was a central constituency of the Democratic Party, and its leaders strongly supported the enactment of civil rights legislation.

In paragraphs 4–6, Kennedy introduces an important theme of the address—that the "worldwide struggle to promote and protect the rights of all who wish to be free" was connected with the successful practice of the ideal of freedom for all in America. During World War II, many civil rights partisans raised the idea that eliminating racial discrimination at home was a logical and practical counterpart to the struggle against Fascism abroad, particularly against the Nazi ideology of Aryan racial superiority. In the ensuing cold war between the United States and the Soviet Union, the issue of the connection between freedom at home and freedom abroad loomed in a new way. The Soviet Union, and indeed the world Communist movement, had long criticized racial oppression in the United States and the imperialist oppression of peoples in the developing world. In advocating a heightened struggle against Communism and for the U.S. concept of freedom around the world in his Inaugural Address, Kennedy was aware of the need for the United States to improve its civil rights record at home and the quality of its interactions with nations in the developing world. In his commencement address at the American University (delivered on June 10, 1963—the day before his Civil Rights Speech), in which he promoted a new approach to the cold war, Kennedy called on Americans to "examine our attitude towards peace and freedom here at home. The quality and spirit of our own society must justify and support our efforts abroad.... Wherever we are, we must all, in our daily lives, live up to the age-old faith that peace and freedom walk together. In too many of our cities today, the peace is not secure because freedom is incomplete."

Noting in paragraph 4 that "we do not ask for whites only" when "Americans are sent to Viet-Nam or West Berlin," Kennedy then argues that Americans "of any color" should be able to attend any public university without needing backup from troops, to register to vote without "interference or fear of reprisal," and to receive "equal service" in public places. In the sixth paragraph, Kennedy couples the theme of equal rights with an allusion to the Golden Rule: "Every American ought to have the right to be treated as he would wish to be treated." A secular person, Kennedy nevertheless included in the address a few spiritual references.

In paragraphs 7 and 8, the president summarizes statistics on the vast economic, educational, and health gaps between blacks and whites and expresses concern about "a rising tide of discontent that threatens the public safety." The perception within the Kennedy administration that deterioration in the Birmingham situation could lead to uncontrollable outbursts by African Americans was, indeed, a major factor in the president's deciding to take to the public airwaves on the spur of the moment.

The president stresses in paragraph 8 that the issue of civil rights is neither a sectional nor a partisan issue. Although the central issue of equal access to public accommodations was primarily a problem in southern states, in keeping with his sense of responsibility as the leader of the entire country, the president asserts that "difficulties over segregation and discrimination" exist in every city and state. His references to the nationwide racial gap and to discontent in cities throughout the country place the issue of southern segregation in its larger national context—perhaps to reduce white southerners' feeling that their section was being unfairly targeted. Kennedy's emphasis on nonpartisanship reflected the reality that the strongest opponents of civil rights were white southerners in his own party and evinced his determination to work with Republican leaders in Congress on his civil rights legislative proposal.

Paragraphs 9–11 are among the most important passages in the speech. After stating in paragraph 9 that the country is "confronted primarily with a moral issue," the president calls on all Americans to do the right thing, to put fairness above partisanship, sectionalism, and comfort with the racial status quo. Kennedy makes clear that the basis of his moral appeal is fairness and a concern for others and their rights when he links a religious reference with an allusion to a central secular document of the U.S. polity: "It is as old as the scriptures and is as clear as the American Constitution." As a secular politician, Kennedy personally confronted the issue of anti-Catholic prejudice in his run for the presidency in 1960 when he spoke before Protestant ministers in Houston, Texas, and assured them that he advocated "an America where the separation of church and state is absolute." In this instance, Kennedy used a nondenominational appeal to religious values to reinforce his attempt to inspire the country on a moral issue. Kennedy, like other presidents, had referred to God in his Inaugural Address.

In paragraph 10, Kennedy refers to the obligations of the Golden Rule—"The heart of the question is ... whether we are going to treat our fellow Americans as we want to be treated"—and issues a creative call for white people to imagine how they would feel if they were black. What would you think, he asks, about being denied service at restaurants, access to the best public schools, the right to vote, and "the full and free life which all of us want"? The paragraph closes with an incisive critique of the moderate approach that he himself had earlier followed and which Martin Luther King, Jr., had so sharply criticized two months earlier in his "Letter from Birmingham Jail." The president asks, "Who among us would then be content with the counsels of patience and delay?" Kennedy is asking Americans to look beyond the sometimes disconcerting and disruptive means used by civil rights activists to see the justice of their cause. As the president himself had only recently come to perceive, the time for incremental changes that essentially left the Jim Crow system intact had passed. Those who saw the issue as a struggle between two extremes, violent racists and civil rights activists, were mistaken. Rather, the struggle was between justice and injustice.

To reinforce the notion that the time for ending racial equality had come, Kennedy notes in paragraph 11 that one hundred years had passed "since President Lincoln freed the slaves," yet "their heirs ... are not fully free." A few years prior to the anniversary of the Emancipation Proclamation, the National Association for the Advancement of Colored People had begun a "Free by '63" campaign. On the occasion of Lincoln's birthday in 1963, the president and the first lady hosted a reception for African American leaders and their spouses and distributed to the guests the U.S. Commission on Civil Rights report *Freedom to the Free: Century of Emancipation, 1863–1963*. In Paragraph 11, Kennedy also reiterates the opening theme from paragraph 3, the interconnection of one person's freedom with another's, remarking that the nation "will not be fully free until all its citizens are free."

Paragraph 12 focuses on the interconnection between the consequences for the U.S. advocacy of "freedom around the world" and for U.S. foreign policy brought about by the treatment of African Americans as "second-class citizens." As concerned as he was about foreign policy, the president maintains that a bigger problem is that people can "say ... to each other that this is the land of the free except for the Negroes." Kennedy emphasizes the heinousness of this situation by alluding to Nazi ideology with the use of the term "master race." For Kennedy, who had fought in World War II, and for all those over the age

President John F. Kennedy discussing civil rights with more than two hundred lawyers on June 21, 1963, at the White House (AP/Wide World Photos)

of thirty-five or so, memories of the struggle against Nazi Germany and the other Axis powers were still vivid.

In paragraphs 13–17, Kennedy emphasizes that crisis conditions are at hand, calling for immediate action. The "cries for equality" are too great to ignore; the president declares in paragraph 14 that with "legal remedies" unavailable, people are taking to the streets in protests that "create tensions and threaten violence and threaten lives." The opponents of civil rights, of course, were the ones who committed the acts of violence. Although civil rights activists' decisions to violate the laws of segregation and to protest in the streets certainly contributed to confrontations, they were committed to nonviolence. Kennedy was worried, however, that spontaneous eruptions of anger among members of the black community could lead to violence. This is the only moment in the speech where the president seems to tilt against the civil rights movement. In the next paragraph he returns to the underlying positive theme of the address, asserting, "We face, therefore, a moral crisis as a country and as a people." He notes that he opposes "repressive police action." While the president says that the situation "cannot be left to increased demonstrations in the streets," he also calls for substantive action, not "token moves or talk," at all levels of society.

In paragraph 16, Kennedy calls on the nation to avoid both sectionalism and attempts to place blame. He characterizes the vast change needed as a "revolution" but notes that it should be "peaceful and constructive for all."

In paragraphs 18–21, Kennedy focuses on the need for civil rights legislation and announces that he will submit a proposal to Congress for equal access to public accommodations, which he characterizes as "an elementary right." He notes that without legislation, the only remedy that African American citizens have for wrongs inflicted on them "is in the street"; "in too many communities, in too many parts of the country," no "remedies at law" could be found. Kennedy maintains that the denial of access is "an arbitrary indignity that no American in 1963 should have to endure, but many do," thus appealing once again to white viewers and listeners to empathize with African Americans and to see that the recognition of equal rights is long overdue.

In paragraph 22 the president reports that he has met with many business leaders and is pleased that they have responded to his call for "voluntary action" to end discrimination in public accommodations. Kennedy comments that despite progress in more than seventy-five cities in the past two weeks, legislation is nevertheless needed because "many are unwilling to act alone."

In paragraphs 23–26, Kennedy outlines additional features of the civil rights legislation that he will propose, including federal government involvement in lawsuits to promote desegregation in schools and "greater protection for the right to vote." He notes that "too many" black students who entered segregated grade schools at the time of the *Brown v. Board of Education* Supreme Court decision "will enter segregated high schools this fall." Only a small percentage of black students had yet moved from segregated to desegregated schools. The consequence of this delayed desegregation, the president argues, is lost job opportunities.

In paragraph 26, the president again emphasizes the need for action "in the homes of every American in every community," while in paragraphs 27 and 28 he praises the "honor" and "courage" of those working for civil rights. Kennedy asserts that these individuals have acted "out of a sense of human decency" and compares them with "our soldiers and sailors" because "they are meeting freedom's challenge on the firing line." This was high praise, indeed, given the importance Kennedy attached to foreign policy and the stress that he placed on political and moral courage in his book *Profiles in Courage*.

In paragraph 29, the president highlights the economic gap between blacks and whites throughout the country. Kennedy argues that this is a problem that "faces us all," in "the North as well as the South." Describing in detail the crisis facing the nation, Kennedy again calls on "every citizen" to care and to act.

In paragraphs 30 and 31, Kennedy makes an appeal based on cultural pluralism, national unity, and equality: The United States "has become one country because all of us and all of the people who came here had an equal chance to develop their talents." He reiterates the need to give the "10 percent of the population" constituted by African Americans alternatives to discrimination and to demonstrations as the only means of gaining rights. The issue, he insists, is one of basic fairness and in the interests of all: "I think we owe them and we owe ourselves a better country than that."

In paragraph 32 the president makes an explicit appeal for people's help and reiterates the theme of treating people as one would want to be treated. In this and the following paragraph, the president emphasizes the theme of equality of opportunity and the importance of treating children right—"to give a chance for every child to be educated to the limit of his talents." Kennedy uses exclusively male pronouns here and throughout most of the address.

In paragraph 34 Kennedy speaks of the reciprocal obligation to be held by black citizens ("be responsible ... uphold the law") and by society ("the law will be fair ... the Constitution will be color blind"). In advocating a color-blind Constitution, Kennedy alludes to John Marshall Harlan's use of this terminology in his dissent in the *Plessy v. Ferguson* separate-but-equal Supreme Court decision of 1896. In the closing paragraph, the president states that basic principles are at stake—what the country "stands for"—and again asks for the support of "all our citizens."

Audience

President Kennedy's audience for his Civil Rights Speech was the entire population of the United States. The address was carried on television and radio, so the vast majority of the population was in a position to hear the president's words. He asked the three major television networks for airtime for the address, and all readily agreed. As part of their licenses to use the public airwaves, the broadcast companies in the period prior to deregulation were expected to be responsive to such requests.

Although the president was speaking to all "fellow Americans," he was particularly addressing white Americans. For example, he asks people to put themselves in the place of a black person and imagine how they would feel about having their rights denied. Kennedy also says that "we" expect things of the black community but that "they" expect to have equal rights.

Kennedy directed his remarks to people of both parties, of all regions, and of all classes. His remarks included praise for businesspeople responding to his call for voluntary action to desegregate as well as for those working on the front lines of the struggle for racial justice. By appealing to fairness, Kennedy hoped to expand support for his civil rights initiative beyond the ranks of liberals and the left.

In using male language at several points, the president addresses himself primarily to men (as in "one-third as much chance of becoming a professional man," "law alone cannot make men see right," and "if an American, because his skin is dark"). In referring to the effort to secure the admission of two African American students to the University of Alabama, one of whom was female, the president uses gender-neutral language ("clearly qualified young Alabama residents"). In referring to student potential in the close of the address, he shifts between male ("his talents") and gender-neutral language ("their talent").

Impact

Civil rights movement leaders and activists were thrilled by President Kennedy's national address of June 11, 1963. Martin Luther King, Jr., immediately sent Kennedy a message praising the speech. The Kennedy administration had been lending assistance to the civil rights movement and was now staking its own political success on the achievement of fundamental reform in the civil rights arena; the administration acted as a good if imperfect ally of the movement. In fact, when civil rights leaders met with the president on June 22, 1963, the president acknowledged that he did not think that the planned march on Washington, D.C., was a good idea. The difference of opinion was resolved, and Kennedy ended up supporting the march. Although the Student Nonviolent Coordinating Committee leader John Lewis was pressured into modifying his address, the march of two hundred and fifty thousand people from the Washington Monument to the Lincoln Memorial was a great success and further expanded positive public attention for the movement.

Essential Quotes

> "Today we are committed to a worldwide struggle to promote and protect the rights of all who wish to be free. And when Americans are sent to Viet-Nam or West Berlin, we do not ask for whites only. It ought to be possible, therefore, for American students of any color to attend any public institution they select without having to be backed up by troops."
>
> (Paragraph 4)

> "It ought to be possible for American consumers of any color to receive equal service in places of public accommodation … without being forced to resort to demonstrations in the street, and it ought to be possible for American citizens of any color to register to vote in a free election without interference or fear of reprisal."
>
> (Paragraph 5)

> "It ought to be possible, in short, for every American to enjoy the privileges of being American without regard to his race or his color. In short, every American ought to have the right to be treated as he would wish to be treated, as one would wish his children to be treated. But this is not the case."
>
> (Paragraph 6)

> "We are confronted primarily with a moral issue. It is as old as the scriptures and is as clear as the American Constitution."
>
> (Paragraph 9)

> "The heart of the question is whether all Americans are to be afforded equal rights and equal opportunities, whether we are going to treat our fellow Americans as we want to be treated. If an American, because his skin is dark, cannot eat lunch in a restaurant open to the public, if he cannot send his children to the best public school available, if he cannot vote for the public officials who will represent him, if, in short, he cannot enjoy the full and free life which all of us want, then who among us would be content to have the color of his skin changed and stand in his place? Who among us would then be content with the counsels of patience and delay?"
>
> (Paragraph 10)

The Kennedy administration did experience some immediate negative political repercussions after the address, as southern Congress members withdrew support from other administration proposals. Also, disagreements with the National Association for the Advancement of Colored People occurred over the details of the civil rights bill, with the administration seeking a more moderate version than was sought by the civil rights coalition. Kennedy met with Democratic and Republican House leaders on October 23 to craft a compromise that proved stronger than the administration's bill. The House Judiciary Committee approved the civil rights bill on November 20, 1963, but whether the bill would be successfully processed by the House Rules Committee, chaired by the segregationist Howard W. Smith, was uncertain. Kennedy would not have the opportunity to work on that problem because of his assassination. President Lyndon B. Johnson took up the banner, however, and worked effectively to secure the passage of the Civil Rights Act of 1964. As vice president, Johnson had urged Kennedy to take a moral stance on civil rights. As segregationists left the Democratic Party in the wake of the passage of the Civil Rights Act and the Voting Rights Act of 1965, the party's stance as an ally of the civil rights movement and of African Americans became a permanent fixture of the political landscape.

See also Emancipation Proclamation (1863); *Plessy v. Ferguson* (1896); *Brown v. Board of Education* (1954); George Wallace's Inaugural Address as Governor (1963); Martin Luther King, Jr.: "Letter from Birmingham Jail" (1963); Martin Luther King, Jr.: "I Have a Dream" (1963); Civil Rights Act of 1964.

Further Reading

■ Books

Branch, Taylor. *Parting the Waters: America in the King Years, 1954–63*. New York: Simon & Schuster, 1988.

———. *Pillar of Fire: America in the King Years, 1963–65*. New York: Simon & Schuster, 1988.

Bryant, Nick. *The Bystander: John F. Kennedy and the Struggle for Black Equality*. New York: Basic Books, 2006.

Dallek, Robert. *An Unfinished Life: John F. Kennedy, 1917–1963*. Boston: Little, Brown, 2003.

Giglio, James N. *The Presidency of John F. Kennedy*. 2nd ed. Lawrence: University Press of Kansas, 2006.

Hampton, Henry, and Steve Fayer, eds. *Voices of Freedom: An Oral History of the Civil Rights Movement from the 1950s through the 1980s*. New York: Bantam Books, 1990.

Lawson, Steven F. *Running for Freedom: Civil Rights and Black Politics in America since 1941*. 2nd ed. New York: McGraw-Hill, 1997.

Questions for Further Study

1. Compare Kennedy's responses to civil rights crises with those of President Dwight D. Eisenhower to the Supreme Court's *Brown v. Board of Education* decision, to the rise of massive resistance, and to the 1957 Little Rock crisis.

2. In referring to the Supreme Court justice John Marshall Harlan's concept of a color-blind Constitution, was President Kennedy concerned with ending systematic discrimination against African Americans or with eliminating any reference to race in American law and practice, or with both?

3. Kennedy highlighted economic disparities between whites and African Americans in his address. Overcoming economic privation was one of the goals of the March on Washington for Jobs and Freedom of August 28, 1963, and the goal of the Poor People's Campaign, which Martin Luther King, Jr., was leading at the time of his assassination. Examine the extent of economic disparities in society today. To what degree would the universal implementation of affirmation action or a program of reparations contribute to substantially closing racial socioeconomic gaps? Might a modern-day president committed to civil rights take other initiatives to eliminate such gaps?

4. In the 1990s a trend toward the resegregation of public schools began taking place. The 2007 Supreme Court decision in *Parents Involved in Community Schools v. Seattle School District No. 1* against the use of race in assigning students to schools further undermined the promise of the *Brown v. Board of Education* decision that schools would be equal and integrated. What measures might be taken today to restore the goal of establishing equal educational opportunity championed by Kennedy in his Civil Rights Address to the nation?

Rorabaugh, W. J. *Kennedy and the Promise of the Sixties*. Cambridge, U.K.: Cambridge University Press, 2002.

Sorensen, Theodore C. *Kennedy*. New York: Perennial Library, 1988.

Strober, Deborah Hart, and Gerald S. Strober. *The Kennedy Presidency: An Oral History of the Era*. Washington, D.C.: Brassey's, 2003.

U.S. Commission on Civil Rights. *Freedom to the Free: Century of Emancipation, 1863–1963; A Report to the President*. Washington, D.C.: U.S. Government Printing Office, 1963.

Watson, Denton L. *Lion in the Lobby: Clarence Mitchell, Jr.'s Struggle for the Passage of Civil Rights Laws*. New York: Morrow, 1990.

Wofford, Harris. *Of Kennedys and Kings: Making Sense of the Sixties*. Pittsburgh: University of Pittsburgh Press, 1992.

■ Web Sites

"John F. Kennedy: American University Commencement Address." American Rhetoric "Top 100 Speeches" Web site.
   http://www.americanrhetoric.com/speeches/jfkamericanuniversityaddress.html.

—Martin Halpern

John F. Kennedy's Civil Rights Address

Good evening my fellow citizens:

This afternoon, following a series of threats and defiant statements, the presence of Alabama National Guardsmen was required on the University of Alabama to carry out the final and unequivocal order of the United States District Court of the Northern District of Alabama. That order called for the admission of two clearly qualified young Alabama residents who happened to have been born Negro.

That they were admitted peacefully on the campus is due in good measure to the conduct of the students of the University of Alabama, who met their responsibilities in a constructive way.

I hope that every American, regardless of where he lives, will stop and examine his conscience about this and other related incidents. This Nation was founded by men of many nations and backgrounds. It was founded on the principle that all men are created equal, and that the rights of every man are diminished when the rights of one man are threatened.

Today we are committed to a worldwide struggle to promote and protect the rights of all who wish to be free. And when Americans are sent to Viet-Nam or West Berlin, we do not ask for whites only. It ought to be possible, therefore, for American students of any color to attend any public institution they select without having to be backed up by troops.

It ought to be possible for American consumers of any color to receive equal service in places of public accommodation, such as hotels and restaurants and theaters and retail stores, without being forced to resort to demonstrations in the street, and it ought to be possible for American citizens of any color to register to vote in a free election without interference or fear of reprisal.

It ought to be possible, in short, for every American to enjoy the privileges of being American without regard to his race or his color. In short, every American ought to have the right to be treated as he would wish to be treated, as one would wish his children to be treated. But this is not the case.

The Negro baby born in America today, regardless of the section of the Nation in which he is born, has about one-half as much chance of completing a high school as a white baby born in the same place on the same day, one-third as much chance of completing college, one-third as much chance of becoming a professional man, twice as much chance of becoming unemployed, about one-seventh as much chance of earning $10,000 a year, a life expectancy which is 7 years shorter, and the prospects of earning only half as much.

This is not a sectional issue. Difficulties over segregation and discrimination exist in every city, in every State of the Union, producing in many cities a rising tide of discontent that threatens the public safety. Nor is this a partisan issue. In a time of domestic crisis men of good will and generosity should be able to unite regardless of party or politics. This is not even a legal or legislative issue alone. It is better to settle these matters in the courts than on the streets, and new laws are needed at every level, but law alone cannot make men see right.

We are confronted primarily with a moral issue. It is as old as the scriptures and is as clear as the American Constitution.

The heart of the question is whether all Americans are to be afforded equal rights and equal opportunities, whether we are going to treat our fellow Americans as we want to be treated. If an American, because his skin is dark, cannot eat lunch in a restaurant open to the public, if he cannot send his children to the best public school available, if he cannot vote for the public officials who will represent him, if, in short, he cannot enjoy the full and free life which all of us want, then who among us would be content to have the color of his skin changed and stand in his place? Who among us would then be content with the counsels of patience and delay?

One hundred years of delay have passed since President Lincoln freed the slaves, yet their heirs, their grandsons, are not fully free. They are not yet freed from the bonds of injustice. They are not yet freed from social and economic oppression. And this Nation, for all its hopes and all its boasts, will not be fully free until all its citizens are free.

We preach freedom around the world, and we mean it, and we cherish our freedom here at home, but are we to say to the world, and much more importantly, to each other that this is the land of the free except for the Negroes; that we have no second-class citizens except Negroes; that we have no class or caste system, no ghettoes, no master race except with respect to Negroes?

Now the time has come for this Nation to fulfill its promise. The events in Birmingham and elsewhere have so increased the cries for equality that no city or State or legislative body can prudently choose to ignore them.

The fires of frustration and discord are burning in every city, North and South, where legal remedies are not at hand. Redress is sought in the streets, in demonstrations, parades, and protests which create tensions and threaten violence and threaten lives.

We face, therefore, a moral crisis as a country and as a people. It cannot be met by repressive police action. It cannot be left to increased demonstrations in the streets. It cannot be quieted by token moves or talk. It is time to act in the Congress, in your State and local legislative body and, above all, in all of our daily lives.

It is not enough to pin the blame of others, to say this a problem of one section of the country or another, or deplore the fact that we face. A great change is at hand, and our task, our obligation, is to make that revolution, that change, peaceful and constructive for all.

Those who do nothing are inviting shame as well as violence. Those who act boldly are recognizing right as well as reality.

Next week I shall ask the Congress of the United States to act, to make a commitment it has not fully made in this century to the proposition that race has no place in American life or law. The Federal judiciary has upheld that proposition in the conduct of its affairs, including the employment of Federal personnel, the use of Federal facilities, and the sale of federally financed housing.

But there are other necessary measures which only the Congress can provide, and they must be provided at this session. The old code of equity law under which we live commands for every wrong a remedy, but in too many communities, in too many parts of the country, wrongs are inflicted on Negro citizens and there are no remedies at law. Unless the Congress acts, their only remedy is in the street.

I am, therefore, asking the Congress to enact legislation giving all Americans the right to be served in facilities which are open to the public—hotels, restaurants, theaters, retail stores, and similar establishments.

This seems to me to be an elementary right. Its denial is an arbitrary indignity that no American in 1963 should have to endure, but many do.

I have recently met with scores of business leaders urging them to take voluntary action to end this discrimination and I have been encouraged by their response, and in the last 2 weeks over 75 cities have seen progress made in desegregating these kinds of facilities. But many are unwilling to act alone, and for this reason, nationwide legislation is needed if we are to move this problem from the streets to the courts.

I am also asking the Congress to authorize the Federal Government to participate more fully in lawsuits designed to end segregation in public education. We have succeeded in persuading many districts to desegregate voluntarily. Dozens have admitted Negroes without violence. Today a Negro is attending a State-supported institution in every one of our 50 States, but the pace is very slow.

Too many Negro children entering segregated grade schools at the time of the Supreme Court's decision 9 years ago will enter segregated high schools this fall, having suffered a loss which can never be restored. The lack of an adequate education denies the Negro a chance to get a decent job.

The orderly implementation of the Supreme Court decision, therefore, cannot be left solely to those who may not have the economic resources to carry the legal action or who may be subject to harassment.

Other features will also be requested, including greater protection for the right to vote. But legislation, I repeat, cannot solve this problem alone. It must be solved in the homes of every American in every community across our country.

In this respect I want to pay tribute to those citizens North and South who have been working in their communities to make life better for all. They are acting not out of a sense of legal duty but out of a sense of human decency.

Like our soldiers and sailors in all parts of the world they are meeting freedom's challenge on the firing line, and I salute them for their honor and their courage.

My fellow Americans, this is a problem which faces us all—in every city of the North as well as the South. Today there are Negroes unemployed, two or three times as many compared to whites, inadequate in education, moving into the large cities, unable to find work, young people particularly out of work without hope, denied equal rights, denied the opportunity to eat at a restaurant or lunch counter or go to a movie theater, denied the right to a decent education, denied almost today the right to attend a State university even though qualified. It seems to me that

Document Text

these are matters which concern us all, not merely Presidents or Congressmen or Governors, but every citizen of the United States.

This is one country. It has become one country because all of us and all the people who came here had an equal chance to develop their talents.

We cannot say to 10 percent of the population that you can't have that right; that your children cannot have the chance to develop whatever talents they have; that the only way that they are going to get their rights is to go into the streets and demonstrate. I think we owe them and we owe ourselves a better country than that.

Therefore, I am asking for your help in making it easier for us to move ahead and to provide the kind of equality of treatment which we would want ourselves; to give a chance for every child to be educated to the limit of his talents.

As I have said before, not every child has an equal talent or an equal ability or an equal motivation, but they should have an equal right to develop their talent and their ability and their motivation, to make something of themselves.

We have a right to expect that the Negro community will be responsible, will uphold the law, but they have a right to expect that the law will be fair, that the Constitution will be color blind, as Justice Harlan said at the turn of the century.

This is what we are talking about and this is a matter which concerns this country and what it stands for, and in meeting it I ask the support of all our citizens.

Thank you very much.

Glossary

equity law	the application of principles of fairness in the absence of rules
public accommodation	facilities serving the public

Martin Luther King, Jr., addresses marchers during his "I Have a Dream" speech in 1963. (AP/Wide World Photos)

Martin Luther King, Jr.: "I Have a Dream"

"From every mountainside, let freedom ring."

Overview

On August 28, 1963, nearly a quarter of a million people arrived in the District of Columbia for the March on Washington for Jobs and Freedom. They had been summoned by the veteran African American labor leader A. Philip Randolph to urge the federal government to broaden economic opportunities for low-income families and to pressure Congress to pass the Civil Rights Act, which was then being debated. Delegations of civil rights supporters from cities across the United States thus joined together for a massive one-day protest.

The orderly crowd assembled in front of the Lincoln Memorial and listened as representatives of labor, religious, and civil rights organizations delivered short addresses. The day's final speaker was Martin Luther King, Jr., the nation's preeminent civil rights leader. The demonstrations against segregation led by King in Birmingham, Alabama, four months earlier had raised the issue of racial equality to the top of the national agenda. Sensing a changing mood in the country, President John F. Kennedy responded by proposing comprehensive civil rights legislation.

King reminded his listeners that day of African Americans' legitimate grievances and promised that they would not rest until full equality was won. As he neared the end of his speech, King departed from his prepared text to deliver his most memorable words: "I have a dream," he thundered, in the powerful preaching cadence of the black Baptist tradition. Using a series of riveting images, King shared his vision of a country free of racial hatred, in which black and white Americans would live as equals. His oration eclipsed the remarks of all other speakers that day and is among the most quoted American public addresses. The "I Have a Dream" speech has come to epitomize the aspirations of the modern civil rights movement.

Context

Gathering in the nation's capital to petition Congress is a time-honored tradition of American political movements. In 1894 Jacob Coxey led an army of unemployed workers to Washington, demanding that the government create more jobs. Thirty thousand World War I veterans seeking early bonuses for their military service camped outside Washington for forty days in 1932, until routed by army troops. In 1941 A. Philip Randolph, the president of the Brotherhood of Sleeping Car Porters, threatened to lead one hundred thousand African Americans down Pennsylvania Avenue, forcing President Franklin D. Roosevelt to act against racial discrimination in defense industries.

As civil rights protests gained momentum in the early 1960s, Randolph revived the idea of a march on Washington. Because he was concerned primarily about African American poverty and unemployment, Randolph proposed a two-day demonstration for jobs to be held in October 1963. He maintained that a massive assembly of black citizens was needed to prod a reluctant President Kennedy into action. Randolph's idea initially drew a lukewarm response from other black leaders—until Martin Luther King, Jr., lent his support. King had just finished a successful campaign to desegregate stores and lunch counters in Birmingham, Alabama. Nationally televised scenes of police dogs and fire hoses battering youthful demonstrators roused public sympathy behind the crusade for equal rights. King was looking for a way to sustain the energy of his movement and press for needed civil rights legislation. When he announced his intention to participate in the march, rival civil rights leaders felt compelled to join. After Kennedy submitted his civil rights bill to Congress, the event was renamed the "March for Jobs and Freedom," the date was changed to late August, and the emphasis shifted from economic issues to support for the proposed legislation.

At a meeting at the White House in June, Kennedy tried to convince march organizers that a mass protest would actually derail support for his civil rights bill. When Randolph and King declared their determination to go ahead with the demonstration, the president offered the assistance of federal agencies to ensure that the march proceeded smoothly. In the weeks leading up to the event, Randolph's chief aide, Bayard Rustin, worked around the clock to nail down the smallest details. Marchers would arrive by chartered buses and trains on the morning of August 28 and depart that afternoon; they would carry only signs approved by the march committee; no sit-ins or civil disobedience would be staged; thousands of sandwiches

Time Line

1963

- **January**
  A. Philip Randolph announces plans for a demonstration in Washington, D.C., to force legislative action on economic problems facing African Americans.

- **April–May**
  Police attacks on civil rights demonstrators in Birmingham, Alabama, capture the attention of the nation and increase pressure for federal civil rights legislation.

- **June 11**
  In a nationally televised address, President John F. Kennedy announces that he will send a comprehensive civil rights bill to Congress.

- **June 18**
  Kennedy delivers what will become the Civil Rights Act to Congress.

- **June 22**
  Civil rights leaders meet with Kennedy, who tries to persuade them to drop plans for their march.

- **June 23**
  Martin Luther King, Jr., leads one hundred and twenty-five thousand marchers through the streets of Detroit in a "dress rehearsal" for the March on Washington.

- **July 2**
  Bayard Rustin presents a detailed plan for the march. To ensure that the march will be racially integrated, four prominent whites are added as cochairs of the event.

- **August 27**
  King toils late into the night preparing his address for the march.

- **August 28**
  Some two hundred and fifty thousand demonstrators arrive in Washington, D.C. King delivers his "I Have a Dream" speech, which is broadcast live by all of the major television networks.

- **November 22**
  Kennedy is assassinated in Dallas, Texas. Lyndon B. Johnson becomes president.

would be prepared to feed the hungry throngs; and security would be provided by off-duty New York City police officers and federal personnel.

King began composing his speech four days before the march, asking advisers to prepare drafts for his consideration. When King arrived in Washington on August 27, he still did not have a version that he felt was satisfactory. That evening he retired to his room at the Willard Hotel to work on revisions; at four o'clock the next morning King handed his final handwritten text to aides for typing and distribution to the press.

The day's events began with a program of entertainment on a stage erected near the Washington Monument. Musicians performed, and celebrities were introduced to the well-dressed marchers, but the crowd grew restive. Around eleven o'clock people spontaneously began moving toward the Lincoln Memorial, and the assembled dignitaries had to scramble to catch up with the people they were supposed to be leading. As the huge crowd congregated on either side of the memorial's Reflecting Pool, the speakers took their turns at the podium in the shadow of the Great Emancipator's statue. John Lewis, the young head of the Student Nonviolent Coordinating Committee, delivered the day's most militant address, calling for a "great revolution" to "splinter the segregated south into a thousand pieces." Mahalia Jackson roused the crowd when she sang the traditional spiritual "I've Been 'Buked and I've Been Scorned." Then, Randolph introduced "the moral leader of our nation," Dr. Martin Luther King, Jr., whose address sounded the climactic final note for the day's celebration.

When King concluded his speech, the throngs quickly dispersed, carrying a message of hope back to their home communities. Leaders of the march, in turn, adjourned to the White House, where they ate a hastily prepared lunch and were congratulated by President Kennedy, who was relieved and delighted that the event had gone off without serious controversy or disorder of any kind.

About the Author

Martin Luther King, Jr., was born and raised in Atlanta, Georgia, where both his father and grandfather pastored the Ebenezer Baptist Church. At the age of fifteen he entered Morehouse College to study sociology. He prepared for the ministry at Crozier Theological Seminary, in Pennsylvania, and then earned a doctorate in philosophy from Boston University. While he was in Boston he met and married Coretta Scott, an aspiring concert singer from Marion, Alabama.

In 1953 King returned to the South to become pastor of the Dexter Avenue Baptist Church in Montgomery, Alabama. When Rosa Parks was arrested in 1955 for refusing to give up her seat to a white passenger, King emerged as the leader of a year-long boycott of city buses. His application of Gandhian nonviolent resistance to fight Jim Crow laws and the successful outcome of the Montgomery protest thrust him into the national spotlight. In 1957 he founded the Southern Christian Leadership Conference to carry his fight for civil rights to other southern communities. Over the next decade King remained at the forefront of the rapidly growing civil rights movement. In 1963 he led a campaign of civil disobedience against segregation in Birmingham, Alabama—one of the most violent southern cities. His "Letter from Birmingham Jail," written following his arrest while leading a demonstration, is an eloquent defense of his nonviolent tactics.

King's "I Have a Dream" speech at the March on Washington helped build public support for the landmark Civil Rights Act that was passed by Congress in 1964. In turn, the Voting Rights Act that became law the following year was enacted largely because of his efforts to dramatize the disenfranchisement of African American citizens in Selma, Alabama. In 1966 King turned his attention to the North, where he attacked slum conditions and segregated housing in Chicago. King's growing opposition to the Vietnam War put him in the front ranks of the antiwar movement. At the time of his assassination in 1968, he was preparing to lead the Poor People's Campaign, a multiracial effort to spur government action against poverty.

King received the Nobel Peace Prize in 1964. His birthday is commemorated by a national holiday, and his bust stands in the U.S. Capitol.

Time Line

1964
- **July 2** Congress passes the Civil Rights Act, which Johnson signs into law.
- **December 10** Martin Luther King, Jr., is awarded the Nobel Peace Prize in Oslo, Norway.

1968
- **April 4** King is assassinated in Memphis, Tennessee. Riots follow in more than one hundred cities, including Washington, D.C.

1983
- **November 2** A bill establishing a national holiday to commemorate King's birthday is signed by President Ronald Reagan.

Explanation and Analysis of the Document

After a brief salutation, King reminds his listeners of the symbolic importance of the ground they occupy. By locating their rally in the shadow of the Great Emancipator's memorial, march organizers hoped to call attention to Abraham Lincoln's unfinished agenda; a century after the end of slavery, African Americans still were not free. King's use of the archaic "fivescore years ago" is an obvious echo of Lincoln's Gettysburg Address. He briefly mentions the triple problems of segregation, discrimination, and poverty that mark the unequal status of black Americans. King emphasizes the long gap between the Emancipation Proclamation's promise of equality and the lingering reality of pervasive racism by repeating "one hundred years" four times.

Using the words of the Declaration of Independence, King advises his listeners that African Americans are seeking only the rights guaranteed to all citizens. He accuses the United States of bad faith in delivering its pledge of freedom. The Constitution, then, can be viewed as a "promissory note" that has not yet been redeemed for people of color. King employs the metaphor of a bad check to describe the unrealized assurance of full citizenship. In the only trace of humor in this otherwise solemn declamation, he claims that the government's check has bounced owing to "insufficient funds." King does not dwell on past injustices, however. Rather, he concludes this passage on a hopeful note, stating his belief that the United States will soon honor its commitment to its black citizens.

King proceeds to assert that America cannot afford to wait any longer; its black citizens are demanding change now. Many critics were accusing the civil rights movement of impatience, of pressing too hard for reform, but King rejects this argument. He underscores the urgency of African American demands for equal rights by reiterating "now is the time" four times. The United States cannot afford to continue "business as usual," as the stakes are too great. He threatens that "there will be neither rest nor tranquility" until these demands are granted.

Lest he be accused of fomenting violence, King abruptly changes gears and admonishes his fellow African Americans to refrain from bitterness and a desire for revenge. They must conduct themselves with dignity and self-restraint; nonviolence must continue to be the hallmark of their movement. He acknowledges the presence of white supporters, estimated to be about 10 percent of the march's participants. White allies are essential for the movement's success, he insists, because "we cannot walk alone."

King then resumes a more militant tone, listing some of the top priorities of the civil rights movement: an end to police brutality, access to public accommodations, the elimination of housing segregation, the removal of Jim Crow signs, voting rights, and meaningful participation in political affairs. He repeats "we cannot be satisfied" or "we can never be satisfied" seven times as he enumerates black grievances. King then enlists biblical support for his position, ending this litany by paraphrasing the Old Testament prophet Amos in saying that blacks will not be satisfied until "justice rolls down like waters and righteousness like a mighty stream."

This section illustrates King's favorite literary device, anaphora—a frequently repeated word or phrase. Drew Hansen, in his text *The Dream: Martin Luther King, Jr., and the Speech That Inspired a Nation*, observes that by using anaphora, "King could create a series of parallel images, which allowed him to suggest connections between seemingly unrelated topics."

King next turns his attention to those battle-scarred veterans of the civil rights movement in the audience; those who have suffered beatings and imprisonment for the sake of freedom. He salutes their sacrifices and courage. Some of them have questioned the effectiveness of Gandhian civil disobedience, but King encourages them to keep faith in nonviolence. They should return to the South to continue their work with confidence that victory is in sight.

If King had concluded at this point, as he had planned, his address probably would have been little remembered. As Hansen remarks, "There was nothing particularly unusual about the substance of the first ten minutes of King's speech." Many other politicians and activists had covered the same ground. Here, however, King departs from his prepared text to deliver an extemporaneous oration describing his vision for the future of America. David Garrow quotes King's recollection of this moment: "I started out reading the speech ... and all of a sudden this thing came to me that I have used—I'd used it many times before, that thing about 'I have a dream'—and I just felt I wanted to use it here." This is a set piece he had used several times previously—most recently in Birmingham in April and in Detroit in June—but never more effectively than on this day. Indeed, the speech metamorphoses into a sermon at this point, with King switching to his role as preacher and with the massive audience as his spirited congregation. Using the distinctive call-and-response style perfected by his Baptist forbears, he enlists the crowd as a chorus to affirm and endorse his prophecy. Every time King reveals a new facet of his dream, the crowd replies with affirmation, clamoring for more. Each response sends King to a higher level of emotional intensity.

In the first glimpse of his dream, King refers again to the Declaration of Independence, asserting his belief that one day Americans truly will honor the words "all men are created equal." King then presents a series of vivid images describing what this new reality will look like. In outlining his vision, he utilizes a series of paired contrasting ideas: slavery and brotherhood; oppression and freedom; segregation and integration; despair and hope; and "jangling discord" and "a beautiful symphony." He foresees a society where the barriers of segregation dividing the races no longer will be enforced—where blacks and whites will be able to sit down and eat together. Jim Crow laws and southern custom widely prohibited the sharing of meals by black and white people at the same table because this sharing would symbolize equal status and inclusion. King thus anticipates the day when blacks and whites in his native Georgia will be able to break bread together.

King's dream also extends to the state of Mississippi, home to some of the most violent defenders of white supremacy. King does not need to remind the assembled marchers of past injustices committed in the Magnolia State; they well know the names of African Americans lynched for alleged transgressions of the Jim Crow code, including fourteen-year-old Emmett Till, who was abducted from his uncle's home and then beaten and drowned, and Medgar Evers, the martyred leader of the National Association for the Advancement of Colored People, who was shot in the back with a high-powered rifle just ten weeks earlier. Despite this sorry record, King asserts that Mississippi will become "an oasis of freedom and justice."

King next makes the dream very personal by including his four young children. He maintains that one day, instead of being considered inferior beings and denied opportunities to develop their full human potential because of the color of their skin, they will be judged by "the content of their character."

Alabama would also be transformed in this renewed nation. King knew very well how difficult it was to bring change to this state, having led the Montgomery bus boycott and, more recently, having defeated hard-core segregationists in the streets of Birmingham. Without mentioning him by name, King attacks the state's governor, George C. Wallace, who made national headlines earlier that summer with his futile defiance of the federal government while trying to prevent black students from enrolling at the University of Alabama. King offers a vision of a time when "little black boys and black girls" will not be isolated from their white peers. Not only will they see each other as equals, but they will also join hands "as sisters and brothers." The physical intimacy King suggests by this simple act was no doubt offensive to rabid racists but presented a powerful image of innocent fraternity to those in his audience.

King turns back to the Old Testament for the next facet of his vision. Quoting the book of Isaiah, he recalls the prophet's description of the kingdom of God. It is a place where earthly imperfections will disappear; where the mighty will be humbled and the lowly will be exalted; and where "the glory of the Lord shall be revealed" for all to see. King embraces the prophetic role, testifying that the quest for civil rights is part of God's divine plan for America and equating the coming victory over segregation with the arrival of the millennium.

At this point King briefly returns to his prepared text for a few sentences affirming his faith in this vision. This faith gives him strength to resume the struggle for freedom in the South with hope for victory despite entrenched opposition; it gives him confidence that America can overcome its bitter divisions and emerge "into a beautiful symphony of brotherhood." Then, improvising again, he claims that the knowledge that "we will be free one day" is enough to sustain him and other civil rights activists through the difficult battles that undoubtedly lie ahead.

King continues spontaneously, describing a coming era when "all of God's children" will win their freedom. On that day, African Americans will be able to sing the patriotic hymn "America the Beautiful," confident at last that the verses apply to them. Here, King paraphrases a well-known address delivered by the Chicago minister Archibald Carey at the 1952 Republican National Convention. He seizes on the refrain "from every mountainside, let freedom ring," once again using anaphora to launch a series of references to specific geographic regions of the United States. The first five are mountain ranges outside of the South—in New Hampshire, New York, Pennsylvania, Colorado, and California. The final three, then, are more poignant because they locate the need for freedom in the Deep South: King speaks of Georgia's Stone Mountain, Lookout Mountain in Tennessee, and even "every hill and molehill of Mississippi," a state without notable mountain ranges.

At this point the crowd in front of the Lincoln Memorial was cheering wildly. King's rhetoric had brought them to the emotional peak of his oration. He summons a vision of the day when freedom will ring "from every village and every hamlet" and when this message will be embraced by "all of God's children." He offers a closing image of blacks and whites, Jews and Gentiles, Protestants and Catholics all joining hands in brotherhood. Finally—as he spoke, he raised his arm in a blessing—King invokes an African American spiritual for his benediction: "Free at last, free at last, thank God Almighty, we are free at last."

The final seven minutes were what made King's speech a triumph of American oratory. These are the words that schoolchildren memorize, because King "added something completely fresh to the way that Americans thought about race and civil rights. He gave the nation a vision of what it could look like if all things were made new."

Audience

The immediate audience for King's speech was the approximately two hundred and fifty thousand people gathered on August 28, 1963, in front of the Lincoln Memorial and around the nearby Reflecting Pool. Additional millions listened on the radio and watched on television. King's words were aimed at all Americans. For black listeners they carried a message of hope with the promise that the goals of freedom and equality were within reach. For whites, King articulated the aspirations of African Americans, placing them squarely in the context of the American dream. Each year, on the national holiday commemorating his life, King's message is passed on to new generations.

Impact

King's words were broadcast live by the three major television networks into homes across the United States. Millions of people for whom King had been only a name in the news were thus able to witness the power of his oratory firsthand. One of the many who were impressed was President Kennedy, who remarked while viewing coverage of the march in the White House, "That guy is really good." Despite his privately expressed admiration, however, the chief executive was unwilling to praise King in public for fear of drawing the ire of die-hard segregationists.

Public reaction to the speech was largely favorable. The next day's edition of the *New York Times* was generous in its praise, with a front-page headline reading, "Peroration by Dr. King Sums Up a Day the Capital Will Remember." The

A view of the crowd that gathered for the March on Washington on April 28, 1963 (Library of Congress)

Motown Company released an unauthorized recording of King's speech that sold briskly in African American record stores. A few black militants, however, chided march organizers for not taking a more critical stance toward the Kennedy administration. One of these naysayers was Malcolm X, who acidly lampooned the day's events as "the Farce in Washington."

King's powerful message undoubtedly helped build support for Kennedy's pending civil rights legislation. According to Drew Hansen, "by delivering a message of hope, and not something that was likely to be labeled as angry or extremist, King's speech could only help the civil rights bill." Nonetheless, while the success of the march boosted the morale of civil rights backers, it probably did not influence any congressional votes. The historian Lerone Bennett has pointed to the lack of concrete accomplishments flowing from the march. In his *Confrontation: Black and White*, he states, "It led nowhere and was not intended to lead anywhere. It was not planned as an event with a coherent plan of action. As a result, the march was a stimulating but detached and isolated episode." It would take ten months of bitter partisan wrangling and skillful political maneuvering by President Lyndon B. Johnson to secure the passage of the Civil Rights Act in July 1964.

Essential Quotes

"Now is the time to make real the promises of democracy. Now is the time to rise from the dark and desolate valley of segregation to the sunlit path of racial justice. Now is the time to lift our nation from the quicksands of racial injustice to the solid rock of brotherhood. Now is the time to make justice a reality for all of God's children."

(Paragraph 6)

"No, we are not satisfied and we will not be satisfied until 'justice rolls down like waters and righteousness like a mighty stream.'"

(Paragraph 10)

"I have a dream that my four little children will one day live in a nation where they will not be judged by the color of their skin but by the content of their character."

(Paragraph 16)

"I have a dream that one day down in Alabama ... little black boys and black girls will be able to join hands with little white boys and white girls as sisters and brothers."

(Paragraph 17)

"Let freedom ring from Stone Mountain of Georgia. Let freedom ring from Lookout Mountain of Tennessee. Let freedom ring from every hill and molehill of Mississippi. From every mountainside, let freedom ring."

(Paragraphs 26–29)

"When we allow freedom [to] ring ... we will be able to speed up that day when all of God's children, black men and white men, Jews and Gentiles, Protestants and Catholics, will be able to join hands and sing in the words of the old Negro spiritual, 'Free at last! Free at last! Thank God Almighty, we are free at last!'"

(Paragraph 30)

King's heightened public profile following the March on Washington inflamed the Federal Bureau of Investigation director J. Edgar Hoover's animus toward the civil rights leader. Where others saw eloquence, Hoover perceived demagoguery. Richard Gid Powers speaks of the "campaign to utterly discredit King, to destroy him personally and as a public figure" that was touched off by the "I Have a Dream" speech. The bureau had been monitoring King's activities for several years, but "after the March the bureau shifted from a hostile but relatively passive surveillance of King to an aggressive—at times violently aggressive—campaign to destroy him." The bureau's wiretaps, bugging of hotel rooms, and leaks to the press would continue until King's 1968 assassination in Memphis.

Although King's speech was widely hailed in the days following the march, by the time of his death, in Hansen's words, it "had nearly vanished from public view." In his cogent historical analysis of the speech, Hansen maintains that between 1963 and 1968 "few people spent substantial time talking or thinking about what King had said at the march." One reason for this was the increasingly militant stance taken by the black liberation movement. The Watts riot of 1965 in Los Angeles, in reaction to police brutality and widespread discrimination, and the periods of urban revolt that followed made the interracial harmony prophesied by King seem increasingly unattainable. Whites were offended in 1966 when the young radical Stokely Carmichael proclaimed that "Black Power" should replace "Freedom Now" as the motto of the movement. King himself also became more radical in his views. Faced with the intractable problems of poverty and the Vietnam War in addition to pervasive racism, he also grew increasingly pessimistic. In speeches after 1965 King began saying that his dream had turned into a nightmare. By the time of his death in 1968, the upbeat spirit of the "I Have a Dream" speech seemed hopelessly out of date. Only after King's murder was his speech elevated to the exalted position it now occupies.

According to Hansen, politicians focused on the "I Have a Dream" speech because it helped them "forget King's post-1965 career." Although the speech twice mentions racial problems in the North, its major emphasis is on the Jim Crow discrimination of the South. By the time a nation-

Questions for Further Study

1. On April 3, 1968, the day before he was assassinated, Martin Luther King, Jr., delivered a speech in support of striking Memphis sanitation workers. Known as his "I See the Promised Land" speech, or "the Mountaintop" speech, it is second only to the "I Have a Dream" speech in popularity among King's speeches. Compare the two addresses. How do they differ in tone? How do they differ in content?

2. There is no substitute for watching a film of King's "I Have a Dream" speech. View the speech and closely observe the interaction between King and his audience. At what points of the speech do his listeners react most enthusiastically? How does the audience's response affect King's delivery? In what ways does the impact of the film version differ from the effect of the written document?

3. John Lewis also delivered an important address at the March on Washington. Both King and Lewis were working in the southern civil rights movement, and both came from strong religious backgrounds, yet their speeches are quite different. After reading Lewis's words, compare the two documents. How do they differ? What are the points of agreement? Why is King's speech remembered today while Lewis's is largely forgotten?

4. In 1895 the African American educator Booker T. Washington delivered a memorable speech—the Atlanta Exposition Address—at the Cotton States and International Exposition in Atlanta. Following his address, Washington was hailed—as King would be—as the unquestioned leader of his people. The thrust of Washington's words, however, is almost totally contradictory to that of King's. Compare the two speeches and identify the different historical circumstances that shaped them.

5. In 1852 the black abolitionist Frederick Douglass spoke at a rally commemorating the Declaration of Independence. His "What to the Slave Is the Fourth of July?" explored several of the same themes covered by Martin Luther King, Jr.'s "I Have a Dream" speech. Compare these two documents and discuss the historical circumstances that produced them.

al holiday in King's name was declared in 1983, corresponding with his mid-January birthday, "whites only" signs had disappeared, and discriminatory voting laws were safely in the past. The recycling of King's speech thus allowed the nation to celebrate the elimination of legally sanctioned segregation while ignoring the widespread racial inequality that remained unaffected by civil rights legislation. In an ironic twist, conservative commentators began to quote King's admonition to judge people not by the color of their skin but by "the content of their character" in arguing against affirmative action, a program King himself endorsed.

See also A. Philip Randolph's "Call to Negro America to March on Washington" (1941); Martin Luther King, Jr.: "Letter from Birmingham Jail" (1963); John F. Kennedy's Civil Rights Address (1963); Civil Rights Act of 1964; Stokely Carmichael's "Black Power" (1966).

Further Reading

■ Articles

Alvarez, Alexandra. "Martin Luther King's 'I Have a Dream': The Speech Event as Metaphor." *Journal of Black Studies* 18, no. 3 (March 1988): 337–357.

Garrow, David J. "King: The Man, the March, the Dream." *American History* 38, no. 3 (August 2003): 26–35.

Mills, Nicholas. "Heard and Unheard Speeches: What Really Happened at the March on Washington?" *Dissent* 35 (Summer 1988): 285–291.

Powers, Richard Gid. "The FBI Marches on the Dreamer." *American History* 38, no. 3 (August 2003): 42–47.

Reed, Harry A. "Martin Luther King, Jr.: History and Memory, Reflections on Dreams and Silences." *Journal of Negro History* 84, no. 2 (Spring 1999): 150–166.

■ Books

Bennett, Lerone. *Confrontation: Black and White*. Chicago: Johnson Publishing, 1965.

Garrow, David J. *Bearing the Cross: Martin Luther King, Jr., and the Southern Christian Leadership Conference*. New York: Vintage Books, 1986.

Hansen, Drew D. *The Dream: Martin Luther King, Jr., and the Speech That Inspired a Nation*. New York: HarperCollins, 2003.

Johnson, Charles, and Bob Adelman. *King: The Photobiography of Martin Luther King, Jr.* New York: Viking Studio, 2000.

Lischer, Richard. *The Preacher King: Martin Luther King, Jr., and the Word That Moved America*. New York: Oxford University Press, 1995.

Miller, Keith D. *Voice of Deliverance: The Language of Martin Luther King, Jr., and Its Sources*. New York: Free Press, 1992.

■ Web Sites

"I've Been to the Mountaintop." The Martin Luther King, Jr., Research and Education Institute Web site.
http://mlk-kpp01.stanford.edu/index.php/encyclopedia/documentsentry/ive_been_to_the_mountaintop/.

"March on Washington for Jobs and Freedom (1963)." King Encyclopedia Web site.
http://mlk-kpp01.stanford.edu/index.php/encyclopedia/encyclopedia/enc_march_on_washington_for_jobs_and_freedom/.

—Paul T. Murray

Martin Luther King, Jr.: "I Have a Dream"

I am happy to join with you today in what will go down in history as the greatest demonstration for freedom in the history of our nation.

Fivescore years ago, a great American, in whose symbolic shadow we stand today, signed the Emancipation Proclamation. This momentous decree came as a great beacon light of hope to millions of Negro slaves who had been seared in the flames of withering injustice. It came as a joyous daybreak to end the long night of their captivity.

But one hundred years later, the Negro still is not free. One hundred years later, the life of the Negro is still sadly crippled by the manacles of segregation and the chains of discrimination. One hundred years later, the Negro lives on a lonely island of poverty in the midst of a vast ocean of material prosperity. One hundred years later the Negro is still languished in the corners of American society and finds himself an exile in his own land. And so we've come here today to dramatize a shameful condition.

In a sense we've come to our nation's capital to cash a check. When the architects of our republic wrote the magnificent words of the Constitution and the Declaration of Independence, they were signing a promissory note to which every American was to fall heir. This note was a promise that all men, yes, black men as well as white men, would be guaranteed the "unalienable Rights of Life, Liberty, and the pursuit of Happiness." It is obvious today that America has defaulted on this promissory note insofar as her citizens of color are concerned. Instead of honoring this sacred obligation, America has given the Negro people a bad check, a check which has come back marked "insufficient funds."

But we refuse to believe that the bank of justice is bankrupt. We refuse to believe that there are insufficient funds in the great vaults of opportunity of this nation. And so we've come to cash this check, a check that will give us upon demand the riches of freedom and the security of justice.

We have also come to this hallowed spot to remind America of the fierce urgency of now. This is no time to engage in the luxury of cooling off or to take the tranquilizing drug of gradualism. Now is the time to make real the promises of democracy. Now is the time to rise from the dark and desolate valley of segregation to the sunlit path of racial justice. Now is the time to lift our nation from the quicksands of racial injustice to the solid rock of brotherhood. Now is the time to make justice a reality for all of God's children.

It would be fatal for the nation to overlook the urgency of the moment. This sweltering summer of the Negro's legitimate discontent will not pass until there is an invigorating autumn of freedom and equality. Nineteen sixty-three is not an end, but a beginning. And those who hope that the Negro needed to blow off steam and will now be content will have a rude awakening if the nation returns to business as usual. There will be neither rest nor tranquility in America until the Negro is granted his citizenship rights. The whirlwinds of revolt will continue to shake the foundations of our nation until the bright day of justice emerges.

But there is something that I must say to my people, who stand on the warm threshold which leads into the palace of justice: In the process of gaining our rightful place, we must not be guilty of wrongful deeds. Let us not seek to satisfy our thirst for freedom by drinking from the cup of bitterness and hatred. We must forever conduct our struggle on the high plane of dignity and discipline. We must not allow our creative protest to degenerate into physical violence. Again and again, we must rise to the majestic heights of meeting physical force with soul force. The marvelous new militancy which has engulfed the Negro community must not lead us to a distrust of all white people, for many of our white brothers, as evidenced by their presence here today, have come to realize that their destiny is tied up with our destiny. And they have come to realize that their freedom is inextricably bound to our freedom. We cannot walk alone.

And as we walk, we must make the pledge that we shall always march ahead. We cannot turn back. There are those who are asking the devotees of civil rights, "When will you be satisfied?"

We can never be satisfied as long as the Negro is the victim of the unspeakable horrors of police brutality. We can never be satisfied as long as our bodies, heavy with the fatigue of travel, cannot gain lodging in the motels of the highways and the hotels of the cities. We cannot be satisfied as long as the Negro's basic mobility is from a smaller ghetto to a larger one.

Document Text

We can never be satisfied as long as our children are stripped of their selfhood and robbed of their dignity by signs stating "for whites only." We cannot be satisfied as long as a Negro in Mississippi cannot vote and a Negro in New York believes he has nothing for which to vote. No, no, we are not satisfied and we will not be satisfied until "justice rolls down like waters and righteousness like a mighty stream."

I am not unmindful that some of you have come here out of great trials and tribulations. Some of you have come fresh from narrow jail cells. Some of you have come from areas where your quest for freedom left you battered by the storms of persecution and staggered by the winds of police brutality. You have been the veterans of creative suffering. Continue to work with the faith that unearned suffering is redemptive. Go back to Mississippi, go back to Alabama, go back to South Carolina, go back to Georgia, go back to Louisiana, go back to the slums and ghettos of our northern cities, knowing that somehow this situation can and will be changed. Let us not wallow in the valley of despair.

I say to you today, my friends, so even though we face the difficulties of today and tomorrow, I still have a dream. It is a dream deeply rooted in the American dream.

I have a dream that one day this nation will rise up and live out the true meaning of its creed: "We hold these truths to be self-evident, that all men are created equal."

I have a dream that one day on the red hills of Georgia, the sons of former slaves and the sons of former slave owners will be able to sit down together at the table of brotherhood.

I have a dream that one day even the state of Mississippi, a state sweltering with the heat of injustice, sweltering with the heat of oppression, will be transformed into an oasis of freedom and justice.

I have a dream that my four little children will one day live in a nation where they will not be judged by the color of their skin but by the content of their character. I have a dream today.

I have a dream that one day down in Alabama, with its vicious racists, with its governor having his lips dripping with the words of "interposition" and "nullification," one day right there in Alabama little black boys and black girls will be able to join hands with little white boys and white girls as sisters and brothers. I have a dream today.

I have a dream that one day "every valley shall be exalted, and every hill and mountain shall be made low; the rough places will be made plain, and the crooked places will be made straight; and the glory of the Lord shall be revealed, and all flesh shall see it together."

This is our hope. This is the faith that I go back to the South with. With this faith we will be able to hew out of the mountain of despair a stone of hope. With this faith we will be able to transform the jangling discords of our nation into a beautiful symphony of brotherhood. With this faith we will be able to work together, to pray together, to struggle together, to go to jail together, to stand up for freedom together, knowing that we will be free one day. This will be the day, this will be the day when all of God's children will be able to sing with new meaning:

> My Country, 'tis of thee, sweet land of liberty, of thee I Sing.
> Land where my fathers died, land of the pilgrim's pride
> From every mountainside, let freedom ring!

And if America is to be a great nation, this must become true.

And so let freedom ring from the prodigious hilltops of New Hampshire.

Let freedom ring from the mighty mountains of New York.

Let freedom ring from the heightening Alleghenies of Pennsylvania.

Glossary

interposition and nullification	a discredited legal theory holding that states can nullify federal laws that they consider unconstitutional, as used by segregationists trying to reverse the Supreme Court's *Brown v. Board of Education* decision
promissory note	a written promise to pay a specific amount on demand or at a specific time
fivescore	one hundred—a "score" being twenty

Document Text

Let freedom ring from the snowcapped Rockies of Colorado.

Let freedom ring from the curvaceous slopes of California.

But not only that: Let freedom ring from Stone Mountain of Georgia.

Let freedom ring from Lookout Mountain of Tennessee.

Let freedom ring from every hill and molehill of Mississippi.

From every mountainside, let freedom ring.

And when this happens, when we allow freedom to ring, when we let it ring from every village and every hamlet, from every state and every city; we will be able to speed up that day when all of God's children, black men and white men, Jews and Gentiles, Protestants and Catholics, will be able to join hands and sing in the words of the old Negro spiritual:

Free at last! Free at last!
Thank God Almighty, we are free at last!

An Act

To enforce the constitutional right to vote, to confer jurisdiction upon the district courts of the United States to provide injunctive relief against discrimination in public accommodations, to authorize the Attorney General to institute suits to protect constitutional rights in public facilities and public education, to extend the Commission on Civil Rights, to prevent discrimination in federally assisted programs, to establish a Commission on Equal Employment Opportunity, and for other purposes.

Be it enacted by the Senate and House of Representatives of the United States of America in Congress assembled, That this Act may be cited as the "Civil Rights Act of 1964".

TITLE I—VOTING RIGHTS

SEC. 101. Section 2004 of the Revised Statutes (42 U.S.C. 1971), as amended by section 131 of the Civil Rights Act of 1957 (71 Stat. 637), and as further amended by section 601 of the Civil Rights Act of 1960 (74 Stat. 90), is further amended as follows:

(a) Insert "1" after "(a)" in subsection (a) and add at the end of subsection (a) the following new paragraphs:

"(2) No person acting under color of law shall—

"(A) in determining whether any individual is qualified under State law or laws to vote in any Federal election, apply any standard, practice, or procedure different from the standards, practices, or procedures applied under such law or laws to other individuals within the same county, parish, or similar political subdivision who have been found by State officials to be qualified to vote;

"(B) deny the right of any individual to vote in any Federal election because of an error or omission on any record or paper relating to any application, registration, or other act requisite to voting, if such error or omission is not material in determining whether such individual is qualified under State law to vote in such election; or

"(C) employ any literacy test as a qualification for voting in any Federal election unless (i) such test is administered to each individual and is conducted wholly in writing, and (ii) a certified copy of the test and of the answers given by the individual is furnished to him within twenty-five days of the submission of his request made within the period of time during which records and papers are required to be retained and preserved pursuant to title III of the Civil Rights Act of 1960 (42 U.S.C. 1974–74e; 74 Stat. 88) : *Provided, however,* That the Attorney General may enter into agreements with appropriate State or local authorities that preparation, conduct, and maintenance of such tests in accordance with the provisions of applicable State or local law, including such special provisions as are necessary in the prepara-

The Civil Rights Act of 1964 (National Archives and Records Administration)

Civil Rights Act of 1964

"All persons shall be entitled to the full and equal enjoyment ... of any place of public accommodation ... without discrimination or segregation on the ground of race."

Overview

Enacted on July 2, 1964—in the year after President John F. Kennedy's assassination; the bloody campaign to integrate Birmingham, Alabama; and the first March on Washington, which featured Martin Luther King, Jr.'s "I Have a Dream" Speech—the Civil Rights Act of 1964 was the most important piece of civil rights legislation passed since the Reconstruction era. It outlawed discrimination on a number of bases, including race, color, religion, national origin, and, with respect to employment, sex. Also of importance was the breadth of areas in which discrimination was outlawed, as the act prohibited discrimination in places of public accommodations, public facilities, federally assisted programs, employment, and voting. It also pushed for the full desegregation of schools and expanded the U.S. Commission on Civil Rights, which had been created by the Civil Rights Act of 1957. Last, the 1964 act created institutions for monitoring and facilitating the advancement of civil rights, such as the Equal Employment Opportunity Commission, to enforce Title VII of the act, and the Community Relations Service, to assist "communities and persons therein in resolving disputes, disagreements, or difficulties relating to discriminatory practices based on race, color, or national origin."

In requiring equality, the Civil Rights Act of 1964 arguably provided many of the freedoms that African Americans should have already enjoyed as a result of the Fourteenth Amendment, extending that amendment close to its logical limit. However, the act went further than Fourteenth Amendment doctrine allowed in regulating purely private conduct in some instances. The regulation of private conduct required that the act be based on Congress's commerce clause power in addition to whatever authority Congress had under its Fourteenth Amendment enforcement power. The act's continual mention of interstate commerce is a nod to that requirement. In truth, without the regulation of private conduct, the act would not be nearly as important as it was and continues to be. Simply put, it remains the broadest, most effective, and most important civil rights bill passed since Reconstruction.

The 1964 act and the debate around it signaled a changing of the guard: Discrimination was officially repudiated, and equality was required in more places than previously imagined. The filibuster of the act by southern senators arguably represented the last-ditch efforts of desperate men who wished to hew to a bygone era. Those who wished to protect and perpetuate the old order were duly told to stand aside, as the United States entered a new era in which all of its citizens were to be treated as equal under the law and as full members of the polity.

Context

The Civil Rights Act of 1964 was passed in the middle of the turmoil and upheaval in American society of the 1950s and 1960s. Seminal events such as the Montgomery bus boycott, the Supreme Court case *Brown v. Board of Education of Topeka*, the integration of Little Rock Central High School, and the March on Washington for Jobs and Freedom had already occurred. Many other events—including the attacks in Selma, Alabama; the passage of the Voting Rights Act of 1965; the assassinations of Martin Luther King, Jr., and Malcolm X; and the riots in major American cities—were yet on the horizon.

The events that immediately precipitated the 1964 act's introduction in Congress and its eventual passage are fairly clear. President Kennedy originally sent the bill that would become the act to Congress on June 19, 1963, as a reaction to the violence that accompanied the civil rights movement's attempt to integrate Birmingham. The bill had not moved far at the time of President Kennedy's assassination in November 1963. In the immediate aftermath of Kennedy's death, President Lyndon B. Johnson called on Congress to pass the law as a fitting tribute to his predecessor. During the legislative debate on the bill, President Johnson used many of the favors he was owed from his longtime service in Congress to move the bill forward. In addition to Johnson's favors, the supporters of the civil rights legislation used many parliamentary maneuvers, voting power, and sheer will to shepherd the bill through Congress. The need for resolve intensified when the bill was significantly strengthened in the House Judiciary Committee after prodding by civil rights groups. Following passage in the House of Representatives, the bill was sent to the

Time Line

1947
- **December**
  The President's Committee on Civil Rights issues *To Secure These Rights*, urging Congress to pass civil rights legislation.

1954
- **May 17**
  In *Brown v. Board of Education*, the Supreme Court outlaws segregation in public schools.

1955
- **December 1**
  Rosa Parks refuses to vacate her bus seat for a white person, sparking the Montgomery bus boycott.

1957
- **September 4–25**
  Central High School in Little Rock, Arkansas, is integrated in a process that requires that federal troops protect African American students and escort them to classes.
- **September 9**
  The Civil Rights Act of 1957, the first civil rights act since 1875, is signed by President Dwight D. Eisenhower, creating the Commission on Civil Rights and attempting—fairly weakly—to protect the voting rights of African Americans.

1960
- **May 6**
  The Civil Rights Act of 1960 is signed by President Eisenhower.
- **November 8**
  John F. Kennedy is elected president of the United States.

1963
- **April–June**
  Civil rights groups attempt to integrate Birmingham, Alabama, and are met with police dogs and fire hoses.
- **June 11**
  The University of Alabama is integrated.
- **June 12**
  Medgar Evers, Mississippi director of the National Association for the Advancement of Colored People, is slain.

Senate on February 17, 1964; after the longest filibuster on record in the U.S. Senate—eighty-two days—the act passed in amended form by a vote of 73–27. The Senate bill then passed unamended in the House of Representatives by a vote of 289–126. President Johnson signed the bill on July 2, 1964.

About the Author

The Civil Rights Act of 1964 was shaped by a host of people. The original bill was crafted and drafted in the Department of Justice, headed by Attorney General Robert Kennedy. The drafting group almost certainly included Robert Kennedy and his assistant attorneys general, Burke Marshall and Nicholas Katzenbach, as well as the Justice Department lawyer Harold Greene (who later became a judge). As the bill moved through the committee process in the House of Representatives, it was significantly redrafted and strengthened by members and staff of the House Judiciary Committee, including the Democratic representative Emanuel Celler of New York and the Republican representative William McCulloch of Ohio and their aides. Many amendments were added from the floor of the House, with one of the most momentous being offered by the Democratic representative Howard W. Smith of Virginia, chairman of the House Rules Committee. Smith added the provision including sex discrimination to Title VII of the act as a prohibited mode of discrimination, apparently in an effort to derail the bill. The amendment passed, and the bill ultimately passed the House. On the Senate side, a number of amendments were offered and passed, but the bill was not overwhelmingly altered in substance; Everett Dirksen, a Republican senator from Illinois, was the Senate's most active amender of the bill.

Explanation and Analysis of the Document

The Civil Rights Act of 1964 begins with a simple recitation of its purpose, indicating the range of substantive areas it touches, the federal commissions it creates, and the methods of enforcement it provides. Title I (Voting Rights) is an amendment of the Civil Rights Acts of 1957 and 1960. It applies to federal elections, requiring that all voters be held to the same qualification standards and prohibiting discrimination on the basis of race, color, religion, or national origin. However, this title does not outlaw some of the methods that were being used to discriminate against African Americans, including literacy tests. Regarding such tests, Title I instead attempts to ensure that they are applied as equally as possible. For example, it requires that literacy tests be administered in writing and allows the attorney general to negotiate with state and local authorities regarding their use. This title also allows the attorney general to request that a three-judge panel hear allegations of voting rights violations arising under its statutes. Appeals from the three-judge panel would be directed to the Supreme Court.

Title I was largely superseded by the Voting Rights Act of 1965, which generally prohibited methods of discriminating against minorities, including literacy tests, and strengthened the right to vote in general. The Voting Rights Act was passed pursuant to the Fifteenth Amendment rather than to the Fourteenth Amendment.

Title II (Injunctive Relief against Discrimination in Places of Public Accommodation) prohibits discrimination on the basis of race, color, religion, or national origin in the provision of goods, services, facilities, privileges, advantages, and accommodations at any place of public accommodations. Title II also prohibits attempts to prevent any persons from attempting to enjoy their rights under its terms. Places of public accommodations are held to include lodging places of all kinds other than owner-occupied establishments with five or fewer rooms for rent or hire. Also included under the title's terms are restaurants, theaters, sports arenas, and all establishments located inside of such places if they serve the customers of those places. The title does not cover private clubs and other places not open to the public.

Title II was one of the act's most controversial titles because it struck at the heart of what some thought were the legitimate prerogatives of business owners. By elevating the right of minority patrons to receive equal treatment above the right of business owners to refuse service to anyone, the title became a public expression of the nation's new equality—and made sit-ins at lunch counters unnecessary.

Rights granted under Title II could be vindicated in a number of different ways. If rights were violated or about to be violated, aggrieved individuals would be permitted to directly sue for injunctive relief, and under certain circumstances the attorney general could intervene in support of the plaintiff. However, if the activity held to be a violation were to occur in a state or locality that allowed local officials to "grant or seek relief from such practice or to institute criminal proceedings with respect thereto," those local officials had to be given the opportunity to address the issue before an action for federal injunctive relief could be brought. If the violation were to occur in a state or locality that did not authorize local officials to redress the activity, the aggrieved person could sue, although the court might refer the matter to the Community Relations Service, established in Title X of the act, to see whether voluntary compliance might be possible.

Title II tracks the public accommodations provisions of the Civil Rights Act of 1875, which were deemed unconstitutional in the Civil Rights Cases (1883), although the 1964 act's provisions are somewhat narrower. In the 1964 act, Congress limited actionable discrimination to discrimination that involves state action or establishments whose operations affect commerce. In doing so, Congress guaranteed that the title was clearly within either Congress's Fourteenth Amendment enforcement power or its commerce clause power. Nonetheless, two challenges to Title II arose immediately after the 1964 act was passed, with both *Heart of Atlanta Motel v. United States* and *Katzenbach v. McClung* challenging the constitutionality of Title II that

Time Line

1963
- **June 19** President Kennedy sends the civil rights bill that would become the Civil Rights Act of 1964 to Congress.
- **August 28** Martin Luther King, Jr., leads the March on Washington and delivers his "I Have a Dream" Speech.
- **November 22** President Kennedy is assassinated in Dallas, Texas.
- **November 27** President Lyndon B. Johnson calls for the passage of the civil rights bill to honor President Kennedy's memory.

1964
- **July 2** The Civil Rights Act of 1964 is signed by President Johnson.
- **November 3** Lyndon B. Johnson is popularly elected president.

1965
- **February 21** Malcolm X is assassinated in New York City.
- **March 7** The march from Selma to Montgomery for voting rights ends with Alabama state troopers attacking marchers.
- **August 6** The Voting Rights Act of 1965 becomes law.

1968
- **April 4** Martin Luther King, Jr., is assassinated in Memphis, Tennessee.
- **June 5** Robert F. Kennedy is assassinated in Los Angeles.
- **November 5** Richard M. Nixon is elected president of the United States.

same year. In both cases, the Supreme Court determined that Title II was an acceptable exercise of Congress's commerce clause power. Once those cases were settled, the constitutionality of the 1964 act was not in doubt, and the task of fully integrating the country could begin.

Title III (Desegregation of Public Facilities) authorizes the attorney general to file suit on behalf of the United States against a state or locality under certain circumstances when the attorney general has received a complaint from an individual indicating that he or she is being denied equal protection rights because he or she is being denied equal use of a public facility. If the individual is unable to litigate the case fully or properly and if suit by the United States "will materially further the orderly progress of desegregation in public facilities," the attorney general may intervene. This title simply puts the resources of the federal government behind those who attempt to integrate public facilities that should have already been desegregated.

Title IV (Desegregation of Public Education) provides technical and financial assistance to school districts that experience problems with desegregation. It also provides help to those persons whose children are being denied the equal protection of the law by a school board or public college because of race, color, religion, or national origin and who are unable to fully and adequately prosecute the litigation. However, the title makes clear that it is not to apply to cases in which busing is sought to resolve issues of racial imbalance in schools. As with Title III, the resources of the federal government were being made available so that established constitutional requirements, in this case the desegregation of schools, could be met.

Title V (Commission on Civil Rights) renews and retools the mandate of the Commission on Civil Rights, which was created by the Civil Rights Act of 1957. The commission is authorized to investigate allegations related to voting rights and voting fraud allegations. In addition, it is tasked with studying and collecting information and appraising the laws and policies of the federal government regarding denials of equal protection based on race, color, religion, or national origin in the administration of justice. Last, the commission is to "serve as a national clearinghouse for information in respect to denials of equal protection of the laws because of race, color, religion or national origin, including but not limited to the fields of voting, education, housing, employment, the use of public facilities, and transportation, or in the administration of justice." However, the commission is restricted from investigating the membership practices of fraternal organizations, fraternities, sororities, private clubs, and religious organizations.

Title V's passage was not without problems, as debate occurred regarding whether merely to extend the life of the Commission on Civil Rights or to make it permanent. The 1964 act simply extended the life of the commission, but it has continued to exist through various extensions and reauthorizations.

Title VI (Nondiscrimination in Federally Assisted Programs) focuses on guaranteeing that federal tax money does not go to programs that discriminate on the basis of race, color, or national origin. It directs federal agencies and departments to issue rules and regulations consistent with the principles underlying Title VI and the act as a whole. Title VI was largely intended to discontinue the funds that were being provided to segregated schools in the South. However, the title clearly applies to all sorts of programs that receive federal funding, including hospitals, building projects, and road construction. Indeed, regulations stemming from Title VI may have been the biggest benefit to minority contractors in the country's history.

Title VII (Equal Employment Opportunity) is by far the longest title of the 1964 Civil Rights Act and possibly the act's most controversial. As originally submitted by the Kennedy administration, Title VII merely allowed the president to establish a commission on equal employment opportunity to regulate companies with government contracts. As finally enacted, the title dealt with guaranteeing equality in employment, an area that was historically thought to have been controlled by the prerogative of the employer. The limitation on how employment decisions could be made was arguably second only to the requirement that public accommodations be equal in its effect on the psyche of those whose actions were regulated by the act. The title restricts not only how employers can fill jobs but also how employment agencies can refer people for employment and how labor organizations can include and exclude people from membership. Simply put, under the terms of the act, none of these entities could discriminate against people and employees based on their race, color, religion, sex, or national origin. In addition, none of the entities would be permitted to retaliate against those who formally or informally opposed employment practices made unlawful by Title VII.

The most momentous aspect of Title VII was its inclusion of sex discrimination as a prohibited ground for discrimination. Sex was added as an amendment by the Democratic representative Howard Smith of Virginia. Although he was the powerful chairman of the House Rules Committee, he was outmaneuvered and overruled by those who were determined to pass the 1964 act. As one of his final attempts to derail the bill, he proposed the addition of sex to the terms. Rather than reject the proposal, the House, with the support of most of its female members, accepted the amendment and eventually the entire act. However, because sex was added to the terms near the very end of the legislative process, little legislative history exists to interpret what constitutes the clause. Consequently, courts have had a more difficult time determining what constitutes sex discrimination under Title VII than what constitutes race discrimination under Title VII.

Title VII also creates the Equal Employment Opportunity Commission and gives it primary responsibility for investigating and processing discrimination claims, although the process of adjudicating such claims is largely left to the federal courts. In addition, the commission is to provide technical assistance to those employers and others who wish to properly discharge their responsibilities and duties under Title VII.

Title VII was controversial not only for what it did but also for what some believed it would do. Many claimed that Title VII's provisions would eventually require that businesses maintain quotas to ensure the racial balance of the workforce. A number of representatives and senators disputed this reading of the bill. Nevertheless, specific language was added to the bill to make clear that Title VII would never require a preference for one race based solely on a racial imbalance in the workplace.

Title VIII (Registration and Voting Statistics) authorizes the secretary of commerce to gather voting data on populations and parse the data based on race, color, and national origin. Rather than parsing data for the entire country, the data is to be gathered for whatever geographic areas are suggested by the Commission on Civil Rights. Given that the Bureau of the Census gathers statistics and is a part of the Department of Commerce, the act unsurprisingly tasks the commerce secretary with the responsibility outlined here.

Title IX (Intervention and Procedure after Removal in Civil Rights Cases) is purely procedural in nature. It dictates what is to occur when a case that was filed in state court and then removed to federal court is sent back to the state court. It also addresses when the federal government is allowed to intervene in a civil rights case and the implications of the intervention.

Title X (Establishment of Community Relations Service) creates the Community Relations Service to provide conciliation and mediation in local communities when issues of equality arise that can be solved through means less formal than court filings. The service is purely a problem-solving entity; it is not supposed to be involved in any litigation that might arise out of the matters it handles. The Community Relations Service can be thought of as a mechanism to turn down the heat on a community dispute before it boils over into discord or violence.

Title XI (Miscellaneous), as its title suggests, addresses various issues not dealt with anywhere else in the statute. For example, it addresses rules for criminal contempt in cases brought pursuant to the act. It also notes that nothing in the act should be construed to affect the ability of the attorney general or anyone acting in his stead from intervening in cases based on laws passed prior to the act. Last, the final title notes the severability of any part of the act found to be invalid—meaning that if a part of the act were to be deemed unenforceable, the rest of the act would remain valid.

Audience

The intended audience for the 1964 act was the country as a whole. The message was to be sent to all citizens of the United States that discrimination would no longer be acceptable if the government could prevent it. Although the government could not change the hearts and minds of its citizens, it could guarantee equality in the most important spheres of life. People could not be required to think in a certain way; however, they could be influenced in their

President Lyndon Johnson signs into law the Civil Rights Act in ceremonies July 2, 1964, in the East Room of the White House. (AP/Wide World Photos)

thinking by the country's collective thoughts on an issue, as expressed in its laws.

Of course, many of the nation's citizens did not need to have their mindsets changed by the act. According to Gallup and Harris polls taken in 1964, the bill had the support of more than half of the American public as it was moving toward passage. Consequently, the act did not have to be sold wholesale to the American people. Rather, the sale needed to be made to certain parts of the country—and perhaps to certain segments in every part of the country—that were quite vocal in their opposition to equality. Eventually, the chorus for equality drowned out the voices for inequality.

Impact

The Civil Rights Act of 1964 changed the landscape of American race relations forever by indicating that discrimination would no longer be the order of the day. The symbolic significance of the act cannot be overstated. By delving into the realm of private conduct and requiring equality in areas that many thought Congress would never regulate, the 1964 act made equality in public areas the new paradigm. It afforded African Americans everyday dignities that had been owed but not granted to black citizens. The act did not cure racial strife, but it helped make American life significantly more hospitable for minorities. The law may not have altered mindsets as much as it gave voice to the attitudes of the more progressive among the citizenry.

Essential Quotes

"An Act: To enforce the constitutional right to vote, to confer jurisdiction upon the district courts of the United States to provide injunctive relief against discrimination in public accommodations, to authorize the Attorney General to institute suits to protect constitutional rights in public facilities and public education, to extend the Commission on Civil Rights, to prevent discrimination in federally assisted programs, to establish a Commission on Equal Employment Opportunity, and for other purposes."

(Introduction)

"All persons shall be entitled to the full and equal enjoyment of the goods, services, facilities, and privileges, advantages, and accommodations of any place of public accommodation, as defined in this section, without discrimination or segregation on the ground of race, color, religion, or national origin."

(Section 201)

"Each of the following establishments which serves the public is a place of public accommodation within the meaning of this title if its operations affect commerce, or if discrimination or segregation by it is supported by State action: (1) any inn, hotel, motel, or other establishment which provides lodging to transient guests…; (2) any restaurant, cafeteria, lunchroom, lunch counter, soda fountain, or other facility principally engaged in selling food."

(Section 201)

"It shall be an unlawful employment practice for an employer—(1) to fail or refuse to hire or to discharge any individual, or otherwise to discriminate against any individual with respect to his compensation, terms, conditions, or privileges of employment, because of such individual's race, color, religion, sex, or national origin; or (2) to limit, segregate, or classify his employees in any way which would deprive or tend to deprive any individual of employment opportunities or otherwise adversely affect his status as an employee, because of such individual's race, color, religion, sex, or national origin."

(Section 703[a])

Equally important, it removed the cover of law for those with discriminatory views. In the end, the law was accepted, grudgingly or not, and most calls to obey were heeded. Indeed, the law and its sanctions made it almost impossible for businesses to fail to comply.

In many ways, the 1964 act finished much of the work of the Reconstruction amendments. Those amendments provided a constitutional structure that was supposed to make all citizens equal before the law and full members of American society. While the Reconstruction amendments made minority Americans legal citizens, the 1964 act helped allow those citizens to enjoy their full rights of citizenship. Equality finally became the glue that is supposed to hold all Americans together.

The 1964 act was a powerful sequel to the Civil Rights Acts of 1957 and 1960. The 1957 act had been the first significant civil rights bill passed since the Reconstruction-era Civil Rights Act of 1875. However, the 1957 act focused on voting rights and did not have nearly the breadth and importance that the 1964 act would have. Similarly, the Civil Rights Act of 1960 was fairly weak. The 1964 act, to the contrary, opened the floodgates of change. In its immediate wake, Congress passed the Voting Rights Act of 1965, and additional strong antidiscrimination measures were passed soon after. Some, like the Age Discrimination in Employment Act of 1967, targeted the hiring practices of businesses. Others, such as the Fair Housing Act of 1968 and the Equal Credit Opportunity Act of 1974, targeted discrimination more broadly. Beyond the 1960s civil rights era, antidiscrimination legislation continued to be passed, both in the form of revisions, such as those to the 1964 act that occurred in 1972 and 1991, and in the form of new acts, such as the Americans with Disabilities Act of 1990. Thus, the Civil Rights Act of 1964 paved the way for many other laws that have made America even more hospitable to all of her people.

See also Fourteenth Amendment to the U.S. Constitution (1868); *Brown v. Board of Education* (1954); Martin Luther King, Jr.: "I Have a Dream" (1963).

Further Reading

■ Books

Gillon, Steven M. *That's Not What We Meant to Do: Reform and Its Unintended Consequences in Twentieth-Century America.* New York: W. W. Norton, 2000.

Grofman, Bernard, ed. *Legacies of the 1964 Civil Rights Act.* Charlottesville: University Press of Virginia, 2000.

Halpern, Stephen C. *On the Limits of the Law: The Ironic Legacy of Title VI of the 1964 Civil Rights Act.* Baltimore, Md.: Johns Hopkins University Press, 1995.

Klarman, Michael J. *From Jim Crow to Civil Rights: The Supreme Court and the Struggle for Racial Equality.* New York: Oxford University Press, 2004.

Kotz, Nick. *Judgment Days: Lyndon Baines Johnson, Martin Luther King, Jr., and the Laws That Changed America.* Boston: Houghton Mifflin, 2005.

Questions for Further Study

1. The Civil Rights Act of 1964 was justified both as an extension of the Fourteenth Amendment and as a proper application of the commerce clause. Would the Civil Rights Act of 1964 have been reasonable law if it had been passed during the Reconstruction era? How similar are some of its sections to laws passed during Reconstruction?

2. To ensure passage, the Civil Rights Act of 1964 underwent significant changes. In fact, the act as finalized proved stronger than the civil rights bill sent to Congress by President Kennedy in 1963. Does this circumstance reveal anything about President Kennedy's commitment to civil rights, or does it reveal his ability to divine Congress's tolerance for a strong civil rights bill, or does it reveal something entirely different?

3. What effect, if any, do you believe the Civil Rights Act of 1964 has had on the electoral results of the Democratic Party in the South from the 1960s to the present?

4. What might the United States have come to look like had the Civil Rights Act of 1964 not been passed? Would the act have passed had President Kennedy not been assassinated?

5. Arguably, the Civil Rights Act of 1964 was the culmination of the first stage of the civil rights era. Which act was more important to civil rights, the Civil Rights Act of 1964 or the Voting Rights Act of 1965?

Loevy, Robert D., ed. *The Civil Rights Act of 1964: The Passage of the Law That Ended Racial Segregation.* Albany: State University of New York Press, 1997.

Sokol, Jason. *There Goes My Everything: White Southerners in the Age of Civil Rights, 1945–1975.* New York: Alfred A. Knopf, 2006.

Whalen, Charles, and Barbara Whalen. *The Longest Debate: A Legislative History of the 1964 Civil Rights Act.* Cabin John, Md.: Seven Locks Press, 1985.

Zietlow, Rebecca E. *Enforcing Equality: Congress, the Constitution, and the Protection of Individual Rights.* New York: New York University Press, 2006.

■ Web Sites

Rhodes, Henry A. "An Analysis of the Civil Rights Act of 1964: A Legislated Response to Racial Discrimination in the U.S." Yale–New Haven Teachers Institute Web site.
http://www.yale.edu/ynhti/curriculum/units/1982/3/82.03.04.x.html.

"Teaching with Documents: The Civil Rights Act of 1964 and the Equal Employment Opportunity Commission." National Archives "Educators and Students" Web site.
http://www.archives.gov/education/lessons/civil-rights-act/.

—Henry L. Chambers, Jr.

Civil Rights Act of 1964

An Act: To enforce the constitutional right to vote, to confer jurisdiction upon the district courts of the United States to provide injunctive relief against discrimination in public accommodations, to authorize the Attorney General to institute suits to protect constitutional rights in public facilities and public education, to extend the Commission on Civil Rights, to prevent discrimination in federally assisted programs, to establish a Commission on Equal Employment Opportunity, and for other purposes.

Be it enacted by the Senate and House of Representatives of the United States of America in Congress assembled, That this Act may be cited as the "Civil Rights Act of 1964".

Title I—Voting Rights

SEC. 101. Section 2004 of the Revised Statutes (42 U.S.C. 1971), as amended by section 131 of the Civil Rights Act of 1957 (71 Stat. 637), and as further amended by section 601 of the Civil Rights Act of 1960 (74 Stat. 90), is further amended as follows:

(a) Insert "1" after "(a)" in subsection (a) and add at the end of subsection (a) the following new paragraphs:

"(2) No person acting under color of law shall—

"(A) in determining whether any individual is qualified under State law or laws to vote in any Federal election, apply any standard, practice, or procedure different from the standards, practices, or procedures applied under such law or laws to other individuals within the same county, parish, or similar political subdivision who have been found by State officials to be qualified to vote;

"(B) deny the right of any individual to vote in any Federal election because of an error or omission on any record or paper relating to any application, registration, or other act requisite to voting, if such error or omission is not material in determining whether such individual is qualified under State law to vote in such election; or

"(C) employ any literacy test as a qualification for voting in any Federal election unless (i) such test is administered to each individual and is conducted wholly in writing, and (ii) a certified copy of the test and of the answers given by the individual is furnished to him within twenty-five days of the submission of his request made within the period of time during which records and papers are required to be retained and preserved pursuant to title III of the Civil Rights Act of 1960 (42 U.S.C. 1974-74e; 74 Stat. 88): Provided, however, That the Attorney General may enter into agreements with appropriate State or local authorities that preparation, conduct, and maintenance of such tests in accordance with the provisions of applicable State or local law, including such special provisions as are necessary in the preparation, conduct, and maintenance of such tests for persons who are blind or otherwise physically handicapped, meet the purposes of this subparagraph and constitute compliance therewith.

"(3) For purposes of this subsection—

"(A) the term 'vote' shall have the same meaning as in subsection (e) of this section;

"(B) the phrase 'literacy test' includes any test of the ability to read, write, understand, or interpret any matter."

(b) Insert immediately following the period at the end of the first sentence of subsection (c) the following new sentence: "If in any such proceeding literacy is a relevant fact there shall be a rebuttable presumption that any person who has not been adjudged an incompetent and who has completed the sixth grade in a public school in, or a private school accredited by, any State or territory, the District of Columbia, or the Commonwealth of Puerto Rico where instruction is carried on predominantly in the English language, possesses sufficient literacy, comprehension, and intelligence to vote in any Federal election."

(c) Add the following subsection "(f)" and designate the present subsection "(f)" as subsection "(g)": "(f) When used in subsection (a) or (c) of this section, the words 'Federal election' shall mean any general, special, or primary election held solely or in part for the purpose of electing or selecting any candidate for the office of President, Vice President, presidential elector, Member of the Senate, or Member of the House of Representatives."

(d) Add the following subsection "(h)":

"(h) In any proceeding instituted by the United States in any district court of the United States under this section in which the Attorney General requests a finding of a pattern or practice of discrimination pursuant to subsection (e) of this section the Attorney General, at the time he files the complaint, or any defendant in the proceeding, within twenty days after service upon him of the complaint, may file with the clerk of such court a request that a court of three judges be convened to hear and determine the entire case. A copy of the request for a three-judge court shall be immediately furnished by such clerk to the chief judge of the circuit (or in his absence, the presiding circuit judge of the circuit) in which the case is pending. Upon receipt of the copy of such request it shall be the duty of the chief justice of the circuit or the presiding circuit judge, as the case may be, to designate immediately three judges in such circuit, of whom at least one shall be a circuit judge and another of whom shall be a district judge of the court in which the proceeding was instituted, to hear and determine such case, and it shall be the duty of the judges so designated to assign the case for hearing at the earliest practicable date, to participate in the hearing and determination thereof, and to cause the case to be in every way expedited.

"An appeal from the final judgment of such court will lie to the Supreme Court.

"In any proceeding brought under subsection (c) of this section to enforce subsection (b) of this section, or in the event neither the Attorney General nor any defendant files a request for a three-judge court in any proceeding authorized by this subsection, it shall be the duty of the chief judge of the district (or in his absence, the acting chief judge) in which the case is pending immediately to designate a judge in such district to hear and determine the case. In the event that no judge in the district is available to hear and determine the case, the chief judge of the district, or the acting chief judge, as the case may be, shall certify this fact to the chief judge of the circuit (or, in his absence, the acting chief judge) who shall then designate a district or circuit judge of the circuit to hear and determine the case.

"It shall be the duty of the judge designated pursuant to this section to assign the case for hearing at the earliest practicable date and to cause the case to be in every way expedited."

Title II—Injunctive Relief against Discrimination in Places of Public Accommodation

SEC. 201. (a) All persons shall be entitled to the full and equal enjoyment of the goods, services, facilities, and privileges, advantages, and accommodations of any place of public accommodation, as defined in this section, without discrimination or segregation on the ground of race, color, religion, or national origin.

(b) Each of the following establishments which serves the public is a place of public accommodation within the meaning of this title if its operations affect commerce, or if discrimination or segregation by it is supported by State action:

(1) any inn, hotel, motel, or other establishment which provides lodging to transient guests, other than an establishment located within a building which contains not more than five rooms for rent or hire and which is actually occupied by the proprietor of such establishment as his residence;

(2) any restaurant, cafeteria, lunchroom, lunch counter, soda fountain, or other facility principally engaged in selling food for consumption on the premises, including, but not limited to, any such facility located on the premises of any retail establishment; or any gasoline station;

(3) any motion picture house, theater, concert hall, sports arena, stadium or other place of exhibition or entertainment; and

(4) any establishment (A)(i) which is physically located within the premises of any establishment otherwise covered by this subsection, or (ii) within the premises of which is physically located any such covered establishment, and (B) which holds itself out as serving patrons of such covered establishment.

(c) The operations of an establishment affect commerce within the meaning of this title if (1) it is one of the establishments described in paragraph (1) of subsection (b); (2) in the case of an establishment described in paragraph (2) of subsection (b), it serves or offers to serve interstate travelers or a substantial portion of the food which it serves, or gasoline or other products which it sells, has moved in commerce; (3) in the case of an establishment described in paragraph (3) of subsection (b), it customarily presents films, performances, athletic teams, exhibitions, or other sources of entertainment which move in commerce; and (4) in the case of an establishment described in paragraph (4) of subsection (b), it is physically located within the premises of, or there is physically located within its premises, an establishment the operations of which affect commerce within the meaning of this subsection. For purposes of this section, "commerce" means travel, trade, traffic, commerce, transportation, or communication among the several States, or between the District of Columbia and any State, or between any foreign country or any territory or possession and any State or the District of Columbia, or between points in the same State but through any other State or the District of Columbia or a foreign country.

(d) Discrimination or segregation by an establishment is supported by State action within the meaning of this title if such discrimination or segregation (1) is carried on under color of any law, statute, ordinance, or regulation; or (2) is carried on under color of any custom or usage required or enforced by officials of the State or political subdivision thereof; or (3) is required by action of the State or political subdivision thereof.

(e) The provisions of this title shall not apply to a private club or other establishment not in fact open to the public, except to the extent that the facilities of such establishment are made available to the customers or patrons of an establishment within the scope of subsection (b).

SEC. 202. All persons shall be entitled to be free, at any establishment or place, from discrimination or segregation of any kind on the ground of race, color, religion, or national origin, if such discrimination or segregation is or purports to be required by any law, statute, ordinance, regulation, rule, or order of a State or any agency or political subdivision thereof.

SEC. 203. No person shall (a) withhold, deny, or attempt to withhold or deny, or deprive or attempt to deprive, any person of any right or privilege secured by section 201 or 202, or (b) intimidate, threaten, or coerce, or attempt to intimidate, threaten, or coerce any person with the purpose of interfering with any right or privilege secured by section 201 or 202, or (c) punish or attempt to punish any person for exercising or attempting to exercise any right or privilege secured by section 201 or 202.

SEC. 204. (a) Whenever any person has engaged or there are reasonable grounds to believe that any person is about to engage in any act or practice prohibited by section 203, a civil action for preventive relief, including an application for a permanent or temporary injunction, restraining order, or other order, may be instituted by the person aggrieved and, upon timely application, the court may, in its discretion, permit the Attorney General to intervene in such civil action if he certifies that the case is of general public importance. Upon application by the complainant and in such circumstances as the court may deem just, the court may appoint an attorney for such complainant and may authorize the commencement of the civil action without the payment of fees, costs, or security.

(b) In any action commenced pursuant to this title, the court, in its discretion, may allow the prevailing party, other than the United States, a reasonable attorney's fee as part of the costs, and the United States shall be liable for costs the same as a private person.

(c) In the case of an alleged act or practice prohibited by this title which occurs in a State, or political subdivision of a State, which has a State or local law prohibiting such act or practice and establishing or authorizing a State or local authority to grant or seek relief from such practice or to institute criminal proceedings with respect thereto upon receiving notice thereof, no civil action may be brought under subsection (a) before the expiration of thirty days after written notice of such alleged act or practice has been given to the appropriate State or local authority by registered mail or in person, provided that the court may stay proceedings in such civil action pending the termination of State or local enforcement proceedings.

(d) In the case of an alleged act or practice prohibited by this title which occurs in a State, or political subdivision of a State, which has no State or local law prohibiting such act or practice, a civil action may be brought under subsection (a): Provided, That the court may refer the matter to the Community Relations Service established by title X of this Act for as long as the court believes there is a reasonable possibility of obtaining voluntary compliance, but for not more than sixty days: Provided further, That upon expiration of such sixty-day period, the court may extend such period for an additional period, not to exceed a cumulative total of one hundred and twenty days, if it believes there then exists a reasonable possibility of securing voluntary compliance.

SEC. 205. The Service is authorized to make a full investigation of any complaint referred to it by the court under section 204(d) and may hold such hearings with respect thereto as may be necessary. The Service shall conduct any hearings with respect to any such complaint in executive session, and shall not release any testimony given therein except by agreement of all parties involved in the complaint with the permission of the court, and the Service shall endeavor to bring about a voluntary settlement between the parties.

SEC. 206. (a) Whenever the Attorney General has reasonable cause to believe that any person or group of persons is engaged in a pattern or practice of resistance to the full enjoyment of any of the rights secured by this title, and that the pattern or practice is of such a nature and is intended to deny the full exercise of the rights herein described, the Attorney General may bring a civil action in the appropriate district court of the United States by filing with it a complaint (1) signed by him (or in his absence the Acting Attorney General), (2) setting forth facts pertaining to such pattern or practice, and (3) requesting such preventive relief, including an application for a permanent or temporary injunction, restraining order or other order against the person or persons responsible for such pattern or practice, as he deems necessary to insure the full enjoyment of the rights herein described.

(b) In any such proceeding the Attorney General may file with the clerk of such court a request that a court of three judges be convened to hear and determine the case. Such request by the Attorney General shall be accompanied by a certificate that, in his opinion, the case is of general public importance. A copy of the certificate and request for a three-judge court shall be immediately furnished by such clerk to the chief judge of the circuit (or in his absence, the presiding circuit judge of the circuit) in which the case is pending. Upon receipt of the copy of such request it shall be the duty of the chief judge of the circuit or the presiding circuit judge, as the case may be, to designate immediately three judges in such circuit, of whom at least one shall be a circuit judge and another of whom shall be a district judge of the court in which the proceeding was instituted, to hear and determine such case, and it shall be the duty of the judges so designated to assign the case for hearing at the earliest practicable date, to participate in the hearing and determination thereof, and to cause the case to be in every way expedited. An appeal from the final judgment of such court will lie to the Supreme Court.

In the event the Attorney General fails to file such a request in any such proceeding, it shall be the duty of the chief judge of the district (or in his absence, the acting chief judge) in which the case is pending immediately to designate a judge in such district to hear and determine the case. In the event that no judge in the district is available to hear and determine the case, the chief judge of the district, or the acting chief judge, as the case may be, shall certify this fact to the chief judge of the circuit (or in his absence, the acting chief judge) who shall then designate a district or circuit judge of the circuit to hear and determine the case.

It shall be the duty of the judge designated pursuant to this section to assign the case for hearing at the earliest practicable date and to cause the case to be in every way expedited.

SEC. 207. (a) The district courts of the United States shall have jurisdiction of proceedings instituted pursuant to this title and shall exercise the same without regard to whether the aggrieved party shall have exhausted any administrative or other remedies that may be provided by law.

(b) The remedies provided in this title shall be the exclusive means of enforcing the rights based on this title, but nothing in this title shall preclude any individual or any State or local agency from asserting any right based on any other Federal or State law not inconsistent with this title, including any statute or ordinance requiring nondiscrimination in public establishments or accommodations, or from pursuing any remedy, civil or criminal, which may be available for the vindication or enforcement of such right.

Title III—Desegregation of Public Facilities

SEC. 301. (a) Whenever the Attorney General receives a complaint in writing signed by an individual to the effect that he is being deprived of or threatened with the loss of his right to the equal protection of the laws, on account of his race, color, religion, or national origin, by being denied equal utilization of any public facility which is owned, operated, or managed by or on behalf of any State or subdivision thereof, other than a public school or public college as defined in section 401 of title IV hereof, and the Attorney General believes the complaint is meritorious and certifies that the signer or signers of such complaint are unable, in his judgment, to initiate and maintain appropriate legal proceedings for relief and that the institution of an action will materially further the orderly progress of desegregation in public facilities, the Attorney General is authorized to institute for or in the name of the United States a civil action in any appropriate district court of the United States against such parties and for such relief as may be appropriate, and such court shall have and shall exercise jurisdiction of proceedings instituted pursuant to this section. The Attorney General may implead as defendants such additional parties as are or become necessary to the grant of effective relief hereunder.

(b) The Attorney General may deem a person or persons unable to initiate and maintain appropriate legal proceedings within the meaning of subsection

(a) of this section when such person or persons are unable, either directly or through other interested persons or organizations, to bear the expense of the litigation or to obtain effective legal representation; or whenever he is satisfied that the institution of such litigation would jeopardize the personal safety, employment, or economic standing of such person or persons, their families, or their property.

SEC. 302. In any action or proceeding under this title the United States shall be liable for costs, including a reasonable attorney's fee, the same as a private person.

SEC. 303. Nothing in this title shall affect adversely the right of any person to sue for or obtain relief in any court against discrimination in any facility covered by this title.

SEC. 304. A complaint as used in this title is a writing or document within the meaning of section 1001, title 18, United States Code.

Title IV—Desegregation of Public Education Definitions

SEC. 401. As used in this title—(a) "Commissioner" means the Commissioner of Education.

(b) "Desegregation" means the assignment of students to public schools and within such schools without regard to their race, color, religion, or national origin, but "desegregation" shall not mean the assignment of students to public schools in order to overcome racial imbalance.

(c) "Public school" means any elementary or secondary educational institution, and "public college" means any institution of higher education or any technical or vocational school above the secondary school level, provided that such public school or public college is operated by a State, subdivision of a State, or governmental agency within a State, or operated wholly or predominantly from or through the use of governmental funds or property, or funds or property derived from a governmental source.

(d) "School board" means any agency or agencies which administer a system of one or more public schools and any other agency which is responsible for the assignment of students to or within such system.

◆ **Survey and Report of Educational Opportunities**

SEC. 402. The Commissioner shall conduct a survey and make a report to the President and the Congress, within two years of the enactment of this title, concerning the lack of availability of equal educational opportunities for individuals by reason of race, color, religion, or national origin in public educational institutions at all levels in the United States, its territories and possessions, and the District of Columbia.

◆ **Technical Assistance**

SEC. 403. The Commissioner is authorized, upon the application of any school board, State, municipality, school district, or other governmental unit legally responsible for operating a public school or schools, to render technical assistance to such applicant in the preparation, adoption, and implementation of plans for the desegregation of public schools. Such technical assistance may, among other activities, include making available to such agencies information regarding effective methods of coping with special educational problems occasioned by desegregation, and making available to such agencies personnel of the Office of Education or other persons specially equipped to advise and assist them in coping with such problems.

◆ **Training Institutes**

SEC. 404. The Commissioner is authorized to arrange, through grants or contracts, with institutions of higher education for the operation of short-term or regular session institutes for special training designed to improve the ability of teachers, supervisors, counselors, and other elementary or secondary school personnel to deal effectively with special educational problems occasioned by desegregation. Individuals who attend such an institute on a full-time basis may be paid stipends for the period of their attendance at such institute in amounts specified by the Commissioner in regulations, including allowances for travel to attend such institute.

◆ **Grants**
SEC. 405. (a) The Commissioner is authorized, upon application of a school board, to make grants to such board to pay, in whole or in part, the cost of—

(1) giving to teachers and other school personnel inservice training in dealing with problems incident to desegregation, and

(2) employing specialists to advise in problems incident to desegregation.

(b) In determining whether to make a grant, and in fixing the amount thereof and the terms and conditions on which it will be made, the Commissioner shall take into consideration the amount available for grants under this section and the other applications which are pending before him; the financial condition of the applicant and the other resources available to it; the nature, extent, and gravity of its problems incident to desegregation; and such other factors as he finds relevant.

◆ **Payments**
SEC. 406. Payments pursuant to a grant or contract under this title may be made (after necessary adjustments on account of previously made overpayments or underpayments) in advance or by way of reimbursement, and in such installments, as the Commissioner may determine.

◆ **Suits by the Attorney General**
SEC. 407. (a) Whenever the Attorney General receives a complaint in writing—

(1) signed by a parent or group of parents to the effect that his or their minor children, as members of a class of persons similarly situated, are being deprived by a school board of the equal protection of the laws, or

(2) signed by an individual, or his parent, to the effect that he has been denied admission to or not permitted to continue in attendance at a public college by reason of race, color, religion, or national origin, and the Attorney General believes the complaint is meritorious and certifies that the signer or signers of such complaint are unable, in his judgment, to initiate and maintain appropriate legal proceedings for relief and that the institution of an action will materially further the orderly achievement of desegregation in public education, the Attorney General is authorized, after giving notice of such complaint to the appropriate school board or college authority and after certifying that he is satisfied that such board or authority has had a reasonable time to adjust the conditions alleged in such complaint, to institute for or in the name of the United States a civil action in any appropriate district court of the United States against such parties and for such relief as may be appropriate, and such court shall have and shall exercise jurisdiction of proceedings instituted pursuant to this section, provided that nothing herein shall empower any official or court of the United States to issue any order seeking to achieve a racial balance in any school by requiring the transportation of pupils or students from one school to another or one school district to another in order to achieve such racial balance, or otherwise enlarge the existing power of the court to insure compliance with constitutional standards. The Attorney General may implead as defendants such additional parties as are or become necessary to the grant of effective relief hereunder.

(b) The Attorney General may deem a person or persons unable to initiate and maintain appropriate legal proceedings within the meaning of subsection

(a) of this section when such person or persons are unable, either directly or through other interested persons or organizations, to bear the expense of the litigation or to obtain effective legal representation; or whenever he is satisfied that the institution of such litigation would jeopardize the personal safety, employment, or economic standing of such person or persons, their families, or their property.

(c) The term "parent" as used in this section includes any person standing in loco parentis. A "complaint" as used in this section is a writing or document within the meaning of section 1001, title 18, United States Code.

SEC. 408. In any action or proceeding under this title the United States shall be liable for costs the same as a private person.

SEC. 409. Nothing in this title shall affect adversely the right of any person to sue for or obtain relief in any court against discrimination in public education.

SEC. 410. Nothing in this title shall prohibit classification and assignment for reasons other than race, color, religion, or national origin.

Title V—Commission on Civil Rights

SEC. 501. Section 102 of the Civil Rights Act of 1957 (42 U.S.C. 1975a; 71 Stat. 634) is amended to read as follows:

"Rules of Procedure of the Commission Hearings: SEC. 102. (a) At least thirty days prior to the commencement of any hearing, the Commission shall cause to be published in the Federal Register notice of the date on which such hearing is to commence, the place at which it is to be held and the subject of the hearing. The Chairman, or one designated by him to act as Chairman at a hearing of the Commission, shall announce in an opening statement the subject of the hearing.

"(b) A copy of the Commission's rules shall be made available to any witness before the Commission, and a witness compelled to appear before the Commission or required to produce written or other matter shall be served with a copy of the Commission's rules at the time of service of the subpoena.

"(c) Any person compelled to appear in person before the Commission shall be accorded the right to be accompanied and advised by counsel, who shall have the right to subject his client to reasonable examination, and to make objections on the record and to argue briefly the basis for such objections. The Commission shall proceed with reasonable dispatch to conclude any hearing in which it is engaged. Due regard shall be had for the convenience and necessity of witnesses.

"(d) The Chairman or Acting Chairman may punish breaches of order and decorum by censure and exclusion from the hearings.

"(e) If the Commission determines that evidence or testimony at any hearing may tend to defame, degrade, or incriminate any person, it shall receive such evidence or testimony or summary of such evidence or testimony in executive session. The Commission shall afford any person defamed, degraded, or incriminated by such evidence or testimony an opportunity to appear and be heard in executive session, with a reasonable number of additional witnesses requested by him, before deciding to use such evidence or testimony. In the event the Commission determines to release or use such evidence or testimony in such manner as to reveal publicly the identity of the person defamed, degraded, or incriminated, such evidence or testimony, prior to such public release or use, shall be given at a public session, and the Commission shall afford such person an opportunity to appear as a voluntary witness or to file a sworn statement in his behalf and to submit brief and pertinent sworn statements of others. The Commission shall receive and dispose of requests from such person to subpoena additional witnesses.

"(f) Except as provided in sections 102 and 105 (f) of this Act, the Chairman shall receive and the Commission shall dispose of requests to subpoena additional witnesses.

"(g) No evidence or testimony or summary of evidence or testimony taken in executive session may be released or used in public sessions without the consent of the Commission. Whoever releases or uses in public without the consent of the Commission such evidence or testimony taken in executive session shall be fined not more than $1,000, or imprisoned for not more than one year.

"(h) In the discretion of the Commission, witnesses may submit brief and pertinent sworn statements in writing for inclusion in the record. The Commission shall determine the pertinency of testimony and evidence adduced at its hearings.

"(i) Every person who submits data or evidence shall be entitled to retain or, on payment of lawfully prescribed costs, procure a copy or transcript thereof, except that a witness in a hearing held in executive session may for good cause be limited to inspection of the official transcript of his testimony. Transcript copies of public sessions may be obtained by the public upon the payment of the cost thereof. An accurate transcript shall be made of the testimony of all witnesses at all hearings, either public or executive sessions, of the Commission or of any subcommittee thereof.

"(j) A witness attending any session of the Commission shall receive $6 for each day's attendance and for the time necessarily occupied in going to and returning from the same, and 10 cents per mile for going from and returning to his place of residence. Witnesses who attend at points so far removed from their respective residences as to prohibit return thereto from day to day shall be entitled to an additional allowance of $10 per day for expenses of subsistence including the time necessarily occupied in going to and returning from the place of attendance. Mileage payments shall be tendered to the witness upon service of a subpoena issued on behalf of the Commission or any subcommittee thereof.

"(k) The Commission shall not issue any subpoena for the attendance and testimony of witnesses or for the production of written or other matter which would require the presence of the party subpoenaed at a hearing to be held outside of the State wherein the witness is found or resides or is domiciled or transacts business, or has appointed an agent for receipt of service of process except that, in any event, the Commission may issue subpoenas for the attendance and testimony of witnesses and the production of written or other matter at a hearing held within fifty miles of the place where the witness is found or resides or is domiciled or transacts business or has appointed an agent for receipt of service of process.

"(l) The Commission shall separately state and currently publish in the Federal Register (1) descriptions of its central and field organization including the established places at which, and methods whereby, the public may secure information or make requests; (2) statements of the general course and method by which its functions are channeled and determined, and (3) rules adopted as authorized by law. No person shall in any manner be subject to or required to resort to rules, organization, or procedure not so published."

SEC. 502. Section 103(a) of the Civil Rights Act of 1957 (42 U.S.C. 1975b(a); 71 Stat. 634) is amended to read as follows:

"SEC. 103. (a) Each member of the Commission who is not otherwise in the service of the Government of the United States shall receive the sum of $75 per day for each day spent in the work of the Commission, shall be paid actual travel expenses, and per diem in lieu of subsistence expenses when away from his usual place of residence, in accordance with section 5 of the Administrative Expenses Act of 1946, as amended (5 U.S.C 73b-2; 60 Stat. 808)."

SEC. 503. Section 103(b) of the Civil Rights Act of 1957 (42 U.S.C. 1975(b); 71 Stat. 634) is amended to read as follows:

"(b) Each member of the Commission who is otherwise in the service of the Government of the United States shall serve without compensation in addition to that received for such other service, but while engaged in the work of the Commission shall be paid actual travel expenses, and per diem in lieu of subsistence expenses when away from his usual place of residence, in accordance with the provisions of the Travel Expenses Act of 1949, as amended
(5 U.S.C. 835-42; 63 Stat. 166)."

SEC. 504. (a) Section 104(a) of the Civil Rights Act of 1957 (42 U.S.C. 1975c(a); 71 Stat. 635), as amended, is further amended to read as follows:

"Duties of the Commission: SEC. 104. (a) The Commission shall—

"(1) investigate allegations in writing under oath or affirmation that certain citizens of the United States are being deprived of their right to vote and have that vote counted by reason of their color, race, religion, or national origin; which writing, under oath or affirmation, shall set forth the facts upon which such belief or beliefs are based;

"(2) study and collect information concerning legal developments constituting a denial of equal protection of the laws under the Constitution because of race, color, religion or national origin or in the administration of justice;

"(3) appraise the laws and policies of the Federal Government with respect to denials of equal protection of the laws under the Constitution because of race, color, religion or national origin or in the administration of justice;

"(4) serve as a national clearinghouse for information in respect to denials of equal protection of the laws because of race, color, religion or national origin, including but not limited to the fields of voting, education, housing, employment, the use of public facilities, and transportation, or in the administration of justice;

"(5) investigate allegations, made in writing and under oath or affirmation, that citizens of the United States are unlawfully being accorded or denied the right to vote, or to have their votes properly counted, in any election of presidential electors, Members of the United States Senate, or of the House of Representatives, as a result of any patterns or practice of fraud or discrimination in the conduct of such election; and

"(6) Nothing in this or any other Act shall be construed as authorizing the Commission, its Advisory Committees, or any person under its supervision or control to inquire into or investigate any membership practices or internal operations of any fraternal organization, any college or university fraternity or sorority, any private club or any religious organization."

(b) Section 104(b) of the Civil Rights Act of 1957 (42 U.S.C. 1975c(b); 71 Stat. 635), as amended, is further amended by striking out the present subsection "(b)" and by substituting therefore:
"(b) The Commission shall submit interim reports to the President and to the Congress at such times as the Commission, the Congress or the President shall deem desirable, and shall submit to the President and to the Congress a final report of its activities, findings, and recommendations not later than January 31, 1968."

SEC. 505. Section 105(a) of the Civil Rights Act of 1957 (42 U.S.C. 1975d(a); 71 Stat. 636) is amended by striking out in the last sentence thereof "$50 per diem" and inserting in lieu thereof "$75 per diem."

SEC. 506. Section 105(f) and section 105(g) of the Civil Rights Act of 1957 (42 U.S.C. 1975d (f) and (g); 71 Stat. 636) are amended to read as follows:

"(f) The Commission, or on the authorization of the Commission any subcommittee of two or more members, at least one of whom shall be of each major political party, may, for the purpose of carrying out the provisions of this Act, hold such hearings and act at such times and places as the Commission or such authorized subcommittee may deem advisable. Subpoenas for the attendance and testimony of witnesses or the production of written or other matter may be issued in accordance with the rules of the Commission as contained in section 102 (j) and (k) of this Act, over the signature of the Chairman of the Commission or of such subcommittee, and may be served by any person designated by such Chairman. The holding of hearings by the Commission, or the appointment of a subcommittee to hold hearings pursuant to this subparagraph, must be approved by a majority of the Commission, or by a majority of the members present at a meeting at which at least a quorum of four members is present.

"(g) In case of contumacy or refusal to obey a subpoena, any district court of the United States or the United States court of any territory or possession, or the District Court of the United States for the District of Columbia, within the jurisdiction of which the inquiry is carried on or within the jurisdiction of which said person guilty of contumacy or refusal to obey is found or resides or is domiciled or transacts business, or has appointed an agent for receipt of service of process, upon application by the Attorney General of the United States shall have jurisdiction to issue to such person an order requiring such person to appear before the Commission or a subcommittee thereof, there to produce pertinent, relevant and nonprivileged evidence if so ordered, or there to give testimony touching the matter under investigation; and any failure to obey such order of the court may be punished by said court as a contempt thereof."

SEC. 507. Section 105 of the Civil Rights Act of 1957 (42 U.S.C. 1975d; 71 Stat. 636), as amended by section 401 of the Civil Rights Act of 1960 (42 U.S.C. 1975d(h); 74 Stat. 89), is further amended by adding a new subsection at the end to read as follows:
"(i) The Commission shall have the power to make such rules and regulations as are necessary to carry out the purposes of this Act."

Title VI—Nondiscrimination in Federally Assisted Programs

SEC. 601. No person in the United States shall, on the ground of race, color, or national origin, be excluded from participation in, be denied the benefits of, or be subjected to discrimination under any program or activity receiving Federal financial assistance.

SEC. 602. Each Federal department and agency which is empowered to extend Federal financial assistance to any program or activity, by way of grant, loan, or contract other than a contract of insurance or guaranty, is authorized and directed to effectuate the provisions of section 601 with respect to such program or activity by issuing rules, regulations, or orders of general applicability which shall be consistent with achievement of the objectives of the statute authorizing the financial assistance in connection with which the action is taken. No such rule, regulation, or order shall become effective unless and until approved by the President. Compliance with any requirement adopted pursuant to this section may be effected (1) by the termination of or refusal to grant or to continue assistance under such program or activity to any recipient as to whom there has been an express finding on the record, after opportunity for hearing, of a failure to comply with such requirement, but such termination or refusal shall be limited to the particular political entity, or part thereof, or other recipient as to whom such a finding has been made and, shall be limited in its effect to the particular program, or part thereof, in which such noncompliance has been so found, or (2) by any other means authorized by law: Provided, however, That no such action shall be taken until the department or agency concerned has advised the appropriate person or persons of the failure to comply with the requirement and has determined that compliance cannot be secured by voluntary means. In the case of any action terminating, or refusing to grant or continue, assistance because of failure to comply with a requirement imposed pursuant to this section, the head of the federal department or agency shall file with the committees of the House and Senate having legislative jurisdiction over the program or activity involved a full written report of the circumstances and the grounds for such action. No such action shall become effective until thirty days have elapsed after the filing of such report.

SEC. 603. Any department or agency action taken pursuant to section 602 shall be subject to such judicial review as may otherwise be provided by law for similar action taken by such department or agency on other grounds. In the case of action, not otherwise subject to judicial review, terminating or refusing to grant or to continue financial assistance upon a finding of failure to comply with any requirement imposed pursuant to section 602, any person aggrieved (including any State or political subdivision thereof and any agency of either) may obtain judicial review of such action in accordance with section 10 of the Administrative Procedure Act, and such action shall not be deemed committed to unreviewable agency discretion within the meaning of that section.

SEC. 604. Nothing contained in this title shall be construed to authorize action under this title by any department or agency with respect to any employment practice of any employer, employment agency, or labor organization except where a primary objective of the Federal financial assistance is to provide employment.

SEC. 605. Nothing in this title shall add to or detract from any existing authority with respect to any program or activity under which Federal financial assistance is extended by way of a contract of insurance or guaranty.

Title VII—Equal Employment Opportunity Definitions

SEC. 701. For the purposes of this title—

(a) The term "person" includes one or more individuals, labor unions, partnerships, associations, corporations, legal representatives, mutual companies, joint-stock companies, trusts, unincorporated organizations, trustees, trustees in bankruptcy, or receivers.

(b) The term "employer" means a person engaged in an industry affecting commerce who has twenty-five or more employees for each working day in each of twenty or more calendar weeks in the current or preceding calendar year, and any agent of such a person, but such term does not include (1) the United States, a corporation wholly owned by the Government of the United States, an Indian tribe, or a State or political subdivision thereof, (2) a bona fide private membership club (other than a labor organization) which is exempt from taxation under section 501(c) of the Internal Revenue Code of 1954: Provided, That during the first year after the effective date prescribed in subsection (a) of section 716, persons having fewer than one hundred employees (and their agents) shall not be considered employers, and, during the second year after such date, persons having fewer than seventy-five employees (and their agents) shall not be considered employers, and, during the third year after such date, persons having fewer than fifty employees (and their agents) shall not be considered employers: Provided further, That it shall be the policy of the United States to insure equal employment opportunities for Federal employees without discrimination because of race, color, religion, sex or national origin and the President shall utilize his existing authority to effectuate this policy.

(c) The term "employment agency" means any person regularly undertaking with or without compensation to procure employees for an employer or to procure for employees opportunities to work for an employer and includes an agent of such a person; but shall not include an agency of the United States, or an agency of a State or political subdivision of a State, except that such term shall include the United States Employment Service and the system of State and local employment services receiving Federal assistance.

(d) The term "labor organization" means a labor organization engaged in an industry affecting commerce, and any agent of such an organization, and includes any organization of any kind, any agency, or employee representation committee, group, association, or plan so engaged in which employees participate and which exists for the purpose, in whole or in part, of dealing with employers concerning grievances, labor disputes, wages, rates of pay, hours, or other terms or conditions of employment, and any conference, general committee, joint or system board, or joint council so engaged which is subordinate to a national or international labor organization.

(e) A labor organization shall be deemed to be engaged in an industry affecting commerce if (1) it maintains or operates a hiring hall or hiring office which procures employees for an employer or procures for employees opportunities to work for an employer, or (2) the number of its members (or, where it is a labor organization composed of other labor organizations or their representatives, if the aggregate number of the members of such other labor organization) is (A) one hundred or more during the first year after the effective date prescribed in subsection (a) of section 716, (B) seventy-five or more during the second year after such date or fifty or more during the third year, or (C) twenty-five or more thereafter, and such labor organization—

(1) is the certified representative of employees under the provisions of the National Labor Relations Act, as amended, or the Railway Labor Act, as amended;

(2) although not certified, is a national or international labor organization or a local labor organization recognized or acting as the representative of employees of an employer or employers engaged in an industry affecting commerce; or

(3) has chartered a local labor organization or subsidiary body which is representing or actively seeking to represent employees of employers within the meaning of paragraph (1) or (2); or

(4) has been chartered by a labor organization representing or actively seeking to represent employees within the meaning of paragraph (1) or (2) as the local or subordinate body through which such employees may enjoy membership or become affiliated with such labor organization; or

(5) is a conference, general committee, joint or system board, or joint council subordinate to a national or international labor organization, which includes a labor organization engaged in an industry affecting commerce within the meaning of any of the preceding paragraphs of this subsection.

(f) The term "employee" means an individual employed by an employer.

(g) The term "commerce" means trade, traffic, commerce, transportation, transmission, or communication among the several States; or between a State and any place outside thereof; or within the District of Columbia, or a possession of the United States; or between points in the same State but through a point outside thereof.

(h) The term "industry affecting commerce" means any activity, business, or industry in commerce or in which a labor dispute would hinder or obstruct commerce or the free flow of commerce and includes any activity or industry "affecting commerce" within the meaning of the Labor-Management Reporting and Disclosure Act of 1959.

(i) The term "State" includes a State of the United States, the District of Columbia, Puerto Rico, the Virgin Islands, American Samoa, Guam, Wake Island, The Canal Zone, and Outer Continental Shelf lands defined in the Outer Continental Shelf Lands Act.

◆ **Exemption**

SEC. 702. This title shall not apply to an employer with respect to the employment of aliens outside any State, or to a religious corporation, association, or society with respect to the employment of individuals of a particular religion to perform work connected with the carrying on by such corporation, association, or society of its religious activities or to an educational institution with respect to the employment of individuals to perform work connected with the educational activities of such institution.

Document Text

◆ **Discrimination Because of Race, Color, Religion, Sex, or National Origin**

SEC. 703. (a) It shall be an unlawful employment practice for an employer—

(1) to fail or refuse to hire or to discharge any individual, or otherwise to discriminate against any individual with respect to his compensation, terms, conditions, or privileges of employment, because of such individual's race, color, religion, sex, or national origin; or

(2) to limit, segregate, or classify his employees in any way which would deprive or tend to deprive any individual of employment opportunities or otherwise adversely affect his status as an employee, because of such individual's race, color, religion, sex, or national origin.

(b) It shall be an unlawful employment practice for an employment agency to fail or refuse to refer for employment, or otherwise to discriminate against, any individual because of his race, color, religion, sex, or national origin, or to classify or refer for employment any individual on the basis of his race, color, religion, sex, or national origin.

(c) It shall be an unlawful employment practice for a labor organization—

(1) to exclude or to expel from its membership, or otherwise to discriminate against, any individual because of his race, color, religion, sex, or national origin;

(2) to limit, segregate, or classify its membership, or to classify or fail or refuse to refer for employment any individual, in any way which would deprive or tend to deprive any individual of employment opportunities, or would limit such employment opportunities or otherwise adversely affect his status as an employee or as an applicant for employment, because of such individual's race, color, religion, sex, or national origin; or

(3) to cause or attempt to cause an employer to discriminate against an individual in violation of this section.

(d) It shall be an unlawful employment practice for any employer, labor organization, or joint labor-management committee controlling apprenticeship or other training or retraining, including on-the-job training programs to discriminate against any individual because of his race, color, religion, sex, or national origin in admission to, or employment in, any program established to provide apprenticeship or other training.

(e) Notwithstanding any other provision of this title, (1) it shall not be an unlawful employment practice for an employer to hire and employ employees, for an employment agency to classify, or refer for employment any individual, for a labor organization to classify its membership or to classify or refer for employment any individual, or for an employer, labor organization, or joint labor-management committee controlling apprenticeship or other training or retraining programs to admit or employ any individual in any such program, on the basis of his religion, sex, or national origin in those certain instances where religion, sex, or national origin is a bona fide occupational qualification reasonably necessary to the normal operation of that particular business or enterprise, and (2) it shall not be an unlawful employment practice for a school, college, university, or other educational institution or institution of learning to hire and employ employees of a particular religion if such school, college, university, or other educational institution or institution of learning is, in whole or in substantial part, owned, supported, controlled, or managed by a particular religion or by a particular religious corporation, association, or society, or if the curriculum of such school, college, university, or other educational institution or institution of learning is directed toward the propagation of a particular religion.

(f) As used in this title, the phrase "unlawful employment practice" shall not be deemed to include any action or measure taken by an employer, labor organization, joint labor-management committee, or employment agency with respect to an individual who is a member of the Communist Party of the United States or of any other organization required to register as a Communist-action or Communist-front organization by final order of the Subversive Activities Control Board pursuant to the Subversive Activities Control Act of 1950.

(g) Notwithstanding any other provision of this title, it shall not be an unlawful employment practice for an employer to fail or refuse to hire and employ any individual for any position, for an employer to discharge any individual from any position, or for an employment agency to fail or refuse to refer any individual for employment in any position, or for a labor organization to fail or refuse to refer any individual for employment in any position, if—

(1) the occupancy of such position, or access to the premises in or upon which any part of the duties of such position is performed or is to be performed, is subject to any requirement imposed in the interest of the national security of the United States under any security program in effect pursuant to or admin-

istered under any statute of the United States or any Executive order of the President; and

(2) such individual has not fulfilled or has ceased to fulfill that requirement.

(h) Notwithstanding any other provision of this title, it shall not be an unlawful employment practice for an employer to apply different standards of compensation, or different terms, conditions, or privileges of employment pursuant to a bona fide seniority or merit system, or a system which measures earnings by quantity or quality of production or to employees who work in different locations, provided that such differences are not the result of an intention to discriminate because of race, color, religion, sex, or national origin, nor shall it be an unlawful employment practice for an employer to give and to act upon the results of any professionally developed ability test provided that such test, its administration or action upon the results is not designed, intended or used to discriminate because of race, color, religion, sex or national origin. It shall not be an unlawful employment practice under this title for any employer to differentiate upon the basis of sex in determining the amount of the wages or compensation paid or to be paid to employees of such employer if such differentiation is authorized by the provisions of section 6(d) of the Fair Labor Standards Act of 1938, as amended (29 U.S.C. 206(d)).

(i) Nothing contained in this title shall apply to any business or enterprise on or near an Indian reservation with respect to any publicly announced employment practice of such business or enterprise under which a preferential treatment is given to any individual because he is an Indian living on or near a reservation.

(j) Nothing contained in this title shall be interpreted to require any employer, employment agency, labor organization, or joint labor-management committee subject to this title to grant preferential treatment to any individual or to any group because of the race, color, religion, sex, or national origin of such individual or group on account of an imbalance which may exist with respect to the total number or percentage of persons of any race, color, religion, sex, or national origin employed by any employer, referred or classified for employment by any employment agency or labor organization, admitted to membership or classified by any labor organization, or admitted to, or employed in, any apprenticeship or other training program, in comparison with the total number or percentage of persons of such race, color, religion, sex, or national origin in any community, State, section, or other area, or in the available work force in any community, State, section, or other area.

◆ **Other Unlawful Employment Practices**

SEC. 704. (a) It shall be an unlawful employment practice for an employer to discriminate against any of his employees or applicants for employment, for an employment agency to discriminate against any individual, or for a labor organization to discriminate against any member thereof or applicant for membership, because he has opposed, any practice made an unlawful employment practice by this title, or because he has made a charge, testified, assisted, or participated in any manner in an investigation, proceeding, or hearing under this title.

(b) It shall be an unlawful employment practice for an employer, labor organization, or employment agency to print or publish or cause to be printed or published any notice or advertisement relating to employment by such an employer or membership in or any classification or referral for employment by such a labor organization, or relating to any classification or referral for employment by such an employment agency, indicating any preference, limitation, specification, or discrimination, based on race, color, religion, sex, or national origin, except that such a notice or advertisement may indicate a preference, limitation, specification, or discrimination based on religion, sex, or national origin when religion, sex, or national origin is a bona fide occupational qualification for employment.

◆ **Equal Employment Opportunity Commission**

SEC. 705. (a) There is hereby created a Commission to be known as the Equal Employment Opportunity Commission, which shall be composed of five members, not more than three of whom shall be members of the same political party, who shall be appointed by the President by and with the advice and consent of the Senate. One of the original members shall be appointed for a term of one year, one for a term of two years, one for a term of three years, one for a term of four years, and one for a term of five years, beginning from the date of enactment of this title, but their successors shall be appointed for terms of five years each, except that any individual chosen to fill a vacancy shall be appointed only for the unexpired term of the member whom he shall succeed. The President shall designate one member to serve as Chairman of the Commission, and one member to serve as Vice Chairman. The Chairman shall be responsible on behalf of the Commission for the administrative operations of the Commission, and shall appoint, in accordance with the civil service laws, such officers, agents, attorneys, and employees as it deems necessary to assist it in the performance of its functions and to fix their compensation in accordance with the Classification Act of 1949, as amended. The Vice Chairman shall act as Chairman in the absence or disability of the Chairman or in the event of a vacancy in that office.

(b) A vacancy in the Commission shall not impair the right of the remaining members to exercise all the powers of the Commission and three members thereof shall constitute a quorum.

(c) The Commission shall have an official seal which shall be judicially noticed.

(d) The Commission shall at the close of each fiscal year report to the Congress and to the President concerning the action it has taken; the names, salaries, and duties of all individuals in its employ and the moneys it has disbursed; and shall make such further reports on the cause of and means of eliminating discrimination and such recommendations for further legislation as may appear desirable.

(e) The Federal Executive Pay Act of 1956, as amended (5 U.S.C. 2201-2209), is further amended—

(1) by adding to section 105 thereof (5 U.S.C. 2204) the following clause:

"(32) Chairman, Equal Employment Opportunity Commission"; and

(2) by adding to clause (45) of section 106(a) thereof (5 U.S.C. 2205(a)) the following: "Equal Employment Opportunity Commission (4)."

(f) The principal office of the Commission shall be in or near the District of Columbia, but it may meet or exercise any or all its powers at any other place. The Commission may establish such regional or State offices as it deems necessary to accomplish the purpose of this title.

(g) The Commission shall have power—

(1) to cooperate with and, with their consent, utilize regional, State, local, and other agencies, both public and private, and individuals;

(2) to pay to witnesses whose depositions are taken or who are summoned before the Commission or any of its agents the same witness and mileage fees as are paid to witnesses in the courts of the United States;

(3) to furnish to persons subject to this title such technical assistance as they may request to further their compliance with this title or an order issued thereunder;

(4) upon the request of (i) any employer, whose employees or some of them, or (ii) any labor organization, whose members or some of them, refuse or threaten to refuse to cooperate in effectuating the provisions of this title, to assist in such effectuation by conciliation or such other remedial action as is provided by this title;

(5) to make such technical studies as are appropriate to effectuate the purposes and policies of this title and to make the results of such studies available to the public;

(6) to refer matters to the Attorney General with recommendations for intervention in a civil action brought by an aggrieved party under section 706, or for the institution of a civil action by the Attorney General under section 707, and to advise, consult, and assist the Attorney General on such matters.

(h) Attorneys appointed under this section may, at the direction of the Commission, appear for and represent the Commission in any case in court.

(i) The Commission shall, in any of its educational or promotional activities, cooperate with other departments and agencies in the performance of such educational and promotional activities.

(j) All officers, agents, attorneys, and employees of the Commission shall be subject to the provisions of section 9 of the Act of August 2, 1939, as amended (the Hatch Act), notwithstanding any exemption contained in such section.

◆ **Prevention of Unlawful Employment Practices**

SEC. 706. (a) Whenever it is charged in writing under oath by a person claiming to be aggrieved, or a written charge has been filed by a member of the Commission where he has reasonable cause to believe a violation of this title has occurred (and such charge sets forth the facts upon which it is based) that an employer, employment agency, or labor organization has engaged in an unlawful employment practice, the Commission shall furnish such employer, employment agency, or labor organization (hereinafter referred to as the "respondent") with a copy of such charge and shall make an investigation of such charge, provided that such charge shall not be made public by the Commission. If the Commission shall determine, after such investigation, that there is reasonable cause to believe that the charge is true, the Commission shall endeavor to eliminate any such alleged unlawful employment practice by informal methods of conference, conciliation, and persuasion. Nothing said or done during and as a part of such endeavors may be made public by the Commission without the written consent of the parties, or used as evidence in a subsequent proceeding. Any officer or employee of the Commission, who shall make public in any manner whatever any information in violation of this subsection shall be deemed guilty of a misdemeanor and upon conviction thereof shall be fined not more than $1,000 or imprisoned not more than one year.

(b) In the case of an alleged unlawful employment practice occurring in a State, or political subdivision of a State, which has a State or local law prohibiting the unlawful employment practice alleged and establishing or authorizing a State or local authority to grant or seek relief from such practice or to institute criminal proceedings with respect thereto upon receiving notice thereof, no charge may be filed under subsection (a) by the person aggrieved before the expiration of sixty days after proceedings have been commenced under the State or local law, unless such proceedings have been earlier terminated, provided that such sixty-day period shall be extended to one hundred and twenty days during the first year after the effective date of such State or local law. If any requirement for the commencement of such proceedings is imposed by a State or local authority other than a requirement of the filing of a written and signed statement of the facts upon which the proceeding is based, the proceeding shall be deemed to have been commenced for the purposes of this subsection at the time such statement is sent by registered mail to the appropriate State or local authority.

(c) In the case of any charge filed by a member of the Commission alleging an unlawful employment practice occurring in a State or political subdivision of a State, which has a State or local law prohibiting the practice alleged and establishing or authorizing a State or local authority to grant or seek relief from such practice or to institute criminal proceedings with respect thereto upon receiving notice thereof, the Commission shall, before taking any action with respect to such charge, notify the appropriate State or local officials and, upon request, afford them a reasonable time, but not less than sixty days (provided that such sixty-day period shall be extended to one hundred and twenty days during the first year after the effective day of such State or local law), unless a shorter period is requested, to act under such State or local law to remedy the practice alleged.

(d) A charge under subsection (a) shall be filed within ninety days after the alleged unlawful employment practice occurred, except that in the case of an unlawful employment practice with respect to which the person aggrieved has followed the procedure set out in subsection (b), such charge shall be filed by the person aggrieved within two hundred and ten days after the alleged unlawful employment practice occurred, or within thirty days after receiving notice that the State or local agency has terminated the proceedings under the State or local, law, whichever is earlier, and a copy of such charge shall be filed by the Commission with the State or local agency.

(e) If within thirty days after a charge is filed with the Commission or within thirty days after expiration of any period of reference under subsection (c) (except that in either case such period may be extended to not more than sixty days upon a determination by the Commission that further efforts to secure voluntary compliance are warranted), the Commission has been unable to obtain voluntary compliance with this title, the Commission shall so notify the person aggrieved and a civil action may, within thirty days thereafter, be brought against the respondent named in the charge (1) by the person claiming to be aggrieved, or (2) if such charge was filed by a member of the Commission, by any person whom the charge alleges was aggrieved by the alleged unlawful employment practice. Upon application by the complainant and in such circumstances as the court may deem just, the court may appoint an attorney for such complainant and may authorize the commencement of the action without the payment of fees, costs, or security. Upon timely application, the court may, in its discretion, permit the Attorney General to intervene in such civil action if he certifies that the case is of general public importance. Upon request, the court may, in its discretion, stay further proceedings for not more than sixty days pending the termination of State or local proceedings described in subsection (b) or the efforts of the Commission to obtain voluntary compliance.

(f) Each United States district court and each United States court of a place subject to the jurisdiction of the United States shall have jurisdiction of actions brought under this title. Such an action may be brought in any judicial district in the State in which the unlawful employment practice is alleged to have been committed, in the judicial district in which the employment records relevant to such practice are maintained and administered, or in the judicial district in which the plaintiff would have worked but for the alleged unlawful employment practice, but if the respondent is not found within any such district, such an action may be brought within the judicial district in which the respondent has his principal office. For purposes of sections 1404 and 1406 of title 28 of the United States Code, the judicial district in which the respondent has his principal office shall in all cases be considered a district in which the action might have been brought.

(g) If the court finds that the respondent has intentionally engaged in or is intentionally engaging in an unlawful employment practice charged in the complaint, the court may enjoin the respondent from engaging in such unlawful employment practice, and order such affirmative action as may be appropriate, which may include reinstatement or hiring of employees, with or without back pay (payable by the employer, employment agency, or labor organization, as the case may be, responsible for the unlawful employment practice). Interim earnings or amounts earnable with reasonable diligence by the person or persons discriminated against shall operate to reduce the back pay otherwise allowable. No order of the court shall require the admission or reinstatement of an individual as a member of a union or the hiring, reinstatement, or promotion of an individual as an employee, or the payment to him of any back pay, if such individual was refused admission, suspended, or expelled or was refused employment or advancement or was suspended or discharged for any reason other than discrimination on account of race, color, religion, sex or national origin or in violation of section 704(a).

(h) The provisions of the Act entitled "An Act to amend the Judicial Code and to define and limit the jurisdiction of courts sitting in equity, and for other purposes," approved March 23, 1932 (29 U.S.C. 101-115), shall not apply with respect to civil actions brought under this section.

(i) In any case in which an employer, employment agency, or labor organization fails to comply with an order of a court issued in a civil action brought under subsection (e), the Commission may commence proceedings to compel compliance with such order.

(j) Any civil action brought under subsection (e) and any proceedings brought under subsection (i) shall be subject to appeal as provided in sections 1291 and 1292, title 28, United States Code.

(k) In any action or proceeding under this title the court, in its discretion, may allow the prevailing party, other than the Commission or the United States, a reasonable attorney's fee as part of the costs, and the Commission and the United States shall be liable for costs the same as a private person.

SEC. 707. (a) Whenever the Attorney General has reasonable cause to believe that any person or group of persons is engaged in a pattern or practice of resistance to the full enjoyment of any of the rights secured by this title, and that the pattern or practice is of such a nature and is intended to deny the full exercise of the rights herein described, the Attorney General may bring a civil action in the appropriate district court of the United States by filing with it a complaint (1) signed by him (or in his absence the Acting Attorney General), (2) setting forth facts pertaining to such pattern or practice, and (3) requesting such relief, including an application for a permanent or temporary injunction, restraining order or other order against the person or persons responsible for such pattern or practice, as he deems necessary to insure the full enjoyment of the rights herein described.

(b) The district courts of the United States shall have and shall exercise jurisdiction of proceedings instituted pursuant to this section, and in any such proceeding the Attorney General may file with the clerk of such court a request that a court of three judges be convened to hear and determine the case. Such request by the Attorney General shall be accompanied by a certificate that, in his opinion, the case is of general public importance. A copy of the certificate and request for a three-judge court shall be immediately furnished by such clerk to the chief judge of the circuit (or in his absence, the presiding circuit judge of the circuit) in which the case is pending. Upon receipt of such request it shall be the duty of the chief judge of the circuit or the presiding circuit judge, as the case may be, to designate immediately three judges in such circuit, of whom at least one shall be a circuit judge and another of whom shall be a district judge of the court in which the proceeding was instituted, to hear and determine such case, and it shall be the duty of the judges so designated to assign the case for hearing at the earliest practicable date, to participate in the hearing and determination thereof, and to cause the case to be in every way expedited. An appeal from the final judgment of such court will lie to the Supreme Court.

In the event the Attorney General fails to file such a request in any such proceeding, it shall be the duty of the chief judge of the district (or in his absence, the acting chief judge) in which the case is pending immediately to designate a judge in such district to hear and determine the case. In the event that no judge in the district is available to hear and determine the case, the chief judge of the district, or the acting chief judge, as the case may be, shall certify this fact to the chief judge of the circuit (or in his absence, the acting chief judge) who shall then designate a district or circuit judge of the circuit to hear and determine the case.

It shall be the duty of the judge designated pursuant to this section to assign the case for hearing at the earliest practicable date and to cause the case to be in every way expedited.

◆ **Effect on State Laws**

SEC. 708. Nothing in this title shall be deemed to exempt or relieve any person from any liability, duty, penalty, or punishment provided by any present or future law of any State or political subdivision of a State, other than any such law which purports to require or permit the doing of any act which would be an unlawful employment practice under this title.

◆ **Investigations, Inspections, Records, State Agencies**

SEC. 709. (a) In connection with any investigation of a charge filed under section 706, the Commission or its designated representative shall at all reasonable times have access to, for the purposes of examination, and the right to copy any evidence of any person being investigated or proceeded against that relates to unlawful employment practices covered by this title and is relevant to the charge under investigation.

(b) The Commission may cooperate with State and local agencies charged with the administration of State fair employment practices laws and, with the consent of such agencies, may for the purpose of carrying out its functions and duties under this title and within the limitation of funds appropriated specifically for such purpose, utilize the services of such agencies and their employees and, notwithstanding any other provision of law, may reimburse such agencies and their employees for services rendered to assist the Commission in carrying out this title. In furtherance of such cooperative efforts, the Commission may enter into written agreements with such State or local agencies and such agreements may include provisions under which the Commission shall refrain from processing a charge in any cases or class of cases specified in such agreements and under which no person may bring a civil action under section 706 in any cases or class of cases so specified, or under which the Commission shall relieve any person or class of persons in such State or locality from requirements imposed under this section. The Commission shall rescind any such agreement whenever it determines that the agreement no longer serves the interest of effective enforcement of this title.

(c) Except as provided in subsection (d), every employer, employment agency, and labor organization subject to this title shall (1) make and keep such records relevant to the determinations of whether unlawful employment practices have been or are being committed, (2) preserve such records for such periods, and (3) make such reports therefrom, as the Commission shall prescribe by regulation or order, after public hearing, as reasonable, necessary, or appropriate for the enforcement of this title or the regulations or orders thereunder. The Commission shall, by regulation, require each employer, labor organization, and joint labor-management committee subject to this title which controls an apprenticeship or other training program to maintain such records as are reasonably necessary to carry out the purpose of this title, including, but not limited to, a list of applicants who wish to participate in such program, including the chronological order in which such applications were received, and shall furnish to the Commission, upon request, a detailed description of the manner in which persons are selected to participate in the apprenticeship or other training program. Any employer, employment agency, labor organization, or joint labor-management committee which believes that the application to it of any regulation or order issued under this section would result in undue hardship may (1) apply to the Commission for an exemption from the application of such regulation or order, or (2) bring a civil action in the United States district court for the district where such records are kept. If the Commission or the court, as the case may be, finds that the application of the regulation or order to the employer, employment agency, or labor organization in question would impose an undue hardship, the Commission or the court, as the case may be, may grant appropriate relief.

(d) The provisions of subsection (c) shall not apply to any employer, employment agency, labor organization, or joint labor-management committee with respect to matters occurring in any State or political subdivision thereof which has a fair employment practice law during any period in which such employer, employment agency, labor organization, or joint labor-management committee is subject to such law, except that the Commission may require such notations on records which such employer, employment agency, labor organization, or joint labor-management committee keeps or is required to keep as are necessary because of differences in coverage or methods of enforcement between the State or local law and the provisions of this title. Where an employer is required by Executive Order 10925, issued March 6, 1961, or by any other Executive order prescribing fair employment practices for Government contractors and subcontractors, or by rules or regulations issued thereunder, to file reports relating to his employment practices with any Federal agency or committee, and he is substantially in compliance with such requirements, the Commission shall not require him to file additional reports pursuant to subsection (c) of this section.

(e) It shall be unlawful for any officer or employee of the Commission to make public in any manner whatever any information obtained by the Commission pursuant to its authority under this section prior to the institution of any proceeding under this title involving such information. Any officer or employee of the Commission who shall make public in any manner whatever any information in violation of this subsection shall be guilty of a misdemeanor and upon conviction thereof, shall be fined not more than $1,000, or imprisoned not more than one year.

◆ **Investigatory Powers**

SEC. 710. (a) For the purposes of any investigation of a charge filed under the authority contained in section 706, the Commission shall have authority to examine witnesses under oath and to require the production of documentary evidence relevant or material to the charge under investigation.

(b) If the respondent named in a charge filed under section 706 fails or refuses to comply with a demand of the Commission for permission to examine or to copy evidence in conformity with the provisions of section 709(a), or if any person required to comply with the provisions of section 709(c) or (d) fails or refuses to do so, or if any person fails or refuses to comply with a demand by the Commission to give testimony under oath, the United States district court for the district in which such person is found, resides, or transacts business, shall, upon application of the Commission, have jurisdiction to issue to such person an order requiring him to comply with the provisions of section 709(c) or (d) or to comply with the demand of the Commission, but the attendance of a witness may not be required outside the State where he is found, resides, or transacts business and the production of evidence may not be required outside the State where such evidence is kept.

(c) Within twenty days after the service upon any person charged under section 706 of a demand by the Commission for the production of documentary evidence or for permission to examine or to copy evidence in conformity with the provisions of section 709(a), such person may file in the district court of the United States for the judicial district in which he resides, is found, or transacts business, and serve upon the Commission a petition for an order of such court modifying or setting aside such demand. The time allowed for compliance with the demand in whole or in part as deemed proper and ordered by the court shall not run during the pendency of such petition in the court. Such petition shall specify each ground upon which the petitioner relies in seeking such relief, and may be based upon any failure of such demand to comply with the provisions of this title or with the limitations generally applicable to compulsory process or upon any constitutional or other legal right or privilege of such person. No objection which is not raised by such a petition may be urged in the defense to a proceeding initiated by the Commission under subsection (b) for enforcement of such a demand unless such proceeding is commenced by the Commission prior to the expiration of the twenty-day period, or unless the court determines that the defendant could not reasonably have been aware of the availability of such ground of objection.

(d) In any proceeding brought by the Commission under subsection (b), except as provided in subsection (c) of this section, the defendant may petition the court for an order modifying or setting aside the demand of the Commission.

SEC. 711. (a) Every employer, employment agency, and labor organization, as the case may be, shall post and keep posted in conspicuous places upon its premises where notices to employees, applicants for employment, and members are customarily posted a notice to be prepared or approved by the Commission setting forth excerpts from or, summaries of, the pertinent provisions of this title and information pertinent to the filing of a complaint.

(b) A willful violation of this section shall be punishable by a fine of not more than $100 for each separate offense.

◆ **Veterans' Preference**

SEC. 712. Nothing contained in this title shall be construed to repeal or modify any Federal, State, territorial, or local law creating special rights or preference for veterans.

◆ **Rules and Regulations**

SEC. 713. (a) The Commission shall have authority from time to time to issue, amend, or rescind suitable procedural regulations to carry out the provisions of this title. Regulations issued under this section shall be in conformity with the standards and limitations of the Administrative Procedure Act.

(b) In any action or proceeding based on any alleged unlawful employment practice, no person shall be subject to any liability or punishment for or on account of (1) the commission by such person of an unlawful employment practice if he pleads and proves that the act or omission complained of was in good faith, in conformity with, and in reliance on any written interpretation or opinion of the Commission, or (2) the failure of such person to publish and file any information required by any provision of this title if he pleads and proves that he failed to publish and file such information in good faith, in conformity with the instructions of the Commission issued under this title regarding the filing of such information. Such a defense, if established, shall be a bar to the action or proceeding, notwithstanding that (A) after such act or omission, such interpretation or opinion is modified or rescinded or is determined by judicial authority to be invalid or of no legal effect, or (B) after publishing or filing the description and annual reports, such publication or filing is determined by judicial authority not to be in conformity with the requirements of this title.

- **Forcibly Resisting the Commission or Its Representatives**

SEC. 714. The provisions of section 111, title 18, United States Code, shall apply to officers, agents, and employees of the Commission in the performance of their official duties.

- **Special Study by Secretary of Labor**

SEC. 715. The Secretary of Labor shall make a full and complete study of the factors which might tend to result in discrimination in employment because of age and of the consequences of such discrimination on the economy and individuals affected. The Secretary of Labor shall make a report to the Congress not later than June 30, 1965, containing the results of such study and shall include in such report such recommendations for legislation to prevent arbitrary discrimination in employment because of age as he determines advisable.

- **Effective Date**

SEC. 716. (a) This title shall become effective one year after the date of its enactment.

(b) Notwithstanding subsection (a), sections of this title other than sections 703, 704, 706, and 707 shall become effective immediately.

(c) The President shall, as soon as feasible after the enactment of this title, convene one or more conferences for the purpose of enabling the leaders of groups whose members will be affected by this title to become familiar with the rights afforded and obligations imposed by its provisions, and for the purpose of making plans which will result in the fair and effective administration of this title when all of its provisions become effective. The President shall invite the participation in such conference or conferences of (1) the members of the President's Committee on Equal Employment Opportunity, (2) the members of the Commission on Civil Rights, (3) representatives of State and local agencies engaged in furthering equal employment opportunity, (4) representatives of private agencies engaged in furthering equal employment opportunity, and (5) representatives of employers, labor organizations, and employment agencies who will be subject to this title.

Title VIII—Registration and Voting Statistics

SEC. 801. The Secretary of Commerce shall promptly conduct a survey to compile registration and voting statistics in such geographic areas as may be recommended by the Commission on Civil Rights. Such a survey and compilation shall, to the extent recommended by the Commission on Civil Rights, only include a count of persons of voting age by race, color, and national origin, and determination of the extent to which such persons are registered to vote, and have voted in any statewide primary or general election in which the Members of the United States House of Representatives are nominated or elected, since January 1, 1960. Such information shall also be collected and compiled in connection with the Nineteenth Decennial Census, and at such other times as the Congress may prescribe. The provisions of section 9 and chapter 7 of title 13, United States Code, shall apply to any survey, collection, or compilation of registration and voting statistics carried out under this title: Provided, however, That no person shall be compelled to disclose his race, color, national origin, or questioned about his political party affiliation, how he voted, or the reasons therefore, nor shall any penalty be imposed for his failure or refusal to make such disclosure. Every person interrogated orally, by written survey or questionnaire or by any other means with respect to such information shall be fully advised with respect to his right to fail or refuse to furnish such information.

Title IX—Intervention and Procedure after Removal in Civil Rights Cases

SEC. 901. Title 28 of the United States Code, section 1447(d), is amended to read as follows:

"An order remanding a case to the State court from which it was removed is not reviewable on appeal or otherwise, except that an order remanding a case to the State court from which it was removed pursuant to section 1443 of this title shall be reviewable by appeal or otherwise."

SEC. 902. Whenever an action has been commenced in any court of the United States seeking relief from the denial of equal protection of the laws under the fourteenth amendment to the Constitution on account of race, color, religion, or national origin, the Attorney General for or in the name of the United States may intervene in such action upon timely application if the Attorney General certifies that the case is of general public importance. In such action the United States shall be entitled to the same relief as if it had instituted the action.

Title X—Establishment of Community Relations Service

SEC. 1001. (a) There is hereby established in and as a part of the Department of Commerce a Community Relations Service (hereinafter referred to as the "Service"), which shall be headed by a Director who shall be appointed by the President with the advice and consent of the Senate for a term of four years. The Director is authorized to appoint, subject to the civil service laws and regulations, such other personnel as may be necessary to enable the Service to carry out its functions and duties, and to fix their compensation in accordance with the Classification Act of 1949, as amended. The Director is further authorized to procure services as authorized by section 15 of the Act of August 2, 1946 (60 Stat. 810; 5 U.S.C. 55(a)), but at rates for individuals not in excess of $75 per diem.

(b) Section 106(a) of the Federal Executive Pay Act of 1956, as amended (5 U.S.C. 2205(a)), is further amended by adding the following clause thereto:

"(52) Director, Community Relations Service."

SEC. 1002. It shall be the function of the Service to provide assistance to communities and persons therein in resolving disputes, disagreements, or difficulties relating to discriminatory practices based on race, color, or national origin which impair the rights of persons in such communities under the Constitution or laws of the United States or which affect or may affect interstate commerce. The Service may offer its services in cases of such disputes, disagreements, or difficulties whenever, in its judgment, peaceful relations among the citizens of the community involved are threatened thereby, and it may offer its services either upon its own motion or upon the request of an appropriate State or local official or other interested person.

SEC. 1003. (a) The Service shall, whenever possible, in performing its functions, seek and utilize the cooperation of appropriate State or local, public, or private agencies.

(b) The activities of all officers and employees of the Service in providing conciliation assistance shall be conducted in confidence and without publicity, and the Service shall hold confidential any information acquired in the regular performance of its duties upon the understanding that it would be so held. No officer or employee of the Service shall engage in the performance of investigative or prosecuting functions of any department or agency in any litigation arising out of a dispute in which he acted on behalf of the Service. Any officer or other employee of the Service, who shall make public in any manner whatever any information in violation of this subsection, shall be deemed guilty of a misdemeanor and, upon conviction thereof, shall be fined not more than $1,000 or imprisoned not more than one year.

SEC. 1004. Subject to the provisions of sections 205 and 1003(b), the Director shall, on or before January 31 of each year, submit to the Congress a report of the activities of the Service during the preceding fiscal year.

Title XI—Miscellaneous

SEC. 1101. In any proceeding for criminal contempt arising under title II, III, IV, V, VI, or VII of this Act, the accused, upon demand therefore, shall be entitled to a trial by jury, which shall conform as near as may be to the practice in criminal cases. Upon conviction, the accused shall not be fined more than $1,000 or imprisoned for more than six months.

This section shall not apply to contempts committed in the presence of the court, or so near thereto as to obstruct the administration of justice, nor to the misbehavior, misconduct, or disobedience of any

Document Text

officer of the court in respect to writs, orders, or process of the court. No person shall be convicted of criminal contempt hereunder unless the act or omission constituting such contempt shall have been intentional, as required in other cases of criminal contempt.

Nor shall anything herein be construed to deprive courts of their power, by civil contempt proceedings, without a jury, to secure compliance with or to prevent obstruction of, as distinguished from punishment for violations of, any lawful writ, process, order, rule, decree, or command of the court in accordance with the prevailing usages of law and equity, including the power of detention.

SEC. 1102. No person should be put twice in jeopardy under the laws of the United States for the same act or omission. For this reason, an acquittal or conviction in a prosecution for a specific crime under the laws of the United States shall bar a proceeding for criminal contempt, which is based upon the same act or omission and which arises under the provisions of this Act; and an acquittal or conviction in a proceeding for criminal contempt, which arises under the provisions of this Act, shall bar a prosecution for a specific crime under the laws of the United States based upon the same act or omission.

SEC. 1103. Nothing in this Act shall be construed to deny, impair, or otherwise affect any right or authority of the Attorney General or of the United States or any agency or officer thereof under existing law to institute or intervene in any action or proceeding.

SEC. 1104. Nothing contained in any title of this Act shall be construed as indicating an intent on the part of Congress to occupy the field in which any such title operates to the exclusion of State laws on the same subject matter, nor shall any provision of this Act be construed as invalidating any provision of State law unless such provision is inconsistent with any of the purposes of this Act, or any provision thereof.

SEC. 1105. There are hereby authorized to be appropriated such sums as are necessary to carry out the provisions of this Act.

SEC. 1106. If any provision of this Act or the application thereof to any person or circumstances is held invalid, the remainder of the Act and the application of the provision to other persons not similarly situated or to other circumstances shall not be affected thereby.

Glossary

civil action	a lawsuit that seeks relief for a wrong
complaint	the opening plea filed in a lawsuit that seeks relief for a wrong
equal protection of the laws	concept drawn from the Fourteenth Amendment that all persons should be treated equally by and under the laws of the government
executive session	the convening of a public body that is closed to the public because of the subject matter to be discussed
injunction	equitable relief granted to a party, requiring that the opposing party perform a specific act or refrain from performing specific acts; also called injunctive relief
literacy test	test of reading or comprehension, such as those that have historically been given to prospective voters specifically to prevent African Americans and members of other minority groups from voting
rebuttable presumption	presumption that arises after specific facts are proved and that can be disproved if contrary evidence is presented
restraining order	order from a court stopping a party from doing a particular act, usually until an action on an injunction is heard
State action	behavior that is done by or on behalf of the state and is required to trigger the protections of the Fourteenth Amendment
subpoena	document requiring that a witness provide evidence in a court case or proceeding

Fannie Lou Hamer testifying at the Democratic National Convention (Library of Congress)

Fannie Lou Hamer's Testimony at the Democratic National Convention

1964

"All of this is on account we want to register, to become first-class citizens."

Overview

In 1964 at the Democratic National Convention, Fannie Lou Hamer testified before the party's Credentials Committee to explain the atmosphere of fear in which civil rights workers lived in Mississippi and to challenge the moral legitimacy of the state's "regular" delegation to the convention. Hamer and her colleagues from the Mississippi civil rights movement had generated momentum that year through the Freedom Summer project, which accomplished widespread education and registration of African American voters. The activists used this momentum to launch a new political institution, the Mississippi Freedom Democratic Party (MFDP), to challenge the legitimacy of the state's traditional Democratic Party. (In the one-party Solid South, the Democratic Party was the only one that mattered.) They did so in part simply to bring national attention to Mississippi, but they also held hopes that their gambit would result in the national Democratic Party's stripping the state's traditional branch of its status and recognizing MFDP members instead as the representatives of the Magnolia State.

Hamer emerged as the group's most eloquent spokesperson. She had distinguished herself as a homegrown leader in the civil rights movement, one who excelled at describing the plight of rural black Mississippians—and the changes they sought to bring about—in vernacular to which rural black Mississippians themselves responded. When the Democratic National Committee held its quadrennial convention in Atlantic City, New Jersey, at the end of the summer, Hamer was a natural choice to speak on behalf of the MFDP. The Freedom Democrats lodged a formal complaint with the national party over the seating of the "regulars"; the complaint would be adjudicated by the national convention's Credentials Committee. The labor lawyer and Democratic Party insider Joseph L. Rauh, Jr., of Washington, D.C., who represented the MFDP in Atlantic City, called on Hamer to testify before the committee on August 22, 1964.

Context

Fannie Lou Hamer was forty-four years old when she first learned she was even eligible to vote. She made two attempts to register at the courthouse in Sunflower County, Mississippi, before her name finally appeared on the voter rolls in early 1963. At the time, fewer than 3 percent of black Mississippians over the age of twenty-one had been allowed to register to vote in the congressional district that included Hamer's home, and the numbers were little better in the rest of the state. Mississippi's schools were completely segregated—providing separate and not even close to equal educational experiences for white and black students. The black schools in Hamer's part of the state, known as the Delta, had school years that were only half as long as those of the white schools, with long breaks for various cycles in cotton production. There were few jobs outside of farming available to African Americans; the separate and unequal system constrained their opportunities. As Hamer once said, "We Negroes know Mississippi education hasn't prepared us to live in any other state."

Mississippi blacks who dared challenge the system found themselves the victims of unimaginable amounts of violence. The state government itself was run by white supremacists for the interests of white supremacists. Indeed, many, if not all, of the most essential Mississippi institutions, from the educational to the political, actively worked to the detriment of black interests. African American activists decided that the state's Democratic Party was in many ways the worst of those institutions. Thus, while black activists worked to create better educational opportunities for their children, desegregate public accommodations, and register more black voters, they also organized to confront the state party.

The 1963 Freedom Vote initiative, also called the Freedom Ballot, was an effort to prove to the rest of the nation that black citizens in the state had been systematically denied the franchise but would exercise it if given the chance. The Council of Federated Organizations, an umbrella group coordinating the efforts of various civil rights groups in Mississippi, organized the Freedom Vote to collect and tally ballots cast by unregistered African American voters. The council accepted the volunteer efforts of several dozen white students from elite colleges to assist with the initiative. In the state's official gubernatorial election that year, with over three hundred thousand ballots cast, the segregationist Democratic lieutenant governor

Time Line

1962
- **August**
  Fannie Lou Hamer attends her first civil rights meeting and makes her first attempt at voter registration in Sunflower County, Mississippi.
- **December**
  Hamer becomes a paid field worker for the Student Nonviolent Coordinating Committee (SNCC).

1963
- **January**
  Hamer's name is added to county voter rolls following her second attempt to register.
- **June**
  Returning from a citizenship-education and voter-registration workshop in South Carolina sponsored by the Southern Christian Leadership Conference, Hamer is arrested for attempting to desegregate a restaurant in Winona, Mississippi, and badly beaten by town police.
- **November**
  Mississippi's Council of Federated Organizations conducts the Freedom Vote initiative to demonstrate the political will of the state's African Americans.
- **December**
  The Council of Federated Organizations agrees to spearhead the 1964 Freedom Summer project, which would include alternative schools, voter-registration drives, and the organization of a shadow party to contest the "regular" Mississippi Democratic Party.

1964
- **August 6**
  The Mississippi Freedom Democratic Party (MFDP) holds a state convention and announces its intention to challenge the state's "regular" party at the Democratic National Convention, to be held later that month. Hamer is elected vice chair of the MFDP delegation.

Paul B. Johnson, Jr., defeated the surprisingly strong Republican nominee, Reubel L. Phillips. The shadow vote, which was for obvious reasons unsanctioned by the state, gathered more than eighty-three thousand ballots, nearly all of which went for the "Freedom Ticket" of Aaron Henry for governor and the Reverend Edwin King for lieutenant governor. Henry, a black Clarksdale pharmacist, and King, a white chaplain at the integrated Tougaloo College, would both be active in the MFDP.

The Freedom Vote proved the point that black Mississippians wanted to practice the rights of citizenship and provided an organizational model for the following year's Freedom Summer project, but it had few other short-term practical effects. Its long-term effects, while admittedly difficult to quantify, were greater. Black Mississippians had been told all along that they were incapable of being citizens—that they were not worth the time and resources it would take to educate them into knowledgeable voters. The Freedom Vote stripped that varnish away and revealed that voting was not, as the terminology of the time put it, simply "white people's business."

During the Freedom Summer of 1964, black and white college-aged volunteers associated with the Student Nonviolent Coordinating Committee (SNCC) and the Congress of Racial Equality spent the summer building and teaching in "freedom schools" throughout the state and registering voters. The freedom schools served a variety of students, from the young to the elderly, and taught a radically alternative curriculum that emphasized the development of critical thinking skills in addition to voter education. It was during this time that the Mississippi Freedom Democratic Party was created as a parallel institution to the state's white-dominated Democratic Party. The MFDP was one of the most significant outcomes of the Freedom Summer project. As a demonstration of the political will of Mississippi's African Americans, the MFDP challenged the status of the delegation elected by the nearly all-white "regular" Mississippi Democrats as the rightful representatives of the state at the 1964 Democratic National Convention, held that summer in Atlantic City, New Jersey. Hamer was among the MFDP representatives in attendance at the convention, and regarding the Freedom Democrats' challenge, she was chosen to testify before the convention's Credentials Committee to address the matter.

About the Author

Fannie Lou Townsend was born on October 6, 1917, the last of twenty children to her impoverished sharecropping parents. She first worked in the cotton fields of the Mississippi Delta at the age of six and dropped out of school after the sixth grade to work full time in the fields to help support her family. She married Perry "Pap" Hamer in 1944, and they would sharecrop on the Marlow plantation, on the outskirts of the Sunflower County town of Ruleville, for nearly twenty years. Fannie Lou Hamer's Delta was a land of contrast: She and millions of other blacks endured staggering poverty throughout their lifetimes, but the Delta's cotton economy, made possible by their labors, allowed plantation owners—men like the U.S. senator James O. Eastland, Hamer's neighbor—to live opulent lifestyles.

Young activists associated with the SNCC and the Southern Christian Leadership Conference moved into the Delta in the early 1960s and began holding community meetings to build support for voter-registration drives among the region's huge African American population. Hamer attended one of the meetings in the summer of 1962 and learned for the first time that she herself was eligible to vote. Hamer's mind began to race while she sat in the meeting, she later recalled. If she could vote, she could improve her community: "I could just see myself votin' people out of office that I know was wrong and didn't do nothin' to help the poor." She traveled with several others from Ruleville to the county seat of Indianola to attempt to register in August 1962; all were denied, and on their return to Ruleville the group was harassed by a state trooper, an Indianola policeman, and several local white segregationists. Because she refused to apologize for or revoke her attempt to register, Hamer was evicted from the Marlow plantation that night. She then decided to take her life into her own hands and threw herself into organizing for the SNCC.

After her eviction from the Marlow plantation, Hamer lived with a succession of friends, never spending more than a few nights at a time in the same place—and with good reason, as on September 10, 1962, night riders blasted the homes of three Ruleville families that had stood up for their civil rights. The bullets that ripped into the house of Mary Tucker, the woman who had first introduced Hamer to civil rights work, struck the wall of the bedroom where Hamer had been sleeping only nights before. The incident was one of many in the Delta that fall. James Meredith's attempt to enter the University of Mississippi in nearby Oxford had emboldened white racists to defend segregation and white supremacy by any means necessary. They used horrific amounts of violence and intimidation to keep African American children out of previously all-white schools and deny all blacks their basic rights as citizens.

Hamer would not be intimidated, however. She began speaking and singing to small groups of blacks who showed an interest in standing up for their rights, and before long she embarked on a national fund-raising tour for the SNCC. Hamer's stories about the violent retaliation being inflicted on black would-be voters helped the SNCC raise the profile of its work in Mississippi. Her singing—which she invariably included in any public presentation—added a religious dimension to the crusade being waged by the civil rights workers. Hamer appropriated and repurposed hymns from the black church, some of which dated back to the struggle against slavery, and used them to share with others her strength for the fight. "This Little Light of Mine" was a particular favorite.

Hamer returned to Ruleville later that fall and dedicated herself to civil rights organizing, accepting full-time employment as a field worker for the SNCC. Hamer devoted herself to the work of distributing food and clothing that had been donated by friends of the SNCC in cities all over

Time Line

1964
- **August 22**: At the Democratic National Convention in Atlantic City, New Jersey, the MFDP formally challenges the state's "regulars"; Hamer testifies on behalf of her party.
- **November–December**: Hamer, Victoria Gray, and Annie Devine, all members of the MFDP, run against the "regular" Democrats in the election for the U.S. House of Representatives; they challenge the validity of the election after losing.

1965
- **January**: The U.S. House of Representatives votes to presently seat the three men that Hamer, Gray, and Devine challenged; the three women are granted guest seats in the chamber.
- **September 17**: Hamer, Gray, and Devine lose their challenge for the House seats.

1966–1968
- Hamer joins MFDP negotiations with liberal whites, labor union officials, and others to form the Loyal Democrats of Mississippi, which aims to unseat the "regular" Democrats at the party's 1968 national convention.

1968
- **August**: Mississippi sends an integrated Loyalist delegation to the Democratic National Convention.

the country to African Americans in Sunflower County. Many black farmworkers in the county relied on federally funded, locally administered social welfare programs to make it through the winter (the fallow period of the cotton calendar). When blacks associated with Hamer began agitating for their rights as citizens, local officials made it difficult for them to receive the needed commodities. The SNCC stepped into the breach to provide the supplies, but Hamer, somewhat controversially, imposed a condition: She would dispense food and clothing only to black adults who attempted to register to vote and paid their poll tax. As a result, the number of blacks making the trip to the registrar's office in Indianola skyrocketed.

Hamer attended her first citizenship education course at Dorchester, Georgia, in April 1963. Described by a fellow participant as a workshop for people like Hamer who had been deeply involved in civil rights work to "unbrainwash themselves," the citizenship education course taught local people skills they could then take back to their communities. For instance, the course provided basic literacy-education techniques that would help African American would-be voters pass registration tests. Hamer, the Greenwood teenager June Johnson, the Greenwood Southern Christian Leadership Conference activist Annelle Ponder, and a handful of other black Mississippians were selected to attend a second course, in South Carolina, the following month.

Vincent Harding, a civil rights movement participant and later one of its finest historians, was among the instructors at the South Carolina course. He encouraged the workshop attendees to begin living the changes they wanted to create in society. If they wanted to desegregate Mississippi, they had to refuse to be segregated themselves. If they wanted equality in society, they had to refuse to be treated as inferiors. Hamer's group took the lesson to heart. On their way home to the Delta they sat down at a lunch counter reserved for whites only in the town of Columbus, Mississippi. To their surprise, they were served without incident. They repeated the action in the town of Winona, but instead of being served they found themselves arrested and confined to the Montgomery County jail. Hamer's description of the group's treatment in the jail formed the basis of her testimony to the Democratic National Convention's Credentials Committee.

By 1964, when the SNCC, the Southern Christian Leadership Conference, the Congress of Racial Equality, and the National Association for the Advancement of Colored People coordinated efforts for what became known as the Freedom Summer project, Hamer was an experienced organizer and spokesperson for the SNCC. She epitomized the group's motto, "Let the People Decide": SNCC workers were to go into southern communities and help local blacks define for themselves the problems they faced and design their own solutions. Rather than acting as outside experts, SNCC workers facilitated and encouraged the development of local leaders. The SNCC helped Hamer develop her own abilities, and she reciprocated by taking the group's philosophy into new communities. Blessed with the ability to speak eloquently within the rhetorical tradition of the rural black church and the American political protest tradition, using simple language that anyone could understand, Hamer connected black Mississippians' struggles "to live as decent human beings"—as phrased in her testimony—with their collective desire to practice their rights as American citizens.

Hamer remained active in the MFDP after the disappointment of Atlantic City, and following four more years of dedication to political work, she was rewarded in being named one of the representatives in the integrated Loyalist coalition sent as the state's delegation to the Democratic National Convention in 1968. In the ensuing years, though she did run for elected office again and supported other black candidates for office, for the most part Hamer turned to alternative strategies for change. She founded Freedom Farm, a cooperative enterprise with high ambitions, in Sunflower County. In its short existence Freedom Farm succeeded in feeding dozens of families who would otherwise have gone hungry, but it proved to be an organizational challenge beyond Hamer's best efforts. She was hospitalized for nervous exhaustion at least twice in the early 1970s as she tried to sustain the farm's operations. Having survived polio as a girl and having fought diabetes, hypertension, and breast cancer as an adult, Hamer finally succumbed on March 14, 1977, to heart failure.

Explanation and Analysis of the Document

Hamer used plain speech at the Democratic National Convention to describe the hardships she had endured simply because she wanted to exercise the rights of citizenship. She "testified" before the Credentials Committee in two senses of the word: In some ways her speech reads like a legal affidavit attesting to her suffering as a civil rights worker, but she performed as though it were religious testimony. Hamer's appearance was but one part of a multipronged effort to persuade the members of the committee to award Mississippi's seats at the convention to the MFDP, an effort that would take most of an afternoon. Joseph L. Rauh, Jr., handled the legal arguments, and others would also testify as to the electoral benefits the party would reap in the South if the MFDP were seated. Hamer was to inject morality into the equation, and out of the dozens of hours of testimony heard by the Credentials Committee that year, it was Hamer's that everyone remembered.

In her testimony, Hamer recounts the indignities and horrific beatings she endured because she wanted African Americans in Mississippi to be able to vote. Her stories serve as illustrations not only of the determination of African Americans in the Deep South to be treated as equal citizens and human beings but also of the violence it took to maintain the region's system of white supremacy. Would national Democrats stand with the blacks of Mississippi and defend their rights? Hamer put them on the spot and demanded that they do so.

The testimony does include one minor inaccuracy: While the U.S. senator James O. Eastland did live and own a plantation empire in Sunflower County, Senator John C. Stennis did not (as Hamer seems to suggest in her introductory sentence). Everything else stated by Hamer was all too sadly true. The provocation with which she concluded her testimony may not have immediately won the case for the MFDP in the 1964 seating challenge, but it echoed into future conventions, all of which would demand that state delegations be integrated.

Audience

Hamer testified immediately following Aaron Henry and Edwin King, the victors of the Freedom Vote; Rita Schwer-

Aaron Henry, chair of the Mississippi Freedom Democratic Party delegation, speaking before the Democratic National Convention (Library of Congress)

ner (the widow of the slain civil rights organizer Michael Schwerner), the National Association for the Advancement of Colored People executive secretary Roy Wilkins, and Martin Luther King, Jr., followed her. Hamer spoke specifically to the 110 members of the Credentials Committee, but because her appearance was to be nationally televised, she delivered her testimony in a way that was intended to bring pressure from Democrats throughout the country on members of the committee and on party leaders, ideally forcing them to recognize the Freedom Democrats as the rightful Mississippi delegation.

President Lyndon B. Johnson, who was worried that white southern voters would break with the party over his handling of civil rights issues and fearful of the scene that would result if the Credentials Committee sided with the MFDP over the "regulars," attempted to defuse the situation by calling a press conference while Hamer testified. His plan backfired. The national television networks ended up broadcasting Hamer's dramatic testimony in full in prime time before a much larger viewing audience than would have been able to see her testify live in the daytime. The attention Hamer's testimony generated made her arguably the most famous poor woman in America at the time.

Impact

If Johnson had hoped that he could ignore the MFDP or sweep the party's concerns under the rug, he was sorely mistaken. Hamer's dramatic testimony brought an emotional dimension to what were normally dry proceedings turning on legalisms. The question of how democratic the Democratic Party's process of selecting state delegations was and the subject of civil rights more generally suddenly became the defining issues of the convention. The president tasked U.S. senator Hubert H. Humphrey, whom Johnson was considering as his nominee for vice president, with fashioning a compromise to satisfy both the MFDP's moral claim for the seats and the national party's desire not to drive white southerners out of the party.

Humphrey settled on a solution whereby Mississippi's "regulars" would be seated, the MFDP would be granted two at-large seats in the convention hall, and all parties concerned would agree to reforms that would democratize and desegregate state delegation procedures in the future. Tellingly, however, the "compromise" dictated that Henry and King would receive the two seats and provided no real chance for the rank and file of the MFDP to vote on whether or not to accept it, much less elect their own rep-

Essential Quotes

> "Mr. Chairman, and the Credentials Committee, my name is Mrs. Fannie Lou Hamer, and I live at 626 East Lafayette Street, Ruleville, Mississippi, Sunflower County, the home of Senator James O. Eastland."

> "The plantation owner came, and ... he said, 'If you don't go down and withdraw your registration, you will have to leave.... You will—you might have to go because we are not ready for that in Mississippi.' And I addressed him and told him and said, 'I didn't try to register for you. I tried to register for myself.' I had to leave that same night."

> "I was carried to the county jail, and ... after I was placed in the cell I began to hear the sound of licks and horrible screams, and I could hear somebody say, 'Can you say, yes sir, nigger? Can you say yes, sir?' ... She says, 'I don't know you well enough.' They beat her, I don't know how long, and after a while she began to pray, and asked God to have mercy on those people."

> "All of this is on account we want to register, to become first-class citizens, and if the freedom Democratic Party is not seated now, I question America, is this America, the land of the free and the home of the brave where we have to sleep with our telephones off of the hooks because our lives be threatened daily because we want to live as decent human beings, in America?"

resentatives. The compromise was accepted for them, but that did not stop the MFDP's membership from debating the settlement among themselves and with leaders from the national party and civil rights establishment. Those debates opened divides that eventually convinced many MFDP members that their interests would be best served outside of traditional electoral politics, or at least outside of the two existing parties. Hamer, for one, rejected the arrangement out of hand: "We didn't come all this way for no two seats," she announced, rejecting the argument that the arrangement at least comprised a moral victory.

Hamer's initial foray into electoral politics left a bad taste in her mouth, but it did not prevent her from returning to Mississippi to campaign for Johnson. She also continued to press for change via the traditional political process. Four MFDP candidates—Hamer, Annie Devine, Victoria Gray, and Aaron Henry—ran for three U.S. House seats and a U.S. Senate seat in the 1964 election. State officials, however, refused to place their names on the ballot, even though their candidacies met the specifications of state election laws. The officials' decision was foolish; the MFDP candidates could not have won a fair election because there were so few black registered voters at the time, and striking their names from the ballot opened an avenue to legal disputes.

Hamer, Devine, and Gray indeed challenged the seating of the three white U.S. representatives they had tried to run against, through both a federal suit and a House of Representatives rules challenge sponsored by the Democrat William Fitts Ryan of New York. Neither challenge had much hope of succeeding—and, in fact, neither did—but together they provided another national platform for Hamer and the MFDP. At the very least, Hamer, Devine, and Gray kept the issue of black disenfranchisement in the national spotlight and helped to build momentum for the legislation that would become the Voting Rights Act, signed into law by Johnson in 1965.

The most ignored plank of Humphrey's 1964 compromise—the stipulation that state delegations would have to be integrated by 1968—provided what may have been the most important and long-lasting outcome of the 1964 convention challenge. In the months leading up to the 1968 national party convention, Hamer and the MFDP worked in coalition with white liberals, union organizers, and the state civil rights establishment to form the Loyal Democrats of Mississippi, or Loyalists. Again in 1968, the "regulars" systematically excluded blacks from their ranks and demonstrated how undemocratic the state Democratic Party machinery truly was. Again the challengers pressed their case before the national convention's Credentials Committee. This time the rules were indisputable, and the committee sided with the challengers, recognizing the Loyalists as the rightful representatives of Mississippi. The episode's outcome fundamentally altered the operations of the Democratic Party. Just as significantly, coming as it did on the heels of the 1965 Voting Rights Act, which brought millions of blacks into the political process for the first time, it changed Democratic intraparty politics in the South forever.

For many Americans, nearly all of whom were introduced to Fannie Lou Hamer via her Atlantic City testimony, the humble civil rights activist was the embodiment of the physical courage and emotional strength demonstrated by black Mississippians in their decades-long efforts to kill Jim Crow. Her testimony offered a powerful moral rebuke to Mississippi officials and helped to convince Americans outside the state that what happened there affected them, too. By demanding to know "Is this America?" as she plaintively wondered, Hamer forced national officials and citizens everywhere to take a side. Ultimately, they took hers.

See also Roy Wilkins: "The Clock Will Not Be Turned Back" (1957); Martin Luther King, Jr.: "I Have a Dream" (1963).

Further Reading

- **Books**

Asch, Chris Myers. *The Senator and the Sharecropper: The Freedom Struggles of James O. Eastland and Fannie Lou Hamer*. New York: New Press, 2008.

Carson, Clayborne. *In Struggle: SNCC and the Black Awakening of the 1960s*. Cambridge, Mass.: Harvard University Press, 1981.

Dittmer, John. *Local People: The Struggle for Civil Rights in Mississippi*. Urbana: University of Illinois Press, 1994.

Hogan, Wesley C. *Many Minds, One Heart: SNCC's Dream for a New America*. Chapel Hill: University of North Carolina Press, 2007.

Lee, Chana Kai. *For Freedom's Sake: The Life of Fannie Lou Hamer*. Urbana: University of Illinois Press, 1999.

Mills, Kay. *This Little Light of Mine: The Life of Fannie Lou Hamer*. New York: Plume, 1994.

Moye, J. Todd. *Let the People Decide: Black Freedom and White Resistance Movements in Sunflower County, Mississippi, 1945–1986*. Chapel Hill: University of North Carolina Press, 2004.

Payne, Charles M. *I've Got the Light of Freedom: The Organizing Tradition and the Mississippi Freedom Struggle*. Berkeley: University of California Press, 1995.

Questions for Further Study

1. What was the "Solid South," and what role did it play in politics during this time period? What effect did the Solid South and concern about it in Washington, D.C., have on African Americans?

2. What impact did Fannie Lou Hamer and her colleagues have on the civil rights movement? What future events could be said to have grown out of her efforts?

3. Given the experiences that Hamer narrates, it seems almost unimaginable that by the end of the first decade of the twenty-first century, Mississippi had more black elected officials than any other state in the Union. What do you think accounts for this remarkable turnaround?

4. Compare this document with Sojourner Truth's "Ain't I a Woman?" speech. In what ways are the documents similar? How did the two women exercise the same kind of moral authority?

5. Make the argument that if it were not for the growing prevalence of television in American homes beginning in the 1950s, the civil rights movement would have been delayed.

■ **Web Sites**

"Civil Rights Movement Veterans." Civil Rights Movement Veterans Web site.
http://www.crmvet.org.

"The Hamer Institute." Jackson State University "Fannie Lou Hamer National Institute on Citizenship and Democracy" Web site.
http://www.jsums.edu/~hamer.institute/.

"Oh Freedom over Me." American RadioWorks Web site.
http://americanradioworks.publicradio.org/features/oh_freedom/.

"An Oral History with Fannie Lou Hamer." University of Southern Mississippi Libraries "Civil Rights in Mississippi Digital Archive" Web site.
http://www.lib.usm.edu/~spcol/crda/oh/hamer.htm?hamertrans.htm~mainFrame.

—J. Todd Moye

Fannie Lou Hamer's Testimony at the Democratic National Convention

Mr. Chairman, and the Credentials Committee, my name is Mrs. Fannie Lou Hamer, and I live at 626 East Lafayette Street, Ruleville, Mississippi, Sunflower County, the home of Senator James O. Eastland, and Senator Stennis.

It was the 31st of August in 1962 that 18 of us traveled twenty-six miles to the county courthouse in Indianola to try to register to try to become first-class citizens. We was met in Indianola by Mississippi men, highway patrolmens and they only allowed two of us in to take the literacy test at the time. After we had taken this test and started back to Ruleville, we was held up by the City Police and the State Highway Patrolmen and carried back to Indianola, where the bus driver was charged that day with driving a bus the wrong color.

After we paid the fine among us, we continued on to Ruleville, and Reverend Jeff Sunny carried me four miles in the rural area where I had worked as a timekeeper and sharecropper for eighteen years. I was met there by my children, who told me that the plantation owner was angry because I had gone down to try to register.

After they told me, my husband came, and said that the plantation owner was raising cain because I had tried to register, and before he quit talking the plantation owner came, and said, "Fannie Lou, do you know—did Pap tell you what I said?"

And I said, "yes, sir."

He said, "I mean that," he said, "If you don't go down and withdraw your registration, you will have to leave," said, "Then if you go down and withdraw," he said, "You will—you might have to go because we are not ready for that in Mississippi."

And I addressed him and told him and said, "I didn't try to register for you. I tried to register for myself." I had to leave that same night.

On the 10th of September, 1962, sixteen bullets was fired into the home of Mr. and Mrs. Robert Tucker for me. That same night two girls were shot in Ruleville, Mississippi. Also Mr. Joe McDonald's house was shot in.

And in June, the 9th, 1963, I had attended a voter registration workshop, was returning back to Mississippi. Ten of us was traveling by the Continental Trailway bus. When we got to Winona, Mississippi, which is in Montgomery County, four of the people got off to use the washroom, and two of the people—to use the restaurant—two of the people wanted to use the washroom. The four people that had gone in to use the restaurant was ordered out. During this time I was on the bus. But when I looked through the window and saw they had rushed out, I got off of the bus to see what had happened, and one of the ladies said, "It was a state highway patrolman and a chief of police ordered us out."

I got back on the bus and one of the persons had used the washroom got back on the bus, too. As soon as I was seated on the bus, I saw when they began to get the four people in a highway patrolman's car. I stepped off of the bus to see what was happening and somebody screamed from the car that the four workers was in and said, "Get that one there," and when I went to get in the car, when the man told me I was under arrest, he kicked me.

I was carried to the county jail, and put in the booking room. They left some of the people in the booking room and began to place us in cells. I was placed in a cell with a young woman called Miss Euvester Simpson. After I was placed in the cell I began to hear the sound of licks and horrible screams, and I could hear somebody say, "Can you say, yes sir, nigger? Can you say yes, sir?"

And they would say other horrible names. She would say, "Yes, I can say yes, sir."

"So say it."

She says, "I don't know you well enough."

They beat her, I don't know how long, and after a while she began to pray, and asked God to have mercy on those people.

And it wasn't too long before three white men came to my cell. One of these men was a State Highway Patrolman and he asked me where I was from, and I told him Ruleville, he said, "We are going to check this." And they left my cell and it wasn't too long before they came back. He said, "You are from Ruleville all right," and he used a curse work, and he said, "We are going to make you wish you was dead."

I was carried out of that cell into another cell where they had two Negro prisoners. The State Highway Patrolmen ordered the first Negro to take the blackjack. The first Negro prisoner ordered me,

Document Text

by orders from the State Highway Patrolman for me, to lay down on a bunk bed on my face, and I laid on my face. The first Negro began to beat, and I was beat by the first Negro until he was exhausted, and I was holding my hands behind me at that time on my left side because I suffered from polio when I was six years old. After the first Negro had beat until he was exhausted the State Highway Patrolman ordered the second Negro to take the blackjack.

The second Negro began to beat and I began to work my feet, and the State Highway Patrolman ordered the first Negro who had beat to set on my feet to keep me from working my feet. I began to scream and one white man got up and began to beat me my head and told me to hush. One white man—my dress had worked up high, he walked over and pulled my dress down—and he pulled my dress back, back up.

I was in jail when Medgar Evers was murdered.

All of this is on account we want to register, to become first-class citizens, and if the freedom Democratic Party is not seated now, I question America, is this America, the land of the free and the home of the brave where we have to sleep with our telephones off of the hooks because our lives be threatened daily because we want to live as decent human beings, in America?

Thank you.

Glossary

blackjack	a baton or truncheon used by police as a weapon; a billy club
Medgar Evers	a Mississippi civil rights activist assassinated outside his home on June 12, 1963